*This book
is dedicated to the late
Sir V. T. Krishnamachari,
a firm believer in planting
the roots of democracy in the
villages of India
through Community Development*

PREFACE

INDIA, like the other newly-developing countries, has, since Independence, had to create and then strengthen free institutions, initiate programmes to raise the level of living of her people, and stimulate increased agricultural and industrial productivity. She has had to attack widespread poverty, hunger, and disease.

India's progress in this task since 1947 stands as one of the historic examples of human advancement. Proceeding through a programme of planned social and economic development, India has increased her food and agricultural production by some forty-two per cent, has raised her low industrial output by an average of ninety-three per cent, and has moved ahead with formation of the numerous policies and institutions, including education and community services, that are required for realizing her goals of future growth. These achievements are monumental and deserve recognition. It is probably safe to say that no other great nation has ever before made so many and so great gains in the short period of time that has passed since India began her first planned "decade of development".

This does not mean, of course, that India's development task is finished, or even that it is keeping pace with the goals of its planners or the imperatives of current needs. Despite the gains being made, poverty, hunger, and low levels of living and of income still persist, owing to the rapid rise in population. It is clear that India's achievement of a modern productive society, with steadily rising incomes and improvements in living standards, will require long years of patient building, phase by phase. Yet it is equally clear that India has already made worthwhile gains toward her goals, and that these gains may be expected to continue with gathering force and speed. This expectation is conditioned upon the continuation of strong economic and technical assistance from abroad, within a context of freedom from foreign aggression and war.

India is an overwhelmingly agricultural country, village-centred; this fact not only determines the nature of much of the development work needed, but also the nature of the entire society. Because development of the rural sector is of towering significance to national development, furnishing the environment and the base for other phases of growth, this book is focused on the conditions and problems of rural people, their institutions, their ways of life and living. It is also directed to the problems and processes of planning, especially in the Community Development Programme, the principal official vehicle of rural development.

India's Roots of Democracy is written for planners and directors of development programmes of newly-developing countries, as well as those of assisting countries, who may find profit in an objective but critical analysis of the first decade of experience of the most giant, planned rural development programme in the free world; for the numerous persons everywhere who want to learn about what India is attempting to do, and why; and for the considerable and increasing number of social scientists who dedicate themselves to the task of understanding the purposes and the problems of the economic, social, and political development of newly-developing countries.

Finally, and with great feeling, this book is written for (and dedicated to) that wider spectrum of the Indian people—her planners, political leaders, teachers and scientists, administrators and field workers—upon whom have fallen the burdens of raising a new nation from its well-established roots. It is our hope to provide these people with the vital one-step-back objective view of their progress and methods in an effort to understand the process of change, to appreciate their vast progress to date, and to provide encouragement for these dedicated people to stand by their commitments and continue in their unassailable faith in the capacity of India's people to overcome the burdens of disease, ignorance, and poverty. For it is these commitments alone which will bear the fruit of a half-billion self-reliant citizens capable of making wise decisions and contributing their full share to the development of the new India.

The first eight chapters of this book describe the setting with which Indian planned development began, that is, the major conditioning factors and identifiable situations, inherited from the past which would inevitably condition the processes of planned change. The next ten chapters discuss the various rural development programmes and give the authors' critical assessment of the trials, errors, and successes of those programmes. The last nine chapters present analyses of observed experiences in the operation of India's rural development programme which we trust will make some contribution to what might be called the sociology of development.

Our interpretations are based on personal and professional observation, buttressed by a great diversity of interviews and conversations with persons on all levels of Indian society, from national and State leaders to village people. To have cited the many persons from whom we obtained knowledge and insight would be impossible, and in many cases inappropriate. In some chapters, we have depended heavily on other authorities, which are listed at the end of these chapters. At the end of all other chapters, we give only enough sources to assist readers to pursue further study of the areas of experience we have discussed.

The views expressed in this volume are those of the authors and do not represent official policies or positions of any institution or agency.

TABLE OF CONTENTS

Chapter P<small>AGE</small>

CHAPTER 1

WHAT INDIA PLANNED TO DO

WHEN India assumed full authority for national development in 1947, what she planned to do was more audacious, and more idealistic, than any non-Communist country has ever planned. She started with less, and planned to do more than most other underdeveloped countries. Because of the size of her population and her strategic location geographically, what she accomplishes within the next generation is bound to be of great importance in world affairs for generations to come. Because she has decided to use only democratic methods in her giant, planned development programmes, her experiences over the first ten years toward an avowed "Sovereign Democratic Republic" provide an unprecedented social, economic and political laboratory.

Analyses of these experiences require an understanding of all the positions or situations from which development planning started. The most obvious of these situations to be discussed are as follows: (1) *widespread poverty* represented by one of the lowest levels of *per capita* income in the world, resulting in near-starvation diets for millions of persons; (2) *an illiteracy rate* of 84 per cent for the total population and probably more than 90 per cent in most villages; (3) a largely *self-sufficient agriculture* with one of the lowest production yields in the world; (4) overwhelmingly a rural population, 83 per cent living in villages; most of the villages highly isolated physically and socially; (5) a *decadent village industry* and *meagre urban industry;* (6) the majority of village people psychologically oriented more to survival than to hope and expectations; (7) a *rigidly stratified social structure*, with hundreds of castes, and some fifty-five million persons in the so-called "scheduled castes" (untouchables); (8) *great diversity of ethnic and cultural types of people*, speaking fifteen different major languages and some 800 other languages or dialects; (9) a *meagre transportation system* and a still more *inadequate communication system;* (10) political leadership attuned to organization of activities designed to frustrate British rule; and (11) an administrative structure oriented to police, tax collection, and regulatory functions.

Behind these conditioning factors lay historical, political, and cultural factors of equal or greater importance. The first and most basic of these was the fact that the geographic areas which it was expected would constitute the Indian Union were not, and never had been, completely under one sovereignty. A corollary to this was the tremendous diversity of peoples, languages, and cultures of the 357 million persons who constituted the people of India in 1950. Third was the fact that Great Britain, although it had decided to grant independence to India, was not in a position to hand over complete sovereignty to the government of India which was to be formed. In addition to the nine Governors' Provinces which constituted British India, there were nearly 600 Indian States that had not been annexed by the British Crown. About half of these were Estates or Jagirs given to individuals or families by Muslim rulers in the past. The other half were ruled by hereditary chiefs, who considered themselves sovereign. Some persons who presumed that they knew India well, reckoning with these cultural facts, seriously questioned whether the Indian people, with their immense diversity, overwhelming poverty and illiteracy, and living under a complicated administrative system, could ever be a nation. But the die was cast in 1947, and the task of building national unity became the first major task of national development.

The Constitution adopted in 1949, two years after Independence was granted, like all written constitutions, was a charter for the kind of government, indeed the kind of society, the leaders of India desired and determined to build. It stated some things to be done immediately, other things as long-term or ultimate objectives. Its preamble stated,

> "We, the people of India, having solemnly resolved to constitute India into a Sovereign Democratic Republic and to secure to all its citizens: *Justice*, social, economic and political; *Liberty* of thought, expression, belief, faith and worship; *Equality* of status and opportunity; and to promote among them all *Fraternity* assuring the dignity of the individual and the unity of the Nation; in our Constituent Assembly this twenty-sixth of November, 1949, do hereby adopt, enact and give to ourselves this Constitution."

As the basic law of the country, the Constitution took some steps in the direction of eliminating immediately some of the most prevalent injustices and inequities. It removed religion, race, caste, sex, and place of birth as qualifications for political citizenship, and made it a penal offence to restrict the access to any public place "maintained wholly or partly out of State funds or dedicated to the use of the general public." It removed the same disabilities to admission "into any educational institution maintained by the State or receiving aid out of State funds." It declared that "untouchability is abolished and its practice in any form is forbidden."

India's Constitution declared objectives which went beyond a guarantee against discrimination among or between citizens and classes. It not only declared the right of every citizen "to work, to education and to public assistance in cases of unemployment, old age, sickness and disablement, and in other cases of undeserved want," but it also made a number of provisions "for the advancement of any socially and educationally backward classes of citizens or for the Scheduled Castes and the Scheduled Tribes". It made special provisions for women and children. India could not, however, as no other nation can, by constitutional provisions, guarantee the consummation of the objectives she thus set forth. She was not by declarations of the Constitution even yet sociologically a national society.

It is not our purpose here to tell the story of the origin of the "crazy quilt" which constituted the political map of India in 1947, or to describe in any detail the fantastic speed with which the total territory was consolidated into seventeen states and ten centrally administered areas by 1949 when the Constitution was adopted. But it is important for the reader to have some understanding of the diversity of these political organizations, as well as of the elements of political and cultural unity with which India started to build a nation. The diversity was incontrovertible, and had Indian leaders not recognized and believed in the over-riding importance of the elements of cultural unity inherent in her people, the goal of creating national unity out of the complex pieces of her colonial past would have been thought impossible to achieve.

The liquidation of the Princely States and Estates was consummated before the Constitution was adopted. It was such a tremendous first step toward national unity that its significance cannot be understood without some knowledge about the origin of these States and their past history, their status during British rule, and the methods by which their liquidation was accomplished. There were some 562 of these Indian States, some of them with larger populations than some of the British States or Governors' Provinces; many of them were only small estates. Only a brief description of their origins is presented here.

India, like other politically underdeveloped countries, had for centuries been ruled by numerous feudal lords. These local rulers came to be known as Princes, and their domains as Princely States. When Great Britain became the Paramount Power in India, these Princely States were legitimized and, as a consequence, increased in number. Akbar, the great Mogul Emperor (1556-1605), had attempted to weld the strongest of these local feudatories into his central government by sending provincial governors out from Delhi. Panikkar says the British reversed this plan when they "discovered a method by which political power could be exercised through puppet monarchs." These so-called "puppets" were the "Princes", many of whom had been provincial officials under the Mogul Empire, and most of whom had gained their power in wars with other Princes. Beginning with the East India Company's first guarantee of the right of. a contending Prince to rule a given territory to 1835, when the British government assumed complete responsibility for all British affairs in India, negotiations with Princes had been primarily to guarantee peaceful conditions under which British trade could be pursued. At first, the agreements with the Princes were little more than that the British would collect the taxes due to the Central Mogul Government, for which, as a matter of fact, the East India Company was a Zamindar[1] and for which services the Princes' tenure and right to rule would be guaranteed. Thus each local area was, so to speak, under a dual system of government, the East India Company responsible for the collection of taxes, the Princes for all other responsibilities.

Because the treaties negotiated with the Princely States

[1] A Zamindar was originally only a tax collector. Later he came to be a proprietor and a landlord.

guaranteed the States not only against external aggression, but also against internal rebellion, British responsibility came gradually to be much wider and greater than that of collecting taxes. British troops, in fairly large numbers, were stationed in the larger States, and the rulers were themselves required to maintain sizable armies. British "Residencies" were located throughout the country to guarantee the effective discharge of increased and increasing responsibilities of British paramountcy in all Princely States which had accepted "subsidiary alliances" with Britain. The "Paramount Power" in the hands of the British Resident was, in addition to defence and protection, gradually extended to supervision of transportation and communication, customs, coinage of currency, limitations of armaments, and even the right to sanction succession of power in the case of natural heirs. As Menon says,

> "The Indian States thus became part and parcel of the British empire in India. In the words of Lord Canning, 'The territories under the sovereignty of the Crown became at once as important and as integral a part of India as territories under its direct domination. Together they form one direct care and the political system which the Moghuls had not completed and the Mahrattas never contemplated is now an established fact of history.'"

"British India", organized into nine Governors' Provinces and three Chief Commissioners' Provinces, covered only 56 per cent of the total territory of the country which now constitutes the nations of India and Pakistan. The other 44 per cent of the territory was divided among the 562 Princely States or Estates. None of these Indian States was subject to British parliamentary legislation. Their people were not British subjects. Undoubtedly millions of persons living in isolated villages in these "Princely States" had never heard of the British Empire and knew nothing about the prospect that with Independence they would become citizens of India, no longer mere subjects of feudal rulers and zamindars. Notwithstanding these facts, the leaders of India were faced with the necessity of qualifying all of them as citizens of India, as the first necessary step in building a nation.

One of the most important issues, therefore, when Great Britain decided in 1946 to quit India as a colonial power was:

what was to be the status of the rulers of the Indian Princely States. Some of these States were large, Hyderabad having a population of more than 16 million people, and Mysore a population of almost 8 million people. Some of them had been ruled by the same dynasties for many generations. The rulers of such States considered themselves to be sovereign and their States to be independent political entities. The contracts, or treaties, of some of them with the British Paramount Power were, in fact, in perpetuity. Some of the rulers argued that no matter who governed the rest of India, Great Britain should honour these treaties or contracts. Such an agreement would have made impossible a unified India. This idea could not be countenanced by Indian leaders and was not countenanced by Great Britain. The sovereignty of all Princes was liquidated, and when the Constitution was adopted, it provided for only seventeen States. Three of the largest and oldest Indian States were among them. All Indian States were either incorporated into one or another of the nine old British States (Governors' Provinces) or were grouped into three new States and five so-called Unions of States.

As we have seen, Great Britain had gradually, over more than two centuries, made India a dual administrative unity—one part, "British India", the other part, the "Indian States". The decision to consolidate them into seventeen States was, of course, a political and administrative act of a relatively few leaders. Millions of Indians were completely oblivious of the fact that such a decision had been made and such an act consummated. Each of them was, however, aware of and deeply conscious of the fact that he was a member of a local village community. And however much the integrity of village self-sufficiency had been diluted politically and socially by British District administration, and its economy jeopardized by the competition of the British factory system, the Indian village remained as the foundation of Indian society. The coming and going of one empire after another, over the centuries, had not greatly changed the manner of life in villages. The rulers of Princely States had not disturbed village organization. The very immobility of village people had made the nearly 300 million peasants the most abiding, and therefore the most stable, element in the continuity of Indian society, an elemental foundation equal to any other cultural inheritance upon which India could quite surely start to build a national society. No matter what the historic or ethnic origins of village people, or in what part of the vast country of India their village was located, village organization and village manners of life were pretty much the same. No small part of the things for which India's leaders planned was based upon an understanding of this fact.

Despite the elements of cultural unity found in the villages, it appeared that the 562 separate political parts of India might be a prime stumbling block to the successful establishment of a unified nation. Indeed this was predicted by some persons who did not wish India well in her attempt to do so. They, like Indian leaders themselves, were astounded at the speed with which the Princely States were liquidated.[2] The task was completed well before the Constitution was adopted in 1949. The low state of development which existed in most of these States, the custom of non-participation of the people in government, and the "privy purses" and pensions granted to the Princes will for some time be drags on national development. But the anomalous relationships between the people and their government were abolished, and the leaders of India were free to build a new government on the basis of foundations which they believed were inherent in the people of India.

The content and scope of the Constitution reflect many of the problems which India faced in forming a union of Indian States. Its provisions reflect the problems inherent in the diversity of people living in the sub-continent, and it deals in some detail with a number of problems inherent in building a democracy out of probably the most highly stratified society in the world. The nine old British provinces had for some time been autonomous units, under responsible governments. The eight "Indian States" now to be incorporated into the Union had been under the autocratic rule of Princes. The ten new States had previously had no autonomy. In the face of these facts, the Constitution of India, unlike the Constitution of the United States, became a constitution of both the Union and the States. It not only provided

---

[2] Those who are interested in learning more about the masterly way in which this was done will want to read two books by V. P. Menon, who did most of the detailed negotiating with the rulers of the Indian States: *The Story of the Integration of the Indian States*, and *The Transfer of Power in India*.

"Directive Principles" for legislation by the States, but prescribed, in considerable detail, the administrative structure for and within the States. As Basu says, it prescribed "citizenship, namely the citizenship of India", that "either Union or State officials shall administer both Union and State laws," that all courts "are headed by the Supreme Court of India," and that "a large concurrent legislative list insures uniformity of legislation in common affairs." In commenting upon whether such an arrangement establishes a federal union or a unitary State, Basu concludes as follows: "Our new Constitution is not an alliance between democracies and dynasties, but a real union of Indian people, built on the basic concepts of the sovereignty of the people."

A constitution is a charter, not a plan for development. A Planning Commission was set up in March, 1950, three months after the Constitution became fully operative. The scope of its work was defined as follows:

> "The Constitution of India has guaranteed certain Fundamental Rights to the citizens of India and enunciated certain Directive Principles of State Policy, in particular, that the State shall strive to promote the welfare of the people by securing and protecting as effectively as it may a social order in which justice, social, economic and political, shall inform all the institutions of the national life, and shall direct its policy towards securing, among other things,—(a) that the citizens, men and women equally, have the right to an adequate means of livelihood; (b) that the ownership and control of the material resources of the community are so distributed as best to subserve the common good; and (c) that the operation of the economic system does not result in the concentration of wealth and means of production to the common detriment."

"Having regard to these rights and in furtherance of these principles as well as of the declared objective of the Government to promote a rapid rise in the standard of living of the people by efficient exploitation of the resources of the country, increasing production, and offering opportunities to all for employment in the service of the community. The Planning Commission will:

> (1) make an assessment of the material, capital and

human resources of the country, including technical personnel, and investigate the possibilities of augmenting such of
these resources as are found to be deficient in relation to the
nation's requirements;

(2) formulate a Plan for the most effective and balanced
utilization of the country's resources;

(3) on a determination of priorities, define the stages in
which the Plan should be carried out and propose the
allocation of resources for the due completion of each stage;

(4) indicate the factors which are tending to retard
economic development, and determine the conditions which,
in view of the current social and political situation, should
be established for the successful execution of the Plan;

(5) determine the nature of the machinery which will
be necessary for securing the successful implementation of
each stage of the Plan in all its aspects;

(6) appraise from time to time the progress achieved in
the execution of each stage of the Plan and recommend the
adjustments of policy and measures that such appraisal may
show to be necessary; and

(7) make such interim or ancillary recommendations as
appear to it to be appropriate either for facilitating the discharge of the duties assigned to it; or, on a consideration of
the prevailing economic conditions, current policies, measures
and development programmes; or on an examination of such
specific problems as may be referred to it for advice by Central or State Governments."

The Constitution could, and did, state the long-term objectives of the type of society which India desired to evolve. The
Plan needed to prescribe the first steps to be taken towards that
ultimate objective, and to attempt to select as first steps programmes which would gain quick, obvious objectives, that is, objectives which could be carried out with available resources, and
programmes which, in their operation, would generate physical,
economic, and human resources for the successful undertaking of
next steps. The Constitution could, and did, state objectives which,
if pursued immediately, would require revolutionary methods. The
Plan had to reckon with the necessity of using evolutionary methods
as a means to accomplishing ultimate revolution. The Constitution
had prescribed that India shall be a democratic republic. The Plan

had to prescribe the democratic means to be used in all development programmes. The Constitution prescribed equality of status and opportunity for all citizens. The Plan had to devise projects which would help to develop equality, create employment opportunity for the greatest number of persons, and welfare programmes which would, in so far as possible, alleviate living and working conditions of those for whom employment was not immediately available. The Constitution had prescribed that, within ten years, compulsory and universal education should be provided to all children up to 14 years of age. The Plan had to develop an additional type of education, one which would provide training for tens of thousands of adults in order that the development programmes might have even semi-competent personnel to operate them.

The First Five Year Plan set forth some of the objectives to be attained in early programme operation and the means which had to be used if the ultimate objectives prescribed by the Constitution were to be attained. The Planning Commission submitted a "Draft Outline" in July, 1951, and expressed a desire that there should be widespread public participation in development planning. The final Plan was submitted to the Prime Minister eighteen months later, in December, 1952. A sociological description, or analysis, of India's First Five Year Plan requires not so much a recording of the "social projects" proposed or the funds allocated as it does the story of the extent to which various groups participated in the planning process and the recognition on the part of the planners of the processes and problems involved in using democratic means and methods of development.

The Draft Outline, which had already been discussed with the central Ministries and the State governments, was submitted for general public discussion with the following comment: "Planning in a democratic State is a social process in which, in some part, every citizen should have the opportunity to participate." Because of the conditions of isolation, lack of communication, and great illiteracy, it, of course, could not be discussed by the great mass of villagers. It was, however, discussed by State governments, labour unions and other groups, in university seminars, and it received wide comment and debate in newspapers.

That the Planning Commission clearly recognized that there

are many problems inherent in the use of democratic methods in rapid development is evidenced by many statements made in the Plan. It said, "The task of organizing a democracy for rapid and co-ordinated advance along several lines is one of special difficulty. ... The rights of free expression of opinion and of freedom of organization inhere in the very concept of government by consent." It, however, apparently had faith that India at that moment could count on that consent. The Plan also said, "Under pressure of crisis such as war, democracies have proved capable of effective action on a mass scale, and there is no doubt that once the community has come to appreciate the vital significance of the tasks in hand, it will rise to similar heights for constructive purposes also." It expressed the conviction that, "The crucial factor in organizing the community for action is leadership, and, in a democracy, not merely leadership at the top but at all levels."

These statements, and a number of others which could have been quoted, expressed the faith of Indian leaders that the basic unity of Indian society was great enough to make them believe that if the consent of the masses was obtained for the launching of development programmes, the entire Indian "community would be energized" for the tasks to be undertaken. They believed that the prospect for improvement on all levels of society would create a national animus equivalent to that engendered by war; that development would become a great national cause. They believed that "stagnant villages" could and would become dynamic through aided self-help programmes, and that leaders would emerge at village levels, as well as at all other levels of society, if permitted and helped to do so. Whether idealistic or naive, development programmes were launched on these beliefs and with these faiths.

India's poverty at that moment was almost beyond imagination. The long-standing existence of this poverty reflected itself in practically every aspect of Indian life and living. Relative stagnation, that is absence of change in the conditions of the masses, had induced something like a fatalistic outlook on the part of the millions of peasants and other poverty-stricken persons. The relative lack of mass means of communication, including rural roads, sharply isolated some 300 million villagers from all agencies and agents of change. The local self-sufficiency of agriculture and cottage industries buttressed this isolation. The rigid class structure of Indian society, more rigid in rural than in urban areas, sabotaged not only economic vertical mobility, but also free communication between different segments of the population. Most isolated from the rest of the population were some 27 million tribal people. In the face of these facts, planned democratic development was to be put to the test in India as it had never been put to the test in any other time or place.

Planning in India did not start de novo in 1950; it had been in process by the Indian Congress for more than ten years, and a number of State plans were already in operation. There are, in fact, those who say, "The First Five Year Plan was not a plan at all; the Planning Commission simply took all the schemes which had been formulated by the States and the National Congress, accepted their recommendations as targets, and put them together as a Plan." Such a statement is an over-simplification, but another statement is undoubtedly valid, namely, that, "The making of the Plan was only one stage, a very important stage, in the whole process of planning which had been going on in India for a number of years."[3]

Probably no other newly-independent country had, for so long a period, looked forward with so sure a conviction that it would in due time inherit the responsibility for planning the course of its own development. Most of the sixty-five-year period, which intervened between 1885 when the Indian National Congress was organized, and 1950 when the Planning Commission was appointed, looked at in retrospect, can be said to have been a period of planning. This planning took definite form with the appointment by the Indian National Congress, in 1937, of a National Planning Committee. The General Secretary of this Committee could report in 1948 that 23 of the 25 sub-committees had made published reports. Not only these reports, but the persons who worked on them, were available to the Planning Commission. The General Secretary of the over-all Congress Committee was a member of the new Commission, and Jawaharlal Nehru, its Chairman, late Prime Minister, was Chairman of the new Planning Commission. A thorough-going study of all State

---

[3] These statements were made to the authors by outstanding Indian leaders in private conversations.

plans was made, and many of the projects already in operation or formulated were inculcated in the new national Plan. But, however great the contribution of these earlier planning bodies, the First Five Year Plan was not merely borrowed from them, nor was it borrowed from some other country. It was formulated by those persons who constituted the official membership of the national Planning Commission, who made the decisions about the objectives of the Plan, and directed the methods of planning. The Commission was appointed in March, 1950, completed work on a "Draft Outline" by June, 1951, and presented the final Plan in December, 1952. Its records are sufficiently ample to make possible analysis of its work and methods.

A 68-page edition of the Plan, entitled "The Five Year Plan —A Short Introduction", was issued by the Publications Division of the Ministry of Information and Broadcasting of the Government of India, in December, 1951. The following direct quotations from it are offered as documentation of Indian planners' decisions, and the reasons for the decisions concerning methods of planning. Under the sub-head, "Democratic Planning", it said.

"Now, what kind of an economic system do we need to achieve our aims? The prevailing inequality, economic stagnation and poverty indicate the necessity for change.

What are the alternatives?

At one extreme is some kind of totalitarianism. To many its appeal lies in its promise to satisfy quickly the basic human needs. It achieves results because under a totalitarian system the mobilization and direction of resources are in the hands of an all-powerful central authority. We know, however, that totalitarianism brings in its train violence, conflict, regimentation and the suppression of the individual. Now these things are repugnant to our national instincts and tradition. We cannot, therefore, give up the democratic ideal even if it were less profitable from the practical point of view. But is it really so?

Economic progress under democratic planning is perhaps less spectacular, but surely more enduring. It is achieved through the willing sacrifice and co-operation of the people. To carry out a plan in a democratic state means hard work and participation by every individual. It is a process of education which, while it secures the progress of the country,

also raises the quality of the individual. Moreover, the incidence of sacrifice which democratic planning demands is
equitably distributed in the society. On the whole, therefore, the democratic way is more advantageous even from a
narrow point of view. . . . "

The sociological rationale of the planners was quite clear.
It was thus cogently stated in the *Review of the First Five Year
Plan* :

"The first five year plan had a two-fold objective.
Firstly, it aimed at correcting the disequilibrium in the economy caused by the War and the partition of the country.
Secondly, it proposed to initiate simultaneously a process
of all-round balanced development which would ensure a
rising national income and a steady improvement in living
standards over a period. While the investment pattern envisaged in the plan was worked out with due regard to the
immediate objective and the resources immediately in sight,
the approach to the problems of mobilization and deploy-
ment of resources was formulated in the light of the long-
term objective. It was also emphasized that the aim was not
merely to plan within the existing socio-economic framework but to change this framework progressively and by
democratic methods in keeping with the larger ends of policy
enunciated in the Constitution. The first five year plan was
thus a step in a new direction, a step which involved greater
direct responsibility for the State in promoting development
and a greater degree of coordination of developmental activity in all economic sectors and at all levels."

While the statement just quoted says that the First Five Year
Plan took a step in a new direction, in terms of greater State
responsibility for promoting development and a greater degree of
co-ordination of development in all economic sectors, the Plan
itself said that in the area of social action, individuals and groups
would themselves have to decide what "contribution they are
best able to make." The planners expressed a conviction, " . . . that
in the process of development, the forces of growth from within
are not stifled by attempts abruptly to superimpose preconceived
patterns of life and activity." It said that "many in the adminis-

tration realize that official machinery by itself cannot carry out those development programmes which call for a great deal of initiative and participation on the part of the people themselves." And furthermore, that whatever financial assistance government could provide would be more effective if joined by the organized effort of local communities. The Plan spoke of generating human, as well as physical and economic, resources for the successful undertaking of next steps. Although it testified that, "In spite of the considerable developments in economic and social sciences in the last few decades, our knowledge of human motivation and of social processes is but limited," and that, "Responses of individuals or of groups of individuals and of classes cannot always be predicted in advance," the planners were nevertheless convinced that these components of a development programme, as well as all others, had to be planned.

There has at no time been any doubt on the part of most Indian leaders about the necessity of planning. To use their own expression, they were "plan-minded". They not only recognized the necessity of husbanding meagre resources, but they trusted the processes of intellectual and logical reasoning. The First Five Year Plan was the product of an attempt to strike a balance between the stern realities of prevailing conditions and situations, and ideals or models for the type of society which India desired to evolve. The necessity of solving some immediate problems was reflected in changes in, or modifications of, the Plan during the period between the completion of the Draft Outline in June, 1951, and the completion of the final Plan in December, 1952.

It is not easy to assess the influence of the wide public discussion of the Plan during this eighteen months' period, but it is relatively easy to identify the influence of the actions taken between the publication of the two Plans to solve the emergency problem of increased agricultural production. In spite of more than ten years of Grow-More-Food Campaigns, and because of the failure of monsoons over several seasons, the most urgent problem in 1950-51 was a great shortage of food grains. An agreement by the United States Government to provide food-grain loans, and the offer of the Ford Foundation to provide funds for pilot experimental programmes in village development, had led to the establishment of 15 pilot agricultural extension projects during

the period over which the Plan was being formulated. The negotiations were in process, but had not been consummated when
the Draft Outline was published. Instead of the community development programme which was launched before the final Plan
was published, the chief community-development-type programme proposed was "co-operative village management". A few
statements will serve to indicate the difference between the plan
proposed earlier and the one which was elaborated in the final
Plan.

"The Five Year Plan, A Short Introduction" said,

> "According to the Commission, co-operative village
> management should be regarded as the ultimate objective of
> agricultural reorganization. Under the scheme the entire area
> of a village becomes a single unit to be managed by the vil-
> lage. The holdings of cultivators are pooled, but their owner-
> ship rights are recognized and they receive compensation in
> the shape of ownership dividends to be paid to them at each
> harvest. Having thus provided for ownership, land is to be
> cultivated on a co-operative basis to the maximum advantage
> of the community. As a matter of convenience, however,
> it may be divided into blocks, each block to be cultivated by
> a family or a group of families. All workers, owners and non-
> owners, will be paid on the basis of the work done by
> them.
>
> Co-operative management is to be introduced in those
> villages where at least two-thirds of the owners or permanent
> tenants, who own not less than half the cultivated area of
> the village, are in favour of the scheme."

This must be recognized as a rationalization of planners, who
themselves would admit that it was not based on evidence that
villagers would accept it. Greater understanding of community
development processes was evidenced by many statements in the
final Plan which recognized that the Plan for two reasons had to
be pragmatic; first, because of the absence of precise data, some
estimates or assessments could not be firm; and second, because
popular enthusiasm for the changes proposed, which it was expected
would develop, would alter many situations and thus require
adjustment in the Plan in order that it might not lag behind the
dynamics which development itself would generate. Therefore,

while Indian planning, as all planning, tended to be more predictive than is possible, it has tended to become more pragmatic
in the light of programme experiences. This was to be expected,
for if the Plan provided "a sense of new direction", it would
generate forces too dynamic to be predicted with surety. This
pragmatism as a definite method or philosophy of planning is one
of the unique characteristics of the Indian Plan as contrasted with
five and seven-year plans of most other countries.

We offer a broad summary of the sociological rationale of
the Plan from the final First Five Year Plan:

> "The problem of development of an underdeveloped
> economy is one of utilizing more effectively the potential
> resources available to the community, and it is this which
> involves economic planning. But the economic condition of a
> country at any given time is a product of the broader social
> environment, and economic planning has to be viewed as an
> integral part of a wider process aiming not merely at the
> development of resources in a narrow technical sense, but at
> the development of human faculties and the building up of an
> institutional framework adequate to the needs and aspirations
> of the people.... Precisely for the reason that the develop-
> ment of a country is a somewhat long-term process, the insti-
> tutional and other factors which affect it can be changed to
> the desired extent and in the desired direction through con-
> scious effort."

This pretty clearly states the basic concept of the task of
planning as that of balancing what is to be desired with what
is feasible, balancing ideals with necessity. The Plan contemplated rapid change, but also deep and fundamental change.
In selecting socio-economic fields in which rapid change would
be possible, planners could afford to be pragmatic, even opportunistic. In areas of fundamental change, there was the necessity
of reckoning with the historic roots of Indian society. India's
planners as thoroughly assessed the historic societal forces which
had created the conditions in which India at the moment found
itself as they did the physical and economic resources of the
country.

Nothing was more apparent, or more widely recognized,

than the stagnation of village life and village organization and the traditional conservatism, if not the apathy, of the hundreds of millions of village people who constituted some 83 per cent of the nation's population. But these masses of people were assessed as one of the major potential resources for development, not only as manpower, but as the chief entrepreneurs of all local improvement undertakings, leaders of all local groups and institutions, and, for some time to come, the chief producers of the wealth of the country. Plans for developing and using these resources were a major component of the Plan.

Plans for increasing agricultural production were given first priority, not only because of the dire need for food supplies, but because agricultural producers constituted the majority of the working population of the country and because, as the Plan stated, it would be schemes for mobilizing local effort for local development which would activate these human resources. The community development programme was designed to provide the method by which millions of village people would be activated, and by which these schemes would spread all over the country. This programme was to be "practised democracy" in action, not only in terms of widespread participation of the masses, but in terms of local initiative and local responsibility. One of the Plan's statements could be said to be a maxim for democratic organization, namely, that, "It is a good general rule for any authority to try and pass the responsibility for a project to the authority immediately below it if, with a measure of help and guidance, the latter can do the job equally or nearly as well."

There would be no greater error than to assume that because Indian society is highly stratified by a caste structure that it is thereby, or ever has been, a totalitarian society. We doubt that the significance of the decision of Indian leaders to use democratic methods in planning and to prescribe democratic methods for development programme operation is adequately appreciated. We doubt that it is widely understood that these leaders had a deep conviction that the use of any other than democratic methods would violate the deepest value beliefs of Indian tradition and would run counter to the village socio-economic structure of the major portion of Indian society. The plans designed for a rural development programme contemplated the strengthening and use of the village community as the foundation and the grass roots institution or agency for carrying out all rural improvement programmes within the over-all, national democratic framework.

With respect to the process of national planning, between 1951 and 1961, the Planning Commission had had time and opportunity to develop its own planning assets. During that ten-year period, there had become available a great volume of information, much of it empirical data. Even more important, a rapidly increasing number of persons had become "plan-minded". By the late 1950's, a large number of intellectuals, not only university professors but others, were available and anxious to lend their research and analytical abilities to the problems of planning. In India, as in other newly-developing countries, before planning began, economists, for instance, had attempted to understand and explain their nation's economics. Their analyses, however, had been chiefly in terms of such matters as imports and exports on which they could assemble gross statistics. Such analyses were descriptive, not prescriptive. The rapidity with which the focus of economic analysis has changed is a measure of the rapidity with which the intellectual planning resources of India have been mobilized and expanded during the first ten years of planning. By the time the Third Five Year Plan was being formulated, a large number of economists who ten or fifteen years earlier would have eschewed research conducted with the objective of formulating prescriptions for change, were assiduously serving this objective. The authors' earlier personal observation was that universities, presumably the capstone of every nation's intellectual competence, were not mobilized or utilized in India to serve planning. This had changed markedly by 1960.

The prospect that India's intellectualism will be increasingly focussed more on the future than on the past is probably the greatest new asset which has developed over the past ten years in India. However, there have been developed over the period of national planning other more easily measurable planning assets. Series of quantitative facts and other types of information, not available when the First Five Year Plan was formulated, were available to the formulators of the Third Plan. More of them will be available for use in future planning. A National Sample Survey has made possible the formulation of a number of such series of data. Other series are being established as Ministries and other administrative bodies are accumulating and systematically recording information for future planning. The Programme Evaluation Organization, an arm of the Planning Commission, has made not only annual reports, but has conducted an increasing number of specific studies on one or another of the on-going planned programmes. The melting pot into which go all these data, information, judgments or opinions, and the recommendations of those employed in these activities, is the national Planning Commission. The Chairman of the Planning Commission is and always has been the Prime Minister, who serves as a direct link between the Planning Commission, the government Cabinet, and the national Parliament.

Most so-called developed countries aver that they do not practise national planning. As a matter of fact, some of them eschew such planning because they believe it smacks of totalitarianism. The only other two giant developing countries, Russia and China, whose plans were well known, have plans for developing totalitarian societies and governments. The prime purpose of India's planning is to develop a democratic society and democratic government. In that development, the means employed are part and parcel of these ultimate objectives. The purpose of our brief discussion of India's machinery, or organism of planning, is to present a description of a giant demonstration of democratic methods in national planning. We do not have the intimate information or competence to interpret the interplay between the great variety and differences of ideas and viewpoints which are bound to have been expressed within the national Planning Commission; the interplay between the Planning Commission and members of the Union Cabinet; between the State Legislatures and the national Parliament; or in the public press. We shall attempt only to make it clear that the Planning Commission is an organ of, not a substitute for, legislative and "popular", or people's planning. The Planning Commission has no responsibility for executing action programmes. It has no administrative or legislative authority or power. It is an advisory body, primarily to the Cabinet, and through the Cabinet to Parliament. It is an independent body, not beholden to any political party, nor indeed to Parliament. Its members are appointed by the government for indeterminate periods of tenure.

The resolution by which the Planning Commission was established made it responsible for continuous study and improvement of planning techniques, for appraisal of progress, and for evaluation and research. On its own initiative, it may seek the counsel of any Indian specialist, or of any outside specialist whose knowledge or skills it believes would be of assistance. The Commission's members themselves study planning techniques of other countries. They are professional, studious, scholarly, objective planners, and are implemented by an increasingly ample staff.

The basic elements of democracy in India's planning are the relationships between the various groups or bodies which are involved in formulating, reviewing, and finally adopting each Five Year Plan. These groups or bodies range from the Planning Commission which is responsible for analytically and objectively assessing the resources of the country, making recommendations, and periodically appraising progress, to Parliament which by necessity must be politically responsive to all sections of the nation's citizens. Under the Panchayati Raj system of government, there is another set of relationships; between local, district, State and national planning bodies.

As we noted above, planning by the national Planning Commission is continuous. As we implied, its planning methods have been increasingly skilful. While its basic role in national development has been the same, and while it has remained an independent and integral body, its membership has been altered as experience indicated it should. We describe briefly its organization and methods of work as of 1962.

The full-time members of the Planning Commission have varied from three to five, one of whom is Deputy Chairman. The Commission is related to Parliament through a Minister for planning. The number of part-time members has also varied. Each full-time member assumes responsibility for one or more broad but specific fields of development: national resources, agriculture, industry, social services. Each part-time member works on the specific field for which he was selected. All members are served by the technical staff of the Planning Commission. While differences among the judgments or opinions of the Planning Commission are not recorded, the fact that all recommendations are made by the whole Commission is evidence that discussion of what it will and does recommend is arrived at by democratic methods. Furthermore, its recommendations are made only after repeated discussions with members of the Union Cabinet and with the States.

Rather than to trust ourselves to describe accurately the working relationships between the different bodies which participate in planning, we present a number of quotations from Sir V. T. Krishnamachari's recent book on *Fundamentals of Planning in India*. Mr. Krishnamachari was Deputy Chairman of the Planning Commission from 1953 to 1960. He says:

> " ... The Planning Commission prepares papers for the Cabinet in the light of conclusions reached at its meetings on such matters, making its recommendations and bringing out the issues for decision. The Deputy Chairman and Members of the Planning Commission are invariably asked to the meetings of the Cabinet Committees or of the Cabinet at which these papers are discussed and given opportunities of explaining their views. The fact that the Prime Minister and the Finance Minister have been in touch with the thinking from the initial stages is of great value in ensuring that there is full knowledge of the implications. When proposals for changes in social and economic policies are made by Ministries, the Planning Commission is given an opportunity of expressing its views on them, before the Cabinet or the Cabinet Committee concerned considers them. The Deputy Chairman and the Members of the Planning Commission concerned are also invited to such meetings. In these ways, there is continuous touch between the Planning Commission on the one hand and the Ministries and the Cabinet and Cabinet Committees on the other....
>
> The link with the Cabinet also exists at the secretariat level. The Planning Commission is part of the Cabinet Organization and the 'demand for grants' for the Planning Commission is included in the budget demand for the Cabinet Secretariat. The Cabinet Secretary is also Secretary to the Planning Commission. In this way, coordination with Ministries is secured....
>
> ... Parliament constitutes a Consultative Committee con-

sisting of about 80 members to be in touch with the Commission at all stages commencing from the stage of formulation of the Plan. The Planning Commission meets the Consultative Committee frequently....

...In every State, there is a Cabinet Committee which is in close touch with the preparation of the plans and the manner in which they are carried out. This Committee is assisted by a committee of officials working under it for co-ordinating plans made by different Ministries and supervising implementation. In many States there are Advisory Committees of non-officials consisting of Members of Legislative Assemblies and others whose advice is likely to be useful...."

Once a national Plan is adopted, it is also a plan for each of the States, but a plan which is not made solely by the Planning Commission, or even solely by the Planning Commission with the types of interchange with the Union Cabinet which has just been described. The States do have a systematic voice in every stage of planning. There is a National Development Council, composed of the Prime Minister, members of the Planning Commision, and the Chief Ministers of all States. The National Development Council, like the Planning Commission, is only an advisory body. However, it greatly enlarges and distributes the right systematically to advise on all programmes for national development. Mr. Krishnamachari records that the National Development Council held nineteen meetings, generally two days each, between the first meeting in November, 1952 and May, 1961. He says that "The Union Ministers in charge of subjects that come up for discussion are invariably invited to meetings of the National Development Council. The Planning Commission prepares papers for the Council on subjects included in its agenda, in consultation with the Ministries concerned. Ministries are also requested to prepare papers relating to their own subjects whenever this is necessary...." The national plannnig organism of India is not, and cannot be, anything approaching central government domination to any greater extent than national parliamentary government is domination.

The national Parliament takes full responsibility for the adoption of each Five Year Plan. The role of the Planning Commission is primarily that of seeing that Parliament is informed in as great detail as possible of the resources which will be available for the following five-year period of national development, and that Parliament may be advised, by recommendations, of the best-reasoned list of, and priorities among, development programmes to be supported during that period.

For the period of the first two Plans, revisions have been made both up and down: in budget allocations, in new projects to be initiated, in project or programme target dates, or even in priorities. No Plan adopted on a given date is static. Based on the experiences of ten years of development in planning skills, the Third Five Year Plan, while just as specific and just as detailed for a given five-year period (1961-65), was formulated as a basis for long-term development. We quote from the chapter on "Long-Term Economic Development".

"A long-term plan of development embodying specific programmes and policies is an essential condition of successful planning for a country with deep-rooted social and economic problems, a large and growing population and widely varying conditions. Such a plan should be conceived not merely in broad national terms but should take into account the possibilities of development of resources in different regions of the country so as to spread the benefits of development as widely as possible without slowing down growth itself. The long-term plan should therefore supply a general pattern of economic and social development which would take into consideration the needs and possibilities of different areas and harmonise these into an integrated endeavour for national advancement. For working out a long-term plan on these lines, there is need for close and continuous collaboration between various Government agencies at the Centre and in the States and leading institutions engaged in scientific, economic and social research. The outline of the long-term plan will be filled in as more data and knowledge become available, and the Plan itself will be adjusted from time to time, in keeping with technological developments, greater knowledge of resources and the progress achieved in different branches of the economy. Work along these lines has already been initiated in the Planning Commission as well as by independent research institutions, and in the course of the next three years it is proposed to devote substantial resources to the preparation of an overall plan of development covering the period up to the end of the Fifth Plan."

The paragraph just quoted reflects the greatest lesson learned out of ten years of planned programme operation, namely that national planning must not only be continuous but integral. While it must be opportunistic in providing for improvement projects which will yield early, obvious results, it must foresee and provide for types of action which will yield less obvious but much greater long-term results. Some of the necessary long-term results cited in the paragraph above are: the development of resources of the various regions of the country, and the need for continuous collaboration between Centre and State government agencies and leading institutions engaged in scientific, economic and social research. An even greater requisite for long-term planning and accomplishment is not identified, namely, the increasingly more effective participation of local people and local groups in programme planning and programme operation responsibilities. This is probably the greatest long-time need and will without question be the most slow-developing planning asset. That this is an essential asset has been recognized since the beginning of planning, but not until the Panchayati Raj system of local government was instituted were effective steps taken to develop this asset. The First Five Year Plan said:

"Unless a village agency can assume responsibility and initiative for developing the resources of the village, it will be difficult to make a marked impression on rural life, for, only a village organization representing the community as a whole can provide the necessary leadership.... Legislative provisions may undoubtedly be helpful, but it is by arousing local enthusiasm for improving village conditions and promoting common effort that village panchayats can secure the largest measure of participation by the people in various programmes of development."

The Second Five Year Plan stated that:

"... The activities comprised within the community development and national extension programme should be regarded as an integral part of a programme for improving all aspects of rural life ... the essence of the approach is that villagers come together for bringing about social change are assisted in building up a new life for themselves and participate with increasing awareness and responsibility in the planning and implementation of projects which are material to their well being. If the programme provides them with new opportunities, in turn, through their active participation in its execution, they give it a distinctive quality and enlarge its scope and influence. . . . "

The Third Five Year Plan said:

"Although efforts were made in several States to prepare block plans specially in agriculture, in the main, the plans of States have been prepared independently of local plans. The inference to be drawn from this is that much more effort will be needed before local plans can become a distinctive stage in the initial preparation of a Five Year Plan. . . . "

District, block, and village planning as a part of, and in some fields of activity the most basic part of, national planning has long been contemplated. But those who are counted on to do this planning will, like national planners, have to learn by doing. It is exceedingly doubtful that they will learn very rapidly unless and until locally-organized groups are permitted, as the First Five Year Plan said, to accept major responsibility for their own development. To do, or attempt to do, what a group, whether voluntary or statutory, decides to do will provide any group its first lesson in planning.

This would not be to expect local people to lift themselves by their own bootstraps. It would be to expect, and know, that local face-to-face groups will develop both in confidence and competence if offered more assistance and less so-called "guidance" in carrying out what they want to do and have decided to do. To permit them to do this constitutes the great experiment of Panchayati Raj.

Panchayati Raj is based upon the assumption that tens of thousands of smaller-than-regional areas will be integrated in an effort for national advancement. To accomplish this may in some ways be more difficult, but in other ways easier, than regional or inter-regional integration. National planners and leaders, by selective allocation of funds, can guarantee the development of regional physical resources. They cannot by mere allocation of funds guarantee the development of millions of people and hundreds of thousands of local village groups and larger-than-local village groups. It is this task that Panchayati Raj hopefully will accomplish.

Panchayati Raj, a three-tier system of local government, is also a three-tier system of organization and action. It is expected that it will be a three-tier system of planning. In long-term development, it will provide a greatly-needed element in national planning, in which its primary role will be the effective development of the greatest undeveloped natural resource of the nation—the energized and effectively-mobilized human resources of the hundreds of millions of Indian rural people. India's planners and leaders have always known and appreciated this fact, as the above short quotations from the First, Second, and Third Plans indicate. There has, however, been inadequate evidence that they have realized the necessity that local planning, as a part of national planning, must develop from the bottom up. There is need that they more systematically prove the validity of the statements they have made in each of the three Five Year Plans.

In a way, Panchayati Raj is an end-product of community development. Sociologically and historically, it is an advanced step in community development, which is a body of methods based on a knowledge and employment of social skills. Social skills deal with the most dynamic, or potentially dynamic, resource in any society. The effective employment of these skills depends as much upon the validated findings of research as does the effective use of fertilizers or irrigation water. If the objective research already begun on the operation and functioning of Panchayati Raj is assiduously pursued and its findings utilized during the Third, Fourth and Fifth Plans, there is every reason to expect that the long-recognized missing link in national planning, namely local planning, will, like the other necessary aspects of planning mentioned in the long paragraph quoted from the Third Plan, have been supplied by 1975.

MAIN AUTHORITIES QUOTED OR CITED

Basu, Durga Das, *Annotated Constitution of India,* Das Gupta & Co. Ltd., Calcutta, June, 1953.

Basu, Durga Das, *Commentary on the Constitution of India,* Third Edition, S. C. Sarkar & Sons Ltd., 1-C, College Square, Calcutta-12, Vol. I, June, 1955; Vol. II, March, 1956.

The First Five Year Plan, Planning Commission, Government of India, December 1952.

Krishnamachari, V. T., *Planning in India,* Orient Longmans, Calcutta, 1961.

Krishnamachari, V. T., *Fundamentals of Planning in India,* Orient Longmans, Calcutta, 1962.

Menon, V. P., *The Story of the Integration of the Indian States,* Orient Longmans, Calcutta, 1955.

National Planning Committee (Indian Congress), Twenty-three Volumes on Various Areas of Development Planning, Vora & Vora, Bombay, 1948.

Panikkar, K. M., *A Survey of Indian History,* Asia Publishing House, Bombay, 1954.

Review of the First Five Year Plan, Planning Commission, Government of India, May, 1957.

Second Five Year Plan, Planning Commission, Government of India, 1956.

The Five Year Plan—A Short Introduction, Ministry of Information & Broadcasting, Government of India, New Delhi, December, 1951, (68 pp.).

The First Five Year Plan, A Draft Outline, Planning Commission, Government of India, July, 1951.

Third Five Year Plan, Planning Commission, Government of India, 1961.

CHAPTER 2

THE VILLAGE AS A SOCIAL STRUCTURE

OF the three major elements in the social structure of Indian society, the village is most important in the programmes of rural development. There is no plan to use the caste structure as a vehicle by means of which to carry on development activities. The same is true of the joint family. The village, however, is the grass roots organization through which the Community Development-Extension Programme is expected to operate. This is because India is a society of villages and will be for decades to come. More than 80 per cent of the total population of the nation, about 350 million people, live in rural villages. More than 50 per cent of national production comes from agriculture and an additional substantial per cent comes from village industries, both of them managed and operated by the people who live in villages. Nothing was more definitely stated in the First Five Year Plan and more universally accepted than the purpose to strengthen and use the village as a unit of action in the development programme.

It is believed that each ancient Indian village was as self-sufficient a local society as ever existed any place in the world. Sir Charles Metcalfe, writing in 1832, said, "The village communities are little republics, having nearly everything they want within themselves, and almost independent of any foreign relations. They seem to last where nothing else lasts. Dynasty after dynasty tumbles down; revolution succeeds revolution . . . , but the village community remains the same. This union of village communities, each one forming a separate little state in itself, has, I conceive, contributed more than any other cause to the preservation of the people of India, through all the revolutions and changes which they have suffered, and is in a high degree conducive to their happiness, and to the enjoyment of a great portion of freedom and independence."

Sir Henry Maine, Administrator of the Indian Empire, said in 1871, this "brotherhood (the village), besides the cultivating families who form the major part of the group, comprises families hereditarily engaged in the humble arts which furnish the little society with articles of use and comfort. It includes a village watch and a village police, and there are organized authorities for the settlement of disputes and the maintenance of civil order."

The statement just quoted, and many others which could be cited, many of them made in the early days of national planning, are indexes to the widespread belief that each village was a ready-made social unit which could be utilized and, with some assistance, be made largely responsible for its own economic and social development. To the extent that this were true, it would favourably condition the possibility of rapid local development. To the extent that there was any fallacy in this belief, such units could negatively condition the operations of rural development, the basic objective of which was to be the transformation of old, traditional social structures.

Germane to the question of whether the unity and solidarity of the ancient village, described by Metcalfe and Maine maintained in 1950, when development planning began, were two significant, known facts. First was the fact that each village in the past was far more highly isolated from other units of social action than it is today. Second was the fact that the otherwise Utopian picture of village unity was marred by the existence of castes. In India, as in all other countries, small population centres, which were economically and socially viable under conditions of physical and social isolation will not be viable under the impact of improvements in transportation and communication facilities. The average population size of Indian villages in 1950 was 500, but many villages had already grown into population centres with more than 2,000 dwellers. This trend would be bound to continue. Under the impact of developed means of transportation and communication and under the necessity for increased State and Central government services to local people, it was inconceivable that India would long remain so completely a society of villages, each village a self-sufficient, viable socio-economic unit.

It was, of course, known that few if any of India's more than 500,000 villages were viable economic units and therefore could not be integral social units. For a long time there have been many inter-village relationships. Within-village relationships were therefore not the only, and in a number of ways were not the dominant, set of social relationships between individuals and families. Marriage and caste relations were inter-village. There was, therefore, the probability that loyalty to these other systems of human relationships would be greater and more demanding than loyalty to the village community in which an individual or a family resides. Added to this was the question of whether the village had ever been the integral and self-sufficient social unit which it was presumed to have been in ancient times. Even if that had been true, facts about the changed status of Indian society over time were well known. Mogul and British administrations had not only established units of administration larger than villages, but had taken over and made government officials out of some village leaders who in the past had been wholly accountable to the village panchayat (council of village elders.). The patwaris (village accountants) and often the headmen (chairmen of the village councils) thus no longer owed their sole allegiance to the local community. District courts were established, to which villagers could appeal against decisions made by village panchayats. In addition to these forces of erosion in village integrity was the fact that, over the centuries of feudal and colonial rule, changes in the field of economic, social, and political life were continuous, even if slow. Equally important with these secular trends was the fact that old caste and joint-family groups remained strong and in some ways divisive, in villages. Villages were more social organizations than they were organisms. Village factions, like local groups of feuding families in many local areas of the world where people have lived generation after generation under the imperious control of tight local social organization, were rife in many villages.

In the light of these facts, and the fact that village people and villages as units of social action were expected to play such prominent roles in India's development programme, it would have been pertinent to raise such questions as the following: To what extent and in what ways can old social structures which, for at least a century, have not played a role in the national society's progress be utilized in planned future national development. Assuming a high degree of validity in the statements of Metcalfe and Maine, what is known about changes in the functioning of the old traditional village structure, and in that structure itself, in the many decades which have intervened between the time when these statements were made and the present. Are there sources of information to prove the validity or invalidity of Metcalfe's and Maine's descriptions of the old traditional village structure and functions. Have any of the changes in village structure and function, which are known to have occurred during the last century, made village communities more effective social units for promotion and administration of action programmes, or less effective units, than they were when they were highly self-sufficient little folk societies. What can be contributed to the answers to some or all of these questions from knowledge developed in the experiences of other nations or societies which, in the past, have moved steadily from an economy and culture of villages toward a national economy and culture. It would appear that questions like these were not raised and answers to them sought in the same assiduous manner as were questions about the economic structure of Indian society; that a knowledge of what sort of social structures villages were seems to have been taken for granted.

It is, of course, impossible to know, with any precision, the social structure of the villages of ancient India, but the story of the changes which have taken place in that structure since ancient times can probably best be visualized by first describing what may be called a model structure of the traditional ancient Indian village; follow this by a description of the most universal and consistent modifications which are known to have occurred in that model; and then describe the typical Indian village social structure of 1950. Such an analysis would probably lessen the faith that the old pristine village still exists in India. The description of the model of the traditional village could not, of course, take into account variations in village structure in the different regions of India. It would assume the integrity of the Hindu caste hierarchy and describe the structure of the ancient village as if it were predicated solely on the structure of that hierarchy. Maybe also the information on changes which have taken place over time could not have easily been obtained by those who counted so strongly on the village and village panchayat as agencies of social change. Most of our information on village structure and village change, as of 1950 and since, comes from recent detailed anthropological studies made since or near that date.

The traditional village would be represented in the model as having had a perfect division of labour among the various caste groups that lived in the village, every group dependent on all other groups and depended on by all other groups. Every resident of the village was an active and loyal member of some one, but only one, of these caste groups. Because each village was relatively isolated from all other villages, it was by necessity, and in reality, an integral economic and ritual unit and therefore an integral social unit. In its organization, the priests and the teachers, the Brahman caste, were at the top and the scavengers, an untouchable caste, were at the bottom of the hierarchy. Changes in the occupational division of labour, based on castes, can be fairly precisely observed, and it can be sociologically taken for granted that these easily identifiable changes have been accompanied or followed by important but not so easily observed cultural and psychological changes.

In this traditional village system, each caste was a specialized occupational group, in fact had a monopoly in that occupation. The member of no occupational caste was permitted to work at any other occupation. The system was an accepted and sanctioned arrangement by which members of all castes, and thus every person living in the village, was guaranteed a complement of the services and goods which the village as a whole provided. These services and goods ranged from the physical to the spiritual necessities of life. In the case of united village action, which was completely controlled by ritual, each caste provided persons for its role in each ceremony or on each occasion. In the case of interrelations and interdependencies which did not require united village action, each caste made its own arrangements with other castes. The Brahman, who provided no physical goods and did no manual labour, spiritually and educationally served some families of each of the other castes and in turn was supplied with all the physical necessities of life. Similarly the scavenger, even though an untouchable, was guaranteed by the whole village which he served in a number of ways, a place to live, and was provided goods and even some services by families which he had arranged permanently to serve. These inter-family relations, passed down from generation to generation, were not precarious or arbitrary, but a complete system of social relationships.

Whether or not this traditional mode of the perfect, economically self-sufficient organization of the village existed everywhere in India, it was at one time sufficiently prevalent to lead a number of students of castes to conclude that this established set of relations was as much, if not more, the foundation of the caste system as it was a proliferation of that system. Cox, for instance, said, "The caste structure is fundamentally a labour structure, a system of interrelated services originating in specialized groups and traditionalized in a religious matrix." Whatever the merits of the age-old arguments about the cause and effect relationships between castes and occupations, it is a well-documented fact that caste and inter-caste social relationships, and occupational and inter-occupational economic relationships provided the organic structure of the ancient Indian village. Furthermore, there can be no doubt that these two major components of village socio-economic structure, more than anything else, served to perpetuate the hundreds of thousands of village societies which today exist in India. To the extent that they are dysfunctional elements in planned programmes of change they negatively condition villages as effective social organizations, vehicles, or agencies for development programme implementation.

Notwithstanding the conserving and conservative influences of village caste and occupational structures, it is not historically tenable to believe they have not been gradually changing for a long time. Documentation of change in castes is more ample than documentation of occupational structure. But Professor Ghurye's analytical account, gleaned from sacred literature from the Vedic period to Indian independence, relates not only the rise of new occupations but also the rise and decline of the sanctions which fixed the status of the different castes in the caste hierarchy, even during ancient times. His review of continuing changes under British rule brings our information up approximately to the period during which detailed village studies have been made.

The British administration enacted a number of laws which weakened caste rule, such as permitting Hindu widow marriage, removal of "caste disabilities", and legalizing caste inter-marriages. But it also did some things that tended to emphasize caste lines.

British administrators, following the popular practice, used caste names as a convenient mode of description of persons. Professor Ghurye says, "This procedure reached its culmination in the Census of 1901 under the guidance of Sir Herbert Risley of ethnographic fame. With a view to helping 'us towards presenting an intelligible picture of the social grouping of that large proportion of the people of India which is organized, admittedly or tacitly, on the basis of caste' the Census Commissioner changed the classification of 1891 into one based on 'social precedence as recognized by the native public opinion at the present day and manifesting itself in the facts that particular castes are supposed to be the modern representatives of one or other of the castes of the theoretical Hindu system'." More important from the standpoint of village organization, was the fact that British administration as was said above, weakened the integrity of village-functioning unity by superseding the jurisdictions of caste and village panchayats by establishing the jurisdictions of district and State courts. It took over, as government servants, some of the officials of the village who previously had been accountable to the village panchayats.

Professor Ghurye also says, "To sum up, social and religious privileges and disabilities born of caste are no longer recognized in law and only partially in custom. . . . Caste no longer rigidly determines an individual's occupation, but continues to prescribe almost in its old rigour the circle into which one has to marry. One has still to depend very largely on one's caste for help at critical periods of one's life, like marriage and death. One's closest companions and friends are mainly delimited by the circle of one's caste. . . . Caste has thus become the centre of an individual's altruistic impulse and philanthropic activities. The existence of definite organization has rallied round the caste the feelings of consciousness of kind."

The influence of caste hierarchical organization on village social unity is essentially that the caste hierarchy established its ideological, and to a considerable extent its practical, domination in ancient times. Modifications in both practices and ideologies have continuously occurred ever since. There has been modification and proliferation of caste occupational groups. Caste boundaries have been violated by caste inter-marriages. Vertical mobility upward of some members of the lower castes has occurred, and vertical mobility downward of many members of higher castes has been prevalent. British administration introduced rules and practices which violated old caste boundaries; instituted a number of measures to raise the status of members of lower castes; and established legal jurisdictions which weakened caste and village panchayat positions. But caste is still a dominant influence in the grouping of persons in villages.

The typical Indian village is not now a *gemeinschaft*. The typical joint family is. In many ways the Indian village is not an integral community. Castes in most villages are communities. As Ghurye makes clear, the great changes in the caste organization rationalized by intellectuals have not been dominant realities in most villages. The influence of these rationalizations has not been great in the hundreds of thousands of villages where the great mass of Indian citizens lives. But it is not an abnormal social phenomenon that caste structure and casteism are strongest in relatively isolated local communities.

In recent years a number of anthropological studies have focussed fairly sharply on an analysis of village unity or lack of unity. From the findings of these studies we summarize categorically our interpretation of what Indian village social structure now approximately is. S. C. Dube says: "Village communities all over the Indian sub-continent have a number of common features. The village settlement, as a unit of social organization, represents a solidarity different from that of the kin, the caste, and the class, and plays a vital role as an agency of socialization and social control. Each village is a distinct entity, has some individual mores and usages, and possesses a corporate unity. Different castes and communities inhabiting the village are integrated in its economic, social, and ritual pattern by ties of mutual and reciprocal obligations sanctioned and sustained by generally accepted conventions. Inside the village, community life is characterized by economic, social, and ritual co-operation existing between different castes. Important administrative functions are performed by the village council composed generally of village elders and village officials. Notwithstanding the existence of groups and factions inside the settlement, people of the village can, and often do, face the outside world as an organized, compact whole. . . . "

M. N. Srinivas also states why it is assumed that the village has unity, but he also raises questions which will provide the focus for our attempt to contribute to the answers to the five questions raised earlier in this chapter. He says, "The unity of the village is a point made by many of the contributors to this series. A body of people living in a restricted area, at some distance from other similar groups, with extremely poor roads between them, the majority of the people being engaged in agricultural activity, all closely dependent upon each other economically and otherwise, and having a vast body of common experience, must have some sense of unity. The point is so simple and obvious that it seems hardly worth making it but for the existence of the institution of caste. Caste is even today an institution of great strength, . . . (and caste) ties are so powerful that a few anthropologists have been led into asserting that the unity of the village is a myth and that the only thing which counts is caste." He concludes with the following statement: "The unity of the village is not then an axiom to be taken for granted, but something that has to be shown to exist." But in his full report on The Social Structure of a Mysore Village, Srinivas says, "The village is a unity in several senses of the term. It is, firstly, a physical unity. If the monsoon fails, it fails for everyone. Formerly, when there was an attack of cholera or plague or small-pox, the entire village acted as one, and moved away to a different place. . . . They all joined together to propitiate the deities presiding over these diseases. The disease was ritually driven out of the village—the village boundary has a certain ritual significance."

The following are quotations from authors of other chapters in this same book. C. Rosser says of a Himalayan village, "Malana is essentially a 'hermit' village. It has developed an almost fanatical sense of difference, of village cohesion, and of intense group loyalty." Kathlun Gough says of a Tanjore village, the "unity of the whole village overrides the separateness of each caste." F. G. Bailey, who studied an Oriya village, records that "The factors which underline such unified actions" of villages which he observed are, "Firstly, the majority of the villagers have a common background. They have grown up with one another and have a common experience which goes back for generations. This is an imponderable factor, but nonetheless real. Secondly, they have a common interest in their economic life." These studies, and others from which no quotations are presented here, name a number of other unifying factors or functions of the village, such as the existence of a village shrine, common propitiation of the same gods, celebration of national holidays, ceremonials which enlist the services of all or most castes, emergencies of different kinds that jeopardize all residents, the existence of village panchayats, and village pride on the part of all who live in the village and all others who were born and reared there.

A number of those making these research reports, and they were persons each of whom had lived in a given village for from nine months to a year and a half, however, cite many situations and types of behaviour which, when continuously and meticulously observed, raise questions about the functional, and even the structural, unity of village social organization. For example: E. J. Miller says, "Whatever internal self-subsistence there may have been in the *desams* of the eighteenth century and earlier, it is very difficult nowadays in Kerala to point to any unit as a clearly demarcated, coherent, independent village community." W. H. Newell says of the Gaddi Village in Punjab which he studied, "In spite of the fact that nearly every village consists of only one caste, caste-consciousness is much stronger than village-consciousness." Miss Gough, who was quoted concerning the unity of a Tanjore village, says, "Today, however, the village structure presents no longer a nice balance of unities and antagonisms between caste and kinship groups in a self-sufficient little republic. For obviously, the economic basis of the system has been fundamentally upset within the last fifty to seventy years." McKim Marriott, in reporting his study of "Social Structure and Change in a U.P. Village", goes deeper than most of the others in the analyses of the various groupings of the village. After reporting on his analysis of "economic, kinship, rank and prestige, and convivial groupings," he concludes, "The many tiny and frail convivial gatherings on ceremonial occasions in Kishan Garhi maintain a minimal net-work of positive inter-group connections among people across the ordinary formal lines of economic, caste and kinship divisions. But at no time in the knowable past has there been any more comprehensive organization than that which they provide. There seems never to have been any form of associational behaviour which regarded the village as a unit in which all groups have a shared equity, or which looked on village problems as the problems of all."

It is not presumed that these quotations from a relatively few detailed village studies provide answers to the five questions we posed above. Nor is it presumed that complete answers can be given from any and all available sources of information. The authors of the present book, even though they have visited hundreds of villages in all parts of India and visited with thousands of villagers, know that they cannot answer the questions from their relatively surface observations. They do not believe that the intellectuals of India, few of whom were born and reared in villages, can be expected to know all the subtle human relationships of the people who live in the villages. While, therefore, researchers are generally not too apt in providing practical answers to problems which arise in current action programmes, their findings on the currently functioning social structure of villages, together with objective, historical accounts, should provide the most trustworthy understanding upon which to base an answer to the question of how village social structure conditions rural development. We catalogue our interpretations of what research findings have to contribute as an answer to that question.

1. Every village studied has a degree of social unity. This unity is most pronounced in villages like the Himalayan village of Malana studied by Rosser, which are fairly isolated both physically and culturally, and is most tenuous in villages like a Mysore village reported in the same volume by Alan R. Beals, whose residents have many, almost daily, contacts with urban centres.

2. Wherever village unity is easily identifiable, it is of various kinds and textures. The most pronounced village unity is based on the sentiments of families whose ancestors have long lived in a given village, and who, no matter to which caste they belong or to what extent they are in some ways segregated from other castes, each and all think, and know, that this is their village. This unity is greatly diluted in villages many of whose members spend much of their time outside their home village and have a number of interests which are served by participation with nonlocal village persons who share their interests.

3. Even then, on many ceremonial occasions, all or most

persons who were born and reared in a given village, participate if possible in these ceremonies and play their roles in the rituals which are a part of many of the ceremonies. Furthermore, many, if not most of them, worship their old village and family gods.

4. Local village unity, however, is not the only social unity or solidarity in which they participate. Their caste loyalties and caste participation are not confined to their home village. Occupational, business, and political activities require functioning in wider than local village groups and require a degree of loyalty to these groups and their objectives. All such loyalties in one way or another compete with loyalties to and practices of village solidarity.

The elements which have tended to dilute and even weaken old village solidarities and loyalties, like those which cement them, have developed out of the day-by-day life and living in local villages. The basis of old solidarities is traditional and emotional. Most of the trends which tend to weaken this solidarity are of fairly recent origin. These trends are moving with increased acceleration, most of them being encouraged and promoted by development programmes. Some of the old solidarities like that of castes are being officially discouraged. Some of the old instruments of village organization, like the jajmani system, are not encouraged and hereditary village panchayats are no longer sanctioned. These provided the village leaders in the past. Now, new bases for leadership are being sought and activities requiring new types of organization and new types and levels of leadership are being promoted. The village is expected to develop and provide all of these. The sociological problem is a compound of the questions of what the village has inherited from the past by way of social organization which can assist development, and what is required of the village if it is to play the roles expected of it in the development programme.

It would appear that the typical Indian village possesses the following qualifications of a local community, as a vehicle, instrument, or agency for promoting and operating local development programmes. Its residents think of the village as a local entity. It has a well and long-established social structure or organization. It has a recognized set of local leaders. But as a social organization it is based primarily on the caste hierarchy, and the leaders are primarily caste and faction leaders. While it is not assumed in the Community Development programme that all old, local leaders will be shunned, there is a determination that many new leaders, irrespective of caste status, shall be developed and thereby be given new local community status. Furthermore, it is definitely determined that nothing shall be done to strengthen the caste structure and everything possible shall be done to transcend caste boundaries. It is also determined that village leaders and village groups must now assume different kinds of responsibilities and exercise initiative for types of undertakings which, in the traditional past, were not a part of village activities.

The present village structure is a favourable conditioning factor because most villages are organized social structures. It will be unfavourable to the extent that old tendencies to be self-sufficient socio-economic structures will impede the inevitability and necessity of larger, more functional socio-economic structures. The factors making for change will increase. Those making for preserving old village structures will diminish in their influence. India will, for some time, continue to be a society with a predominant village structure, but village structure will not escape the necessity and inevitability of change. One problem of over-all economic, social, and political development will be not only how to make village social structure more democratic, but how to develop inter-village associations, even inter-village institutions, which will be required as villages by necessity become more interdependent and more co-operative with those who live beyond their old local socio-economic village boundaries. There are research findings which can be utilized to provide some guidance for both of these accomplishments. These findings provide information on why and how persons previously not associated together intimately do form new action groups, how they select and utilize their own chosen leaders; and what factors operate to enhance group solidarity and continued effective group action. The researches have been on the processes of new group formation, local community mobilization by means of multiple-group co-ordination, the development of local leaders from various types and levels of group action, the development of local self-governing institutions, and the use of democratic methods, as objectives in themselves, for the accomplishing of all of these other objectives.

Practically all of these studies have, however, been made in open class societies where there are few, if any, social barriers to an individual's participation in any and all types of special interest and special purpose groups. The necessity for the formation of such groups was not foreseen by development programme planners and directors because of their assumption that each village was an integral social group and also because of their unawareness of the roles played by special interest and special purpose groups in mobilizing those living in local communities for effective local action. As we shall see in later chapters, it took a number of years of programme operating experience to reveal to directors that their administrative structure would have to be accommodated to today's functioning village social organization rather than to an assumed village organization which, if it ever existed, does not now exist.

Under the necessity of maximum local group responsibility and initiative, and the greatest possible effectiveness of local group action, India's Community Development programme is, and will for some time to come be, the greatest group dynamic laboratory in the world. In this laboratory, increased understanding of group processes will develop, and, as would be expected, some processes that have been thoroughly validated will be violated or not used as effectively as they could be. These experiences will be assessed at a number of places in this book which describe programme operation. They will be discussed in more formal sociological frames of reference in later chapters on planned social change which discuss the process and problems of community develop-ment. It will also be noted at various places that development programme experiences have developed a surer knowledge of what the Indian village is and what it is not than development planners had in 1950. But none of the things which either research or development experience shows, reveals anything other than that the village structure of Indian society conditions both favour-ably and unfavourably all programmes for rural development.

MAIN AUTHORITIES QUOTED OR CITED

Cox, O. C., *Caste, Class and Race,* Doubleday and Company, Inc., New York, 1948.

Dube, S. C., *Indian Village,* Routledge and Kegan Paul, Ltd., London, 1956.

Dube, S. C., *India's Changing Villages,* Routledge and Kegan Paul, Ltd., London, 1958.

Ghurye, G. S., *Caste and Class in India,* Popular Book Depot, Bombay, 1957.

Lewis, Oscar, *Village Life in Northern India,* University of Illinois Press, Urbana, 1958.

Maine, Sir Henry, *Village Communities in the East and West,* New Edition, John Murray, London, 1890.

Marriott, McKim, (Ed.), *Village India,* University of Chicago Press, 1955.

Mayer, A. C., *Caste & Kinship in Central India,* University of California Press, 1960.

Metcalfe, Sir Charles, Report of the Select Committee of the House of Commons, 1832, Vol. III, Appendix 84, p. 331, cited in Srinivas, M. N. (Ed.). *India's Villages.*

Srinivas, M. N. (Ed.) *India's Villages,* Asia Publishing House, Bombay, Second (Revised) Edition, 1960.

Series of Indian Village Studies, Mimeographs, University of California, Berkeley, 1958-59.

Wiser, W. H., *The Hindu Jajmani System,* Lucknow Publishing House, Lucknow, 1958.

CHAPTER 3

CASTES AND THE CASTE SYSTEM

THREE basic social structures—villages, castes, and joint families—importantly condition programmes of change and development in India. Castes and casteism pervade all types of human relations and dominate many sentiments. It is primarily an understanding of these human relationships and the sentiments which buttress them, not the caste system itself, to which we shall, as sociologists, turn our attention.

For those who have not had the opportunity to read much of the immense, and diverse, literature on castes, we shall quote liberally from that literature and cite additional sources. Otherwise we shall describe the caste system in broad sociological generalizations which we believe are valid. Even if these generalizations are valid, they, like all generalizations, will have both strength and weakness. Their strength will be that they do not become so involved in the tremendous diversities which exist as to fail to emphasize the common denominators of all castes. Their weakness will, of course, be that they disregard the many variations, the great diversities, which exist among the three thousand or more castes which are in India. It is our judgment, however, that the many and repeated attempts to relate the diversity of details about the great varieties of castes in India have tended to obscure rather than reveal the fact that caste is little, if anything, more than a universal historical phenomenon of social stratification in all developing societies. Whether or not the doctrine about the sanctity of castes in India was more firmly established, and more widely accepted, than in other countries, it was this doctrine and not the physical existence of hundreds of thousands of separate kinship and occupational social groups which constituted a conditioning factor to development when the great programme of change was launched in India in 1950.

The first and foremost prevailing condition was that a person's caste membership not only directed all his interpersonal relationships, but dictated his concept of who he was as a human being. This would automatically be an obstacle to the development of an egalitarian society. Compounded with the joint-family system, a person's caste would condition the opportunity he had to secure employment and determine the kind of jobs which would be open to him. Castes also constitute the socio-economic structure of villages, in which eighty-three per cent of the people of India live. Castes constitute the most universal social structure of Indian society, and no society in the world is more highly structured or stratified. If, therefore, we are to attempt to show a measure of the influence of the caste system on national development, we must attempt to describe that system and show how deep and firm its roots are.

Until fairly recent years, the chief contributions students have attempted to make to an appreciation of the depth and strength of the social and psychological roots of India's caste system were to document its antiquity and its original religious sanction. Those scholars who have attempted to document the antiquity of castes and those who have demonstrated that castes are primarily kinship groups have made great contributions to an understanding of what might be called the social psychology of casteism. Each of the many scholars offers his own definition of caste. Risley says that caste is "a collection of families or groups of families bearing a common name, claiming a common descent from a mythical ancestor, human or divine; professing to follow the same hereditary calling; and regarded by others who are competent to give an opinion as forming a single homogeneous community." Ketkar says that a caste is a "social group having two characteristics: (1) Membership is confined to those who are born of members and includes all persons so born; (2) the members are forbidden by inexorable social law to marry outside the group." Hutton says, "From the point of view of the individual member of a caste, the system provides him from birth to death with a fixed social milieu from which neither wealth nor poverty, success nor disaster can remove him unless, of course, he so violate the standards of behavior laid down by his caste that it spews him forth—temporarily or permanently."

Professor Ghurye, a lifelong student of Indian castes and himself an Indian, does not so much presume to define caste as the others we have quoted, but in Chapter I of his book, *Caste and Class in India,* discusses "features" of the caste system. He says there are six of these features which we synopsize:

1. Castes were groups each with a well-developed life of its own, the membership whereof, unlike that of voluntary associations and classes, was determined not by selection, but by birth.
2. Everywhere in India, there was a definite scheme of social precedence among the castes, with a Brahman at the head of the hierarchy.
3. There are restrictions on feeding and social intercourse; ... there are minute rules as to what sort of food or drink can be accepted by a person and from what caste.
4. Segregation of individual castes or groups of castes in a village is the most obvious mark of civil privileges and disabilities, and it has prevailed in more or less definite forms all over India.
5. There was a "lack of unrestricted choice of occupation: ... caste or a group of allied castes considered some of the callings as its hereditary occupation, to abandon which in pursuit of another, though it might be more lucrative, was thought not to be right."
6. There are "restrictions on marriage—most of the groups, whose features I have attempted to characterize above, are further divided into a number of sub-groups, every one of which forbids its members to marry persons from outside it. Each of these groups, popularly known as sub-castes, is thus endogamous."

As we said above, it is not our intention to discuss caste structure except as this structure conditions human relationships and sentiments. We have not found any more complete and vivid description of how caste membership does this than Hutton's quotation from Wilson, which follows:

"Caste gives its directions for recognition, acceptance, consecration and sacramental dedication, and vice versa, of a human being on his appearance in this world. It has for infancy, pupilage, and manhood, its ordained methods of sucking, sipping, drinking, eating, and voiding; of washing, rinsing, anointing, and smearing; of clothing, dressing, and ornamenting; of sitting, rising, and reclining; of moving, visiting and traveling, of speaking, reading, listening, and reciting; and of meditating, singing, working, playing, and fighting. It has its laws for social and religious rights, privileges, and occupations; for instructing, training, and educating; for obligation, duty, and practices; for divine recognition, duty and ceremony; for errors, sins, and transgressions; for intercommunion, avoidance, and excommunication; for defilement, ablution, and purification; for fines, chastisements, imprisonments, mutilations, banishments, and capital executions. It unfolds the ways of committing what it calls sin, accumulating sin, and putting away sin; and of acquiring merit, dispensing merit, and losing merit. It treats of inheritance, conveyance, possession, and dispossession; and of bargains, gain, loss, and ruin. It deals with death, burial, and burning; and with commemoration, assistance, and injury after death. It interferes, in short, with all the relations and events of life and with what precedes and follows . . . life."

The above compact, yet detailed, summary of how completely the behaviour of a member of a caste, no matter of what caste, is dictated still does not include the many prescribed intercaste relationships which were just as rigidly enforced, in many cases by law. It was upon the rules for these intercaste relationships that the whole caste hierarchy was built. It was the elaborate proliferation of these rules and the meticulous enforcement of them that guaranteed the separateness, and the integrity, of each caste. It was this complete separation of the various social strata which made India's class structure unique. It was the rules prescribing degrees of separation which constituted the sociology and psychology of the caste hierarchy. The enforcement of physical distance between castes was the index to the enforced social distance between status classes which came to constitute India's greatest obstacle to the development of the kind of society which the Constitution declared in 1949 India would seek to build.

Neither the universality of the caste system nor its influence on future national development rests on whether its origin was based on differences in colour, whether or not it was of Aryan origin, or whether all sub-castes are in and of themselves real castes. It rests fundamentally on the extent to which caste influences the prospective economic, social, and political opportunities of hundreds of millions of Indian citizens. Theories about its origin have, however, not only served to perpetuate but also to proliferate the caste system over the centuries. To the extent that these theories, formulated by intellectuals, were accepted by the masses, they dictated the day-by-day relationships between individuals and groups and became the sanctions for what was right and proper and the taboos for what was wrong. Socio-religious sanctions and taboos which have existed for centuries cannot be abolished by mere constitutional or legislative enactment. To have an appreciation of the immense task which India prescribed for itself when its Constitution abolished untouchability, we present as real and vivid a picture as possible of the extent to which inequalities among castes had become not only socially practised but socially sanctioned. While students of comparative culture cannot accept Hutton's belief that there was no other system of social stratification like India's caste system, all will probably accept his judgment that taboos, prevalent in all societies, and especially prevalent in primitive societies, were the basis for the meticulous classification of all groups of people in India into a hierarchy of castes. What the members of a caste were not permitted to do almost automatically became prescriptions for what they must do; and, therefore, what it was their bounden duty to do. Even a brief, and incomplete, description of the do and don't prescriptions which controlled the behaviour of members of different castes and their relationships to and inter-relationships with other castes will serve to show how thoroughly caste rights and duties structured every facet of Indian society.

The most functionally fundamental among the prescriptions were those which determined what occupation each member of each caste must pursue. The caste member was as definitely initiated into his occupation by birth as he was born into a given family and into a given caste. The least functionally fundamental were those which prescribed untouchability. It is not socially abnormal, however, that these less functional prescriptions were the most rigidly enforced because they served to safeguard the status system of the whole society. To violate them would compromise the status of the very person whose position, whether in local communities or national affairs, was the most important thing in the world to him. The superior person in each social contact was sure to insist on the outward manifestations of inferiority on the part of any other person whose status was below his.

It is impossible to exaggerate the extent to which prescriptions for maintaining the social distance between various castes were proliferated. The whole set of gradations prescribed among castes was based on the idea of purity of the Brahman and the utter impurity of the untouchables. Most fantastic was the belief that the breath, or even the shadow, of an untouchable would pollute another person. In some places untouchables were required to wear cloths over their mouths in order that their breath might not pollute. In Poona they were not permitted within the city walls between 3 p.m. and 9 a.m. because during the early morning and late afternoon sun their bodies cast long shadows. In at least one area there were not only untouchables but unseeables. A caste of washerwomen had to do their work between midnight and daybreak and not show themselves except during the hours of darkness. All castes other than Brahmans were graded in terms of their purity by the extent of provisions to safeguard them against pollution by untouchables. The untouchable who could not, for instance, come closer than 124 feet to a Brahman might come within half that distance to an intermediate caste person and as near as seven feet to some lower caste person. In another area the specified gradations of distance were 96 feet down to 36 feet, the specified distance from Brahmans always being the greatest. Wells were polluted if a low caste man drew water from them. The water of a stream was polluted if a Sudhra was permitted to walk across a bridge over it. A low caste man could pollute an idol in a temple if he came closer than seven feet and if he did not cover his mouth and nostrils with his hands. Even the glance of a man of low caste, falling on a cooking pot would necessitate throwing away the contents of the pot. Public roads which came near temples could not be travelled by untouchables. There were places where untouchables were required to carry sticks or brooms not only so that they might be easily identified but to designate their status. There were places where all castes except Brahmans were especially forbidden to cover that part of their body above the waist. In rules for purification after one had been polluted, water for purification could not be brought by a Sudhra. Those of lower castes could accomplish purification much easier than could Brahmans.

The list of specifications for physical distance, and therefore for social distance, between the castes, especially between the untouchables and the Brahmans, could be extended almost indefinitely. Even the short list we have given here was not universal. Some of the specifications prevailed in one area and some in another. Our purpose has been only to illustrate the fantastic extent to which these rules went, but even more to identify the historic fact that a group of persons who had lived under these rules for generations cannot be expected quickly or completely to rid themselves of the attitudes and feelings which had been engendered in them because of the practice of these rules.

The Wisers, who for years lived and worked among untouchables, and whose observations were exceptionally perceptive, in speaking of the revulsion of others to those who were compelled to do revolting work say: "Although occasioned by the work of scavenging which the bhangi men and women are expected to do, untouchability has attached itself to the group as a whole. Not only are they untouchable during the hours or during the years when they are engaged as scavengers, but from the time they are born until they die. They become so accustomed to being creatures to be avoided that they feel no resentment. Many a time when we have winced under the scorn or rebuff which we have suffered because of the bhangis we had in our tent or in our car, we have observed that those who gave rise to the scorn accepted this situation complacently."

It was this lack of resentment, this acceptance of their lot in life, by the members of each caste, which subsumed the social status of each caste, high or low, into the caste system. It was only this high degree of fixity, buttressed by religious sanction, which made the Indian caste structure different from the status structure of other highly stratified societies. There was, however, this difference, and it was at the heart of this difference that the new Constitution struck when it declared that untouchability must be abolished. As is the case with all social and socio-psychological phenomena, their antecedents have not only caused them but are a part of them. An analysis of the phenomena, therefore, requires an analysis of their causes. Such an analysis is the answer to the question of how such a system of human relationships as was dictated by the Indian caste system came into existence.

An attempt to trace the development of the theories about the origin of castes, to trace the growth in rigidity or flexibility of the caste system, or even to cite approximately the entire record of its baneful results in Indian society, would be to synopsize thousands of pages written by dozens of eminent Indian and non-Indian writers. We propose instead to state what is known from comparative analyses about social processes or social evolution, which is undoubtedly as generally true of the Indian caste system as it is of many other status structures in the world. We believe that the following ten broad generalizations are validated by a comparative study of the class structures of a great many societies.

1. There are two basic units of social organization which have been found in all simple societies—the family and the local community.

2. Division of labour is the most universal basis or principle by which functions have been assigned to, and obligations accepted in, both community and family life.

3. As societies have become more complex and new functions become necessary, the division of labour between different groups in the society has become more complex.

4. Societies had not reached any high degree of complexity and advancement when two functions other than the tasks essential to guarantee food and shelter arose. One of these was government, a secular function. The other was the task of maintaining and promoting the folkways and mores, and may be thought of as a sacred or religious function.

5. There were many societies (and still are some) where the secular function of the king, and the sacred or religious function of the priest were performed by the same person or family.

6. By and large, however, the first highly-specialized function of increasingly complex societies, other than that of the king or the warrior, was the function, and therefore the profession, of the priest.

7. In most, if not all, feudal societies, these two functions or functional groups, the rulers and the priests, were set apart, so to speak, from those who performed other divisions of labour.

8.   Where trade and commerce had developed, a third class quite often evolved. This was usually called the trader or business class. Most often the persons who constituted this class were more nearly retainers of the rulers than they were a separate class in and of themselves.

9.   In due time, practically every society which has evolved among people who have lived continuously in approximately the same geographic area has come to be organized into two broad classes, those who performed functions which were deemed essential to the maintenance of the overall society, and those who performed the many menial functions of supplying themselves and the functionaire classes with the physical necessities of life and living.

10.   The statement that all societies have in due time become stratified into what might be called the "elite" and the "masses" is too simple a generalization to explain many different ramifications of the class structure of many societies. It is, however, a valid generalization.

We cannot adequately even summarize the evolution and devolution of the model Hindu caste hierarchy. Because, however, the story relates not only the rise of new occupational castes, but also the rise and decline of the sanctions which fixed the status of these castes in the hierarchy, we will synopsize the evidence. Professor Ghurye presents his analysis in terms of three periods: The Vedic period, ending about 600 B.C.; the post-Vedic period, extending to about the third century of the Christian era; and the period which ends with the 10th or 11th century A.D. He says, "In the Rig-Veda the earliest literature of the first period, three classes of society are very frequently mentioned and named Brahman, Kshatriya and Vis. The first two represented broadly the professions of the poet-priest and the warrior-chief. The third division apparently was a group comprising all the common people;" that the Sudras, the fourth class of the model hierarchy occurred only once in the Rig-Veda. It seems the class represented "domestic servants approximating very nearly to the position of slaves." He says that the Brahmin is definitely said to be superior to the Kshatriya because he is said to insure the king's safety by his prayers. The Kshatriya seems to have included only the chiefs and the nobles and the Vaisya "figures singularly little in Vedic literature. The Sudra is described as "the servant of another, to be expelled at will, and to be slain at will;" that the Brahmin and the Kshatriya were the two important orders in the society and that the former was "steadily gaining exclusive influence with the increasing complexity of the sacrificial ritual." "The prohibition of dining in the company of others is not laid down in connection with these orders, though the general idea is there." He says the doctrine was taught that God created the Sudra to be the slave of all, that he was supposed to be fed and clothed with castoffs of food and raiment, that the Veda must not be recited in his presence, the holy law must not be expounded to him and that of all the rules of society, only the sacrament of marriage was explicitly applicable to the Sudras.

The second, "post-Vedic", period saw a great consolidation of the position of the Brahman class. The Kshatriyas were downgraded and the status of Vaisyas came to approximate that of Sudras. During this period of some nine hundred years, the number of named occupations increased greatly and the doctrine was that each caste stemmed from one of the four original varnas and that each varna possessed a dharma. The varnas originated in the process of the divine creation of man, in which the Brahman sprang from the head of God (Brahman), the Sudras from his feet, the Kshatriyas from his trunk or chest, and the Vaisyas from that portion of the body which lies between the chest and the feet. The theory of dharma was that it was the sacred duty of each class to fulfil its divinely-created task and by doing so fulfil its mission in life and guarantee its future life. Ghurye says that it was during this period that "the three lower castes are ordered to live according to the teaching of the Brahmin, who shall declare their duties, while the king is exhorted to regulate their conduct accordingly." This theory of salvation will be recognized as the heart of Hindu religion. As Ghurye says, "this philosophy of caste takes the sting off the institution and thus skilfully stereotypes it."

During this long period of social evolution, many new occupations evolved and each of the four varnas came to have many subdivisions. The logic of the stereotype made it easy to assign the duty of each of them. Professor Ghurye summarizes the logic and the practice of this system as follows:

"The ideal theory of castes laid down certain duties as common to all of them and some as specific to each. Out of these some were prescribed as the authorized modes of gaining livelihood, and were generally peculiar to each caste and ordinarily forbidden to others. The Brahman must subsist on teaching and officiating as priest at the sacrifices of the castes that were entitled to offer such religious worship and by accepting gifts. The Kshatriya was to live by administration and the profession of arms. Agriculture, trade and pastoral pursuits were to be exploited by the Vaisya, while the one occupation prescribed for the Sudra was service of the other castes."

We can best rapidly summarize developments of the third period by quoting short passages from Professor Ghurye's account. He says, "The occupational diversity was far greater than the one contemplated in the old scheme. . . . The traditional assignment of occupations to four castes is very largely modified. . . . While in the last period it was only the Sudra who was enjoined to serve the varnas, and particularly the Brahmin, now all three varnas are exhorted to serve the Brahmin, the theory being that each lower caste owes subservience to all the higher castes. . . . The solidarity of a caste as a unit of social organization is more and more acknowledged. . . . There is no doubt that there was some defined scheme of the status of different occupations which depended not so much on their lucrativeness as on their ceremonial purity. . . . It appears that in reality new occupational groups having the characteristics of castes had arisen, and . . . account of their origins was a mere theory based on permutations and combinations of the four original castes which bounded the Brahmans' mental horizon. . . . In the treatment of the outcaste section of society this period witnesses a development which is in keeping with the ideas of ceremonial purity. Untouchability is graded according to the supposed impurity of the object. A Brahmin should keep a distance of one yuga, two, three and four yugas between himself and a degraded person, a woman in her period, a parturient woman, and a Chandala respectively in order that he may not catch pollution from them."

The last quotation above describes the origin of a practice resulting in the social distance described earlier. Since this social distance was a function of prescribed physical distance in order to avoid pollution, it prescribed and described the emotional attitudes between persons who were socially distant from each other. It would be foolish for us to attempt to thread our way through, or even to comprehend, all the meanings of purity and impurity which have been expounded, or at least exposed, in Indian writings. We need not do so, for it is the common phenomenon of inward revulsion to that which is outwardly repulsive. As the Wisers say about this phenomenon, "without the fostering of this inner revulsion, the outward expression could not have survived these many centuries." Nor could any system which degrades large classes of persons be maintained anywhere in the world. Those who maintain, and foster, the status system of all societies tend to, and often actually do, rationalize that those who do the necessary dirty work in society, are of a different social order from themselves. It is rationalized that there must be "hewers of wood and drawers of water" in all societies; that the willingness of some persons to do menial work is proof that they are menial personalities; that even though one recognized the imperative need that such work be done, this does not mean that they should personally associate with those who do this work, much less that they should permit one of their daughters to marry a person who does such work. The consciences of high-status persons in societies which practise slavery quite generally rationalize that slaves have no souls, are not really human beings. It is more than probable that the chief difference between India and most other societies is the extent of the detail with which these rationalizations were logically thought through and recorded.

Hocart attempts to document this idea by comparative analysis of a number of societies, among them India. He says, "They mostly describe the creation of the world and man in general, but sometimes they account for the divisions of the people somewhat on the lines of the Visnu Purana and Manu. . . . The gist of them is that the ancestor, the god, at his installation assigns to each branch of his family in order of seniority the duties it will have to perform in the State ceremonial." He says, "We are faced with two alternatives: either all these myths were derived from India after the composition of the Purusa hymn; or else that hymn is merely the Indian version of a much older myth . . . .

The first alternative does not appear to fit the facts, so we are left with the second." He shows that such theories still prevail in some ` primitive societies and that they at one time prevailed in what are now known as advanced societies. He adds "In a country where learning is as arrogant as it is in India, it is not surprising that potters have sunk while the scholars have soared." Such social and mental processes are not, however, unique to India. There have been these same processes in one developing country after another in order, probably, to justify social orders which had evolved long before some group of philosophers rationalized them.

Dr. Irawati Karve makes a major contribution to an analysis based not so much on historical documentation as on current field studies. She says concerning the caste hierarchy in India, "This order is of two types. One is an order in a small area (a village or a group of villages) where a given number of castes are arranged in an order which is recognized by the majority. Secondly, there has been in existence for at least 2,500 years an order which rests historically on a classification of society by ancient Hindu theoreticians." Because Dr. Karve presents a parallel analysis of the historic structure of castes and the evolution of the rationalizations about castes, her theories warrant some exposition. To us, her two above-quoted statements accord with two bodies of easily validated facts: *First*, that there were literally hundreds of thousands of small groups in India, each so isolated that it wrought out its own social order. *Second*, that as in many other societies, so in India, as far back as 2,500 years, there developed a class of intellectuals who theorized about all known aspects of life. From such groups have come explanations of creation, expositions of the social order, the nature of differences between all known classes of people, and the order of relationships between these classes. Dr. Karve says, "The mention of castes and the theory of their origin from the varnas is itself a proof that castes existed before Aryans and that the Aryans tried to fit them into the class structure known to them." She says also that "in turn the philosophy (that is, the theory of the varna) justified the existence of such a society and helped to maintain it." She says, "The matter for thought is not why a society split continuously into ever smaller units, but why Hindu society retained the autonomy of these groups while other higher civilizations were able to merge smaller groups into larger ones." Her reasoning, and she believes her evidence, is that local groups created in the past were not subdivisions of larger groups; they were not the product of splitting up of larger kinship, occupational, or racial groups, much less "formed by continuous fission or cutting up of something which was a cohesive whole." The fission theory of caste origins would fit the logic of the four varnas all of which spring from the body of God, each of which by fission became many different castes or sub-castes, but it does not fit what appears to be the historic fact that each of the thousands of local and diverse groups was isolated physically and socially from other groups, and these groups were far more isolated in the ancient past than they have been for many centuries. We believe that Dr. Karve herself answers the question of why Hindu society retained the authority of these local groups, and that the answer is that it never destroyed their indigenous autonomy, in fact fixed and maintained that autonomy by sanctioning and perpetuating it long after these groups might have accommodated themselves to, or as she says, "emerged into," larger groups. If it be assumed that such a generalization has validity, it must then be concluded that caste, and joint families, of which castes are composed, while they gave greater stability to hundreds of thousands of local groups, by doing so stultified these groups and sabotaged the societal evolution of increasingly larger groups. To the extent that this was true, it helps to identify one of the ways in which the caste system was, and is, a conditioning factor of overall societal development.

This, however, is not the only way in which castes are conditioning factors in economic, social, and political development. They have contributed to the personal degradation of millions of individuals, which constitutes a hurdle in the path of developing the democratic society which India is attempting to build, and they have contributed to the development of a system of statuses and ranks which sabotages the dynamics of new roles, not all of which can be played by high-caste persons. It is only to an analysis of these three basic conditioning factors of development that we seek to make a contribution. Such an analysis makes no contribution to the detailed structure of the caste system. It

has, however, the possibility of making a contribution to an understanding of the social and psychological problems which confront
Indian leaders, and all Indian people, in eliminating, or at least
alleviating, the negative conditioning influence of casteism. Incidentally, it is natural that the term casteism has come into vogue
in India only recently. Now it is used to identify the negative
aspects of the caste system. So long as the system was taken for
granted, that is, accepted without question, its negative influences
were not emphasized. Now they are.

That India has retained hundreds of thousands of small
groups is a patent fact. Dr. Karve, in some of the findings of her
own and others' field studies, feels that there prevails in each of
these groups practically every type of behaviour and practice for
which caste philosophy has laid down prescriptions. She does not
believe, however, that it was these prescriptions which have controlled the behaviour of local groups. She says that each local
group has its own type of food, its own food taboos, wears its
own type of garments, uses its own type of cooking utensils, has
its own type of family organization, controls its own type of
inheritance, and worships its own gods. Each of these systems of
behaviour and practices is different from the system of practices
in other local areas. Each "group itself sets the boundaries and
each member of such groups moves within rather narrow boundaries of traditional behavior."

How far back in the past these local groups were, or came
to be, castes may never be accurately known. How a similar local
social order, varying greatly between local groups, came to be
something that could be, and is, called a caste system, will
probably never be precisely known. But Dr. Karve's definitive
characterization of such groups helps the reader to understand
what such groups still are today. She says, "A caste is a group
which practices endogamy, has a particular area (generally within
one linguistic region) of dispersion, may have one or more traditional occupations and has a more or less determined or flexible
position in a hierarchical scale." Each caste has "a certain traditional behavior pattern, which is enforced in many cases by a
caste council made up of caste elders. Castes live together with
other castes without mingling except on certain occasions only.
The intercourse of castes is peripheral or tangential. Castes almost

never interlock in such a way that their internal autonomy is jeopardized." That such groups are pretty firmly fixed social structures, she has no doubt, and comments, "the names of castes may suggest only one item of differentiation from the others, but investigation shows that the differences embraced almost the whole fabric of life and are very deep-going." These facts are known and emphasized by every* other student of castes. They are recognized by the members of the castes themselves and by the leaders of India who are convinced that the caste system must be broken. To know the processes by which they can be broken requires an attempt to analyze the forces which have made caste lines so deep.

We do not analyze the historical development of the values and attitudes which, on the one hand, cement the internal structure of each local caste, and on the other hand completely separate each caste from all other local castes because neither of these has been a universal product of the evolution of local village life. They have, however, been very prevalent in countries other than India, and we would suspect that they are products of the reasonings or the ratiocinations of intellectuals who believe that they must find, and have found, meaning in what they have seen around them, and that they have found that meaning in the concept of a natural, even a divine, origin. We would speculate that this is what happened in India and that once such doctrines or theories were wrought out, they were propagated and came to be accepted even by local people as an explanation of the division of labour and the separation of kinship groups, which, in fact, are a natural, and/or a universal, phenomenon in simple societies. If there is any difference between the Hindu caste system and philosophy and the doctrines which maintain marked differences in the social strata of other societies, it is probably in the elaborated theory of degrees of spiritual purity and/or impurity which buttress the caste system. Theoretically the physical, social and cultural distances prescribed by the caste hierarchical model are categorized into absolute attitudes and values which are not only accepted, but felt deeply by the members of all castes. It is the testimony of Brahmans who have freed themselves from these attitudes and values that Harijans (untouchables) both vocally and physically manifest feelings of guilt when they are asked to disregard old inhibitions to interpersonal interactions between themselves and those whom they have always believed to be their superiors.

The above body of sociological reasoning is intended to reveal how emotionally deep the roots of casteism are. We have inferred that the struggle even to induce untouchables to seek higher status will not be easy because their own attitudes are laden with a feeling of guilt when they violate what they and everyone else have long recognized as right. It may be still more difficult to change the attitudes of members of higher castes because, in addition to holding these same philosophies of natural differences, they are the recipients of many advantages because of their superior social status.

If one is aware that members of the lower castes, especially the "scheduled castes" (untouchables), because of almost countless generations of practice and also because of preachment, became unwilling to violate old caste boundaries, he will be able to appreciate the inhibitions to upward mobility on their part. If he will recall the specifications for the physical distances which had to be maintained between various castes, and if he sees clearly that the maintenance of social distance was also a purpose of these specifications, and especially if he appreciates the deep avoidance (taboo) psychology which such practices and preachments were bound to develop, he will realize the personality adjustments with which members of the higher castes must struggle. Social distance is a phenomenon of all societies. In India's society, the specifications of these distances were absolute. As Kimball Young says, "The term social distance expresses the idea of a gradation of one's own group and its values with respect to those of another group. Social distance implies subordination and superordination. . . . Social distance signifies not merely spatial isolation but, more importantly, isolation of ideas and attitudes." Of these two, ideas and attitudes, it is attitudes and, later, values which must be emphasized. Many careful and detailed studies of social distance have been made in open-class societies. So far as we are informed, no detailed study of social distance has been made in an intensively-stratified society. It would be difficult to make such a study if for no other reason than the fact that the replies of respondents to questions about degrees of social distance would be made in terms of cultural stereotypes, not in terms of personal emotional reactions. A great enough number and variety of such studies have, however, been made in other societies that their findings can help us intelligently to understand this phenomenon in India.

We report two important general facts which are revealed in the findings of all of these studies. One is that most of the variations in the degree of social distance which correspondents expressed, and apparently felt, were based much more on stereotyped views than upon personal experiences; also, that the degree of distance correlated with the degree of prejudice which the correspondents had about the other group of persons. If prejudice is assumed merely to be pre-judgment, this, too, would be little more than a stereotype. But as Allport says, "Pre-judgments become prejudices only if they are not reversible when exposed to new knowledge. A prejudice, unlike a simple misconception, is actively resistant to all evidence that would upset it." Psychologically, the orthodox beliefs about castes were as irreversible as revealed truth, and the belief was that to break down the sacred distance between castes, was to defy an order ordained by Providence. Let it be repeated, however, that this theory was not unique to India, but in India it was so completely stereotyped by repeated rationalizations that it had no element of prejudice in it. It did not violate any of the important norms or values accepted in the culture. There was, therefore, no feeling of guilt on the part of either party in the habitual, practised relationships between castes. Everyone did not only the right but the expected thing.

It is the orthodoxy of these beliefs and these norms of behaviour, and the sentiments which have buttressed them for generations, which are now called casteism in India. This term is used in an opprobrious sense, in resolutions of political parties and in editorials and newspaper columns. No leader objects to its opprobrious use, nor would any leader openly defend the historical model of the caste hierarchy. We would ourselves have doubt about the validity of our observations if we failed to recognize these facts. We would also cast doubt on the validity of our observations, and the observations and judgments of many Indian leaders, if we did not say that the generations-old practices of prescribed and sanctioned inter-caste relationships, and the deep attitudes which these practices and sanctions have induced, will not give way quickly.

Millions of low-caste persons, even though they may raise their expectations, will not quickly or necessarily insist on vertical mobility. Nor will many high-caste persons, even with dedicated purposes, relinquish their professional status and the influences which, in the past, have been advantageous to them. We would be something less than objective social analysts if we could not see the problems which confront India because of the widespread and deep conditioning influence of casteism on the task of raising hundreds of millions of low-caste persons to the status of equality in citizenship. We would not, we believe, be intelligent interpreters of social processes if we assumed that caste separateness is as completely a fixed system of social relationships and organization as many persons assume it to be. Every student of castes over the ages has cited the many ways in which new castes (or sub-castes) have been formed; ways by which orthodox caste boundaries have been transcended; and the rise and wane of especially the intermediate castes. Evidence produced by recent research studies shows that in local community practices, caste social separation never was so fixed as caste doctrines declared it to be. If one carefully reads the rather ample number of village studies made over recent years, looking for evidences of social change, he will find many descriptions of forms of human association which violate, or do not strictly follow, caste lines. Not only do members of castes follow other than their traditional occupations, but they cross caste boundaries in various types of informal associations.

Members of various castes, for example, have entered commerce, operating stores and other business. Members of various castes now work side by side in local factories. Convivial groupings, play groups of children, and gossip groups of adults cross caste boundaries. Children from all castes generally attend the same schools. School teachers and government employees living in local areas do not cater to caste lines. Local leadership patterns tend to change as new occupations emerge and persons and groups gain prestige because of newly-gained status based on wealth and/or education. Detailed studies of villages over the past decade document the facts just cited and many other facts which show that caste social boundaries are not totally rigid. Some dozen other recent village studies document even more marked changes. We cite only four of them: Alan Beals' "Study of Leadership in a Mysore Village", John T. Hitchcock's "Leadership in a North Indian Village: Two Case Studies", William C. McCormick's "Mysore Villages—View of Change", each a working paper presented at a seminar in 1956. The other is a detailed report of a study by Mayer of a village and its region in Central India.

We give special atttention to Mayer's study because, while the object of his study was an analysis of castes and kinship, his approach to the analysis was the observable behaviour of current human groups, and the ways in which these groupings were conditioned by caste and kinship relationships and organization A few examples of his findings will show how factors other than caste conditioned the everyday behaviour of local groups. Some "wards", which are the geographic subdivisions of the village, contain only one caste, but some contain members of two or more castes. Mayer says that the people of the ward "may have informal everyday contacts which overlay otherwise existing differences of caste or kinship." . . . "People from the same ward, though of different castes, may more easily attend small rites than fellow-caste mates at some distance in the village." "Sitting groups," a common phenomenon of Indian villages, while not formal social structures, are groups of men who meet at given places and talk. He says, "I think these spots" (meeting places) "represent places of fairly permanent . . . visiting." They do not follow caste lines. He describes one of them as a place "where there is a craftsman; his clients will gather there and passers-by will stop, too." . . . "Other sitting-places are set in the middle of wards," convenient places for many nearby residents to gather. Members of various castes, except Harijans, sit together. He lists the main factors conditioning attendance as, "relations with other people, pressure of work, time of day, etc." Of these groups he says, "In many cases there is a feeling of common neighbourhood as contrasted with 'those people over there'." He lists as another universal form of co-operation among castes the threshing floor and says, "The time at the threshing floor is pleasant for the entire family—it is a sort of a camp—for the women, of course, bring their children with them." He says these interpersonal types of relationship lay the ground for "ritual kinship", by which persons unrelated by kin become brothers and sisters and even ritual fathers and mothers.

Mayer makes some statements the validity of which, if widely accepted, does much to alleviate the notion that caste structure is inexorable. He says, "While the caste is recognized by society at large and many sub-castes make up a caste, this means little more than that caste is a *category* composed of sub-castes, rather than a group in its own right." Sub-castes are local groups they are traditionally assumed to be. They are not status groups or even always, though they tend to be, socio-geographic groups. They are very often not effective social units. All of this is not to say that kinship and caste do not influence the forms of behaviour of all these groups. It is to say that to study social structure in terms of systems of human relationships comes nearer to making a contribution to the understanding of living social structures than do repeated reviews of traditionalized structural categories.

We have viewed the Indian caste system as the model, partly real and partly theoretical, of the Indian class structure. We are not competent to assess the merits of any of the controversies about the origin or antiquity of the caste system, nor would we deem it any great contribution if we could do so. What little we have presented on the history and the evolution of the caste system was only for the purpose of discussing ideologies and attitudes which to some extent still exist. Our understanding is that the caste system is, as Mrs. Karve says, of two orders, one local, the other society-wide. Panikkar calls it a parallel organization of society. Ghurye says that "though it is the caste that is recognized by the society . . . it is the sub-caste that is regarded by the particular caste and individual." Panikkar says that it is the sub-caste, which is synonymous with the joint family or extended family, which controls the behaviour of the individual, and to which the individual's loyalty is dedicated. Mayer calls "caste a rather shadowy category outside the village" and says, "it need not encompass a group of inter-acting members as does the sub-caste." In other words, we are assuming the caste hierarchy is chiefly a logical construct, but that the sub-castes or extended family groups are living social entities. They are, however, local organizations.

Audacious as it is, we are inclined to express the judgment that far more can, or could, be learned about how caste structure conditions development programmes if analyses were made of the day-by-day behaviour of that overwhelming majority of the Indian people who live in local communities. If such studies were to be made by social analysts who had never heard the word caste, their findings would undoubtedly be as follows: (1) Those who live, and for generations have lived, in highly-isolated local communities are "locality groups"; that is, the overwhelming proportion of their inter-personal or social interactions is with other persons who similarly live within the borders of small geographic areas; (2) There are various kinds of sub-groups among the persons who live in these local communities, the most universal of which are kinship groups; (3) The second most prevalent type of sub-groups is composed of those who do the same kinds of work, have the same occupations; (4) There are conviviality groups, children who play together, adults who visit much more with some than with other members of the community; (5) When there is an overall community celebration or ceremonial, most, if not all, of these different groups take part in it and each group plays that part in which, according to its own judgment, and the judgment of other groups, it can best perform.

Such almost certain, objective findings would provide guidance to community development workers who are supposed to carry out and interpret all development programmes for village people. They would provide these workers with a knowledge of a living, functioning social structure of local communities in which people are already mobilized, in one way and another, for almost every kind of group action. Local development workers would need pay even less attention to the "shadowy" influence of the exterior caste relationships of local people than local people themselves do. They would, however, be compelled to recognize and deal with the living reality of sub-castes—joint and extended family groups and loyalties. More will be said about the joint-family structure and influence in the succeeding chapter. More needs to be said here about other aspects of caste organization and caste attitudes which condition development programmes and problems.

In sharp contrast to the fairly complete and adequate analysis

which was made of economic problems and processes, there was
nothing said publicly in the First Five Year Plan or elsewhere
which identified the socio-psychological problems or discussed
socio-psychological processes. This may have been partly due to
the paucity of social and psychological research findings in the
field of caste attitudes and values, but it was undoubtedly also
partly due to an inadequate appreciation of the inevitable inter-
relationships between economic and socio-psychological factors in
human behaviour. Development programme experiences, as in
many other fields in India, have gradually developed an awareness
of these inter-relationships. Indian sociologists have not been
totally unaware of the need for socio-psychological studies of
castes and caste relationships. In a symposium on castes and the
joint family, Professor Aiyappan said, "The depth of the caste
sentiment that forms part and parcel of the personality of individuals of the various castes should be investigated by social psychologists." In that same symposium, Professor H. Acharya said,
"Caste is a unique social institution. It is unique not only because
of its immense hold on the people, but also because of its power
to influence the personality of the individual member in one way
or another." He said further, "The study of castes can be fruitful
only if we do not confine ourselves to what it was and what it is
today but study sentiments and attitudes of the people who
preserve the institutions through the ups and downs of history in
its early formation." He might, of course, have added: and who
preserve it yet today. Indian sociologists and psychologists have
begun to make the type of studies which they themselves recognize as valuable for programme development guidance, but here
again this experience will be reported in a later chapter.

Among the adverse conditioning influences of the caste
system on programmes and processes of development, the outstanding one which Panikkar identifies is such a fragmentation of
social feeling as to make the building of a national community
difficult. This fragmentation of feeling is the result of the intense
loyalty of persons to their joint families—sub-castes. He says that
small cohesive groups render "the development of any common
social feeling impossible . . . it is a negation of the idea of society."
Another adverse conditioning factor is what some have called
"casteism', that is, insistence on the practice of super-ordination

and subordination in all walks of life, even in day-by-day development programme administration. Neither of these conditioning influences is so easily recognized as the influence of the existence of some fifty million untouchables and at least an equal number of others whose levels of life and aspirations have for generations been little higher than those of untouchables. Because of the physical and economic, the educational and political attack on the problems of this great mass of disadvantaged people, it is easier to identify and assess the programmes which have been launched for the alleviation of this condition. The actual alleviation, or overcoming of the "fragmentation of feeling", will probably have to be assessed in terms of the evidence of participation of local people in wider-than-local programmes and plans. The alleviation of "casteism" can probably be assessed only in terms of evidences of the extent to which it does or does not still impede various programmes of change.

MAIN AUTHORITIES QUOTED OR CITED

Dube, S. C., *India's Changing Villages*, Cornell University Press, Ithaca, N. Y., 1958.

Ghurye, G. S., *Caste and Class in India*, Philosophical Library, New York, and Associated Advertisers and Printers, Bombay, Revised Edition, 1950.

Hocart, A. M., *Caste, A Comparative Study*, Methuen & Co., London, 1950.

Hutton, J. H., *Caste in India*, Oxford University Press, London, 2nd Edition, 1951.

Karve, I., Papers presented at Centre for South-Asian Studies (Mimeographs) Institute of International Studies, University of California, Berkeley.

Mayer, A. C., *Caste and Kinship in Central India*, University of California Press, Berkeley, 1960.

Panikkar, K. M., *Hindu Society at Cross Roads*, Asia Publishing House, Bombay, 3rd edition (rev.), 1961.

Srinivas, M. N., (Ed.) *India's Villages*, Asia Publishing House, 2nd edition (rev.), 1960.

Symposium: *Caste and Joint Family*, Reprint in Indian Sociological Bulletin, Vol. IV, No. 2, September, 1955.

Wiser, William and Charlotte, *Behind Mud Walls*, University of California Press, 1963.

Young, Kimball, *Handbook of Social Psychology*, Routledge & Kegan Paul Ltd., London, Revised ed., 1957.

CHAPTER 4

THE JOINT-FAMILY SYSTEM

THE joint-family system in India is as universal as the caste system. The model we use is the "traditional Hindu joint family". There are variations of this pattern all over India today and there have always been many different patterns in the past. We deal only with the special facets of this type of extended family having relevance to the social and economic planning of development in India, in which all social institutions become formidable factors in either promoting or inhibiting change.

The principal features of the joint family of tradition are: that it is three-generational in depth, that its members live under the same roof, and that property, of whatever kind, is shared by all. It is a self-sufficient unit socially and economically, the centre of the universe for the whole family, the arbiter of life's important decisions, the supplier of daily and lifetime needs, the reservoir of deep loyalties and bonds of affection. It is a kinship group that serves at once as place of abode and centre for social, recreational, and religious activities. It is within this family circle that all momentous decisions are made—of education, career, marriage—and all important events take place—worship, weddings and other celebrations, births and deaths and their appropriate ceremonies.

It is because of these elements of what might be called the structural aspect of the joint family that the functional side has great significance, and this also helps to explain why the joint family has been a part of the Indian scene since recorded time. Because of the communal, co-operative nature of joint-family life, a special kind of familism has been developed which involves duties and obligations accepted without question by the family as a whole and by its individual members. Roles within the family and the inter-relationships between them are clearly defined. Responsibility for the young, the aged, the indigent within the large kinship group is assumed by the family; assistance is expected to be given and returned whenever needed as a part of family obligation and duty. Given centuries of this kind of close-knit family living, it is easy to see that deep and abiding loyalties and kinship ties would be outstanding characteristics of joint-family life in India.

There are other reasons why this particular family form has for so long retained a strong position in Indian life. The joint family is peculiarly a product of an agricultural economy in which land, as a necessary base, is highly valued. In this context, sonship is of primary importance in the patriarchal family to guarantee the continuity of land ownership through inheritance from one generation to the next. In the joint family, it has been the custom for centuries, sanctioned by law through what is called a "coparcenary", for all sons to inherit equally at birth. Although the eldest male is regarded as the manager and trustee of the family property, most decisions are jointly made and executed. This shared responsibility for safeguarding and perpetuating the family enterprise, whatever it may be, binds the male members of the family together in a lifelong concern for the welfare of their inheritance and contributes very heavily to the values engendered by this unique type of extended family. It also gives support to the attitudes and sentiments surrounding the practices of providing protection and security to the young, the unmarried or widowed females, the aged parents, grandparents, and other kin, the sick and indigent—and all within the family circle who are in need of assistance. In Hindu philosophy, this is embraced in the concepts of dharma (sense of duty) and karma (deeds) which give greater depth and intensity to what would otherwise be simply practices of familism found in family circles everywhere, but which in Western society are obligations which have gradually been taken over in large part by outside agencies.

In India, the powerful combination of social, economic, and religious or philosophical functions within the joint family has made this ancient and respected institution continue to survive in the face of strong forces playing on it to weaken its hold. As a social structure especially adapted to conservative village life, in a folk society, a peasant agricultural economy, it stands in a vulnerable position at this stage of India's development as this nation moves towards a secular society through vast programmes of change. As an old, conservative institution, it will probably tend to inhibit changes of various kinds.

It is not our purpose here to say, as some have, that the joint family has "broken up", that it has "disappeared", nor to predict what the future will bring. We shall attempt to describe the probable role of the joint-family system as a factor conditioning the rate and direction of change in India's programme of development during this crucial period of transition from a folk to a secular society.

Change in the direction of industrialization will move people from their customary places of habitation and from their usual roles in society. Many village people, as industrialization and urbanization accelerate, will seek jobs and further education in towns and cities. As employment opportunities multiply and become more diversified, both men and women, of whatever station in life, will be enabled to equip themselves, through education and training, to rise in social and economic status to better positions. Mobility, both horizontal and vertical, is an essential component of all programmes of development. We have seen in the previous chapter in what ways the caste system affects programmes of development. Here we shall look at what influence the joint family may have on bringing about or impeding necessary change.

Within the framework of horizontal and vertical mobility as an integral part of India's programmes of development now under way, the role of the joint family as an important conditioning factor may be considered, on the one hand, from the point of view of the family as well-established social structure—a self-sufficient, all-embracing kinship circle, in many cases a sub-caste. We may also think of the influence of this family pattern in terms of the kinds of individuals it produces because of the inter-relationships imposed on the family members and the values, attitudes and sentiments they foster among them. Particular kinds of personality traits grow out of customary joint-family operations which may or may not lend themselves to the typical single-family or nuclear household known to secular societies in the West.

A further dimension to be taken into account is the role of the joint family in promoting or inhibiting the formation of extra-familial relationships, such as memberships in youth clubs, women's organizations, business associations, all of which are important in developing a viable pluralist society that will cut across the narrow boundaries of local village, caste, and family. The joint family stands in a strong but vulnerable position across the path of change which will tend to lead its members away from the home or ancestral place, up the social and economic ladder, and into new groups based on common interests rather than caste or kinship or local village residence. The old family pattern and practices will either bend to the winds of change through accommodation to new circumstances or will likely lose their hold more and more in the face of a frontal assault by new ways of doing and thinking.

As development programmes grow and proliferate, both in size and diversity, an increasing number of people from rural villages all over India will be needed in the towns and cities to man the factories, teach in the expanding number of schools, serve in the health centres and hospitals, and help to conduct the many new kinds of activities required in a modern economy. The people who answer these calls will need training of various kinds, higher education, and in many cases adaptability to a new way of living. It is in relation to this necessary mobility, both horizontal and vertical, that the joint-family system, or the joint family as a well-established social structure, poses problems for the programmes of social change. Because the joint family is an ancient institution, is self-contained and all-embracing for its members, and places supreme importance on the ancestral home —land and other property and all they produce—strong pressure is exerted on all members of the family to remain at home. This is particularly true, of course, in agriculture where all hands are needed and where it is economically more fruitful to farm all shares of land as one piece. The pressure to remain with the family enterprise is not only external to the individual members, that is, coming from the family as a whole, but also internal as the individual views his share in the whole as something to safeguard for himself and his progeny and as his responsibility as a contribution to the success of the joint undertaking. Thus for any person to "break away" from the family farm or business means the possible sacrifice of an inherited share of property and also abandonment of management and family responsibility. This is a difficult step for a man to take. And yet programmes of economic and social development must draw on the reservoirs of rural man-power for new recruits in all fields—business, industry and the professions.

The institutional aspect of this family system is a powerful force in and of itself in inhibiting to some degree the mobility of individuals required in periods of transition from folk to secular society. Looked at from the point of view of the individual members of such a kinship group, we see that inherent in its operation as a social and economic unit certain personality traits are fostered which are not the same as those characteristic of the single-family pattern as we know it in the West. The role-playing expected of each member in a joint family is not only clearly defined, but is intrinsic to the inter-relationships necessary to the performance of this group as a self-sufficient unit—in work, in play, in worship. The eldest male is the manager or trustee of the joint-family property, but his decisions are usually made on the basis of the views of the other adult male members of the household (brothers, sons, cousins) and jointly carried out by all. This may be a matter of what crop to plant on a given piece of land, how much to invest in fertilizer or improved seed, or what to do about that old bullock that needs to be retired. In a com-mercial or business family, the procedure would be similar, but the questions would likely have to do with credit, equipment, prices, and improvement of skills. The women in the household are not necessarily subordinate, although they have only recently acquired property rights, but their domain is clearly that of domestic duties—cooking, cleaning, caring for the children, some-times light field work and feeding animals and poultry in the compound. Even quite young children play their part in a farm family by helping with younger children and animals, gathering wood and dung for fires, and doing other light chores.

As a truly co-operative enterprise, the joint family operates for the benefit, security and protection of all its members. The individual's contribution to the success of the undertaking is more important than his success as an individual. While this gives rise to personality traits of co-operativeness and self-sacrifice, it does not tend to develop some of the attributes needed by individuals in a modern, competitive secular society, such as individual initiative, aggressiveness, independent decision-making, and even acquisitiveness. Nor do the values engendered in the joint family prepare individuals well for the somewhat different set of values and attitudes that spell success in an industrialised, urbanized society. Social status in a folk society rests heavily on family position, whereas in a secular society, with free horizontal and vertical mobility, it tends to be measured by individual achievement gained through education, training, development of skills, and accumulation of material rewards.

In addition to the influence of the joint-family system on the kinds of individuals it produces, the customs and practices of its social life create attitudes concerning extra-familial associations which are out of tune with a modern, secular society. Strictly family affairs—births, deaths, weddings, worship ceremonies, religious festivals—represent almost the total social and recreational life of the members. Even those who are working away from the home place try to return for all special family occasions. Since all business and political discussions and decisions take place in the family circle, and all social, recreational, and religious activities are centred there, it is small wonder that associations based on other than family concerns find it difficult to grow. In a model joint family, even young children feel no great need for outside contacts because families are typically large and provide an adequate number of playmates at home. Women lead busy lives with their domestic affairs, have other women in the household for company, and do not therefore feel the need for much outside association with women's groups. This is appropriate to a folk society. In a secular society, however, many groups need to function to serve varied interests. These groups are based on common interests of all kinds and go beyond the narrow boundaries of family, and even of local communities. Such groups serve to break down barriers of language and locality and are crucial to the development of a truly national society. The joint family with its self-containment stands in the way of the flowering of these new kinds of associations.

Because India is in a period of transition from folk to secular society, and because India's leaders recognized from the beginning of planning the necessity of fundamental change in her social and economic life, it is possible fifteen years after Independence to observe certain accommodations to change in even so basic an institution as the joint family. We shall discuss briefly only three factors as they bear on the modifications already apparent in the joint family, namely: more widespread education; new legislation concerning marriage and women's property rights; and the national policy favouring industrialization and urbanization. We shall attempt to relate these forces of change to what appears to have happened to both the structure and functions of this family system. Both are important, are inter-related, and are probably changing, but they do not necessarily change in the same way nor to the same degree, nor even for the same reasons. It is only when we consider both structure and function that we can say that the joint family has modified in degree of jointness rather than "broken up" or disappeared."

The impact of greater educational opportunity during the past fifteen years has touched young people from elementary school up through higher education. India's Constitution set forth the principle of universal education, and vigorous efforts have been made since Independence to make at least elementary education available to all boys and girls up to the age of fourteen. Special attention has been given to bringing more girls into the school-going population despite resistance from many parents who do not see its value. But even the forward looking Third Plan does not provide for as many girls as boys in school. Substantial increases in total enrolment have, however, not only greatly augmented the numbers in school at all levels, but have significantly increased the demand for qualified teachers, calling for thousands of women to enter professional employment for the first time.

One effect of the heroic effort to educate the young and to prepare a proportion of the students for technical and professional careers is to remove young people of all ages from the home for a longer period of time for schooling, to make them more mobile horizontally and vertically, and to give them greater freedom to pursue lines of activity independently of family and caste predilection. It is also seen to be having the effect of postponing, and therefore raising the age of, marriage. As the marriage age rises, and particularly as the sexes come to mix more freely in the academic and business worlds, young people will doubtless want to choose their own marriage partners, gradually displacing, for many, the arranged marriages of the typical joint family. More education as a preparation for adult life has its economic aspects too, as parents more and more appreciate its value as the road to advancement and security, a kind of insurance for the future, rather than relying simply on the combined strength of numbers within the kinship group. For girls, education is coming to have economic as well as social value, not only as a necessary step to employment in ever-increasing numbers of fields, but also as an asset in preparation for marriage, sometimes as a valuable dowry consideration and sometimes as a desirable feminine accompaniment to an educated young man's climb up the social and economic ladder after marriage. An education represents to both young men and young women a favourable factor in satisfactory adjustment to marriage, to new peer groups in school and business, and to a new way of life that promises greater social and economic opportunity in the future.

The joint-family system has responded to the pronounced trend toward more education for its young people by modifications in both structure and function. The actual composition of the household is reduced in size as the younger members leave the village for towns and cities to seek additional schooling, training or jobs. Young people may, and often do, return for special family occasions and holidays, but they do not generally return to stay or to resume farming the home place. Their physical removal from the joint family alters its functional aspects also. The duties and obligations traditionally assumed by the younger members of the family to perform certain chores, to learn from the elders of the family, and to grow into responsible carriers of the family name, traditions, customs, and enterprise for the continuation of the family, generation to generation, are displaced by new concerns, new interests, and possibly different values. Many retain a feeling of obligation to support the family, financially or otherwise, even though living and working away from home. But the major responsibility for carrying on the family's business devolves upon the elder members who may eventually have to partition, lease, or lose the property if there is no one to take it over from them when their working days are over.

The customary inter-relationships involved in caring for the very young, helping to arrive at business decisions, conducting family worship and other ceremonials, assisting the sick and aged, all these are disturbed by a shrinking number at home to observe them. The roles that would have been taken over gradually and automatically by younger members of the family as they matured must be fulfilled by the elders. The young son who has gone off to the city to study engineering cannot help with the planting and the harvesting, the care of the animals, the arrangements for his sister's marriage. The young daughter who is taking training as a nurse or teacher cannot tend her younger brothers and sisters, help with the domestic chores, wait on the sick or the aged grandparents. With the young people away, the joint family may still be three-generational and therefore structurally joint, but functionally it becomes quasi-joint as fewer of the duties are shared. The degree of jointness will depend, according to the view of some scholars in this field, not upon the actual numbers represented in the household, but upon the extent to which the bonds of affection, dependence, and responsibility are retained by those who have moved away from home. It is contended that even after these young people have married and established their own homes elsewhere, many still retain ties with their family's home and enterprise and thus remain a part of the original joint family.

Hindu marriage and family life have always been governed more by ancient custom and religious practice than by established law. Although two distinguished schools of judicial thought, the Mitakshara and the Dayabhaga, which have interpreted ancient Vedic literature concerning marriage, inheritance, and contract, have heavily influenced Hindu practices, nevertheless there has been great variation between religious communities, geographic areas, castes, and language groups all over India as to what customs prevailed. Custom and usage in local areas dealt primarily with caste endogamy, village exogamy, degree of kinship permitted in marriage, and appropriate rites to be performed. This was mostly a matter of prohibiting inter-caste marriage and at the same time extending the kinship circle beyond the immediate village. Custom frowned on the remarriage of Hindu widows and disapproved of divorce. The joint family was held responsible for arranging the marriages of daughters and providing suitable dowries; it was also expected to maintain all minor children and other dependents in the family. Where established law has taken a position on these matters, whether by the British when in power or by the courts of India since Independence, it has apparently been an accepted principle that the law promulgated would take into account local custom and usage.

Such major pieces of recent legislation as the Hindu Marriage Act of 1955 and the Hindu Succession Act of 1956 represent attempts to codify laws relating to these matters rather than to regiment all religious and other cultural groups whose customs are so greatly varied. Local practices are still observed and respected, but the new, comprehensive laws do deal with rights and social problems long neglected.

The Hindu Marriage Act regulates the conditions of marriage, including legal age, degree of kin relationship permitted, and consent required; it provides for marriages to be registered by the State; it specifies the grounds for judicial separation by petition and grounds for divorce by either party. This law also makes bigamy punishable under the Indian Penal Code and gives the Court the responsibility to decide on divorce charges and maintenance, including the power to make interim and final orders regarding custody, maintenance, and education of minor children. The Hindu Succession Act dealt with intestate succession and women's property rights for all religious communities which had been operating everywhere under their own personal laws and different family systems. Under the new law, the determination of heir was based on secular tests of consanguinity and affinity, without any discrimination on the ground of sex. This represented a new charter for women who, under this Act, acquired full and absolute ownership and control of all property they possessed, whether acquired by inheritance or gift. Thus these new laws, although Hindu, attempt to legislate for various religious communities, to use the secular courts of law to interpret their meaning and intent, and to deal with longstanding social problems such as child marriage, ban on widow remarriage, and lack of women's property rights. The recent anti-dowry law is another example of a legislative effort to remove a social evil which has been an overwhelming financial burden to parents for centuries. These old practices do not, however, give ground quickly.

Laws such as these provide greater freedom and protection concerning marriage, divorce, inheritance and succession, and control of property. At the same time they weaken the hold of the joint family on its members and the customs of the joint-family system make law enforcement difficult. As the marriage age rises, either because of longer periods of schooling or the higher legal age of marriage, young people tend to exercise greater freedom of choice in their own marriage partners, thus removing the ancient joint-family function of arranging marriage of daughters. The widow who can inherit and control joint-family property is no longer at the mercy of her husband's heirs for maintenance and support. Established recourse to secular courts of law may eventually remove the settlement of many family quarrels from the limited circles of village or caste panchayats and joint-family councils where judicial functions of many kinds have customarily been performed in the past. Change in the joint family due to legislation of this kind is therefore found in the functional aspects of its operation more than in its structure. It can be taken for granted that the structure will tend to resist the change.

While India has established a national policy of industrializing, and therefore urbanizing, her economy, the impact of these processes on the joint family is not yet very great. India's rural population in 1961 was still about eighty per cent, and it is among her rural village people that the joint family has traditionally had its deepest roots. As the movement to industries and to towns and cities accelerates, more and more young and middle-aged people, particularly males, will leave the rural areas to seek greater economic opportunity than is afforded in non-urban, non-industrial areas. They will leave behind the ancestral joint-family residence, and eventually establish new homes of their own, in many cases of the nuclear type predominant in the West.

The absence of the migrating members of the household will alter both the structure and functions of the family they leave behind. Because they will probably follow the typical Western single-family pattern in the urban setting, the structure and function of the new household will be different from the old. It will begin with a married couple who will play all the roles formerly carried by several adults in the joint family. The husband and wife will share the responsibility of starting a new branch of the older family from which they came. When their children come into the household, there will be no grandparents, aunts or uncles, to assist in caring for them. The children will later find their playmates among peer groups in school or in the neighbourhood instead of among siblings and cousins living under the same roof as in the large joint family. The nuclear family will be an independent entity embracing the roles of bread-winning, household management, and adjustment to a new kind of life outside of the family.

Both the structure and the functions of this small family will be different from the traditional joint family. There will, however, for some time be a degree of jointness, or connection with the stem family. What the new branch retains will be determined by the ties which the ancestral home still nurtures. It will also depend on the extent to which new nuclear families may include under their roof their aged parents, younger brothers or sisters who come to town for schooling or jobs, or dependent kin who need their assistance and protection for whatever reason. It is too early to judge the extent of accommodation to change that has already taken place in the joint-family system due to such factors as those we have briefly discussed.

There are, of course, many other forces playing on this social institution besides those of education, new legislation, industrialization and urbanization. Since development programmes require change and mobility, it becomes important to look at the ways in which modifications of so basic a social institution as the joint family promote or inhibit these processes. One way to do this is to consider the attributes inherent in the traditional joint-family system which can be preserved as values in a developing secular society and which could be turned to the promotion of change without destroying the institution itself. Against these qualities, our focus must also be directed to the particular ideas, attitudes and customs which, if unchanged, would tend to inhibit change and mobility. This cannot be done in the sense of striking a credit and debit balance, but would be to recognize that the joint-family system has within it certain assets and liabilities in this transitional period of India's history. We do not attempt to predict the future of this ancient family form, nor even precisely to assess its present position, but simply to point out, on the basis of experience elsewhere in moving from folk to secular society, the aspects of this kind of family life which may contribute to change and those which are likely to be inhibitions to change.

Probably the most outstanding characteristic of the joint-family system is its stability. In a conservative, peasant economy, it stands as a bulwark of security, of continuity, of orderly relationships between old and young, a link from the past to the future. It guarantees the protection of all its members and their progeny on the land which goes from father to son, generation after generation. It clearly defines the roles of those who live under the same roof or on the same land, the roles of men and women, of young and old. Familism is more highly developed here than in any other kinship system. All facets of life are encompassed—social, economic, religious, recreational, political. Certain personality traits of genuine sharing and co-operativeness are developed and highly valued. It is a complete way of life, with its own traditions, customs, values, loyalties, duties and obligations. The joint family is revered and cherished by its members who are bound together by deep ties and strong emotions. The joint-family system has been functioning with attributes of this kind for centuries. It is ancient, respected, admired. It has been as much a part of the Indian scene as the bullock cart, the Hindu temples, and the Ganges. It is probably as deeply embedded in Indian life as the caste system.

How does a social system of this antiquity, and with these characteristics, fit into the modern world of change? Is it an anachronism? How can a family system of this kind adapt itself to promote change and mobility instead of standing in the way? We have already indicated that some accommodations have been made where migration has taken place, particularly in urban areas. We have also suggested that the joint family has some plus values worth preserving even under changed circumstances. There are, however, some aspects of joint-family life which will tend to inhibit change or will at least make the adjustment to a new way of doing and thinking difficult for those who break away from the family temporarily or permanently.

The major handicaps to joint-family members in playing their necessary roles in a developing country will be in terms of the individual traits fostered by joint-family life, which will be inadequate in a different setting, and the exclusiveness of this kind of living which is a poor training ground for the multiple contacts and extra-familial associations that will be required. This is not to say that joint-family life nourishes undesirable traits; it is to say that certain other traits will be more suitable in another context. For example, the young man who accepts without question the decisions of others, strives for group welfare rather than individual competence, and counts on the family circle to supply all his wants and needs is ill-prepared to strike out on his own in unfamiliar surroundings, make his own decisions, or compete with peers for advancement. The young woman who has never learned to manage a household by herself and never been trained for any career other than marriage, who has never looked outside of the family circle for companionship, has not developed the talent necessary to operate a single-family household, much less to compete as an individual in occupations and professions. The drive, initiative, aggressiveness and even acquisitiveness which generally underlie successful adaptation in a modern, competitive, secular society are not normally fostered by typical joint-family life. Even different sets of values and attitudes are presupposed in the measurement of success in a secular setting which are not necessarily the values and attitudes cherished in the joint family. Individual achievement, professional or technical competence, and even accumulation of material gains will tend to become measuring sticks of attainment of secular goals.

Perhaps of equal importance with the kind of individual traits fostered by joint-family life are the attitudes toward the outside world which are bred by the exclusiveness and all-encompassing nature of its operations. As an institution which caters to all the needs of its members, the joint family discourages participation in peer groups, social clubs, business associations, political organizations which are so much part of modern society. Since the Hindus have no organized church or congregation, as in the Christian religion, even worship is largely an individual and family matter and does not lead to regular association with others on the basis of religious interests, except on the occasions of large festivals and special holidays. Political decisions seem to be made quite often on the basis of agreement within the family circle; independent, active, local-level political party groups therefore do not flourish in villages. Because of the joint family's assumption of responsibility for its own sick, aged, and indigent, few welfare agencies have come into existence and the family members feel reluctant to surrender these responsibilities to outsiders since they are regarded as a true part of life's fulfilment of duty to the ancestors and to the ongoing family—good deeds (karma) to be performed as one's mission in this life and as preparation for the next life. Family members turn inward on themselves for the satisfaction of all their wants and needs.

In order to perform the multiple functions of joint-family life, the role of each member is clearly defined and certain inter-personal relationships are stressed. Because these roles and relation-ships are especially well adapted to the purposes of co-operative joint-family operation, they are not necessarily suited to single-family living in a modern, especially non-rural, context. The eldest male who, with the concurrence of the men in the house-hold, assumes responsibility as trustee or manager of the whole family does not consult his wife on business affairs; she has her own purely domestic concerns. In a single-family dwelling, the husband and wife share the full management role as partners, without any other adults available for guidance and assistance. In the joint family, the wife's relationship with her sons is stronger than with any other members of the family, even after the sons have married and brought their wives into the household. It is the mother of the family who traditionally supervises the fledgling families, teaches her sons' young brides their places and duties in the household, and holds a tight rein on their affection, obedience, and loyalty. Her bond with her sons is usually stronger than that with her husband and tends to take precedence over the loyalty of her sons to their wives.

In the nuclear family, the husband-wife relationship must be a strong partnership bond of mutual understanding and shared responsibility for the family they have founded. If the pattern of the single-family household continues, both sons and daughters will again establish new families of their own when they marry. When this phase of the family cycle arrives, the father and mother are alone again, and it will be important that the husband-wife relationship be a strong one. This represents the typical life-cycle of the nuclear family found in most urbanized, industrial countries. It is for this type of family living that the structurally-large, function-sharing joint family lays little foundation. Those who venture into the unaccustomed ways of urban life, whether attracted by the prospect of greater social and economic opportunity or pushed out of rural areas by the pressure of population, will need to stand on their own feet, cultivate friendships among their peers on the basis of other than family connections, and compete for economic success by developing individual competence. This will constitute a whole new way of living, doing and thinking. For many, accustomed and attached to the joint family's way of life, it will be a difficult adjustment and a difficult step to take to embrace it. In this sense, the hold of the joint family will doubtless act as a brake on the mobility required by programmes of change.

Even after approximately eleven years of development planning and programmes of change, it is impossible to determine in the vast and diversified society that is India what has happened to the traditional form of the Hindu joint family. Recent research in this field has been limited in the main to relatively small samples of college students and to residents of urban areas, while the principal stronghold of the joint family is, and has always been, in the rural areas. That the pattern is changing in the large towns and cities there is little doubt. That it has yet changed substantially in the rural areas we have considerable doubt.

As an ancient, conservative institution with its network of loyalties, duties and obligations, the joint family may well slow down mobility and change because of its hold on potential migrants. The security and protection of the ancestral home and enterprise will act as a counter-force to horizontal and vertical mobility. The love and loyalty of the large family circle, embracing so many of life's activities and interests, may overshadow the possible lure of the strange new ways of the city. If, however, the traditional joint family can modify its structure and role-playing functions, or division of labour within the household, and still retain some of the old loyalties, values and sentiments, it may be able to make an accommodation to the pace of change and development in a more modern, secular society. This will require more schooling for the young, higher status and more responsibility for the women, more freedom and independence for young people in the choice of marriage partners and careers, more association of all members of the family in extra-familial groups, and gradually more reliance on outside agencies for the care of the sick, indigent and aged. This will, of course, take place first in urban areas and only slowly permeate to the rural village population. If the joint family can adjust itself to the new forces inherent in developing the kind of modern society India envisions for herself, it may, for some time to come, retain for its members many of the values associated with its kinship ties while it yields to the structure and changed functions of a new day. Whether or not it can ultimately adapt itself to new conditions, it is a widespread, venerable social institution still very much alive in rural India today. As such, it constitutes a significant conditioning factor in India's social and economic development.

If what we have said about the joint family in India in some ways seems to be a brief for the personal and social values which contribute to what may be called familism, this is because sentiments are the cement of all social institutions and the joint family is one of the most ancient and revered institutions of Indian society. As such, the joint-family system will probably be more resistant to change than the caste system. It would be difficult to imagine that India, or any other society, would pass legislation outlawing familism, as India has literally outlawed casteism. Familism is an *ism* in all societies; parents assist their children to get started, as adults, in all walks of life. Brothers and sisters recognize greater obligations to each other than they do to other persons. Family obligations in India are honoured above all other obligations. That sentiments in behalf of these obligations would ramify practically every social, economic and political relationship should be clear from what has been said in this chapter. But neither the laws nor the customs of secular societies sanction nepotism in government or business relationships. In government employment each individual must qualify for appointment and advancement by purely secular criteria and standards. In business, with relatively few exceptions, the same is true. In a society where familism is as dominant a sentiment and practice as it is in

India, family sentiments induce nepotism as a deep moral obligation.

This sentiment prevails so widely that it even colours the interpretations of some of the increasing number of studies of what is happening to the joint family in India. As often as not the reports of research findings smack of attempts to show that while the joint obligations of members of joint families are less easily practised, sentiments concerning these obligations are still universal. Interpreters of the meaning of these facts should know that such facts are not unique to joint-family relationships. They are true of personal relationships of all types of families. It is the type of family institutions, units of organization for action, which they buttress and sustain, which will dictate the extent to which the institution of the joint family in India will impede the development of the many other kinds of units of organization for action which the development of a pluralistic social order requires.

MAIN AUTHORITIES QUOTED OR CITED

Anshen, Ruth Nanda, Ed., *The Family : Its Function and Destiny*, Science of Culture Series, Vol. V, Harper & Bros., New York, 1949 (especially Chapter V, "The Family in India", by David G. Mandelbaum).

Bailey, F. G., "The Joint Family in India", A Framework for Discussion, *Economic Weekly*, 20 February, 1960, pp. 345-352.

Cormack, Margaret, *The Hindu Woman*, Asia Publishing House, Bombay. (Teachers' College, Columbia University, 1953, First Indian Edition, 1961).

Derrett, J. Duncan M., "Law and the Predicament of the Hindu Joint Family", *Economic Weekly*, 13 February, 1960, pp. 305-311.

Ghurye, G. S., *Family and Kin in Indo-European Culture*, University of Bombay Publications, Sociology Series, No. 4, Oxford University Press, London, 1955.

Karve, Irawati, *Kinship Organisation in India*, Deccan College Monograph Series: 11, Deccan College Post-Graduate & Research Institute, Poona, 1953. (Printed at the G. S. Press, Mount Road, Madras).

Mayne, John D., *A Treatise on Hindu Law and Usage*, 6th Edition, Revised and Enlarged, Higginbotham & Co., Madras, 1900.

Murphy, Gardner, "*In The Minds of Men*, The Study of Human Behavior and Social Tensions in India", Basic Books, Inc., New York, 1953 (Based on the UNESCO Studies by Social Scientists Conducted at the Request of the Government of India.)

Panikkar, K. M., *Hindu Society at Cross Roads*, Asia Publishing House, Bombay, 3rd Edition, 1961. (With a new introduction.)

Prabhu, Pandharinath H., *Hindu Social Organization*, A Study in Socio-

Psychological and Ideological Foundations, Popular Book Depot, Bombay, 3rd Revised Edition, December, 1958.

Ross, Aileen D., *The Hindu Family In Its Urban Setting*, Oxford University Press, Indian Branch, 1961.

Shah, B. V., "Joint-Family System", An Opinion Survey of Gujarati Students, *Economic Weekly*, 24 December, 1960. pp. 1867-1870.

"*Social Legislation*—Its Role in Social Welfare", issued on behalf of the Planning Commission, Government of India, New Delhi, 1956.

Sociological Bulletin, Indian Sociological Society, Bombay, Vol. IV, No. 2, Sept., 1955; Vol. V, Sept., 1956; Vol. VIII, No. 2, Sept., 1959; Vol. IX, No. 1, March, 1960; Vol. XI, Nos. 1 and 2, March and September, 1962.

CHAPTER 5

LOCAL RURAL INSTITUTIONS

LOCAL village self-government in India, the panchayat or village council, is probably more ancient than any other in the world. The story of its origin is buried in antiquity. It has, however, been more completely preserved than any other because its social, economic and political structures were over the centuries preserved by a caste system which was buttressed by religion. It therefore has always been a real social institution. This institution, however, for more than a hundred years at least, has been overlaid, and modified, by other local government or administrative structures. These structures were not indigenous; they were imposed by colonial rule. Whether or not such administrative structures can be called institutions, they have become well established and both their purposes and procedures thoroughly rationalized. They were not built on the foundations of the hundreds of thousands of indigenous, folk self-governments of villages. As a matter of fact, there were few functional relations between the two systems by which the hundreds of millions of rural people were governed, their own local panchayats and government District officials. The result was that when the new government of India was formed in 1949 and rural development programmes launched in 1951, India had no system of government in which the village panchayat was part and parcel of its total government structure.

To build or evolve such a system was one of the basic tasks of the new government. The new Constitution declared that "the States should take steps to organise village panchayats and endow them with such powers and authority as might be necessary to enable them to function as units of self-government." The First Five Year Plan also said, "As the agencies of the State Government cannot easily approach each individual villager separately, progress depends largely on the existence of an active organisation in the village which can bring the people into common programmes to be carried out with the assistance of the administration."

Local government institutions were bound to condition the planned programmes of rural development in two ways. They were organizations which could be used as instruments or vehicles for development, but they were also institutions whose inertias were strongly buttressed by traditions and sentiments. New institutions, or the realignment of old institutions, could be and were rationally prescribed by a national Plan. But the change of traditions and sentiments, which provided the adamancy of old institutions, could not be prescribed. As is always the case with planning, the question may be raised as to whether programme planners and directors realize how much, and all the ways in which, sentiments about old, established social institutions are sure to condition progress toward the objectives which planning prescribes. In this, as in all other fields of activity, much more has been learned from ten years of programme operating experience in India than could have been known in advance. At this point it is our purpose only to analyze the social forces which local government structures represented, and to describe the historic events by which these forces had been developed. We do this because history cannot be revoked, but also because it is always inevitably a part of the function of development not only to utilize the end-products of history but in various ways to alter the forces which created those end-products.

The recorded history of village panchayats is both voluminous and diverse. The best we can do is to accept, and briefly relate, what has been most widely accepted by scholars who have attempted to write this history. Sir Henry Maine, who—probably justifiably—has been more widely quoted than any other authority on Indian villages, describes their social organization and customary practices in the light of his knowledge of similar folk governments in other societies. He says:

> "At the outset they seem to be associations of kinsmen, united by the assumption (doubtless very vaguely conceived) of a common lineage. Sometimes the community is unconnected with any exterior body, save by the shadowy bond of caste. Sometimes it acknowledges itself to belong to a larger group or clan. But in all cases the community is so

organised as to be complete in itself. . . . " It, in fact, includes "a nearly complete establishment of occupations and trades for enabling them to continue their collective life without assistance from any person or body external to them. Besides the Headman or Council exercising quasi-judicial, quasi-legislative power, they contain a village police, now recognised and paid in certain provinces by the British Government. They include several families of hereditary traders; the Blacksmith, the Harness-maker, the Shoemaker. The Brahmin is also found for the performance of ceremonies, and even the Dancing Girl for attendance at festivities. There is invariably a Village Accountant."

He says that:

" . . . if I may trust the statements of several eminent Indian authorities, it is always the fact or the fiction that this council merely declares customary law. And indeed, while it is quite true of India that the head of the family is supposed to be chief of the household, the families within the village or township would seem to be bound together through their representative heads by just as intricate a body of customary rules as they are in respect of those parts of the village domain which answer to the Teutonic common mark and arable mark. . . . "

At other places, Maine describes the complete acceptance by all villagers of panchayats' decisions that custom has been violated; that the offence of one person is not considered an offence against another person, but an offence against the integrity of the entire community.

" . . . It would be altogether inappropriate to speak of a political superior commanding a particular course of action to the villagers. The council of village elders does not command anything, it merely declares what has always been. Nor does it generally declare that which it believes some higher power to have commanded; those most entitled to speak on the subject deny that the natives of India necessarily require divine or political authority as the basis of their usages; their antiquity is by itself assumed to be a sufficient reason for obeying them . . . a person aggrieved complains not of an individual wrong but of the disturbance of the order of the entire little society. . . . "

It is in no sense our purpose to document the evolution of Indian village society. Others far more competent than we have not successfully done so. Our purpose is merely to present some of the justification for the belief, on the part of many Indian leaders, that the roots of local government were very old, very deep, and still living. Wavell said, "The old Vedic ideal, with its theory of dharma, and the Indo-Aryan village community, more democratic than the free cities of Greece, had for many centuries provided India, both north and south of the Vindhyas, with the spiritual and economic ties which create a sense of nationality."

Jayaswal said, "Going back to the oldest literature of the race, we find from the Vedas that national life and activities in the earliest times on record were expressed through popular assemblies and institutions." Law said, "The Mahabharata expatiates on the policy that should be followed by the monarch in regard to the Ganas, and by the Ganas themselves for self-preservation. These Ganas appear to have been self-governing communities." Sir Malcolm Darling presented evidence that the basic ethos of the village panchayat was still living in the Punjab as late as 1930. He quoted a villager as saying, "How could a man venture to tell a lie before his brotherhood?" and adds, from another villager, "It is a Hindu belief that where five sit together God himself is present and no one would dare to lie in His presence." Mahatma Gandhi said, "My idea of village swaraj is that it is a complete republic."

No one can doubt the wholeness, the self-sufficiency and competence of the village panchayat in ancient times. Similar folk-governing groups existed as the antecedents of all modern societies, except those peopled by immigrants from other relatively-advanced societies. The question in India was not how far back in the evolution of its society this form of local government existed, but the question of how completely it could be taken as a model for the reconstruction of villages.

The Planning Commission said that the economic and social structure of villages had been weakened under British rule. Some of the authors we have quoted earlier recorded the ways in which village self-sufficiency had been diluted over the centuries of feudal and colonial rule. Moreland and Chatterjee, like a number of authors who attempted to trace the evolution of the Indian village back through sacred literature, said that, " . . . most villages, but probably not all, contained a resident community or brotherhood, held together by the tie of common ancestry, and managing, as a body, the affairs of the village, subject to whatever orders the administration might give." The last clause of this quotation probably identifies the first modification or dilution of complete village self-sufficiency, namely, that they were always in some ways subject to overhead administration. Others, outstanding among them Sir Henry Maine and Baden-Powell, attempt to document in some detail the factors and the processes by which Indian villages had, far back into the past, been diluted by overhead government interference and interposition.

Both Maine and Baden-Powell describe, and fairly well document, the development of feudalism as a system of rule which appeared between the era of primitive folk societies and the time when the attempt to revive village panchayats began. Maine seemed to postulate this as an automatic stage in social development. He said that feudalization in India was in process when British rule began, and described how it was moved forward by the English Settlement Acts. Baden-Powell did not philosophise about any inevitability of social evolution, but did document the widespread existence of the local rule of "aristocratic classes and dominant families", in most, if not in all, sections of India. Furthermore, he severely criticized the evidence upon which Maine based his broad conclusions that joint—or village—ownership of land prevailed widely in India. He traced in detail the various, specific, historic administrative acts which served to dilute old primitive village self-sufficiency and to curtail the role of panchayats as units of local government. He cited one type of case after another in different parts of India where "revenue farmers" had grown into "proprietors"; how "cadets and scions", to whom life grants had been made, "became co-sharing owners of whole groups of villages"; and where the holdings of a clan had "become a district of the empire, but was covered with villages often held by bodies of descendants of the former rulers." Other less careful scholars have presented more lurid descriptions of the feudalism which had developed, not only during the period of the British and Moghul rulers, but even before that. From these historic accounts, one can only arrive at the judgment that for a long time before Indian independence and national planning, feudal rule had compromised the pristine folk communities which Metcalfe seemed to think were still not only self-sufficient, but efficient units of local government.

Overhead government interference with, and interposition in, village life and organization was, however, not the only force which had tended to dilute the integrity of old, folk village life and organization. Village self-sufficiency, for a long time, had been gradually supplemented by trade with other villages and with traders from more distant centres. Maine cites a case where grain traders, as a class, were not permitted to be a part of the occupational organization of village structure. Traders and money-lenders, as well as government servants and their functions, had become a steadily-increasing part of village life. Some resident villagers had shifted from old, past occupations to these new functions and thus became parties to trade and other types of interaction with extra-village functions. This has happened in all societies as they have moved out of local self-sufficiency into the edges of the price and market system of society. Whether or not this shift can be chronologically documented, it is known to have happened in India.

It is, however, not necessary to depend solely upon conclusions derived from comparative analyses of other societies and from such nineteenth-century authorities as we have quoted, to document the ways in which village life and organization had departed from the patterns of simple folk societies. We discussed in considerable detail the findings of current anthropological studies of Indian villages in Chapter 2. On the basis of the information which all of these sources provide, we venture a summary of what could be known about the assets and liabilities of Indian village communities as local entities upon which, on the one hand, to base the development of democratic local government and, on the other hand, as effective agencies for promoting and executing programmes of local development.

The first liability, or weakness, was that the typical Indian village, while it was a highly-structured social entity, was not a democratic community or in any way a *gemeinschaft*. The second weakness was that extra-village kinship and caste rights and obligations in some ways took precedence over local village obligations. The third general weakness was that, to the extent that village panchayats still functioned, their function was far more that of settling local disputes between persons and families than it was of directing local government. Even then caste panchayats more often than village panchayats, settled these disputes, and caste loyalties were probably stronger than village loyalties. The fourth weakness was the overweening influence of what Baden-Powell called "dominant families" and Dube called "elite classes". Finally, an equally if not more important weakness, partly the result of other weaknesses, was the fact that villages had not for decades, even generations, been socio-economic, self-sufficient communities.

There were, however, assets of villages as social entities which could be woven into a system of local self-government and used as agencies for local development projects. Each village was a geographically-separated and considerably-isolated population group. Each recognized that, notwithstanding its inter-village kinship and caste responsibilities, it did have local village responsibilities. Even though it had for generations not been permitted completely to govern itself, it had always been dealt with as a unity by overhead government, even by feudal owners and administrators. At the moment of Independence, overhead government was, through its district and sub-district offices, dealing with villages as living social entities. In spite of all of its weaknesses, the result of long periods of decay, village settlement was and is sure to be for a long time to come one of the most basic social structures of Indian society.

Local governments, while not buttressed by the same traditions and deep sentiments as were village panchayats, had evolved on the basis of a rationale which many believed had been historically validated. This system of local government, however, had not been closely inter-related with the ancient village panchayat system, and because of this fact, had contributed to the weakening of local self-government.

Concerning the origin and evolution of the system of district government, it is enough to say that the evolution of the Collectors' district system began in Bengal as early as 1872, before the British Empire began taking over from the British East India

Company, and that by the beginning of the nineteenth century, districts were well-established institutions in all of British India. They were at first primarily tax-collection districts and the officers in charge of them were called "Collectors". To this original function was soon added the function of maintaining and administering law and order. Districts became not only the basic overhead units of local government in all British provinces, but prevailed in a modified form in all other areas where Great Britain established and maintained "paramount power". It was natural, therefore, as the Princely States were liquidated, and zamindars and jagirdars were eliminated as tax farmers, that districts and their sub-districts should constitute a complete system of local government.[1]

Tinker, in his meticulous analysis of local administrative units as units of local government, deals in detail with panchayats. But in the first chapter of his book, he says: "Local government in present-day India, Pakistan and Burma has inherited but little from indigenous local institutions." Because we expect to follow Tinker's account fairly closely, a brief sketch of the organisation of the government units which he is discussing is in order.

The basic administrative unit of local government was the magisterial district. Above the district was the province or State and below it were the sub-districts—talukas or tehsils. This administrative organization was first established wholly for purposes of revenue administration, a little later for administration of law and order, and still later for administering of welfare programmes. At the time the new national government was established, there were something like three hundred districts, most of them still called Collectors' districts and their administrative officers called Collectors. Each district had from three to five sub-divisions. Had the almost three hundred million people who lived outside the towns and cities been equally divided among the three hundred districts and their sub-districts, each district would have had a population of approximately one million, and each sub-district approximately 250,000. As a matter of fact, some districts

---

[1] The reader interested in local government administrative units of earlier dynasties, and the art of government in very early times in India is pointed to Altekar, A. S., State and Government in Ancient India From Earliest Times to A.D. 1200, Motilal Banarasi Das, 1949; and Shamasastry, Dr. R., Kautilya's Arthasastra, Mysore Printing and Publishing House, Mysore, India, Sixth Edition, 1960.

had more than three million population and some sub-districts more than one million population. In most countries such large units would not be considered as *local* units of government.

The highlights of Tinker's account are that district administrators were primarily interested in efficiency in carrying out their assigned responsibilities, not in local self-government. There were repeated attempts to temper what in the beginning was almost absolute power of the district officers, by establishing district boards. These bodies of citizens were, however, little more than tools of the district officer. In some ways they strengthened rather than diluted his absolute authority, and in many cases, members of district boards were representatives of personal vested interests, most often landlords. Never in the early days of the system, and seldom in the latter days, were representatives of village panchayats members of district boards. Furthermore, for a long period, the gradual expansion of district jurisdictional responsibilities steadily diluted the responsibilities and thus the privileges of local village panchayats.

As we interpret Tinker's account, from the time the British government took over from the East India Company until 1864, the trend was steadily in the direction of expanding district administrative authority and a steady dilution of old panchayat jurisdictions. This had begun under Moghul rule. Tinker says, however, that:

"The Mughuls had interfered very little with the ancient customs of village government; they incorporated the village into the administration as a unit for revenue and police purposes only. The state dealt through the headman or muqaddam who was held responsible for the maintenance of law and order and the restitution of theft within the area of his authority. The judicial powers of the village council, the panchayat, were considerably curtailed under the Mughuls, otherwise local affairs remained unregulated from above, and the village officers and servants were answerable primarily to the panchayat."

After 1864, there were repeated attempts to construct, or rehabilitate, local self-government. A brief, and sketchily-documented, account of each of these long periods reveals the difficulty experienced in the changing of direction and the forces which sabotaged this change that were still resident in India when India herself took over the reins of government planning and administration. The contest was between those who favoured greater responsibility for local units of government and those who believed that evidence showed that village people would not accept responsibilities and had not done so in fields such as sanitation which they could themselves greatly improve if they were willing to do so. We shall telescope the history of this contest by citing briefly the few major attempts to encourage and strengthen the development of village self-government.

A Resolution of 1862 was issued by Lt.-Governor Sir Robert Montgomery of the Punjab which provided for the setting up of municipal committees. Tinker says, "District officials seem to have remained entirely in the background." Nevertheless, a great many local governments for municipalities, that is, towns and small cities, were established as a result of this Resolution. Another Resolution was issued by the Lawrence government in 1864 which, in part, read as follows:

"The people of this country are perfectly capable of administering their own local affairs. The municipal feeling is deeply rooted in them. The village communities ... are the most abiding of Indian institutions. They maintained the framework of society while successive swarms of invaders swept over the country. In the cities also, the people cluster in their wards, trade guilds and panchayats and show much capacity for corporate action. ... Holding the position we do in India, every view of duty and policy should induce us to leave as much as possible of the business of the country to be done by the people. ... and to confine ourselves to ... influencing and directing in a general way all the movements of the social machine."

The so-called Mutiny of 1857 also apparently gave a considerable lift to the desire for local self-government. But again, this registered itself largely in the towns. Tinker says village life was hardly touched by the new district committees which had been set up, and the extent of municipal control left to the local citizens (town councils) was only in those types of action which could be supervised by the government-appointed Commissioners.

Lord Ripon had urged that provincial legislation be passed providing for a two-tier system, with district boards and sub-district boards based either upon the sub-division or the tehsil. Tinker records, however, that " . . . every province except Assam, Burma, C.P., and Madras entrusted the district boards with all the funds and almost all the functions of local government." Lord Ripon had contended, as Sir Henry Maine had contended long before him, that "if local government is to have any vitality, then it should evolve out of local circumstances; if it has to be created artificially, at least it should be planned in detail by local administrators, and not be imposed ready-made by the central government."

The famous Resolution on Local Self-Government of May, 1882 stated: "It is not primarily with a view to improvement in administration that this measure is put forward and supported. It is chiefly designed as an instrument of political and popular education." Tinker observed that the vast majority of the local Anglo-Indian officials were conservatives, supported by a single "paternal" administration, so that the reforms projected by Ripon were attenuated, or even ignored, by provincial governments and district officers who were responsible for putting them into practice. He records the optimism which developed ten years later when in Parliamentary debate, on the Indian Council Act, Prime Minister Gladstone had argued that "from the training school of local government might emerge the future leaders of India."

In 1907, the British Government set up a Royal Commission on Decentralisation which made its report in 1909. This report was not especially forward-looking. It said that the Commission had "heard a mass of evidence which tended to confirm that the ancient 'solidarity' and community-bonds had long disintegrated," and said, "We do not think it possible to restore the ancient village system." The recommendations were that the village head-man should become "sarpanch" (chairman of the village council) and that other members be "informally elected". It listed functions for which the village council might be made responsible and said, "They should not be saddled with taxation." If further said that, "They should be supervised by district officers, not district boards, and they should not be subject to the petty tyranny of petty officials."

The Government of India, in a Resolution in May, 1918, declared that, "Both urban and rural boards were to contain a majority of elected board members ... and it listed what criteria should be used for those eligible to vote for board members. It stated that boards should be free to raise and lower taxes and that grants should not be allowed to specify items of expenditures, and that pioneer panchayats "should be given a portion of the district cess." The Resolution urged all provincial governments to pass the legislation essential to the implementation of these recommendations. Upon this recommendation, a number of provinces enacted various types of panchayat legislation, some of them to make newly-formed panchayats identical with old district sub-divisions, others to be over a "circle" (a local group of villages or a single large village). Some States provided for transference of control over village schools, village works, and management of cattle farms from districts to panchayats. Panchayats, however, largely had to depend on grants for the financing of these undertakings. When, therefore, these grants were not made by higher authorities, as Tinker said, "The allotment or withholding of financial grants was potentially a powerful instrument of ministerial control ... " and that while, "Local bodies resented the supervision of their activities by departmental officers" they, as in the past, expected "Government to provide the money for schemes of expansion."

Not all of the provinces attempted to follow these recommendations with the result that, in some instances, overhead supervision was only slightly lessened. In other cases, it was so completely abandoned that village government was in chaos, riddled by local factions, sterile in leadership, controlled by nepotism, or dominated by landlords. We do not present illustrations of each of these, which Tinker provides, for the long period of thirty years in which the Government of India was a dyarchy, in which India and Britain shared in the control. Nor do we make little more than passing reference to Tinker's exposition of how the national independence movement not only failed to consolidate the ground which local government had so painfully gained, but how it directly or inadvertently weakened the continued growth of local government. There was, however, nothing anomalous in what occurred. Britain was a party to the gains which over the last few decades had been made in the field of local government, and was a party to the further planned progress in this field. Tinker's remark concerning the Resolution of 1918 was as follows: "Excellent sentiments, but to the Indian politician, merely the confirmation of his fears that he was to be offered local authority as a bait, to induce him to relinquish his national aspirations."

Whether or not this was true, the non-co-operation of the Independence movement led national, provincial, and even local leaders to non-participation in local as well as national government. They repudiated all government authority. They refused even to accept educational grants, and persons who took part in district board activities were ostracized. It was by these tactics, as well as by going to jail by the thousands, that the Indian Congress won Independence. As Tinker says, " . . . it was only logical for Congress to order those of its followers who were members of local bodies to carry out parallel disruptive tactics. If as a result local bodies were disorganised, and local board staff demoralised, Congress policy can only be accounted successful. But while this may have been effective political tactics, it was disastrous to the stability of local government. . . . "

The legacy of this disaster was not, however, as great as the legacy of the long period of neglect, even sabotage, of local government which was bequeathed to India's leaders when, immediately following Independence, they made the reconstruction of village life as effective local governments a prime objective of national development. Whether or not Metcalfe's idyllic picture of the village panchayat was a true picture, it was undoubtedly true that at a much earlier date each village had its own self-contained local government. There is no doubt that this kind of government had been overlaid by government structures established by colonial powers. Nor can there be any doubt that the main objective of these superimposed layers of district, provincial, and national government had not been to strengthen or even to preserve the local self-government of village panchayats.

This brief synopsis represents more than a century of an historic period in which new government structures were built and old village government structures decayed. The Royal Commission on Decentralisation in 1909 said, "The scant success of the efforts hitherto made to introduce a system of rural self-government is largely due to the fact that we have not built from the bottom. The foundation of any stable edifice which shall associate the people with administration must be the village, one in which the people are known to one another and have interests which converge on well-organised objects."

Moves had been made to decentralize government administration by re-establishing sub-district governments and thus bring responsible administrative officials closer to village people. District and sub-district boards, composed at least partially of citizens, were intended to bring local administrators closer to villages. Increased grants had been made to these local bodies. Such bodies had in some States been allocated part of the land tax and permitted to levy other kinds of taxes. Some provincial governments had passed village panchayat laws. Provincial departments of education, health, etc., had been granted the right to promote and make grants for local improvements. It is probably too strong a generalization to say that all these acts, and others, constituted consistent progress in the rehabilitation or strengthening of local self-government. They constituted gains in local education, health, and to some extent in transportation, but they were all on the initiative of higher administrators and statesmen, not on the initiative of the village people themselves.

This was largely true even when the organization of village panchayats was encouraged. A statement by Tinker probably well states the constructive rationale of all of these attempts at improvement. He says that, "The plans for new types of village authorities which were embodied in the legislation after the First World War were nowhere intended to reproduce the characteristics of the old-time panchayats, but were designed to fulfil one of three purposes; to provide a smaller area as a basic unit for the existing structure of rural local government, to provide a rudimentary municipal framework for large villages or small towns, or (and sometimes in conjunction with one of the previous types) to form a simple judicial tribunal. In each case there was a hope that the new bodies would be able to mobilise that local community spirit to which the larger, more artificial units of administration could not appeal." He summarizes the gains of a later period when he says, "The idea of this experiment" (the establishment of village authorities) "was to attempt to associate local government with the life of rural communities—in which the more artificial district boards had manifestly failed. There is evidence that the new village councils, although there were many failures, did awaken many country dwellers to the meaning of local government in villages in all parts of the sub-continent."

If, however, the view is accepted that district, sub-district, and even "circle" units of government administration were not units of real local self-government, there were then left only a little more than 80,000 panchayats which existed in 1950-51. There were more than 550,000 villages. Few of the panchayats were real local governments. They were granted only limited powers, had few sources of finance, were either strictly supervised or neglected by district administrators. They were often dominated by locally-posted government officials or by local leaders who catered to district and sub-district officers. Few of them were democratically-organized. They were quite universally composed of the various representatives of past panchayats, and were councils of village elders, each of whom came to his position by inheritance. Thus local government, in so far as it existed, was a by-product of two other local institutions, the caste and the joint family.

This discussion has been partly to describe existent local government institutions as potential instruments of local and national development. We are aware that this cannot be adequately done by the attenuated acount we have presented. But as was stated earlier, the greater purpose has been to discuss these institutions as factors which conditioned development programmes. This purpose could be served only by presenting the history of these institutions and the ideas and inertias which had developed out of this history. One body of ideas buttressed the conviction that the ancient village panchayat provided the foundation, and the great potential, for the construction or reconstruction of local self-government. The other body of ideas was centred on the conviction that efficient administration required not only assistance but firm guidance, even if that meant the domination of local government by overhead government.

MAIN AUTHORITIES QUOTED OR CITED

Baden-Powell, B. H., *The Origin and Growth of Village Communities in India*, Swan-Sonnenschein & Co. Ltd., London, 1889.

Darling, Sir Malcolm, *Wisdom and Waste in the Punjab Village*, Humphrey Milford, Oxford University Press, London 1934.

Jayaswal, K. P., *Hindu Polity*, A Constitutional History of India in Hindu Times, The Bangalore Printing & Publishing Co. Ltd., Bangalore City, 1955.

Law, N. N., *Aspects of Ancient Indian Polity*, Clarendon Press, Oxford, England, 1921.

Maine, Sir Henry, *Village Communities in the East and West*, New Edition, John Murray, London, 1890.

Moreland, W. H. and Chatterjee, A. C., *A Short History of India*, Longmans, Green & Co., London, 4th Edition, 1957.

Nanavati, M. B. and Anjaria, J. J., *The Indian Rural Problem*, 5th Edition, The Indian Society of Agricultural Economics, Vora & Co. Publishers Ltd., Bombay, 1960, Chapter XIV.

The First Five Year Plan, Planning Commission, Government of India, December, 1952.

Tinker, Hugh, *The Foundations of Local Self-Government in India, Pakistan and Burma*, University of London, Athlone Press, 1954.

CHAPTER 6

POPULATION AS A CONDITIONING FACTOR OF DEVELOPMENT

THE overall objective of India's planning—to raise the standards of living of her people and guarantee them fuller employment opportunities—is complicated by the necessity to accelerate economic development to match the pace of population growth. The increase in India's population between 1951 and 1961 has been nearly as large as the increase in the two preceding decades. This chapter will present some general facts concerning the size and characteristics of India's population, in the context of population as a basic conditioning factor in a developing country.

There are some reasons to doubt that the experiences of other countries, both developed and underdeveloped, in terms of the pattern of population growth will be replicated in India. Conditions involved in development have been different in some countries from those under which India's development started. Size of country and natural resources, stage of industrial development, presence or absence of immigration possibilities, and many other factors help to determine the direction and speed of population growth. China, the only country in the world with a larger population than India's, has a far greater land base on which to support her people and, because of a different political ideology, is moving toward her objectives through methods different from those India has chosen. Japan has become very rapidly industrialized and is therefore less dependent than India on agriculture as the principal support of her people. Although population has been steadily increasing in the United States, the land base is large, physical and economic resources are great, and industrialization and urbanization have largely replaced the agricultural character of the economy with which she began her development. Although the United States is still a young country, the period in which she evolved from a frontier, agricultural economy to a modern, industrialized nation was far longer than the period in which India is attempting to move from a peasant society to a modern developed economy.

The United States started with an advantage in terms of an immigrant population from Europe, typically young and male, already in possession of certain basic techniques and technologies which were applied to developing a new country. India, on the other hand, started her development programme with a large, agricultural population, poor and illiterate, on a limited land base, and ill-prepared to cope with the problems of building a prosperous agriculture or industries large or small. India is a large country, a sub-continent, but the amount of arable land available is not extensive enough for so large an agricultural population. Because her level of agricultural yields is among the lowest in the world, her people are poor and she cannot accumulate adequate savings to invest in industrial or other enterprises. With continuing, rapid increases in population, too large a proportion of national income must go to survival rather than investment for progress. To attain her stated goal of raising the standards of living of her people, given her physical, economic, and human resources, India is faced with "population pressure" of forbidding dimensions.

India's population has historically been large, although its growth was somewhat erratic until 1921. Since then, growth has been steady and the rate of growth has increased in nearly every decade. Her population which was some 235 million in 1901 rose to nearly 250 million in 1921, and jumped to about 317 million in 1941. It grew from 359 million in 1951 to more than 436 million in 1961. This represented an increase in decennial growth rate from about 6 per cent in the 1901-11 decade to about 21 per cent during 1951-61. The decade 1911-21 was the only decennial period since 1901 which showed a net decrease in population and rate of growth. This decrease was due primarily to plagues, economic disorganization after World War I, crop failures, and an epidemic of influenza which caused a devastating death toll all over India. This past decade has shown a rate of growth of about 2 per cent per year, nearly twice the rate of the preceding three decades. Population during 1951-61 grew 61 per cent faster than the rate at which it grew between 1941-51.

While India's growth rate does not appear to be high compared with other underdeveloped, or even developed, countries, the population base to which she has been adding is so large that the increase in absolute numbers is very high indeed. In absolute numbers, her population increased by 39 million from 1931 to 1941, by 42 million between 1941 and 1951, and by 77 million between 1951 and 1961. These large increases are not attributable entirely to a high birth rate; they are also due to a falling mortality and morbidity rate, due to widespread immunization, development of an indigenous supply of drugs and medicines, and to other health and sanitation measures. No longer do disastrous plagues and epidemics of earlier decades take toll of millions of India's people. Improved methods of preventing or controlling epidemics, use of DDT and antibiotics, more efficient disaster relief programmes, and faster communication facilities all have helped to reduce the death toll of former years. Thus India faces the paradoxical situation of aggravating her own population problem by adopting modern and humane measures for protecting her people from the ravages of disease and increasing their welfare and span of life. In order to raise the standards of living and increase *per capita* incomes, India needs to stabilize her population growth as she has emphatically stated in her Five Year Plans, but as a developing country she cannot turn her back on improved health and sanitation measures for her people.

Although the overall increase in population has been very great, there were in 1961 only seven cities in all India of more than a million population. Greater Calcutta, including all contiguous urban areas, had a population in 1961 of five and one-half million, one of the ten largest metropolitan areas in the world. Calcutta City proper had a population just under three million. Greater Bombay had slightly more than four million people, ranking fifth in the list of the world's largest cities. Density of the total population increased markedly in every State, and in the country as a whole from 316 per square mile to 384. Two States, Kerala and West Bengal, went over the 1,000 mark in density. While the urban population was growing by 16 million people between 1951 and 1961, the rural population added 61 million to her numbers and made up 82 per cent of the total population. This meant that India in 1961 was still primarily a nation of rural villages. The shrinking of the man-land ratio over the decades indicates that agriculture and rural areas, mainly villages, have become steadily more crowded. India not only has a large rural village population, overwhelmingly dependent upon agriculture, but the age distribution of the people reveals a heavy dependency factor both in and outside of agriculture. The 1951 Census figures on age structure, based on a total population of about 350 million, showed that 41 per cent of this total fell within what may be called the "dependent ages"—below 14 and over 65 years of age, a total of about 145 million in these two dependent groups.

In 1951, there were about 134 million infants and young people in the age group up to 14, all of them still presumably on the receiving end for the basic necessities of food, clothing and shelter and at least minimum education and health services. The oldsters in the population, 65 and over, numbered some 11 million, requiring at least the minimum essentials of life, with additional health and welfare services supplanting educational needs. This is a heavy burden on the 204 million men and women in the productive ages of 15 to 65. In developed countries, the ratio of dependent people is high among those of 65 and over, whereas in India and other underdeveloped countries the ratio is high among those who have not yet reached their productive years. In 1951, 92 per cent of the dependent groups, up to 14 and 65 and over, were in the age group 0 to 14 in India; this is in contrast to 76 per cent in the United States and only 67 per cent in the United Kingdom.

Based on information concerning the various livelihood classes, numbers of self-supporting persons and dependents in a total population figure of 357 million, the 1951 Census of India stated that in India each self-supporting, gainfully employed person must support himself and two and one-half other persons, compared with one and one-half persons in the United States and one plus in Great Britain. Because of the larger portion of young people under 15 in India than in the United States or Great Britain, it is estimated that on the basis of 1,000 self-supporting, gainfully employed persons, the figures on dependency would be 1317 in India, 702 in the United States, and 496 in Great Britain. These comparisons show the relatively heavy burden borne by the Indian worker in his productive years.

The high dependency ratio in India is a significant factor in development not only for the load it places on the productive age groups, but also because it requires a disproportionate expenditure of income for the bare essentials of maintaining life. In a low *per capita* income country such as India, where the accumulation of savings and productive investment capital is so urgently needed, this factor is particularly important. Too high a percentage of total expenditures, for example, must go for food—two-thirds in India in 1950 and less than one-third in the United States. A recent study showed that three highly developed countries—Belgium, West Germany and Switzerland—had less arable land per person than India, but all three had less than 50 per cent as many in the normally dependent age groups (under 15 and over 65). Whereas in India the ratio of dependent to productive age groups was 69.9 per cent, in Belgium it was 45.5 per cent, in Western Germany 48.9 per cent, and in Switzerland 49.5 per cent. Six other countries had a dependency ratio of less than 60 per cent.

Looking at India's population from the point of view of occupational groups, we have seen that the great majority, some 70 per cent, were agriculturists, living primarily in rural villages. The character of the various classes of agriculturists, owners to landless, and the contribution they make to the national economy in India are discussed in some detail in the following chapter. We shall, therefore, turn our attention here to the remaining 30 per cent. or 107.6 million people, who earned their livelihood outside of agriculture. They were divided by the Indian Census into four main groups as follows: (1) non-agricultural production such as mining, quarrying, processing, and manufacturing, (10.5 per cent of the general population); (2) commerce, (6 per cent); (3) transport, (1.6 per cent); and (4) non-agricultural "rentiers" pensioners, etc., (12.1 per cent). Although 107.6 million of the total 1951 population were classified as non-agriculturists, only 33.4 million of them were listed as self-supporting. Self-supporting non-agriculturists represented 32 per cent of all self-supporting persons. Slightly more than half of these were employers and self-employed persons, about 44 per cent were employees, and a very small number were pensioners and miscellaneous income receivers. The great majority of these self-supporting non-agriculturists were in industry and services, almost equally divided between processing and manufacturing 28 per cent; in commerce (trade), transport, and communication 24 per cent. The principal types of processing and manufacturing in which they were engaged involved the primary products of cultivation and animal husbandry; cotton textiles; metal and chemical products; wood and wood products; glass and pottery. Most of the workers in commerce were carrying on retail trade and selling of foodstuff. In both processing and manufacturing industries and in retail trade, the base was agriculture because the products of cultivation and animal husbandry were the chief ones involved.

If we consider only the 104.4 million self-supporting persons in the general population, leaving out all non-earning and earning dependents, it is seen that while 68 per cent of the agricultural classes were self-supporting, only 32 per cent of the non-agricultural classes were described as self-supporting. Even more striking was the fact that against the total general population of 356.6 million people, 19 per cent of the agricultural classes, but only 9 per cent of the non-agricultural classes were self-supporting.

The population picture thus far drawn portrays in broad outline a massive, rural village people, devoted mainly to agriculture as a means of livelihood. Increasing density of population has increased pressure on the land. The agricultural composition of the population together with figures showing the proportion of people who are self-supporting reveal a heavy dependency factor operating in both the agricultural and non-agricultural sectors. All of these aspects of the population situation have great significance in planning India's economic and social development. But these factors relate mainly to size of population.

India's development plans also carry along with them the necessity of building a nation which will unify the many and diverse elements in her population. The sociological implications and processes involved in nation-building will be discussed in a later chapter. Here we look briefly at the various cultural groups in India which have a marked influence on the success of development plans because of their separatism and the need to integrate them in a unified effort to build a modern nation. The three principal cultural groups which we shall discuss are: language groups, religious groups, and tribal or scheduled castes, sometimes designated as "backward classes". The fact that they are diverse cultural or social groups in the Indian population is an important conditioning factor in economic and social development. The Census of 1951 enumerated a total of 845 languages or dialects, 14 of which were major language-culture groups. Out of a total population of some 357 million for which this information on languages was reported in 1951, the overwhelming proportion of the people, 324 million or 90 per cent, spoke these 14 specified languages. Of these 324 million, about 150 million, or 46 per cent, spoke the four principal specified languages of Hindi, Urdu, Hindustani, and Punjabi. Telugu was reported by about 33 million, Marathi and Tamil by about 27 million each, and Bengali by 25 million. Some 12 million persons reported speaking 23 different tribal languages or dialects, and about 18 million others reported that they spoke 24 other Indian languages or dialects. This potpourri of languages has made communication difficult even between regions and neighbouring peoples in India and has increased the isolation of rural people.

The various religious or communal groups have also presented problems to India's planners and leaders. While the proportion of the Indian people who professed the Hindu religion was exceedingly large, 85 per cent, as reported in the 1951 Census, there were several other religious groups which claimed a substantial number of adherents. The Muslim religion was professed by some 35 million persons in 1951, or nearly 10 per cent of all the persons enumerated. There were about 8 million Christians, a little over 2 per cent of the total, and 6 million Sikhs, slightly under 2 per cent. Jains and Buddhists each claimed about 2 million persons, and Zoroastrians or Parsis about 1 million.

The presence of these religious and communal groups is significant to India's development to the extent that they operate on the basis of their communal interests in cases where these interests either do not contribute to the national effort or actually hamper it. Where the two largest groups, Hindu and Muslim, have found themselves in conflict with each other, divisive and even destructive efforts for supremacy in a particular area have contributed to national disunity. Even the minor religious groups, numerically small, play a larger role than might be expected because they are among the most literate, most prosperous, and most urban of all Indian societal groups and are able to make their voices heard.

Another large category in the Indian population is designated as "Scheduled tribes, scheduled castes, and other backward classes". As is implied by this terminology, the people in these groups are set apart from the rest of the community, are economically weak and socially disadvantaged. Because of their large numbers and their special problems, they play a role as a somewhat separate population group in India's plans and programmes for economic and social development. All suffer disability either socially or economically or both. The 1961 Census enumerated these "backward classes" under three classifications and estimated their number as follows: (1) scheduled tribes, 22.5 million; (2) scheduled castes, 55 million; and (3) "denotified" tribes (formerly "criminal" tribes), about 4 million, a total of about 82 million.

The general and specific problems of the so-called backward or depressed classes are legion. India's Constitution set aside for them certain privileges or reservations in government posts and educational institutions to protect them from social injustice and exploitation for a period of ten years after Independence, later extended another ten years. Many feel that this policy has accentuated their isolation from the larger community and proved to be a divisive influence. In any case, the vast majority of the tribals are dependent upon agriculture, forestry, or fishing and are therefore not in the market for positions in government or in educational institutions. Economic development programmes in the fields of irrigation, power, and industry have often contributed to the problems of tribal population by using land and water on which they have depended for their shifting cultivation or fishing and forestry occupations. The economic problems of the backward classes can be quickly summarized by saying that they include disadvantages arising from poverty, unemployment and underemployment, and prevailing indebtedness. The social problems can be listed as: isolation, lack of schooling, health and communication facilities; differences among themselves in addition to differences from those around them; social disability, accentuated in the case of scheduled castes by the stigma of untouchability. The incorporation of a sizable population group such as the backward classes—tribals and scheduled castes—nearly 82 million people—into the developing society India is promoting is a significant challenge.

These diversities of the population—mainly language and religious groups and backward classes—have been a characteristic of India's population for a long time, and the steady increase in total size of the population is not a new phenomenon. This is not, however, to say that India's population has been static. Changes have been taking place in terms of internal and external migration, the growth of cities, and the imbalance in manpower utilization, which have resulted in widespread unemployment and underemployment.

Of the two broad types of migration, internal and external, we shall be concerned here mainly with the former because the latter has never been a highly significant factor in the Indian population picture in extent, and it has been steadily decreasing in numbers and importance. India has been neither a receiver of heavy immigration nor a sender of migrants to other countries in large numbers for many decades. A large part of Indian emigration has not been for permanent settlement abroad, but has been a highly male-selective movement for employment in such countries as Burma, Ceylon and British Malaya, which could be easily reached from India's seacoast. This kind of emigration was stimulated by great economic pressure in the source areas of migration, but this flow has been almost entirely stopped since the 30's. Figures for the five-year period 1954-58 showed that emigration from India was almost offset by the number returning, the net number of emigrants being only about 5,000 persons.

A reliable estimate of the extent of internal migration in India is difficult because of the scarcity of precise census information, but most informed observers seem to agree that the Indian population is, and has been for a long time, largely immobile. Various reasons have been advanced for this lack of mobility— some social, some economic, and some cultural. Among the social and cultural causes of immobility are the joint-family system which encourages early marriage and strong home and family ties; the deep attachment which the Indian peasant cultivator has characteristically and historically felt for his home village; and the existence of the various ethnic, language, religious, and caste groups which tend to hold their members within the boundaries of their "own kind". At the same time that all of these groups offer security and protection to their own "in-groups", they act as an inhibition to movement outside of their limits of authority and power and as a barrier to those who may wish to enter. They exercise a strong hold on people to remain where they are. Added to these are certain economic factors such as: heavy rural indebtedness which keeps cultivators from being free to move elsewhere, the absence of vacant land to which to move, and the low wages and insecurity of the unskilled jobs in towns and cities, the only kinds of jobs for which most rural people would be eligible. In the absence of a real pull from larger towns and cities, with the prospect of better income and improved living conditions, any one of these factors can operate as a real inhibition to long-distance or permanent migration for the vast majority of cultivators.

This is not to say that there is *no* moving about in India. Because of the sheer size of the population, a relatively small proportion of the people migrating for whatever reason would add up to an impressive number. A great deal of the movement that occurs is short-distance, for marriage, religious, or political reasons or for seasonal or temporary employment. Marriage migration, chiefly of women, is quite extensive but is mainly inter-village, due to the marriage customs of caste endogamy and village exogamy, in which a bride must marry within her caste but outside of her own village. In a country of almost universal marriage, this particular tradition calls for considerable travel between villages. Many people, both men and women, also go some distances to religious festivals, commercial fairs, and political gatherings as well as to special family rites and ceremonies. Males who move to towns and cities or to plantation or other agricultural areas generally travel alone, leaving wives and families behind in their villages, themselves expecting to return after a season away from home.

Vertical mobility in India is hampered by some of the same social and economic factors that have acted as barriers to horizontal mobility. As was noted earlier, the three basic social structures or institutions—the village, the joint family, and the caste system—have roots deep into the past. Each of these in its own way tends to keep people in a peasant agricultural society such as India's immobile vertically as well as horizontally. The village holds the cultivator not only because his land is there, but because in it is the home place of his family. His kinship ties are there, and the caste group to which he belongs gives him a sense of security and protection. From the same set of social institutions, his occupation in life is largely determined—by the needs of the village, the traditional occupation of his family, or the occupation assigned to him by his caste. In a society with a highly-stratified class structure, where thousands of villages are isolated and largely stagnant, where illiteracy in the rural areas is well above 80 per cent, and where vocations are generally handed down from generation to generation with little change or improvement, there is little likelihood or opportunity for vertical mobility. Without conclusive scientific measurement of this phenomenon available from research, it is impossible to say that *no* vertical mobility has taken place in a given period or that any particular number of people have or have not moved up the ladder. As sociologists, we can only observe that, given the social structure of Indian rural society and an understanding of the behaviour of its components discussed earlier, it is probably safe to assume that relatively little vertical mobility exists in India as a whole. It is probably also true that some of the same economic factors which inhibit horizontal mobility, such as lack of money to invest in education or business enterprises, or even to pay off debts so that alternatives to current occupations might be available, operate to inhibit vertical mobility. Many of these social and economic factors are so closely interwoven that it could be said that the common denominators underlying the immobility found in much of Indian rural society are poverty, illiteracy and isolation.

Some internal migration has taken place, by far the most important of which is rural-urban migration. One of the factors operating to draw rural people to towns and cities is the high degree of rural unemployment and underemployment, especially among young people with some education and skill. They want better opportunities for education, employment, and social services, and grow impatient with the difficulties involved in making a living in agriculture on low incomes and low standards of living.

As Tarlok Singh put it, " . . . rural communities cannot develop at a rate at all commensurate with the rate of growth of the urban economy. They are not only unable to provide the minimum employment opportunities and livelihood for the bulk of the rural population but are also unable to keep within their fold those sections of the population which are progressive and are able to take advantage of opportunities for better education and training. Without reorganization in a basic sense and the creation of a socially just and economically viable structure, in the midst of poverty the tensions and conflicts of rural life tend to be accentuated and become a further factor in driving progressive elements away from the village. . . . "

While conditions in the larger towns and cities are far from ideal for rural emigres, nevertheless, it is believed by demographic scholars that rural-urban migration has steadily increased, having begun even before Indian Independence, and will continue to increase in the decades ahead. Coale and Hoover stated: "It is appropriate to note here that there has been a steady trend toward urbanization of the Indian population even prior to the development effort of the Five-Year Plans. Data for recent decades suggest that the urban population has tended to grow somewhat more than twice as fast as the total population." In 1901, for example, cities with over 1 million population had only 0.6 per cent of the population; by 1961, they had nearly 3 per cent. If we include all cities of 100,000 or more, this urban sector is about 9 per cent of the total 1961 population. At the same time, however, that cities have been growing because of increasing industrialization, trade and commerce, and have been increasing largely at the expense of rural areas, the rural sector of the population, most of it in centres of 5,000 or less, still represented four-fifths of the total 1961 population. Clearly, the growth of cities has made a relatively small dent in the rural population.

Tarlok Singh believes that, "The distinguishing marks of recent urban growth are its continuity and the steadily increasing rate at which it occurs," and he points out that until late in the nineteenth century most towns in India were either local trading and marketing centres or places of administrative and cultural importance. Commercial centres have grown with the increase in foreign trade, particularly with Western countries. Industrial towns, on the other hand, are of comparatively recent origin and have experienced rapid growth.

Some light on the nature of the push and pull that are operating to stimulate internal migration is afforded by a recent study by Gosal of the regional sex composition of the population. Attention here is focused primarily on two opposite types of areas which, based on their sex composition, are revealed as having considerable in-migration or out-migration. Certain regions are designated as having a low female ratio, compared to the norm for the country as a whole, and others as having a high female ratio. An area of low female ratio (less than 950 females per 1,000 males) is described as one which has a male excess at birth, a higher mortality among women, especially in infancy and early childhood, and one which is either a developing agricultural area attracting workers to expanding plantations or other types of agricultural production, or a highly industrialized and urbanized area with potential job opportunities for men. The opposite extreme, an area of high female ratio (over 1,000 females to 1,000 males), is an area of male out-migration, one which males have left for employment elsewhere in large enough numbers to affect the sex composition of the source area. A region in which the ratio of females is below the national norm is generally one of meagre resources, high density of population, and scarcity of food, with accompanying chronic malnutrition. It is an area too poor to support its population, and the males therefore leave for agricultural or industrial employment elsewhere. This kind of emigration is highly male-selective because it is toward cities or industrial areas where there are no jobs for women and where the acute housing shortage and high cost of living discourage men from bringing their wives and families.

This helps to account for the lower sex ratio in urban than rural areas in India, unlike the situation in the United States where farming is largely a male occupation and many women find employment in cities and even in industry. In India, women remain in the villages and on the farms and men seek employment in the cities and industrial centres. The growth of cities and the rise of new industries and newly-developing agricultural areas have thus stimulated a highly-selective male migration out of poor agricultural areas, in sufficiently large numbers to alter the sex composition of both the areas they leave and the areas to which they go. The rural areas of poverty and heavy pressure of population are areas of male emigration leaving behind a larger number of women than men. On the other hand, the areas where cities are growing, industries are starting or expanding, and new plantations and irrigated or rich valley lands are opening up, attract male immigrants and become areas where women are outnumbered. There are, of course, many areas in India in an intermediate position between these two extremes where migration in or out has not been sufficiently great to alter the sex ratio within them. A generalization that is probably justified by the findings of this study is that the streams of internal migration in India are fed primarily by males, as was true in the early industrializing, urbanizing period in the United States.

One of the major purposes of India's economic development programmes is to create productive job opportunities for all levels and classes of workers. The exact dimensions of the complex unemployment problem in India are not known. They are very difficult to ascertain in the rural areas because the nature of the work is seasonal, the household is the prevailing unit of production, and the extent of unpaid family labour is not easy to measure. Estimates made by the Planning Commission have been based mainly on sample surveys in urban areas. On the basis of available data, it was estimated that early in 1956 there were about 5 million unemployed persons in the country, almost evenly divided between urban and rural areas. This figure gives a totally inadequate picture of the situation because the unemployed worker in India does not customarily register himself in an employment exchange office, even where these offices exist. At best, these exchanges are found only in a few large cities. The situation in the rural areas is immensely magnified by almost universal underemployment in agriculture. Ashish Bose has said this runs as high as 31 million for 7 months of the year. Coale and Hoover say that, "On the average, the Indian agriculturalist is occupied for only about three months in the year, and many of the landless labourers even less than that ... 'Indian economists estimate conservatively that a quarter of the rural population is surplus, in the sense that its removal from the land would make no difference to agricultural output. This is equivalent to having some 20 million people permanently unemployed.' " A surplus of rural manpower has so long been true of Indian agriculture that there has been little demand for mechanization or other labour-saving methods.

From the scanty urban data available, based on trends observed in the period 1953-57, it would appear that the largest group of unemployed were the "unskilled services" category, with "clerical services" second largest, followed in order of size of the group by skilled and semi-skilled services, educational services (teaching), domestic services (manual work in public institutions such as hospitals), and industrial supervisory services. Of all these groups, during this same period, those whose rates of placement were highest were teachers, followed by the clerical services, with no increase for skilled and semi-skilled persons, and a monthly decline in the number of unskilled persons placed. The industrial supervisory group, on the other hand, seemed to be absorbed in employment fairly well.

In the rural areas, the category of personnel in short supply is of administrative and technical officials—competent, well-trained leaders who understand agriculture and rural people. As Coale and Hoover have pointed out, it takes a substantial part of the funds allocated to the Community Development-National Extension Service programme to pay for the training, salaries, and administration of those officials who run the programme "to promote more effective use of India's surplus rural manpower." They say further that, "Both unemployment and underemployment are high. With increasing industrialization, urbanization and monetization of the economy, and the weakening of extended-family ties that will accompany these trends, it is to be expected that the non-utilization of manpower will become more and more manifest as unemployment rather than in the present semi-concealed form of underemployment. This will increase the urgency of efforts to promote fuller employment, which already is a policy objective of the same order of priority as the increase of overall output."

The Third Five Year Plan states that, "Lags in development in a country with a large population and heavy pressure of population on land are reflected most acutely in the problem of unemployment. Until the economic structure is strengthened and the economy is able to meet its growing requirements of equipment and raw materials largely from its own resources, it is difficult to absorb even the entire addition to the labour force into increasingly productive work at a reasonable level of wages."

It has been estimated in an article by K. N. Raj that at the present rate of annual population growth, about 2 per cent per year, and assuming that the ratio of those seeking work out of increases in the population will be the same as that of estimated total "working force" to total population, additional employment will have to be•found, at a minimum, for 2.5 to 3 million persons every year, nearly a third of them in manufacturing industries.

A corollary of an overcrowded agriculture, and a newly-developing industrial economy unable as yet to absorb an appreciable number of either surplus rural people or the annual increase in the labour force, is an imbalance in manpower resources, the paradox of excess manpower on the one hand, and scarcity of skilled and trained workers on the other, added to the further paradox of a large number of educated unemployed. Villagers who move to towns and cities because they are surplus in agriculture or because they seek better working and living conditions are untrained for mechanical and industrial jobs. Rural development programmes, on the other hand, cannot find, in rural or urban areas, enough competent, technically trained personnel to carry on their work among villagers. Those who have been educated in institutions of higher learning have been surplus because most of them have not been taught the administrative and technical skills needed by the development programmes India has set in motion.

Heavy unemployment in urban areas and underemployment in rural areas are exacerbated by the annual increase in the number entering the labour force. S. N. Agarwala stated recently that even if it were possible to stop all births for the next 15 or 18 years, the labour force would continue to increase, and that a decline in the growth of population would have no effect on unemployment or underemployment for the next decade or two. The urban labour force is made up not only of rural migrants, but also of those from other urban areas, workers going from one city to another in search of employment. A sample survey in 1953 showed that as much as 40 per cent of the urban labour force were migrants. More than half of those had come from villages, about one-sixth from other urban areas; the rest were displaced persons, many of them from rural areas. The so-called "educated unemployed" numbered about 300,000 in the urban sector in 1955 (a significant element in the population). More than three-fourths of them were reported to be looking only for non-manual or "white collar" jobs.

Underemployment as well as unemployment are probably more noticeable in rural than urban areas because there is a higher proportion of the population in the labour force in rural areas, where men and women both work and where the young and old are usually pressed into service. A survey in the fall of 1956, reported by Agarwala, showed that nearly 46 per cent of the rural population was in the labour force as opposed to about 36 per cent for the urban population. In both rural and urban areas, more girls than in the past have been entering the labour market, partly because of the rising marriage age and partly because of the general search among young people for better standards of living and more social and economic opportunities which they believe can be theirs by having independent sources of income or moving to new situations.

India's population is large, growing, and overwhelmingly rural. Second only to China in size of population, India must support about 15 per cent of the world's population on 2 per cent of the total land area. Her people have been steadily growing in numbers for 4 decades. This past decade, to the immense population base of 359 million, she has added another 77 million people. Despite substantial growth of cities, India was still more than 80 per cent rural in 1961. This means that most of the people were living in villages. An age structure of population with a disproportionate number of very young and very old, and a people nearly three-fourths of whom are dependent on agriculture for a livelihood, contribute to a heavy dependency on those who are in their productive years. India's population is also diverse, containing multiple language and religious groups and a large section of socially and economically disadvantaged peoples, sufficiently set apart from each other to be non-communicative and divisive in India's nation-building efforts. Added to these conditioning factors is the structure of Indian society in which the long-standing social institutions of the joint family, the village pattern of settlement, and the caste system have inhibited mobility both horizontally and vertically. Taken all together, these population facts have constituted important conditioning elements in India's development and will continue to do so for some time to come.

MAIN AUTHORITIES QUOTED OR CITED

Agarwala, S. N., Ed., *India's Population,* Some Problems in Perspective Planning, Asia Publishing House, Bombay, 1960.

Bose, Ashish, "The Population Puzzle in India", *Economic Development and Cultural Change,* Vol. VII, No. 3, Part 1, April, 1959, Research Centre in Economic Development and Cultural Change, University of Chicago.

Burdick, Dr. E. Douglass, "India's Population Problem; A Deterrent to India's Progress", Health Div., U. S. TCM to India, Sept., 1959, Mimeo.

Census of India, 1951, Vol. I, Part I-A, Report; Vol. I, Part II-A, Demographic Tables, Appendix II, C-III, Government of India.

Coale, Ansley J. and Hoover, E. M., *Population Growth and Economic Development in Low-Income Countries,* A Case Study of India's Prospects, Princeton University Press, Princeton, N. J., 1958.

Davis, Kingsley, *The Population of India and Pakistan,* Princeton University Press, Princeton, N. J., 1951.

Gosal, G. S., "*The Regionalism of Sex Composition of India's Population*", Rural Sociology Journal, Vol. 26, No. 2, June, 1961.

India 1960, A Reference Annual. Ministry of Information and Broadcasting, Government of India, April, 1960.

Provisional Population Totals, 1961 Census, Government of India, Ministry of Home Affairs.

Raj, K. N., "Employment and Unemployment in the Indian Economy: Problems of Classification, Measurement & Policy", Economic Development and Cultural Change, Vol. VII, No. 3, Part I, April, 1959, Research Centre in Economic Development and Cultural Change, University of Chicago.

Singh, Tarlok, "Some Implications of Recent Rural-Urban Trends in India", Mimeo.

Third Five Year Plan, Planning Commission, Government of India, 1961.

CHAPTER 7

PEOPLE AND THE LAND

THE phrase "teeming millions" springs almost automatically to one's mind when one first sees and experiences the mass of diverse and tangled traffic which jams the streets and the sidewalks of Calcutta or Bombay. But these are not the people who provide most of the pressure of population on the resources of the country. In 1951, only a little more than 17 per cent of the people of India lived in urban areas; about 82 per cent lived in villages. Furthermore, most of these village people depended for their livelihood on the cultivation of the land. Population pressure in India, as in a great many other underdeveloped countries, is pressure on the agricultural land.

Population per square mile of geography is much greater in a number of other countries than it is in India, but less than a dozen countries of the world have a greater population per square mile of cultivated land than has India. Urban industrial development has not yet moved far enough to provide an economic alternative to those engaged in agriculture, and thus has not been able to siphon off much of this pressure on the land. There is also traditionally very little occupational interchange between farm people and other village people. Under these conditions, it has been inevitable that cultivators practise chiefly subsistence agriculture.

In 1951, cultivators and the members of their families constituted 249 million farm people, approximately 70 per cent of the nation's people.[1] More than 33 millions of these persons were agricultural labourers and members of their families. Farm labour families, together with owner and tenant operator families, who tilled holdings of less than two and one-half acres, constituted a rural slum far greater than the combined slums of all the cities of India, and probably greater than the combined slums of all the so-called advanced nations of the world. Some of the conditions under which they worked and lived steadily deteriorated over the

[1] At the time of writing this book, detailed 1961 Census data were not available on rural and agricultural population.

last few decades. Cultivated land *per capita*, for instance, had declined from 1.11 acres in 1921 to only .84 of an acre in 1951. Statistics are not available to prove it, but the level of living, at least of these lowest-income families in agriculture, must have deteriorated also, and the low level of living of farm people, together with the nation's need for increased food grains, served to make the development of agriculture a first priority in the First Five Year Plan.

It is the first purpose of this chapter to describe the bench marks from which that development had to start. We say *had* to start because it was the land that was there and the people who lived on it that provided the only conditions of, and the chief potentials for, rural development.

The rural population of India had increased steadily over the last few decades, by approximately 50 per cent (100 million), between 1921 and 1951. The urban population had increased percentage-wise also (about 53 per cent), but had absorbed less than 10 per cent of the increased national population. Thus, population pressure on the land was steadily growing greater. Agricultural labourers had increased by 11,500,000 in the last twenty years, slightly more rapidly than the agricultural population as a whole. To the extent that these two trends prevailed, a larger percentage of the rural population in 1951 than ever before were nearer the bottom of the agricultural ladder. Not only had differentials between rural and non-rural people widened, but differentials between the various segments of the rural population had widened. An increasing percentage of all agricultural workers were becoming landless and an increasing percentage of land-owners and tenants were being compelled to eke out a living on impossibly small holdings.

Agriculture was providing almost 70 per cent of all "self-supporting" persons and more than 80 per cent of the "earning dependents" who constituted the nation's working force of more than 143,000,000 persons. It was providing 51.3 per cent of the total national income, more than three times as much as mining, manufacturing, and small business enterprises, but it was not yielding the output required for even a start in national development or enough to support an above-poverty level of living for the agricultural workers and their families. Among the eight gainfully employed classes, only domestic servants had a lower net economic output than agriculture. The vast majority of cultivating families did not have enough cultivable land, enough working capital or credit, or indeed the technical agricultural know-how to force higher yields out of the land they tilled. Millions of farm families had lived under these conditions for so many decades that they were said to be stagnant, to be apathetic, even fatalistic, in their lack of expectations or even their hopes. If such attitudes prevailed, they were induced by stern and long-standing conditions.

A National Sample Survey, made in April-June, 1951, showed that 5.9 per cent of all agricultural households were not operating any agricultural holdings. They were landless agricultural labourers. The 63.5 per cent of agricultural owners and tenants who were farming holdings of less than 5 acres were operating only 18.7 per cent of all the cropland. At the other end of the scale, the 5.3 per cent who were operating holdings of 25 acres or more were managing 33.4 per cent of all cropped land. The remaining 48 per cent of the cropped areas was distributed among the 14.3 per cent whose holdings were more than 5 but less than 10 acres, and who managed 18.6 per cent of all cropped land, and the 11 per cent with holdings of more than 10 acres but less than 25 acres who were managing 29.3 per cent of all cropped land.

In terms of an agricultural ladder of four steps, the following table offers a visual picture:

	Percentage of cultivators per size of holdings	Percentage of cropped area
Landless	5.9	0
Less than 5 acres	65.5	18.7
5-10 acres	14.3	18.6
10-25 acres	11.0	29.3
25 acres or more	5.3	33.4

An agricultural ladder, constructed in terms of types or kinds of tenure, as is done in Western society, would not have the same meaning for India. Nevertheless, Professor M. L. Dantwala constructed such a table from the 1931 Census. Even though there has been some landlord abolition legislation passed between 1931 and 1951, and even though Professor Dantwala's table was only for

British India, the percentages were probably not so different in 1951 from what they were in 1931. Starting at the bottom of the ladder, Dantwala's statistics were as follows: Agricultural labourers, 32.7 per cent; cultivating tenants, 35.4 per cent; cultivating owners, 27.7 per cent; non-cultivating owners, that is, landlords, 4 per cent.

It is unfortunate that there are no data by which adequately to measure any of the important economic or social consequences of various-sized holdings and tenure status. Crop yields times the number of cropped acres should determine economic output and thus determine farm-family income. Income, in turn, should determine farm-family levels of living. Some data are available on consumption expenditures from which some broad comparisons can be made between the level of living of rural and urban families and between agricultural labour and other farm families.

The Third Round, National Sample Survey, reporting data gathered in August-November, 1951, showed consumption expenditures per person per month as follows: in villages, Rupees 24.2 (approximately $5); in towns, Rupees 31.55 (approximately $6.84); the average for the four cities of Calcutta, Bombay, Madras, and Delhi was Rupees 54.80 (approximately $11.50). To the extent that these data are representative, they show that village levels of living were approximately 77 per cent of town levels of living, but only 35 per cent of consumption expenditures in cities.

Mr. V. Gopalan, of the Programme Evaluation Organisation, in 1956-57 attempted to make more detailed analyses of data available from all studies of the National Sample Survey and the Labour Inquiry Committee. These studies were of the *annual* expenditures of families for consumption goods and services. The amount of annual expenditures for rural families varied in the different areas of the country from 35 per cent to 60 per cent of those for large cities. They were slightly less than 60 per cent of the expenditures of all middle-class families in the cities which were included in the Survey. When the expenditures of farm labour families were compared with those of industrial labour families, they showed that agricultural labour families spent about 90 per cent as much as labourers in cottage industry, but less than 52 per cent as much as industrial labourers in Ahmedabad, a highly industrialized city. Expenditures of farm labour workers' families for the different geographic areas of the country varied from less than $200 per year to slightly more than $255 per year. While the samples from which these data were gathered, and upon which these calculations are made, were thin, they probably were not unrepresentative. Their trustworthiness is enhanced by the fact that detailed data on the distribution of expenditures among consumption items manifest the same characteristics as they do in detailed levels of living studies throughout the world, about the validity or representativeness of which there can be no question.

We need present very little information on expenditures for various consumption items to illustrate this fact. None of the farm labour family groups spent less than 80 per cent of their total consumption budget for food, and some groups spent as much as 87 per cent. There was no case and no group of farm labour families which had as much as $50 per family to spend on all other items of consumption, the average being approximately $25 per year. As best we can gather from the available data, this $25 was distributed approximately as follows: $10 for clothing, $2 for fuel, $1 for housing, and the remainder for all other purposes. Probably next above farm labour families in levels of living are the 29 million cultivator families who till less than two and one-half acres of land, and above them, the 9½ million cultivator families who till between 1½ and 5 acres of land. It is probably safe to conclude that among the total population of the nation, farm labour families are at the very bottom of the level of living ladder; that those with 2 acres of tilled land are next above them; and that those who have higher levels of living are graduated upward in accordance with the increasing acreage they have in tilled land, this irrespective of their tenure status.

Data of this kind are given to help describe the factors which condition development. That these conditioning factors are stern facts it is easy to grasp, but neither their magnitude as development problems nor their meaning to the people whose lives they depict is easy to grasp. To make these facts more vivid, we present a short synopsis of a detailed case study of a cultivator family which, by no measure, can be counted as below a middle-class agricultural family. This is to say that this family is above the average.

Nathu owns five acres of land. He is 35 years old, his wife,

26. He has a household of six members, including 2 children of his own and his sister's son who is part of his family. His mother also lives with him. (His nephew is 15 years of age, his son is 5 years of age, and his daughter 2 years of age). They live in a two-room, mud-wall, thatched-roof house, which has an attached cattle shed, roofed but otherwise open in the front. The two rooms, separated by bamboo matting plastered with mud, are used as combined kitchen and storeroom and as a sleeping room. At the back of the house is a compound in which enough bamboo is grown to supply all housing repair needs.

Nathu's chief crop is paddy (rice), but he also grows jowar (millet and sorghum) and pulse (peas). He and his family, and his animals, eat all that he grows. In poor crop years, this is not enough; in good years, he has some surplus to sell. He has two buffaloes and a cow and a calf, also two chickens.

It was not possible accurately to calculate either the income or the expenditures of the family, but Nathu and the interviewer estimated that the annual cash expenditures were Rupees 225 (slightly less than $48) per year. He paid the carpenter 48 seers (96 pounds), the blacksmith 8 seers (16 pounds), and the barber 8 seers (16 pounds) in terms of crops which he grew. His house has to be rethatched each year. He grows or gathers his own thatch and he and his neighbours join hands in doing most of the work, but he needs some lumber and carpenter work. His plough is wooden and he therefore needs little blacksmithing.

Nathu is so deeply in debt that he can no longer borrow from the co-operative credit society, because he has borrowed and not yet paid back the loans already received and for which he pledged his land as security. The secretary of the credit society, however, makes him personal loans at interest rates which Nathu does not think are excessive. He also borrows from a professional money-lender who, he says, charges very high interest rates, probably 60 per cent. He borrowed Rupees 300 ($63 approximately) from the credit society a few years back to buy a bullock for Rupees 200 (about $42). He has repaid only about Rs. 100 (about $21) on this, but has paid nothing to reduce his debt of Rupees 300 during the past two years. He owes now, all told, not less than Rupees 400 (about $84). He wants to buy more land, and probably will when his nephew is older and his son old enough to work in the field. He will, of course, have to borrow money to buy more land, but seems not to doubt that he will be able to do so. When asked about his debt, his reply was, "How do you live without debt?" He is anxious to get his nephew married, but knows that he would have to borrow money to finance the wedding ceremony and has therefore delayed the marriage for which he feels a deep obligation.

The diet of the family is chiefly rice, jowar, and pulses, no butter (ghee). The two children have some milk. The family has meat (chicken) probably twice a year, always shared with friends. They spend about Rupees 105 (approximately $22) per year for clothing. Their housing costs are very little more than what they pay the carpenter each year. Nathu literally spends nothing for health. His mother cares for all illnesses and injuries and acts as midwife. When a cure is beyond her talents, the ailing person is taken to the village priest for magical treatment. In extreme cases, the patient can be taken to the "mission dispensary". This has happened once, with his mother, and they were charged Rupees 2 (approximately 43c) for an injection for influenza.

The family has no costs for education now that they have no child who is in school. His nephew went to school for four years, but did not like it; he would run away and beg to be allowed to help with field work. About his son, he says that he will let the boy decide how far he will go in his schooling, but added, "How can I force him to go to school? If he does not like school, he will never pass, and then all the money spent on sending him to school will go to waste .... How can people like me spend on his going and coming and for books, etc.? Our children should better stick to the fields."

Very little is spent on recreation, which consists chiefly of visiting and gossip and to help support troupes of travelling singers and dancers who come to the village from time to time. Nathu contributes Rupees 5 (about $1) per year to help bring these singers and dancers to his village.

Nathu is a landowner, not a tenant or an agricultural labourer. He farms more land than do 65 per cent of the agricultural families in India. He is a long way from the bottom of the agricultural ladder, or from the bottom of the rural level of living ladder, but he is poor. His family is not one of the millions of cultivator families inhabiting the widespread rural slums of India, but is typical of that great body of cultivators who contribute nothing to commercialized agriculture. He knows something about the value of better seed, chemical fertilizer, better farm implements, and better farm practices, but he makes no use of any of them.

There are 60 million agricultural households in India. Nathu's family probably has a level of living above the average. It is not chronically hungry; it does not want for clothing; and its house is livable. He produces most of what his family consumes. He gets along as well as he does because he is a self-sufficient, subsistence farmer. But even as a subsistence farmer, Nathu is in debt. As a subsistence farmer, he will never get out of debt. He must grow more products for sale, and if he is ever going to be able to secure the extra land he wants to buy, in order adequately and efficiently to utilize his family labour supply, he will have to grow an increasing amount of products for sale. If he had more land, at least part of it irrigated, he would produce more products for the market. He would probably use more up-to-date farm machinery also; if not he, then his son, would probably use more modern farm methods. But there isn't enough land for every agricultural family to have twice as much land as Nathu now has. There isn't that much land in India. There are too many farm families trying to make a living by farming.

Why does so large a portion of the nation's population still live on the land, and such a high percentage of the gainfully employed work in agriculture? The simplest answer is that the Industrial Revolution has not yet fully developed in India. But this answer does not explain why India's economy is still an overwhelmingly agricultural and village, not an industrial and urban, economy. The answer to this question is to be found in the story of why India did not keep pace with the industrial development which took place in many other parts of the world. The percentage of India's population which was rural was no greater 150 years ago than it was in the United States. But in the United States, there was a rapid and accelerating shift from agriculture to industrial employment as from rural to urban residence. The same has been true of every so-called advanced country in the world. In other words, the answer, we

PEOPLE AND THE LAND

believe, is found primarily in an analysis of two basic historical conditions: *first* the landlord system of tenure, and, *second* the fact that India's once-famous fabricating (manufacturing) enterprise did not provide, or was not utilized so as to provide, a base for the initiation of an industrial revolution. Each of these was, to a large extent, due to the fact that economic development in India, for one to two centuries, was directed by a colonial power.

Thousands of pages have been written on the land tenure and land revenue system which was evolved during the period of British administration. Because it is our primary purpose to describe the evolution of landlordism, we shall not describe the differences between the various tenancy systems, but discuss only zamindari, under which is quite often included also a number of other systems which lead very largely to the same results. Zamindars were government tax-collectors who became landlords.

Government land-revenue systems dated far back into the period of Hindu kings and had been perpetuated by the Moguls. The land tax had, however, apparently not been excessive or very burdensome to the cultivator. He paid his taxes in kind, which was about one-sixth of the gross product of his land. Zamindars, when first installed by the British administration, were not landlords at all but only tax-collectors. As government agents, they were supervised by government. They were paid in terms of a percentage of the taxes they collected, but the amount of the tax was determined by the government, not by the tax-collectors. How these persons were selected to perform these government functions, and to receive these emoluments for collecting taxes, seems not to be too specifically known. Sir Henry Maine and others, however, say that they were chiefs of clans, barons, and probably the same persons who had been used by previous political regimes. In all cases, however, they apparently were the native aristocracy in the various areas where they became tax-collectors.

It is quite often averred by Indian historians, and by some British historians, that it was the purpose of the British to establish a class of landlord gentry, in the expectation that these gentlemen-landlords would accept and exercise the same responsibilities as such a class of citizens did in the British Isles. It must have also been expected that tenants, the actual cultivators of the land, would have a status similar to the British tenants. But because of the differences in historic backgrounds and the looser administration, no such development occurred. Contracts of zamindars required that they collect the land tax, but it was, by and large, left to the zamindar to determine what the tax rate would be. It is said that in the earlier days, zamindari rights were sometimes auctioned to the highest bidder. No matter by what method these rights were obtained, the roles of zamindars as government tax-collectors and administrators of large allotments of land developed into an elaborate system of sub-feudation. Cultivator families who had lived from time immemorial with unquestioned rights of occupancy, and as tenants of the government, became tenants of zamindars, who now determined the amount of taxes they must pay and the sort of tenancy rights they would be granted.

Few zamindars lived on the land, and many of them did not even live within the area they administered. They sub-let their rights and sub-allocated their responsibilities. Thus tax farming became the business profession of an increasing number of persons who competed with each other for the sub-feudal rights which zamindars had to dispense. This was a financial benefit to the zamindars who could now allocate as small a percentage of their share of the tax-collection to sub-collectors as was made possible by competition between would-be sub-tax-collectors. It was detrimental to the cultivator taxpayers because the sub-collectors could exact higher taxes from them than they needed to remit to the zamindars. Those sub-tax-collectors or sub-landlords, who dealt directly with zamindars, in turn sub-let the lands for which they had become responsible to still others. Thus the lands of a given zamindar might have from one to many intermediary tax farmers between him and the cultivators. There were cases in which there were known to be 50 or more levels of such intermediaries. They were all middlemen, between the cultivator at the bottom and the zamindar at the top, the economic support of all resting on the produce of the land. Naturally, those at the bottom felt the full impact of this weight. They were at an impossible disadvantage in bargaining. Many of them lost their rights to occupy the land which their ancestors had occupied for centuries. More and more of them, and most new competitors for land, were required to become "tenants at will", with no guarantee of continued occupancy. Others became share-croppers, and still others became agricultural landless labourers. Thus there developed pronounced gradients in the agricultural population. Among the cultivators, if not in economic status, then in social status, stood first the owner-operator, next the "permanent occupancy tenant", then "tenants at will", and at the bottom of the agricultural ladder, landless labourers. All the evidences available indicate that there had long been a steady drift of numbers down this agricultural status ladder, a larger and larger percentage of all cultivators becoming tenants, a larger percentage of all tenants becoming tenants at will, and an increasing percentage of all agricultural workers becoming landless labourers. Over the long period during which these trends were moving with increased acceleration, isolated, illiterate cultivators were impotent to do anything about their deteriorating conditions. Worse still was the deterioration of these millions of persons as human beings, who appeared to those who became acquainted with them for the first time, and many of those who have participated in their exploitation, as mere animals on treadmills.

This brief description of the landlord system depicts one of the sternest factors which, in 1950, conditioned rural development in India. During the period for which it was a system of revenue administration, for which zamindari was instituted, it not only oppressed taxpayers, but subverted government. As a long-standing land management system, it contributed to every rural problem described above. We summarize the ways in which it contributed to these problems in the following four categorical statements: (1) The economic value of land which increased because of increasing competition for its use went to persons who contributed little or nothing to that value. (2) As the agricultural enterprise was gradually commercialized or monetized, the money went to zamindars, and other intermediaries, and therefore created no incentives in cultivators whose incomes were controlled, as it were, by the "iron law of wages". (3) As a long-standing system of feudal control, workers on the land, even though they were horizontally mobile, were not vertically mobile. They remained, and multiplied, where they were, and they remained in the same or lower position instead of rising in economic and social status. (4) Two extremely different classes of citizens were developed.

One was a relatively small, elite group of landlords whose social and political dominance became very great. The other was a large class of persons whose economic and social status was so low that it had no political power, not even in its own local communities.

We said above that the second most general cause for population pressure on the land, with all its attendant conditions, was that the Industrial Revolution had not fully entered India. This was in spite of the fact that India was at one time one of the great industrial and trading nations of the world. In general, India's once industrial and commercial ascendancy was based on products fabricated by hand, the world's market demand for which depended upon a relatively small, wealthy clientele, not on the demands of millions of people. When factory production did start in India, it met domestically the competition of one of the most completely self-sufficient systems of local economy that the world has ever known. This was an institutionalized, complex, local barter system by which each village supplied all its own essential goods and services. There is a legitimate question of whether, as factory goods penetrated this local market and displaced local handicrafts, it may not have for some time increased population pressure on the land rather than alleviating it. While some handicraftsmen moved from villages to cities and towns in response to increasing industrial employment opportunities, many village artisans who had previously been fully employed in weaving, leather working, and other village non-agricultural jobs, entered agriculture and thus increased competition for tillable land. It is as part of the explanation of why population pressure on the land increased, why distribution of available land among an ever-increasing number of cultivator families, resulted in hundreds of thousands of small holdings, and why low *per capita* and low farm family incomes resulted, that we relate the story of the evolving industrial economy of India.

Gadgil in *The Industrial Evolution in India* undoubtedly provides the most objective, detailed, and analytical account. He cites trends and events which show why India did not effectively catch step with the Industrial Revolution which developed in most Western societies; which gave direction to an increasing percentage of the working force in non-agricultural occupations;

and, which moved an increasing percentage of their population off the land.

Following Gadgil's account, the first step in the actual decline in the handicraft markets was in domestic sales which had in the past been substantial. These sales were, however, chiefly to the retainers and the hangers-on of the native Indian courts. As these courts gradually disappeared under the British political regime, these markets gradually diminished. Then followed an increased adoption of British textile goods and patterns. Finally, factory-produced goods became prevalent in urban centres. The fine handicrafts which India had made for hundreds of years are still produced and were produced all during this period of decline, but rather than providing a steadily increasing volume of products to expanding markets, they provided a declining percentage. What industrial production India had in 1950 had not been built on the foundations of her handicrafts which had once made her famous as an industrial and trading country.

In countries where the Industrial Revolution moved rapidly, with all its attendant results, it has been built upon both an expanding domestic, and an expanding foreign, market. It has not yet reached any wide domestic market in India. This is not to say that there has not been a great expansion in production, especially of textiles, as the population of India has increased, but this has not been solely of factory-fabricated textiles. The overwhelming portion of it was, and still is, both produced and consumed in villages. The institutionalized barter system (jajmani system) made each village community such a completely self-sufficient economic unit that raw products produced in these communities were fabricated and consumed there; they did not flow into external trade. Furthermore, because of this local village self-sufficiency, the great mass of rural people provided no market for factory-fabricated goods. Indian villages never had participated in either the production or consumption of the products which had made India famous in the past. As millions of potential purchasers of factory-made products, India's rural population has not yet joined the Industrial Revolution.

Isolated as Indian villages were, village people had not remained totally unaffected by what had happened in other sectors of Indian society. Their lands were taxed by the government, and gradually more and more taxes were collected in terms of money rather than farm and other village-produced goods. It may be too simple to say that the government, through its taxes, initiated monetized village production, because there had slowly grown up some village trade with non-village persons, and Indian agriculture had become slowly more commercialized. As with the Industrial Revolution, Indian cultivators have not yet thoroughly joined the price and market system in agriculture. But much of the commercialized agriculture promoted under the British administration had been for the purpose of furnishing raw products for British factories—jute, tea, and cotton, the first two of which were expanded by plantation farming. Thus much of the increased market for agricultural products had little effect on the old self-sufficient village economy. Roads and railroads were constructed by the British from the interior of the country to ports, but roads from villages to highway and railroad receiving points were not constructed. Villages thus remained pretty well isolated from the increased foreign trade, and old traditional types and methods of production changed only slightly.

The first successful factory development in India was in the 1850's in the field of cotton textiles. Cotton had been produced in India for centuries, and while it had provided some of the raw materials from which the fine fabrics which were exported and the goods for the elite domestic market were made, most of it was used to supply village weavers and spinners. An increasing quantity of it had been shipped to England to supply British factories. The earliest factories established in India were chiefly spinning mills, and their first influence on indigenous textile fabrication was to supply yarn to village weavers. This was followed by dyes and then woven goods. Contemporaneously with these developments was a gradual displacement of old Indian cloth patterns by English factory-produced fabrics. Gadgil analyzes and describes these trends in considerable detail, first the decline in the elite domestic demand for fine handicraft products, and then the growing competition of factory production with village handicraft production. Gadgil explains that the increased demand for new types of cloth and tourist demand for cheap Indian handicrafts gradually diluted the excellence of old Indian fabrics. Both of these things weakened the competitive position of those products upon which India's industrial and trading status had been built.

Neither of the trends just cited greatly affected the village market for textiles. How it later did so is the story of the influence of urban manufacturing on village industry and the extent to which this, in turn, affected rural to urban migration. Village employment in spinning and dye-compounding diminished as mill yarn displaced village-spun yarn, and aniline dyes displaced old vegetable dyes. This trend is best measured by the growth of the spinning-mill industry. There were in 1879, 58 mills which employed about 40,000 persons. By 1895, there were 144 mills which employed 139,600 persons. By 1914, cotton mills had increased to 264 and were employing approximately 260,000 persons. The 1911 Census, which included all establishments which employed as many as 20 workers, reported 7,113 factories. The total number employed in them was 2,105,824. Included among these industries were plantations, mines and collieries, railroad workshops, brick factories, etc. This Census made a special analysis of four groups which employed more than 100,000 persons and which together employed 1,717,200 persons, almost 82 per cent of all industrially employed. Plantation employment accounted for almost 50 per cent of this employment. Textiles, which ranked second, employed slightly less than 33 per cent. If plantations are not counted as industries, textiles would have accounted for more than 60 per cent of all those who were employed in large industries. It is clear that even if all of these factory workers had come from villages, employment in textile processing and manufacturing would have done little to reduce population pressure on the land. Because it cannot be known what per cent of factory workers did come from villages, we shall not pursue further, at this point, the increase in factory employment, but instead turn to an analysis of available data on changes in the percentage of population which resided in different-sized population centres.

In those economies which have evolved steadily from self-sufficient local economies to commercialized and industrialized economies, increase in commerce has preceded increase in industry, and somewhat in the following pattern. Increased commercialization of agriculture requires, and develops, a class of middlemen—marketers—who reside in larger than small-village centres, in order that they may handle products from a number of villages. In every place in the world, these market towns have developed. To the extent that agricultural producers sell their products for cash, they purchase goods not produced in country areas. The merchants who sell these goods are also located in market towns. A third trend which has always helped to increase the population of these town centres has been the shift of much, later all, of processing from farms to towns—tanning, wagon-making, black-smithing, etc. These are, of course, simple manufacturing processes. By and large, these smaller industries themselves have helped to develop larger population centres.

There is a positive correlation between commercial development and the growth of all sizes of population centres which are larger than local self-sufficient villages. Available data do not make it possible to measure the precise influence of either commercialization or industrialization on the growth of towns and cities, the magnitude of which growth would, of course, lessen population pressure on the land. Available data, while by no means adequate, do make possible some analysis of the growth of different-sized population centres. Gadgil made this analysis for the period 1872 to 1921. He also presented all available data on factory development and, in the absence of statistical data, discussed in some detail the known shifts of village handicraftsmen and artisans to towns. From census data, it is possible to follow his line of analysis to 1951, when planned national development began. The following table presents information for the period 1881-1951.

PERCENTAGE OF TOTAL POPULATION IN VARIOUS-SIZED
TOWNS & VILLAGES

Population-size Centre	1881	1901	1921	1941	1951
100,000 to over 1,000,000	2.08	3.9	4.3	5.6	7.3
50,000 to 100,000	.82	1.2	1.2	1.5	1.8
20,000 to 50,000	1.32	3.0	2.1	2.5	2.9
10,000 to 20,000	1.12	2.0	2.0	2.2	2.5
5,000 to 10,000	1.12	1.8	2.0	2.3	2.3
	6.46	11.9	11.6	14.1	16.8
Below 5,000	93.54	88.1	88.4	85.9	83.2

From the preceding table, it is seen that urban population (the population of all centres with 5,000 or more inhabitants) increased from 6.5 per cent to 16.8 per cent of the national population. The increase in the percentage of the total population in the largest cities was the most rapid. The increase in cities from 20 to 50,000 was second highest. The increase in cities from 50 to 100,000 was least. The increase in population of the two smaller population-size centres was not great, and the percentage of population in centres of under 5,000 decreased. But two important analyses are not revealed by these data; the relative increase of commerce and industry, and the movement of population in that portion which was in rural areas (centres with less than 5,000 population). Through most of the period under review, the major increase in large-city population was due more to increase in trade and commerce than it was to industrial development. From all that can be learned about the so-called rural population, there was a relative increase in the number of people in rural trade centres, and also in political or government (district) towns. Furthermore, there was an absolute increase in the population of centres with less than 5,000 inhabitants. If, therefore, there was to be any lessening of population pressure on the land, it had to come from migration from villages to towns within rural areas. There are few statistical data by which to analyze the extent to which there was such a shift. We must therefore depend upon less precise information.

We first briefly report Kingsley Davis' analyses and conclusions about the increasing effect that developing industry had on the size of large population centres during this period. His analyses are much more definitive than any that can be made from the crude census data presented in the table above. He says that the cities which developed in the pre-British period in Asia "did not rest primarily on industry and commercial development, but rather on political and religious functions," and that when cities began to appear in fairly large numbers in many places, their chief functions were to serve trade and commerce. A number of them were provincial capitals. As some cities pulled away from others in their rates of growth, two of Davis' conclusions are germane to the topic we are discussing: first, that a substantial part of the increase in large-city populations came from persons who were not born in these cities; and second, that many of these cities did become industrial as well as trade centres in due time. Most of them were ports, but whether ports or railway centres, they were in a good position to be assembly points for raw products and shipping points for factory products.

We are not sure that valid conclusions can be drawn about the relative influence of either industrialization or in-migration on different-sized cities. The rate of industrial growth was pretty closely correlated with the increasing size of cities. This might be interpreted to mean that as the stream of migration moved from rural areas toward cities, it was swelled by recruits from towns, small and intermediate cities. This, with exceptions, was probably true. To the extent it was true, it followed the normal, wave-like, or step-by-step, migration from rural to urban centres in Western countries. It was, however, moving too slowly to lessen population pressure on the land. There were approximately 90 million more people living in rural areas in 1951 than there were in 1901, an increase of 43.2 per cent. Cultivated land during this period had increased by less than 2 per cent. The answer to how much over-all industrial development, or even town development, had served to alleviate population pressure on the land, therefore, depended upon the volume of people who had moved out of small villages into occupations located in town centres with less than 5,000 population. As we attempt to appraise data on this movement, we will be looking more at commercial than at industrial development.

Unfortunately there are no comparable decade-by-decade data on what portions of the total rural population (in centres of less than 5,000) were in various-sized population centres. Based on data provided by the 1941 Census, Chandrasekhar presents a table (below) which shows that of the 654,396 classified population centres, 450,926 were villages with less than 500 inhabitants.

Population Group	Number of Villages	Population in Millions (1941)
Under 500	450,926	94.2
500 to 1,000	123,911	86.9
1,000 to 2,000	57,408	79.3
2,000 to 5,000	22,151	63.4
	654,396	

The table shows the number of villages by population-size group and the population in each grouping.

We are undoubtedly justified in assuming from the data given in the percentage distribution on page 136 that there had been within the rural areas a steady, and probably an accelerating, increase in the percentage of the rural population who were living in villages of increasing size. We are probably justified in assuming that the smallest-sized villages, those with less than 500 population and probably most of those of less than 1,000 population, were primarily agricultural villages, and that those with populations of 2,000 to 5,000 were largely non-agricultural populations. If these assumptions are correct, it is then clear that there were still many more persons and families living in almost purely agricultural communities than there were in those communities which were developing urban characteristics. As we said above, these urban characteristics were, however, more commercial than industrial.

The causal factors which appeared to be involved in the movement of population from small villages to larger villages and towns were: (1) an increasing commercialization of agriculture and, for that matter, of other village products; (2) highway and railroad development, which provided channels for the outward flow of village produce; (3) the movement of village craftsmen to country market centres; (4) an increase in marketing middlemen, sellers of village products, and merchants of city or large-town products to village people. All of these were far more commercial than they were industrial developments. Furthermore, it probably can be said that the growing commercialization of the rural economy was a greater factor in stimulating urban industrial development than urban industrial development was in stimulating rural commercial development. Our focus at this moment, however, is not so much on this issue as it is on the question of the extent to which the increase in the number of large-sized centres within the rural areas served to lessen population pressure on the land.

There are evidences that in spite of the movement of a large number of persons from small villages to large villages and towns, the number of people who depended for their livelihood' on agriculture increased. Gadgil's generalizations on what happened to village occupational groups as rural commercialization increased are about as follows: ... Village weavers were no longer also dyers. Factory-produced textiles had entered country markets. Some village weavers had moved to market towns where they could have a wider clientele than a local village could provide. Other occupations had done the same thing. Some villages thus no longer had all the occupational groups which in the past had sustained a self-sufficient village economy. Thus the economic position of craft and artisan occupations in the village was weakened. Those who remained in small villages had no alternative but to turn to agriculture, the only occupation which had not changed. One of Gadgil's summary statements is, "The growth in the numbers of those for whom there was no longer any place in their hereditary industry was shown by the increasing diversity between the caste and occupation statistics. These statistics generally indicate that artisans were giving up their occupations for agriculture or ordinary labour."

Wiser, in his detailed study of The Hindu Jajmani System, included in his analysis what each of the traditional occupational caste groups in the village which he studied were doing. A few sentences from his down-to-earth account illustrate what was happening. He said, " ... there are residents in Karimpur who have begun to take advantage of transportation facilities and venture to the cities to make their purchases where they claim they can get better rates." "The Chamars (leather workers) are called upon to do all kinds of field work, from the hauling and spreading of manure, through every process, up to the carrying of the winnowed grain into the house." "The 'kam karnewala' ... [2] gets opportunities for agricultural work. At the time of sowing, weeding, irrigating and harvesting when labour is scarce and his own work is not pressing, he can find opportunities for supplementing his food store." One of his summary statements is, "It has already been pointed out that with the exception of the barber and washerman, who are constantly kept busy, all castes engage in a certain amount of agriculture." Wiser presents an elaborate table which shows that "out of 161 families who might be potential members of the Hindu Jajmani System with a symmetrical service relationship, only 80 function on this basis .... Of the 80 families, only 14 draw their entire income from their occupation...."

[2] Term used in jajmani system to identify "those who serve".

These are sketchy bits of information, but the kinds of sources from which they are taken are the only ones available from which to learn what was happening in villages as commerce and industry developed in large population centres. The generalization that the British factory system destroyed the once-famous handicraft industry and threw most village craftsmen into agricultural occupations is altogether too broad. All available evidence is that as industrial production increased and competed with village handicraft production, there was a shift on the part of the village population to larger population centres, but that this shift out of small villages was not directly to large urban centres but to relatively small cities and larger towns within what the census called rural areas. Furthermore, even the volume of this movement did not lessen population pressure on the land. As a matter of fact, the net effect was to throw an increasing number of persons into agriculture for a livelihood.

A paragraph from Gadgil seems to us to summarize the relationship of the developing industrial revolution in India to the problem of population pressure on the land. He says, "The whole survey emphasizes . . . the very slow growth of new industries and the partial decay of old ones; the increasing pressure of the population on the land; the very small progress made in agricultural improvement—especially in the introduction of labour-saving appliances. The considerable change that has come about is neither in agriculture nor in industry but in trade. Methods of trading have been revolutionized, and the volume of both internal and external trade has increased enormously. Markets are now both wider and better organized. But the progress of industry has not gone hand in hand with this commercial revolution. The lines which the small progress that has been achieved have taken are not, indeed, peculiar. They follow in almost every respect the lines of industrial evolution in most other countries. The only thing, then, remarkable about this industrial evolution of India, has been its slowness."

This chapter has presented the historic causes for so high a percentage of India's steadily-increasing population remaining on the land. The account we have briefly chronicled is that neither the commercial nor industrial revolution had fully developed in India by 1950. Commercialization of the rural economy had been much more rapid than industrialization of the whole economy. But even the benefits of a degree of commercialization of the agricultural economy had not accrued to the people on the land. What amounted to a feudal system of landlordism had, for generations, reaped the benefits of monetized agriculture and increased land values. Furthermore, as has been the case with all feudal regimes, the increased wealth accumulated by landlords was left in the rural sector, or spent in luxury living; it was not shifted to the development of industrial enterprises. There was, therefore, no industrial development commensurate with the development of capital within the country. Feudalism not only sabotaged industrial development, thus permitting population to pile up on the land, but intermediary landlords fostered the division of land into small holdings because they collected higher rent from the many small cultivators who competed for tillable land. Furthermore, the whole zamindar feudal system did more than any other one thing to develop the wide economic, social, and cultural gap which came to exist between a relatively thin layer of the elite at the top and millions of poverty-stricken, illiterate peasant masses at the bottom of the socio-economic, political structure of Indian society.

With such a social structure, other elements in a steadily-evolving economy and society failed to develop. Channels of transportation and communication in and out of rural areas were not developed. Peasants not only remained illiterate, but developed no hopes or aspirations, which inevitably must provide the chief dynamics of development in a society in which they constitute the overwhelming portion of the total population. The development of industry was, and had to be, at the hands of foreign capitalists, and, as in all colonial regimes, these foreign capitalists were more interested in developing their own country than they were in developing one of their country's colonies. We quote from the summary of Nanavati and Anjaria, two eminent Indian economists, on the over-all trends which we have briefly described:

> " . . . These factors were: the rapid growth of population with increasing pressure on the land; the growth of a money economy, which led to extensive alienation of land from the agriculturists to non-agricultural classes; the de-industrialisa-

tion of the country-side, which was a characteristic feature during the period of the economic transition in India; and the prestige attaching to the ownership of land, combined with the notion that actual work on the land was degrading, which led the well-to-do classes to invest in land and become absentee landlords. In this process, the erstwhile owner after selling off his land to a money-lender often went on bended knees to him asking to be allowed to cultivate his old plot of land on terms which were necessarily unfavourable to him."

We believe that the above is a fairly accurate description of the situation which existed in India in 1950. What the two authors just quoted call "the economic transition in India" had, however, begun before 1950. What has been done since 1950 to hasten this development will be discussed in Chapter 12 on Land Reform Programmes.

MAIN AUTHORITIES QUOTED OR CITED

Baden-Powell, B. H., *Land Systems in British India*, Oxford Press, London, 1892.

Chandrasekhar, S., *India's Population*, The John Day Co., New York, 1946.

Dantwala, M. L., "Problems in Countries with Heavy Pressure of Population on Land: The Case of India," in *Land Tenure*, Proceedings of the International Conference on Land Tenure and Related Problems in World Agriculture, Edited by Parsons, K. H., Penn, R. J. and Raup, P. M., University of Wisconsin Press, Madison, Wisconsin, 1956. (Table 8, p. 135).

Davis, Kingsley, *The Population of India and Pakistan*, Princeton University Press, Princeton, N. J., 1951.

Gadgil, D. R., *The Industrial Evolution in India in Recent Times*, Oxford University Press, 4th Edition, Calcutta, 1954.

Nanavati, M. B. and Anjaria, J. J., *The Indian Rural Problem*, 5th Edition, The Indian Society of Agricultural Economics, Vora & Co. Publishers Ltd., Bombay, 1960, Chapter VIII.

Wiser, W. H., *The Hindu Jajmani System*, Lucknow Publishing House, 2nd Printing, Lucknow, U.P., India, 1958.

CHAPTER 8

STATUS OF SOCIAL SERVICES AND FACILITIES

THE position of India's services in 1950 in the fields of education, health, and welfare as well as transportation and communication facilities, imposed serious obstacles to development planning and action. It was not only that woeful deficiencies existed in all of these areas of social and community service, but that great improvement in all of them was regarded as essential to what India wanted to do for her people in the various development programmes. To raise the standards of living of her citizens required better educational facilities, improved health and nutrition standards, and alleviation of poverty, poor housing, and social injustice. To promote a dynamic, modern economy necessitated an efficient transportation system and more nearly adequate community facilities. India's planners recognized these urgent needs but were also aware of the very low base from which they had to start to build their network of social and community services.

In every index by which various countries are ranked as underdeveloped, illiteracy—always a component on such an index —correlates more highly with the total ranking than any other. India is ranked low on every development index as much because of her high rate of illiteracy as any other one factor. When India achieved her independence, she had somewhere between 80 and 85 per cent illiteracy; in villages probably from 90 to 95 per cent. Furthermore, in 1950-51 only 43 per cent of all children six to eleven years of age were in school; that is, only 19 million out of 45 million of these young school-age children were in school. This represented in rural areas only 38 per cent, in urban areas, 57 per cent in this age-group.

In general, the States which had been included in British India were far better off than others. Princely States and tribal areas were worse served. In the tribal areas of the North-East Frontier Agency, a territory covering almost thirty thousand square miles, not a school existed before 1947. Indeed, the scant proportion of rural children everywhere in India attending school was in part a direct reflection of the shortage of schools. As late as 1949 an estimated 300,000 villages—50 to 60 per cent of all villages—had no schools at all.

Another grave problem was that perhaps as many as two-thirds of the children who entered primary school dropped out by the fifth grade, although educators estimate that four or five years of primary schooling are necessary to attain even functional literacy. In some States nearly four out of five did not complete the fifth grade. And the wastage was always higher for girls. While no exact figures are available, it is presumed that drop-outs were higher in rural than in urban areas. The economic factor accounted for some, perhaps a large part, of the drop-outs. Even though primary education was generally free, children—especially rural children—were needed to earn money for the family. However, one can justifiably assume that another important factor in the high rate of drop-outs was the poor quality of education and its divorcement from the life of the people.

If primary education was so scant and it reached so few, its content was also unsuited to India's needs. Obviously, as a Ministry of Education Report said in 1953, the model provided by the Westernized urban school was "unsuited to the needs of the masses and to the conditions of life in rural areas. And yet, when the pressure of awakening public opinion demanded the extension of education to rural areas, this model was transplanted into the new environment without any attempt to study rural conditions or to modify the school curriculum and teaching methods to suit the rural ways of life." Or as a high Education official put it, "The child does not see the purpose of the education he receives... (and) remains a passive and in many cases an unwilling subject who submits to, rather than receives an education."

In addition, the teachers of the primary schools were neither trained nor able to alter their methods. Only one primary teacher in ten had a high school education. Minimum qualifications for a primary teacher were a middle school "pass", so that their general educational level was not much higher than the pupils they were expected to teach. A fairly large number had not even completed the primary course. In 1950-51, only about 60 per cent had had teacher training. The proportion of trained teachers varied widely between States, ranging from 20 per cent to 92 per cent.

According to a UNESCO report, the average pay of teachers in Government schools in 1944 was as little as $5 to $6 a month, and in private schools generally lower; in one large province, the average was less than Rs. 10 per month (about $2.00). This report said further that "their living and working conditions were far from enviable.... The school buildings are generally inadequate and unsatisfactory.... The equipment is often of the poorest type. The standard of instruction, therefore, is generally poor and sometimes shockingly low." The teachers "discontented and dispirited, somehow emphasize in their talk as well as in their life the dull mechanical aspects of teaching." The low status of the teacher in the Indian social scheme, his lack of prestige and influence as well as financial reward, was indeed one of the most serious problems with which India had to cope. Teaching school, particularly in the villages, was viewed as the "last resort for those who had failed everywhere else."

Compulsory education had been tried by 1947 in a few areas in a few States. In 1950-51 it was estimated to cover 5.4 million children and to have succeeded in those areas in bringing 77 per cent of the six to eleven age-group to school, about double the national average. This reported figure for attendance is probably very high. The First Plan confessed that, "The experiment of compulsion, which is generally regarded as the only remedy for improving the position (of wastage) has not made much progress. ... most of the States expressed their inability to enforce it." The famed 1944 Sargent Report on primary education felt that it would take forty years to make primary education compulsory and universal.

If primary education reached only a relatively few, secondary education was even more restricted. Only 13 per cent of the relevant age-group (11-14) went on to middle or junior high school, and only 8 per cent (about 2 million out of 27 million in the 14-17 age-group) attended secondary school. In all of India in 1950-51, there were, moreover, only some 20,500 middle and secondary schools for the 47 million potentially eligible pupils, 11-17. Most secondary school pupils were boys. Only about 3 per cent of all the girls went past primary school, as compared with 15 per cent of all boys.

While it is difficult to get exact figures, certainly the upper levels of secondary education were largely urban. Only a little over a third of the students in higher secondary schools were rural children. "Secondary (and higher) education of girls was almost exclusively confined to urban areas." In any case, the cities had 60 per cent of the higher secondary schools. Of the middle or junior high schools, (11-14) about three-fourths were in rural areas. Perhaps this is not surprising, since secondary education was and is not free. Most secondary schools in India were (and are) privately run. Even in 1958, an analysis showed that 71.5 per cent of all high/higher secondary schools were run by private agencies, and 20 per cent of these received no grants from Government or local bodies. Inevitably, therefore, these schools catered largely to the urban and the well-to-do. Thus, just as inevitably, the scant few who did get to secondary school were not necessarily the most qualified but simply those who could afford it. By and large, these were from urban families.

In secondary schools, as in the primary schools, most of the teachers had little better education than their pupils. For middle schools, minimum qualifications were high school graduation or an intermediate pass, for higher secondary schools an intermediate pass or a B.A. In 1950-51, 17 per cent of the secondary school teachers were not even matriculates (high school graduates) and only a fourth were college graduates. Barely more than half of them had been trained for the job, and there were only 53 teacher training colleges in India, turning out about 6,000 teachers a year. Pay scales averaged Rs. 40-70 (about $8 to $14) per month for middle school teachers, and only a little more for the high schools.

The most fundamental defect of India's educational system was that the universities dominated the entire field of education, and primary and secondary education were subservient to their needs. India's university system, begun in 1857 with the founding of major universities in Calcutta, Madras, and Bombay, was extensive by 1950-51 and consisted of 27 universities and 798 affiliated or non-affiliated colleges. University enrolment had been rising with unhealthy speed over the previous decades; it rose from 225,00 in 1947 to 373,000 in 1950-51.

In part, this rapid increase was due to a policy of "indiscriminate" and "unlimited" admissions and in part to public pressure.

Depending on how we calculate it, one out of every three or four high school pupils went on for higher studies—compared to about one in seven in England or Germany at that time. According to the Sargent Report of 1944 on Post-War Educational Development in India, however, assessment of the total number of students in colleges and universities, in relation to the whole population, shows "that India is perhaps the most backward of all the principal nations of the world in university education." Even in 1950-51 only 1 per cent of all the young men and women in the relevant (17-23 years) age-group were in college. Moreover, only about a fourth of those students were from rural areas. Only about an eighth of them were girls, although the proportion of girls going to college was definitely rising.

Liberal Arts courses still claimed the vast majority. Yet a change was beginning to set in. The available figures are not strictly comparable, but we know that the war and wartime industry and other needs had stimulated considerably more attention to professions related to development. In 1941-42 the preferred professions were law, commerce, medicine in that order, with engineering far down the list (about a third as many students as in law). In 1950-51 the order had markedly changed, to bring medicine first, engineering second, with commerce and law following. In agriculture, there had been almost no increase even in numbers, and the proportion to total college level registration had certainly fallen. In 1951, there were only an estimated 19 agricultural colleges turning out about 1,000 graduates a year. As a university education commission cogently stated it, "The vast rural population of India has been scarcely touched by secondary or higher education, except by the permanent withdrawal from village life of those able young people who have left the village for the University."

The 1944 Sargent Report gives an illuminating picture: "The gravest (of the university problems) is their failure to relate their activities sufficiently closely to the practical needs of the community as a whole.... Hundreds of young men who have received a purely literary education go about knocking at every office door without any clear idea as to where their proper vocation lies.... A great deal too much importance is attached to examinations (which) .... put a premium on book learning of a narrow kind at the expense of original thinking and real scholarship. . . . Overcrowded lecture rooms and over-worked lecturers are not conducive to that personal contact between students and teachers from which the greatest benefits of a university life may often be derived. The tutorial system is in a very embryonic stage . . . nor do colleges and universities as a rule excite the same spirit of loyalty and obligation as is usual in other countries. . . . While in many universities and many faculties, notably science, work of the first-class standard is being done, it cannot be said on the whole that Indian universities are yet producing either in quantity or quality the leaders and experts in all phases of national life whom this country is likely to need urgently in the near future.

The real trouble lies in the fact that neither private benefactions nor grants from public funds have yet been on such a scale as to place universities in a position of financial stability. So long as they remain largely dependent on student and examination fees, they can hardly be expected to put such restrictions on admissions as would allow high standards to be maintained. . . . Many (students) are there not because they have been found fit for higher education or have a thirst for knowledge, but because they found no opportunities for employment on leaving school and their parents gambled on the chance that their sons might discover a successful career after obtaining a university degree. . . . The large number of failures in University examinations is by itself an indication. . . . Probably nowhere among the universities of the world is there so large a proportion of failures in examinations as in Indian Universities."

But dark as the picture was, it would be a mistake to assume that the system of university education built up under British rule over the preceding century had completely failed to provide India with at least some of the leaders and elite she needed to create and head a nation. The First Five Year Plan put the problem in almost moving terms: "In spite of their grave defects, the existing universities are the only repositories we have of the tradition of organised knowledge and the course of wisdom is to improve their working while we attempt to build a system or systems better suited to our needs."

The low status of all levels of educational attainment and the inadequacies of educational institutions and services conditioned the process of development in many ways. The rural development programme was to require 50,000 young men and women to work in villages alone, as agents of change, aside from those needed by the various technical aid Ministries of the government. All these village-level workers were to be selected from villages and to be high school graduates. Obviously, these requirements could not possibly be met. The cadre of programme personnel immediately above these village workers were to be college graduates in the fields of agriculture, health, education etc., and more than 25,000 of them were needed. They were to technically "back-stop" village-level workers and thus guide the programme of technical assistance to village people. Clearly, few of these technical back-stoppers could have had practical village experience and also gained a college education.

The basic over-all weakness of educational services was that there did not exist in India anything like a normal pyramid of educational institutions. Although the number and proportion of children reaching for education had been rising very sharply over the previous several decades before Independence, there were still simply not enough primary schools in which numbers of millions of youth could be prepared to enter secondary schools, and thus to enter institutions of higher learning and technical education. A comparison between what we may call the pyramids of education of Japan and India, as of 1951, will reveal the tremendous importance to development of this basic fact. More than 80 per cent of all the people of India in 1950-51 could neither read nor write, whereas in Japan there was almost no illiteracy. Only 43 per cent of India's children of school age were in primary schools at that time; in Japan about 90 per cent. In India, only 7 per cent were in high schools; in Japan 42 per cent. In India only about 1 per cent were in higher institutions; in Japan 3 per cent.

Moreover, very few of those in India attending and graduating from institutions of higher learning had ascended the pyramid of education by the process of vertical social mobility. The vast majority of university graduates in India came from families who had been either intellectuals or the favoured status group for many generations. They were not only ill-trained for assisting in the technical know-how which development programmes would require, but were even less well equipped emotionally to assist in a giant rural development programme, which by necessity had to play a large part in national development.

The First Five Year Plan recognized and commented upon many of these educational problems that faced the country. It pointed out the lack of proper distribution of schools between rural and urban areas, the "lack of balance between provision of facilities for different sections of society", the problem of backward tribes and scheduled castes, the "neglect of women's education," and the disturbingly large "wastage" that occurs at different stages.

With especial significance, the Plan noted that, "The absence of adequate facilities for technical and vocational education results in a much large number of students going in for general education than is justified by the requirements of the country or the tastes and aptitudes of the pupils. The undue emphasis on the academic and theoretical aspects of education retards the development of the practical sense, initiative and resourcefulness among large numbers of students. One result of this is that educated people tend to depend too much upon employment by Government or commercial concerns, which can absorb only a limited number." The validity of these statements was almost immediately proved by the discovery that even with all the new development programmes there were something like 500,000 so-called "educated unemployed". What was undoubtedly meant was that in a forward-going programme they were unemployable.

The need for, but lack of, persons trained for playing essential development programme roles was by no means the only adversely-conditioning factor of the state of education in India in 1950. Success of practically all the processes of development would require effective communication between programme planners and directors and the masses. The low level of literacy, especially of the rural masses, would be hurdles in the channels of communication. That the social distance between the university-educated persons, who by necessity would have to plan and direct development programmes, and the masses would be an equally ominous hurdle was revealed when the planned development programme was thrown into gear.

Improvement of the educational system to attune it more closely to the needs of development was, then, of the highest urgency as India entered upon her "great and tremendous journey" towards development. What gave such improvement an even more immediate urgency was the already rising tide of demand for education from primary school through college. The fast-growing pressures for education—rising from village as well as city—were already in themselves creating educational problems of overwhelming proportions—problems which, as planning began, may have been only dimly seen, but which over the next decade enormously influenced what India did and could do to improve her educational system.

The paucity of India's health services in 1950 was also an important conditioning factor in development plans. In the absence of detailed data on the health status of the people of India on Independence, probably life expectancy is the best over-all measure of health. According to Kingsley Davis, who wrestled heroically to document what official Indian statistics reveal, life expectancy at birth in 1941 (the latest year at that time for which data were available) was 32.09 years for males and 31.37 years for females. Davis' calculations on life expectancy for older age-groups show that only about 55 per cent of all males ever reached twenty years of age and less than 13 per cent had the probability of living to age 60.

For purposes of identifying the nation's health problems, even more important than these figures on life expectancy were the major causes of death. An assessment of the health and health services in India had been made by the famous Bhore Committee only a few years before national development programmes were planned and launched. The four-volume report of this Health Survey and Development Committee was published in 1946. Its findings provided a basis for assessing the health problems and needs of India as of 1950.

In its study of pre-independent India, the Bhore Committee found that half of all deaths in India were of children under 10 years of age and half of these children died in the first year of life. Maternal mortality was at least four times that of England at the same period. Approximately one hundred million people suffered each year from malaria, a preventable disease, and two million people died of it, directly or indirectly. Half a million died of tuberculosis. Dysentery and diarrhoea killed over a quarter million annually. Leprosy and elephantiasis incapacitated hundreds of thousands. Taken as a whole, India's death rate was higher than that of any other country in the world except Egypt.

The Bhore Committee assessed what it thought were the chief causes of this low state of health in India. Foremost among these were the lack of safe drinking water and environmental sanitation in both city and village. It said "the wide prevalence of unsanitary conditions in rural and urban areas is so well known that it seems hardly necessary to provide any evidence in support of it." For the country as a whole, not 10 per cent of the people in any province had assurances of water safe to drink; in the vast United Provinces, (now Uttar Pradesh) only 4 per cent. Even in the relatively prosperous and well-administered province of Punjab, less than 1 per cent of the village people had safe water supplies. Furthermore, only 7 million out of British India's population of some three hundred million in the early 1940's lived in areas served by sewers. A few of the larger cities had modern disposal systems, but the Committee said "in the rural areas it may be stated as a broad generalization that no system of collection and disposal of excreta exists."

To cope with the illness arising from poor nutrition, impure drinking water, and unsanitary conditions, India had neither enough personnel nor adequate health services. The country had been turning out doctors since the first medical colleges opened in 1835 and yet by 1945 there was still only one doctor per six thousand people, against a United Kingdom average of one per thousand at that period, and one nurse in India to 43,000 people (U.K. average was one to three hundred). Most of the doctors —perhaps nearly three-fourths—served in the cities. Estimates for 1947 showed that in rural areas as a whole there was only one doctor for twenty-five thousand people.

Although the majority of all deaths in India were those of mothers and children, there were only five thousand practising, trained midwives against a minimum need for twenty times that number, and only 70 to 80 women doctors in the whole country with special training in maternity and child welfare work. Only one province (Madras) had organised maternity and child welfare work on systematic lines; school health services did not exist.

Hospitals and dispensaries were few and the rural population was everywhere less adequately provided for than the urban. The Bhore Committee said "only the outermost fringes of such public health services and amenities as the country enjoyed may come within the orbit of the cultivator's daily life." In the cities, in 1942 one medical institution (either hospital or dispensary) was available to an average of some sixteen thousand persons. In the rural areas of India, one such institution had to serve on the average, 49,000 people. The number of hospital beds available was 0.24 per one thousand population as against 7.14 in England and Wales and 10.5 in the United States. Even by 1949, in the villages, the ratio of beds was 0.09 per one thousand.

Not only were there too few institutions, but as the Committee said, "the services rendered by these institutions leave much to be desired. . . . In most dispensaries and out-patient departments, the time devoted to patients was so short (48 seconds to one minute per person) as to make it perfectly obvious no adequate medical service was given to the people." Moreover, it said, "The medical officers in charge of many dispensaries have, for long periods, been out of touch with modern medical practice without an opportunity to work in a well-conducted hospital. The quality of the medical aid given by such men must necessarily be low."

With particular significance, the Bhore Committee said that "the poorer classes have grave difficulties in securing medical aid in public hospitals and in dispensaries, although they often must come from great distances to seek help. The sympathetic attention and courtesy which they are entitled to expect from the hospital staff are often absent. . . . A radical change in the existing state of affairs is necessary to insure the success of future health programmes drawing on the support and co-operation of the people."

It is hardly surprising that the Committee reported that "the people view with apathy the large amount of preventable sickness and mortality which exists. . . . The outlook has no doubt been largely due to continuance of the existing state of affairs through many generations to which the inadequacy of available health services has been an important contributing factor." The Committee concluded that "if it were possible to evaluate, with any degree of exactness, the loss India suffers annually through avoidable waste of human material and the lowering of human efficiency through malnutrition and preventable morbidity, the result would be so startling as to arouse the whole country and create and enlist an awakened public opinion in support of the war against disease."

The First Five Year Plan stated only one of the basic conditions of national growth when it said, "Health is fundamental to national progress in any sphere. In terms of resources for economic development, nothing can be considered of higher importance than the health of the people which is a measure of their energy and capacity as well as the potential of man-hours for productive work in relation to the total number of persons maintained by the nation. For the efficiency of industry and of agriculture, the health of the worker is an essential consideration."

Progress has been made since 1950 in some areas of the health field and emphases have accordingly changed. The campaign against malaria, for example, has been so strikingly effective that the focus is now on total eradication of that disease. Immunizations of other preventable diseases are gradually gaining wide acceptance. Safe drinking water in rural and urban areas, on the other hand, is still a critical problem. Acute awareness of the heavy burden to development and to the welfare of the country of the rapidly-increasing population has brought the family planning programme of the Ministry of Health to the fore in the last few years. Nutrition, sanitation, and many other health problems of considerable magnitude are still unsolved.

It is difficult to assess what may be called the welfare of the people of India in 1950, not only because of the absence of statistical data, but also the absence of anything approaching a precise definition of welfare. Hundreds of millions of people were living in dire poverty, ill-fed, ill-clothed, and ill-housed; malnutrition bordering on starvation was the lot of millions; and social injustice pervaded very large segments of the Indian population.

In the early 1950's, before modern welfare programmes became a part of planned national development, national and public concern had been with injustices which created disabilities, while the care for those who suffered disabilities was left primarily up to local communities. Another way of stating this dichotomy of responsibility would be to say that government and the general public had been held responsible for social reforms, but local communities were held responsible for social work. It was also true that institutional care, as we know it in the West, had not been developed because the joint family traditionally cared for its own sick, aged, and disabled.

We know that India had behind her a century of social reform during which she had attacked with considerable success some of the worst social ills of reactionary Hinduism prevalent in the eighteenth and early nineteenth centuries. Among these reforms had been laws abolishing suttee (the burning of a widow upon her husband's funeral pyre) and legislation to permit widows to re-marry and inherit, to prevent female infanticide and child marriage, and to discourage exploitation of child labour; efforts had also been made to gain acceptability for women's education. The earliest of these reforms, led largely by Hindus in Bengal, was religious in character and part of the Indian struggle to liberalize Hinduism itself.

An analysis of the social welfare agencies in the three major cities of Calcutta, Bombay, and Madras indicated that child welfare was one of the oldest fields for social work, beginning with charity schools and orphanages; then toward the end of the nineteenth century with some work for handicapped children. Charitable hospitals were another effort started in the mid-nineteenth century, and late in the century, charitable trusts and educational societies began, some of them founded by communal and regional reforms associations.

Many of the earliest and most vigorous leaders of the freedom movement had taken part in the religious and secular movements toward social reform. The freedom movement itself, therefore, and especially under Gandhi, had in it a strong bias to social reform in the broadest sense of the term. However, some of those concerned with social welfare today find it difficult to assess Gandhi's influence on social welfare because he made welfare work subordinate to political agitation and social reforms. Others feel that what Gandhi did was to give social welfare a wider perspective, a new orientation, to include the welfare of the people as a whole, and very particularly of the villages.

The 1920's and 1930's were marked by the initiation and growth of activities in the field of women's welfare, as well as, after 1930, by the development of the concept of what India calls "Constructive Work" (community improvement, especially "rural uplift"), Harijan welfare, and adult education. Indeed, the inclusion of women in the political movement, specifically in *satyagraha* (civil disobedience activities), and Gandhi's strong espousal of women's equality and women's education, his encouragement of Constructive Work by women as well as men, were perhaps the greatest legacy of the freedom struggle to the future of Indian social welfare work.

The "magna carta" for women in India was the resolution of the historic Karachi meeting of the Indian National Congress in 1931. The declaration read: "All citizens are equal before the law, irrespective of religion, caste, creed or sex. No disability attaches to any citizen by reason of his or her religion, caste, creed or sex, in regard to public employment, office of power or honour, and in the exercise of any trade or calling." The National Planning Committee subsequently "gladly endorsed" this declaration of fundamental rights, adding that although "the freedom of women is still to be achieved. . . . a degree of understanding and an appreciation of the difficulties she has to face in her effort for equal citizenship is growing in the public mind." There was a similar assertion of the rights of children.

Thus by the time India became independent, welfare work had made a strong beginning. An estimate made early in the First Plan period put the number of already-existing voluntary social welfare organisations at 8 to 10,000, although no formal registration of such agencies was required and there was no complete record nor any clear idea of what their main fields of work were. It was known, however, that most of these organisations were urban and perhaps more than half of them were in the three major cities of Calcutta, Bombay, and Madras, where the early reform movements had gained most strength.

A beginning had also been made in the late 1920's in formal training for social work in Bombay. Subsequently Baroda University began formal studies in social work, and the Delhi School of Social Work, offering the first graduate-level studies, opened in 1946. Training facilities for Gandhian "Constructive Workers" were also started during this period.

It should be noted moreover that, especially after the 1919 Montagu-Chelmsford Act delegating authority to the Provinces for various "state subjects", there had also been considerable social legislation passed by the Provincial Legislatures, much of it to protect women and children, regulate social vice, and safeguard inheritance rights. In general, however, enforcement was poor to non-existent, lacking both staff and administrative organization, court facilities, and correctional institutions. For example, a Labour Investigation Committee in 1946 and 1947, found that particularly in small industries child labour laws were "openly disregarded" and that in some cottage industries, even children 3 to 5 years old were employed.

The significant point about the pre-Independence reform and welfare movements was that they were popular and voluntary, and were carried out almost entirely without the Government being an active partner. An early exception, the abolition of suttee, was done by order of the British Government in India with the support of voluntary social reform groups. A later exception was the initiation in Madras in the early 1940's, under British rule but with Indian leadership, of one of the first statewide and official women's welfare programmes. Initially, this was in part because of the then British Government's specific policy of not intervening in the religious affairs of its subjects; later, it was also due to the more political character of the reform movement.

Although government action had been chiefly legislative, India had not followed to the excess common among many newly-developing countries, the attempt to provide welfare services to its people by a plethora of social legislation which could not be implemented. Her legislation was—and today still is—largely confined to basic social reforms which government action could enforce. The new Constitution specified a number of such reforms, chiefly those which provided for strengthening the status of the weaker or most disadvantaged members of Indian society—scheduled castes and tribes, but also women and children.

The First Five Year Plan, although it gave some consideration to social work of various kinds, followed the same course. It, however, said, "Social legislation can be better enforced by associating social service agencies with agencies set up by the State." It also presented some account of the beginning of modern social welfare work, especially among women and children, and said, "There are a few agencies dealing exclusively with the problems of the family in India, and they cater mainly to local needs." Under the heading "Community Approach in Social Welfare", the Plan said, "The field of social welfare will expand in the measure in which local communities accept responsibility for solving their own problems. The State has undoubtedly a vital role to play and, as its functions develop, an increasing field of social work becomes linked in one way or the other with programmes initiated or supported on behalf of the State. Community welfare programmes embody four inter-linked ideas, namely (1) self-help and mutual service, (2) maximum use and development of local resources through organised community life, (3) economic betterment and cultural development through social participation in co-operative effort, and (4) achievement of community objectives through the minimum amount of assistance from the State." Modern social welfare leaders in India have had to struggle heroically and persistently to force State and national agencies to provide their share in co-operation between official and local voluntary "welfare undertakings".

We believe the generalization to be valid that the magnitude of social services is the ultimate measure of the development status of all countries. This magnitude is measured by the percentage of: professionally employed persons who are teachers, librarians, and others engaged in educational work; those professionally employed in health and welfare work; and those professionally employed in other fields of social and cultural improvement. The percentage of all employed persons thus engaged is highly correlated with the affluence of societies, their capacity economically to support a large corps of real social servants. India's capacity to do this was severely limited before Independence and will be limited for some time to come.

There is no greater disparity between underdeveloped and highly developed countries than that revealed by differences in the facilities for transportation and communication. Geographic areas over which, and various levels of social life between which, persons communicate with each other, have meanings which are difficult to grasp. Communication is the opposite of isolation, and the isolation of millions of persons is as pronounced a characteristic of underdeveloped areas as is poverty.

Needless to say, it is very difficult to portray the state of isolation in underdeveloped countries. The only data available for comparisons between countries are on mass media of transportation—miles of highways and railroads per population quantums—and mass media of communication—radios, telephones, circulation of newspapers per population units, etc. These are the very instruments or means of communication which the vast majority of the population of a developing country uses least. Contrasted with this fact, persons living in local communities, highly isolated from other sectors of a country's population, undoubtedly have more inter-personal contacts than do those who daily read one or more newspapers and use the telephone many times each day.

In order to visualize the ways in which, and the extent to which, the paucity of mass media of transportation and communication was, and still is, a conditioning factor of development, we shall present some statistical data on the status of communication and transportation in India in 1950. But it is necessary to go much beyond statistics to lay the ground for consideration of what needs to be done, and what has been done over the first ten years of planned development in India to improve means and methods of transportation and communication.

Whether for communication between rural areas themselves, or between rural and urban areas, the relative importance of transportation development in some underdeveloped areas of the world ranks as the first priority in development programmes. There is no better illustration of this than in countries like Haiti in the Western Hemisphere, where there is such a low ratio of miles of highways and railroads to population that one is inclined to think that development of transportation should outrank the development of education as a means of alleviating social isolation of the masses. A country like Laos in the Eastern Hemisphere would equally well illustrate the problem of the need for developing means of transportation. We are not, however, discussing transportation and communication targets for development, but rather the inadequacies of both transportation and communication in 1950 as they constituted a conditioning factor of development in India.

A trunk highway system from north-west India to Calcutta, built by the Moguls, was greatly expanded by the British and, according to estimates made in 1943, included 229,000 miles of roads. If one were to calculate this road mileage per some unit of population, there would be 1 mile of highway for each 1,300 population. It would thus appear that India's people were fairly well served by major highways. Such data do not, however, reveal the inadequacy of highway transportation in the rural areas of India. There were hundreds of thousands of villages in India in 1950 the only access to which was still by footpath and crude bullock-cart tracks. Major highways, during this period of expansion, had been built and used chiefly for moving raw products to ports where they would be shipped to British manufacturers, only incidentally for purposes of internal economic development of the country. This is in sharp contrast to highway systems which have been built in other countries to serve the needs of their own people rather than the needs of a colonial power.

Once a system of highways had been built in India to serve the purpose of the export of raw materials, there had been very little expansion. Available data for British India, including Burma but not including Princely States, show an increase of only 14 per cent in road mileage from 1926 to 1944. Once the development of facilities of transportation gets going, it tends to outrun purely economic development. After the advent of automobiles, a good-road movement developed in the United States which reached all segments of the population. "Farm-to-market" roads were a part of this movement. The basic objectives of highway transportation development in India have had little concein for the millions of cultivator families who lived in villages.

Road improvement throughout history has been in response to the need to accommodate road vehicles. The early roads built by the Roman Empire were to accommodate heavy war vehicles. The early paved roads in Europe were in no small way built to accommodate bicycles and were later greatly improved to facilitate automobile traffic. In the United States, the "good-roads" movement came with totally unpredictable speed in the decade before 1920, when automobiles became prevalent. The increase in traffic vehicles in India has without question far outrun road development to accommodate them. Motor vehicles have tripled in the past fifteen years, having increased by approximately 45 per cent in just the four years 1947 to 1951. These motor vehicles are, however, almost altogether urban-owned and used for inter-urban travel. But in inter-urban travel they traverse not only the good roads of India, but any and every type of road. Motor lorries by the thousands ply between urban centres. But transportation from villages to local markets is still chiefly by bullock cart.

The first railroad was built in 1853. The mileage of 10,000 in 1883 multiplied by more than 300 per cent during the next 50 years. In 1951, India had the fourth most extensive railway system in the world. It, like trunk highways, was built primarily to carry raw products from the interior to ports where they could be shipped to England. In 1951, 70 per cent of railway tonnage was coal, ores, cement, iron and steel. Not all of this was for export; an increasing percentage of it was for feeding the developing factory system in India. Only 19 per cent of the tonnage was of raw agricultural products, and about two-thirds of these products were food-grains chiefly for urban consumption, the other one-third to feed the growing factory system.

Railroad mileage in 1951 was 1 mile per 2,559 square miles. This would be a very abnormal ratio in a country where there is anything approaching an advanced rural road system, but the railroads, even more than trunk highways, had been built to transport raw agricultural products for shipment to British factories. They were not built to provide transportation and communication between the rural and urban populations of India, much less between rural communities, or even between villages and rural trade centres.

The fact that data on all the components of communication are not available in many underdeveloped countries makes comparisons between India and other so-called underdeveloped countries difficult. Most indexes include only a few components. They all, however, reveal a high correlation between the status of communication and the status of total development. One study accepted the boundary between developed and underdeveloped countries on the basis of whether or not 50 per cent or more of the gainfully-occupied males were engaged in agriculture, and used only one component of a communication index—the percentage of illiterates in the total population. Another study analyzed in detail the relations between each of five components of a model communication index—newspaper circulation, radios, telephones, cinema seats, and literacy. A number of rankings of countries have used all of these elements and others by which to array the countries of the world on a continuum from "underdeveloped" to "highly-developed" status. To assess the status of communication in India in 1950 when planning for national development began, we shall use these studies as background data.

The data here, from the 1952 Statistical Yearbook of the United Nations, are not systematically arrayed because they are presented only to show how low India ranked in means of mass communication even among other underdeveloped countries. She ranked lower in literacy (20 per cent) than any other heavily-populated country of the world except Indonesia and Pakistan. She ranked on an equality with Ghana and Bolivia. In circulation of newspapers she had only 8 per 1,000 inhabitants as compared with Ghana (19), Southern Rhodesia (16), Guatemala (19), Bolivia (23), Vietnam (9). In number of radio-receiving sets, India in 1952 had only 2 per 1,000 inhabitants. She was outranked by such countries as: in Africa, Tunisia (23), Egypt (11), Kenya (3), Southern Rhodesia (9); in South America by El Salvador (12), Haiti (11), Nicaragua (15), Brazil (15), Paraguay (25); in the Middle East by Jordan (5), Iraq (8), Syria (14); in South Asia, she outranked Afghanistan (1), Cambodia (1), Burma (1), and Pakistan (1).

An analysis of data from United Nations Yearbooks, for both developed and underdeveloped countries, was made of the relationship between each of six types or kinds of communication. The status of each type of communication correlated highly with the relative status of total development, highest with literacy, followed in order by newspaper circulation, cinema seats, radios, television, telephones, and school attendance. The major implications of the findings are that communication development is part and parcel of total development. The fact that in both developed and underdeveloped countries the status of communication development correlated highly with the status of total development does not, of course, establish causal relationships between communications and other forces or agencies of development. It does, however, provide the justifiable assumption that literacy in some ways is more causally related than the other means of communication to total development.

Shannon's study dealt directly with literacy. Because the analysis was only of relationships between literacy and degree of industrial development was not a serious weakness in light of the ample evidence of the relations of industrial development to so many other indices of total development. Since the data for this study were for developed as well as underdeveloped countries, and spanned a great many decades, the analyst was able to equate the experiences and status of underdeveloped countries now with the experiences of advanced countries which had in the past been in that same stage of development. More important, the analyst was able to learn what happened to the relationship of literacy development and industrial development as advanced nations passed beyond the stage of development in which underdeveloped countries now are. Findings on the experiences of five nations subjected to this analysis were presented in the table reproduced here, entitled "Actual and Expected Decline in Illiteracy in Selected Countries" (Shannon).

PERCENTAGE OF ILLITERATES IN THE POPULATION AGED 10 AND OVER

Country and year	Actual	Expected	Difference (Actual Percentage Minus Expected)
India :			
1911	93	64	29
1931	91	64	27
1951	80	61	19
Egypt :			
1907	93	67	26
1927	86	56	30
1947	75	51	24
USSR :			
1926	49	80	— 31
1939	19	39	— 20
Brazil :			
1940	57	61	— 4
1950	52	52	0
USA :			
1870	20	37	— 17
1910	7	5	2

It will be noted that three of the countries studied, India, Egypt, Brazil, are universally classified as underdeveloped. The United States is always classified as a developed country. Development in the USSR has been very rapid in recent decades. In the case of three of the countries, the period of development has been recent, ending in each case around 1950. The period used for the United States was from 1870 to 1910, to make it more comparable with the other four countries. Brazil had lagged in its literacy progress in relation to industrial development in 1940, but had balanced literacy performance with expectations by 1950. In Egypt, industrial development outran that expected of literacy from 1907 to 1927, but then increased literacy began to work toward balance with industrial development. In both the United States and Russia, literacy development consistently outran expectations. In India alone, did progress in literacy in each decade from 1911 to 1951 lag constantly behind predicted expectations. In 1951, India's literacy rate was 19 per cent below what the past experience of countries which had earlier moved down the road to development gave cause to expect. This was in spite of the fact that total educational development in India over the period had been greater than industrial development. It is our judgment that neither the intellectual elite nor the members of the civil service of any country listed in the table above outrank these groups in India. Because we believe this is true, it is difficult to escape the conclusion that India's low rank, not only in literacy but in all means of communication, is due to inadequate communication between those who rank high in intellectual attainments—literature, philosophy, science, and statecraft—and the great mass of her population which participates very little in mass means of communication.

We do not mistrust the data of statistical analyses on the status of communication in various underdeveloped countries nor do we question the validated conclusion that communication development is highly correlated with total development, nor the well-established fact that industrial development is the sine qua non of total development of underdeveloped countries. But we submit that the analyses which have established these facts have contributed little by way of specifications for remedies which can deal with the basic causes of India's low status in media of communication. The analysis needed is of types and characteristics of communication which are not reflected in data on participation in mass types of communication. Such an analysis is not easy, but it is imperative if it is to provide an understanding of needed priorities in communication development. It is also needed if agents of change are to be effective in their contacts with the communication fabric and practices of the masses who live in villages.

Communication in its simplest and most effective form is reciprocal two-way interaction (s) between persons. In its more complex forms, it is largely one-way communication, the reading of published news or listening to radio broadcasts, to which the reader or listener can make no response except in terms of his own aroused emotions and thoughts. Of all means of mass communication, only the telephone provides the opportunity for reciprocal interaction between persons. Communication by radio broadcasting is not reciprocal. Whether it is communication at all depends upon whether or not the broadcaster understands the percepts of the listeners and is thus able to convey thoughts to them through words and concepts which they understand. Newspapers require that the user be able to read. In the case of both radio and newspapers, the effectiveness with which these mass media of communication reach the masses depends primarily upon the capacity of the masses to receive such communications. The only other variable in the situation is the capacity of the communicator, whether he be a news-writer or a radio broadcaster, to understand the percepts and the language of the reader or listener. The great social distance between the originators of such communications and their prospective receivers in India, as in most other underdeveloped countries, has in the past been so great that the volume of mass communication has been small. The measure of participation in mass media in communication has therefore ranked India low on the communication index.

There is not, and never has been, any marked lack of communication within Indian villages, where reciprocal interactions between persons are easy and constant. But we cannot mistrust the evidences which rank India low, even among other underdeveloped countries, on the indices which measure participation in mass media of communication. The solution to the problem these validated facts raise, is not to be found solely in increasing the volume of mass communication, for an increased number of newspapers would not, and could not, be read, and increased news broadcasts over the radio would not be news at all unless it was real to the listeners. It is news to a listener only when it arouses or heightens some interest or concern which he already has. Otherwise, it is bizarre, and possibly confusing. Increased participation in all means of mass communication, much to be desired, awaits substantial improvement in other than mass means and methods of communication.

Mass means of communication will be relatively ineffective until literacy has greatly increased. Until then, communication with illiterates will have to be by word-of-mouth, face-to-face communication. This will, of course, require great numbers of personnel in development programmes. Because most of this personnel will, by necessity, come from the top down, there will be little, or ineffective, communication from the bottom up. This was in 1950, and still is, a conditioning factor of the first importance in total social and economic development. Progress in literacy has been slow, and extension of mass media of communication has been relatively slight, constituting very real obstacles in getting the messages on how to improve agriculture, health, industry, education and standards of living out to the masses of the Indian people who need to receive them.

MAIN AUTHORITIES QUOTED OR CITED

Basic Facts and Figures, UNESCO, Paris, 1952.

Education in India, 1951-52, Vol. I, Ministry of Education, Government of India.

Educated Persons in India, 1955, Planning Commission, Government of India, 1959.

India, A Reference Annual, Ministry of Information & Broadcasting, Government of India, 1960 and 1961.

Kabir, Humayun, *Education in New India*, George Allen & Unwin, London, 1956.

Literacy and Educational Standards, 1951 Census, Paper II of 1954, Census Commissioner, Government of India.

Post-War Educational Development in India, Report of the Central Advisory Board of Education, Bureau of Education, Government of India, January, 1944.

Report of Health Survey and Development Committee, Sir Joseph Bhore, Chairman, Government of India Press, Calcutta, 1946.

Shannon, L. W., *Underdeveloped Areas*, Harper and Bros., New York, 1957. (Chapter IV).

Statistical Yearbook, 1952, United Nations, N. Y., 1953.

Summary of Proceedings of the Center/Provincial Health Conference, New Delhi, October 1946, Department of Health, Government of India, April, 1947.

The First Five Year Plan, Planning Commission, Government of India, December, 1952.

CHAPTER 9

THE COMMUNITY DEVELOPMENT-EXTENSION PROGRAMME

INDIA was by no means the first country to establish a national extension service. Nor was she the first country to use community development methods. She was the first country to say clearly that she was going to use community development as an extension method, and the first to avow that her great mass of illiterate, poverty-ridden villagers are a development resource. A statement made at the time the community development-extension programme was launched, in October, 1952, was repeated two months later in the First Five Year Plan. That statement was that, "Community Development is the method and Rural Extension the agency through which the Five Year Plan seeks to initiate a process of transformation of the social and economic life of the villages." If we were to rationalize this statement, it implies a knowledge, or belief, that the technical know-how of science and the potential capacities of the masses of villagers are the two main forces of rural development, and that a government community development-extension system would bring these great forces into effective conjunction.

At no place in the Plan or in the early, published programme literature, however, was an analysis of the experiences of other countries in community development ever presented, as was done in a number of the other fields of development. The pattern of agricultural extension of Western countries was known to Indian leaders and was already, to some extent, being used in India. It is, therefore, easy to see where the concept of rural extension, to be used to extend not only agricultural but health, sanitation, and adult educational technical know-how to rural people, came from.

An analysis of the origins of the concept of community development in Indian planning is more difficult to trace. The First Five Year Plan said, "... the concept is not a new one...." It cited a few of the rather numerous experiments in community development which had, over the fairly recent past, been tried in India. It gave as the cause of the limited success of past experiments the lack of adequate financial assistance. In its Draft Outline, community development was not a major element in the Plan. The shift in concept and design, so far as the Plan was concerned, came between the dates when the "Draft Outline" and the final Plan were issued. Changes made in the proposed Plan reflected what was happening in the rapidly-moving events during this interim, but do not adequately account for the more fundamental ideas which probably provide an explanation of why India adopted a community development-extension programme. It was not merely as a method for doing extension work, but also a method to be used in the reconstruction of Indian rural society.

One of the chapters in the final Plan dealt with "Community Development and Rural Extension". After a brief discussion of "Basic Principles", this chapter describes the complete administrative organisation of the national "rural extension agency" to be established, and describes the "main lines of activity" which were to be "undertaken in a community project". One of these basic statements was, "While on the subject of organisation, it is necessary to stress the importance of ensuring, right from the start, the people's participation, not merely in the execution of the Community Development Project but also in its planning. This in fact is the very essence of the programme." And it said, "The Community Development Programme aims at the establishment of a suitable organ to ensure participation of the villagers at the planning stage." The programme was started seven months before the Plan was issued, and six months after a Technical Co-operation Programme Agreement was entered into between the governments of India and the United States. This agreement was signed by the two governments in May, 1952. It provided for a "community development programme".

If there is any importance in identifying then current projects or activities as influence which helped to crystallize the concept and design of a community development programme, Chester Bowles probably does so when he says that work in the two refugee colonies, Faridabad and Nilokheri, had demonstrated that village people could generate their own capital and reconstruct their own villages with their own labour, and when he said that the Etawah Project had demonstrated "that a single worker could be trained as a generalist" and could be an effective extension worker if technical specialists were located where he could get their ready assistance when he needed it. The projects named by Bowles were not the only ones on whose experiences Indian leaders could draw. There had been, in various parts of India, over the previous two or three decades, a number of community development-type programmes, and there was in the ideas of Indian leaders the conviction that this type of programme was an expression of the customs and traditions of Indian rural life upon which could be built a programme of rural change and progress. The most basic conviction was that India's village culture and village organisation were sound bases upon which to build a programme of rural reconstruction.

Probably the most widely known of these early experiments was a project initiated by F. L. Brayne, a British District Magistrate in the Punjab. Brayne's plan made provision for everything which villagers needed to do to improve their lot in life, from improved agricultural practices to family and community welfare. His project was advertised widely and watched carefully by Indian leaders. It, however, did not succeed for any period of time. As a matter of fact, it could be questioned whether it succeeded at all. But it contributed considerably to community development thinking. Brayne's blueprint for improvements was good, but chiefly what he demonstrated was that self-effort could not be, or was not, easily catalyzed by administrative directives. It is commonly said, and is undoubtedly correct, that his project after all was administered from the top down. Spencer Hatch's rural reconstruction project in Travancore-Cochin was also well known, and while it was backed by considerable outside funds, was nevertheless a true community development programme. Sevagram, Gandhi's ashram in Madhya Pradesh, was also a community development project and is such today. An institution known as the Panchayatgar was evolved in the United Provinces (now Uttar Pradesh) and initiated a number of experiments which were not too different from the Etawah Project later started in that same province. All of these projects are cited not because it is easy to trace their direct influence upon the thinking which lay back of the community development programme, but because they demonstrate that wherever any individual or official or group had attempted to start a community development-type project in India, it had nearly always met with the ready co-operation of the local people.

Another community development-type project was the Firka programme in the State of Madras. It was a State programme, promoted and directed by a "Firka Development Department", which, though not a full-fledged department of the State government, did have a provincial firka development officer, and regional and village development officers. Furthermore,, it had a complete plan of work, in agriculture and village industry, sanitation, health, housing, village education, village organisation, and village culture. It announced, "This has to be done by using local initiative and local responsibility to the utmost extent possible in the economic, political and social fields of reconstruction on co-operative lines."

We cite one other programme the influence of which on the community development programme that was launched can probably be fairly clearly identified. It was the Rural Reconstruction Centre at Kasamba, Baroda, promoted and guided by Sir V. T. Krishnamachari, then the Dewan of Baroda. He was later the Chairman of the Grow More Food Campaign Enquiry Committee and was Deputy Chairman of the Planning Commission from shortly after that commission was appointed until he retired in 1961. Mr. Krishnamachari, in his Annual Reports as Dewan of Baroda, as far back as 1932-33, recorded his plans for, and results of, a programme which must be identified as part of the roots of the community development programme. As early as 1928 in a speech to the District Baroda Cooperative Conference, he had said, "This cannot be achieved by the efforts of official agencies alone. There should be in every taluka or in a smaller unit if possible, a band of enthusiastic workers who would form a link between the department and the people and carry on educative propaganda among the people." In a speech at the opening ceremony of a Rural Reconstruction Centre in 1932, he said, "The success of a centre like this depends entirely upon the co-operation of enlightened agriculturists in the area, and I appeal to all here today, and to those who have been unable to be present here, to do their best to spread the benefits of this movement widely, so that in the next few years we may be able to start more and more centres like this in all parts of the State." In his Annual Report, 1933-34, he said, "The Centre should aim at effecting an improvement in all aspects of rural life—changing, in fact, the outlook of the agriculturists, the problem being the development of the desire for a higher standard of living."[1]

The last sentence quoted above gives expression to a fundamental doctrine of India's community development programme. Grow More Food campaigns had been in existence since 1942. The Grow More Food Enquiry Committee was appointed to analyze the experiences of these campaigns and make recommendations concerning future policy. Its recommendations are the most easily identified ideological antecedents of the community development programme design, because they represent the well-known and almost universal differences in two approaches to rural development, one being a straight-out drive for increased production of food, the other based upon the conviction that increased agricultural production can best be accomplished as part of a total rural community development programme, in which increased agricultural production will automatically be a major, and probably a priority, undertaking. It is therefore germane to set forth briefly what the observations and recommendations of the Grow More Food Enquiry Committee were.

Anyone seeking authoritative documentation for the first clear-cut, and detailed, statement of India's emerging community development programme will find it in the following quotations from the report of the Grow More Food Enquiry Committee: "The economic aspects of village life cannot be detached from the broader social aspects; and agricultural improvement is inextricably linked up with a whole set of social problems . . . all aspects of rural life are inter-related, and . . . no lasting results can be achieved if individual aspects of it are dealt with in isolation." The Committee followed this statement with specific recommendations for a national extension system, a block or taluk team of extension specialists, village workers who "should know and be known to all families in their villages," who would discuss and make plans for improvements with village groups, in order that

[1] Transcript of these speeches and reports was provided to the authors by Sir V. T. Krishnamachari, then Deputy Chairman, Planning Commission, Government of India, Delhi.

improvement projects "may command the largest measure of support... (and) bring into existence for villages or groups of villages, leadership of the best quality."

On the continuum from those antecedents which were an abiding part of Indian culture to those which had appeared at the time Independence was gained, or immediately thereafter, it is of course easier to identify the influence of those of the present or the immediate past, even though those of longer standing may be more important. The historically intermediate antecedents were chiefly those represented in the work of Mahatma Gandhi, his "Constructive Work" in villages, and his insistence upon the worth of the masses and the fundamental structure and integrity of village life. In the immediate past, there were the demonstrations of rather numerous community development projects or programmes, the major ones of which were briefly described above. Very recently launched and currently operating were the two refugee colonies of Faridabad and Nilokheri and the Etawah project, mentioned by Bowles.

The two large rehabilitation projects of Nilokheri and Faridabad did not provide the blueprint for local village community development projects, nor was extension an element in their methods. What they had proven was that seemingly helpless persons could be mobilized, and would mobilize, to lift themselves by their own bootstraps, so to speak, if given some material and technical assistance. Etawah was a real pilot project in local community development which clearly demonstrated what needed to be done, and could be done, in one local community after another if the methods which it employed were intelligently and patiently used. But probably more important than these experiments, as reasons for launching a community development programme, was the conviction on the part of many national and State leaders that they must at the earliest possible moment launch programmes which would reach all villages and involve village people themselves in development programmes. Community development was, and still is, believed to be the one programme which could, and will, utilize all the resources of government, and all the resources of village people in organised efforts to remove the burden of poverty, ignorance, and ill health from the rural masses.

The design of the programme that was launched was for a

nationwide rural extension programme which would use community development methods in one village after another as soon as each could be included in the development programme. The rural extension programme was to channel the technical and material assistance from all "nation-building departments" to village people. Community development methods were to be used to catalyze village groups to work on organised self-help improvement undertakings and to join hands with nation-building departments in all aspects of rural development. It was clearly foreseen that this would require a great expansion of government personnel and probably some alteration, modification, or addition to government administrative machinery.

India's government administrative structure had been largely organised by the British and, although it was now manned entirely by Indians with years of administrative experience, it was not considered to be completely adequate for the administration of a dynamic rural development programme. Doubts were expressed especially concerning district and sub-district administration, which were the lowest rural units of the government's hierarchical administration. The doubts were whether district and sub-district officers could be expected to overcome the habits of mind which they had developed as collectors of taxes and as court magistrates. Furthermore, the functions of local government were to be greatly expanded in the new programme. Great faith was placed in the possibility of rebuilding village panchayats. But even if this was accomplished, there would be great physical distance, and even greater social distance, between the existent local units of government and village panchayats. There was also fear that the red tape of hierarchical State administration would be cumbersome and slow-moving and would need to be supplemented or by-passed as far as possible. The design for a system of rural development administration was made in the light of these conditions.

Because each State had the right to establish its own administrative organisation, what might be called the blueprint recommended by the Central Committee and sanctioned by the conference of State Development Commissioners was not meticulously followed in all States. What is recorded here, therefore, is a description of the model for a community development-extension organisation and administration which, while not faithfully followed in all States, represents the general design for the rural development programme.

Starting with the State level, the recommendations were that something like a State Development Board be instituted, composed of representatives of State cabinet ministers; that the Board or Commission be chaired by the State's Chief Minister; and that a new officer, a State Development Commissioner, be appointed who would be secretary of the State Development Board or Commission and the Director of the State Development Programme which that body formulated. It was stated that "in view of the difficult nature of the work with which the Development Commissioner is entrusted, it is necessary for him to be a very senior and competent officer."

At the district level was to be a District Development Committee, composed of officers of the various development departments on the District Officer's staff, with the District Officer (the Collector) as chairman. The departments which normally posted officers in the District office were Agriculture, Education, Health, and Public Works, and in some Districts others. There was to be posted in each District a special Development Officer who would play the same role in the District as the Development Commissioner did in the State. Over the years, States have been encouraged to add two deputies to the Collectors' top staff, one to assist the Collector in the field of law and order, the other to assist him in development programmes.

At the Block level, it was said that the same pattern might be reproduced in gradual stages; that a Project Advisory Committee, "as representative as possible of all non-official elements within the project area," would be included, in addition to the principal government officials serving in the area—Members of Parliament and State Legislatures, representatives of co-operative societies, social workers, principal agriculturists, etc. The Block Development Officer would be the administrator of all programmes in his area of 100 villages. He would have posted on his staff technical specialists in agriculture, health, education, co-operatives, village panchayats, etc., who were technically accountable to their respective Ministries, but in development programmes would be accountable solely to the Block Development Officer.

As members of his staff, there would also be 10 to 20 multiple-purpose village workers.

At the village level, each multiple-purpose village-level worker would serve either 5 or 10 villages, depending on whether the programme in the Block was intensive or extensive. These workers were to be selected from among village-born and reared young persons with a minimum of high school education, who would be given training in all technical fields, more in agriculture than in other fields. Each worker would live in one of the villages of his circle of 5 or 10 villages, but would work in all of these villages. He would render first aid technical assistance, catalyze and help organise village groups for self-help undertakings, and be the agent through which village needs could be made known to the Block Development Officer and his specialists. Through him, Block technical specialists could channel their proffered technical aid to villagers. Great emphasis was laid on the importance of selecting village-level workers from among village people and on the vital role of these village-level workers in the programme.

A communication sent to all State governments as early as June, 1952 said that, while "the village-level worker will be required to take interest in all different lines of activity which will be undertaken in the community project area, the primary emphasis will necessarily be on agriculture." A following communication said that "in the selection of village-level workers, local talent should be utilized as far as possible, as it will tend to harness the enthusiasm of the people of the local area;" and one of the basic criteria specified for the selection of village-level workers was that "he must be capable of meeting villagers at their own level, before he can ever hope to win the confidence and extend to the field and home new and better ideas and practices." It was emphasized on all sides and repeatedly that the village-level worker, the grassroots agent of change among villagers, was the key man in the whole development programme, and that all personnel and echelons of administration above him would serve the activities which he was attempting to promote.

The programme, briefly described above, was fully crystallized by May, 1953, when the Community Projects Administration presented its first report to Parliament. This programme was thoroughly reviewed by the National Development Council in its second annual meeting held in October of that year. By that time, 472 blocks had been allotted, and work had been started in 417 of them. These blocks included 43,350 villages and almost 35 million people. It was planned to increase the coverage to 120,000 villages, about one-fourth of the country. The Third Five Year Plan provides for complete coverage of the country with development blocks by October, 1963.

During the First Plan period, the logic of development stages, represented in three types or classes of development blocks, had been crystallized. The logic was that as many blocks as could be staffed with trained personnel and supported by adequate funds would initiate and carry out an extension programme by *intensive* community development methods. These intensive blocks would be staffed by 20 village workers and a full quota of block extension specialists, and would be granted a little more than $31,600 over the first year of operation. A series of *less intensive* (National Extension Service) blocks, would be staffed by about one-half as many personnel and supported by one-half as much funds over a three-year period. A third type of block, which would emerge out of three years of intensive work in community development blocks, would be *post-intensive* blocks; with respect to personnel and financial support, they would revert to less intensive (NES) block status. It was planned that an increasing number of NES blocks would, year by year, be converted into community development blocks, and each community development block would, at the end of 3 years' operation, become a *post-intensive* block. The presumption inherent in this development logic was that the successful use of community development methods, after three years, would develop such widespread participation of village people and such effectively-organised village groups, with enough competent local village leaders, that local development projects and programmes would be locally self-generated and locally supported by experienced village personnel, largely supported by village-generated funds.

A review of the events, over the first five years of programme operation, revealed that by the end of the first year, programme leaders were exceedingly well pleased, and somewhat surprised, at the ready and widespread response of the villagers to the programme. They and many others who visited widely in villages were thrilled with the teeming activities they witnessed in village after village. Before the programme had been operating three years, it was being called a "community development movement", which meant that it was so highly sanctioned by everyone from villagers to national leaders that a faith in its progress had become a national contagion.

During the high tide of the so-called "community development movement", practically all levels of government personnel were in one way or another participating in the "movement". There was a serious attempt to channel this participation. There were regional seminars, State seminars, and in large States, district seminars. Each year, more than 2,000 persons spent an average of 5 days in regional seminars, most of whom had already participated in district and State seminars. An agenda of topics, stated in terms of pertinent and current issues, was prepared well in advance and discussed at all seminars. There was a welter of ideas and opinions presented and debated. An analysis of them provides an understanding of the animus of the programme and an explanation of the course which it took during the early years.

In the records of seminar discussion, there appear suggestions for practically every reform in programme organisation and operation which was later adopted. The authors, as observers, and sometimes participants in the seminars, were interested in attempting to discover the extent to which seminar discussions revealed an awareness of certain basic practices in programme planning and operation which were later reported by the Programme Evaluation Organisation as not being consonant with the original programme design and expectations. The reader of seminar reports will have difficulty in discovering much awareness by seminar discussants that basic community processes of the type extolled and expected to be used were being jeopardized by planners and programme directors, and by failure to work through local village groups. On the issue of whether or not there was a lessening of reliance on government finance and direction of improvement projects, quite often responses were in terms of how this would be accomplished in the future. At one series of annual seminars, specific questions were asked about the influence, on developing self-reliance and local responsibility of village people and village groups, of targets handed down from above, and of improvement-project selection being influenced by the amount of subsidy offered. By and large, the responses were either that targets weren't handed down from above, or it didn't make any difference so long as villagers accepted them and worked to accomplish them.

The insight that we as analysts gathered from reading the published reports of the discussions in these seminars, and by listening to a fairly large number of these discussions, was an insight into what some development leaders described as "the smug complacency of administrators who always had directed programmes which had been assigned to them from above, but who had never worked with village people and village groups." In keeping with the universal practice, those who were highest on the administrative chart had most to say in the seminars. Village-level workers always constituted a very minor percentage of the attendants, and a far smaller percentage of those who participated actively in seminar discussions. Junior administrators at many seminars made some very progressive suggestions and rather brashly criticized some trends in programme operation, but they were not high enough in the administrative hierarchy to have very much influence. While, therefore, the seminars were designed as conferences between those playing roles at the top, at the bottom, and in intermediate positions of programme operation, they were dominated by highly-positioned administrators. Although some of these administrators saw quite early in the programme's operation that not all was being accomplished that had been expected, they undoubtedly represented the widespread conviction that more was being accomplished in all phases of village improvement than had ever before happened. They were justifiably proud of this fact, but it rested on others to measure the degree of accomplishment not by the past but by the goals set by those who planned and launched the community development-extension programme.

This broader and more forward mode of thinking is best represented at the annual Development Commissioners' Conference which is, so to speak, the capstone of all seminars. It is, in fact, an annual review and policy-making body, on which sit not only all State Development Commissioners and members of the Planning Commissions, but representatives of the Central Government, Ministries, and officers of the Community Development Programme administration. It reviews all sorts of reports, including those of the Programme Evaluation Organisation, and it makes specific recommendations for programme action. Its published documents are therefore the best record from which to ascertain the opinions and judgements of the leaders of India about how well the programme is working.

Year after year, the conference keynote address had been delivered by Sir V. T. Krishnamachari, then Deputy Chairman of the Planning Commission, who, it must be remembered, had been the chairman of the Grow More Food Enquiry Committee, and whose official 1952 report first stated the rationale of a community development programme. In his annual address to the conferences, he repeatedly emphasized this rationale. Some of his remarks were:

"We must make them (villagers) realize that it is only by community self-help that improvements on the scale needed can be brought about. . . . The villagers should feel that it is only by their own efforts that they can get all of these needed supplies. The government may assist with grants and loans to some extent, but the main effort should be theirs. . . . I have talked to you about a change in the outlook of the rural population. But there is another factor equally important. There should be a change in our outlook as well. . . . We should give up the idea that we are here to force our programmes and plans on the villagers. It is for the villagers to tell us what they want and for us to assist them . . . we must see that our officers work as a team all over the district. They should bring before the villagers the basic idea that village life is one and indivisible and that self-help is at the root of all improvement. . . . I would remind Development Commissioners that the National Extension movement is essentially a people's movement. It should not be allowed to deteriorate into a series of official projects or schemes, but should continue to be a dynamic movement representing the efforts made by the people to improve their own condition."

The Administrator of Community Projects, in his addresses, set forth the difficulties he was experiencing because of old administrative rules and procedures. In the 1953 Conference, he said:

> "The old Governmental rules do not permit us to function in the new way. It is with the co-operation of the executive departments that those rules should be amended to fit in the new context. The people of India, the servants of the Government of India and the leaders of the Government of India are not here to subserve rules. On the contrary the rules are to serve the new masters."

Two years later, in the 1955 Conference, he said:

> "The people can be brought in if only we take a move simultaneously to pick up and train the people's leaders and then give shape to the organisation and see that the organisation is vested with responsibilities for both planning as well as for execution. This way alone we can expand the government activities till they cover every phase of life, and yet not complicate the machinery of government with the extra burden of planning and supervision, which, so far as the details of local operations are concerned, can be adequately taken care of by local agencies."

In the Third Development Commissioners' Conference, 1954, a great deal was said about the necessity of developing people's organisations and making them responsible for carrying out local improvement projects, even public works projects. The sub-committee on "People's participation in programme execution" said, "The village plans should be drawn up after consulting the general assembly of the entire village. . . . Wherever the voluntary organisations irrespective of political complexion are doing useful constructive work and are effective, they should be associated in the programme and their representatives should have representation in all Advisory Bodies at all levels." This conference diligently studied and expressed approval of most of the critical judgments expressed by the Programme Evaluation Organisation concerning over-emphasis on targets handed down from above, the necessity of village groups setting their own targets, and of cultivators being taken into counsel concerning all proposed agricultural improvement programmes.

The 1955 Conference made specific recommendations concerning the delegation of power to local authorities and recommended that panchayats be allowed to levy taxes and be authorized to plan and execute works projects to the limit of 2,000 rupees, (about $400) worth of expenditures. It also recommended the training of the members of local bodies. It specifically suggested that "people's participation in the programme" should be one of the main criteria for the achievements of project blocks.

The First Five Year Plan period had come to an end before the fifth annual meeting of the Development Commissioners' Conference was held. Instead, therefore, of attempting to analyze the trend in thinking about, and plans for, adjustment in the community development programme from the records of the State Development Commissioners' Conferences, we turn to the annual reports of the Programme Evaluation Organisation, which, as an arm of the Planning Commission, had been set up during the first year of official programme operation. Its establishment and its continuing and expanding support is an index to the conviction of Indian planners that systematic, constant review of programmes in action would be imperative for constant programme improvement.

The first Programme Evaluation Report, published in 1954, was an evaluation of what had transpired in the programme from the day it was started to the end of the year 1953. This report said, "The response of the village community to schemes of extension and improvements has been uniformly good. . . . As a rule, where extension has been attempted with the requisite competence there has been no lack of public participation." But it also said that there was a tendency for community projects to take over some functions that normally belonged to village organisations, and that, "There is a growing realization in all States that targets handed down from above have little validity in them." It also noted that some roads built in the great enthusiasm of shramdan (organised voluntary labour) were already falling into disrepair. The second annual report said that, "Initially participation was intended to imply popular initiative and sharing in the whole process of development of a rural community. As, however, the governmental organisation became the most noticeable outward expression of the developmental effort, and as proformas of schemes intended to be illustrative came to be put to people as suggestions, plans took the character of state or governmental rather than community or local plans."

The fourth annual report of the Programme Evaluation Organisation listed forthrightly what its authors believed Indian leaders had learned during the first five years of programme operation. Five of its conclusions are most pertinent to an analysis of the success and/or failure in the use of community development methods up to that time. The report said:

> "Items involving change in social attitudes such as readiness to go in for or maintain community centres, youth clubs, and women's organisations are, generally speaking, not particularly successful. . . . Items involving change in organisational attitudes in the political field such as better understanding of the objectives and responsibilities of panchayat membership and readiness to use panchayats for planning and executing village development programmes are comparatively unsuccessful. The objective of inducing public participation and positive support has been comparatively successful in the case of constructional programmes, but not in the case of institutional programmes. While there has been considerable increase in rural consciousness of economic, and to a smaller extent, of social needs, the objective of stimulating continuing and positive effort based on self-help for promoting economic or social development has been comparatively unsuccessful. Too much dependence on Government initiative and assistance is still being exhibited by the vast majority of the rural population affected by the programme. The rural population in project areas is, generally speaking, now developing a feeling that Government is there not merely to rule but also to help. In fact, expectation of what Government can do to help has perhaps reached a stage beyond the current resources of Government. On the other hand, there has not taken place an equally strong sentiment of self-reliance and initiative, whether individual or cooperative."

This report did not fail to list programme accomplishments, but it directed attention to lack of success in the very areas to which community development processes were presumed to make their greatest contribution—developing self-reliance and initiative on the part of villagers, lessening dependence on government assistance and direction, and the failure to develop local institutions and local leadership. It was to remedy these shortcomings that a move for "democratic decentralization" was later proposed and initiated.

Interviews with a number of persons who from the beginning had not only daily observed the programme, but had prominent roles in programme direction, testify that between two and three years of programme operation had shown that not all of the obvious village improvements were being accomplished by sound community development methods, that the programme had become, as they said, an "amenities", a "construction", and even an "administrative" programme, rather than a "production", a "self-help", and a "people's" programme.

These leaders were asking, "Is the outlook of village people being changed? Is the programme becoming more and more a people's programme and less and less a government programme; are village organisations and institutions and village leaders emerging? Are community development-extension methods yielding adequate increases in agricultural production?" These and other questions of similar import became so widespread that within five years from the time the programme was launched, it was being subjected not only to widespread public criticism, but subjected to official government scrutiny, the results of which were proposals and plans for programme-corrective measures.

The Introduction of the 1956 Programme Evaluation Report, entitled "The Process of Development", commented at considerable length on this theory of programme organisation for development. It commented on the—up to this time—accepted idea that,

" ... the process of intensive development of an area, which has been called 'community development', is composed of at least two stages. In the first stage, the primary emphasis may be on provision of amenities but in the second, it must shift to intensive efforts in development of agriculture and village industries and strengthening the institutional structure. In the case of the first community projects, only the first stage is being completed and they are now ready for undertaking the more intensive effort needed for the second. ....
While the fundamental objectives of the programme continue

to be defined in terms of producing economic, social and, in particular, psychological changes among the rural people, and the physical accomplishments are seen as means towards producing these changes, there is a distinct change—gradual but nevertheless definite—in the way in which the programme is being carried out in the field. The emphasis on physical and financial accomplishment—getting targets achieved, expenditure incurred, buildings constructed—is definitely on the increase.... Even among physical accomplishments, preference in many areas is distinctly for the spectacular as against the less noticeable though more lasting and fundamental improvements. Construction activities are especially favoured.... Undoubtedly there has been a great, almost phenomenal increase in expenditure in most projects, but whether all this has been an advantage from the point of view of the programme is problematical."

These excerpts state in essence that the practice of placing first emphasis on the development of amenities had resulted in a steady drift toward making the whole programme a construction rather than an extension programme; furthermore, that construction had absorbed so much of the village-level workers' time that they had lost sight of the objectives of the programme and would feel sincerely frustrated that they must turn their hands and minds to real extension work at the end of three years of so-called intensive development. These were not merely opinions; they were judgments derived from the findings of detailed field studies made by the Programme Evaluation Organisation.

The Programme Evaluation Organisation, as was said above, is an arm of the Planning Commission and is its official evaluating agency. It was supplemented, in 1956-57, by a special committee appointed by the National Development Council, which may be thought of as a review committee of the Planning Commission. This committee was directed to study and report on (1) the content of the programme and the assignment of priorities to different fields of activity; (2) arrangements for the execution of the programme; (3) assessments of requirements for personnel; (4) the extent to which the programme had succeeded; (5) the method adopted for reporting results; and (6) any other recommendations that the team may like to make in order to insure economy and efficiency in the working of the community projects and the national extension service.

This committee, or "Study Team", made maximum use of all of the quantitative findings of the Programme Evaluation Organisation and made elaborate qualitative field analyses of its own. Its analyses and recommendations were quite comprehensive and detailed. Its three-volume report covered 416 pages and included 322 recommendations. Our review of it, at this point, is confined to its analysis and comments on the operation of the community development-extension programme, the roles of the programme's various cadres of personnel, their relationships with each other, and the administrative direction of the programme.

In a chapter entitled, "Work Study of a Few Typical Blocks", the committee reported findings on the various roles played by different cadres of personnel. We first report its findings on what we have called the line of extension communication, as measured in terms of the number of extension workers, and then in terms of their capacities to play effectively the roles which the extension programme required. Since the village-level worker and the agricultural extension specialists in the block are the primary agricultural extension personnel, who are supposed to work directly with cultivators, we emphasize especially the committee's report on these two cadres of personnel.

The committee reported on the findings of a study of 20 blocks, located in 6 States. The full quota of personnel prescribed for intensive blocks was 20 village workers, one each to serve 5 villages; 7 block extension specialists; and, of course, a chief Block Development Officer. Only 14 of the blocks were in the intensive stage of development, but it is important to evaluate actual performance in terms of the programme which was designed to do a complete community development-extension job. It reported that 18 of the 20 blocks had only one block agricultural specialist, and that there were approximately 240 village-level workers, an average of 12 instead of 20 per block. Its analysis showed that what was admittedly a thin line of extension communication between the sources of technical knowledge and cultivators was seriously deficient in terms of posted personnel. It showed further that only one-third of the village-level workers had been trained in basic agriculture and one-half of them in extension, and that most of the agricultural specialists were untrained in practical field extension methods. It said also that 25 per cent of the Block Development Officers were untrained. All of this was to say that many of the persons functioning on the extension line of communication were untrained or inadequately trained.

The committee undoubtedly recognized that some, if not most, of these deficiencies were inevitable, due to the rapidity with which the programme had expanded and due to the paucity of trained personnel. It knew that it would take time to remedy these types of deficiencies. There were other deficiencies, however, that it believed could and should be remedied by early action. It reported that the block specialists spent some 30 to 50 per cent of their time at headquarters, and that village-level workers spent 25 to 40 per cent of their time at block headquarters or their own village circle headquarters. It analyzed the causes for these two cadres of personnel not effectively playing their prescribed roles in agricultural extension. The block agricultural specialists were being used to assist in administrative tasks of the block and the village-level workers were giving about 20 per cent of their time to "construction" work and were required to spend approximately $3\frac{1}{2}$ months, or 94 working days, per year, to complete all the records and reports required of them by higher administrative officials. They were spending a great deal of their time in distributing seeds and fertilizers and negotiating and collecting loans. The committee said of the agricultural extension specialists that the time of college-trained men was being utilized for routine office work, and that the village-level worker, if he did all the detailed things assigned to him, would have very little time to work with cultivators.

These diversions of the work-time of extension workers were, in the committee's mind, no more serious than what it called the "built-in character" of the community development programme. It said it meant by this phrase that the limits of the programme were being fixed by the "schematic budget" which allocated funds for the support of undertakings which planners and programme directors presumed would, in the development process, follow in sequence one step after another. The committee's criticism was not only that the built-in programme set limits to the type of projects for which both personnel and financial support were provided, but that the effect of such a built-in character robbed local workers and village people of being in any measure self-directive.

Closely related to, as a matter of fact part of, the "built-in character of the programme" was its domination by administrators. The committee made many comments and a number of recommendations concerning programme administration; in fact, had a whole section discussing "administrative difficulties". But the chief difficulties with which the committee dealt were lack of co-ordination of the contributions of nation-building agencies at the block level and below, and the ineffective co-operation of technical personnel of the departments in the block and below. It said some of the difficulties are "endemic to our administrative procedures and have been repeatedly pointed out by Indian as well as foreign critics." The committee's report and recommendations dealt not only with agricultural extension, but with the whole community development-extension programme. Its discussion of the necessity for decentralization of administration and its detailed recommendations for establishing village and area institutions for programme promotion and administration were undoubtedly its greatest contribution to programme reorientation and reorganisation, but it also made many recommendations for action which it believed would improve the agricultural extension programme.

There were some other significant notes sounded in the committee's discussion which had not received much consideration in the First Plan and which the study team believed had not received the emphasis which they deserved in a rural development programme. We have already mentioned the necessary balance between projects to develop amenities and projects to increase production. The report gave, for almost the first time, due recognition to the importance of improved agricultural practices as a component of all other prescriptions for increased agricultural production, whether these other specifications were for more irrigation water, better seeds, or more chemical fertilizers. The committee made the important point that no one of these other prescriptions would yield the results which had been assigned to it unless cultivators were taught improved agricultural practices.

It is exceedingly doubtful that any development programme, whether planned or unplanned, even in so-called advanced countries, and certainly no other planned programme of development in newly-developing countries, has ever been submitted so constantly and so thoroughly to analysis by persons and organisations,—the Planning Commission, its Programme Evaluation Organisation and other bodies it appointed,—as was the community development-extension programme of India during the formative years of its operation. The changes which resulted from these self-examinations were reported in the Third Five Year Plan.

From our own observations, and from a study of official and non-official sources, we are reporting here the experiences of a giant evolving programme. India's first ten years of experience in implementing and operating the largest extension programme in the world, and conducting the greatest experiment in community development ever staged, offers an unparalleled opportunity for such an analysis. The programme is so young and has moved so fast that we have been able to observe its total evolution. We have recorded what has happened to, or in, a splendid, rationally-designed programme for widespread action when it was subjected to the necessity of operating under varying and rapidly-changing conditions.

We have made it clear that Indian leaders believed there was no alternative to launching a programme of giant proportions; that to launch a few pilot projects would have meant that what was learned from these projects would have had little influence by way of leavening a stagnant rural economy and a traditional body of some 300 million local village people. India was a newly-free and sovereign nation and because of this, there were widespread expectations, even among the masses, that something would be done to improve their conditions. It was imperative that these expectations be nurtured. In the absence of mass means of communication, the only way to nurture these hopes and expectations was to initiate improvement projects in a great many local areas where locality-bound villagers could not only know about them, but participate in them.

Those observers from Western nations who have witnessed the struggles with, and the shortfalls in the performance of,

India's community development-extension programme, and who believe a more effective programme would be modelled on the agricultural-extension system of the United States or the agricultural advisory system of England, fail to understand that India did not have one-tenth enough agricultural technicians to staff a nationwide agricultural-extension programme. Such critics, or theorists, fail to reckon with the fact that such a nationwide agricultural-extension programme would have required some 60,000 agricultural agents even to supply one agent to each 1,000 cultivators. Indian leaders and planners did recognize and reckon with this fact, and decided that it would be far better to supply some 60,000 first-aid technical assisters to villages and technically backstop this corps of local village workers with some 6,000 better-trained agricultural technicians located physically near enough to village-level workers to assist them. Perhaps of greatest importance in understanding why India's planners decided in favour of the community development-extension approach was the deep conviction that the prerequisite for national rural development was the development of the people's competence to learn, to solve their own problems through the development of village institutions, the strengthening of village leaders, and the motivation of people to want and accept new ways of thinking, new standards of living, and new methods of securing their livelihood. This is what their blueprint provided.

It was inevitable in a programme of such magnitude, which had to be so rapidly staffed, that there were many village-level workers who did not meet the criteria of the programme blueprint in terms of either training or practical experience, and that there were not enough college-trained technicians to effectively backstop village-level workers. There were undoubtedly some programme shortcomings which were not inevitable. It has been only gradually recognized that there have been shortcomings in both community development and extension technical know-how. Furthermore, there have been an inadequate understanding and some false theories about how to motivate individuals and local groups. There has been a failure to understand that such a widespread, diversified, fast-moving programme could not be meticulously directed by State and national government administrators; that dynamic, democratic local groups won't develop and grow in either competence or confidence if they are told in detail what they are and are not permitted to do. There has been an outstanding failure to use community development methods in agricultural-extension where they are most needed if great numbers of cultivators are to be stimulated to adopt improved agricultural practices and these practices are to be widely diffused in one rural community after another.

The recently-initiated Panchayati Raj is an avowed move in the direction of decentralizing programme administration. If it fulfils what is expected of it, it will not only encourage but need to use good community development methods. To do so will automatically dilute the dominance of bureaucratic administration. The Intensive Agricultural Districts Programme, or so-called "Package Programme", which will be discussed in Chapter 11, should, if it uses good community development methods, not only demonstrate how to increase agricultural production by better use of science and technology, but how effectively to catalyze and mobilize groups of farmers to adopt and use better methods of farming. What these two programmes are expected to accomplish was provided for in the original design of the community development-extension programme. Indian leaders have had to learn, and have learned, out of practical programme operation experience, how better to implement what they rationally designed.

MAIN AUTHORITIES QUOTED OR CITED

Evaluation Report on First Year's Working of Community Projects, Programme Evaluation Organisation, Planning Commission, Government of India, May, 1954.

Evaluation Report on Second Year's Working of Community Projects, Vol. I, Programme Evaluation Organisation, Planning Commission, Government of India, April, 1955.

Evaluation Report on Working of Community Projects and N.E.S. Blocks, Programme Evaluation Organisation, Planning Commission, Government of India, April, 1956.

Evaluation Report on Working of Community Projects and N.E.S. Blocks, Vol. I, Programme Evaluation Organisation, Planning Commission, Government of India, April, 1957. (P.E.O. Publication, No. 19.)

Krishnamachari, V. T., *Community Development in India,* Publications Division, Government of India, October, 1962 (Rev. ed.)

Ministry of Community Development, Panchayati Raj and Co-operation, *Evolution of Community Development Programme in India*. Government of India, Delhi, 1963.

Report for 1952-53, Community Projects Administration, Planning Commission, Government of India, 1953.

Report of the Team for the Study of Community Projects and National Extension Service, Committee on Plan Projects (COPP), Vols. I and II, New Delhi, November, 1957.

Report of The Grow More Food Enquiry Committee, Ministry of Food and Agriculture, Government of India, June, 1952.

Summary Record of Second Development Commissioners' Conference on Community Projects, (16th April to 19th April, 1953), Community Project Administration, Planning Commission, Government of India Press, 1955.

Summary Record of Third Development Commissioners' Conference on Community Projects at Ootacamund (27th May to 31st May, 1954), Community Projects Administration, Planning Commission, Government of India, March, 1955. (CPA Series, No. 26).

The General Plan for Firka Development Work, A Subcommittee Report, J. Ramachandran, Chairman, Government of Madras, India, 27 October, 1947.

The Five Year Plan, A Short Introduction, Publications Division, Ministry of Information & Broadcasting, Government of India, December, 1951.

The First Five Year Plan, Planning Commission, Government of India, December, 1952.

CHAPTER 10

TRAINING PERSONNEL FOR COMMUNITY DEVELOPMENT

THE story of India's training programmes for community development is in itself an analytical story of the process and growth of the community development programme. In launching this programme India took the position that she would learn from her experiences in development what categories of people would need to be given specific types of training. The only exception to this was the decision to start training village extension workers (Gram Sevaks or Village-Level Workers) at the same time the decision was made to launch a community development programme.

The merits of this decision can now be reviewed with the perspective of ten years of experience. It must be remembered that India's projection of her community development programme was based on her faith in the people's capacity and readiness to participate in a government-sponsored, village-oriented, self-help programme. As we stated in Chapter 9, in conceiving her community development programme, India drew not only on Gandhi's and Tagore's teaching and experience—several pilot projects of pre-Independence days, including the projects involved in building new communities for refugees—but also drew on experience from the world community. India, therefore, approached the task of launching her community development programme with a broad-based philosophy and not with a blueprint. Even after ten years of experience, India is still without a blueprint for the future. To be sure, she can more clearly project the future course of action in 1964 than when the programme was launched in 1952. India's planners can therefore, today, with a fair amount of certainty, forecast the number and types of training centres that will be needed after the nation has been blanketed with community development blocks. The fact that India did not, at the time the programme was conceived, also forecast its training needs for the years ahead, has provided

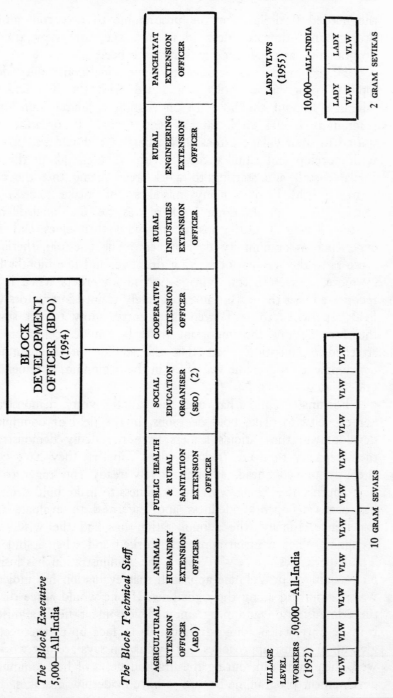

TRAINED PERSONNEL IN A COMMUNITY DEVELOPMENT BLOCK

The Block Executive
5,000—All-India

BLOCK
DEVELOPMENT
OFFICER (BDO)
(1954)

The Block Technical Staff

| AGRICULTURAL EXTENSION OFFICER (AEO) | ANIMAL HUSBANDRY EXTENSION OFFICER | PUBLIC HEALTH & RURAL SANITATION EXTENSION OFFICER | SOCIAL EDUCATION ORGANISER (SEO) (2) | COOPERATIVE EXTENSION OFFICER | RURAL INDUSTRIES EXTENSION OFFICER | RURAL ENGINEERING EXTENSION OFFICER | PANCHAYAT EXTENSION OFFICER |

VILLAGE
LEVEL
WORKERS 50,000—All-India
(1952)

| VLW | VLW | VLW | VLW | VLW | VLW | VLW | VLW | VLW | VLW |

10 GRAM SEVAKS

LADY VLWS
(1955)

10,000—ALL-INDIA

| LADY VLW | LADY VLW |

2 GRAM SEVIKAS

the needed flexibility for the programme to take root and to project and interpret new ideas, and therefore new training programmes, as experience indicated the need.

Having made the decision to launch her community development programme, India was faced with the hen and egg dilemma. Should she hold up on staffing a limited number of community blocks until training centres could be organised and staffed to train village extension workers? Or should she proceed with development simultaneously with training, taking the best available staff and starting to work, recognizing that the early phases would involve many mistakes and make necessary a learning-by-doing philosophy? There was the functional dilemma of not having available instructors who themselves had field experience in community development. The question, therefore, arose as to the wisdom of starting first five, and five months later 29 more, centres to train village-extension workers when it was recognized that there were not adequately-trained instructors with field experience to staff even one centre. How to get started therefore became the important issue. It can be seen from the attached organisation chart that the staffing of a community development programme was, even in the beginning, a tremendous undertaking.

Fortunately, India has, over the past ten years, demonstrated her capacity to make bold decisions. In the field of community development, the nation's leaders have repeatedly demonstrated their capacity to make "risk decisions", in that they have courageously moved ahead, administratively ready and eager to try new approaches. Along with this readiness to make bold decisions has been an open-mindedness and eagerness to evaluate their experience. Finally, the administration has had the wisdom to recognize when a given approach worked and when it did not. The experiences are few in which the administration has insisted on retaining a programme approach that evaluation has indicated was not moving along the right lines. If one would agree that in the administration and programme development field, a mistake is made only when administration fails to face up to the need to give up or adjust approaches that evaluation says are not working well, then India can, during the first ten years of her community development programme be said to have made few mistakes. That

India has tried many programme approaches which, as originally planned, have not worked out is a part of the record. These programme approaches which experience proved unworkable, and which were therefore either dropped or modified, in the minds of the authors should be classified as essential experience in developing a new programme, not as features of it. If India had been less bold in her readiness to explore the frontiers of new ideas and programme approaches, the community development programme would not have continued to grow as it certainly has grown.

Perhaps the boldest, and to many the greatest, risk decision India has made during the first ten years of community development was the decision to start simultaneously 55 community project areas with an untrained and untried staff, and at the same time to organise 34 centres to train village-extension workers. The 55 Project Executive Officers[1] selected to administer these first 55 community project areas were assembled for one month's orientation in July, 1952. At best, this training was an attempt to have a selected number of people, with views about how to initiate the programme in the field, expound their ideas to the newly-recruited project executive officers. Since those who were lecturing had themselves had limited field experience, and few had any understanding of the new approach which was to be an extension and educational one, the new project executive officers left the training course little wiser about how to proceed than when they had assembled. They did, however, get one important thing from the orientation course, which was an idea of the guide lines of the new programme and a keen sense that, in the final analysis, each was to be pretty much on his own in actually launching the programme in the field. They also departed from the centre with a sense of the importance the new nation placed on developing the human resources of 550,000 villages. The awakening of village people to the significance of India's freedom was to all a challenge. To catalyze village people to be capable and willing to assume

---

[1] A "Project Executive Officer" was placed in charge of the so-called "Community Project Area", each area being composed of 3 blocks in the original programme. When it was decided to make community development a nationwide programme, each block became a "Community Development Block" with a Block Development Officer in charge. The title "Project Executive Officer" was then dropped.

responsibility in the development of the new nation, through the process of rebuilding each of India's villages, gave to these new project executive officers a sense of high purpose.

When it came to the decision to simultaneously organise 34 centres to train village-extension workers, there were many views expressed about how to proceed. Some reasoned that the first step should be to train the new instructors. Others reasoned that the originally-planned five centres of the pilot programme referred to later, should have a chance to get started and gain a year or two years of experience before deciding to set up 29 more. Having made the decision to go ahead with all 34 centres, however, many persuasive arguments were presented to develop a detailed syllabus to help the inexperienced instructors. It represented a courageous decision when it was agreed that the new centres were to be given few directives. Instead of directives, and in the absence of the detailed syllabus many wanted to impose, the decision was made that the village-extension workers were to be trained as multipurpose workers, i.e. to be concerned about, and capable of interesting and helping village people to find, solutions to their multiple problems of agriculture, health, education and the many related problems of making a living as well as learning how to live better. Since the village-extension workers were to use extension educational methods in interesting and motivating village people to take up new programmes, it was agreed that they were to be given training in extension methods. Finally, since the instructors lacked field experience and had not themselves been formally trained in extension methods, it was agreed that about 60 per cent of the training time would be spent in the centre on theoretical lectures, library reading, and discussions and the remaining 40 per cent would be devoted to learning how to apply what had been taught in the classroom lectures to actual village conditions.

With these three basic decisions made concerning the size and character of the training programme, 34 centres were organised during the year 1952 and put on their own resources to experiment for a full year, at which time all the Principals of the training centres were assembled for a national stock-taking evaluation and tuning-up conference. It was interesting to note that as these Principals discussed their year's experience, they found that they had encountered common problems and had met with similar successes. It was, therefore, logical and comparatively easy to give direction to the future about both content and basic methods for carrying on the training programme for the coming year.

In planning for India's community development programme, the senior administrative officers responsible for implementing it regarded people at their level, as well as people who would function as Block Development Officers, as being capable of taking on any new programme responsibilities without requiring additional training. In a very real sense, the attitudes expressed then about who should be trained left no doubt that they thought the only group of people who would need to be specially-trained for community development were the village-extension workers. The fact that the administrative officers had been trained to carry out regulative, law-and-order functions, and that community development, on the other hand, would require people knowledgeable and experienced in human relations and in group skills, and people who had understanding about, and were capable of applying, extension educational methods, in no way presented a challenge to the administrators who had been trained and who were mentally-conditioned to accept all assignments as detached, objective administrators.

Prior to the decision to make community development a national programme, the Government had decided, in November, 1951, to launch fifteen pilot extension blocks and to start five centres to train village-extension workers. As was pointed out earlier, the decision to start 55 "community project areas" and add 29 more extension training centres was made before the first five planned centres were fully organised. The five to six months' planning that went into the first five centres did, however, prove invaluable in, first, deciding to go ahead with the additional 29 centres and, second, in planning for their organisation.

In planning for these first five centres, a number of basic policy decisions were made which were, with few exceptions, applied to the later 29 centres. Among the more important ones was the decision that the VLW (village-level worker) should be trained as a multipurpose extension worker. It was agreed that the minimum qualifications for admission to the training centres would be that: the candidates should be matriculates (high school graduates); they should be of village heritage and from 17 to 25 years of age. The centres were to advertise, inviting young men interested in serving their country to apply for admission. Interested candidates were first to make a written application stating why they wanted to do village work. A selection committee was set up to review the applications and to decide which ones were to be invited to appear before the committee for personal interviews. The interviewers were to concentrate their attention on determining the attitudes, intelligence, motivation, willingness to work with hands, and ability for self-expression of the applicants. Those finally invited to join the centre were given further testing and screening upon their arrival.

To provide for maximum faculty-trainee interaction, and to facilitate organising the "village practicals", it was decided that 50 trainees would be the maximum number accepted at each centre, and that they would be given training for six months. Since the VLWs were to be trained as multipurpose workers, it was agreed that they should have some subject-matter training in public health, literacy education, animal husbandry, co-operatives, agriculture, and extension methods. To help assure the involvement of the technical departments of the government in both training and development in the organised blocks, it was agreed that the instructors should be detailed to the training centres by their parent departments in the States. Since time was of the essence in starting the training centres, and the desire was to hold to a minimum the cost for facilities, the government took every precaution to locate idle buildings which, when renovated, would offer adequate facilities for training centres. By following this policy, India was able to open all of the 34 initial centres without constructing many new buildings.

While India drew upon the experience of the world community in formulating her community development programme, it is important to understand that the programme as launched, and as it has evolved over the past ten years, was, and continues to be, indigenous to India. It is a programme that fits India and offers great hope for the future. From its inception late in 1951, when the decision was made to undertake the organisation of the first fifteen State pilot extension projects and the launching of five training centres, the multipurpose extension worker was

conceived as the key functionary, first in the fifteen pilot extension blocks and later in the national community development
programme. India early recognized that, while she might be able
to staff and finance technical specialists at the block and district
levels, she could not foresee the time when it would be possible
to either staff or finance technical specialists at the village level.
It was for the purpose of providing an extension worker at the
village level who would be sensitive to, and concerned about, all
village needs, and who would be knowledgeable about, and
capable of drawing on, all available outside resources that the
multipurpose extension worker in India came into being. Some
have felt that he should have been called a single-purpose extension worker, in that his central and continuous responsibility is
to help village people find ways and means of solving their problems. This is, of course, true, but there are multiple needs in the
village and therefore many facets to the job of the village-level
worker.

While India has now had ten years of experience in training
the multipurpose extension worker, it cannot in all honesty be
said that she has been more than moderately successful in her
efforts. While there are many explanations for this situation, the
authors feel that two basic reasons are apparent: (1) the Central
government and State Ministries of Agriculture, which are
administratively responsible for the training of the multipurpose
extension worker, by tradition have remained oriented to agriculture and have not fully accepted either the place or philosophy
of community development; and (2) the instructors in the training
centres have never been selected because of their special training
or experience as teachers, or because they have necessarily excelled
in their field of work. They have taught their courses strictly as
technical subject-matter, paying little attention to how the village
workers were to apply what they were taught when they took
up their assignments as multipurpose extension workers. Few
indeed have been the instructors of the basic course in extension
methods, who have themselves had formal training in adult
education and extension methods. In the beginning, this state of
affairs had to be accepted, but today, the same situation exists,
and relatively little effort is being made to train and keep
competent staff in the centres.

A further factor contributing to India's lack of success in coming through on the training of the multipurpose extension worker is that the field-work experience is carried out very much as the instruction, in that it is subject-matter oriented and not village-problem and village-solution oriented. However, in spite of these limitations in training, the multipurpose worker has proved himself sufficiently to assure his permanent place in India's community development programme. Fortunately, the weaknesses in his training are, without any great effort, correctable.

It was pointed out earlier that in the initial discussions and decisions about training staff for community development, the senior, policy-making administrators did not see the need to give special training to the people who were to supervise the village-extension worker. However, immediately after assigning the first trained village-extension workers to the blocks, it became clear that the VLWs and the Block Development Officers (BDOs) were poles apart in their approach to the village people and in the methods to be followed in guiding village people through the process of change. The VLWs had been trained to find out what problems were of paramount concern to the people. Their orientation was toward helping villagers find solutions to their expressed, felt needs. The Block Development Officers, on the other hand, were oriented to giving the VLW orders, and establishing physical targets for the village people to achieve, expecting the VLW to mobilize the people to achieve the BDO-established targets.

Since this early field experience documented the need to give the staff selected as BDOs special training, steps were taken in 1954 to set up training centres for them. Even after eight years of experience in training BDOs, one must conclude that the training is still inadequate and of too-short duration. While the early centres provided for only two months of training, this was later expanded by a six-weeks' additional refresher training course at special Orientation Training Centres. There are, however, at least three basic reasons why the BDO training is still inadequate. First, neither government policy nor the individuals assigned to the BDO post regard the BDO's position as having any degree of permanency. It is the feeling of the authors that India's experience with community development should provide the convincing proof that there is need for far more orientation in the programme to longer tenure for the BDO. Since his job is to give leadership to a people's movement, and to co-ordinate and guide a staff in helping village people develop strong institutions (co-operatives, panchayats, and schools), he can do so only as he himself is accepted as a leader and is both intellectually and emotionally involved in the movement.

A second factor explaining the inadequacy of training is similar to that found in the VLW training centres. The instructors are, with few exceptions, lacking in training in teaching methods, and few indeed are those who have had any specialized training in administration, social psychology, adult education and extension methods, economic growth and social change, or social organisation and institution-building. The third thing is that, as in all positions in India, the instructors are like rolling stones; they are moved in and out of the training centres all too frequently.

It is the view of the authors that if community development is to become a movement, India must provide greater continuity of staff in the community development programme. We further believe it is crucial that the BDO begin to think of making a career as a BDO in one block. When Government policy supports such a decision, then the persons selected as BDOs need to be more carefully chosen. While many excellent BDOs can be found in the existing administrative services and technical departments, the providing of scholarships for superior VLWs to receive advanced training and preparing them to step into BDO positions will pay rich dividends. Such a policy will make possible the promotion of the best VLWs, and bring to the BDO positions young men who know and understand village people and who have had successful experience in serving them.

As shown in the organisation chart presented earlier, the Block Development Officer was to be assisted by a staff of technical, subject-matter extension specialists. Since this staff was conceived as the link between the VLW and the resources of science and technology, it was assumed that this corps of specialists would perform two basic roles. In the first place, they were to provide guidance to the village workers in assisting village people to analyze and find solutions to their agricultural, animal husbandry, health, education, co-operative, panchayat, and other village problems. Second, for the problems that science presently had no answer, they were to be responsible for seeing that the research institutions were informed of the village problems on which research was urgently needed. In guiding and working with VLWs, these block specialists were to respect the multi-purpose role of the village worker and to appreciate that his methods were essentially educational and persuasive.

Since these technical extension specialists who were assigned to the blocks had not, with few exceptions, come out of village life, they lacked an understanding of village culture. Inasmuch as their college training had been purely technical, they knew only the theoretical phases of the village problems they were asked to help solve. Lacking in both their experience and their training was "folk or village knowledge" and an understanding of the methods by which village people would have to be approached if they were to accept the recommendations backed by science and technology. There has been a further factor complicating the effectiveness of the block technical staff, which is that much of their technical knowledge has been outdated. This continues to be the case.

Because of the magnitude of the training problems in the community development programme and the need for special kinds of training of the personnel so far discussed, certain priorities had to be established. As early as 1953, a decision was made to experiment with changing the curriculum of five selected colleges of agriculture, adding courses in rural economics, rural sociology, extension educational methods, and organised village "practicals" (demonstrations and practical field work). While to change college curricula, and get the changes accepted by the universities, proved to be a formidable task, taking some four years, this was finally achieved by the end of 1956. Twelve other colleges on their own initiative have added courses in extension methods since then. The Third Five Year Plan calls for establishing Extension Wings in all of the 39 colleges of agriculture now in existence. Three agricultural colleges added post-graduate training in extension education beginning with the Third Plan. While future agricultural graduates can be expected, therefore, to possess an extension outlook, the older graduates continue to be only partially effective in their block assignments because they have not had this training. There have been many attempts to remedy this situation, including short refresher courses and instruction in extension methods for the block agricultural extension officers. The over-all effort to bring them up to the mark has not been startling.

From the beginning of the training programme, there has been considerable discussion concerning the proper division of training time between theoretical, classroom instruction and so-called practical field work in the villages and in the cultivators' fields. The centres originally set up to train men and women village workers were thought to provide the proper balance between theoretical and practical training. As was mentioned earlier, one of the guide lines agreed to in starting the first five centres, was that about 60 per cent of the time was to be spent in classroom lectures, library reading, and related centre-oriented activities and about 40 per cent in the village learning to apply what had been taught. India's experience since then supports the wisdom of this early decision. The problem, however, is not so much the percentage of time spent on theoretical and practical work as it is assuring that all the time spent in the villages is so carefully organised that each village visit provides a real teaching and learning situation. The same can be said for the organised manual work required about the centre, as well as the time spent working on the training-centre farm or in the kitchen garden.

One could agree that in the early stages of India's experience in launching its community development programme, there was a place for emphasis on the dignity of labour; therefore, programmes which emphasized work for work's sake had a place. Today, however, it is both possible and essential that all field work programmes provide primarily a teaching and learning situation. If this is done, there will and should be less time spent on physical labour, thus leaving more time for reading in the library and studying technical subject-matter. While the training centres continue to provide time for village practicals, much of the time spent is unproductive both to the trainees and to the villages in which they do their field work. This situation will continue until such time as the training centres are staffed with highly-trained, well-motivated instructors who themselves are experienced in extension methods of working with village people.

Two important issues—one philosophical and one administrative—in the community development programme contributed to the fairly early decision to introduce a new cadre of personnel at the block level known as Social Education Organisers. From its inception, the community development programme has been wrestling with a conflict between its philosophy of helping village people to develop basic institutions (co-operatives, panchayats, schools) and its desire to prove its worth through the achievement of physical targets such as building roads, digging drainage ditches etc. While this conflict is still present after ten years, one may expect that Panchayati Raj will mean that the people, through their village institutions, will in the future be the ones who will decide the programme's targets to be achieved. The authors are of the view that in a parliamentary democracy which, in voting new funds, insists on evidence that the previously-appropriated funds have brought concrete results, there was no escape, in the early stages of community development, from the establishment of village and block targets. We would, however, reason that even in the early stages, village people could and should have been more fully involved than they were in the process of setting these targets and that now physical targets should be supplanted by the basic purposes of community-wide development of the village people.

The other issue referred to above involves the rationale of "farming out" supervisory and administrative responsibilities for various categories of training to the Centre and State technical ministries. This policy was based on the desire, on the part of the Ministry of Community Development, directly to involve these other ministries in the programme in all ways which seemed appropriate. The Ministry of Community Development felt, and rightly so, that it must not become another technical ministry nor should it take on functions which the technical ministries could and should do. While there is much to be said for these arguments, the effect has, in general, been to weaken the training, in that the technical ministries have never fully accepted either the place or philosophy of community development. In all too many cases, the technical ministries have assigned their less competent staff to the training centres, reasoning that they should keep their best staff to do the Ministry's work, thus admitting that training for community development was not their job. Even so, the Ministry of Community Development could and should have given stronger leadership to guaranteeing that the training centres were always fully manned with the most competent staff to be found and that the Centres were given the supervision they needed. The effect of this lack of positive leadership has been to settle for mediocrity in training.

While administrative policies and procedures did give dominance to setting and achieving physical targets, as pointed out above, the first two years of the community development programme's operation convinced its top administrators that it was necessary for the block staff to understand that it was the development of the people's competence and village institutions that was the ultimate objective of community development. It was at this point in time that the most controversial of all the block specialists, the Social Education Organiser (SEO), was introduced and special centres were organised to train this new specialist. The very fact that he was injected into the programme was significant, because it revealed the conviction that the programme was not yet really a people's programme. Although the SEO was never fully accepted, the controversy, discussions, and debates which followed in all community development conferences provided the turning point in moving community development from things (targets) to people and from people to their institutions. Since this was a new category of specialist and did not logically fit into the orientation of any of the technical ministries at that time, the Social Education Organisers' training centres were set up and supervised by the Ministry of Community Development and Co-operation.

The function of the Social Education Organisers' training centres was to turn out persons who could assist all of the staff members, take a lead in their orientation to the programme, and help them to increase their competence to assist village people in the successful working of their village institutions. The curriculum, therefore, had to be kept flexible, and it underwent many fundamental changes. While this new block-extension specialist was called a Social Education Organiser, he was in fact a specialist in social organisation, human relations, and extension methods. From the time he was introduced, it was assumed that he would remain as a block specialist, as long as necessary to get all of the block staff socially-conscious and, with sufficient training and experience in extension education methods, to assume the basic staff approach of social education.

Since the other block extension-officers were assigned as technical subject-matter specialists and had been so trained, it was to be expected that each would view his job from the point of view of having the VLW carry out the programme he thought the villagers should have. To the technical specialists, the VLW was there to assist them. While there will probably always be a feeling on the part of each specialist that his subject-matter field is the most important, India has, over the past ten years, largely through a wide range of in-service training courses and continuous staff conferences, done much to get the various technical specialists to view their role as one of assisting the VLW in his basic task of helping village people understand the alternatives available to them in solving their problems. The specialists are also growing in their understanding that villagers differ greatly in the priorities they place on the problems they want solved.

It should not be inferred by the reader that the community development training programme, even in the early days, was limited to the particular personnel thus far described. While community development started with an all-male staff, it was never assumed that the problems of the family and the home were outside of its orbit. Prior to the launching of the programme, India had had substantial experience in social welfare programmes, but was devoid of any village experience in the field of home economics, or home science as it is called in India. In addition to not having any village home-economics work to draw upon, there was a question in the minds of some as to whether or not village men would permit their wives to receive training in home-making activities. Community development programmes had been under way only about two years when it became apparent that the women wanted to be involved and that the men were willing that they should be. Furthermore, some of the more perceptive leaders in community development early visualized that the women could, if they were involved in the programme, become a powerful stimulus to change. There was also recognition of the fact that men and women worked side by side in earning the family living, and that the women in particular should be trained in ways of converting increased incomes, expected from adopting improved family practices, into more effective living.

While male VLWs were, in the blocks organised early, put into the field without any training in extension methods, it was felt that women must be trained before posting them in the fields. Of all the training programmes organised to train staff for community development, none was more difficult than the centres to train young girls and women for village home-economics-extension work. In the first place, India had few women who had been formally trained in home economics, and most of these were Western-trained. Few had themselves worked directly with village families. Furthermore, the few women who had been trained in home economics were urban-bred, and therefore lacked an understanding of, and orientation to, village family life.

Like so many programmes which had to be started without much past experience to draw on, India in 1954 decided to go ahead despite the above difficulties and organised 27 centres to start training village women for home-economics-extension work. These centres, which got under way in July, 1955, were attached to selected VLW Training Centres and were called "Home Science Wings". They were expected to train women to deal with extension work in home economics, including nutrition, housing, clothing, infant care, child development, health, sanitation, and handicrafts. This was a large order.

Since the newly-selected Principals of the Centres themselves had to be oriented and trained in both the content and methods of working with village families, they were first sent to Hawaii and Japan to observe extension programmes for village families. The Instructors recruited for the Centres had varied experience and training, little of which was related to home economics; for them, an Instructors' training programme was organised. Allowing for the time required to train the new instructors and the six months originally allowed for the newly-recruited village women to undergo training, it was about two years from the time the decision was made to train them for village-extension work until the first trained women were ready to be assigned to the blocks. The training period for gram sevikas (Lady Village-Level Workers) was soon changed to 12 months.

Because of the lack of trained home science staff to start with, along with limited research in this field and an almost total lack of Indian literature concerning village family-life, it was natural that the new instructors felt they needed some experience to lean on. Since the early experience and most of the early literature was borrowed from the Unted States, it was inevitable that the initial training was far from satisfactory. The curriculum was more American than village-India-oriented, and the emphasis was on training women for institutional home-economics professions. However, since experience is a great teacher, and since India has always been ready to experiment as a basis for gaining experience, the home-economics-extension programme has, after seven years of growing pains, developed a trained and seasoned staff. This staff has gradually evolved an appropriate curriculum and contributed to the development of outstanding literature in the home science field, so that India is presently turning out graduates capable of doing a first-rate job of working with Indian village families in all phases of their life.

The role of the village people themselves as non-official or non-professional leaders in the community development programme, has long been of concern to programme planners and leaders. It is of interest to note that from the programme's inception there were strong views held and readily expressed, both pros and cons, about the extent of responsibilities which village people were capable of assuming. Early provision was made in policy and enunciated in procedural manuals to involve village people through village panchayats, co-operatives, and block advisory committees. But there was a consistent reluctance on the part of many administrative people to take seriously the suggestion that village people, although largely illiterate, could be counted on to assume increasing responsibility for both the formation and execution of village and block development programmes.

There were, however, a significant number of exceptions, in that a number of the early Project Executive Officers were of the Gandhian school of thought and therefore had great faith in the capacity of village people. Through the years, there were also notable exceptions among block officers. Those who came from the government's administrative services were, in general, reluctant to involve the village people, but the block officers who came from a social welfare background, and those who had been block agricultural extension officers, were inclined to give village people greater opportunity to participate. It was not, however, until the States recently passed Panchayati Raj legislation that village people were in fact brought into a full partnership-relation with the block and district staffs in planning and executing community development programmes.

One of the programmes instituted in 1957-58 by the Ministry of Community Development, which has taken on increased importance since the beginning of Panchayati Raj, is the training programme for village leaders or Gram Sahayaks. This training was carried out in a series of special 3-day sessions in village camps in each Gram Sevak's circle for about 50 leaders at each session. Included with the village leaders at these camp sessions were the Block Development Officer, the Social Education Organiser, the Extension Officer concerned, and one or two Village-Level Workers, all of whom were in charge of conducting the camps, the Block Development Officer having the major responsibility. Priority-emphasis was given to learning ways, through lectures, discussions, and field demonstrations, to increase agricultural production. Other subjects such as Panchayats, Village Industries, Education, etc. were to be included after completion of the first rounds of camp sessions devoted to Agriculture. Each village leader was to be awarded a certificate at the close of the 3-day camp session indicating that he had "undertaken to adopt improved practices", "to educate his brother-farmers in improved agricultural practices", and "to promote all organisational activities leading to increased production". This certificate was to be signed by the District Collector and awarded on the last day of the course.

This training programme has met with considerable favour among the 2,500,000 progressive farmers who have attended the short-term camp programmes in the development blocks all over the country. At the annual conference on Community Development in July, 1959, it was recommended that about 2 per cent of the Gram Sahayaks trained in these camps be given additional training in agricultural subjects in order to improve their own agriculture and that of their neighbours. As a result, a plan has been devised to give intensive training to 250,000 selected progressive farmers for about 2 weeks at certain Extension Training Centres, Basic Agricultural Schools, and Agricultural Colleges. It is hoped to reach from 60 to 65,000 cultivators or village leaders each year during the Third-Plan period, to help them improve their farm skills, increase their efficiency in farm management, and increase agricultural production. This programme will be implemented by the State Governments, with financial assistance from the Central Government. There has also been established now in New Delhi a Central Institute for the training of the teaching staff of the Panchayati Raj Training Centres.

It is hoped, of course, that the short-term camps for Gram Sahayaks will gradually encompass training in all aspects of the Community Development programme and that the Village-Level Worker can count on these village leaders, when they return home, to share the benefits of their training with their neighbours and help to involve the village people generally in planning for and implementing their own improvement measures. Now, with the framework of Panchayati Raj to give the villages the administrative and communication network better to utilize block, district, and Central Government assistance, these trained village leaders are expected to play an increasingly significant role in the nation-wide effort to increase agricultural production and improve standards of living.

The advent of Panchayati Raj adds a new dimension to training for community development, not only because of the importance attached to the role of the villagers themselves in programme planning and execution, but also because of the necessity for smooth working relationships between these "non-officials" and the officials at the block and district levels. In order to make Panchayati Raj successful, the role of each group must be thoroughly understood by the other, and each must be trained in order to be effective in that role. Officials themselves, from experience in the programme, have learned that involvement of the village people is crucial to the success of their efforts. Thus programme experience has again revealed a weakness not earlier apparent, namely the lack of training and experience among villagers that would enable them to participate fully in planning and carrying out programmes for their own villages. Therefore a training programme for non-officials, village workers and leaders, will become increasingly important as Panchayati Raj gives village people and institutions more and more responsibility for their own development.

As a corollary to the training of these village people, the officials in the programme need to understand the full role the people must play and how they can implement them in playing their part. The various training programmes carried on during the past ten years, from the point of view of adequately preparing block and district officials for their roles, reveal a consistent lack of stress on their job of developing people's institutions and training institutional leaders to effectively carry out their roles. We can, therefore, see that with Panchayati Raj a reality, and with the importance the Third Five Year Plan places on co-operatives, all training programmes must, without exception, include appropriate emphasis on training district and block staffs in the philosophy underlying Panchayati Raj and co-operatives. The training must also later prepare them in turn to educate the village people in all phases of developing effective panchayats and co-operatives. Since this will be their primary job in the future, it logically follows that their training must prepare them to offer leadership in the organisation and functioning of people's institutions. Not only must the official staff, through organised training institutions, be prepared to assist village people in this task of running their own institutions, but special organisations must be constituted to train non-officials in their roles as village co-operative and panchayat leaders. The Third Five Year Plan provides for the further development of non-officials' training camps, institutes, and seminars for this specific purpose.

The primary objective in the training of both programme officials and non-official village leaders in the working of co-operatives and panchayats is to make sure that these are regarded as real people's institutions. Their primary purpose in existing is to provide village people with the essential organisations to work together, first, to function as a village community and second, to make full and effective use of the resources of government, both manpower and financial, available to them. The distinction between officials and non-officials, both in the beginning and at the present time, must yield to the concept of a co-ordinated team of village lay leaders and district and block staff working together, each supplementing the other in the common task of rebuilding India's 550,000 villages.

Outside of the main stream of government-sponsored training programmes discussed above, three groups of block-extension officers have been trained through specially-created centres. Beginning in 1953, the Reserve Bank of India set up and operated 5 regional centres to train intermediates and senior co-operative specialists, and the Ministry of Health has organised three centres to orient public health staff to community development. The third group of centres, to train the cadre of extension workers in social education, was set up separately by the Ministry of Community Development and Co-operation as described above.

Concerning the first group, namely the block-extension specialists for co-operatives, it will be remembered that since its inception, community development has had as one of its primary purposes the development of basic village institutions—co-operatives, panchayats, and schools. Since it has been hoped that co-operatives would replace the money-lender in the credit field, it was natural that Government policy should place a high priority on training a new corps of workers in the co-operative field. Furthermore, the Reserve Bank undertook its first Rural Credit Survey as early as 1951-52, to determine village credit needs and get guidance on how the Reserve Bank could play a more dynamic role in helping co-operatives provide the needed credit. It was therefore logical that the Reserve Bank should set up and operate the initial centres to train block and district staffs as specialists in co-operatives.

Following the Conference of Registrars of Co-operative Societies and the Annual Conference of the State Ministers of Co-operation in New Delhi, in October, 1961, when the Report of the Study Team on Co-operative Training was considered, an administrative decision was made to transfer all intermediate and junior co-operative training centres to State Co-operative Unions as of April, 1962 or as soon thereafter as possible. The 13 intermediate training centres (regional as well as block-level co-operative officers' training centres) included the 5 centres operated by the Reserve Bank of India and 8 which had been operated by the Government of India. It was specified that the centres were to be run through special committees of the State Co-operative

Unions appointed with the approval of the State Governments. It was also proposed by the Study Team that the number of intermediate training centres be increased from 13 to 15, to be called "co-operative training colleges", and that the number of junior training centres be increased from 62 to 120.

The role of the Central Government in co-operative training to be carried out by a special committee of the National Co-operative Union of India, was spelled out in some detail, including essentially the following activities: (1) To run a Central Institute for training senior personnel of departments and co-operative institutions on an all-India basis; (2) to arrange for special courses at intermediate training centres on an inter-State basis; (3) to arrange for and co-ordinate a programme of research at the Central Institute and at intermediate and other co-operative institutions, universities, etc.; (4) in some cases, to run intermediate centres until the States are ready to take them over; and (5) to be in charge of over-all co-ordination of the entire programme of co-operative training and education including membership education, at present being carried out by the National Co-operative Union and State co-operative unions; to prescribe the syllabus, methods and conduct of examinations, and to ensure that the standards of training and education are maintained.

The stated purpose of the Study Team's recommended phased programme of decentralization of co-operative training was ultimately to transfer all co-operative training to the co-operative movement itself. All levels of training were considered by the Team, from advanced education at the National Co-operative college at Poona, to the intermediate and junior centres just discussed, to the training of non-officials, that is co-operative members, committee members, and office bearers. This latter group was to be trained in short courses by peripatetic parties of instructors in their own villages or as near as possible to the trainees' place of residence. It was estimated that about 1300 peripatetic parties would be needed, at the rate of 4 per district. While the programme for co-operatives will be greatly expanded in the Third Plan over the Second, thus far only the recommendation of the Team concerning the transfer of intermediate and junior training centres to the State co-operative unions has been implemented. The Reserve Bank of India has agreed to continue to co-operate with the Government of India in decentralizing the training of co-operative personnel.

Regarding the second category of personnel trained independently, the public health workers who were available for assignment to the community development blocks were for the most part "inspector"-oriented. In the pre-Independence period, public health workers had been trained to inspect health conditions and to enforce conformity to administrative rules and regulations. Their task then was primarily to try to check major epidemics. Preventive health and educational methods were foreign to both their training and experience. It was therefore decided early in the programme to set up special centres for the purpose of orienting the existing public health staff to the philosophy and extension educational methods of community development. These three Health Orientation Training Centres, located in the States of Madras, Delhi, and West Bengal, and operated by the Ministry of Health, offer a training course of about two months to the health staff prior to their joining the Extension Team, to "relate their professional skill to field problems". These centres have since been supplemented by some State governments which also give this orientation training. The health personnel for the community development programme include medical officers, sanitary inspectors, lady health-visitors, and midwives.

One of the principal avenues of self-correction of training programmes, besides operating experience, has been the regular and consistent practice of self-evaluation of methods and performance. In fast-moving programmes of social change, the practice of self-evaluation and self-criticism has made possible the introduction of needed correctives. This has been true in the field of community development and in the training programmes for its personnel. Evaluation started early and has continued. The initial thinking behind the decision to set up the Programme Evaluation Organisation simultaneously with the first blocks and training centres was that the results of independent evaluation reports would provide guidance for the policy decisions related to the future emphasis and direction of community development. It was thought that these reports would also indicate the ways in which training programmes would need adjustment to assure training people with the right attitudes and technical and extension educational skills. One need only read the annual Programme Evaluation reports to see that they set high standards in objectivity; their findings were clearly analyzed and backed by recommendations which the data supported.

While the State Development Commissioners, responsible for over-all programmes of rural development, have regularly discussed the Programme Evaluation Organisation's reports in their annual conferences and have made appropriate policy decisions on the basis of them, the technical ministries responsible for the community development training centres have not paid similar attention to these reports. While there are many reasons for this, perhaps the main one is that since the Programme Evaluation reports have been largely focussed on development rather than on training for development, the ministries have not systematically analyzed them for their implications for changes required in training. It is significant, however, that, while those who were responsible for the training centres did not study these reports to see what changes were implied for training, the evidence is clear that their cumulative effect has been to influence training. For example, while many of the reports have brought out clearly the inadequacies of the VLWs in their application of extension methods, the 1961 report highlighted their weakness in the use of the most basic of all extension methods—the result demonstration. This so jolted the extension training centres that it resulted in a re-examination of their training programme in extension methods.

A further avenue for self-evaluation, as well as for a special kind of training experience, was opened to State, District, and Central Government administrative and technical personnel when the Central Institute of Study and Research in Community Development was established in June, 1958, in Mussoorie. During the formative years of community development centres, State and District officials had come together for working-conferences to take stock of the way the programme was taking root in the field and to reach group decisions about future courses of action. In a sense, these regional and State working-conferences were a kind of training programme, in that they provided an opportunity for clarification of understanding about the philosophy underlying the decision to launch a national community development programme and to exchange views on the merits of using democratic and educational methods of interesting and involving village people in a self-help programme.

Gradually, a climate was created to support a national policy decision to establish this Central Institute, to provide an opportunity for key Centre, State and district officials and non-officials, including Members of Parliament, State legislators, and university professors, to come together for a month's study. The orientation of the study has remained on broadening and deepening the understanding of these key functionaries from the administrative services, technical departments, and non-officials in the philosophy, methods, and place of community development in national development and the sciences of human relations, including sociology, social psychology, and social anthropology. The Centre, therefore, has, through free and open group discussions, provided an opportunity to analyze both national and administrative problems, to exchange experiences, and to gain additional knowledge. It has also provided the useful function of bringing officials and non-officials together in their thinking and approach to problems, resulting in each understanding better his dependence on the other.

While the Central Institute was established primarily for this purpose of study and training, a research wing has been added to assist in the analysis of field problems revealed by the operating experience of the community development programme. A competent staff is being developed to sponsor, guide, and co-ordinate research carried on by Orientation and Study Centres, Social Education Organisers' Training Centres, and universities in several States. A scheme of research fellowships has been worked out, and a Clearing House of Information on Community Development set up to collect and disseminate available literature on the programme.

Today, as one looks at some 200 centres which have been organised during the past ten years to train all categories of staff for community development, it is desirable to take another look at the problem, still unsolved, of using what might be called ad hoc centres instead of established colleges and universities for training purposes.

In the formative years of organising community development, the colleges and universities were neither interested in, nor capable of, taking on a practical, field and development-oriented training function which would necessarily have to be kept experimental and free from rigidity. There was also, in these early years, an unexpressed government belief that these centres were temporary, and that they would disappear from the scene once the required number of people had been trained to man enough community development blocks to blanket the nation.

Now, with ten years of experience in training for community development, it is possible to make a number of long-range projections about training requirements for the years ahead. Now that the entire country has been blanketed with organised blocks, it is clear that most if not all of the present centres will continue to be needed. First, there will be need to train replacements; second, there will be need for continuous in-service training of existing staff; and finally, one must face the fact that future training must have greater depth, and therefore must be of longer duration. Training must continue to prepare staff to give competent leadership to the advancement of village people as they move away from a reliance on past traditions to acceptance of science and technology for the solution of their many problems. If India is to continue to strengthen her community development programme, she must in the future not only broaden, deepen, and lengthen the period of training required to provide fresh staff for replacements, but must also systematize her in-service training. By recognising, as India does, that these two training functions must be carried on simultaneously and indefinitely, she has reached a policy decision with the States that the existing centres must be considered from now on as permanent training institutions; some are being designated for training of fresh staff and others for in-service training.

While one can agree that it was necessary in the formative years to set up many training centres outside the orbit of the colleges and universities, one can today visualize the need to put these centres under the guidance of established colleges and universities so that they can have the intellectual environment essential to command the kind of faculty the centres need. It is also clear that by involving the colleges and universities in this training function, they will, in the course of time, include in their regular curriculum the basic training required for community development. That the colleges and universities were not willing nor able either to change their curriculum or directly supervise the many ad hoc training centres set up during the past ten years is understandable. But it would be a mistake to assume that the colleges and universities cannot now be persuaded to train most of the basic staff for community development, either through specially-approved syllabi or supervision of existing training institutions.

Related to this matter of involving established institutions of higher education in the training of community development staff is the necessity of laying a solid foundation for career opportunities in this programme for the personnel employed now and in the future. It is essential that all categories of staff working in community development have, as soon as conditions permit, at least a college education. Central Government, State and district technical staff, and later block technical staff, should be of postgraduate level. All staff recruited as instructors in the training centres should, as rapidly as conditions permit, be M.A. and Ph.D. graduates.

To establish career opportunities in community development, factors other than educational background are also involved. If community development is to become a movement, as it must, and if the block staff is to provide the leadership required to help village people work successfully in panchayats and co-operatives, India should recognize that the present methods of selecting and training BDOs are far from satisfactory. Great care must be exercised in choosing men who are sincerely interested in carving out a career in the field of rural development and who will remain dedicated to this task. They must then be trained, as VLWs are for their jobs, specifically for the technical and personal requirements of the job of Block Development Officers. While it will take time to train people capable of living up to the nation's high expectations of community development, steps must be taken now to provide, within at least selected colleges, the kind of curriculum needed for the BDO of the future. In broad terms, he must have basic training in agriculture, economics, psychology, sociology and social institutions, and adult education and extension methods. He should have at least an M.A. degree.

As far as future preparation for the VLWs is concerned, experience has proved that they are not at present competent to do the job expected of them, largely because they have not been equipped with appropriate training. As one looks at the changes which have occurred in the training programmes for this cadre of personnel during the past ten years, one is impressed by their patchwork nature. The training programmes have not yet provided the proper orientation to multipurpose extension work. As the VLW comes out of the training centre today, he is competent to function neither as a multipurpose nor an extension worker. If community development is to avoid finding itself on a plateau, not progressively providing leadership for continuous change; and if it is to help people take advantage of the new findings of science, it must quickly decide to change drastically the VLW curriculum to encompass both the multipurpose and extension character of the job to be done. Furthermore, in order to provide for intellectual leadership, and to make possible a college degree for the future VLWs, the best approach might be to make the present VLW centres appendages to the colleges of agriculture. The curriculum, however, must be oriented to training a person who will be a college graduate and who will be technically and practically prepared to carry on the functions of a multipurpose extension worker. This will require the future VLWs to have training for a period of four years instead of the present two years.

Since to have a college degree will, in the Indian scene, make the future VLW eligible for advancement, he should be able to anticipate promotion either to a BDO's post or to that of a block-extension specialist, but only after he has returned to college for post-graduate training to prepare himself for this new post. The authors recognize that there will be strong arguments against giving the VLW four years of training and requiring that future BDOs and extension specialists have at least M.A. degrees. The need for this type of training, however, has been amply borne out by a careful examination of India's community development programme.

It is now clear that the task of helping village people to develop and function successfully with village co-operatives and panchayats requires a vastly superior type of VLW and BDO than the present training programmes are providing. It is equally clear that if village people are to take advantage of the advancements in science and technology, the extension specialists serving them must be men of scientific competence. A first step in this direction has already been taken to open the gates for promotion of Village-Level Workers. It has recently been proposed by the Ministry of Community Development and Co-operation, in a meeting with the Ministry of Education, that selected Village-Level Workers with at least 5 years of field experience, and having previously had 2 years of training in Extension Training Centres, be admitted to Rural Institutes with 2 years of credit. This would entitle them to earn the Diploma at the end of 2 years of advanced education in certain prescribed core subjects at the Rural Institutes, and further prepare them for career opportunities at a higher level.

India's ten years of experience in training staff for community development now makes it possible to draw a number of generalizations. We shall point out here quite categorically what we regard as the most significant among the many lessons India has learned as the result of this experience. The following appear to us to be worthy of special attention, even at the risk of repetition:

(1) As the programme of community development itself changes, either in its approach, areas of emphasis, or methods, there is need for similar updating of the job descriptions of each person on the district and block staffs. Only as the policy-makers agree on the job each staff member is to perform can those responsible for training keep it focused on the function each individual is to perform when he joins the district or block staff.

(2) Since the competence of the trainee at the conclusion of his training period will be largely determined by the competence of the instructors, it is impossible to overemphasize the absolute necessity of assuring that only the most competent people available are recruited for teaching assignments in the training centres. They should not, as at present, be assigned by the technical departments of the government. Once selected, steps must be taken to make them fully qualified to teach the subject assigned. Most instructors selected will need special training in the philosophy and objectives of community development, in extension teaching methods, and in relating their specialized subject to an integrated concept of a multipurpose, village-extension worker.

Once adequately trained, the instructors should be given some reasonable security of tenure in the training centres. Transfers of instructors out of the centres should be few and exceptional.

(3) Since the manpower required to staff community development can now be projected for at least twenty years, and since the community development programme itself is an integral part of the governmental, administrative and technical staff-structure, training centres which are, in the future, to turn out the basic staff should be integrated into established colleges and universities. As we have said above, the centres need a richer intellectual base than can be provided through the present arrangement. It seems reasonable and appropriate, however, for the government itself to direct the centres for orientation and in-service training.

(4) Since all staff members who are to have administrative, supervisory, technical, or extension-educational responsibilities must function as an inter-related team, and since the staff team in turn must be inter-related with village people through their local institutions, one cannot emphasize too strongly the need to orient all staff members in the philosophy, objectives, and methods of community development.

(5) Because community development objectives can be achieved only as the staff becomes effective in helping village people to develop strong panchayats and co-operatives, which in turn must motivate village people to give up their traditional ways of thinking, farming, and living, it is imperative that the training process be carefully balanced between the theoretical side and village practicals. The trainees are at the centres to learn and not to do physical labour as such. It is therefore most important that all work which qualifies for trainee time have a teaching-learning value. Inasmuch as most of the people going into community development have not themselves lived and worked as village cultivators' sons and daughters, it is essential that village practicals be so organised as to assure maximum village involvement, in a planned teaching-learning frame of reference.

(6) India's experience in the community development programme needs to be drawn on realistically in setting new and higher standards of performance as a basis for selection of all categories of personnel for community development posts. If

recruitment is vigorously pursued, it should be possible in a country of 440 million to find people with the right attitudes and motivations and who, once they are trained, can be counted on to assure the success of community development.

(7) Even with thorough job preparation and careful selection of personnel, it is essential to continue in-service training at frequent intervals for all categories of staff members, if community development is to remain a vital force in helping village people find new solutions to old problems by applying the ever-growing body of science.

(8) While India has taken considerable pains to orient and train a professional staff, this staff has not as yet carried on vigorous, vital, and purposeful educational programmes among village people to make sure that they, who are to benefit from community development, know and understand its philosophy and objectives. It will in the future, with the advent of Panchayati Raj, be especially important that all co-operative and panchayat leaders be trained so that they will know what the village community has a right to expect of them, and so that they, in turn, will know how to carry out their leadership responsibilities.

(9) Since community development's past strength has been its willingness, if not eagerness, to be evaluated, and to adjust and change as experience has directed, one must hope that this will also be true of training. India's experience supports the need for training to be continuously evaluated and needed adjustments readily made to meet new needs.

With the new element of Panchayati Raj introduced on the Indian rural scene, training programmes for community development must go beyond even this important series of correctives just discussed. The scope of the efforts to reach and to develop the people who live in India's half-million villages is much greater than it was ten, even five, years ago. Not only must a network of technical personnel be trained to man the 5,000 blocks in India, but the villagers themselves must come alive to initiate and help carry out the programmes they want the VLWs and others to implement. They, too, must be taught the techniques and technologies required to improve their agricultural production, get better schools for their children, and raise their levels and standards of living.

In retrospect, we might say that community development is now moving into a new phase, and with it the training programmes to make it effective. The first phase, covering the first two Plan-periods, might be called the foundation-laying stage. During this phase, a whole set of new steps was taken: the structure of the community development agency was built; administration was gradually reoriented from regulatory to developmental; villagers were awakened to their new freedom and its concomitant responsibility for self-help in overcoming poverty, disease, and ignorance; science and technology were introduced into rural India; training institutions for the many and diverse community development personnel were opened; and a backlog of experience in building village institutions was accumulated. At the same time, this phase had another dominant characteristic—the programme was largely created and run by Central and State bureaucracies. The village people, in effect, were invited to participate in village and block programmes dominated by officialdom.

The second phase, now just beginning, will necessarily be different, both in its aims and in its problems. During this phase, there will be an intensification of the development of village institutions such as panchayats, co-operatives, and schools. There will be a growth in understanding between the official bureaucracy and the officers of village, block, and district institutions. Planning and development will be based on the interest, initiative, motivation, and leadership of the people themselves. The economic base for village development will be strengthened by giving priority attention to increases in agricultural production. And finally, staff competence for educating villagers in institution-building and in utilizing science and technology in their lives will increase.

As this new phase begins, and then develops momentum, its success will depend even more than the last one did on the competence of the staff selected, trained, and assigned to the villages, blocks, and districts. The staff of Community Development will, in fact, be faced with a whole new set of demands. It was, after all, one thing to begin the programme and to create devices among the people for improvement; it will be quite another to assure successful execution of the high objectives that have been set and to see that these desires are fulfilled. It was necessary to organise panchayats and co-operatives, but it will also be necessary to make them work effectively. It was not easy to introduce improved agricultural practices; it will be even more difficult to motivate the people to accept the findings of science that support them. It was imperative to build schools, but they must be made vital village institutions, with the teacher an important village leader. It was reasonably acceptable for the Village-Level Worker to be philosopher, guide, and friend of the people, but he must also be competent to help village people succeed in solving their problems through village institutions. It was believed essential to put technical extension-specialists in the block organisation; it is equally important for them to understand village problems and the modifications of science that village situations require. It was one thing for the BDO to be the leader of a team of specialists and village workers; it will be quite another for him to enable his staff to help village people develop their own institutions and use their own initiative to solve their problems.

In view of these new goals and problems, India's Community Development programme must again meet the challenge before it, just as it has in the past. It must evolve new concepts of training to satisfy new needs. We have recommended ambitious proposals for advanced education for the various levels of official personnel and for correctives needed in the training programmes. We believe that India can, and will, rise to meet the challenge of the new day ahead.

MAIN AUTHORITIES QUOTED OR CITED

"Extension Training", Y. N. Verma and J. C. Ramchandani, Directorate of Extension, Ministry of Food and Agriculture, Government of India, New Delhi, March, 1962.

"India's Experience With Training In Extension Education for Community Development", Ford Foundation Program Letter, India, Report No. 118, 15 October, 1960.

"Manual of Village Leaders' Training Camps", issued by Ministry of Community Development & Co-operation, Government of India, 1961.

"Study, Research and Training for the Community Development Personnel", Ministry of Community Development & Co-operation, Government of India, 1960.

Third Five Year Plan, Planning Commission, Government of India, 1961.

"Training for Community Development", Ford Foundation Program Letter, India, Report No. 100, June-October, 1958.

CHAPTER 11

PROGRAMMES TO INCREASE AGRICULTURAL PRODUCTION

SOME slight account of the agricultural situation in India in 1950 was presented in Chapter 7, "The People and the Land". The somewhat expanded, but still brief, account of that situation is presented here as an introduction to a description and analysis of the planned agricultural improvement programme which was launched in 1952. Some of the gross facts were that only 38.6 per cent of the land area of the country was in sown crops, only a little more than 14 per cent was irrigated, and less than 11 per cent of the sown area was double-cropped. The chief limiting factors to high production per acre were lack of moisture, soil exhaustion, pest and parasite damage, inadequate farm tillage implements, limited use of commercial fertilizer and improved seeds, limited credit, and various impediments to systematic crop rotation. Food crops covered a little more than 80 per cent, and commercial crops, such as cotton, sugarcane, and oilseeds covered slightly less than 20 per cent, of the total cropped area. The majority of agricultural holdings were so small that most of the food crops were consumed by subsistence farm families. Most seeds were of poor quality, and animals, which supplied most of the farm power, were generally poor. Cattle, which numbered about 155 million, were of inferior quality and competed with people for food.

The analysis of why Indian agricultural production lagged behind the agricultural production of some other developing countries, and lagged behind its inherent potential will serve to emphasize the depth of the problems to be solved. It can, of course, be summarily said that the most basic cause of India's low state of agricultural development, and the low level of living of farm families and village communities, was that under colonial rule there had been very little development of the industrial sector of the national economy. Not only had excess population, due to natural increase and absence of urbanward migration, increased population pressure on the land, but the incapacity of village craftsmen to compete successfully with British factory production had forced many of these village craftsmen into agriculture. The over-all result of these historic factors was that Indian agriculture had become overwhelmingly subsistence farming. Subsistence farming is, of course, an early stage in the evolution of agricultural economies everywhere in the world. This stage in agricultural economy has rapidly changed in developing industrial societies where it has become more commercialized and more monetized. Furthermore, in rapidly developing industrial societies, there has been a steadily accelerating shift of population from rural areas and agricultural employment to urban areas and into industrial employment.

These historically validated facts are not offered to justify the oft-repeated, obvious, but naive, statement that one, if not the main, solution to basic agricultural problems has been industrial development. Indian planners, of course, knew this. But they also knew they had a second great problem, namely how to convert some sixty million cultivator families, the majority of whom were subsistence farmers, and thus survival-minded, into enterprising commercial producers. The first of these is overwhelmingly an economic problem, the solution of which will, of course, have far-reaching social results. The second is in many ways primarily a social problem. We shall therefore only consider what attention India's planners had been compelled to give, and have given, to the inter-relations of the plans for attacking these two problems concomitantly.

Planning for increasing agricultural production did not start de novo in 1950, with the First Five Year Plan. State plans had been in operation for four or five years. The national Grow More Food Campaign had been in continuous operation for seven to eight years. But what had been done in these programmes, and especially what had been learned in the operation of the Grow More Food Campaign, greatly conditioned the First Five Year Plan. Many of the agricultural programmes launched under State plans were continued in the early part of the First Five Year Plan period. What had been planned, and both what had been accomplished and what had not been accomplished, under these State plans, undoubtedly also greatly influenced the provisions of the First Five Year Plan. We briefly review these State plans not only that the reader may appreciate the ways in which they influenced national planning, but in order that he may follow the various shifts in emphasis which have taken place during the ten years of operation under the national plans.

State agricultural programmes, including the Grow More Food programme, had allotted only 12.3 per cent of their development funds directly to agriculture. They had allotted 16.2 per cent to irrigation. Thus these two combined were given 28.5 per cent of all State-planned development funds. The civil works programme was allotted 24.6 per cent and electricity 14.6 per cent. The remainder of the allocations of funds differed greatly among the various States and reflected the degree of emphasis on various lines of development. The situations in States, of course, differed, but their plans somewhat illustrated their different theories about the role of agriculture in over-all development. Their sub-allotments reflected their theories about how best to stimulate increased agricultural production. While increased use of compost was quite commonly recommended, the composting programme proposed was chiefly that of converting urban refuse and night soils into compost, not programmes for farm composting. Most allocations for agricultural programmes were not for improving the practices of cultivators, but chiefly for land reclamation, seed multiplication, fertilizers, and other supplies. Land reclamation, most of it for de-weeding, required heavy expenditures for tractors. East Punjab allotted 95.7 per cent of its planned funds to economic development, most of it for irrigation, electricity, roads, and buildings. Purely agricultural undertakings got only 2 per cent and this included Grow More Food campaign funds. In over-all development for the five-year period 1946-51, agricultural schemes which required the participation of cultivators ranked fifth among the fields to which funds were allotted. Only the field of health development ranked below it.

Most of the agricultural development programmes required activities in which cultivators were not directly involved. Even a considerable part of the Grow More Food campaign funds were allotted for tubewells, some of which would ultimately be owned by economic entrepreneurs who were not themselves active cultivators. All of these schemes were calculated to, and did, contribute to increased agricultural production, but it was not until a Grow More Food Enquiry Committee was appointed and made its recommendations for an agricultural extension system that agricultural planning began to provide a programme which was calculated to reach those millions of cultivators upon whose practices increased agricultural production must primarily depend.

The Grow More Food programme was started in 1943. There was a distinct evolution in the experiences of this programme which led to recommendations made by the Grow More Food Enquiry Committee in 1952. At a meeting in April, 1942, three main undertakings were suggested, (a) to "switch over from cash crops, mainly from short staple cotton, to food crops, (b) intensive cultivation of cultivated lands through irrigation, better seeds and manures and better farming practices, and (c) extensive cultivation by bringing under plough current fallows, culturable waste lands, etc." This was its programme until 1946 when it was decided to continue the programme for another five years. The recommendations then were for "greater attention to minor irrigation works, development of local manurial resources and distribution of improved seeds; plans for production of fertilisers; survey of ground water resources with a view to undertaking tubewell construction; and setting up of a Central organisation for undertaking reclamation and development of large blocks of culturable waste land." A top-level drive was initiated at that time to accomplish food self-sufficiency by March, 1952. In 1952, the Committee reported that total expenditures during the eight years of the campaign had been Rs. 67.5 crores (about 142 million dollars), but that by and large the campaign had failed.

The Committee diagnosed the causes of its degree of failure. It said the programme had failed because it was a campaign, not a programme ... "the movement has touched only a fringe of the population, viz., the larger holders. ... " Furthermore, that to try to attain food self-sufficiency by a target date, and by means of campaign drives was to use inappropriate methods. The Enquiry Committee cited the experiences of other countries which had demonstrated the efficiency of agricultural-extension methods and recommended that India establish that type of organisation, which it believed could, and would, provide a corps of local village-extension agents to work among the cultivators. Up to that time, India had tried to eliminate the weaknesses in its agricultural production almost solely by promoting and financing large reclamation projects, the establishment of a large number of government seed-multiplication farms, and by demonstration or test farms. It thus duplicated the experiences of practically every developing country in the world which has tried to accomplish rapid development by what might be called miracle-working projects. Unlike some countries which have abandoned some of their giant reclamation and resettlement areas, and even permitted some costly irrigation works to fall into disrepair, India has not abandoned any of these physically necessary projects. She, in fact, has continued and expanded such projects. But since 1952-53, she has recognized that the full and proper utilization of these facilities and materials depends on the education of millions of cultivators in the proper and efficient utilization of the facilities and supplies, which over-all planning has made available to them.

The judgment expressed in the Grow More Food Enquiry Committee's report was that the extension programme had to be more than solely technical and material aid to cultivators; that it had to be a multiple-purpose programme, a programme that would touch all facets of rural life, else it would not quickly make an appeal or challenge the interest of cultivators' families. It said further that it had to be of service to non-cultivator families, millions of them living in rural villages. The Grow More Food Enquiry Report was made between the time of the publication of the Draft Outline of the First Five Year Plan and the final Plan. The Plan reflected this theory of rural development, which theory, with all the ups and downs of the programme, has never been abandoned as the key to India's rural development programme.

As we have said, before the Community Development Programme was officially launched, 15 pilot extension projects were launched, one in each of 15 States. Each project was to cover 100 villages and each project area was to be under the direction of a graduate of a college of agriculture. He was, however, to have not only village-level workers below him but agricultural specialists on his staff. Various State Ministries were to provide specialists in the fields of health, education, etc. Each village-level worker was to be a multiple-purpose worker, giving more attention to agriculture than any other special field, but neglecting no technical aid programme which any self-help, organised group in any one of the 15 pilot project areas might request. Probably the boldest part of the experiment was the decision to recruit high school graduates from village families and train them to be village-level workers.

There were doubts on the part of many as to whether such an experiment would work. They doubted whether village people would be willing to organise themselves into self-help groups; whether high school graduates would volunteer to be village-extension workers; and whether persons with only high school education could be effective village workers, especially in the field of agriculture. The extension systems of so-called advanced countries, after which this experiment was patterned, had never utilized as extension workers persons with so little technical training. The Ford Foundation provided the funds for this bold experiment of organising the five village-level workers' training centres and for starting the 15 pilot-extension projects. Before the end of one year's experience with village-level workers, who were given only 6 months of intensive training, the principal doubts were pretty well dissolved in the minds of those who closely observed the experiment. Far more than the number of required recruits for training volunteered. Village people did organise themselves quite readily in self-help groups to receive the technical and material assistance which the extension agents were ready to provide.

These pilot projects were planned in late 1951, and before July, 1952 when the Indo-American Agreement for greatly-expanded technical assistance was consummated, it was decided that there should be many more such projects established. The trials, errors, and successes in ten years of experience in attempting to prepare millions of cultivators to make maximum use of these facilities and supplies constitute the story of the progress made in the agricultural extension programme.

The rationale of that programme was presented in Chapter 9, as a part of the description of the community development programme which was launched in 1952. Sir V. T. Krishnamachari, then Deputy Chairman of the Planning Commission, clearly stated the rationale of the community development-extension programme as follows. *First*, "there should be organised a National Extension movement covering the entire country within a period of seven or eight years; *Second*, a pattern of both official and non-official organisation should be established at all levels—State, district, sub-district, division and village; *Third*, The Central Government should help all States to establish an extension service." The Grow More Food Enquiry Committee had said there was imperative need for "an organisation for intensive rural work which would reach every farmer and assist in the co-ordinated development of rural life as a whole,"... that, "Extension or advisory services and other allied services have the following indispensable functions—instructing farm people in agricultural and domestic science and in agricultural affairs; bringing them the latest results of research in these fields, on quality and cost as well as on the quantity of production, and teaching them improved techniques of farming and rural living; calling the attention of research institutions to the agricultural and home problems that require study; and providing opportunities for farm people to meet together for the purpose of learning from each other and developing leadership in agricultural affairs."

It can be said that this blueprint, or model, for an extension system or programme, like the model for a community development programme, was constructed out of India's own experience as well as a knowledge of the best experience that the various countries of the world had developed and demonstrated. Like the community development model, and all other models, it was too ideal to be immediately, or quickly, put into execution. The model, however, has never been abandoned as a pattern for action. While its implementation has had to go through trial, error, and success, its nearer approach to success over the years has been wrought out through the process of consistent reappraisal and repeated adjustments.

The design for an agricultural extension programme which would ultimately blanket the country was also presented in Chapter 9. Here we repeat that design, and its specifications, only as they reflect the plan for agricultural extension work. It was expected that there would be, when the programme had blanketed the country, presumably by 1961, at least 50,000 multipurpose village workers, and a corps of extension specialists in each of the 5,000 or more development blocks, more of them specialists in agriculture-agronomy, animal husbandry, and agricultural co-operatives—than in any other technical fields. The block agricultural specialists would be backstopped by the agricultural officers in the district offices, each of whom would be an employee of his State Ministry of Agriculture. This would be by far the most giant agricultural extension programme in the world. But no other country, except China, had such a tremendous number of agricultural families to serve.

The programme was officially thrown into high gear in October, 1952. The steps by which it was thrown into gear were, first, to expand the 15 pilot-extension projects to 55 community development-extension blocks, and then steadily increase the number of blocks to 988 by the end of the First-Plan period, and to 3,100 blocks by the end of the Second-Plan period in 1961. The date set for complete coverage of the country was later moved forward to 1963, because it had been discovered that the programme could not be implemented by either trained technical personnel or funds by the end of the Second-Plan period. As we shall see later, even this expansion of the programme was too rapid for effective implementation. But as was pointed out in Chapter 9, a knowledge of what the programme was accomplishing well before the end of the First Five Year Plan period had become so widespread, and the demand from villages and from officials of the State Governments and Members of Parliament had become so insistent that there was no alternative to an attempt to meet this demand. Rapid expansion not only strained the capacity of the programme directors to select, train, and post technical personnel, but strained the capacities of the country to provide the physical goods required for agricultural improvements—fertilizers, improved seeds, plant protective materials, and also production credit. One of the first things persons from so-called developed countries learn about an agricultural-extension programme in a developing country is that accompanying extension education must be these material and financial aids; and furthermore, that government is the only source from which these aids can be secured.

The Planning Commission in its review of the experiences

India had during the First-Plan period reported shortfalls in some facilities' and supplies' targets. It did not attempt to equate costs of the facilities with gains in production resulting from them. The Commission's reviews of the whole rural programme at the end of the First-Plan period and again at the end of the Second-Plan period could not be as precise in terms of successes and shortfalls in the extension programme as they were of physical projects. Therefore, our summaries of what the experiences in agricultural extension were over the first ten years of development must also be more qualitative than quantitative.

The appraisals made by the Planning Commission of the successes of some of the physical components of the programme were also more qualitative than quantitative. The Plan had contemplated that 8.5 million agricultural acres would be brought under irrigation during the First-Plan period. Its estimate was that water had been made available to 6.3 million additional acres. More than twenty-five hundred tubewells had been sunk and more than eighteen hundred other tubewells had been energised. Fertilizer production had increased from 270,000 tons to 600,000 tons—an increase of more than 220 per cent. Almost 120,000 acres had been "reclaimed", chiefly de-weeded by tractor ploughing. The construction of major and medium irrigation facilities had made great strides, but had fallen short by 2.2 million acres. The Commission reported that the portion of minor irrigation which was to be supplied by new and renovated tanks had been disappointing, and that consumers' demand for phosphatic fertilizers, although subsidized by 25 per cent of the cost, had increased by less than 50 per cent.

The Planning Commission also made a number of qualitative statements bearing upon agricultural extension and programme administration. It said, "Three main problems in the working of the fertilizer programme have been encountered and it cannot be said that in any State an altogether satisfactory approach towards them has been so far evolved. It is recognized that chemical fertilizers should be used as far as possible along with organic manures, including green manure, but work on this latter programme has been on a totally insufficient scale. Secondly, although a variety of distribution arrangements has been tried out, as for instance, through depots of the agricultural department, through private distributors as well as in a few cases through co-operative societies, farmers do not find it by any means easy to obtain the quantities of fertilizers needed by them and instances of supplies running short or arriving late have been by no means uncommon. In the third place except a very limited extent, the distribution of fertilizers has not been supported by supply of agricultural credit." These statements seem to clearly indicate that to some degree what would otherwise have been far more effective agricultural extension work had been handicapped by ineffective administration, primarily of supply lines.

These analyses of the Planning Commission emphasize two major points; first, the difficulty of reaping maximum results from the grassroots work of an agricultural extension programme which depends on effective government action at many levels. This, however, was an inevitable condition under which the agricultural-extension programme in India had to work. There were no supply lines other than those which government programmes could provide. The second point we seek, again, to emphasize, is that national planners and leaders were assiduously evaluating the conditions under which agricultural development programmes were operating and planning to correct the weaknesses in programme operation which their analyses revealed. The Planning Commission Review of the First Five Year Plan which we are at the moment reporting on, was both an analysis of the experiences thus far and plans for the future. It said:

> "The organisation of extension services with the object of securing increased production and raising the standard of village life is a new undertaking. Extension is a continuous process designed to make the rural people aware of their problems, and indicating to them ways and means by which they can solve them. It thus involves not only education of the rural people in determining their problems and the methods of solving them, but also inspiring them towards positive action in doing so."

The Second Plan in its review of the First-Plan period made no detailed appraisal of the community development-extension programme, but did make some very perceptive comments. One of these comments was that, "Once the impulse has been given and the first stages of the journey covered, a programme such as that of community development and national extension grows out of its own experience and momentum. As it expands, it meets old needs and creates new ones. New methods are discovered, deficiencies long ignored come to be recognised, and in content and in the manner of its functioning the programme may succeed in solving the vital problems of the community." Another comment was that, "National extension and community projects should play a large part in promoting the diversification of the agricultural economy and in increasing agricultural production. They should also increase greatly the reserves of skill and the habit of improvisation of new techniques to serve local needs which are a condition of large-scale industrialisation." A further comment was that, "In a programme of such far-reaching significance spread over the entire country, it is essential that at each stage its working should be observed closely and objectively."

The Programme Evaluation Organisation, functioning directly under the Planning Commission, had continuously from 1953 onwards appraised the working, the effectiveness and ineffectiveness, of the community development-extension programme. The first Evaluation Report was on the early workings of the whole Community Development-Extension Programme, but it could not measure the effectiveness of performance over such a short period of time. Therefore, considerable of what it had to say might be called preachments. But these preachments were always about either weaknesses in operation which had been specifically observed or about failures to live up to the purposes, methods, and objectives which had been stated for the programme. They had to do with the competence and performance of different levels of personnel, the co-ordination of the services of these personnel, and to a considerable extent with the shortage of personnel. It also remarked that, "there must be some method of organising the use of total supplies in such a way that for the lack of one item other resources, including that of people's confidence and enthusiasm, do not get frozen."

One problem which it identified and referred to fairly often was the failure to recognize, on the part of the nation-building departments and of their personnel, that the block extension personnel were as important as the VLW. In this and subsequent reports, it mentioned quite often the fact that the personnel deputed by the nation-building departments were not enthusiastic about being posted in the blocks, the fact that they seldom visited the villages, and that they were not participating in the planning. Concerning the VLW, they reported quite early that they felt that he was wasting too much of his time in fortnightly meetings at block headquarters, spending too much time in distributing supplies, and that he could not adequately maintain all the records required of him.

The first and following reports quite often identified the fact that the number and the specific types of personnel which the programme design had contemplated were not posted, that even the very important position of Block Development Officer was quite often vacant for long periods of time, and that in many cases the nation-building agencies had not posted their personnel in the blocks. Most of the first and second, and to some extent the third, annual Evaluation Reports had to do with matters of administration and personnel. After 1957, and especially in 1958, when the Programme Evaluation Organisation made some detailed studies, part of them at the request of the Committee on Plan Projects (COPP), their comments on actual extension performance became much more specific and pointed.

As was mentioned in Chapter 9, the National Development Council constituted in 1956, just at the end of the First-Plan period, a Committee on Plan Projects. This Committee appointed a team to study and report on the Community Projects and National Extension Service. The team made its report in the fall of 1957. It made the sort of objective analyses which the Second Five Year Plan had said were required. Its assessment of agricultural extension work was as forthright as had been the assessment of the Grow More Food Enquiry Committee in 1952. Had its report not included workable recommendations for corrective measures of various kinds, its criticisms would have been devastating. We will only highlight its assessments of the main weaknesses of the extension programme and some of its suggestions for remedying the weaknesses. We do this because the appointment of such a committee and the report of its Study Team so aptly illustrate the process, even the procedures, by which India's planning is made pragmatic and thus progressive.

The process might be described as continuous evaluation and criticism, not only by the Programme Evaluation Organisation but by the National Development Commissioners' Conferences, and by the press, and then every so often the appointment of a commission or committee specifically to assess its operational experiences and, so to speak, introduce a mutation in the evolution of its various development programmes.

The Study Team's analyses of the working of the agricultural extension programme were introduced by the statement that, "Material progress in the agricultural sector can be judged only by the total increase in production." Its first, and probably most pointed assessment of increased agricultural production was that "the all-India average of additional food production in the Community Development and National Extension Service blocks comes to only 10.8 per cent." Its estimates were that this varied from as high as 41.4 per cent to as low as 2.7 per cent. It set itself the task of analyzing in what respect the current procedures and practices had not yielded the desired results. It said that, "Often, the farmer is either unaware of its existence (a strain of improved seeds) or is not convinced of its quality."

This was another way of saying that village and block-level extension agents had not effectively spread the good news of the availability of improved seeds and that they had not staged local demonstrations which proved the superior results which such improved seeds would obviously yield. It recommended that, "Each Gram Sewak should arrange in respect of every new item of improvement—seed, fertilizer, cultural practice, etc., in each of the villages in his circle at least five demonstrations on controlled basis on cultivators' fields and thereby demonstrate its relative merits and superiority over the practice in vogue." Notwithstanding that no Gram Sewak, no matter how technically competent, could stage and supervise such a large number of farm demonstrations, the Study Team identified and emphasized the one sine qua non of effective agricultural-extension work, namely, the necessity of demonstrating the effectiveness, and the profitableness, to cultivators, of the adoption of various improvement elements for increased agricultural production.

The Study Team emphasized another well-validated method for securing the adoption and spread of improved farm practices, namely, that "Even more effective than the demonstration carried out by the Gram Sewak is the actual practices adopted by the neighbour." It not only pointed out the feasibility of village workers persuading cultivators to follow the best practices of progressive farmers in their own neighbourhoods, but suggested that, "Associations of progressive farmers should be encouraged." This, too, has been one of the standard methods of effective agricultural-extension work everywhere in the world. In addition to citing what, in its judgment, were weaknesses in field-extension methods, the Team made a number of comments on the ineffective co-ordination of other elements in the over-all programme for increased agricultural production. It said that it had noted that in some of the major irrigation projects, "there was no experimentation in regard to the cropping patterns, nor of the right use of water newly made available." It pointed out some types of greatly-needed extension education and the need for research to determine what extension agents should teach. Major among those were proper rates of water application to obtain best results, proper rates of fertilizer application, and the feasibility and profitability of double-cropping on irrigated lands. It made it clear that its findings proved that the administration of supply lines, especially for fertilizers, but also for other supplies essential to carrying out the recommendations of extension workers, had failed in many instances. One notable example of failure in supply lines was of improved poultry-breeding stock. The significance of this failure was that the promotion of increased and improved poultry production was believed to have such easy, wide application.

The Study Team's report was exceedingly forthright. We know of no such analytically-devastating report on a going programme in any other developing country. The Team's report was discussed in detail in Parliament and discussed widely in the press. The Second-Plan period was well advanced when the Team's report was published. The Third Five Year Plan reflected the influence of the criticisms and recommendations of this report, the influences of the annual and special reports of the Programme Evaluation Organisation, and the ample discussion in the public press, of the issues which these reports had raised about the programme for increasing agricultural production.

If we were to summarize the suggestions made by the Study Team, measured by validated standards of effective agricultural extension organisation and practices, we would catalogue them as follows: (1) That the first task of an agricultural-extension worker is to make farmers aware of the existence of knowledge of ways to increase agricultural production; and second, by field demonstrations, prove to farmers the superiority of the new kinds of agricultural practices. (2) That the spread, or diffusion, of an improved agricultural practice, once it has been adopted by one or a few cultivators in a local community, comes chiefly from the observation and imitation by many others of the practices of these few early adopters. (3) That the failure to mobilize and utilize extension, and even community development, methods in newly-irrigated areas will lessen the possibility of maximum and effective use of irrigation waters to increase yields. (4) That the main job of an agricultural-extension worker, whether village-level worker or block-agricultural officer, is educational, and that to the extent that he is compelled to spend any considerable amount of his time performing routine administrative jobs, to just that extent he is compelled to neglect his educational work. We should probably add, (5) That in a situation such as in India, cultivators can adopt some improved practices only if the needed physical supplies—fertilizers, seeds, etc.—are made available at the exact time they should be used; otherwise, they cannot be used, or else they will be used ineffectively; and unless loan money is available and assured, many cultivators, even if they are convinced of the superiority of improved agricultural practices, cannot adopt them.

The Programme Evaluation Organisation made some special investigations for the Study Team, the findings of which emphasized and validated those of the Team. We record some of the critical issues in day-by-day programme operation which these studies identify. They were: (1) The heavy load VLWs and Block Agricultural Specialists were expected to, and were trying to carry, and the fact that such a large proportion of their time was spent on things other than extension teaching. The studies showed that the average VLW, "stays rather more than four days a month at block headquarters and nearly two-thirds of his nights in his centre village headquarters. Forty-five per cent of non-headquarters villages were visited at the rate of less than once per month. The average block agricultural specialist could visit only two-thirds of the villages under his charge as often as once a year;" (2) There were shortages of personnel posted in the blocks, in comparison with the numbers which the programme implementation prescribed. "About 40 per cent of the blocks studied reported absence of BDOs for varying lengths of time, the average being five months." Nearly 60 per cent of the blocks "had to do without agricultural specialists from five to ten months respectively or about one-fourth of the average period of their operation;" (3) The study discovered what the analysts considered to be quite ineffective day-by-day working relationships between Block Extension Officers and VLWs. In some cases, this was due to the Block Extension Officers' conviction that the VLW was incompetent in the field of agriculture. In other cases, the VLW testified that he received no effective assistance from the Block Agricultural Specialist. Added to this, the analysts reported that the Block Agricultural Officers received very little technical backstopping from the District Agricultural Officers. Most of the assistance they received was in administrative matters; (4) There was the repeated complaint of the failure of supply lines to deliver fertilizers, seeds, etc. at the right time and sometimes in the right amounts. The VLW was reported to have thought that he should be associated with the securing of these supplies, but did not believe that he should be involved in the time-consuming task of distributing the supplies to the cultivators.

Indian planners and leaders, while keeping their eyes on the broadly-stated objectives set forth in the First Five Year Plan for the promotion of increased agricultural production, enhanced their understanding of the detailed tasks of accomplishing these objectives by continuous critical analysis of their programme-operating experiences. Our emphasis has, therefore, been upon weaknesses which they identified and sought to remedy. Some of the weaknesses were in the performance of programme personnel, but most of them were clearly due to the overwhelmingly difficult task of implementing the giant programme which had been undertaken; the task of reaching and serving, as quickly as possible, hundreds of thousands of cultivators and serving them not only with technical agricultural aid, but also with the supplies essential for carrying out recommended, improved agricultural practices. We later describe a revised, we might say new, attack on these problems, the so-called "Package Programme", which was begun in 1960-61 as a part of the Third Five Year Plan.

It will be remembered that increase in agricultural production, especially of food-grains, was given top priority in the First Five Year Plan. That Plan, however, also specified the necessity of the reorganisation of the whole agrarian structure, by which it meant primarily various types of land reform and the development of co-operative credit and other institutions through which farm people could be mobilized and served.

According to the Third Five Year Plan, total agricultural production (excluding cotton and jute) rose from 90.4 million tons in 1950-51, to 133.1 million tons in 1960-61, food-grains (cereals and pulses) from 52.2 million tons to 76 million tons. The index of agricultural production rose from 95.6 (1950-51) to 135 by 1960-61; the food-grain production index rose to 132, the index for other crops to 142. Population increased over this period by about 21 per cent and national *per capita* income increased by about 16 per cent. While no precise estimate can be made concerning which of the various elements contributed to these increases, there are quite accurate statistics presented in the Third Five Year Plan of what had been done to strengthen the capacity of the major elements in the programme for increased agricultural production.

"The net area irrigated is estimated to have increased from 51.5 million acres in 1950-51 to about 70 million acres in 1960-61.... About 4 million acres were reclaimed by the end of 1960-61. Mechanical cultivation was extended to 0.5 million acres and land improvement to about 1.5 million acres. The consumption of nitrogenous fertilisers... increased from 55,000 tons to 230,000 tons; of phosphatic fertilizers... from 7,000 tons to 70,000 tons between 1950-51 and 1960-61."

The personnel posted in the Community Development-Extension Programme, officially launched in 1952, had expanded rapidly. There were 31,000 VLWs, 5,000 Block Extension Specialists in agriculture and animal husbandry and about 2,600 in Co-operation. The programme in 1960-61 was serving 3,100 blocks, 370,000 villages and more than 200 million village people. Ninety-three VLW training centres, 42 training centres for block officers, and 41 (Home Science) extension wings had been established.

The Plan expressed dissatisfaction with progress made in plant protection measures and said that they "have lagged behind several other aspects of the agricultural programme"; that, "the Programme Evaluation Organisation has revealed a number of weaknesses in the existing situation and in the working of seed farms"; and that, "A serious gap in the agricultural programmes undertaken during the First and Second Plans has been in the field of improved agricultural implements."

To increase agricultural production was the main objective of each of the elements in the agricultural programme, from irrigation and reclamation for increasing the size of the agricultural land base, to extension programmes to increase the proficiency of cultivators. There had been recognized from the beginning of the Plan two other major agricultural problems; the creation of economic employment for excess rural manpower and the reorganisation of the agrarian structure toward the end of not only increasing agricultural production, but as issues of equity and justice. The Third Plan said, "The First Five Year Plan included proposals for the settlement of agricultural labour and protection against ejectment from homesteads. Not much progress was made in schemes for land resettlement. . . . " It further said that there had been no positive programmes for effectively utilizing surplus manpower except in shramdan undertakings. The Third Plan proposed "a comprehensive programme of rural works" and "intensive and concentrated effort involving the participation of millions of families in programmes of agricultural development." It said that, "For many years the greatest scope for utilising manpower resources in rural areas will lie in programmes of agricultural development, road development projects, village housing and provision of rural amenities." It also stated that the development of small and village industries provided a larger employment potential than had yet been utilized.

The Third Plan by implication assessed the shortfall in agricultural production from all these measures when it said that the rate of increase in agricultural production during the Third-

Plan period would need to be three times as great as that during the previous ten years if the country was to be self-sufficient in food production by 1965-66. To assist in accomplishing such an increase the Third Plan specified that the net irrigated area should be increased to 90 million acres; that the amount of barren and uncultivated land, and land in current fallow, should be reduced; that the area sown more than once per year should be increased by 15½ million acres and the gross area sown increased by 23.5 million acres. Other measures, such as increased production of commercial fertilizers and plant protection materials and a great increase in production and distribution of improved seed, will be discussed later in connection with the Package Programme.

The Plan also discussed some necessary elements in a programme for rapid increase in agricultural production which would depend upon more effective and efficient assistance from agricultural extension personnel. It said, "In all areas, and specially in the development blocks taken up under the community development programme, these programmes will need to be implemented with the largest measure of participation on the part of local communities and to reach as many families as possible through the village production plans." None of the statements was, however, accompanied by any detailed specification for more effective agricultural extension work which would be required if all the physical facilities and supplies were to yield what was expected of them.

But while the Third Plan was in process of formulation, once again a Study Team was appointed to probe deeply into past performances in India's attempts to increase agricultural production rapidly, and to make recommendations for eliminating such weaknesses as a study would reveal. The Team consisted of thirteen American agricultural scientists and twelve Indian colleagues. The Team spent approximately three months in intensive study and made its report in April, 1959 to the Ministry of Food and Agriculture and the Ministry of Community Development and Co-operation. These were the Ministries which had been in the past, and would be in the future, responsible for agricultural extension work.

The remarkable report of the Agricultural Production Team on "India's Food Crisis and Steps to Meet It" forcefully and cogently stated every programme weakness which India's previous evaluations had identified. It also offered specific and detailed remedies for each of these weaknesses. One fact operating here was that every American member of the joint team was an expert in one or another basic field of scientific knowledge essential to efficient agricultural production and all were from a country which had proved that it knew how to produce agricultural products in abundance. The second fact was that while India too had some top agricultural scientists, either because there were not enough of them, or because they were not strategically placed in programme operation, they had not been able to plan and direct an outstanding programme to increase agricultural production.

The Report on "India's Food Crisis and Steps To Meet It" was written and signed by only the members of the American team. But it is difficult to believe that any group of agricultural scientists could on its own and after such a brief study, so accurately hit every bull's eye of the programme or programmes which India needed if she was to attain the increase in agricultural production which she sought. Indian counterparts of the American Team state that the members of the American Team had not only high competence, but that "they were broad-minded and tolerant." Members of the American Team say that enough of their Indian counterparts were competent scientists and had a sufficiently-detailed knowledge of not only Indian agriculture, but of Indian administrative organisation, to give both balance and sure and practical direction to the recommendations which were made.

This was also true of the process by which the recommendations of the Team were converted into specifications for the "Package Programme," more formally known as the Intensive Agricultural Districts Programme (IADP). As in processes by which the recommendations of the Grow More Food Enquiry Committee were written into the First Five Year Plan, and carried into execution during the First and Second-Plan periods, there were some individuals who participated in the COPP Study Team investigations who were also counterparts of the American Food Team and also participants in formulating the Package Programme. This is an important fact, for ideas originate and are conveyed by persons, and have neither logical sequence nor follow-up if there are no persons who participate actively and influentially in each step in the sequence of the process. This was the case subsequently with some of the American members of the Food Team who are now in India as Ford Foundation consultants on the Package Programme. It is, of course, the case with a number of Indians, some of whom were not only counterparts to the members of the American Team, but who before and since that study were central figures in the planning and administration of India's agricultural programme.

The Food Team stated that in its judgment the target of 110 million tons of food-grains by 1965-66 was reasonable in terms of need, but it said, as did the Third Five Year Plan, that to meet this target would require a rate of increase three times as great as had thus far been accomplished, but added that the target "can be achieved." It also stated that it could be achieved "only if an all-out emergency food production programme is undertaken." Its prescription for such emergency action was not a prescription of what is generally called a "crash" programme. Nor were the methods it proposed those of a "campaign". It was a programme for organising and efficiently directing the material and human resources which are resident in India. The Team believed that a recognition was necessary, on the part of Indian planners and leaders, that a "food crisis" did in fact exist and would become greater unless these resources were effectively mobilized and efficiently directed. The report said:

"India is using only a small portion of its potential water supply, which is one of the largest in the world. India now gets only one-fifth to one-fourth ton increase in crop yields on irrigated lands as compared to non-irrigated lands. Moreover, only about 12 per cent of irrigated acreage grows more than one irrigated crop per year.... Better water management is needed. ... Millions of acres could be reclaimed and made more productive by drainage improvement.... The unemployed and underemployed in the villages represent a waste of resources that should be used to produce more food. ... There are no inherent soil, climatic or other physical reasons for the present low yields. But there are no blanket proposals that can be generally applied to reach the Third Plan target."

There was nothing new, or different, in the recommendations of the Food Team, from those made in the Third Five Year Plan, and as a matter of fact in previous plans, in terms of more irrigation water, intensification of production in irrigated areas, high priorities for chemical fertilizers, need for production and distribution of improved seeds, and more farm production credit. But the Team believed that it was imperative that there be staged outstanding local area demonstrations of the effectiveness of guaranteeing the combined and co-ordinated application of all of these necessary components of agricultural production. It said that specific areas should be selected to demonstrate this fact and that,

> "These areas will, the Team believes, increase India's food production more rapidly than others, if given allocation of fertilizers in combination with other improved practices, such as plant protection measures, improved seeds, and water for irrigation. . . . There are tremendous physical potentialities for increasing production per acre if they can be achieved."

Its recommendations, briefly, were: (1) That the capacity of India to triple the rate of increase in agricultural production could undoubtedly be demonstrated and the Third Plan targets be accomplished, if all the well-known required elements for such accomplishments were mobilized, or assembled, and applied in combination with each other. (2) That the demonstrations could not be too many if all of the elements or factors—improved seeds, water for irrigation, fertilizer application, supervised credit, and extension teaching—were to be properly controlled and effectively directed. (3) That, "More effort should be concentrated on the most promising areas for wheat and rice production, i.e., those which have had the most rapid rate of increase in the recent past, and which have also the highest potential for rapid large increases in the years immediately ahead." (4) That, "Far-reaching centralized authority with a clear line of command and execution alone can meet the challenge of growing more food. . . . The administrative structure, moreover, must be simplified and clear lines of authority and responsibility established at all levels of Government, so that policy decisions are carried out to the village level."

The Team said,

"Community Development and all technical agencies must be geared to mobilization and strengthening of village leaders and organisations, and effective channelling to village people of all information and help necessary to increase food output. The Team believes, therefore, that *all Ministries concerned with any aspect or programme relevant to food production must give top priority to food production now and for the period of the Third Plan.*"

The American team concluded its summary of recommendations with the following encouraging statement: "While the Team has been concerned with India's problems and has highlighted the critical issues, *the Team leaves India confident that it is within the capacity of India's people to mobilize to meet the great crisis before them.*"

The next step in the launching of the Package Programme was a careful analysis of the various recommendations of the Team and the cataloguing of these into a "10-Point Pilot Programme", all points focused on the objective of assisting individual cultivators, in ever-increasing numbers, to increase their agricultural output. While this would require that each cultivator would have made available to him all the elements—fertilizers, good seeds, adequate credit etc.—the primary object was to make some cultivators efficient farmers; then to increase the number of such farmers until "good farming" became a tradition or a value, literally a set of moral standards by which a cultivator judged himself and by which his neighbours and everyone else judged him. This is the sort of status that the farmers of every leading country of the world have attained, not only with themselves and with their neighbours, but with the national society, by efficient agricultural production. Because they have attained this status, they are not downtrodden and not objects of pity, not apathetic or fatalistic. They are legitimately aspiring, and legitimately proud, and beyond question, efficient. In a developing country like India, the climb to such status must start with the first step of developing a number of efficient farmers, followed by steps which will steadily increase the number of such farmers until good farming, not mere survival, is the object of millions of cultivator families.

The social or nation-building objective of the Package Programme emphasizes two important things: First, that this is the historic logic by which the farming sector of every advanced society has gained the socio-economic status which Indian leaders have stated from the beginning of planning as an ultimate objective; and, second, that the first step toward this objective is to plant the leaven of good farming into the practice of enough individual farmers, in enough carefully selected geographic areas, and enough local communities, that both cultivators and planners are convinced of the efficacy of this method of attaining this ultimate objective.

There is no better way by which we can adequately state the prescriptions for the necessary elements in the Package Programme than to quote in toto from the "Suggestions For 10-Point Pilot Programme To Increase Food Production", as follows:

1. Adequate farm credit, based on production potential, made readily accessible through strengthened service co-operatives.

2. Adequate supplies of fertilizers, pesticides, improved seeds, improved farm implements and other essential production needs, made readily accessible through strengthened service co-operatives.

3. Price incentives to participating cultivators through assured price agreements for rice and wheat (and for millets in appropriate Districts) announced two years in advance.

4. Marketing arrangements and services which enable the cultivator to obtain the full market price for his marketed surplus.

5. Intensive educational, technical and farm management assistance made available in every village in every development block in the pilot Districts. (Organisation of entire Pilot District into development blocks as quickly as possible.)

6. Participation of all interested cultivators, both large and

small, in direct individual farm planning for increased food production.

(a) *for all interested cultivators*, a *simple* farm improvement plan to apply minimum recommended combination of improved practices. The goal should be to get 20 per cent of all cultivators participating in the first year, 65 per cent by 5th year.

(b) *for 10-15 selected cultivators*, a *total* farm improvement plan to use *all* available resources of the integrated programme. The goal is 10 cultivators in each VLW circle of 5 villages the last year, 10 in each village in the 5th year.

7. Village planning for increased production, and village improvement to include: livestock improvement programmes; strengthening of village organisations such as co-operatives, panchayats, development councils and of village leadership.

8. A public works programme, using local labour, to undertake drainage, bunding, soil conservation, minor irrigation, building of accessible godowns and roads, and other development works contributing directly to increased food production.

9. Analysis and evaluation of programme from the day of its initiation, to include:

(a) a resource and production "benchmark" study of each District at beginning of programme;

(b) analysis of programme as it proceeds, as to effectiveness of its methods and organisation;

(c) evaluation of results, season by season and at end of five-year period as to increased production and farm income, input-output data, etc.

10. Co-ordination on a priority basis, by village, by Block, District, State and Centre, of all resources—adequate and well-trained staff, adequate administrative facilities, credit and farm supplies, pricing and marketing and godown arrangements, irrigation and soil conservation services, educational and information aids and programmes, etc.— essential to mount and carry out the programme with maximum speed and effectiveness.

The steps to be taken to launch the programme were specifically scheduled. The programme which was launched, and is now operating, included seven districts selected for pilot programme operation. In each district, every element in the Package Programme for increasing agricultural production is provided. The number of agricultural extension and community development personnel is doubled in each district.

After a year of preparatory work, the programme was launched in early 1961 under the Third Five Year Plan. It is a five-year programme in which the Ford Foundation is providing both financial and technical assistance, the latter supplied through a team of Ford Foundation Consultants from the United States. As members of this team, the Foundation has endeavoured to provide a high quality of personnel and to insure their service on the job for the full five years.

The Package Programme as a whole is a community development programme in which intensive emphasis is given to achievement of increases in agricultural production and productivity. Concentration of effort and resources is the key element in the programme's attack upon agricultural development.[1] The emphasis thus far is almost entirely upon increasing food-grain production. The programme provides intensive technical guidance to cultivators in improving farm practices, makes sure that unusually large supplies of fertilizers, improved seed, and other production supplies are available for cultivators to purchase, and sees that adequate credit is available for cultivators to buy the needed supplies. Special emphasis is given to assuring that these supplies are available in local godowns within a short distance of the cultivators' villages, well in advance of the time for their use. The programme includes provision for construction or hire of such godowns, if they are not already in existence.

Development of individual farm plans with cultivators, including simple "package of practices" plans, is an important feature. These individual plans help provide a basis for extension

[1] The reader's attention is called to the Annual Proceedings of the American Farm Economics Association (annual meeting at Storrs, Connecticut in August, 1962) in which the sharpness of focus of this programme was discussed in a paper entitled "Overcoming the Obstacles to Farm Economic Development in the Less-Developed Countries", which was published in the *Journal of Farm Economics,* Vol. XLV, No. 5, December, 1962.

of credit and for advance procurement of production supplies in each area. Even more importantly, they are a means for cultivators to commit themselves to specific improvements in practice. This "pinning down" is highly beneficial.

A most significant feature is the programme's "package approach" to production improvement. Agricultural improvement work in India in recent years has stressed the adoption of single practices, such as use of improved seed, or of green manure, or sowing of paddy rice in rows instead of broadcasting the seed. The Package Programme, however, emphasizes the simultaneous use of a "package" of several related practices, such as use of better seed, seed cleaning and treatment, better seedbed preparation, use of fertilizers at the right times and in the proper quantities, better water use, and suitable plant protection measures. The "package of practices" varies between areas, but always includes a group of inter-acting practices that are much more productive than any single practice can be when applied alone. The practices involved are those that are feasible for cultivators to perform under existing conditions, that can be supported with adequate technical guidance and supplies, and that the cultivators themselves agree to undertake. Altogether, this represents a wholly new departure in India.

The improved practices in each local "package of practices" are those locally recommended as suitable to the area and are based on the already available store of research knowledge in India. As the Food Crisis Report pointed out, India's agricultural research knowledge is already adequate to permit a very large expansion in production and productivity per acre. The basic problem is to extend the known and tested practices to cultivators and ensure their adoption. This is the particular province of the Package Programme. Therefore, the programme does not include provision for research on its own, although it does expect to profit from field experience in its operations and from such new research knowledge as is developed by the experiment stations.

The programme relies heavily upon field demonstrations to educate cultivators in the use of new practices in tillage and planting, application of chemical and organic fertilizers, use of seed treatments and better selection of seed, water use and drainage, plant protection, and harvesting, drying, and storing of grains. From several hundred to several thousand field demonstrations of improved crop production practices were carried out in each of the seven districts during the crop year just past. Extension education work is also carried on by the Village-Level Workers and block and district staffs through individual contacts and village meetings.

In addition, a wider avenue of rural education is now being opened up by the establishment of Package Programme information offices at each of the district headquarters. According to the official plan, the work of these information offices will be conducted as part of an integrated Centre-State-district information service. These units are the first district agricultural information offices to be established in India. It is their function to develop and use the available channels for mass dissemination of technical and programme information to cultivators and the general public. They will produce and distribute simple visuals, leaflets, photographs, posters, and slides for use in their districts, and will aid in training of extension workers. To the extent feasible, they will make use of newspaper and magazine publicity, public speeches, radio programmes, exhibits at fairs and melas, and motion pictures and strip films. They also will assist in activities with schools, youth groups, women's groups, local co-operatives, business groups, and the Panchayati Raj institutions so as to extend programme information as widely as possible.

Further, the Package Programme provides for improvements in storing and marketing of crops and for linkage of credit and marketing. It also supplies an Agricultural Implements Workshop in each of the seven districts to assist in design and development of simple but improved agricultural implements. Then, to make possible the better guidance of fertilizer recommendations, a soils laboratory is being established in or near each of the selected districts. These activities, along with the work of development, testing, and distribution of high quality seed, act as essential backstops and supports for the programme. Although operations to date involve relatively little attention to improvements in livestock production, this phase of the work will become increasingly important.

The programme has been in operation for too short a time for us, or anyone else, to assess its effectiveness in terms of securing increased agricultural production in the seven pilot districts, much less to measure the extent to which, and the ways by which, what will be demonstrated in these districts spreads to other areas. What we can do is to describe how the agricultural programme, and the plans for increasing agricultural production named in the First Five Year Plan as top priorities, have evolved over the first ten years of national development.

We have already described the over-all process of developing ideas and planning as one of continuous analysis of programme-operation experience; also the appointment of a group of experts to appraise what has been learned and to make recommendations for improvements in not only programme methods and procedures, but in some cases programme organisation and administration. The decision to establish a community development-extension programme was something like a mutation in the methods by which India had attempted to grow more food. We have cited the recommendations of the COPP Study Team, many of whose recommendations were adopted, as being a second marked advance in programme orientation. It is now clear to us that the launching of the Package Programme is another such programme reorientation.

In the programme launched with the fifteen pilot projects in 1951, and expanded to 55 community development blocks in 1952, it will be remembered that the First Five Year Plan said that extension would be the agency, and community development the method, by which improvements in all areas of rural life would be accomplished. Increase in agricultural production was named as the first priority for the programme. The village-level workers were given more training in agriculture than in any other field, or in all other fields combined. A minimum of two agricultural extension specialists were to be located in each block and were to be technically back-stopped by their Ministries in each State. In addition to these, the State Ministries had some agricultural assistants operating in the same areas as were the community development-extension block workers. Thus, some 60,000 to 70,000 agricultural extension agents would, as we said earlier, be the greatest body of agricultural extension workers in the world. But even if it had been possible to recruit, train, and post full quotas of personnel, the work-load of each extension worker would have resulted in minimal technical assistance to cultivators. There could, however, be no escape from this element of programme weakness, unless it had been decided to expand the programme very slowly. This, we earlier explained, could not be countenanced in the face of steadily and rapidly increasing demand not only from Members of Parliament and State leaders, but also from village leaders who expressed the desire that their areas be included in the community development-extension programme.

Our analysis is that another weakness, which need not have developed, was that community development methods were employed less in the agricultural sector than in any other sector of the whole programme; thus the whole, sound genius of extending agricultural technical know-how to cultivators, and the effective mobilization of local groups of cultivators to learn about, and to learn, this technical know-how were never adequately implemented. Because it was easier to organise great numbers of village people for shramdan (voluntary work brigades) and to mobilize them for construction projects, for the carrying out of which substantial financial and other material aids were granted, the major portion of the time of village-level workers was given to these types of projects.

The major programme emphasis itself got centred on obvious physical accomplishments and on measurable people's participation. Even if group methods of agricultural extension had been used, which they seldom were, neither the amount of "popular participation" in terms of participating cultivators, nor the immediately-obvious physical accomplishments of agricultural extension could have competed with construction and amenities. The results of effective agricultural extension methods become obvious only as farmers are taught, and themselves meticulously learn, better methods of farming. This is a relatively slow-moving process, but like all learning processes, it is cumulative and constantly more self-generating. As John Dewey said, "Education is the process of learning to learn." The Package Programme is based upon a faith in this process of education and therefore is based on a plan to stimulate farmers to undertake, and to teach them how to adopt and practise, improved farming methods.

To the extent that this programme is implemented and

expanded to other districts having a good agricultural production potential, it will complete the full cycle of adaptation in a country which, aware of its great need for increased agricultural production, especially food production, and aware of a relatively stagnant agriculture, decided from the beginning, as a matter of national policy, to establish a nationwide extension agency and use community development-extension methods. The terminus of this cycle was the launching of the Package Programme for increasing agricultural production, which contains every element of the best agricultural extension programmes in the world, and utilizes to the fullest extent possible the impact of co-ordinated application of extension methods in all agricultural improvements.

In the event, however, that this programme becomes stereotyped, a patented blueprint rather than a programme adapted to the geographic and ecological areas in which it operates, it might fare little better than the community development block programme, which also was a package programme. The only element in the programme which can and should be stereotyped is the guarantee that all the basic elements for maximum agricultural production shall be made available to each package programme district. In each district, the programme must depend upon the administrative machinery that is to deliver these basic elements to the districts and to guarantee their proper distribution within the districts. But even if this is effectively done, the success of the programme will depend ultimately upon the effectiveness of the grassroots agricultural extension work among the cultivators.

The Package Programme's provisions for effective agricultural extension work will not, of course, solve all of India's agricultural problems. For a number of decades, until industrial development is well advanced, there will be more people in rural areas than can be effectively employed in agricultural production. The Third Five Year Plan provides for creating productive public works for as many as possible of the rural unemployed. It has recommended the maximum use of unemployed rural workers in work which would increase the usable land base for agricultural production, not only in irrigation, flood control, land reclamation, and soil conservation, but in local drainage and bunding (field dikes) and minor irrigation canals. The Plan expressed the hope that these types of work would provide about 100 days a year of wage-employment for each of 2,500,000 persons by the last year of the Plan.

Basic land reforms, some of them initiated even before the First Five Year Plan was formulated, but few of them as yet completely implemented, are still stated as a necessary part of the agricultural development programme, as are adequate agricultural production credit and co-operatives. But Indian planners and leaders clearly recognize that the agricultural sector cannot lift itself by its own bootstraps; that there must be a concomitant and increasingly-accelerated development of the industrial sector. They further recognize, and outside observers should recognize, that in attempting to increase agricultural production within the agricultural sector itself, India is dealing with a situation, or a body of socio-economic conditions, different from those which have prevailed in the high agricultural-producing countries of the world. Maximum agricultural mechanization, the twin of maximum use of science, in developing the efficient and profitable agriculture of countries like the United States and Canada, or Australia and New Zealand, cannot work the miracle in production per man in India that it has in these and other countries. It cannot do so because there is no place where displaced rural manpower can go to find employment. The problem in India is how to promote increased agricultural production more by labour-intensive methods of production than by maximum mechanization. Even non-agricultural labour-intensive projects will have to employ as much as possible of excess rural manpower. None of these requirements, however, lessens the need for the use of science and efficient management on the part of Indian farmers.

Planners can, however, from a knowledge of programmes in economically-advanced societies, plot programmes of progress which move much more rapidly than it is possible to move the masses of Indian cultivators. Indian planners and programme directors now know this. It is of some importance that others appreciate what a tremendous undertaking it will be for some time to come to train millions of Indian cultivators in efficient agricultural production. It will take time for Indian cultivators to become as skilful and efficient as most modern Japanese farmers. This type of development is relatively slow, but it is cumulative and ultimately self-generative, if and when individuals or co-operative groups of cultivator families become aware of the fact that they are making steady and accelerating progress in meeting their daily felt needs. This was the gospel of the recommendations of the Grow More Food Enquiry Committee in 1952. It is the rationale of the community development-extension programme launched in 1952-53. It is still the rationale of India's rural development programme.

The Third Five Year Plan looks not only at the period 1961-66, but towards what can ultimately be accomplished. We would say, as do Indian planners, that the outlook need not be discouraging. We believe India can reach her stated objectives if and when she determines to make the organisation and administration of her agricultural programme more efficient than at present. Moreover, if and when 90 to 100 million acres of land are irrigated and millions of Indian cultivators are as efficient irrigation-farmers as are the Japanese, India can not only adequately feed and clothe her own people, but become one of the great agricultural-producing nations of the world. Over the decades it will take to accomplish this seeming miracle, industrialization will have also gained momentum and industrial employment will have alleviated population pressure on the land. It is contemplation of this type of gradual, but accelerating, growth that marks the difference in the approach to the Third Five Year Plan from the approach to the First Five Year Plan. In 1950, the emergency was to achieve a quick increase in food production. The Third Plan still emphasizes the high priority for increased agricultural production. But total economic development has gone far enough that it is now possible to contemplate, and foresee, the possibility of a bright future in agriculture.

MAIN AUTHORITIES QUOTED OR CITED

Evaluation Report on First Year's Working of Community Projects, Programme Evaluation Organisation, Planning Commission, Government of India, May, 1954.

Evaluation Report on Second Year's Working of Community Projects, Programme Evaluation Organisation, Planning Commission, Government of India, April, 1955.

Evaluation Report on Working of Community Projects and N. E. S.

Blocks, Programme Evaluation Organisation, Planning Commission, Government of India, April, 1956.

Evaluation Report on Working of Community Projects and N. E. S. Blocks, Programme Evaluation Organisation, Planning Commission, Government of India, Vol. I, (P. E. O. Publication, No. 19), April, 1957; Vol. II, (P. E. O. Publication, No. 20), May, 1957.

Report for 1952-53, Community Projects Administration, Planning Commission, Government of India, 1953.

Report of the Team for the Study of Community Projects and National Extension Service, Committee on Plan Projects (COPP), Vols. I & II, New Delhi, November, 1957.

Report of the Grow More Food Enquiry Committee, Ministry of Food & Agriculture, Government of India, June, 1952.

Report on India's Food Crisis and Steps To Meet It, by the Agricultural Production Team Sponsored by The Ford Foundation, Issued by The Government of India (Ministry of Food and Agriculture and Ministry of Community Development and Co-operation), April, 1959.

Report 1960-61, Ministry of Community Development and Co-operation, Government of India Press, 1961.

Review of the First Five Year Plan, Planning Commission, Government of India, May, 1957.

Second Five Year Plan, Planning Commission, Government of India, 1956.

"Suggestions For 10-Point Pilot Program To Increase Food Production-Summary", Mimeo., 16 November, 1959—Ford Foundation Team.

Summary Record of Second Development Commissioners' Conference on Community Projects, Community Project Administration, Planning Commission, Government of India Press, 1955.

The Five Year Plan, A Short Introduction, Publications Division, Ministry of Information & Broadcasting, Government of India, December, 1951.

The First Five Year Plan, Planning Commission, Government of India, December, 1952.

Third Five Year Plan, Planning Commission, Government of India, 1961.

CHAPTER 12

LAND REFORM PROGRAMMES

IN an earlier chapter, entitled "People and the Land", there were reported the historical and statistical facts about conditions which were bound, sooner or later, to give rise to demands for various kinds of land reform. India's land problems are discussed here in a comparative frame of reference with similar problems which face all, or most, underdeveloped countries when they decide to launch national development programmes.

The basic economy of all so-called underdeveloped countries is agriculture; from seventy to ninety per cent of their people depend on agriculture as an occupation. To increase agricultural production as quickly as possible is, therefore, one of the first objectives of every national plan with which we are familiar. In all these plans, land reform, in the judgment of the national leaders and planners, is a requisite to gaining this objective. Because of this, there is a fairly large body of information on what has been planned and what has been accomplished by various types of land reform programmes. From this information, more can be learned about the difficulties encountered in carrying out land reform programmes than can be precisely learned about their accomplishments. We cannot objectively assess accomplishments in India without an awareness of the fact that she is bound to have encountered the difficulties that are inherent in land reform programmes.

The most prevalent common denominator consists of a few core problems, or conditions, which have evolved between tribal days and the present, three of which are almost universal in underdeveloped countries. The first is a feudal type of land ownership and/or control of land. Another problem, partly a result of feudal control, is such great population pressure on the land that the majority of cultivator families must attempt to make a living on very small holdings. The third problem is parcellization of holdings, due to the fact that there has been practically no emigration out of rural areas. Family inheritances have been divided and subdivided, generation after generation, until even small holdings consist of from two to many small tracts. Each of these three core problems or conditions affects the central goal of increasing agricultural production.

The abolition of landlord systems of control is generally the first problem identified by national leaders and planners of land reform programmes. In countries where organised peasant revolts have alarmed national leaders and landlords, there have been examples of Government leaders, with even the backing of landlords, who promoted welfare programmes of various kinds—housing, health and sanitation improvements, etc.—in the expectation that these amenities would serve to retain the loyalty of tenants. The other extreme has been that which has been practised in the totalitarian countries, where landlords have been ruthlessly liquidated. Probably the greatest successes have been in countries where what might be called a programme of gradualness was initiated and carried out.

By and large, it can be said that welfare programmes have had little effect, or have had the opposite effect from what was expected, by raising the sights of the tenants who have increased their demands for fundamental land reforms. The expropriation of feudally-owned lands never, in and of itself, solves all problems. In Mexico, where more than 30 years ago large haciendas were expropriated and turned over to illiterate and unskilled tenants, it took 30 years before a new generation of relatively-skilled cultivators could be developed. In Iran, where the tenants had been mere sharecroppers or hired men, the Shah distributed lands to them. But these former tenants had never had to, or been permitted to, make decisions and the programme was in jeopardy until farm management and technical production guidance was provided for them.

It can generally be said that the success of the various land reform programmes around the world, in which the landlords have been eliminated, has depended upon the roles which landlords have played in the past. In Argentina, for example, estancieros (large landowners) are experts in livestock breeding. Some member of the estancia family is generally an agricultural college graduate. In addition to the technical knowledge which he provides, the estanciero employs skilled farm managers (major domos) who are some of the best livestock managers in the world. If and when countries have disregarded these constructive roles which landlords play and have abolished the system, chaos generally reigns for some considerable period thereafter.

As one looks across the board at the land reform programmes which have attacked the landlord system, he is compelled to conclude that there would have been far greater success in many countries if an analysis had been made of what contributions the landlords in the past had made, or had not made. In Buenos Aires Province in Argentina, several hundreds of skilled, top-farming tenants were selected as settlers. Unlike the large cattle ranchers, the owners of large tracts of tenanted cropland had not provided technical knowledge, or even the day-by-day farm management direction. Tenant farmers were the skilled farmers in these areas. They made these colonization projects outstanding successes because they were now able to reap the economic benefits of their own skills in farming. Probably the outstanding reason that the land reform programme in Japan has succeeded to the extent that it has is because it was literate, skilled tenant farmers, not landlords, who in the past had provided the technical know-how of agriculture and who, when given the opportunity to have owner-operated farms, have automatically succeeded.

It can probably be quite dogmatically asserted that the sudden abolition of landlords, irrespective of the roles which they have played in agricultural production, does not in and of itself solve the outstanding agricultural problems which we listed above. It can be just as dogmatically stated that where the landlords have in the past been nothing more than rent collectors, where they have contributed nothing to the management of the land and nothing to the technical knowledge required for the improvement of agricultural production, it is not likely that their immediate and even ruthless elimination will in any way jeopardize the agricultural production of the country. In these cases, their influence in the past has not only been negative, in that it forestalled the development of a system of effective peasant proprietorship, but it has in other ways sabotaged the technical improvement of agricultural production. Furthermore, it has left a legacy of social and political status structure which, in many underdeveloped countries, has proved to be the greatest hurdle to land reform programmes which national plans have specified and sought to implement.

It is recognized by most developing countries that their landlords have made little or no contribution to economic development. They have contributed nothing to the technical knowledge of agricultural production and have contributed nothing to the effective management of agricultural resources. As rent collectors, they have collected most or all of the monetary dividends derived from agriculture, but have poured little of their accumulated capital back into agricultural improvement. Nor have they invested it in non-agricultural enterprises which would create alternative employment opportunities that would help to siphon some of the population pressure off the land. Such landlord systems have contributed to establishing landlord classes. In those countries where landlords are the elite of the society, they refuse to abandon their status, even to the point where they make poor use of their investment capital. Others, who are less affluent, seek to gain status by investment in land. Because of these socio-economic practices, the development of non-agricultural enterprises does not take place. Population piles up on the land and available tillable land is divided into smaller and smaller tracts to accommodate an ever-increasing number of cultivator families. Because non-agricultural enterprises do not develop, land constitutes the only type of family inheritance, and inherited lands over the generations have been parcelled out with a geometric progression.

The social and political status and influence of landlord families which have for generations controlled the chief economic resources of the country, are far more difficult to change than are the economic rights of landlords or the size of agricultural holdings. The negative influence of a powerful group of "first families" of a country is not so often exercised or even manifested in the planning stage of land reform, but it is as unyielding as it dares to be when it comes to implementing the planned programme. This group is far more than proportionately represented in State legislatures and national parliaments, and in some countries it is the power behind public administration which is made responsible for implementing development programmes. Those at the other end of the status ladder, the peasants, are seldom members of legislatures or administrative bodies. They depend on intellectual planners and altruistic national leaders to plead for, and seek to represent, their interests. But no matter how rationally intelligent or how altruistic these leaders are, they seldom if ever realize the degree of fatalism, and thus the resignation, of the peasant masses which have been induced by generations of enforced low status into mental and social inertia which is very difficult to overcome.

The land reform situation in India when the First Five Year Plan was launched, was that approximately fifty per cent of all farm lands were under the control of large landowners, 83.7 per cent of all cultivators farmed no more than ten acres and almost six per cent of all agricultural families were landless labourers. The 5.3 per cent of all cultivator families who had twenty-five or more acres of sown crops had one-third of all the sown crops in the country. The vast majority of landlords were absentee. Between them and those who tilled the soil were many intermediaries. The vast majority of all small holders were in debt to money-lenders. Many had lost their lands because of their incapacity to liquidate or even keep up the payments on land mortgages and other debts. Very few cultivators' holdings were in one piece. In one, not atypical village which one of the authors studied in some detail, the two-acre holdings of one cultivator were in four separate parcels; the thirty-four acre holdings of another family were in sixteen parcels. The alleviation of each of these situations, and first steps in the solution of the problems arising from them, constituted the main planks in the land reform platform which was adopted in India. Other measures such as reclamation of wastelands, increased irrigation, some colonization projects, and co-operative farming are also a part of the land reform programme.

Some measures for land reform had been taken long before the First Five Year Plan was launched. What may be called land reform legislation by various States can be cited as far back as the nineteenth century. Something approaching a land reform movement was initiated around the middle of the twentieth century. For our purposes, there would be little value in recording in detail the legislation of the various States. Furthermore, it is impossible to identify a neat chronology by which legislation was passed by the various States, either in terms of dates or in terms of problems attacked. Nanavati and Anjaria in their book on "The Indian Rural Problem", conclude their discussion of earlier periods of land reform by saying:

"... Tenancy legislation in all the provinces where it had been enacted generally aimed at granting the benefits of the three F's—fixity of tenure, fair rents and free transfer— to tenants. As a result, the privileges of the landlord were no doubt considerably curtailed, but the benefit of the legislation did not reach the actual cultivator. Tenants-at-will and share-croppers received no protection."

These same authors reviewed tenancy legislation after the early period by presenting comparisons between the situation in 1938-39 and the situation in 1950-51. After having summarized what had transpired before 1938-39, they said: "The agrarian problem was too intricate to be solved by tenancy legislation alone. It demanded an overhaul of the system of land tenures and tenancies and the development of a more efficient system of land management." They described the purpose of the legislation from 1938-39 to 1950-51 as follows:

"Within this broad policy, it was held that land should be occupied only for use and as a source of employment. Therefore, the lands belonging to non-cultivating land-holders or to others, who were not for any period able to exercise the right of cultivating them should vest in the village community, the original holder or his successor being entitled to take possession of the land for personal cultivation only. The fixation of a maximum limit to the total holding was also suggested."

The report of the Land Policy and Agricultural Labour and Insurance sub-committee of the National Planning Committee of the Indian Congress, one of twenty-five sub-committees appointed as early as 1939, should be mentioned here. It was a symposium of the opinions, judgments, and recommendations made by different members of the sub-committee in 1948. The chief variance, one might say conflict, between the members of the committee was on the issue of peasant proprietorship and some form of collective control and management of land.

A generalized summary of these two main points of view is presented to show the ferment of opinion and the differences in judgment which prevailed on the part of various Indian leaders before official national planning began. One line of argument was completely rational and presented the position of those who believed completely in national planning as contrasted with what might be called State and local planning. The rationale of the statement supporting a land reform programme of this type was that all available or potential tillable land and all rural manpower should be organised and managed in such a way as to maximize agricultural production, that,

> "A complete programme of all Agricultural work in every aspect must be prepared, side by side with the Census, and by the same Authority. Available workers (or peasants) should be adjusted according to their aptitude, domicile, training and desire, to the total work, whether on the farm or in the factory.... A fair re-distribution of the Population would leave agriculture with 50%, Industry of all kinds and sizes 20%, commerce and the associated service of Banking, Insurance and Transport of all kinds 10%, Services, Utilities and Amenities 10% and general administration including defence 10%=100%."

A "charter" for working out this balance provided for re-adjustment of all available labour force, or total manpower, of the country to the amount of aggregate work, planned in advance, to be done in the country. The organisation of the management of this force would be a system of collectives called "Compulsory Universal Co-operative corporations". Such a complete transformation would be accomplished in some fifty years, or two generations, and would by the third generation be a fait accompli.

Immediate steps would, however, be taken to reclaim all wastelands and all desert lands to which irrigation water was brought. These lands would be operated from the beginning by co-operatives. Individual cultivators, it said, "must be organised into a universal co-operative association for each village.... All produce raised during any given period, year or season, must be distributed or marketed..." through their Council. There would be a whole hierarchical system of councils—Village, Taluqua, District, Provincial, and National. The report said,

> "These Councils must be closely inter-connected, so as to form a federation, and work in constant harmony and co-ordinated programme of land cultivation or development, within its own jurisdiction, framed in advance for a given term of years.... The Councils must be empowered to supervise and control cultivation, irrigation, manuring, harvesting, storing and marketing of crops raised on the land. They must be constituted on a democratic basis, with the representatives of primary units, in each ascending stage of the hierarchy of such Councils, so that the National Council of Agriculture at the top is a really representative and federal body of experienced agriculturists, with proper foresight and vision for a National Planned Economy."

It was believed, however, that what each one of these bodies would do and would not be permitted to do should be "prescribed in the National Land Law on this subject."

The rationale of this proposed plan for land reform makes it evident that, if adopted, landlords of all kinds would be eliminated. There would be no agricultural tenure ladder with farm labourers at the bottom and zamindars at the top. Everyone would be a member of a producing, marketing, in fact a completely self-sufficient, village co-operative. Reclaimed waste and desert land would be colonized and farmed in a collective fashion, with maximum use of science and technology. The author of the statement recognized that local village loyalties would be an impediment to migration into new land areas and that the rendition of equal division of landed property among male heirs would be a sentimental impediment to complete co-operative ownership of land, but he said that, "in one form or another the trammels of private proprietorship, functioning under the shackles of individual initiative and dominated by the research for private profit must be removed and annulled if this ancient land of ours is to yield all that it is capable of."

Two other members of the sub-committee were in sharp opposition to the rationale of such a programme. One statement said,

"Collectivisation of property for joint farming and joint sharing of produce is incompatible with the needs of intensive cultivation in a country of heavy population pressure like India. Cultivation units of economical size should be constituted by re-stripping and consolidation. Co-operation in agriculture and marketing in all forms should be encouraged in order to get the best out of planned peasant farming, and the safeguarding of peasant farmers' rights.... The limited possibilities of large-scale mechanised agriculture in India rule out collective farming as efficient method of land utilisation. To Russian agriculture the machine is everything. Tractors and reaper threshers are looked upon as the most important instruments in the effort to increase agricultural production. Undoubtedly the population factor and agricultural practice both offer little opportunity for the employment of machinery for big-scale collective farming in India.... The amalgamation of the peasants' small holdings into large collectivised units will destroy the farmers' individual initiative and enterprise, and if the farmers' quota of sharing of agricultural produce does not bear direct and immediate relation to their toil, the present unbalance between heedless multiplication and increase of production will be aggravated resulting inevitably in greater poverty and lower standard of living and farming."

This writer took a strong stand on the liquidation of zamindary when he said,

"Unless the evils of under-cultivation and rack-renting in the zamindary provinces are completely eliminated through the transformation of tenancy into farm occupancy ... the landless class will continue to exist and expand as a dangerous sore in the body politic."

Another member of the committee agreed with these viewpoints and in a written statement enlarged upon the arguments in their behalf. Another member of the commission wrote a rather long statement pleading the cause of the landless labourers and made suggestions not only for placing them on the land, but for labour legislation which would give them approximately the same advantages as industrial labourers. The arguments of this committee and the ideas of its various members show the sharp contrast in beliefs between those who supported a high degree of collective organisation and those who pleaded the cause of peasant proprietorship.

Probably no country in the world had a more complex or highly diversified gamut of land problems, or a greater variety of land tenure relationships, than had India. Zamindari systems, even including Jagirdari and other landlord systems, prevailed in only about half of the country. There were also large landlords in the Ryotwari areas, and many small landlords who did not own or control large holdings. Some of them rented all their lands, others personally farmed some of their lands and rented part of them. Some owners, and even some tenants, leased all or part of their lands to sharecroppers. In addition to all of these, there were millions of farm labourers.

When the Planning Commission was appointed in 1950, it had before it not only the report of the Indian Congress sub-committee on land policy, but the legislative acts and experience of a number of States which had already instituted land reform programmes. Some students of land reform, who knew the experience of such countries as Mexico, Japan, and Russia, severely criticized what they called the "milk and water" recommendations of the Planning Commission. We view the efforts of the Commission in a quite different frame of reference which recognizes the great diversity of the land problems that existed, and which recognizes that the Indian Constitution did not provide for the liquidation of estates, but did provide in every way possible for preserving and developing the equal rights of all citizens. In our view, what was said on land policy in the First Five Year Plan is documentary evidence of the intelligence and care with which the newly-founded national Government took its first step in a nationwide land reform programme. The First Five Year Plan's chapter on Land Policy began with, "The future of land ownership and cultivation constitutes perhaps the most fundamental issue in national development." This was followed by the statement that, "the conclusions to be emphasised are: (1) increase of agricultural production represents the highest priority in planning over the next few years; and (2) the agricultural economy has to be diversified and brought to a much higher level of efficiency." It added that,

"From the social aspect, which is not less important than the economic, a policy for land may be considered adequate in the measure in which, now and in the coming years, it reduces disparities in wealth and income, eliminates exploitation, provides security for tenant and worker, and finally promises equality of status and opportunity to different sections of the rural population.... Problems of land reform may be viewed in two ways, namely, (i) from the point of view of agricultural production and (ii) from the point of view of different interests in the land."

The remainder of this chapter in the Plan was a survey of the situation of each of these interested classes, not only on account of what was known about each, but what was not known and needed to be known if planning for land reform was to be based on an analysis of known facts and conditions. The chapter contained few positive and specific recommendations, but in many places fairly positive and strong suggestions were made, such as,

"Keeping in view the limit for resumption of personal cultivation, we suggest that for areas in excess of this limit the general policy should be to enable the tenants to become owners.... While it is difficult to suggest a generally applicable maximum rate of rent, over the greater part of the country, a rate of rent exceeding one-fourth or one-fifth of the produce could well be regarded as requiring special justification."

We interpret the following as either recommendations or strong suggestions for action which should be taken. The State should have "direct contact with the occupier of the land," whether he be an owner or one of the various kinds of tenants. This meant the complete elimination of all intermediaries, legislation to accomplish which had already been enacted in a number of States. It was stated that "there should be an upper limit to the amount of land that an individual may hold." Land available after prior ownership was reduced to these limits, and land thus made available, should be allotted to those who are now tenants on these lands, and each State should enact legislation providing standards for "cultivation and management of land held by an individual owner." The Plan said there probably should be a limit, varying among the different sections of the country, "below which subdivision (of holdings) is not permitted."

There were five suggestions concerning "small and middle farmers" which were expressed in quite positive terms, as was also the suggestion for co-operative village management. One of these statements was:

"... it is important that small and middle farmers, in particular, should be encouraged and assisted to group themselves voluntarily into co-operative farming societies. These societies may be formed on conditions such as the following: (i) The area under a co-operative farming society should not be less than a prescribed minimum. This could be fixed according to circumstances, as, say, four to six times the family holding in an area. It is perhaps not necessary to prescribe a maximum for a co-operative farming society; (ii) Preference should be given to co-operative farming societies in the matter of supplies, finance, technical assistance and marketing; (iii) In undertaking consolidation proceedings, preference might be given to villages in which co-operative farming societies are formed; (iv) Preference should be given to co-operative farming societies in leasing agricultural waste lands belonging to the Government or taken over from private owners with a view to development. Suitable assistance in bringing such lands under cultivation should also be given; (v) It could be provided that so long as a co-operative farming society continues, no adverse tenancy rights would accrue against those of its members who might not engage in personal cultivation. The object of this concession is not to affect in any way the rights of existing tenants (as they should enter the co-operative farming society as members) but to encourage individual small and middle owners to join together to form co-operatives."

Concerning "co-operative village management",

"Apart from sharpening the conflict of interests within the rural community, proposals for further regulation become in effect proposals for sharing poverty. While the objective of family holdings with increasing emphasis on co-operative methods of organisation may represent the most practical method of translating into practical action the principal (*sic*) of 'land for the tiller,' the effective fulfilment of this very principle requires that there should be a more comprehensive goal towards which the rural economy should be developed . . . . For several reasons it has become imperative that at the village level there should be an organisation deriving its authority from the village community and charged with the main responsibility for undertaking programmes of village development. . . . While it is necessary to safeguard the interests of small and middle owners and permit them to resume land for personal cultivation, some way must be found for ensuring that the tenant who is thereby displaced has land to cultivate."

Thus the argument in behalf of co-operative village management was based both upon strengthening the local village community and providing land opportunities, first by farming the "village waste," but later by complete co-operative village management and operation of all village lands.

This chapter of the Plan concluded as it began, with a plea for the development of more adequate and detailed information on which to base the planning of over-all land policy. It said,

"The stage has now been reached when new measures of land reform should be based on objective assessment of the working of measures already introduced. Since land reform affects every aspect of rural life, the evaluation of land reform programmes requires trained investigators. Within each State, therefore, there is need for some machinery for investigating and reporting upon the progress of measures of land reform. In the Central Government also there is need for an organisation which could pool knowledge and experience gained in the States and could suggest lines for further investigation . . . . To assist in the process, we recommend the establishment in the Central Government of a land reforms organisation. The details of the organisation which will be needed in connection with the implementation of a national programme of such vital importance as land reform and co-operative reorganisation of the rural economy will need to be worked out carefully. We believe that such an organisation will prove to be of considerable value both to the Central Government and the States and will help the progress of land reforms."

We look upon the recommendations or suggestions of the First Five Year Plan as the first steps in a continuing, evolving programme for land reform. We attempt to interpret or assess the progress made in the Second and in the Third Five Year Plans and to report, from the best information available, the actual changes which have taken place in land reform during the first ten years of national development planning.

The Planning Commission set up a Panel on Land Reforms in May, 1955, with the objectives of reviewing the progress in the implementation of land policy proposed in the First Five Year Plan and of studying further steps in connection with the Second Five Year Plan. In Chapter 2 of a report on Tenancy Reform entitled "Land Policy in the First Five Year Plan", this Panel stated that, "The main objectives of the First Five-Year Plan were to secure an increase in production and reduction in disparities." It interpreted the First Five Year Plan to have said or implied that, "The transition to this state from the variety of system (*sic*) of peasant exploitation that existed in India could only be by stages" and recapitulated the recommendation of the First Plan's purposes as,

(1) Abolition of intermediaries; (2) Tenancy reforms, e.g. security of tenure to the tenants, provision of fair rents and a right of purchase for the tenants; (3) Fixation of ceiling on land holding and the distribution of the surplus land; (4) Improvement of the conditions of the agricultural workers; and (5) Co-operative organisation of agriculture with the ultimate objective of co-operative village management.

The Panel reported its findings on each of these fields of endeavour, quite often State by State. Its findings were, of course, diverse because legislative provisions were different in the various States. There is more point in showing this diversity than there would be in an attempt to work out statistically-reported accomplishments. For the difference in actions taken by different States portrays the results of the methods of land reform which have been undertaken in India in contrast to national totalitarian programmes. Because reform was not by edict but by legislation (State not national legislation), it was to be expected, as the

Panel reported, that "The implementation of the legislation was delayed in many States due to long drawn litigation by the intermediaries." It reported, however, that, "The legislation has now been fully implemented..." in all except six States.

Some of the specific accomplishments had been that village common lands, wastelands, forests, etc., were acquired in all cases by the States. It said, however, that in certain States, "Certain categories of non-agricultural lands, homesteads and buildings and in some cases tank-fisheries and limited areas of pasture lands were, however, retained by intermediaries." The Panel reported that in most States intermediaries had been permitted to retain their "home-farms". In most of the States, no maximum limit was placed upon agricultural land which intermediaries were entitled to retain, but in most States they were not allowed any land for "personal cultivation" in addition to "home-farms."

We record some of their findings concerning these rights of intermediaries, which rights, of course, varied from State to State. In one State, where land had been under the personal cultivation of the landlord continuously for five years prior to 1948-49, he was permitted to resume up to 30 acres of irrigated land and 90 acres of unirrigated land. In another State, if the landlord held 10 acres or less, he was permitted to resume the entire area; if he held more than 10 acres, he could resume 10 acres or 2/3 of the areas owned, whichever was the greater, subject to the maximum of 33½ acres. In State legislation where it would appear that the tenant's rights were given high priority, the landlord could resume only a portion of the land leased to tenants, or he was permitted to resume the land only when the State Government had provided some alternative land for tenants. Concerning each of these, the Panel reported that there had been a good deal of litigation over the rights of the landlord to resume the land by ejecting tenants, the right of the tenants to retain a minimum holding or to get land from the Government, the right of the tenant to land even if all of it was not resumed by the landlord, and the right of the landlord to eject "tenants at will" and resume the land for personal cultivation.

This kind of litigation illustrates the fact that landlordism, and especially that of intermediate landlords, was quite universally condemned by public sentiment, even though all landlords were not "liquidated", as has been the case in some totalitarian land reform programmes. Tenants were given the right to retain a minimum holding of the lands which they had previously farmed. In one State, "every tenant is entitled to retain at least three-fourths of the area leased. The landlord may resume the remaining one-fourth subject to a maximum of five acres."

Various types of provisions were laid down in State legisla-lation providing the methods by which tenants would be required to pay for the holdings which were made secure to them. In practically all States, there was a difference made between types of tenants. Fairly secure rights of tenure were generally desig-nated for "occupancy tenants", or "protected tenants". Con-trasted with them were "tenants at will" or "ordinary tenants". Then there were the sharecroppers. Of these types of tenants, occupancy and protected tenants were recognized as having been guaranteed superior rights to the other types of tenants. The land farmed by tenants-at-will could be, by and large, resumed by the landlord for personal cultivation, in some States without limitations. The Panel said that in one State, "The tenancies in raiyatwari areas and sub-tenancies in intermediary areas are not regulated by law." Sharecroppers, by and large, were given no protection and provided no rights, although in one State they were permitted to secure land if the landlord failed to resume cultivation within two years, after which the sharecroppers were given first option to purchase. The Panel reported in some detail on the attempt of some States to guarantee "fair rents". In the summary paragraph of this chapter, the Panel said,

"We noticed during our tours that the regulation of rents has not generally been effective. We have described the rights which have been conferred on tenants under the law in various States. In many States, the recommendations made in the First Five-Year Plan have not been implemented or have been only partially implemented."

In Part II of this Panel's report, it came to grips with the problems which its investigations had revealed, in terms of what it called some "fundamental considerations". It said that in the course of its tours, discussions with landlords had revealed that this group argued that agricultural production would suffer if their holdings were divided and allotted to numerous small cultivators:

> "The landlords have made little contribution to the development of land in the past; they did not consider it necessary as they could obtain considerable incomes by letting the land to tenants on extortionate rents. Whatever investments were made went to the acquisition of land and not towards providing facilities for increased production or improvement of the conditions of the cultivators. For a different reason, the present situation is also not conducive to any large-scale investment on land under the personal cultivation of big land-holders who are merely marking time and only desire adequate compensation for the value of their lands."

If, on the other hand, instead of receiving outright compensation, landlords were granted the privilege of personally farming the land, the Panel believed that they might do so by the use of hired labourers or sharecroppers and would thus in fact lead to greater fragmentation of cultivated holdings. It reported its findings on what had happened in a particular State when landlords were permitted to resume lands for "personal cultivation", when it said they had observed,

> "that in all cases personal cultivation admits of cultivation through servants or hired labourers.... Defective definitions of the expressions 'personal cultivation' and 'tenant' have in many cases, rendered the tenancy law very largely ineffective. Many people who had never engaged themselves in actual operation of cultivation and in some cases were living in distant towns, have resumed land by ejecting tenants on the ground of personal cultivation and got the lands cultivated by hired labour or through partners remunerated by a share of the produce."

The Panel laid down its own criteria for personal cultivation, namely, (a) that the cultivator should take the risks of cultivation, (b) should personally supervise cultivation and (c) should be a person who himself is engaged principally in agricultural operations. It said,

"Where an owner meets the entire risk of cultivation but does not reside in the village and exercises personal supervision effectively, he should have an opportunity to take up residence in village. With regard to future arrangements, while the three conditions described above represent the goal which should gradually be achieved, it is not necessary at this stage to insist upon the performance of minimum labour provided the owner meets the entire risk of cultivation, resides in the village and personally supervises agricultural operations."

This sounded as though it were a compromise with the landlords. The members of this expert group, however, apparently felt that if the owner of the land was willing to take a personal interest, that was a great safeguard against purely exploitative landlordism. At the same time it offered some safeguard against the probability that all-out distribution of land to the tillers would, for some time to come, result in chaotic and decreased agricultural production. It was convinced that to follow the widest possible distribution of the land, not only to the tenants but to the landless labourers, would so greatly increase the number of "diminutive holdings" as to reduce all cultivators to the destiny of subsistence farmers and would thus fail to develop capital out of agricultural production or to attract capital investment in agriculture. The committee believed, however, that the argument on behalf of complete resumption of ownership by landlords under the promise of "personal cultivation" was neither honest nor practical. Few landlords had in the past proven proficient in stimulating and directing increased agricultural production, and it was doubted that they had either the personal desire or the technical knowledge to do so.

The Panel had divided itself into four sub-committees, each to deal with an area of land reform which was already under way: Tenancy Reforms; Size of Holdings; Problems of Reorganisation; and Bhoodan. The committees held discussions, made field investigations, and described what had been attempted, what had and had not been accomplished. There was some duplication and some difference between the suggestions and recommendations of the different sub-committees. Not all of the recommendations or suggestions of some of the sub-committees were unanimously agreed to by all of their members. There was quite general consensus in the over-all report of the Panel that the economic and social dividends of cultivation should accrue to the tillers of the soil. It was recognized, however, that an attempt to provide employment opportunity for all available tillers would require the most efficient organisation of both labourers and land. The report said:

"The implementation of the recommendations made by the Committee on Tenancy Reforms and the Committee on Size of Holdings will ameliorate the economic and social conditions of the cultivators. The possibilities of their influencing the social and economic conditions will, however, soon get exhausted.... There is a large under-employed or unemployed population which subsists on land. On the other hand, there is a large employment potential.... Even if the employment opportunities in the urban areas expand more rapidly than can be anticipated, for many years to come any appreciable reduction in the pressure of population on land does not seem feasible. We have, therefore, to think for the immediate future in terms of mobilising the man-power for the development of the available land and the ancillary activities and intensification of agriculture."

The Panel, therefore, reasoned that agriculture should be so reorganised as to utilize the maximum amount of adult labour on the land; to increase in every way possible the amount of available agricultural land; and to bring to both the agricultural worker and the land the best which both science and management could provide. It was the logic of this thinking which led to prescriptions for co-operative farming and co-operative village management.

The first few sentences under the sub-topic, "Co-operative Farming", were as follows:

"The most urgent problem of re-organisation of agriculture relates to a change in the pattern of land use. In a fairly large unit of management several wasteful operations can be eliminated, costs reduced, and better planning and use of land obtained by the application of scientific knowledge and improved techniques. It is easier to secure financial resources for production purposes. If economic holdings are grouped into larger units of operation through co-operative activity the economies and advantages of large-scale organisation become available and it is possible to utilise more fully, with comparatively less capital investment, the surplus manpower in the intensification of agriculture, the improvement of land, houses and roads and other developmental activities. The other advantage would be that a considerable amount of industrial work for self-use could be organised very much better in these co-operatives."

Village management would also, of course, be co-operative, not only for agricultural production and any other type of economic enterprises but for social improvements of all kinds.

No matter what any critic may think of the rationalizations about, and faith in, co-operatives, he must admit that the Panel faced the fact that rural manpower had to be employed in agriculture and such other enterprises as could be developed in villages. The Panel approved both co-operative farming and co-operative village management, not as universal blueprints for the solution of all land problems, but as what was believed to be the only way by which some very large sectors of the rural population could be effectively utilized in the task of increasing agricultural production, and at the same time be free from domination and exploitation by others who, in the past, had made no major contribution to economic production, but had contributed a great deal to the injustice to which these weakest sectors of the rural population had been subjected. While the document containing the reports of the sub-committees of the Panel was not published before the Second Five Year Plan was issued, its work was largely done and its findings known by the Planning Commission. The Second Five Year Plan not only utilized the findings, but largely followed the suggestions and recommendations of this Panel.

The chapter, "Land Reform and Agrarian Reorganisation", of the Second Five Year Plan is a statement of the situation in 1956. This chapter, together with the chapter on "Development of Co-operation" which followed, presented a summary of what at that moment was known about the progress that had been made in every phase of land reform which had been advocated in the First Five Year Plan. It utilized not only the findings of the Panel on Land Reforms, but presented considerable additional factual information. It is, therefore, a restatement of the land policy, an assessment of progress made, and a clear statement of what had become the central core of not only India's land policy, but of her whole agrarian reorganisation. We cite here only a few broad diagnostic and prescriptive generalizations.

Intermediaries had been largely eliminated by the end of the first five-year period. Many varieties of tenancies had been eliminated and many tenants and subtenants had become owners or had been given the right to do so. A number of States had passed laws setting ceilings on holdings. Equities of former landholders had not been expropriated; all of those who could prove ownership were compensated, generally by State bonds, which were to be amortized by land tax revenues on land then in the hands of new owners. All of these steps would, however, when universally accomplished (a step not yet reached), only clear the ground for positive and progressive action for technical improvement of agricultural production and better management of land resources.

Both for purposes of increased agricultural production and equity among those who must be depended upon to provide that increase, the problem of small economic holdings has been found the most difficult to solve. To divide available land equally among all those who needed to be provided with land would lead to an even greater parcellization of holdings. To divide the land into economically viable farm units would not provide more than one-half of the agricultural families with farms. As the Plan said, even if urban employment far exceeds what can be expected in the foreseeable future, there will be no escape from choosing between these alternatives or finding a way to maximize the assets and minimize the liabilities of each. This was the problem with which the Second Plan wrestled. It said:

"Against the background of these considerations, the objectives of land reform are twofold: firstly, to remove such impediments upon agricultural production as arise from the character of the agrarian structure; and secondly, to create conditions for evolving, as speedily as may be possible, an agrarian economy with high levels of efficiency and productivity. These aspects are interrelated, some measures of land reform bearing more directly on the first aim, others to a greater extent on the second."

The widespread and diversified interest of what may be called the "general public" in all problems of land reform, including the issue of co-operative farming, can be gauged by reporting public discussion—by political parties, by newspaper editors and columnists, and in articles in various periodicals. A "land reform" climate created by public discussion and controversy between the issuance of the First and the Third Five Year Plans is difficult to analyze and report because it has been expressed in hundreds if not thousands of published statements. Needless to say, we cannot take space to document what we shall say by citation to all newspaper comments, editorials, reports of public speeches and the like. We shall first restate the basic issues of land reform as they were universally recognized in India and then report in a general way public and newspaper discussion of these issues.

The issues in order of the logic of development were (1) the elimination of intermediaries, (2) the transfer of ownership to tillers of the soil, or those who would take the risks of and supervise agricultural production, (3) ceilings on holdings, to guard against exploitation of others by large holders, and to make the maximum use of land available for distribution. These three were basic issues of equity and justice, but they also involved the issue of the ways to increase agricultural production. There were other issues which had to do primarily with increased agricultural production, but to which justice and equity were corollary issues. All of these issues, by and large, could be grouped under the heading "farm organisation and management", or as the Plan stated it, the "reorganisation of agrarian structure". The sub-issues of this basic issue might be listed as follows: (1) The issue of peasant proprietorship, with each holder managing his own farm enterprise, or collective management of some kind; (2) the maximum utilization of rural manpower versus, if not maximum, at least greater, mechanization. In any case, the necessity of elimination of extreme parcellization by consolidation of holdings was accepted. In addition to these was the question of equity and the maximum utilization of rural manpower, and the issue of justice to those families who had for generations owned land.

Some of the issues or problems relating to land reform, it might be said, were no longer subject to debate. It had been already decided, for instance, that there would be no outright expropriation of the ownership of landlords. Those with property rights would be compensated. The State would issue them bonds, and these bonds would be converted out of the money that new landowners would pay for the land which they were receiving, this to be collected as taxes on their land. There were discussions over the ten-year period between the issuance of the First and the Third Five Year Plans on compensation, but by and large that issue had been settled before the First Five Year Plan was issued.

One of the first positive statements of an issue was that the food crisis required that land reform legislation remove, as controllers of agricultural production, the middle-men-zamindars, jagirdars, and all other intermediaries—who were not real agricultural entrepreneurs, much less tillers of the soil. We have earlier briefly described the provisions under which large holders would be permitted to retain a certain amount of land if they were real agricultural entrepreneurs, the first of the two basic requisites. Before they had had time to prove that they were effectively meeting either of these requisites, however, some of them, and some others with whom they had influence, began to argue that the prescribed ceiling on land holdings would jeopardize agricultural production; that it would lead to even greater parcellization of holdings, and that it would automatically reduce cultivator families to below-poverty levels of living. This argument undoubtedly stated a real problem, but it also reflected the biased opposition of previously large landholders.

Jagirdars were slow in registering their resumption rights and thereby delayed distribution of land to tenants. A newspaper headline as late as 1961 referring to Rajasthan read, "Are Jagirdars Still a Feudal Force?" In one State, large landlord owners organised overtly to promote higher ceilings on land, argued for 40 and 50 acres instead of the 30 acres which was generally advocated, and argued that such holders should be permitted to farm as much land as would yield 5,000 rupees of family income (about $1,000). Side by side with these arguments were the pleas of those who wanted the widest possible distribution of land. Leading this argument were Communist groups and what were generally called "other leftwing organisations".

It was argued that powerful landlord families influenced those who were formulating land reform legislation; that under the influence of these landholders, some State legislators were "prescribing a more than usual tortuous procedure" for the enactment of land reform legislation. One newspaper article in 1957 recorded an instance in which the high court had to override a revenue official who was unduly influenced by powerful landholders. Another headline was, "Reactionaries Bid to Thwart Land Reforms". One newspaper headline during the year 1958 read, "Top Congress Leaders Are Hindering Land Reform." No issue was more thoroughly and more widely debated than that of ceilings on land holdings.

There were reports of various kinds that subterfuge was being practised in the exercise of rights to given amounts of land even under ceilings legislation; that some joint families were exercising the right to maximum holdings under the ceiling for every member of the family, that more distant relatives were claimed to be members of joint families, and that in all of these practices lands which should be distributed to past tenants were being claimed by large holders and the members of their families. One newspaper headline in the middle of the year 1958 read, "Mass Eviction of Harijans".

The other side of the issue of land distribution was, of course, the extent to which land was getting into the hands of tenants who were to be converted into owners. There was a great deal of argument to the effect that the slowness with which State legislatures were passing land reform legislation and the slowness with which cases were being brought to courts to determine the rights of different parties was in and of itself not only slowing up land distribution, but sabotaging the expected increase in agricultural production; that some of the holdings resumed by landlords were lying idle, not being farmed at all; that some tenants were afraid to insist on their rights to holdings for fear they would be ejected and were, therefore, surrendering or at least not claiming their rights. There was agitation that tenants should be granted a longer period of time to claim their allocations and that it should be made clear to them that they had these rights over this longer period of time. It was said that, in some cases, tenants who had been given land allotments were slow to participate in the consolidation of holdings for fear they would lose their rights or because of doubts as to whether they had the right to participate in consolidation. There were arguments that where such small holders had allowed their holdings to be consolidated with others, large holders were being allocated the best lands. One newspaper headline in the middle of the year 1958 was, "Tragic Failure of Consolidation Plan".

We have here only indicated the fact that a climate for land reform had been created in India and that the issues of that reform were being debated widely. Nanavati and Anjaria, in the fifth edition of their book on *The Indian Rural Problem*, in their chapter on the land problem, had this to say:

"Although considerable progress has been made in the enactment of legislation for land reform, it cannot be said that the problem has been satisfactorily solved either in terms of providing an efficient system of land use and management or in terms of evolving a stable social structure in rural areas. The objectives of land reform, according to the Second Five-Year Plan, are: 'firstly, to remove such impediments upon agricultural production as arise from the character of the agrarian structure; and secondly, to create conditions for evolving, as speedily as possible, an agrarian economy with high levels of efficiency and productivity.' The legislative reforms of the last ten years have only cleared the ground, as it were for the more positive steps which will have to be taken to attain the above objectives. Moreover, legislation is one thing, implementation of the reforms, another.... In anticipation of legislative reforms, large-scale evictions and transfers of land have taken place with a view to defeat the provisions of law. From a broader point of view the immediate impact of the spate of land reform legislation must have been to reduce productive efficiency. Land reform measures should, therefore, be accompanied by appropriate steps to increase the productivity of agriculture by promoting more efficient system of land use. A greater degree of co-ordination in the activities of various State Governments in the field of land reforms is also necessary. A beginning in this direction can be made through the Central Committee of Land Reforms, consisting of the members of the Planning Commission and the principal Central Ministers concerned, which reviews from time to time the measures taken by the State Governments."

The Third Five Year Plan reviewed the progress made in land reform during the ten-year period of the First and Second Plans, analyzed the causes for the extent of failures and successes, and made recommendations for strengthening and, where deemed necessary, modification of previously-stated methods for accomplishing objectives. Because we are interested primarily in the effects of accumulated experience on planning for further progress in land reform, we give only such space to reporting the extent of accomplishments as is necessary for an analysis of the whys and wherefores of what was proposed in the Third Five Year Plan.

The chapter of the Third Plan on Land Reform restated the same two objectives of land reform as were stated in the First and Second Plans: namely,

> "to remove such impediments to increase in agricultural production as arise from the agrarian structure inherited from the past," and "to eliminate all elements of exploitation and social injustice within the agrarian system, to provide security for the tiller of soil and assure equality of status and opportunity to all sections of the rural population ... In pursuance of the second object, in particular, it was proposed that steps should be taken to reduce disparities in the ownership of land—a policy widely accepted as being essential for the economic development of countries with limited areas of land and large population dependent on it. It was realised that with the existing pattern of distribution of agricultural holdings and the predominance of small farms, redistribution of land in excess of any given level of ceiling was not likely to make available any large results in the shape of surplus land for distribution. It was considered, however, that such reduction in disparities was a necessary condition for building up a progressive co-operative rural economy."

On the "Abolition of Intermediary Tenures", the Third Plan reported that this part of the programme had largely been implemented; that this reform had "brought more than 20 millions of tenants into direct relationship with the State and improved their social and economic position." It said that because of the heavy burden that had been thrown on the revenue administration, there had been a measure of delay in the shift of ownership to tenants and a delay in the compensation to previous owners.

On "Reduction of Rents," it said that all States had enacted legislation for regulating rents, reducing them from the once-customary rate of one-half to rates varying from one-third to one-sixth, of the produce. It said that in the early years there was "considerable ignorance on the part of tenants of the rights granted by legislation." It suggested that the State Governments could help if they would make it obligatory that past owners furnish receipts for rents received and for tenants to deposit rents due from them with appropriate revenue officials. These rents (in fact taxes) would constitute instalment payments on the purchase of land by tenants.

The chief problem of guaranteeing "Security of Tenure" rested on the rights of previous owners to "resume" land for "personal cultivation" and therefore the right to eject tenants from lands thus resumed. The review said, "On the whole, both legislation and administrative action have fallen short . . . ;" that so-called voluntary surrenders of tenants' rights "are open to doubt as bonafide transactions," and that thus far there had been found no sure way to make owners assume all the farming risks in the operation of lands which they had resumed for personal cultivation.

In the sub-section of the chapter dealing with "Resumption of Tenancies", the review reported that landlords who were generally given five years for resumption of holdings had created sustained insecurity on the part of the tenants who could not know when, or if, they would be guaranteed rights to purchase; furthermore, that rights of resumption varied from State to State. In some States, it appeared that each member of landlord families was permitted to claim a resumption right. Uncertainty about this created even greater insecurity on the part of tenants.

"Rights of Ownership for Tenants" were assumed ultimately to guarantee permanent security. The review of progress toward this objective said that the facts were difficult to obtain because it was difficult to know whether tenants who were still cultivating the same land as previously had legally taken the necessary steps towards ownership, or whether the landlords had in fact relinquished ownership or would later claim resumption rights. There was the issue of whether small tenants who rented all or part of their land should have the right to eject their sub-tenants and resume all or part of their land. This raised the question of whether they would contribute to the pool of land available for new owners or might themselves acquire more land. In some States, the implementation of new legislation had been stayed until some or all of these issues could be legally settled. In the meantime, tenants had little or no guarantee of ultimate ownership.

It is easy to understand how the issue of a "Ceiling on Agricultural Holdings" was bound to become very important because upon what was done depended directly how much land would be available for distribution to tenants. Not all States had passed legislation fixing ceilings on holdings, and the size of holdings permitted by the States which enacted such legislation varied from as low as fourteen acres on irrigated land to as high as 132 acres on dry cropland. In some States, no allowance was made for size of family. Where such allowances were made, the limit placed on total size of holdings which all members of a family might claim was complicated by how widely joint-family relationships would be honoured by law.

In addition to a review of all these issues, this chapter also dealt with the "Exemptions from Ceilings" which the Second Plan had envisaged—tea, coffee, and rubber plantations; orchards; farms engaged in cattle breeding, dairying, wool raising, etc.; sugarcane farms operated by sugar factories; and efficiently managed, farms, "whose break-up is likely to lead to a fall in production." The only positive suggestion made by the planners was "that the integrity of the farms (thus exempted) should be maintained and their levels of efficiency ensured. . . . "

It had been expected that a great deal of land would, by reclamation of various kinds, become available for "Schemes of Resettlement". The Plan stated that,

> "Far-reaching legislation has been enacted and although precise estimates are difficult to make, it would appear that

the total area of surplus lands likely to be available for distribution to the landless might be considerably less than what had been hoped for at one time."

"Consolidation of Holdings," which it was hoped would solve the problem of extreme parcellization, it had been assumed would make rapid progress. The review reported that,

> "By the end of 1959-60 about 23 million acres had been consolidated.... According to indications given by States, the total area likely to be taken up for consolidation in the Third Plan is about 30 million acres."

The Plan said that consolidation would make its greatest contribution to increased agricultural production if accomplished in irrigated land areas, but that the efforts on consolidation and on increased agricultural production had not always been coordinated.

The area upon which the least progress could be reported was "Land Management Legislation". The Plan said that, "Legislation regarding land management has been enacted only in two States and in one Union Territory and even in these it has not been actually implemented." The subhead for the final section of the chapter on Land Reform was, "Problems of Implementation". The content of the discussion was a rapid summary of the findings of the Panel on Land Reforms, which we have previously reviewed, and a statement that further and continued study was necessary and would be made.

If we attempt to assess the influence on the Third Five Year Plan of the experience during the previous ten years of land reform legislation and implementation, we can do no better than to again quote from this chapter on Land Reform, which said:

> "It will be seen that, with the implementation of a programme of land reform on the lines described above, the vast majority of cultivators in India would consist of peasant-proprietors. They are to be encouraged and assisted in organising themselves in voluntary co-operative bodies for credit, marketing, processing and distribution and, with their consent, progressively also for production. To the extent such reorganisation is carried out at the village level, some of

the difficulties arising from small and uneconomic holdings could be diminished and the weaker in each community could be assisted to raise their standards. It has always been stressed that as each phase of land reform is implemented, it will become possible to give fuller assistance to cultivators in increasing agricultural production and in diversifying the village economy. Greater cohesion among cultivators and the strengthening of the village community will also lead to a larger local effort and more rapid economic and social progress.

"As legislation has been enacted in one State after another, there has been greater understanding of the need for land reform and the purposes it is intended to achieve. ... Yet, the total impact of land reform has been less than had been hoped for. For this there are several reasons. In the first place, there has been too little recognition of land reform as a positive programme of development, and it has been only too often regarded as extraneous to the scheme of community development and the effort to increase agricultural production ... there has been insufficient attention to the administrative aspects of land reform. Frequently at the lower levels of the administration, collusion and evasion have gone unchecked, and there has been failure also to enlist the support and sanction of the village community in favour of effective enforcement of legal provisions ... it has not been sufficiently realised that the reform of land tenures and the early enforcement of ceilings are an essential foundation for the building up of the co-operative rural economy."

From the review of the Planning Commission of what had and had not been accomplished in land reform during the first ten years of development, it should be evident that the Commission, as it has done in all of its work, looked critically at past operational performance in order to obtain guidance for future planning. By such a critical review, it was able to focus attention on those fields of action which had thus far not been as successful as was desired. The ever-increasing knowledge of the meaning of land reform on the part of the public, however, also focused the criticism of those who, for one reason or another, opposed some one of the planned reforms.

The review of past performance, recorded in the Third Five

Year Plan, did not discuss all the factors and types of behaviour which influence the climate for land reform. The best gauge of that climate, as we said above, is public debate on the various issues or elements in the proposed land reforms. Such debate has been continuous from 1950, when the Planning Commission was appointed, to the present time. Undoubtedly it has influenced what is planned for the period 1961-66. We cannot presume to measure that influence, but we shall attempt briefly to report the issues of land reform on which there has been publicly expressed the greatest concern.

There was not, from the beginning, much public debate on the issue of the elimination of feudal landlordism with its multiplied intermediaries. An understanding of the need for doing this had long been recognized even by the landlords whose vested interests would be obliterated. The slogan of the transfer of "land ownership to the tillers" so cogently expressed the ideal of guaranteeing justice that no one dared question that goal. The physical impracticability of guaranteeing land to all tillers, and the economic infeasibility of doing so, were issues which were, however, soon subjects of debate. The issue of ceilings to be imposed on size of holdings was debated almost from the beginning of planning. Many persons believed from the first that the decision to pay landlords full compensation for the lands they were to surrender was too easily resolved in favour of the landlords.

The two issues which, from the beginning and ever since, have been most widely debated are ceilings on landholdings and types of farm management. Opposition from zamindars and jagirdars to low ceilings arose early and still continues. The issue of types of farm organisation and management has led to debate on co-operative farming and village management. What ceilings are to be imposed on holdings must and do depend on State legislation, and there has been great diversity in the actions taken by the various States on this issue. Development officials are still pleading with some of the most important States to implement the legislation they have enacted.

It will be remembered that the First Five Year Plan stated that land reforms would seek to accomplish two objectives: (1) Increase of agricultural production, and (2) reorganisation of the agrarian structure. These same objectives have never been modified. They were, in fact, explicitly repeated in the Second and Third Five Year Plans. The First Plan went into some detail in spelling out the types of development undertakings which would most surely move in the direction of these basic objectives. The undertakings would be co-operative farming and village management.

The rationale for village management starts with the knowledge that peasant society is based largely on self-sufficient, individualistic farming and that it universally uses traditional agricultural techniques and technologies. To the extent that it has become monetized, peasants are exploited by those who possess greater social and economic power than do the peasants, landlords, money-lenders, and shopkeepers. Such a system of rural economy and social organisation not only leads to and perpetuates widespread rural poverty, but fails to utilize human and economic resources with a view to efficient production. Farming techniques are traditional, not modern, and village organisation is more social than administrative. Villages are therefore not capable of initiating and carrying out needed economic and social change.

But the great majority of villagers are cultivators. Upon them must primarily depend the transition from traditional to modern methods of agricultural production and the successful transition from a self-sufficient to a monetized agricultural economy. Upon cultivators, and other members of the local village community, depends the successful, and inevitable, transition from local isolation to participation in an evolving communicative society. Because there will be no early escape from over-population in rural areas, there must be plans for maximum utilization of rural manpower and the most effective mobilization and organisation of village communities for more proficient production, primarily agricultural production, but also handicraft and village industrial production. It is still believed by many that joint-village management is the most feasible alternative for accomplishing all these objectives. Co-operative village management, it is believed, is the only alternative to administered, totalitarian management. Furthermore, it builds on the foundations of age-old socio-economic village unity.

This rationale was presented in a small book, entitled *Poverty and Social Change* published as early as 1945, written by Tarlok

Singh of the Planning Commission. It is quite clear that the reasoning presented in this book had far more influence than did the report on Land Policy by the Indian Congress Sub-Committee of the Planning Commission, and this rationale, modified by ten years of discussion in the Planning Commission, still prevailed in the Third Five Year Plan, although not so much was said in this Plan about village management as about co-operative farming.

Sentiment among Indian leaders, especially those of the Congress Party, has made co-operative farming the chief issue of agrarian reform. All other objectives of tenure are still pursued, but more has been said about, and more faith imposed in, co-operative farming than any of the others. The Third Five Year Plan said:

"The role of co-operative farming in the reconstruction of the rural economy was stressed both in the First and in the Second Plan. The goal indicated in the Second Plan was that such essential steps were to be taken as would provide sound foundations for the development of co-operative farming, so that over a period of ten years or so, a substantial proportion of the agricultural lands were cultivated on co-operative lines. With the growth of population and the need to secure rapid increase in agricultural production and rural employment, it is essential to intensify efforts to develop co-operative farming throughout the country and to realise as speedily as possible the objective set in the Second Plan. In the main, co-operative farming has to grow out of the success of the general agricultural effort through the community development movement, the progress of co-operation in credit, marketing, distribution and processing, the growth of rural industry, and the fulfilment of the objectives of land reform. The contribution of co-operative farming to rural progress will be significant in the measure in which it develops as a voluntary mass movement under genuine local leadership and as a logical growth of community development and co-operation at the village level. Given the approach of community development and the acceptance by the village community of its responsibility for the welfare of all its members, the main problems of co-operative farming are organisational, technical and educational."

Elaborate plans have been made, and many of them are

already in operation, for training persons to assist in the operation of co-operative farms. Experimentation on many fronts in co-operative farming is continuing and expanding.

The Bhoodan movement which envisions redistribution of land has made considerable headway. This movement is based on a moral appeal to landowners to make gifts of land to be distributed to landless agricultural workers or to those whose holdings are small. It was initiated in 1955 by Vinoba Bhave, a colleague of Mahatma Gandhi, who believes that,

> "it is highly inconsistent that those who possess land should not till it themselves, and that those who cultivate it should possess no land.... Since they have no right on the yield produced by them they work halfheartedly. Moreover, they are paid in coin and they do not get even sufficient food. Why should this be tolerated?"

One of his disciples analyzes the ends and means of Bhoodan as follows: (1) *Economic*: the ends: removal of poverty; the means: proper production and utilization of land. (2) *Social*: the ends: to vest ownership in the community; the means: redistribution. (3) *Political*: the ends: peaceful transfer of lands; the means: change of character and outlook through possession.

In the case of "Gramdan" villages, another phase of the Vinoba Bhave programme, begun in 1957, all the land and property are to be owned by the community. All of the economic resources and labour of the village are to be owned and managed co-operatively. It cannot be said, however, that Gramdan villages have proven the validity of the type of village co-operative management so long envisioned by Indian planners. But the fact that all members of a large number of villages have agreed to operate as co-operative communities probably does indicate that it will be easier to establish village management in India than in many other countries of the world.

It can be said that there is certainly no fiction in the conviction that land reform, in terms of the reform of the total agrarian structure, is a basic problem. The conviction on the part of some experts in land reform that there does not exist in India "a climate for land reform", we believe is based upon the failure to appreciate the fact that in this, as in all other fields of development, Indian leaders are attempting to accomplish revolutionary ends by means of evolutionary processes. These processes had to start with the fact that there were deep, vested social as well as economic interests in maintaining the old agrarian structure. Notwithstanding this fact, the first step forward was taken when zamindar and jagirdar systems of tax collection were abolished. The peasant's relation to his government is no longer intervened by countless intermediaries who, for generations, have exploited him. It will take time to make the great mass of peasants of India aware of the significance of this fact, and aware of the fact that they need not, and should not, compromise their newly-established legal rights. The fact that many peasants have compromised, or not insisted upon, these rights is a carry-over of generations of time during which they literally had no rights.

In contrast to the Indian peasants' supine attitudes have been the many peasant revolts in other countries and the attempts of Communist leaders to stimulate such revolts in India as well as in other newly-developing countries. Indian leaders know that it may take a number of generations to validate the evolutionary methods they are pursuing, but they consistently eschew revolutionary methods.

For some time to come, millions of families will and must remain on the land. During this time, it can be expected that Indian leaders will justifiably continue to experiment with the evolutionary development of co-operative farming, village industries, and co-operative village management. Over this period of time, industrial development of the nation's economy will create increasing employment opportunities and thus alleviate the extreme population pressure on the land. Hopefully, the development of village industries will strengthen the whole rural economy. There will still be, for some time, the carry-over of old economic, social, and political status and influence of those who for generations have benefited from the old agrarian structure. But their status and influence will decline, and the status and influence of peasants will increase. All of which is to say that land reform will and must be part and parcel of the total economic, social, and political development of the country.

MAIN AUTHORITIES QUOTED OR CITED

Land Tenure, Proceedings of the International Conference on Land Tenure and Related Problems in World Agriculture, Held at Madison, Wisconsin, 1951, Edited by Kenneth Parsons, Raymond J. Penn, and Philip M. Raup, University of Wisconsin Press, Madison, Wis., 1956.

Nanavati, M. B. and Anjaria, J. J., *The Indian Rural Problem*, Fifth Edition; The Indian Society of Agricultural Economics, Vora & Co. Publishers, Ltd., Bombay, 1960, (Especially Chapter VIII).

Reports of the Committees of the Panel on Land Reforms, Planning Commission, Government of India, 1959.

Second Five Year Plan, Planning Commission, Government of India, 1956.

Shah, K. T. and Mukerjee, Radha Kamal, *Land Policy, Agricultural Labour and Insurance*, Vora and Company Publishers, Ltd., Bombay, 1948.

Singh, Tarlok, *Poverty and Social Change*, A Study of the Reorganisation of Indian Rural Society, Longmans, Green and Co., Toronto and New York, 1945.

Studies in Co-operative Farming, Programme Evaluation Organisation, Planning Commission, Government of India, (P.E.O. Publication No. 18), December, 1956.

The First Five Year Plan, Planning Commission, Government of India, December, 1952.

Third Five Year Plan, Planning Commission, Government of India, 1961.

Chapter 13

THE PROSPECT AND PROBLEMS OF DEVELOPING CO-OPERATIVES

It is difficult to describe the development of co-operatives in India with any degree of precision because of the relatively small accomplishment in the direction of what is ultimately planned. To say that India may in due time provide one of the great historic epochs in the development of agricultural co-operatives would be to reckon with possibilities. To say that she has not made as great progress as she had expected in this direction would be relatively easy to document. We shall describe why India's leaders believe that a tremendous development of co-operatives is important and why relatively little progress has thus far been made.

It might be an over-simplification to say that the history of co-operative development in India is the story of a conflict between groups of persons who have attempted to preserve old values and practices of mutual aid and mutual support, which were presumed to have once prevailed in all Indian villages, and the need to catch step with a steadily evolving price and market economy. It is easier, of course, to document the present need for co-operatives than it is to document the social and cultural values out of which widespread faith in co-operatives prevails.

Indian cultivators are moving slowly, but steadily, into a price-market economy. Need for credit and need for well-organised market facilities are a concomitant of a commercialized agriculture. If these needs are not met by organised efforts on the part of cultivators, they will be met by middlemen. They have for a long time been met by middlemen, money-lenders and commission men, in India. As everywhere else and throughout all time, these middlemen have exploited isolated primary producers as they moved out of subsistence farming into commercialized or monetized farming. As cultivators have become more economically enlightened they have, in different countries of the world, overcome this exploitation either by peasant uprisings or by co-operatives. There have been no pronounced peasant uprisings in India. There have been persistent efforts, for more than fifty years, to develop both local co-operatives and a hierarchical superstructure to support local co-operatives.

It is easier to blueprint, and thereby plan, a whole hierarchy of a co-operative system than it is to blueprint methods by which local folk groups, natural units for local co-operation, can be enlarged and thus provide the lowest foundation tier for a whole national co-operative structure, both of which are exceedingly important. Our assessment, however, will not be based on judgments about the desirability of these objectives, or even of the possibility of their attainment. It will rather be a discussion of what has been done and is being done in India to build co-operative institutions.

Experiences in various areas of the world in the development of co-operatives have ranged all the way from what Sir Henry Maine called "primitive communism", small, completely communal village communities, to the outstanding experiences of the Scandinavian nations in their development of almost completely secular co-operative business organisations. Along the path of development there have been various combinations of these two types of co-operatives; local communities, or locally associated communities, as in Nova Scotia, Canada, where the people of local communities first developed maximum mutual aid and then gradually gained influence in secular markets, to giant producers' groups in the United States, which organised for the sole purpose of influencing markets, but have been compelled to conduct educational programmes to make members aware that these giant organisations are also mutual aid associations.

Exceptionally successful demonstrations of co-operatives have been in the Scandinavian countries, where co-operatives were rooted in folk cultures but whose co-operatives have successfully become giant business organisations; and, Israel's co-operative communities, built on a need for mutual aid and mutual support, which are now thorough-going business co-operatives, ranging from co-operative farming to co-operative marketing. The co-operative development experiences of no two of these countries have been identical, but together their experiences provide something approaching criteria for co-operative development by which India's experiences can be observed.

No one of the countries cited as having provided successful demonstrations with co-operatives started its development of co-operatives from the same economic and social benchmarks as did India. Each of them, however, provides one or more elements in the goals which India seeks to gain. Each has contributed valuable knowledge which can be utilized by India as she moves toward these goals. Each has contributed to the authors' capabilities to observe events in India as she strives to reach these goals.

The co-operative movement in India is generally said to have been initiated with the "Co-operative Credit Act of 1904". There were, however, previous acts; the "Land and Agricultural Acts of 1883 and 1884", and there had been a proposal as early as 1882 for the establishment of agricultural banks. The primary purpose of all of these acts was to provide credit for agricultural production. Many other legislative acts were passed between the years 1904 and 1950. The end product of this forty-six-year development was the establishment of more than 180,000 local credit societies with a combined membership of more than 27,500,000 persons.

The findings of an All-India Rural Credit Survey, which reported the co-operative credit situation in 1954, were published by the Reserve Bank of India just as national planning was in process. As we read the findings of this thorough-going survey and the findings of other planning committees, we would characterize the development of agricultural co-operatives over the fifty-year period as follows. First, the enterprise was always and basically a rural credit enterprise which reached down to local people through local credit societies. Second, while it was operated primarily for the purpose of making production loans to small producers, it gradually increased the purposes for which loans could be be made to include not only construction of wells and minor irrigation works, and reclamation, but to support local supply stores. Third, it remained, over the half-century, a government loan enterprise which steadily increased emphasis on the organisation of local thrift and saving societies and urged that as high a percentage as possible of capital for the societies come from savings "among members and neighbours," and that loans should be made only to society members. Fourth, it required that the liability of members for the payment of government loans should be unlimited.

This survey, however, discovered, from detailed questionnaire data, that in spite of the considerable progress which had been made in the organisation of credit societies, co-operatives were providing only 3.1 per cent of the amount of money cultivators borrowed. Governments were providing an additional 3.3 per cent. Cultivators were still securing 93.6 per cent of their borrowed funds from other than government sources such as "professional money-lenders", "agricultural money-lenders", and "traders and commissioned agents". It was thus clear that fifty years of steadily increasing numbers of credit societies had not established co-operatives as local institutions, much less had the supplying of needed agricultural credit been wrested from the hands of economic middlemen. The Credit Survey report summarized the situation as follows:

> "We thus arrive at a picture, of which only the broad outlines emerge from the Survey, of a large body of agriculturist and professional moneylenders, rural and urban; the distinguishing feature of this body is the combination of the activities of moneylending and trading; but, at the margins, this group of trader-cum-lender shades off into a relatively small group of non-trading village moneylenders on one side, and a still smaller group of non-trading urban moneylenders on the other side. Since we have earlier concluded that the larger part of the produce may be assumed to be sold in the village to the trader, it seems reasonable to take that conclusion a step further and make the working assumption that the marketing of agricultural produce is largely in the hands of a body of men who, as distinguished from Government and the co-operatives, represent private interests, and who control both the sources of credit and the disposal of the produce. Often enough, therefore, the cultivator's position is that of having to bargain, if he can, with someone who commands the money, commands the credit, commands the market and comes with the transport."

Although the findings of the "All-India Rural Credit Survey" were not available at the time the First Five Year Plan was being formulated, the Plan summarized the state of co-operative credit societies at that time. It did much more, however. It described the benchmarks of thinking from which co-operative planning started in the early 1950's. We quote from the Plan:

> "In India, as in many other countries, co-operation started as a means of ensuring for the poorly equipped citizens advantages which better placed persons were able to command by their own individual resources. The principle of mutual aid, which is the basis of co-operative organisation, and the practice of thrift and self-help which sustain it, generate a sturdy feeling of self-reliance which is of basic importance in a democratic way of life. By pooling their experience and knowledge and by helping one another, members of co-operative societies can not only find the solutions of individual problems but also become better citizens. ... As an instrument of democratic planning, combining initiative, mutual benefit and social purpose, co-operation must be an essential feature of the programme for the implementation of the (First) Five Year Plan. As it is the purpose of the Plan to change the economy of the country from an individualistic to a socially regulated and co-operative basis, its success should be judged, among other things, by the extent to which it is implemented through co-operative organisations. ... "

The benchmarks from which the development of co-operatives in India had, in 1950, to start, were the following five basic social situations: (1) There was a great excess of people on the land, who needed by some means to become more economically and socially productive; (2) there was a high rate of rural illiteracy, and the economic and social horizons of the majority of village people were very narrow; (3) there was great social distance between villagers and national and State development leaders; (4) there prevailed the belief on the part of most of the Indian leaders, including government officials, that they must and could guide the purposes (even the motives) of the masses; and (5) there was the age-old tendency of socially isolated village people to mistrust outsiders, no matter how good the intentions of the outsiders were. In contemplating what had to be done in the face of these conditions it required first a reckoning with the need for, and inevitability of, change in all of these conditions.

There was the need to be sure that everything possible should be done to speed up the awareness of the masses of their inevitably increasing involvement in what Graham Wallas called "The Great Society". Indian peasants had drifted into their participation in the price and market economy and would inevitably move into this economy with increasing acceleration. There was the high probability that village people could be made more quickly and keenly aware of the significance of this fact and become involved in local credit, marketing, and supply co-operatives, for the organisation and operation of which they would have to accept a high degree of responsibility.

As activities to meet these needs were initiated, it was our recorded observation at the time that in the development of local groups and, thus, the development of local people, there was too great faith placed in the miracle-working capability of co-operatives. This was evidenced not only in the early specification that there should be a multipurpose co-operative in every village, but also in the identification of the problems which co-operatives would be expected to solve. We did not, and we do not now, believe that co-operatives alone or in any substantial way should assume the major responsibility for solving all the problems of all the disadvantaged groups which abound in India. Co-operatives alone cannot lessen the distrust which villagers now have of outsiders, including government officials. These and many other tasks assigned to co-operatives are the responsibility of government itself, and even more of them are the responsibility of the programme of over-all community development. The first evidence of the growing recognition of this fact was seen when the Community Projects Administration was raised to a Central Government Ministry and made responsible for the development of co-operatives and panchayats.

It is chiefly by continuous analysis of her own experiences that Indian programme planners and leaders have made and are making progress in the development of co-operatives. This is not to say that Indian planners and leaders have not attempted to learn from any of the world's experiences with co-operatives all they can from them. Well before official government planning for the development of co-operatives began, Indian leaders began what, over the years, has been a continuous, and in some ways an intensive, study of the co-operative experiences of other countries. As early as 1946, a delegation was sent to Palestine to study Israel's experience in co-operative farming. The Land Policy and Agricultural Labour and Insurance Committee, of the National Planning Committee of the Indian Congress, as early as 1938, gave consideration to, and made recommendations on co-operatives, in a report published in 1948. Since the time official planning began, one commission, working group, or delegation after another has been commissioned to study experiences both in India and other countries. The reports of non-official bodies have been published and widely circulated. We cite only those which have attracted wide attention.

An official delegation was sent to China in 1956 to learn what it could about what was claimed to be the most giant, and most successful, experiment in agricultural co-operatives that the world had ever witnessed. Other small groups have been sent to Scandinavian countries, to Yugoslavia, to Japan, in some cases to study the experiences of all successful co-operative undertakings. The Indian Co-operative Union, a non-official organisation, published a critical analysis of co-operative farming. It published and circulated a brochure in which the recommendations on co-operative farming did not square with official, stated government plans, but which was widely circulated and diligently studied by national planners and leaders. While Indian planners may have, from the formulation of the First Plan to the Third Plan, steadily maintained their ideas about co-operatives, there has been no lack of search for knowledge about, and understanding of, proven demonstrations, wherever they have occurred and of the roles which co-operatives may be able to play in India's rural development programme.

The First Five Year Plan discussed in some detail the merits of "multipurpose" co-operative societies in all villages, co-operative village planning and farming societies, all towards the end of developing co-operative societies as a means for reorganisation of the Indian agrarian structure. The Third Five Year Plan, published at the end of ten years of planned national development, reviewed the achievements and difficulties encountered during the first two Plan-periods and laid down elaborate specifications and targets, not only for the next five years, but for the long-time future development of co-operatives of all kinds. Typical of all other fields of planning and development, there had been continuous analysis of what was occurring in terms of failures as well as successes during the preceding ten years.

In the first annual report of the Programme Evaluation Organisation in 1954—covering the first eighteen months of programme operation—only general statements on co-operatives were made. In its second annual report, 1955, it said, "While progress in quantitative terms cannot be said to have been striking in any area the lines of progress and the variety of tasks attempted by co-operatives are such as should strengthen a feeling of confidence." In 1956, the same organisation reported some satisfactory and some unsatisfactory experiences and said, "For a considerable time to come, it will be necessary to assist the co-operative agencies, especially by providing guidance and trained staff before they can be adequately equipped for taking up these tasks." It identified one special weakness when it said, "There seems to be no effective arrangement by which an advancing agency can check the existing liabilities of a cultivator before advancing a further loan to him, nor has there been any great anxiety towards making such arrangements." The organisation reported in 1957 that some experiences observed by its field men showed the possibility of some advances in credit and co-operative marketing, linking the two and establishing appropriate organisations for both. The 1958 report presented findings on the over-all administration of the community development programme and said little about co-operatives.

In the 1959 PEO report, covering the year 1958, the fifth year of full programme operation, the findings of a special study of local co-operatives were given. The 1960 report covered a study of seven outstandingly successful co-operative societies. The statistics which these two studies presented are not as important as the foci, or purposes, of the studies. The first focus reflected the deep conviction of many Indian leaders that organised mutual aid in local communities had for so long a time been practised in Indian villages that multipurpose local co-operatives would be natural · modern counterparts of ancient village social organisation. The second focus reflected a knowledge of Indian leaders that with village economy becoming steadily more monetized, local village co-operatives would need to be organically related to the wider business world. It has been possible to observe and, in a general way, document activities and publicly-expressed ideas which developed between the issuance of the First Plan in 1951 and the Third Plan in 1961.

In addition to the more precise planning for co-operatives in the Second than in the First Plan, there was a whole series of assessments of what could be learned from programme experiences. Even before the two studies of co-operatives by the Programme Evaluation Organisation referred to above, Sir Malcolm Darling, an international student of co-operatives and a person with elaborate experience in India, was invited in 1957 to again look carefully at Indian co-operatives and make recommendations. In his report, Sir Malcolm did not leave it to the reader to interpolate his findings or guess what his judgments were about the necessity of building strong primary co-operatives and the difficulty of doing so quickly. We present his findings and recommendations in terms of what might be called negative and positive criticisms of the programme as it was operating in 1957.

On the negative side, he said there was too great emphasis on speed, that notwithstanding the argument that India must develop at the pace of totalitarian countries, if India expected to build strong local co-operatives the stimulus would have to "come from below, and on a co-operative basis; otherwise democracy will not survive." He said, "The difference is all-important, for all democratic processes involve a slower pace than authoritarian." He criticized the setting of targets for the organisation of co-operatives because they over-emphasize speed. He criticized overhead pressures and directives because they sabotaged local participation and even led to the registration of some societies as co-operatives which in fact had no co-operative development. He even implied that some societies which were registered were "false co-operatives". He doubted the wisdom of organising large co-operatives because they failed to obtain the active and personal participation of all their members, and furthermore tended towards "uniformity". He criticized the training of co-operative officers and said that, "The first step on recruitment should be to send the recruits not to a training course, but to the field for preliminary training, in order that they may become acquainted with the A.B.C. of Co-operation before hearing lectures on it." He made very positive recommendations for the strengthening especially of local co-operatives, and could be said to have been quite fundamentalist in his doctrine of co-operatives as mutual aid societies. He said:

> "From time immemorial the village in India has been a self-contained unit with strong economic and social ties. It is true that with modern economic and political developments it is becoming less self-contained, but it still provides the best atmosphere for the spirit of mutual help and understanding which should inform every co-operative society. This advantage will be lost if villages with no tie but propinquity are grouped together, especially if, as happens in some cases, the radius of operation is as much as five miles. The disadvantage may be counter-balanced in part by the greater attraction that a large society with limited liability may have for many, especially for the well-to-do. I doubt whether it will have the same appeal for the poorer class of peasant, whom it is particularly wished to benefit. He is unlikely to feel so much at home in the formal surroundings of what will in fact be a bank, as in the familiar informal atmosphere of his own village society."

Sir Malcolm made seventy specific recommendations, each for some particular line of activity. In the struggle between the mutual aid aspects of co-operatives and co-operatives as commercial enterprises, he gave major emphasis to the necessity that local village co-operatives be, in both feeling and practice, mutual aid societies. His report was not incorrect in saying that the sentiment about, and the dedication to, co-operatives would have to become a movement; that is, there would have to come into existence a whole series of ideologies and activities which would develop a public opinion among Indian leaders and Indian farmers about the need for co-operatives.

In our early interviews with a great number of village people we were unable to identify a widespread conviction and knowledge about co-operatives on their part. The average peasant, when queried, favoured the idea of co-operatives but evinced little knowledge about them. He very often did not think of the credit society from which he had been receiving loans as a co-operative. Gradually, however, over the years his awareness of the need for co-operatives has increased. There is a strong probability that it has developed more because of raising co-operatives to the level of a political issue than because of educational work in behalf of them. In the absence of a widespread reading rural public, this may have been the only way the issue of the establishment of co-operatives could be raised to the level of national concern. Doing so through the declaration of political parties has had both positive and negative results. The greatest positive effect has been a growing awareness on the part of rural people that the development of co-operatives should be one of their concerns. The chief negative results have been the extreme and unvalidated statements on the part of disputants of what co-operatives will be able quickly to accomplish.

Public discussion began to reflect itself in newspaper accounts as early as 1955 and 1956 and grew to a crescendo in 1959. Newspaper articles as far back as 1957 and 1958 were chiefly the reports of successful co-operatives. The interesting thing was that from even this early date attention seemed to be mostly upon co-operative farming societies. It was in the year 1959 that the Congress Party passed its now famous resolution on co-operative farming, and it was in that year that the discussion of co-operatives, more often co-operative farms than other types of co-operatives, reached its height. There had, however, been a great deal of discussion, though not so heated, on other issues, such as single-purpose versus multipurpose local co-operative societies, large versus small societies, and what had come to be called "service co-operatives" of various kinds—chiefly marketing and purchasing societies.

It is difficult to assess the progress in the various fields of co-operation in India over the first ten years of national development, for two reasons: first, because many of the newly-formed co-operative societies were, according to Indian leaders themselves, not yet functioning co-operatives; and second, because data are not available to show degrees of success and failure. There can be no doubt, however, that the formulators of the Third Five

Year Plan, for the purposes of intelligent further planning, diligently attempted to assess what had happened during the past ten years.

Agricultural credit societies remained the most prevalent type of agricultural co-operatives. They were the only type of co-operative society on which anything approaching adequate statistics were available to those who formulated the Third Five Year Plan. Primary agricultural credit societies had increased from about 105,000 in 1951 to 210,000 in 1961; membership in these societies increased from 4,400,000 to 17,000,000; short-and-medium-term loans increased from approximately $48,300,000 to approximately $420,000,000. On co-operative marketing and processing societies, apparently no adequate data were available. Some slight beginnings in co-operative marketing societies were noted, some outstanding accomplishments in sugar processing, and a substantial start in cotton processing were reported. The Plan said that out of forty-one co-operative sugar factories which had been organised, thirty were in production in 1960-61, and that 378 co-operative processing units, other than sugar factories, had been assisted during the Second Plan period.

Statistical records on the development of co-operative societies do not provide clues to the basic problems of the future. The first of these problems is that of developing local co-operatives as viable economic institutions. The second is the problem of developing an overhead hierarchical co-operative structure which will service local co-operatives in such a way as to strengthen them as local institutions. In India, at this moment, the overhead hierarchical structure is far more adequate than are local co-operative institutions. For two reasons this is not anomolous: first, because this hierarchy had been built during the fifty years during which local co-operative societies had been given priority in and were receiving credit from government sources; and second, because hierarchical structures can be established by legislative action whereas the development of economically viable local co-operatives, or for that matter any other type of local institutions, requires the education and evolving experience of millions of people. It is to the second of these problems that India is now, and for some time has been, directing major attention. The studies she has made, the facilities she has established for analysing her own experiences, and her steadily more-rational planning for the future are evidences of this major attention. We turn first to the findings of the two studies of the Programme Evaluation Organisation, mentioned previously.

The first study was made at approximately the same time that Sir Malcolm was making his study. It was focused primarily upon comparisons between large and small co-operatives. On the average, the large societies covered eleven villages, the small societies two villages. The large societies had an average of 418 members, the small societies 64 members. As we have seen, Sir Malcolm Darling favoured small societies. He argued that in the over-all history of co-operatives, small societies can more easily practise inter-personal, mutual aid; large societies, however, have the greater possibility of becoming efficient business organisations. The Programme Evaluation study reported that as small societies extended their geographic, (and membership) coverage, they lost some of their homogeneity and previous internal cohesion. The findings also showed that while small societies had a considerable record of prompt loan repayment, the large societies had a better record of the "percentage of overdues". Apparently the hard core of membership in small societies, the 85.9 per cent who repaid their loans on or before they were due, represented a feeling of deep obligation to maintain the integrity of their local societies. The authors of the report were of the opinion that the better record of the large societies in terms of low percentage of "outstanding overdues" was due to the fact that these societies were better staffed and could therefore more effectively process and supervise their loans. This, too, is a common difference between small and large groups. Small human groups, because of a close inter-personal relationship between their members, tend to be tolerant of individual shortcomings. Secular groups on the other hand tend to insist on and take measures to force uniformity of individual membership performance.

The other Programme Evaluation Organisation study was of seven very carefully selected, outstandingly-successful co-operatives. In the final summary of this study, the authors pointed to location, social environment, economic resources, and sound business operations, as the most likely causes of success. We glean from the findings the following social factors and practices

which have obviously conditioned the experiences of these societies and contributed to their vitality as local institutions. All the
societies studied "have developed—in the course of time—from
credit to multipurpose co-operatives." Each society included
among its members "most of the rural classes". Most of them
included in their membership a high percentage of all households
in the village, all but two of them had forty per cent memberships and one had ninety per cent. They all had honest, intelligent
and devoted leaders. They have all had good management. All
but one of the societies had been functioning "at least for a period
of 15 years". We add to these social factors some outstanding
economic facts which the authors recognize as conditioning
factors of success, thus proving that the societies were efficient
business groups. All but one of the societies were located in
villages with five thousand or more population, in villages near
large trade centres, and in villages that were prosperous. Most of
the cultivators had fairly good irrigation facilities and produced a
considerable amount of cash crops. The economic accomplishments
of the societies were good. They had all increased their assets, loans,
and deposits. Four of the seven had depended mainly on their own
resources, had not borrowed from the central bank. Some of the
societies had been especially active in inducing members to deposit
their savings with the society. There had been a steady increase
in members' borrowing for production purposes.

We recognize that it may be precarious to attempt to distil
from these rather few sample studies conclusions about the ways
in which local co-operatives have not been developing as local
institutions, especially when to determine this was not the object
of the studies. To develop co-operatives as local institutions is,
however, in India a fixed objective and is, we are convinced, a
necessity. The studies we have reported upon were made by
objective persons. They were by no means all the studies that
were made of co-operatives preceding the formulation of the
Third Five Year Plan. The Agricultural Credit Department of
the Reserve Bank of India, for instance, issued a report in March,
1960, concerning the co-operative movement from 1956 to 1958,
which also reviewed the findings of the Rural Credit Survey of
1954, the Conference of the State Ministers of Co-operation held
in April, 1955, and the financial outlay of the Second Five Year

Plan in 1956. It discussed the history and growth, and to some extent the difficulties, of every type of co-operative which had played any role in India. We quote from the final paragraph of the report on what had been occurring over the past five years.

"It may ... be stated that the fact that the policies and programmes in regard to co-operative activity have given rise to active thinking, albeit resulting in some cases in controversy, is itself an indication of the dynamic nature and democratic character of the movement which are its chief sources of strength. The ground has been prepared in the country for the development of the movement in all its multifarious aspects and steps have been taken in this regard. It may not be too much to hope that the movement would soon successfully cover the various aspects of our economy and in particular the agricultural sector and help in the economic development of the country."

Nothing is more significant than the continuous and constant planning in India. This is even more readily observable in the field of co-operation than in many other fields. Not only is newspaper and periodical discussion continuous, but as soon as one Five Year Plan has been adopted, commissions and study groups have been engaged to begin assembling additional information on the effectiveness of programmes already in operation and to make recommendations for new and improved programmes. This process is well documented by the records of such activities between the time the Second Plan was adopted and the Third Plan was formulated.

The Programme Evaluation Organisation had begun its study of co-operative farming societies in 1955, in connection with the work of the Panel on Land Reform. It issued its report in December, 1956, just as the First Plan period came to an end. It made a study of local co-operative farming societies in 1959 and published its report in 1960. The annual Conferences of State Ministers of Co-operation reviewed the past performances of co-operation and made recommendations for improvements. A Working Group on co-operative policy was appointed in November, 1958 and rendered its report in 1959. A Committee on Co-operative Credit was appointed in 1959 and made its report in May, 1960. The Working Group on Co-operative Development During the Third Five Year Plan held its first meeting in January, 1960 and issued its report in May of that same year. It is important to note that the assignment to each committee or working party was calculated to bring out, consider, and make recommendations on one or more of the various facets or problems inherent in the development of viable co-operatives.

The 1959 Conference of the State Ministers of Co-operation was in some ways a more systematic review of all the problems encountered and corrective action needed than could be the review of any one of the special committees or study teams. The 1960 Conference was notable not only for its annual review of progress and problems, but for its discussion of suggestions and recommendations made by the expert Committee on Co-operative Credit and its discussion of other programmes and projects which it knew were to be included in the Third Plan. The recommendations of this conference (1960) were, by and large, different from the recommendations made by the expert Committee on Co-operative Credit, although both inquiries were initiated by the Ministry of Community Development and Co-operation. The report of the Committee on Co-operative Credit used a long-time review and critical analysis as the basis for its presentation of what it thought should be done. The Report of the Working Group on Co-operative Development During the Third Five Year Plan was more a preview of what should be done and an expression of hope and faith. It is not an oversimplification to say that the Co-operative Credit Committee chiefly emphasized co-operative production credit. It stated what it believed were clear policies for financial assistance to co-operatives and recommended that the use of external aid be limited as quickly as possible. It believed that external resources should be used only in the growth of new co-operatives like marketing, and co-operatives among especially disadvantaged and backward groups, such as landless labourers and isolated tribesmen. The tone of the Report of the Working Group on Co-operative Development was set by the target it proposed. It started with the hope which had been expressed in the Second Five Year Plan, namely, "that the co-operative movement should be so developed as to bring within its fold all rural families before the end of the Third Five Year Plan."

On the problem of keeping local co-operatives small enough that they could be mutual aid societies and large enough to be viable economic business organisations, the Committee on Co-operative Credit stated that, "The co-operative aspect is as important as that of viability, the co-operative society cannot afford to enlarge itself into an impersonal institution." But it said that "one of the main aims of future endeavour should be the promotion of viable units of co-operative service and business." It spelled out the criteria for judging or measuring viability as follows:

"A viable unit is that which may be expected within a reasonable time to render the more important of the services expected of credit societies both adequately and to as large a number of producers as possible, without depending upon financial assistance from Government except for a limited period. The society should have the ability not only to command the services of competent personnel, but at the end of the stipulated period be able to meet fully the expenditure incurred on such personnel as well as the expenditure on rent, audit and supervision and provide for education fund, reserves and a reasonable return on share capital."

The Committee stated as the requisites for the development and maintenance of the viability of local co-operative societies: "To ensure that the funds supplied are utilised for production, there should be adequate arrangements to watch the use of the loans by the societies themselves as also by the agencies responsible for their supervision." The State government should be satisfied that the society is viable. To these two essentials it added the desirability and possibly the necessity of requiring that members of local co-operative credit societies market their produce through co-operative marketing societies, where payment on loans could be deducted from market sales; that the organisation of societies be on the basis of limited liability; and that at the village level there should be only one institutional agency for the supply of credit. For the future, it said:

"Since the number of inactive societies requiring careful

attention is admittedly large, it will be necessary to appoint special staff for the purpose. Where the number of dormant societies is large, one or more inspectors may be posted in each district to attend to rectification. In States where the total number of societies to be rectified and revitalised runs into 500 or more, one or more Assistant Registrars may be appointed for expediting the work."

The Committee expressed the judgment that not more than sixty per cent of all co-operative credit societies could be made viable in the near future. As we said earlier, the Report of the Working Group on Co-operative Development During the Third Five Year Plan was more prescriptive than analytical. It said in its introductory statement:

"In formulating the plans, we have made certain assumptions. Similarly certain basic conditions are implicit in our proposals. If these assumptions do not materialise or the basic conditions are not fulfilled, it may not be possible to achieve the targets."

The Working Group's Report began with a statement of "Objectives in the Second Plan.—In a country whose economic structure has its roots in the village, co-operation is something more than a series of activities organised on co-operative lines; basically its purpose is to evolve a system of co-operative community organisation which touches upon all aspects of life."

While the Working Group said that, "The programmes of co-operative development should go hand in hand with the programmes of agricultural development," it recognised that even a cultivator has other than production needs, for clothing, shelter and medical care, etc., and raised the question of what source if not co-operative credit societies, could the cultivator get money to pay for these vital necessities of life? It also raised the question of whether or not, if credit-worthiness is to be measured by strict banking criteria, the great mass of small holders would be served at all by co-operatives and said:

"During the Third Five-Year Plan it is proposed to make larger credit available for the production plans of a large number of borrowers many of whom may be marginal or sub-marginal. The risks involved in such lending are obvious and it is not unlikely that co-operative organisations may have to suffer considerable losses. It is also necessary that primary societies and central financing institutions are encouraged to make larger credit available and it is felt that adequate funds should be provided for outright grants as well as for constituting guarantee funds at various levels. Co-operative organisations must also provide fairly large amounts for their bad and doubtful debts funds to take the initial shock of losses. The State Governments may also have to help losses which are beyond the capacity of the co-operative structure."

This committee also gave great emphasis to the necessity of service co-operatives—co-operative marketing and processing—and fisheries, and other than purely credit type co-operative societies. It laid more emphasis on the greater need of the weaker members of local communities than did the Co-operative Credit Committee. It also emphasized the role of non-official organisations, and one of its closing paragraphs said:

"Co-operatives being peoples' organisations, the popular character of the movement should be so developed that ultimately it will become self-regulatory. In this connection, it is necessary to be clear about the functions which the non-official organisations should take over and which of them should continue to be discharged by the co-operative departments. Non-official organisations should be given complete responsibility for promotion and organisation of co-operatives, and training, education, publicity and propaganda. Supervision will also be the responsibility of functional organisations wherever they exist. Statutory functions, e.g., audit, arbitration, execution, cancellation and liquidation should continue to be discharged by the co-operative departments. In regard to registration, however, a section of the Working Group felt that it should be gradually taken over by the non-official organisations, while another section thought that it should continue to be with the co-operative department to prevent spurious growth."

It is not our intention to imply that there was great conflict between the recommendations of the two committees. They were undoubtedly appointed with the knowledge that each would emphasize a somewhat different aspect of the essentials of co-operative organisation. We have presented our review of their findings, at least partially to make clear that both mutual aid and economic viability are essential requisites of co-operatives. Each of these requisites was cogently presented to the Planning Commission in the two reports we have just reviewed. They contain by no means the only information or ideas upon which the final Plan was formulated. The published Plan provides the main source of information for a brief summary of the state of co-operative development in 1962. In a resume of its provisions, in the Planning Commission's document entitled, "Towards A Self-Reliant Economy—India's Third Plan, 1961-66," probably the most generic statement about co-operatives is as follows: "As India sees it, and under a policy agreed upon by the National Development Council, responsibility and initiative for the social and economic development of the village rests equally on the village co-operative and the village panchayat."

The Third Plan further elaborates on what is ahead:

"All villages will be served by panchayats and co-operatives. Through the introduction of democratic institutions at the district and block levels, responsibility and initiative for development are being transferred to the people of each area. Membership in service co-operatives is expected to increase to about 37 millions, that is about two-thirds of all agricultural families. Considerable expansion of co-operative credit is aimed at, the targets being about Rs. 530 crores of short and medium-term advances and Rs. 150 crores (loans outstanding) of long-term credit. The number of co-operative marketing societies will be increased from 1869 to 2470. Nearly 980 new storage godowns at mandi centres will be set up and 9200 smaller godowns will be established in the rural areas on a co-operative basis. Twenty-five new co-operative sugar factories will be set up and greater attention will be paid to the establishment of co-operative processing units for rice, cotton, jute, groundnut, fruits, etc. There is also a programme for setting up 2200 primary consumers' stores and 50 wholesale stores on a co-operative basis. Efforts will be continued to popularise co-operative farming and

3200 co-operative farms will be organised as pilot experiments throughout the country. . . . "

It is thus fairly clear that the intention is to develop all over India two basic local institutions, one of which will be a co-operative, or a group of local co-operatives. The Third Plan says, "Within the rural economy, . . . co-operation is the primary means for raising the level of productivity, extending improvements in technology and expanding employment so as to secure the basic necessities for every member of the community." This last quotation reflects a different approach from that of the First and Second Plans, in that the Third Plan "seeks to relate the next phase of development to the country's basic social objectives and the perspective of long-term economic growth." It seeks to stimulate and accelerate the development of basic democratic institutions at all levels of social organisation and action.

This blueprint for co-operative development prescribes the tasks which India has set for herself. We analyze them mainly in terms of the methods which will be employed if the tasks are to be accomplished. We need say little about the funds to be allocated because the amount of money to be spent will be a relatively minor factor in determining how well the various co-operative undertakings will be accomplished. The task of serving all villages with co-operatives will, of course, require ample loan and probably some grant funds, but the greatest task will be education of the membership, and the prospective membership and managers of local co-operatives.

If what is to be a co-operative sector of the national economy is to be developed, it should be clear that co-operatives will have to be well-established and effectively-functioning economic institutions, and be recognised by rural people as effective instruments for handling their economic affairs and relationships with the other two well-organised sectors of the economy—the official or government sector, and the private sector. The other side of this equation is that co-operatives must be capable of competing in the business world with the private sector and that the government does not make co-operatives "hothouse plants" which cannot survive in this competition. This is not to say that the government may not legitimately render assistance, and will need to render assistance to co-operatives. Governments everywhere in the world seek to build and sustain people's institutions, not only units of self-government, but educational, health, and welfare institutions. But such institutions in democracies survive and grow strong only if they are people's institutions.

In countries like Israel and those of Scandinavia, co-operatives are people's institutions primarily because each local co-operative is organised and managed by the people of each local area. Each local co-operative for business purposes is linked with other local co-operatives in a higher-level co-operative organisation, in which probably only one representative of each local co-operative actively participates. All higher levels of the pyramid of the country's structure of co-operatives are formed in this same way. This means, of course, that the highest level of the co-operative hierarchy is managed by persons few, if any, of whom are known personally to members of local co-operatives. The powerful co-operative sectors of these countries, whose foundations are the many mutual aid societies of many local communities, become thoroughly secular in their business organisation and operation. Equally significant is the fact that it is only in such countries that there has developed what can legitimately be called a co-operative movement. We therefore discuss here the growth or development of local institutions, development of a co-operative movement, and the development of co-operative personnel, especially that corps of personnel which needs to help in the development of local co-operative institutions.

No basic social institution is created by law or decree except law itself. All others are created by social and cultural evolution. It is difficult to observe this evolution except over long periods of time, certainly over longer periods of time than India's ten years of planned development experience. It is not possible to observe, over those ten years, evidences of core practices which are changing in the direction of institutionalisation. Nor is it easy to observe or know about the growth of sentiments which sanction, and are the cement of, institutional relationships. We shall, however, attempt not only to review what evidence we do see, but shall cite historical evidence that there have been in the past in India practices of, and sentiments about, co-operatives and co-operation. In India, and in most other developing countries, which have not yet moved too far out of folk cultures, local institutions have a firm heritage upon which to build. Planners cannot disregard this heritage, and in fact must build upon it if local co-operatives are to be rooted in practices of mutual aid and mutual support.

Indian leaders may have overestimated the amount of sentiment in villages in behalf of mutual aid. They may have underestimated the difficulty of developing the practice of thorough-going, village-wide mutual aid among castes. They, however, know that Mahatma Gandhi had, over a period of many years, done a great deal to develop in millions of village people sentiments about the value, and the necessity, of mutual aid and mutual support, and to encourage the practice of over-all village co-operation. There can be little doubt that there are a goodly number of public leaders in India who share Gandhi's viewpoint, and his viewpoint can be said to be a living tradition in India. Gandhi was deeply devoted to programmes which offered hope of improving the living conditions of the lower economic and status groups. He saw in co-operatives a way of helping the forgotten people of India. To him the practice of co-operation was the only way to make life a little more bearable and to assist the have-nots in their struggle to survive. The insistence on the part of the co-operative leaders of India that co-operatives must serve the interests of the weaker members of the community is probably due more to Gandhi's influence than to any other thing.

From the beginning of planning national development, it was recognised that village economic and social improvement would require the revival or rehabilitation of local village institutions. Village life in the not-too-distant past had been highly institutionalised. Each village as a socio-economic structure was formalised, and sanctioned, by all members of the village. It was the desire of Indian planners and leaders that this institution be revitalised and employed in national development programmes. In so far as co-operatives were institutions in India, they were, however, in general, part and parcel of, not separate from, local folk village government. Because village economy is no longer a self-sufficient economy, has moved some distance into a larger market-price economy, it is believed that two village institutions are now required, a panchayat for village government and a co-operative as a business agent of the village.

The First Five Year Plan did not present elaborate information on the experiences which India had had in the field of co-operatives, but made it clear that co-operatives, like panchayats, were in the future to be counted upon as local institutions. They were no longer to be mere instruments through which government credit could be channelled to village people, but were to be agencies of development. The Second Five Year Plan was formulated after a report of the Rural Credit Survey had been made. It not only followed most of the recommendations made by the Survey but went much further, as this first paragraph of its chapter on Development of Co-operation shows:

> "Economic development along democratic lines offers a vast field for the application of co-operation in infinitely varying forms. Our socialist pattern of society implies the creation of large numbers of decentralised units, both in agriculture and in industry. These small units can obtain the advantages of scale and organisation mainly by coming together. The character of economic development in India with its emphasis on social change, therefore, provides a great deal of scope for the organisation of co-operative activity. The building up of a co-operative sector as part of the scheme of planned development is, thus, one of the central aims of national policy."

We shall concern ourselves at this point only with the Plan's statements as they bear specifically upon the development of co-operatives as local institutions. The two following statements, not too much out of the context in which they were written, describe basic elements in local institutions:

> " ... the co-operative form of organisation ... offers a means of achieving results valuable to the community by drawing equally upon incentives which are social and incentives which are individual.
> Co-operative institutions are the medium through which many activities in the village are to be reorganised and financed."

These two statements get into the edges of the basic issue of modern co-operatives, namely, how local or primary societies can remain mutual aid and mutual support groups and at the same time be sub-units of larger, more secular, groups. The problem identified by these statements is the same as the problem of developing local government, and for the same historic reason. This reason is that one of the main characteristics of societal evolution is the development of a steady increase in larger social, political, and economic units of organisation and action.

While these larger units of organisation and action do not totally eliminate the need for local social and political and economic units of organisation and action, they do modify their functions by taking away some of them and adding others. Institutions, however, are fairly stable social structures; once well-established, they are not easily modified. In dynamic societies, however, re-institutionalisation of systems of human relationships is continuous. Because India intends increasingly to be a dynamic society, the question may be raised of whether her leaders may not be attempting to foster a too rapid change and too early institutionalisation of co-operatives. While it is easy, and necessary, to blueprint a pyramidal structure of a system of co-operatives, it is not easy and probably not desirable to attempt to blueprint the internal relationships between members of local co-operatives. Above all other groups, in co-operatives decisions must be made by the free choice of their members. It is probably too much to expect that co-operatives alone will teach their members to do this and make them willing to do it. A Danish writer states that in the early days of co-operative development in Denmark, it was necessary to dilute the loyalties of members and prospective members to their old traditional folk groups before they could be fairly loyal to their new co-operative groups.

It is highly probable that past loyalties of persons to their own local village societies, to their castes, and to joint families, are a part of the heritage of the past which may be a greater liability than an asset to the development of co-operatives as local institutions. Co-operatives will be undertaking a number of things in which none of the old traditional groups have had experiences. Most co-operative groups will need to be different types of groups than these old traditional groups were, or now are. It is possible, if not probable, that the main difficulty in developing strong local co-operative institutions will be the necessary task of village people to learn how to be loyal members of a number of special-purpose groups; some for the purpose of securing credit, some for the purpose of securing production and consumer supplies, etc. While some co-operative societies may do two or all of these things, they will not thereby serve equally all members of the local community.

No other field or area of rural development so clearly reflects the difficulties of the contribution we are attempting to make to an understanding of rural development programme experiences than has been our attempt to observe, study, and report India's experiences in the development of co-operatives. These difficulties inhere in the attempt to make objective observations. Our study is an attempt to assess not only development accomplishments, but development ideals or objectives. We may be at fault in our judgment that the experiences of other countries can be more largely used than has been the case in India. We doubt that we are incorrect, either sociologically or historically, in our judgment that India is wrestling with a problem which is not unique but universal in the development of modern viable co-operatives. This is the problem of retaining and utilising the practices of mutual aid which have been the basis of co-operatives in simple societies, and the establishment and maintenance of co-operatives which are viable secular business organisations.

There is, however, a difference between sentiments of mutual aid or co-operation among members of a local community, and co-operatives as organisations of one kind of special-interest group or another, whose members join in efforts to accomplish one or several common purposes. We state this difference between the role of community development and co-operatives to indicate our judgment that India will begin to make surer and greater progress in the development of co-operatives if and when each type of co-operative she seeks to develop is recognised, organised, and operated for one, or relatively few, specific purposes. This is the practice in Denmark where some persons are members of ten or more co-operatives. This does not, as might be assumed, completely segment the co-operative movement. All co-operatives are part and parcel of a national co-operative movement, and in most villages there is a well-organised co-operative centre. There is a slogan in Denmark "that every village has three cherished local institutions, the church, the inn, and the co-operative". To the extent that this slogan is a description of a Danish village community, it describes as high a degree of village unity as can reasonably be expected. It also describes the specialised role of co-operatives in that unity. There are efficiency and dynamics but not stultification in this type of unity; a spirit of co-operation pervades village life. The efficient, but separate, organisation of each co-operative contributes to this spirit.

It is our feeling that in India there has unconsciously been confusion between the need, on the one hand, for co-operation among all the people of the local community in order to enlist the organised participation and co-operation of all citizens in socio-economic development, and the need, on the other hand, for viable local co-operatives by which village groups and larger-than-village groups may be influential in the reconstruction of the agrarian economy. There may also be some confusion about the role of Panchayati Raj, by which village groups and larger-than-village groups may be influential in the democratic reconstruction of government.

In India, the purpose is to develop three universal local institutions, panchayats, co-operatives, and schools. Each of these institutions will contribute to village and national development, but each will evolve into a real social institution only as each develops together with, in fact out of, total local community development. This is not to say that there is no need for vigorous promotion of co-operatives. It is to say that the greatest needs for the rapid development of co-operatives in India are, a recognition of the precise role of co-operatives in total rural development, and above everything else, the need for educating prospective members and boards of directors of local co-operatives. This education can be most effectively promoted through discussions among village people themselves, more discussions of how co-operatives work than preachments about, or the detailed prescriptions for, the organisation of co-operatives.

Having made these seemingly critical comments, we hasten to say that there has been real progress in India in the field of the development of co-operatives, and that there are prospects for much greater progress in the future. Some of this progress will result from a recognition that India is not so different from other societies that she cannot, and need not, assiduously attempt to learn about, and even seek technical assistance from, other countries. This is especially true of those countries which, over the last century, have experienced the greatest advance in co-operative development. Some of India's greater progress may very well be made in some types of co-operatives which are not prevalent in other countries, but which may more effectively meet the needs that are peculiar to India. The First Five Year Plan identified and briefly described two such types of co-operation—co-operative village management and co-operative farming societies.

One who has seen not only the low level of living of families who farm the hundreds of thousands of impossibly small holdings, but also the low level of agriculture practised on these farms, is bound to agree with those who wrote the First Five Year Plan, that a major transformation of the "agrarian structure" of India is imperative. He must believe, in fact know, that not only the consolidation of all the small holdings of many individual farm owners, but joint farming of the total owned land of a number of farm families would make a major contribution to the reorganisation of the prevailing agrarian structure. In 1950, more than 63 per cent of all land holdings were five or less acres in size. More than 30 million cultivator families were attempting to make a living on only 18 per cent of the cropland of the country included in these small holdings. India's planning and development leaders have no intention of converting these many, poorly-farmed, starvation farms into collectives and no intention of compelling their occupants to accept employment in a giant programme of forced industrialisation. To them, the rationale of co-operative farming and village management is a more acceptable alternative.

The rationale of co-operative farming is that even small co-operative farms will make possible better and more complete utilisation of the land, better and improved agricultural practices, better patterns of crop rotation, better use of water, profitable use of modern farm machinery, and, hopefully, better business management in farming. These same improvements would be equally or better guaranteed on larger co-operative farms. Better management would be the first requisite. Furthermore, the amount of produce from a few adjacent, large co-operative farms would make it possible for the operators of these farms to group themselves into co-operative marketing societies and even co-operative processing societies. Each of these would in and of itself assist in the development of other needed kinds of co-operatives.

The rationale of business management is that there will be no alternative for some time to come to making the maximum and most effective use of both the physical and the human resources of blighted local village communities. The Bhoodan Movement which envisions complete village management has made some headway. In recent years it has more or less specialised in the mobilisation and development of Gramdan villages. We do not mean to imply that these Gramdan villages can be taken as examples of what the Planning Commission means by "village management," but the fact that the residents of some hundreds of villages have decided to operate their villages as co-operatives, is a reflection of a type of organised mutual aid which could not be expected in societies in which social and cultural values of mutual aid are not as evident as in India.

We do not assume the task of explaining the expressed faith of those who count heavily on the efficiency of co-operative farming and village management to implement a programme of land reform and to help develop an over-all co-operative movement. Our purpose has been to expose the fact that there is the opportunity, and the need, in India for developing some types of co-operatives which are not so greatly needed, and which probably could not easily survive, in countries where extreme population pressure on the land does not exist and where rapidly increasing urban migration alleviates the necessity for the maximum utilisation of all resident physical and human resources in rural areas. Nor is the recognition of this need the only reason for considerable optimism about the possibility that there will be continuous and accelerated progress in the development of co-operatives in India.

As we stated earlier, India is moving steadily out of a self-sufficient rural economy into a price-market economy. The opportunity, if grasped, for the development of what are called "service co-operatives", primarily marketing and purchasing co-operatives, will in due time result in the organisation of tens of thousands of commercial, co-operative societies. These societies will be secular organisations in that eligibility for membership in them will be dictated by what persons desire to sell and buy, not by old traditional groups to which they belong or by where they live. The successful function of these societies will require the joint participation of persons from all levels of economic and social life, all castes, and in many cases, from a number of different local communities. The loyal participation in these societies will not necessarily be fortified by, in fact may be inversely influenced by, super-loyalties to old traditional groups. Anomalous as it may seem, these old group-loyalties may in some ways be blocks to the development of some kinds of co-operatives rather than facilities to be used and built upon. We are, however, convinced that, if co-operatives will grasp the opportunities of gaining and controlling the management of those functions which are essential, and have everywhere developed, between primary producers and ultimate consumers in a price and market economy, loyalties to effective co-operative groups will do more than anything else to lessen the loyalties to old sterile groups.

The primary requisites for developing co-operative marketing, purchasing, and processing societies are: First, training millions of cultivators to become successful farmers; and, second, training a sufficient number of managers to efficiently manage local co-operative societies. The first of these is the responsibility of the community development-agricultural extension programme. The second is part and parcel of this basic rural development programme, not something separate from it. This is to say again that the successful development of local co-operatives, like the successful development of village panchayats, depends on the development of effective, local special-purpose groups.

The Second Five Year Plan wrote the specifications for a local co-operative when it said:

> "Its area of jurisdiction should, on the one hand, be large enough to make it an efficient unit and, on the other, it should not be so large that it might become difficult to secure amongst members the knowledge, the sense of mutual obligation and concern for rehabilitation of the weaker sections of the community and the intimate contact between the committee of management and individual families without which co-operation cannot make a real impact on rural life."

This states, but does not solve, the problem of modern and viable business co-operatives. Nor is the problem solved in any of those countries which have been leaders in all fields of co-operative organisation. It cannot be solved by insisting that the sentiments of mutual aid be equally shared by all members of necessarily large co-operatives. It can be, and is, solved only if and when, or to the extent that, all members understand that no given commercial co-operative can serve the common needs or purposes of all members of a local village society. As was said earlier, the basic struggle, conscious or unconscious, is between, on the one hand, an attempt to preserve, and build upon, the age-old practice and value of local mutual aid and mutual support, which is believed to have been the genius of Indian village life, and, on the other hand, the inevitability of moving steadily into more secular, and wider than local, village units of socio-economic association. We say the inevitability of moving in this direction because this has been the universal experience of evolving national economies and societies. The historic evolution has been, so to speak, unguided or blind. It is the intention of Indian leaders that it shall be guided by rational planning. Planning must recognize the functional division of labour between co-operatives, many of which are organised for purposes of successfully linking the economic interests of local people with the developing national economy, and panchayats, which provide the instruments or organisations by means of which local communities can by self-help and self-direction deal successfully with the problems of local community development. Local co-operatives are essential parts of this development, but at the present, there is, it appears to us, confusion concerning the division of labour between the role of the programme for community development and that for developing co-operatives.

In the final analysis, it should be recognised that India, like all other newly-developing countries, is wrestling with the basic problem of a society which is moving rapidly from an old and relatively self-sufficient local economy and culture toward a price and market economy and a wider range of necessary, secular human relationships. Because co-operatives as human groups require the spread and practice of mutual aid and mutual support, and because co-operatives as economic organisations require secular attitudes and hardboiled business practices, India, like Denmark one hundred years ago, is attempting to solve an apparent dilemma. We therefore briefly discuss the problems which India has encountered in transforming its highly class-structured and village-centred rural people into an open-class society in which its rural people will no longer be sharply isolated from the remainder of their national community. Because the problems of developing co-operatives are similar to, in fact a part of, the development of a democratic social order, we offer some comments on the problems involved and the prospects for the development of a co-operative sector of the Indian economy and the development of a people's co-operative movement.

There will probably be, for some time, the continued lack of understanding, on the part of top leaders, that the assumed unity of Indian villages cannot provide the sure basis upon which to develop viable local and larger-than-local service co-operatives. In fact, there is a high probability that the necessity for, and effective organisation and operation of, service co-operatives will do more than any other one thing to gradually remake the social structure of Indian rural society. We hasten to say, however, that this is not meant to imply that the development of co-operatives is or can be a substitute for all other facets of the community development-extension programmes. It is to say that co-operatives will have a more rapid development, as has been the case in other countries, when they are recognised as part and parcel of total community, and total social and economic, development, rather than thought of as some unique catalytic agent of total economic and social development.

We do not discount the need for planning for co-operatives. We do not discount nor belittle the dedication of leaders to the task and idea, even ideals, of developing co-operatives. We do not discount the need for, or opportunities to build co-operatives in India. We would accept the conclusion of the authors of the Rural Credit Survey that while co-operatives in the past have failed, they must eventually succeed in India.

MAIN AUTHORITIES QUOTED OR CITED

Abrahamsen, M. A., "Observations on Agricultural Co-operatives in India," Farmers' Co-operative Service, U. S. Department of Agriculture, Washington, D. C., July, 1960. (Mimeo.)

All India Rural Credit Survey, Report of the Committee of Direction, Vol. II of The General Report, Reserve Bank of India, Bombay, 1954.

Darling, Sir Malcolm, *Report on Certain Aspects of the Co-operative Movement in India*, Planning Commission, Government of India, 1957.

Evaluation Report on Second Year's Working of Community Projects, Vol. I, Programme Evaluation Organisation, Planning Commission, Government of India, April, 1955.

Evaluation Report on Working of Community Projects and N.E.S. Blocks, Programme Evaluation Organisation, Planning Commission, Government of India, April, 1956.

Mamoria, C. B. and Saksena, R. D., *Co-operation in India*, Kitab Mahal, Allahabad, 1960, (2nd ed.)

Nanavati, M. B. and Anjaria, J. J., *The Indian Rural Problem*, Fifth Edition, The Indian Society of Agricultural Economics, Bombay, 1960.

Report of the Committee on Co-operative Credit, Ministry of Community Development and Co-operation, Government of India, May, 1960.

Report of the Working Group on Co-operative Development During the Third Five Year Plan, Ministry of Community Development and Cooperation (Department of Cooperation) Government of India, May, 1960.

Review of the Co-operative Movement in India 1956-8, Agricultural Credit Department, Reserve Bank of India, Bombay, March, 1960.

Second Five Year Plan, Planning Commission, Government of India, 1956.

Singh, Tarlok, *Poverty and Social Change*, Longmans, Green and Co. Ltd., London, 1945.

State Ministers' Conferences on Co-operatives, 1955-56, 1959-60, Ministry of Community Development and Co-operation, Government of India.

Studies in Cooperative Farming, Programme Evaluation Organisation, Planning Commission, Government of India, December, 1956. (P.E.O. Publication No. 18).

The First Five Year Plan, Planning Commission, Government of India, December, 1952.

Third Five Year Plan, Planning Commission, Government of India, 1961.

Towards a Self-Reliant Economy, India's Third Plan, 1961-66, Planning Commission, Government of India, September, 1962.

CHAPTER 14

THE RECONSTRUCTION AND DEVELOPMENT OF LOCAL GOVERNMENT

OVER ten years of directed development in India, there has been no social development more interesting to observe than the consistent attempt to rebuild decadent local institutions. The First Five Year Plan said,

> "For many decades the village has been the primary unit for revenue and police administration but, as a social and economic organisation, it became weaker under British rule.... The Constitution has provided for democratic institutions at the Centre and in the States, but so long as local self-governing institutions are not conceived as parts of the same organic constitutional and administrative framework, the structure of democratic government will remain incomplete."

Attempts to bring existing local institutions into the organic framework of government, mentioned by the Planning Commission, have revealed an inevitable struggle between the nostalgic idealizing of ancient institutions and rationalized planning. The Planning Commission has been interested not only in developing local institutions appropriate to the inevitability of constant, long-term change, but also as instruments or vehicles for carrying out local development programmes. Those who retained the nostalgic images of the ancient village panchayat, as probably the most perfect example of simple but self-sufficient local government the world has ever seen, were inclined to the belief that all that was needed was to remove the interferences and encumbrances imposed on this perfect folk institution by colonial and feudal rulers, and village revival would be automatic and self-generative.

Local village people revered their local village community and national leaders respected these local sentiments. Planners, however, were convinced that not all local village institutions would, or could, be viable social, economic, or even political units for development undertakings. They were convinced that there would need to be inter-village co-operation and, if a national society was to be built, there would need to be organic relations between local and national institutions. Integration of local units of government with higher units of government is easily accomplished in totalitarian regimes where, for carrying out national development programmes, local action groups are only adjuncts of central government. But India had determined to use democratic, not totalitarian, methods.

In Chapter 5 we presented a brief resume of the history of local rural government; the evolution of District and Sub-District government; and the devolution of village panchayats. We quoted Tinker, who as much as said that, in the more than fifty years of attempts on the part of some British and some Indian leaders to establish more democratic governments in the Districts and even a degree of self-government in villages, the most that had been accomplished was a degree of decentralization of provincial governments. This had, however, strengthened District administration, but had not done much to strengthen local self-government. Even the District Boards, had they been democratically constituted and been given something more than advisory power, would not have been self-government by village people themselves.

We should point out here that the Planning Commission looked beyond the necessity of rehabilitating village panchayats and improving district government. It foresaw the desirability, and probably the necessity, of other levels of local self-government. The First Plan said:

"While the village is the basic unit of *community organisation* (italics ours) over the greater part of the country, for particular purposes it may be found that a larger unit is needed.... How large the area should be and what arrangements should be made for effecting the necessary co-ordination and economy in the provision of services and amenities must depend upon local conditions and requirements. The need for such arrangements, however, exists everywhere and has to be taken into consideration in planning the execution of rural schemes under the Five Year Plan."

Within about seven years after this statement was made, the programme of "democratic decentralization" was launched, which provided for two other levels or tiers of local government between panchayats and district offices. Because the final draft of the First Plan was completed after the Community Development-Extension Programme was launched, the Commission related those elements of its thinking which we have, in the last few paragraphs, been attempting to synopsize, to the development block structure which had been initiated. For a description, and documentation, of what was done to establish village panchayats, and to transform district government into a district development organisation, we turn to what may be called the programme operation's planning and working documents.

We provided in Chapter 9 considerable information on the organisation for the operating of the Community Development-Extension Programme, with a description of the interplay of ideas and attitudes of those who were a part of, and proud of, the district and sub-district system of government, and those who were quite distrustful of the capability of that system and its officials to change what they called "revenue-mindedness" to "development mindedness".

The Planning Commission had said that district personnel needed to be more competent and greater in number; that the technical staffs of the districts were so weak and so thinly-spread that technical departments of government were bypassing them and attempting to go directly to the people; and that there needed to be a greater number of sub-districts in order that officials might travel and "be able to acquire intimate knowledge of the people". In discussing the new development block, it suggested that "sub-collectors", or, where the sub-division system is not developed, other officers closely associated with the district administration, might head the block staff, and it spoke of the "Collector" as head of the extension movement. To the extent that these suggestions have been implemented, the implementation has been wrought out by trial and error in programme experience. It is not possible to present a straight-line chronology of this experience as it evolved toward a clearer recognition of the necessity of developing a real system of local government if the millions of people who live in villages were effectively to make their maximum contribution to the rural development programme. Development in this direction started with the conviction on the part of planners that district government was not responsive to needs of local people, much less that village people had any effective voice in local district government. In the plans to remedy these defects, there was the obvious tendency, if not to bypass, at least to minimize the part which district officers would play in working out the remedy.

There was no organised conflict, or even any overt struggle, between local government bureaucrats—district and sub-district officials—and those who doubted that these officers should be entrusted with the many new enterprises which development required. The local government bureaucrats, in fact, remained pretty much on the sidelines in planning the development programme. The planning and launching of the programme was largely by negotiations between the Centre and State Governments. Those Collectors who sat in conferences or seminars during the first few years of programme operation, for the most part, volunteered very little participation. Visits with them in their own districts and offices, revealed that some of them were deeply interested in, and sympathetic with, the new order. Others, mostly older men, seemed to be sitting back waiting either for the programme to fail or until they reached retirement.

The new community development programme was placed directly under the Planning Commission. All early programme negotiations were between State governments and, at first, the Central Committee of the Planning Commission, later the Community Projects Administration. From the public documents of these organisations can be traced the evolution of the accommodation being wrought out. In retrospect, it can be generalized that there were three phases in the evolution of the accommodation which was finally accomplished. First was a trend in the direction of setting up and operating a development programme administration which paralleled the old district government administration. Second was a slow but gradual coalescing of the two lines of administration. Finally, there was something approaching the establishment of a whole new system of local government. It would be incorrect, however, to say that the rural development programme administration evolved was a completely new line of administration, because the new administrative positions established were placed in the State and district offices. Such was by no means universal in the case of the below-district-level units of development programme operation, where day-by-day development activities were carried out.

One of the first communications (25 March, 1952) from the Planning Commission to all State governments said that, "At the State level there should be a State Development Committee consisting of the Chief Minister and Ministers in charge of the Development" and various technical programmes. It said that, "The Development Commissioner/Development Secretary of the State should act as Secretary of this Committee;" and "be the officer responsible for ensuring co-ordination at the headquarters of the State Government...." that at the district level there should be a District Development Officer with the status of an Additional Collector. This communication was followed in less than a month (18 April, 1952) with a communication from the Administrator of the Community Projects Administration which had now been established, notifying all State governments that a new cadre of Project Executive Officers, each in charge of some 300 villages, with two assistant Project Executive Officers, each of them in charge of 100 villages, was being set up. The communication said that it was intended that these officers would respectively have the status of Sub-Divisional Officer and Deputy Collector. It did not specify that they should have been district or sub-district officers. In practice, it turned out that most of them were recruited from these cadres. The communication said that those selected to be Project Officers would be given a short course training for their jobs.

Thus something approaching a second line of command for development programme administration was to be established. This line of command was clearly described by the Second State Development Commissioners' Conference when it said,

> "There will be a direct link from the Development Commissioner to the Village-Level Worker in the following way: Development Commissioner - District Development/ Planning Officer—Block Extension Officer—Agricultural Extension Officer at the Block level—Village-Level Worker."

In November of that same year, a letter from the Deputy Secretary to the Government of India, addressed to All Development Commissioners, said, "With regard to the administrative procedure to be followed in the drawing up and execution of the schemes, while there is nothing to be gained by duplication of staff, and there can be no doubt that the existing agencies should be utilised as far as possible, it is desirable that the normal administrative procedure should be adapted as far as possible to the special requirements of community projects, in the interest particularly of speedy execution." When development blocks were substituted for chief project areas, and Block Development Officers were substituted for Project Executive Officers, block administration in some States operated fairly free from district office direction.

The First Five Year Plan, in a section on the "Role of Local Bodies in Development Programmes", pointed out the vital role that local self-governing bodies should play in development. A statement which might be interpreted as predictive of the third phase of development was, "It may also be necessary to work out suitable arrangements for linking local self-governing bodies at different levels with one another, for instance, village panchayats with district or sub-divisional local boards." Such boards or advisory committees were later established at block and district levels, but they were not linked to each other. Furthermore, the evidences are that they had little influence on district and block administration. The members of these committees were expected to be active participants in development work at all stages, from planning to execution, but the first Evaluation Report said, "There are very few instances indeed in which these committees have worked as they were intended to work." And further, that "Even after the lapse of a year advisory committees had not been set up in some states. Few committees met regularly." The second Evaluation Report said,

> " ... by and large the present pattern of district and project advisory committees cannot be said to have been a proved success. The main points for consideration are (1) whether advice is appropriately sought from representatives of district and project opinion or from legislators whose representative claims are based on wider and somewhat different grounds,

and who in most cases are too much preoccupied to take a continuous interest in the development of particular project areas; and (2) whether departmental officers in the District and Project areas are given an opportunity to share authority with responsibility or they are merely expected to be collaborators of project officers. . . . "

From the third Evaluation Report:

"While Advisory Committees continue to be ineffective in a large number of the projects, there has been improvement in several cases, largely as a result of such organisational improvements. . . . Steps for re-organisation of these committees should therefore be seen as part of the arrangements contemplated for improving inter-departmental coordination, and especially for securing effective association of popular institutions in the development programme."

The fourth (1957) Evaluation Report said,

"Advisory committees at the block and district levels are still to play the role that was expected of them in the development programme. This is due partly to defective membership and partly to continuing reluctance of the official machinery to make full and positive use of the Advisory Committees."

It is only for analytical purposes that we describe the second phase of programme administration evolution, which was not a result of one but of many decisions. Furthermore, various of these decisions were made by different States at different times. The product of all these decisions was an increasing participation of district officers and offices in development programme operation. The result of various types of accommodation to the necessities of a steadily-expanding development programme was stated in the fourth Evaluation Report, as follows:

" . . . coordination at the block level is now becoming more a by-product of coordination at the district level, with the District Collector—directly, or assisted by a District Development Officer—exercising more coordination over the technical heads of development departments in the district and more control over the development work of the project staff in his district. The district officer is thus tending to become the king-pin of the development programme. . . . "

But even if this statement is taken at face value, it was not adequate evidence that local self-government was being evolved. District and block officials were all still employees of State governments. Advisory committees and boards were not in and of themselves governments. It remained for the third phase of evolution to initiate the development of real units of local self-government.

The third phase was a real evolution, based on both foresight and hindsight. The Planning Commission had evidenced foresight in the First Five Year Plan when it said that it would probably be found necessary to have larger units of local organisation than village panchayats. It went much further in the Second Plan when it pointed out that there were 380,000 villages in India with populations of not more than 500, and an additional 104,268 with populations of not more than 1,000, and said, the "question of combining existing villages into units with a population of about 1000 deserves to be examined." This was a forthright recognition that the stereotyped concept of a panchayat in each of the 550,000 villages would not alone provide an efficient nationwide system of local government.

The Planning Commission gave a whole chapter in the Second Plan to "District Development Administration" and laid down five criteria or guide lines for the reorganisation of district administration. The following two of these five were especially germane to the establishment of local government. They were, "establishment for development at the village level of an appropriate agency which derives its authority from the village community;" and "linking up, in relation to all development work, of local self-governing institutions with the administrative agencies of the State Government."

Typical of India's practice of continuous self-examination of its own programme operating experience was a recommendation that a special investigation under the auspices of the National Development Council be made of the experiences of different States. Part of the main focus of this investigation would be a study of "the future structure and functions of district boards with reference to the functions of village panchayats and to those of various administrative agencies functioning in the district."

Such an investigation was instituted. Its findings provide the pattern for the development of what we see as the third phase of planning for the establishment of a system of real local self-government. The findings and recommendations contained in the three-volume published report of the "Team for the Study of Community Projects and National Extension Service", were so cogent and so pointed that we offer liberal quotations from that report. In relation to the weaknesses of district administrative units as units of local government, the report said:

> "The district boards ... have also been handicapped by having too large a charge to receive their detailed attention. ... The very size of its charge compels delegation of a very large area of authority and discretion to its own officers, so that the effect is to replace State officers drawn from larger cadres by officers of limited experience in restricted fields. The tendency has been for the States to take over many of the functions of the district boards; even so, there is a sort of overlapping dyarchy prevailing in certain aspects of administration. ... Nor will it be easy, convenient or practicable to link the village panchayat directly to the district board. In many States a district consists literally of hundreds of village panchayats and even in those where the village panchayats are large in jurisdiction, their number is inconveniently large. Under these circumstances the link between the district board and its constituent village panchayats cannot be a live one."

The above quotations state fairly clearly two significant things—one, that the district unit of administration encompassed so large a number of villages that it could not effectively relate itself to panchayats; and second, in essence it said, as the development programme had increased in magnitude, administrative officials above the district had further centralized administration by taking over many functions which normally would have gone through district administrations. After a brief discussion of existing rural self-governing bodies, the report stated:

> "With this background, we have to consider whether

the time has not arrived to replace all these bodies by a single representative and vigorous democratic institution to take charge of all aspects of development work in the rural areas. Such a body, if created, has to be statutory, elective, comprehensive in its duties and functions, equipped with necessary executive machinery and in possession of adequate resources. It must not be cramped by too much control by the Government or Government agencies. It must have the power to make mistakes and to learn by making mistakes, but it must also receive guidance which will help it to avoid making mistakes. In the ultimate analysis, it must be an instrument of expression of the local people's will in regard to the local development. . . . It is not theory or dogma which is impelling us to make these recommendations but practical considerations. Democracy has to function through certain elective machinery but the democratic government operating over large areas through its executive machinery cannot adequately appreciate local needs and circumstances. It is, therefore, necessary that there should be a devolution of power and a decentralisation of machinery and that such power be exercised and such machinery controlled and directed by popular representatives of the local area."

The detailed recommendations of the Study Team were for a three-tier system of local government, the first tier to consist of village panchayats; the second tier, of panchayat samitis (blocks); and the third, of zila parishads (districts). The pivot or hinge in the three-tier system, for development programme operation, would be the panchayat samiti. The Study Team recommended, "that all Central and State funds spent in a block area should invariably be assigned to the panchayat samiti to be spent by it directly or indirectly, except to an institution, assistance to which is either beyond the panchayat samiti's functions or its financial resources." Since panchayat samiti areas would generally, if not always, be identical with development block areas, this recommendation implied that the panchayat samiti, a democratically-elected body, but an administrative unit of State government, would direct local development programmes.

The Team's proposal was that "the panchayat samiti should be constituted by indirect elections from the village panchayats." It said, "The panchayats within the block area can be grouped together in convenient units, which can be Gram Sewaks' circles, and the panches of all the panchayats in each of these units shall elect from amongst themselves a person or persons to be a member or members of the panchayat samiti." It, of course, must be recognized that this would be a far cry from the idea of each village, large or small, having its own presumed self-contained local government. It would, however, mean that each local area, with a population of from 5,000 to 10,000, would be almost completely self-governed. It would not mean that the "little folk village societies" would be disregarded or would have no semblance of local self-government. It would mean that each of them would have a mediator between it and a distant district office.

The Team listed the different sources of financial support for samiti government, including "voluntary public contribution" and "grants made by government". It said, "we suggest that . . . the land revenue assigned to the panchayat samiti and the village panchayat should not be less than forty % of the State's net land revenue." Village panchayats would then not only still exist, but be granted definite shares of land tax revenue and would have such other taxes as they levied on themselves. They would be both financially and technically assisted by the panchayat samiti to carry out local improvement projects. The Team said, "As we contemplate that the village panchayat will receive substantial grants from the panchayat samiti and that its budget should be approved by the latter, it would be a workable arrangement to prescribe a smaller number of compulsory functions and permit the panchayat to undertake any other developmental work with the approval of the panchayat samiti—such approval being automatic with the approval of the budget." It was contemplated that for planning and carrying out local development programmes, it might be wise for groups of local villages, and thus village panchayats, to work together. It specifically suggested that judicial panchayats cover something like 10 to 30 villages.

The Team's recommendations concerning the composition and role of the zila parishads, whose areas of governance would be identical with districts, bore directly upon the issues which dominated what we have called the first and second phases of accommodation. It said:

"We have already indicated the reasons why in the matter of developmental activities village panchayats and the panchayat samitis should be the main local bodies. Having assigned to them functions in various fields, we feel that there is very little left for any higher administrative executive body other than the Government. The district board, the district school board and the janapada sabha become superfluous, as local interest, supervision and care, necessary to ensure that the expenditure of money upon local objects conforms with the wishes and needs of the locality, are provided by the panchayat samiti, which we consider a body of size adequate in population and area.... To ensure the necessary co-ordination between the panchayat samitis, we suggest a zila parishad of which the members will be the presidents of the panchayat samitis, all members of the State Legislature and of the Parliament representing a part or whole of a district whose constituencies lie within the district and district level officers of the medical, public health, agriculture, veterinary, public health engineering, education, backward classes welfare, public works and other development departments. The Collector will be the chairman of this parishad and one of his officers will be the secretary."

This would mean that the samiti members would be a small minority of the parishad. But the Study Team said,

"We do not contemplate that this parishad will have executive functions; that way lies danger to the initiative and, therefore the effectiveness of the panchayat samitis in their early years. Nor do we consider that the district level officers on the panchayat samitis should be members of the parishad without the power to vote; that would be the surest insurance for indifference. The time is long past when we could think of the officers' interest in rural development as something different from or contrary to that of the non-officials.

It is possible on the basis of the experience of the working of this panchayat samiti that we may decide to decentralise the administration further; possibly, it may be necessary to alter the composition, scope and powers of the zila parishad. Again, there is little doubt that after a few years the powers vested in the Collector and District Magistrate may fall into desuetude and may be statutorily withdrawn."

Notwithstanding this speculation or prophecy, the Team made definite recommendations concerning the role of the parishad, namely, that it would approve the budgets of the panchayat, that

> "Where funds are allotted by the Government for the district as a whole, their distribution between the various blocks will be made by the parishad; it will coordinate and consolidate the block plans, annual as well as quinquennial; where grants for special purposes are needed or demanded by panchayat samitis, these also will be consolidated and forwarded to the Government by the parishad. It will also generally supervise the activities of the panchayat samiti. It will also replace the present District Planning Committees. . . . " It said that the zila parishad, as "a district body will have to be fully empowered by statute, to carry out all developmental activities in the district in the same manner as we have recommended for the panchayat samiti, though on correspondingly a larger scale."

The clearest statement of the rationale of these recommendations was in the last paragraph of Section 2, Vol. I, of the Team's Report. It said:

> "Development cannot progress without responsibility and power. Community development can be real only when the community understands its problems, realises its responsibilities, exercises the necessary powers through its chosen representatives and maintains a constant and intelligent vigilance on local administration. With this objective, we recommend an early establishment of statutory elective local bodies and devolution to them of the necessary resources, power and authority."

The Team said, "In the ultimate analysis, the establishment of the panchayat samitis with a wide devolution of powers by the State Government has to be an act of faith—faith in democracy." It might have said the same thing about the possible ultimate elimination of the zila parishad and thus the de-emphasis of district government. But the Team was writing a blueprint for the future, and it must be said that its blueprint included practically all the requisites of local government.

As has happened in many other areas of decision, the recommendations of the Study Team were given careful consideration, not only by the National Development Council, but by Parliament. These recommendations provided the general blueprint which became the national programme for "Democratic Decentralization". It was, of course, up to each separate State to take such action as it desired. The States, by and large, enacted legislation which provided for a three-tier system of local government. The similarities, and differences, in their systems and in their subsequent operating experience, like so many other components of India's development programme, offer an opportunity to attempt an analysis of democracy in the process of evolution.

This process will not have been working for any great length of time when our assessment of it, by necessity, will be consummated. The programme will, however, have been launched in a number of States and debated not only in State legislatures but in many other places. Such debate began immediately after the COPP report was presented. The issues which were debated and the various opinions expressed can therefore be reported and analyzed. Because these opinions were diverse, we shall need to categorize them but shall first express our own judgment on the issues and problems which were bound to appear out of the past history of rural government.

First, obviously, would be the problem of revitalizing village panchayats which, no matter what they may have been in the ancient past, were now not actual local governing units. Besides that there were not very many of them. They had not only been diluted by interposition of higher levels of government, but were caste and faction-ridden. As we have previously seen, only about ten per cent of the 550 thousand villages had active panchayats. Probably the chief cause for their having fallen into desuetude was that they had been stripped of their once self-imposed authority. They had been denied authority by higher levels of Government, which is to say they had not been permitted to assume any effective responsibility. Now they were to be asked to accept and exercise heavy responsibilities, not only for their own improvement, but for many tasks which would be allocated to them, together with funds to implement the accomplishment of these tasks.

Second, would be the issue of whether District Officers could bring themselves to accept, either rationally or emotionally, the idea expressed by the Prime Minister, "to let village authorities function and let them make a million mistakes." To take this attitude and follow this practice would violate every standardized practice of bureaucracy. Most Block Development Officers installed since the national development programme was established had been trained in the same high standards of administrative efficiency as had district officers. Administrators were now being asked not only to compromise their schooled judgments about good administration but, to some extent, suffer some loss in the elite status which they had enjoyed.

Third, would be the problem of building wholly new inter-village local government units—the samitis. Such inter-village groups as had existed in the past had no government functions. They had been, and still were, "marriage and festival" circles. In the development blocks, village-level workers' circles were administrative and service groupings organised for administrative purposes and not by villagers. In other inter-village relationships, there were probably many more organised inter-village hostility groups than there were inter-village co-operative groups. Now the samiti was not only to be the pivot or hinge of the whole new system, but was to be controlled and directed by village people specifically organised into units of government.

In our judgment, the three basic problems just described were inherent in the revolutionary steps to be taken. They constituted the main issues which had been debated since early 1959 when the decision was made to establish this new system of local government. They have been debated in terms of the recognized need for greater and more efficient rural economic and social development and have been debated as the basic issues of building a democratic, political, and social order. We present here the contents of the debates which were constant and widespread while the programme of democratic decentralization was being adopted, and which have been continued as one State after the other has instituted its programme. The arguments have been presented in daily newspapers, in various periodicals, in reports of parliamentary debates, and especially in the official organ of the Ministry of Community Development and Co-operation,

Kurukshetra. Some of the arguments which we catalogue, however, are synthetic. We offer these arguments as if they were of the opponents of the movement, the proponents of the movement, and those who took a middle ground.

Those who doubted the wisdom, and workability, of so radical a departure from past experience said that the government is apparently going to turn over anything and everything to local panchayats, and if it does, it will reap the same results it did when it turned over anything and everything to village workers. Panchayats are to be asked to do so many different things, none of them clearly understood or defined, that they will do nothing well. It may be all right to make them responsible for local welfare, but not for physical and economic development projects. Village panchayats should assume the responsibility for mobilizing their own manpower, for Shramdan (local public works), but not be asked, or permitted, to manage projects which require funds granted by Government. National and State funds are allocated in terms of graded priorities and targets for accomplishing these priorities, in order that the Government funds shall be spent for specified accomplishments. There must, therefore, be some uniformity in projects to be supported by Government funds. If each village, or even each samiti, is permitted to decide on the projects for which it will spend Government funds, the purpose of national and State planning will be greatly jeopardized, if not completely destroyed. Some expressed doubts about the wisdom of the suggestion that the block organisation (the new samiti) should so nearly supersede the responsibilities of the district organisation, and seriously questioned "subordinating" the Block Development Officer to the "Pradhan" (the president of the samiti). One critic said the BDO would be just a "head clerk" and others said "the popular representative can't ignore the superior wisdom of the civil servant."

Those who had faith in the new venture and were enthusiastic about it argued that village institutions had "long been recognized as essential for the rejuvenation of village life," that the power which district and block officers had in the past exercised had caused them to "ignore the possibility of democratic development of panchayats," and "that many villagers knew and understood things which college graduates could well afford to learn from them." Probably their most telling argument was that the old bureaucratically organised and operated community development extension organisation had not accomplished what had been expected of it, and that the evidences were that the degree of failure was due to its incapacity to elicit, mobilize, and harness the great potential for dynamic democratic development action which resided in village people and village groups. They said, "decentralization means not only the creation of a few institutions and revamping already existing ones to suit the expanding needs of development, it means a total transformation in the outlook upon the power-relationships, and the radical reorientation of attitudes toward the power structure." They further said, "The local community organisation subsists not by virtue of grant and exercise of power conferred by the Centre, but by virtue of the loyalty of the community toward them."

There were those who took what might be called a middle position on all these issues. They said that the local government system had not, in the past, in the development programme, "on the whole been hierarchical" and that by training all levels of personnel, official and non-official, in the roles they should play, they would, under the experience of responsibility and systematic "guidance", play their roles well and with enthusiasm. They said, "Till sufficient experience is gained, a continued central guidance and period of tutelage may not only be justified but felt necessary, but the role of Centre vis-a-vis the small community organisations should not be misunderstood even at this stage." They recognized, however, that "budget control" by high authorities might tend to frustrate the experimental attempts of non-conforming localities by "compelling them to confirm the central idea of political policy." They did not think that this would be altogether bad. Some of them expressed their optimism through the following logic: that the district level organisation would be responsible for government funds and responsible for overseeing and training the leaders of the lower unit—the samiti; that the samiti would inspect, guide, and stimulate village panchayats and that there need be no conflict between administrative or executive systems of relationships between the popular governments which were to be established; that the village-level worker would be the executive secretary of the panchayat, the BDO the executive secretary of the samiti; and the district officer chairman of the district organisation, the parishad.

The last-cited line of argument amplifies the model prescribed by the COPP group for a three-tiered system of local government which was systematic and would appear to guarantee step-by-step guidance of programme operation by experienced government officials, from the top down, but at the same time permit and invite initiative from the bottom up. To those who had consummate faith in village people and their leaders, this blueprint seemed to open the gate for too much administrative domination. To those who had consummate faith in the efficiency and wisdom of government administrators, it seemed to open the gate for all kinds of ill-conceived local schemes and probably a great waste of scarce government money. For the social analyst, it provided the opportunity to observe the extent to which, and the ways in which, the legislation of different States attempted to provide for the maximum of initiative of village people and/or the safeguards of administrative guidance. A study of the State panchayat laws reveals wide differences. Some States provided for a great deal of local initiative and some States provided for a great deal of administrative supervision and control.

It should be kept in mind that it was not expected that States would suddenly annul old local government institutions and in no State was there complete absence of some system of local government. Indeed some States had quite elaborate systems of local government and had much experience in the administration and operation of well-established local government institutions. A few States already had, a number of years earlier, established well-organised systems of local government not too different from the new Panchayati Raj system. There were other newly-established States in which local government institutions had been minimal. In some of them, government had been largely in the hands of rajahs and zamindars and other intermediaries who made no pretence at seeking popular approval. As we review the legislation establishing or re-aligning local government institutions, and later attempt to summarize the experiences under these different situations, we must necessarily back away from the detailed provisions of the laws of the various States and make our observations in terms of a few generalized categories.

We expressed our own judgment that there were problems which would automatically arise out of past historic practices and attitudes. The practices had been different in different States and it would be natural to expect that there would be different attitudes towards, and ideas about, the newly-proposed scheme of local government. But in all States, the problems were different from those in countries where for a long while there had been local community or local village self-government. In those countries, the jurisdiction of local community government was almost complete for the handling of all matters for which the local people were willing to accept responsibility. Each higher level of government interceded only in inter-relationships between local jurisdictions and by adding services to local people, none of which annulled local jurisdictions. In such countries, the problem quite often has been to convince people in local areas that they would forfeit none of their rights of local self-direction by accepting services from higher levels of government.

The issues in India were how to establish a desire, or demand, on the part of local communities for self-government direction, and how, once local communities had accepted this responsibility, they could be helped while they were gaining experience in, and developing judgment about, how to be self-directive. Too much overhead help would raise the issue of too much outside domination; too little assistance would leave most units of local government helpless. It was almost certain that local governments would request assistance from higher levels of government, but shun any direction by them. Higher levels of government would probably be willing to grant assistance only if they could provide some direction for its use.

A review of the provisions of the various State laws reflects these different points of view by State legislatures. Their viewpoints expressed their faith or lack of faith in the capacities of village people to be self-governing which was reflected in the amount of authority they granted to village panchayats, for self-governance and for development projects. It is reflected in how much authority, which in the past had resided in the district officials, would be transferred to parishad officials and how much

transferred to samitis. It was reflected in how much of the authority transferred from the district to the samitis would be exercised
by samiti officials and how much by government block officials.

One of the first State laws, which quite faithfully followed
the recommendations of the Committee on Plan Projects (COPP)
for a three-tiered system of local self-government, was: "The
Rajasthan Panchayat Samitis and Zila Parishads Act, 1959", which
was passed by the Rajasthan State Legislature and approved by
the President on the 9th day of September, 1959. The major purpose of the Act was to establish Panchayat Samitis, as units of
local government between district governments (parishads) and
village or village circle panchayats. Each established development
block was to be a samiti, with the proviso that "the State Government shall define, and may alter, the limits of every block." The
membership of each samiti was to consist of the Sarpanches
(chairmen or presidents) of all village or Tehsil panchayats. Its
elected officers were to be a Pradhan (president), Up-Pradhan
(vice-president), and chairmen of standing committees. The
BDO of the block (Vikas Adhikari) was to be secretary. Thus
the members of the samiti were elected indirectly by the village
people, in that each Sarpanch elected by each local panchayat
automatically became a voting member of the samiti.

In addition to these elected members of the samiti, there
were to be some "co-opted" members from persons residing in
the block; "one Krishi Nipun" (a person assigned by the district),
two women, one person belonging to the scheduled castes (untouchables), one person belonging to the scheduled tribes (if the
population of such tribes in the block exceeded five per cent of
the total population of the block), one person from among the
members of the managing committees of co-operative societies
in the block, and "two persons whose experience in administration, public life or rural development would be of benefit to the
Panchayat Samiti." These two administrative persons might reside
outside the block, but must reside within the district where the
block is located. Each member of the Legislative Assembly of the
State, so long as he held such office, was to be an "associate member". Such members could attend any meeting of the samiti and
take part in the deliberations, but could not vote, be elected

Pradhan or Up-Pradhan, or be a member or act as chairman of any standing committee.

It can thus be seen that the samiti was not to be a local parliament to which each member was elected directly by his local constituents. The members from scheduled castes and tribes and women were co-opted to guard against traditional discriminations. The provision for a member from the co-operatives expressed a bias which was widespread in circles of Indian leaders. The co-opting of persons with administrative and/or public experience was a safeguard against what was bound to be the considerable confusion or lack of decorum in open and free debate by inexperienced village Sarpanches. Some other provisions of the rules apparently had the same objective.

The prescribed functions of the samiti were delineated in a "schedule" which listed sixty-five specific activities in seventeen different fields. They included all development activities from agriculture and education to management of forests and grazing land, and all public welfare activities from management of trusts to emergency relief. In addition were such other powers and functions as might be conferred on or delegated to it by the State government. It was granted the right to levy taxes and thus create a Panchayat-Samiti fund with which to support any and all the activities for which it was made responsible. Into this fund were to go grants from the State government, grants for liabilities transferred to it by the State government, and annual ad hoc grants by the State government. It was to have a share of the land revenue, calculated at the rate of twenty-five paise (approximately five cents) per head of the population of the block.

The samiti's relationships with constituent village panchayats were to be exceedingly important if for no other reason than because it was to carry out all of its works and programmes through these panchayats. The samiti would supervise such programmes and enforce compliance with any agreements with panchayats. The standing committees of the samitis were to be the technical advisers and the supervisors of works and programmes carried out by panchayats. Many of the tasks and powers of supervision previously exercised by the State were now transferred to the samiti.

Its organic relationship with the parishad (district organisation) was that its Pradhan, together with the Pradhans from all other samitis in the district, were to constitute the voting members of the parishad. It would receive ad hoc grants from the parishad and would in general be supervised by it. Especially its budget would be reviewed by the parishad. In addition, the parishad was commissioned to "watch over all agricultural and production programmes, construction programmes, employments and other targets laid down for the district and see that they are being properly carried out, accomplished and implemented and review at least twice a year the progress of such programmes and targets." The Pramukh of the parishad was to "encourage the growth of initiative and enthusiasm in the Panchayats and provide to them guidance in the plans and production programmes undertaken by them and the growth of co-operative and voluntary organisations therein."

In addition to all the Pradhans of the Panchayat-Samitis in the district, there were to be included as members of the parishad: the members of the Council of States and House of the People (the members of the two Houses of the National Parliament who resided in the district); the members of the State Legislatures elected from the district; the president of the Central Co-operative Bank in the district or serving the district; two women; one person belonging to the scheduled castes and one from the scheduled tribes; and two persons with experience in administration, public life or rural development. The District Development Officer could attend all meetings of the parishad but had no right to vote. The officers were to be a Pramukh (president) and Up-Pramukh (vice-president), to be elected by the voting members. The State government was to appoint as secretary of the parishad a member of the State Service. It will thus be seen that the same logic was to maintain as in the samiti, even to making a State official the secretary, just as the BDO was to be the secretary of the samiti.

Let us now see how the first State (Rajasthan) to initiate a programme or system of "democratic decentralization" by legislative decision, resolved the issues which had been debated for approximately two years after the COPP recommendations were made. Local panchayats, each a State-incorporated body, were established throughout the State, most of them including a circle of villages. The members of the panchayats, elected by complete adult suffrage were not to be less than five nor more than fifteen in number, to be decided by the State government. Panches could not be less than twenty-five years of age. The Sarpanch must be able to read Hindi. All issues coming before the panchayat were to be decided by majority vote, except that decisions on such construction projects as wells, tanks, roads, new buildings, etc., which involved considerable expenditure of funds, must be by a two-thirds majority. The panchayat had authority to require conformity to all sanitary and health regulations and to assess penalities for nonconformity. It could levy taxes to support community services and charge fees for licences and permissions. It was to prepare an annual budget of receipts and expenditures and submit it to the samiti for approval or modification. When its budget was approved, it was granted funds and technical assistance by one or more of the standing committees from the samiti.

Above the village or village-circle panchayat is a samiti which now performs all the development functions previously performed by the development block. But in addition to being a development block, it is a statutory unit of local government which can levy taxes, receive grants, make and collect loans, execute contracts on its own behalf, exercise supervision over its own officers, including the accounts of the BDO, and exercise supervision over all village panchayats in its jurisdiction.

Above the samiti is also a people's government, the parishad, which operates under its own elected officers. While it stands between the samiti and the State government, it does not completely supervise panchayats, although it does review and approve all samiti budgets. Its main tasks are those of planning and coordination. It advises the State government on all matters concerning the implementation of any statutory or executive order referred to it by the State government and on the implementation within the district of national planned schemes; it collects data and publishes statistics, encourages the development of cooperatives and other voluntary associations, organises conferences and seminars of Sarpanches, Panches, and Pradhans. While it may require any local authority to furnish information regarding its activities, and its Pramukh and Up-Pramukh are admonished to visit blocks and offer advice to samitis, it has no power, other than budgetary, to direct the programme or activities of samitis. When there is conflict between samitis, a Commissioner (regional officer) calls and presides at the meeting to settle the dispute. The Commissioner calls and conducts the parishad meeting at which co-opted members are selected.

If we now look at the three problems which we said earlier were bound to appear when the new system replaced the old, long-standing system of local government—the problems of re-vitalizing local panchayats, of diluting the bureaucratic power and practice of district officers, and of establishing units of inter-village local government—we would probably conclude about as follows: *First,* that the Rajasthan law provides definitely for lessening the administrative authority not only of the district officers but also of the Block Development Officers; *second,* that it provides for covering the States with local panchayats, provid-ing for democratic elections of their members and granting them some powers of decision-making which they had not previously had; and *third,* that its outstanding provision was the creation of samitis, as the pivotal organisation for directing development and as units of local government close enough to the people that their elected village leaders can constitute its governing body. It did not provide for as much initiative on the part of local panchayats as the enthusiastic proponents of the new system had advocated. An article in the *Economic Weekly* cites especially a provision of the law which permits the samiti to receive appeals from "any order of a panchayat against which there is a complaint," and argues that to grant the samitis such jurisdiction brings it "much nearer to the Soviet model" than to the model of self-governing local democracies. How successfully the not-too-ample legal jurisdictions of local panchayats could thwart the legitimate desire better to mobilize the enthusiasm of village people and develop local village leadership will have to await the experience of programme operation after the provisions of the law have been put into practice.

By providing for rather wide and strong jurisdiction and powers of the samiti, with only slight supervision by the parishad, even though that jurisdiction did compromise the expectations of some for thousands of little village democracies, it did bring local government much nearer to the people than district government had ever been or could possibly be with present communication and transportation facilities. Even though the average samiti jurisdiction would cover about thirty panchayats, there would be some five or six times as many samitis as districts between the State government and village panchayats.

Concerning the third issue of decision-making and direction of development programme activities by government administrative officials or "popular" bodies, the Rajasthan Act went further than the suggestions of the COPP report. That report had suggested that the gram sevak be made the "development secretary of the village panchayat"; that he "should submit his progress report to the village panchayat," and that the panchayat should forward its comments to the Block Development Officer. The only provision for panchayat secretaries provided in the law was that a panchayat might request authority to employ a secretary. The committee had suggested that during the first two years after the creation of the panchayat samiti "it might be well for a sub-division officer to be chairman." The law made no such provision. It even made the BDO and his staff subject to the administrative control of the Panchayat-Samiti and the standing committees thereof, and required his presence and the presence of his staff at their meetings. The law further provided that, "The Pradhan shall, at the end of every year, send a confidential report as to the work of the Vikas Adhikari (BDO) during that year to the District Development Officer who shall send a copy of that report to the State Government along with his own confidential report." The COPP report made about the same suggestion concerning the position of the district officer in the parishad during the early years of programme operation. The law specifically provided that the district officer should hold no office in the parishad. The report suggested that the parishad have standing committees. The law specified such standing committees for samitis, but said only that "every Zila Parishad may constitute for the performance of its functions . . . such subcommittees as it may deem necessary."

The Andhra law was also passed in September, 1959 and provided for a three-tier system of local rural government. The title of the Act was "The Andhra Pradesh Panchayat Samithis and Zilla Parishads Act, 1959". It contained no provisions for village panchayats because panchayats already existed. Our interpretation of the law is that it provides for relatively greater authority of the panchayat, vis-a-vis the samiti, than does the Rajasthan law. It provides that the parishad shall have "standing committees" and that "the District Collector shall be the Chairman of every Standing Committee." An understanding of the prescribed functions of the standing committees, which in the Rajasthan law were prescribed only for samitis, would indicate that the parishad is assigned greater authority in Andhra than in Rajasthan. Its supervision over samitis is spelled out in greater detail, even to mentioning that the Collector may attend samiti meetings. It is also more specifically emphasized that the government may assign or transfer even greater powers to the parishad.

The "Assam Panchayat Act, 1959" also specifically provided for a three-tier system of local government. Its lowest tier, the Gaon Panchayat, is in fact the executive committee of the Gaon Sabha which is composed of all eligible voters in the village or village area. The Anchalik Panchayat is similar to the samiti in Rajasthan and the Mohkuma Parishad is the district unit of government. Assam illustrates the case of a number of other States which have State, and in some cases District, officers who supervise all levels of local government. It has a State "Inspector of Local Works". The State may also appoint Project Executive Officers and commission Deputy Commissioners and Sub-divisional Officers as Inspectors. Like most other States, the government names the secretary of the parishad. Because of these State-wide and district-wide government officials, there is not a pyramidal order of inspection and supervision, as in Rajasthan and Andhra, in which each higher level of local government is granted the powers and made responsible for the supervision of those units of government which are below it.

The State of Orissa established Zilla Parishads and Panchayat Samitis throughout the State in early 1961. Its law specifies about the same relationship between units of government as do the laws of Rajasthan and Andhra. As in these other States, it specifies that a government servant shall be appointed secretary of the parishad and the Block Development Officer as Executive Officer of the samiti. It, however, goes much further in specifying the roles of other overhead government servants. As in a number of other States, all members of the national Parliament and all members of the State Legislature residing in the area are made members of the parishad. In addition, the Collector of the District and other District Officers of Medical, Education, Public Health, Agriculture, Veterinary, Panchayat, Forest, Welfare, Works, Co-operation, and other departments are included in the membership of the Parishad. Sub-Divisional Officers exercising jurisdiction within the District are also members of this, assumed-to-be, people's government. In the part of the Act dealing with "control", we are impressed with the repeated cautions about, one might say expressed fears of, granting authority to local, popularly elected bodies. Cautions are expressed in other State laws, and it may be precarious to assume that such words as "the Collector of the district may require," "the Samiti is bound to comply," "the Government may supersede" a samiti "for any period they may deem fit," and other such phrases have meanings different from less forthright statements. Our only purpose in quoting the language of this Act is to present an outstanding illustration of the super awareness of some higher authorities that the devolution of long-established central power to lower, newly-established units of government was a matter which they thought needed to be managed with very great caution.

There are a number of States which not only had had panchayats for some time, but also had thoroughly institutionalized State and district services in local areas. The type of adjustments these States made in order to further the movement for greater decentralization of government could be illustrated in any one of the following States: Uttar Pradesh, Madras, Mysore, or Punjab as an outstanding example. We select the State of Bombay[1] because it had more panchayats than any other State, because its panchayat laws were the end products of repeated amendments of past panchayat legislation, and because it had a gamut of technical State departments upon which it could depend to provide services to local areas, which services newer States had to provide by new legislation. It was also one of the old, well-organised States which

[1] Now divided into the States of Gujarat and Maharashtra.

expressed willingness to realign its already well-operated institutions and services in such a way as to prove the feasibility of granting greater powers to local village panchayats.

Its realigned system is described in the Bombay Panchayat Act of 1958. There were more than 54,000 villages in Bombay. A 1956 law had made it obligatory for the State government to establish a panchayat in every village with a population of 2,000 or more. In order to blanket the State with local panchayats, villages might be combined into panchayat areas. Such areas were declared to be villages, and all persons living in each area who were eligible to vote constituted the Gram Sabha (popular assembly) of the village area. The village panchayat, elected by the Gram Sabha and consisting of from seven to fifteen members, was the administrative unit of local government. The executive officer of the smallest unit of local government was a Sarpanch (president), or in his absence the Up-Sarpanch (vice-president), elected by the members of the panchayat.

Next above the village panchayats were Panchayat Mandals. They were constituted as "district village panchayat mandals" by State law and are therefore district level units of local government. The members of each mandal were: the Collector, the President of the District Board, where there is one, the Chairman of the District School Board, where there is such a body, the Vice-Chairman of the District Development Board (a creation of the State government), seven to twelve members to be elected from among the sarpanches in the District, and four other persons elected by the District Local Board, at least one from scheduled castes or scheduled tribes. The Collector is the chairman. The vice-chairman is elected by the members. The District Village Panchayat Officer is secretary. The duties of the Panchayat Mandal are to establish village panchayats; supervise and control them; and perform such other functions as the State government may assign to it. It may delegate certain of its budgetary and supervisory duties to subcommittees. It makes reports to the Collector.

There is no third level of local rural government between village people and the State government, but the Panchayat Mandal is, as we have seen, a body composed, on the one hand, of the district officials and officials of other district or State established institutions and, on the other hand, members elected from village panchayat sarpanches. It, therefore, performs some of the functions of both the parishad and the samiti of certain other States. The unit of local government which is accorded greater power and responsibility, and therefore increased emphasis, is the village panchayat. It performs many other functions and as many of the powers as are assigned to samitis in States which follow the three-tier system. This in a way obviates the necessity of establishing an intermediate level of government between the village panchayat and the mandal (the district panchayat). This was made feasible because the village panchayat had been strengthened over past years and there were many such panchayats in the State of Bombay at that time. There were also in the State a number of other special-function boards, agencies, and officials whose assigned duties and responsibilities led them to operate vertically from the district, and even the State government levels to village levels.

The few States whose panchayat legislation we have discussed by no means reflect all the differences which exist between the State laws. They do, however, represent the common denominators, rather than the differences, in the legislative provisions of all the States in their attempt to establish everywhere, and for the first time, a system of rural local government which includes tiers of local units, each with far more than a semblance of local self-government. Furthermore, each unit or level forms a link in a chain of government from villages to State Commonwealths. We, therefore, summarise what those main common denominators are.

First, we would say, no matter what the various States defined or declared to be villages, there are now universally-established village panchayats as statutory bodies. Second, no matter what the differences among the State provisions, some local panchayat officials are everywhere members of the next higher level of governing bodies. Third, there is the devolution of power in all States from higher to lower units of government. Fourth is the significant fact that in all States, village panchayats retain some of their traditional rights and practices as judicial bodies. There are varying rights of appeal from panchayats to the courts and courts have the right to intervene, but always within prescribed limits. Village panchayats are, however, made responsible for monitoring the behaviour of village residents in those inter-personal relationships which affect the morale and equanimity of local village life.

The provisions of laws could not, of course, even if they were identical in all States, guarantee identity of experience in the administration and operation of local government. There are great differences among the traditional experiences of the people in the various areas of India. There are marked differences in the amount of experience which various States have had in local government. There are bound to be differences in the organisation and administration, as well as in the institutions of local self-government. Some of the problems will probably turn out to be only episodic. Others may prove to be generic, but together they illustrate what is happening in India as she attempts to carry out her programme of "democratic decentralization" of the Pancha-yati Raj system of local government.

MAIN AUTHORITIES QUOTED OR CITED

Chaudhuri, P. K., "Decentralisation or Delegation of Power? The Rajas-than Panchayat Samitis and Zila Parishad Act, 1959," *The Economic Weekly*, Vol. XI, No. 40, October 3, 1959, Bombay.

Evaluation Report on First Years Working of Community Projects, Pro-gramme Evaluation Organisation, Planning Commission, Government of India, May, 1954.

Evaluation Report on Second Year's Working of Community Projects, Vol. I, Programme Evaluation Organisation, Planning Commission, Government of India, April, 1955.

Evaluation Report on Working of Community Projects and N.E.S. Blocks, Programme Evaluation Organisation, Planning Commission, Government of India, April, 1956.

Evaluation Report on Working of Community Projects and N.E.S. Blocks, Vol. I, Programme Evaluation Organisation, Planning Commission, Gov-ernment of India, P.E.O. Publication No. 19, April, 1957.

Important Letters Issued by Community Projects Administration, (Period April 1952 to October 1953), Community Projects Administration, Government of India, March, 1955. (C.P.A. Series 35).

Legislation on Panchayati Raj (A comparative study on), Ministry of Community Development & Co-operation (Department of Community Deve-lopment), Government of India, New Delhi, June, 1961.

Report of the Team for the Study of Community Projects and National Extension Service, Committee on Plan Projects (COPP), Vol. I, Planning Commission, Government of India, November, 1957.

Second Five Year Plan, Planning Commission, Government of India, 1956.

Summary Record of Second Development Commissioners' Conference on Community Projects (16th April to 19th April, 1953), Community Project Administration, Planning Commission, Government of India Press, 1958.

The Andhra Pradesh Panchayat Samithis and Zilla Parishads Act, (Act No. XXXV of 1959), Printed at the Government Press, Hyderabad, 1959.

The First Five Year Plan, Planning Commission, Government of India, December, 1952.

The Rajasthan Panchayat Samitis and Zila Parishads Act, 1959, (Act No. 37 of 1959), Law and Judicial (A) Department, Government of Rajasthan, Published by Authority, Government Central Press, Jaipur.

Tinker, H., *The Foundations of Local Self-Government in India, Pakistan, and Burma,* University of London, Athlone Press, 1954.

CHAPTER 15

DEVELOPMENT OF RURAL INDUSTRIES

As we have seen earlier, the continued growth of population has created pressure on the land which has made agriculture increasingly insufficient as a means of income for many rural people. Furthermore, seasonal fluctuations in work-load leave most cultivators with no occupation for a large portion of the year, and for the landless labourers in particular, underemployment is an acute problem. One economic aspect of the rural industries programme is to help this group by providing new sources of employment to the unemployed and the underemployed. It was evident from the beginning that improvements in agricultural production, however massive, would not be sufficient to create the hoped-for increases in rural employment and income. Other avenues also had to be opened. Among them, rural industries held possibilities for helping to mitigate the growing rural unemployment and underemployment resulting from continued pressure on the land. The case for rural industries in India, however, has never been purely economic. The social motivations have also been of prime importance, and in reviewing the arguments for a rural industries programme, we shall have to account for both of these aspects.

One economic facet of the rural industries programme has been the attempt to revive languishing artisans' crafts and the desire to support various agricultural-processing industries which have been hurt by competition with large-scale, mechanized industry. With the gradual industrialization of the sub-continent, numerous rural artisans and craftsmen had been hard hit by the competition. Another important aspect of the rural industries programme has, therefore, been to assist this segment of the rural population through support, stimulation, and protection of their industries. Thus we see that a primary economic aim of the programme has been both to encourage and to create new sources of employment and to protect old sources threatened by other aspects of development. Furthermore, the proponents of rural industries argue that the growth of this sector, besides adding to over-all national output, will be a more effective way of utilizing scarce national resources than uncontrolled expansion of large industry. An often-used example is cloth. In this case, it is argued that *per capita* consumer demand is not increasing, and new demand comes only from an expanding total population. Since this growth in demand can be met by goods produced by cottage industries, it is felt that this labour-intensive form of industry should be encouraged rather than the more capital-intensive textile mills. A natural corollary of this argument is a demand for restrictions on expansion of mill capacity, an argument which, as we shall see, has been reflected in national policy.

To these various economic aspects, there are wedded a number of rather disparate social ideas. The most important of these is the concept of balanced national economic growth. Not the least of the disparities in India is that of income and wealth between the towns and cities on the one hand and the rural areas on the other. Average urban incomes are substantially greater than rural incomes. A suggested means of correcting this is by providing new employment through rural industries and increasing the income of those already engaged in them. A prominent member of the Khadi and Village Industries Commission said that the gulf between rural and urban incomes will be narrowed down when opportunities in agricultural production are open to the rural population through work in cottage or subsidiary industries or through supplementary occupations near home. He goes on to add that this pattern of development will also check the increasing tendency to migrate from rural to urban areas, with its concomitant high social costs.

The statement above leads us to the next of the social arguments, that it is more desirable for a worker to be self-employed in his own home, to be a member of a co-operative, or to be employed in a small unit than it is for him to work in a large factory. It is argued that the mere dispersal of large-scale industries to rural areas would not be a sufficient solution. Rather, policy must be such that the pattern of rural industrialization allows the workers to own and control the enterprises and "to enjoy the full fruits of their industry". The proponents of this argument feel that, just as true democracy must be based on a decentralized pattern that grows upward from the village, so the pattern of production, particularly for consumer goods used throughout the countryside, must be similar if the producer is to secure "the blessings of democracy".

The Gandhian overtones of this argument are very strong. An important aspect of Gandhi's ideas for the social reconstruction of the polity after Independence was the self-sufficient village community. He described it as "a complete republic, independent of its neighbours for its vital wants, and yet interdependent for many others in which dependence is a necessity." This community would manufacture its own cloth, do much of its own agricultural processing, and particularly for consumer goods, interact with only the immediate area. This idea has had particular influence on the ideology and programme of the Khadi and Village Industries Commission. Although the possibility of self-sufficiency at the village level has been generally recognized as unworkable, self-sufficiency within a small area has still been a principal object. And, as we have seen above, this idea has had great influence on many people's ideas of the basic purpose of rural industries.

We must also keep in mind the importance of khadi[1] as both an economic weapon and an emotional symbol in the struggle against British colonialism. Khadi was a focus of resistance against British economic exploitation, at least as it manifested itself in the textile policy, as well as a particularly significant way of focusing attention on boycott and non-co-operation. As a result, the production of khadi, and by implication a number of the industries in the rural industrialization programme, have been invested with particular emotional significance. The strength of this emotion is reflected in the argument that village industries should be supported even if they are uneconomic and require either subsidies from the State or government doles for the artisans. It is first argued that costs can be brought down through improved techniques, increased credit facilities, and better marketing. Even if these do not work, however, a number of people suggest that the consumer should be convinced that it is worth paying a bit more for the products of cottage industries—in the

---

[1] Khadi is cloth hand-woven of yarn, hand-spun both by the traditional Indian "Charkha", or spinning wheel, and by the improved Ambar Charkha.

spirit of Swadeshi,[2] in the manner of sacrifice that motivated the Independence struggle. Needless to say, however, this motivation has been difficult to develop in the years that have followed Independence, and the argument that villagers should prefer to buy goods made in the village as part of their national function has been without notable success.

Even this superficial review indicates how numerous and diverse are the motivations of the rural industries programme. With so many strands, many of which lead in opposite directions, it is not surprising that the policy for rural industries which has emerged has been without a clear-cut pattern. It has never been decided just what the objectives of the rural industries programme are or how best to reach them. We shall trace the course of these various ideas through the first two Plans, discuss the agencies created to implement them, and look briefly at the programme set forth in the Third Five Year Plan, to see what future direction the rural industries programme might take and what role it may be expected to play in the over-all rural development in India.

The term "village industry" was defined by the First Five Year Plan as those industries concerned "in the main, with the processing of local raw materials for local markets and with simple techniques." This would include such things as oil pressing, hand pounding of rice, handicrafts, and handloom weaving, to name only a few. "Small-scale industry", on the other hand, refers to industries with more sophisticated techniques of production, usually mechanized and often employing power, employing a larger number of people in one industry (or installation) than village industry, and usually dealing with a larger market or working intimately with medium and large-scale industry. For the most part, this chapter will be concerned with village industries, but we shall use the term "rural industries" to denote either village or small-scale efforts, when they are located in non-urban areas. The significance of this distinction will become evident below, when we discuss the efforts to decentralize industrial production and the recommendations that usually-urban small-scale industry be fomented in rural areas. There has been a definite commitment in Indian planning, at least in principle, that modern,

[2] Use of indigenous products.

mechanized small industries be brought to rural areas, if not in villages, then in district towns or large non-urban conglomerates.

Even before the beginning of the First Five Year Plan, much thought and investigation had gone into the question of rural industries. When the Congress party created its National Planning Committee before the war (it was to report in 1948), one of its sub-committees was on Rural and Cottage Industries. Its report was a series of memoranda which suggested certain kinds of action. Although more definite policy trends were to develop only at a later stage, the report is worth reviewing since the controversies it mirrors are indicative of the early intellectual and emotional climate that invested this topic.

We have already mentioned the influence of Gandhi and the importance of khadi in much of the thinking about rural industries. There are a number of controversies, however, and one in particular, which emerge. Gandhi did not wish to support khadi and village industries as a replacement for large-scale industry, or even necessarily as competition. Rather, he wanted them to be a means of providing spare-time employment for the rural populace, increasing their incomes, and keeping their hands from idleness. Unfortunately, however, the pull of supply and demand would not allow such a peaceful form of co-existence and the hand spinners and weavers were the ones who stood to lose. Thus Gandhi's arguments had often to become not merely in favour of hand production; they also became, in fact, anti-industrialization. "Our concern is therefore to destroy industrialism at any cost," he said at one point; and at another, "Industrialism is, I am afraid, going to be a curse for mankind." This is not to say that Gandhi was "against progress," but he conceived of progress in terms of technological improvements in the implements and devices used in cottage production, and he stressed that they must not displace village workers when they were introduced. In short, Gandhi's attitude was to favour those improvements which would reduce the drudgery and strain of the village worker, but which would not reduce his employment or his income.

For our purposes, Gandhi's own points of view are important mainly for the attitudes to which they gave birth in his followers, and the influence they have had on rural industries. There are many in India who argue that Gandhi would have changed his views about technology in the light of the problems facing the new India, had he lived to see them. But in many of his followers, the interpretation of Gandhi's ideas became merely one of "hate the machine" and resist its introduction at all costs. The result has been that a segment of Indian opinion and planning has opposed the rapid and extensive introduction of modern technology into rural industries on the ground that its effect on the problem of unemployment has been under-estimated.

This is not to say that the problem of technological unemployment is not real. It doubtless is, and considering the fate of many of the rural industries during the later nineteenth and early twentieth centuries, there is good reason why many Indians would be hypersensitive about its implications. Nor is this to say that the question of technological advance in rural industries has been hampered by merely ideological opposition. Definite and large problems of power, transport, and technique have also been an important question. Even if all Indian planners had *wanted* to introduce rapid technological progress in rural industries, the sheer physical and social obstacles would have been grave deterrents. But those who have thought about and planned for rural industrialization in India have never clarified a policy for the question of technological innovation and advance. Nor has possible conflict with the desire to preserve at whatever social or economic cost existing rural industries, utilizing only slightly modified techniques, ever been resolved. As a result, a pattern of ideas for development has never become clear, and in trying to pay homage to both an ideal and a necessity, real service has been paid to neither.

This dichotomy of thought was evident in the National Planning Committee's sub-committee report on "Rural and Cottage Industries." On the one hand, certain members used phrases such as "avoiding the evils of industrialism", "producing for use, not exchange," and "irrespective of considerations of comparative cost, in relation to the competing methods of production". On the other hand, some members argued that the principal question was how to achieve maximum output and suggested that turning one's back on the machine was not the way. Phrases like "the problem in India today is production and more production" typified this point of view.

The actual resolutions of the National Planning Committee fell somewhere between these two extremes of opinion. There was, of course, no question about government support of, and assistance to, small and rural industries. There was also no doubt about the need for State regulation of the relationship between large and small industries and their respective rates of production. In attempting to give guide lines, the Committee listed a number of factors to be considered in State programmes for industry. In addition to the expected ones of employment, output, and distribution of income, it also listed "reactions on the health, freedom, initiative, character and culture of the people", thus revealing a mixture of motivations. After much deliberation, the sub-committee mildly stated that "the national plan should provide for the adoption of all measures necessary for relieving these cottage and rural industries from the stress of competition, and for facilitating the expansion of such industries to the desired size, while providing a living wage to the workers engaged in these industries." Obviously no clear-cut policy existed.

At the same time, we must recognize that this was an entirely new field of planning and that the obstacles were great. More important, perhaps, is the very fact of the support which had been assured to village and small-scale industries. This also appeared, at about the same time, in the Industrial Policy Resolution of 6 April, 1948 which said, "Cottage and small-scale industries have a very important role in the national economy, offering as they do scope for individual, village or co-operative enterprise, and means for the rehabilitation of displaced persons. These industries are particularly suited for the better utilization of local resources and for the achievement of local self-sufficiency in respect of certain types of essential consumer goods..."

The First Five Year Plan's remarks and recommendations on village and small-scale industries are the outgrowth of the trends we have been discussing. The principal importance of the Plan's statements is the firm support they gave to village and small-scale industry, thereby setting the stage for definite, and increasing, government assistance and participation in future years. The Plan called this development "as much a matter of State action as the increase of agricultural production". Since the industries were then in rudimentary stages of development, however, and since no mechanisms had yet evolved for support and assistance, actual financial allocations were not very great.

The First Plan devoted one chapter to "Village Industries" and another one to "Small Industries and Handicrafts". As we have seen, village industries were defined as those concerned "in the main, with the processing of local raw materials for local markets and with simple techniques." They were advocated, on the one hand, primarily to utilize surplus manpower while effectively supplying local demand, but, on the other hand, also because of the social and economic significance of rural arts and crafts. Although there is no elaboration of this latter idea, it is evident that it grows from the arguments already outlined.

The chapter on "Village Industries" is important because the section on "State Policy" sets forth certain basic policies which have operated ever since. It is emphatically stated that a programme of village industries "has to be supported both by specific measures of assistance as well as by appropriate State policy," and it goes on to elaborate that the "primary objective of policy should be to provide a field within which each cottage industry may be able to organise itself." This basically meant that government policy would be such that it created favourable conditions in which village industries could grow. This was spelled out as what the Plan called a "common production programme". In effect, this was to be a government programme to rationalize production from large and small sectors; and in its formulation "account would have to be taken of the factors determining the efficiency of large-scale and small-scale production, the scope for development through small-scale methods, the extent to which the social aspect has to be emphasized and the value of any particular course for increasing rural employment." The last consideration, in particular, was to receive emphasis. To implement this, the Plan suggested a number of possible measures, headed by reservation of spheres of production. They would specifically limit certain goods to small or village production units and would curb the output of mill and factory installations. While the First Plan stressed the need for strong State policy and sufficient regulation, it was not wholly, or even primarily, protectionist in outlook. It emphasized the need for improvement in techniques, for more, better, and permanent training facilities, better marketing, and more adequate means of getting finance to the producer.

The chapter in the First Plan on "Small Industries and Handicrafts" dealt with those industries which were not "an integral part of the village economy". On the whole, the over-all recommendations were the same as those for Village Industries, with emphasis on State participation in formulating programmes for the improvement of techniques and facilities. The Plan also stressed the lack of information about either small industries or handicrafts and the need for both the collection of data and a co-ordinated approach based upon the information that was gathered.

· More important were a number of policy statements which appeared in the Plan. On "State Purchase", for instance, the chapter on Small Industries said that the government was to give preference to cottage and small industries' products, when other basic economic considerations were comparable. Furthermore, even in this group, preference was to be given (and later, only) to orders from co-operatives or from an agency approved by the government. This has been an asset primarily to small industries, but for those rural industries which have extra-village markets (especially in the case of cloth), it has also been important. The result has been definite assistance to the industries concerned but at the same time, a number of experts in the field have criticized the resulting tendency to depend on the possibility of government purchase. This outlet, it has been argued, has, on the whole, been a deterrent to attempts to improve normal marketing channels. This question comes up again and again.

Finally, there was a recommendation in this chapter that rural industries outside of the village should concentrate in new townships or in extensions of old towns, not in cities. The idea was to encourage these centres of non-urban industry rather than having all new, small industrial development occur in the cities to which the entrepreneurs would naturally flock. In the First Plan, this was a relatively minor recommendation, but after the report of the Karve Committee, discussed below, it was to become a major part of the nation's rural industries policy.

Concerning the further development of policy, a significant document, the Report on Small Industries in India by the International Planning Team, was published in 1955. This report dealt, in the main, with the problems of small-scale rather than village or rural industrial development. The over-all emphasis was important and has had repercussions on the broad policies affecting rural industrial efforts. This Team, sponsored by The Ford Foundation, made extensive recommendations on a number of subjects which had been discussed and the importance of which was already known, such as marketing, credit, and quality control. But the significance lay in the systematic manner in which the problem was approached, something which had been noticeably lacking before, in the specific nature of the recommendations, and in the prestige which the International Team brought to the subject. The gist of the report was an emphasis on modernization of techniques, both of production and of management. It stressed the absolute need for breaking the "cake of custom" in manufacturing and in marketing and noted the tremendous potential domestic market which might be reached. The Team strongly condemned anti-mechanization attitudes, arguing that cheaper, more efficient ways of making better products would expand markets, and, in the long run, create more rather than less employment. The Team did not, however, urge that small industries be entirely, or even substantially, urban. They believed in the decentralization of industry, in which individual units of production could be brought to rural areas, rather than drawing population to great centres of industry. Finally, the report emphasized the absolute necessity for developing markets and suggested, as others were to do five years later, that too much reliance on government purchase and support was ill-advised.

The Report of the International Team was to have tremendous importance in India, although its direct effect on rural industries was, in fact, not very great. The important thing here is that again one line of policy recommended was in almost direct contradiction with others. Decentralization and rural industrialization for the International Team meant the establishment, in rural areas, of modern, mechanized industry, producing goods for exchange, not use. There was a general feeling that the economic factors of expansion and production would, of themselves, mitigate the problem of technological unemployment. There were some who radically opposed this point of view.

Even more important was another document published late in the same year, the Report of the Village and Small-Scale Industries (Second Five Year Plan) Committee, usually known as the Karve Committee Report. Its principal purpose was to make specific recommendations for allocations during the Second Five Year Plan. The Karve Report reflects virtually all the arguments, counter-arguments, ideas, and contradictions which marked the thinking about rural industries up to this time. In trying to balance and accommodate them, the Committee came up with an umbrella-like series of recommendations under which the proponents of virtually all points of view could take shelter. It was the fullest statement that had been made on industrial decentralization.

In the important chapters, "Basic Approach" and "Principles and Policies", the Committee set up three areas in which it was to make recommendations, namely measures for: (1) halting growing unemployment and underemployment in existing occupations; (2) the progressive provision of additional employment; and (3) creating the "basis for the structure of an essentially decentralized society for the future", which provides also "for progressive economic development at a fairly rapid rate."

The report's stress on employment was stronger than in any of the previous documents and was supplemented by concern about technological unemployment. It stated, for the entire programme, that, "Avoidance of what may be called further technological unemployment may be said to be the starting point of the work," and stressed that the growth of more modern methods of production will only aggravate the problem. "In the peculiar Indian situation the possible compensating effects on total employment of rapid introduction of modern technology are not immediately obtainable." It went on to say that an "important reason for the emphasis laid in the second five year plan on obtaining increased supplies of consumer goods through the village and small-scale industry sector is this desire to prevent a further aggravation of the unemployment and underemployment problem."

These attitudes, of course, left the Committee open to the charge of being against progress, and they defended their point of view at some length by saying that technology itself was not undesirable; "The deliberate regulation of the pace of adoption is related specifically to those spheres where the adoption of such technique is likely to cause unemployment of both existing capital equipment and labour." The Committee went one step further and argued that their approach was an attempt at the most effective utilization of both economic and human resources. It argued that "if existing investment and personnel can produce required results fairly efficiently it might be wiser for the next stage of development to utilise them fully than to utilise scarce resources of capital in creating substitutes for them."

At the same time, the Committee did not suggest investing capital merely for the preservation of old techniques, but said that expediency demanded utilization of the old while sinking money into new methods. Specifically, "when new capital investment has to be made, it should be made as far as possible only in improved equipment or where existing equipment is itself capable of being improved by addition or adaptation. . . . In the adoption of improvements a long period view must necessarily be taken, so that the improvements now effected are capable of being utilised as higher techniques without being rendered obsolete at an early stage in the process of development." And finally, the Committee ended its discussion of techniques by saying that, "So long as the improvement is capable of wide adoption in a decentralised system and so long as it has no deleterious effects on employment its adoption is agreed upon by all."

The core of the Committee's recommendations was its statement on decentralization. Indeed, this report had the strongest policy statement on decentralization yet made, and its words, if implemented, would have had far-flung implications. The report said, "The bias towards decentralisation would mean that in the future programme of technical improvement, the techniques adopted are appropriate to the decentralised pattern, and further that continuous effort is made to adjust existing improved techniques for particular production activities which are ordinarily centralised in modern economies to a decentralised mode of operation or to invent or to discover decentralised substitutes for them." In this case, economic and technical considerations were to be altered to fit an ideological bias, based on a particular set of concepts of social policy and social welfare. The chapter on "Principles and Policies" repeated the emphasis on decentralization when it said, "big villages or small towns" were to be centres of manufacture and production, working in concert with the small villages, on the one hand, and the large cities on the other, the only method by which both the proportion and the absolute numbers of population in agriculture would be reduced. But the consideration was not merely economic. The Committee spoke also of the "essential superiority of the small and medium-sized town as a centre of socio-economic life in an egalitarian democracy," and that, "The principle of self-employment is at least as important to a successful democracy as that of self-government."

The whole concept of decentralization was summed up in a paragraph which was quoted repeatedly as the basic approach to rural industrialization:

"The pattern of industrial activity that should gradually emerge is that of a group of villages having its natural industrial and urban centre. These small urban centres will be similarly related to bigger ones. Thus a pyramid of industry broadbased on a progressive rural economy will be built up. In such an organisation small centres can experience a cooperative interest in the bigger ones, and these latter would develop a genuinely supporting instead of an exploitational relationship towards the smaller towns and the countryside."

It is not clear how the specifics of such a system might work, and as before, the really difficult problems of implementation have been left unsolved. Still, a visionary, oft-to-be-talked-of pattern for rural industrialization had been established. Only the details, then as now, remained to be filled in.

The Second Five Year Plan reflected what the Karve Committee had said. It stated its primary object as developing "small industries in rural areas...to extend work opportunities, raise incomes and standard of living and to bring about a more balanced and integrated rural economy." It went on to say that although technical change would take place and better methods of production eventually replace current techniques, support must be given to assure the stability and growth of the village economy. Specifically, it said, "...the sector of village and small industries is not to be viewed as a static part of the economy, but rather as a progressive and efficient decentralised sector which is closely integrated, on the one hand, with agriculture and, on the other, with large-scale industry."

The Second Plan's discussion of the Karve Committee Report accepted the basic principles which we have already outlined and backed them up by referring to the Industrial Policy Resolution of 30 April, 1956, which assured State support and protection for small industries. In referring to the Policy Resolution, the Plan again repeated the position that "it is essential that the technique of production should be constantly improved and modernised, the pace of transformation being regulated so as to avoid, as far as possible, technological unemployment." This emphasis, and the stress on decentralization were the two most important aspects of the Second Plan's approach to this question.

As far as policy is concerned, we have seen that the concept of rural industries has, from the very beginning, received complete support from India's planners. It has been viewed as a means of creating employment, producing a significant portion of the consumer goods in the country, integrating the rural economy with the urban, ensuring a more equitable distribution of national income, and avoiding some of the evils of unplanned urbanization, in addition to the ideological considerations already discussed. Yet, within this over-all framework of support, there have been diverse opinions about just what "rural industries" meant, what the implications of mechanization might be, and what methods were to be supported by whom, to what degree, and for how long a time. The result has been the noticeable failure of a pattern for rural industrialization to emerge, and a marked tendency for each of the various agencies to proceed without much relationship to any of the other work being done in the field.

One of the greatest problems facing India's planners for small-scale and village industries at the beginning of the First Five Year Plan was organisation. Since some mechanism had to be created through which the various programmes for village and small-scale industries could be implemented, the principal efforts of the First-Plan period were organisational. For this purpose, the establishment or reconstruction of six All-India Boards was the most important step taken for the planned development of village and small-scale industries during this period. These Boards were

for: Handloom, Handicrafts, Coir, Sericulture, Small-Scale Industries, and Khadi and Village Industries. As the Karve Committee
said, each of these boards functioned on a national scale and
tried to evolve, in co-operation with State governments and other
organisations, arrangements for co-ordination, technical training,
facilities for marketing, standardization of designs, and forms of
assistance for artisans. In the case of the Khadi and Village Industries Board, the group not only prepared programmes for the industries with which it was concerned, but also implemented them
through its own registered institutions or through co-operatives.
The other Boards have been concerned primarily with programme
formulation, and the State governments were usually responsible
for implementation. Thus a three-tiered structure was developed,
with the Ministry of Commerce and Industry in the Centre Government, then the All-India Boards, and finally the State Departments of Industries and the State Boards. Co-ordination within
this structure has always been a problem, and remains so today.
Just how the recommendations of the various Boards were to be
carried out has always been a difficult question to answer, and
the hope put on Community Development for this function has
yet to materialize.

It was the Boards, however, which gave village and small
industries much of their original momentum during the First-
Plan period and their significance at this time was less the extent
of their physical accomplishments than the fact of their establishment. The Planning Commission's Review of the First Plan
stated that although much remained to be done at the end of the
Plan period, "Nevertheless ... as a result of programmes undertaken and the institutions established ... small industries have now
an assured place in Indian planning and their key role in diversifying the rural economy and expanding employment opportunities will continue to be emphasised." It is interesting, however,
that the same Review indicated that too much of the initiative
for these developments came from the Centre Government, which
set up the six Boards, provided the bulk of the finance, helped in
the establishment of training and other institutions, and assisted
the States in embarking upon larger programmes. It emphasized
that the vitality of such industries would have to depend upon the
degree to which they became integrated with the development

programmes and the needs of each local area, a fact which had not been widely recognized or accepted.

Other measures during the First-Plan period included steps, however limited, to begin the implementation of a "Common Production Programme". This generally took the form of improving the techniques of production in small industries and restricting the expansion of capacity in large-scale industries, with cloth being the most seriously affected. For this industry, a series of Government notifications, actually beginning in 1950 before the start of the Plan, limited the production of certain kinds of goods to the handloom industry. For example, in 1950 the notification said that the production of certain kinds of garments of prescribed width and border were reserved for the handloom sector. Then in 1952, mills were directed not to produce in any one month more than 60 per cent of the average quantity of certain categories of cloth packed for sale in India during the year 1951-52. And in 1953, an additional excise tax was levied on the production of bordered dhoties[3] by large mills in excess of 60 per cent of their production during 1951-52.

The funds derived from restriction of production and the levy of excise taxes were then made available for various development schemes such as sales rebates for both the handloom and khadi industries. Thus, the costs of the khadi programme and the uneconomic nature of its production were to be subsidized by penalties levied on the large-scale factories for exceeding certain limits of production. In other areas of production, similar measures were suggested, although not always implemented, during the First-Plan period. The village industries involved included matches, leather footwear, furniture-making, sports goods, slates and pencils, and other writing materials. If this did not represent a full-scale approach to the problems of a common production programme, it was a start; and one immediate result was a rise in certain sectors of production due to a growing market for manufactured products of all kinds. The output of handloom cloth rose from 843 million yards in 1951 to 1358 million in 1954-55, to 1450 million in 1955-56. Similarly, the total value of khadi produced in 1950-51 was 2.75 million dollars and in 1955-56, it

---

[3]Full, draped garment, usually white.

was up to 11.25 million dollars. Employment in 1955-56 for khadi production was 557,000 spinners and 43,000 weavers, compared to 307,000 spinners and 18,000 weavers two years earlier. It is probably correct to say that without government support, the handloom industry's share of the total market for cloth would have been considerably smaller.

On the whole, the positive (rather than protective) measures for the promotion of village and small-scale industries during the First-Plan period made less headway, if only because the starting point was so low and so much of the money and energy had to be expended on the creation of procedures for training, establishing co-operatives, expediting finance, etc. The Review of the First Five Year Plan noted that although almost every State had expanded its training programme, the "expansion in training facilities for artisans which has taken place during the past few years ... is still inadequate." Similarly, programmes for government purchase and for improvement of marketing techniques showed only slight progress at best. By the time the Karve Committee reported in 1955, a recommendation for a State purchasing programme was under review by the Government of India, but had not yet been put into action. For marketing, the only evident improvement was the creation of a number of emporia in large urban centres. Industrial co-operatives, on the other hand, showed greater progress and had more than doubled during the period.

During the Second Five Year Plan, measures to assist village and small-scale industries were considerably increased, and they followed the broad policy lines outlined above, but most of the progress appears to have been in "small scale" rather than "village" industries. By the end of the Second Plan, dispersal of industrial growth and significant success in creating viable, functioning rural industries on any meaningful scale had not yet taken place. The scale of assistance during the Second Plan, for both village and small-scale industries was about four times that of the First Plan. With this outlay, a number of programmes were organised, including an expansion of industrial estates (although most were in urban rather than rural areas), a programme for the manufacture and distribution of improved spinning equipment for khadi, a scheme to assist handloom weavers' co-operatives to introduce powerlooms, steps to provide more assured markets for certain industries, reservation of production in certain spheres by limiting large industries, and further elements of a common production programme, although principally in areas which would affect small-scale rather than village production. In addition, a strong effort to relate Community Development and rural industries was made.

As a result of these measures, there were a number of advances. The number of industrial co-operatives continued to grow and by 1959-60 was almost double the number in 1956. Even so, as the Third Five Year Plan mentions, " ... industrial co-operatives did not cover more than a small proportion of those engaged in village and small industries." On other fronts, the Third Plan notes, there were a number of advances. The production of handloom cloth continued to increase, and what the Third Plan called "fuller employment" had been provided for nearly 3 million weavers. Exports of handloom cloth, on an annual average, were about 36 million yards for the last three years of the Second Plan, valued at about 10.5 million dollars. Similarly, the production of traditional khadi (cotton, silk, and woollen) showed an almost seven-fold increase in a decade. Employment in both traditional and Ambar Khadi was provided to about 1.4 million spinners, most of which was part-time; and whole-time employment was provided to about 190,000 weavers, carpenters, and others associated with the programme.

Accomplishments of other programmes, particularly the village industries' efforts, were not encouraging. The only programmes about which information is available are those administered by the Khadi and Village Industries Commission and even for these, it is scanty. During the Second-Plan period, the largest part of financial assistance for village industries was in the form of improved equipment, training, and marketing help for industries such as the processing of cereals and pulses, crushing of oilseeds, tanning of leather, making of non-edible oils and soap, match-making, making of palm gur, bee-keeping, manufacture of hand-made paper, and pottery. The Third Plan indicated that a substantial portion of the funds disbursed remained unutilized during the early years of the Second Plan, and a Working Group which reviewed these programmes during the middle of this period indicated that "the results obtained in respect of both production and employment were not commensurate with the expenditure incurred." During the latter years of the Second Plan, however, there were some improvements. Over-all, the Third Plan indicated that, "Village industry programmes in the Second Plan have provided partial relief to about 5 lakhs (500,000) of artisans and under-employed women workers in villages," and added, "They have also furnished experience which should be useful in working out future patterns of industrial development in rural areas." Thus the progress made by the rural industries programme was sporadic and the results meagre.

The problems of the All-India Boards in coir, sericulture, and handicrafts are so particularized and their contribution to over-all rural industrial development is so limited that we shall not go into details. The sericulture programme, for instance, provides full-time employment to only about 35,000 persons and part-time employment to about 2.7 million. Throughout its work, the industry has been constantly beset by the principal problem of high costs of production, because of low yields of mulberry trees and of cocoons. The programme for the industry has been directed mainly toward improvement in the methods of cultivating mulberry, in the quality of silkworm seeds, in the supply of equipment, and in the organisation of research conducted at the Central Sericultural Research Institute and at a number of its branches. In the decade between 1951 and 1960, production of raw silk rose from 2.5 million pounds to 3.6 million.

In the coir industry progress has been generally slow, according to the Third Five Year Plan, because of organisational deficiencies in coir co-operatives, inferior quality of coir yarn, and competition from substitutes in foreign markets. According to present estimates, the industry provides employment to about 800,000 persons.

Handicrafts, however, have been more successful. During the Second Five Year Plan, four Regional Design Centres and a number of emporia and sales outlets were established. In addition, training and production centres were established for specific crafts; the result of all these measures was an increase in internal sales and in exports of handicrafts. Over-all, the Third Plan said that, "Favourable conditions for stable and fuller employment were created for skilled craftsmen which in turn resulted in considerable improvement in their earnings." Despite this, the Third Plan added, "Progress was somewhat retarded by the shortage of technical personnel and certain basic raw materials and the difficulty in channelling credit to the artisans."

In the handloom industry, we find more pronounced success, but there are also a number of significant problems, indicative of those that do and will face most traditional village industries. Growth in production, employment, and wages in the handloom industry has been significant through the first two Five Year Plans. In large measure, this has been due to the efforts of the All-India Handloom Board and the State governments, the success with which they have fostered the growth of co-operatives and used them for dispensing assistance, and the funds made available from rebates derived from the mill industry.

The handloom industry was one of the hardest-hit by industrialization, and its plight was in no way mitigated by British textile policies. After Independence, the position subsequently worsened until, in 1952, the industry faced an acute crisis and was beset by concurrent unemployment and accumulation of stocks. To offset this, the protectionist measures which we have mentioned above were instituted and with this as a stimulus, the Handloom Board began its work. Early in the First Plan, the Board decided that the only solution was to organise the industry on sound lines to ensure proper marketing of its products. It also decided that because the industry was so dispersed and the primary producer so subject to exploitation, co-operatives were the most feasible mechanism for bringing about consolidation and organisation. As a result of these efforts, the position of the industry became stabilized to some extent during the First Plan. More and more weavers joined co-operatives, production increased, wages improved, and the over-all employment picture was encouraging. During the Second Plan, expenditures were increased and the same hopeful trends continued.

There are still significant problems. The growth of handloom co-operatives, for instance, has been impressive, but the increase in number has not always been matched by the quality of performance. The owned resources of most societies are too scant to permit them to obtain adequate institutional finance, the leadership is generally weak, and managerial staff is in short supply.

Furthermore, significant numbers of the co-operatives have not been functioning for a period of years. The weavers in these defunct societies have been left without sufficient assistance and have again been drawn into the control of master weavers, with all the exploitation that the relationship entails. Thus, the problem of building successful co-operatives remains with the handloom industry. To remedy this, the Working Group which reviewed the handloom situation in 1959 recommended that stress during the Third Plan be placed not on the formation of new co-operatives, but on strengthening the already-existing structure, a recommendation which has been included in the Third Plan.

Another problem facing the handloom industry is marketing. In the fall of 1957, at the invitation of the Government of India, The Ford Foundation sponsored a foreign "Handloom Fabrics Survey Team" to take a close look at the development of India's handloom fabrics, with a particular interest in their marketability both in India and the United States. The Team made two basic recommendations: one in the area of service, the other in sales.

It was suggested that several "Weavers' Service Centres" be established in the main areas of handloom production to serve both co-operative societies and individual weavers. These centres were envisaged as providing a stock service, thereby insuring quality control, and a training-cum-design service, whereby weavers could obtain new designs and increase their technical skill. As seen from 1963, the experimental-design and technical aspects of this recommendation have been implemented very well in almost precisely the manner prescribed by the Team. At present, however, the centres are not distributing-houses, although they do provide a liaison between such houses and individual or co-operative weavers.

The Team's second basic recommendation has not fared as well. They suggested that a sales centre be established in New York, to provide both a wholesale and a retail outlet to the potentially vast American market. The government, perhaps because of the "exclusive contract" nature of the fabric industry (which requires the supplier to grant exclusive purchase rights to the buyer) has only recently established a sales outlet outside of India. On the other hand, sales centres in Bombay, Calcutta,

New Delhi, and Madras, are currently operating and doing a good business with tourists.

But the marketing problem has still to be satisfactorily resolved. The Working Group of 1959, in reviewing the industry's progress, recognized the importance of marketing in the dispersed cottage sector of an industry that faced competition from the mechanized sector; and the question it put was, how do you permit the handloom industries to continue without being forced out of business by the mills. The Working Group suggested three measures: (a) introduction of sales promotion activities; (b) establishment of selling units; and (c) payment of a subsidy on sales. It has always been the idea that traditional industries should be helped until they could get on their feet, as it were, and that measures like (c) would be gradually withdrawn in favour of more positive forms of assistance. And yet, the Working Group, which tended to be protectionist in outlook, did not think it either feasible or possible to remove the subsidy. It answered the argument that technical improvements should make the handloom industry more competitive by saying first, that improved appliances have been supplied to only a limited extent; second, that until full employment is reached, improved appliances by themselves will not reduce or eliminate the handicap; and third, that whatever productive improvements do take place in the handloom industry are more likely than not to be offset by technical advance in the mill industry. So the Working Group concluded that there was little likelihood of this handicap being removed in the near future. Although it did not rule out the importance of positive measures of assistance, it stressed the need for continued, and even increased, protection of the handloom industry, at the expense of the mills.

Programmes for technical improvements have been begun, on a number of fronts, but they have been without notable success. An example of this problem is the attempt to mobilize a programme of powerloom installation. The Textile Enquiry Committee in 1954 recommended a phased programme of conversion of handlooms into powerlooms; and on this basis, the Government of India decided to allow installation of 35,000 powerlooms in the handloom sector during the Second Five Year Plan. The intention was to improve the economic condition of the handloom weavers and also to achieve the production target of 200 million yards of cloth. There were a number of conditions attached, such as location in rural areas, installation by co-operative societies, and the like, but the important fact here is that a major modernization programme was envisaged.

When the Working Group made its report, it stated that as of 31 March, 1959, out of *13,377* looms sanctioned, only *1,118* had been delivered and only *572* had been installed and were working. By the end of the Second Plan, the pace of installation had been stepped up somewhat, and as the Third Five Year Plan indicated, about 3,500 to 4,000 had been installed. Nevertheless, this was not more than 10 per cent of the original target of 35,000, and it will probably take until the end of the Third Plan before the 13,000 first sanctioned, are installed and functioning.

Problems of similar type but even greater magnitude have also been encountered in the work of industries supported by programmes of the Khadi and Village Industries Commission. We have already mentioned how important khadi was to Gandhi, both as a weapon for achieving political independence and as a means for reconstructing society. When the programme continued to function after Independence and during the Plan periods, it therefore had a backlog of workers, a series of organisations, and a definite, if not always articulated, ideology. The objectives of this idealogy were stated clearly by the Working Group which reviewed the progress of the khadi programme in 1959. They were: (a) to establish personal relations between khadi workers, on the one hand, and the spinners, weavers, and the other artisans, on the other; (b) to make khadi an instrument of production on a co-operative basis and make it as far as possible self-initiated and self-directed; (c) to make production for use rather than for sale the primary object of the khadi programme; (d) to make khadi an instrument for developing and transforming the whole economy on the basis of equity, justice, and freedom; (e) to introduce and establish the primacy of social values as distinguished from money values, in the operation of the economy, and make money values and monetary mechanisms a means for realizing social values and not to make them an autonomous force, and (f) to make continuous improvement in techniques an essential part of the implementation of the programme and basis for its development.

The All-India Khadi and Village Industries Board was created by the Government of India in February, 1953, with the purpose of "preparing and organising programmes for the production and development of Khadi and village industries, including training of personnel, manufacture and supply of equipment, supply of raw materials, marketing and research, and study of the economic problems of different village industries." The Board was to function as a clearing-house of information and experience relating to these industries and was to work with the State governments and with other organisations for their promotion. From the very start, however, there were organisational difficulties, and the Board continually felt hampered by the procedural requirements and administrative delays of government machinery. As a result, a statutory commission was set up and the Board continued to function in an advisory capacity. This Commission has supervised programmes for the production of khadi (cotton, woollen and silk) and has also been in charge of a number of traditional village industries, which have been less successful than the khadi programme. Khadi production, in fact, has increased sevenfold in the first two Five Year Plan periods and has provided employment to a number of artisans and wage increases to others.

Nevertheless, the problems which remain are so great as to almost completely overshadow the gains. First there is the problem of what happens to the khadi cloth that is produced. One noticeable trend has been that khadi producers have sought, or have had to seek, markets in urban rather than in rural areas. According to estimates of the 1959 Working Group, about 60 per cent of sales are in urban areas, and the trend is for this to increase rather than decrease. This opposes the ideological khadi consideration of production for use rather than for exchange. Furthermore, national policy for rural industries indicated that cloth of this sort should be used for local consumption and should be marketed within an area near its production centre, not in urban markets. But even more irksome is the fact that khadi stocks in urban areas have far outpaced demands, sales have lagged, stocks of yarn and cloth have grown; and as a result, increases in production have become a cause for concern rather than for satisfaction.

There are a number of reasons for this accumulation. Although it is unlikely that there is any inherent consumer bias against khadi, finer grades of cloth have to be sought elsewhere. Furthermore, and particularly in rural areas, it is possible that the brighter colours and more varied patterns of mill cloth have special appeal. But this consideration pales before the principal problem of the cost of khadi. The fact is that retail prices of khadi are higher than for other varieties of cloth, including handloom. As a result, khadi is not competitive in either rural or urban areas. As the Working Group indicated in its report, although a certain amount of bias in favor of khadi for non-economic reasons can be expected, it certainly cannot neutralize the effect of the price difference. As the price difference has remained for a longer and longer period of time, consumer resistance has grown and stocks have accumulated. A further factor contributing to this surplus has been the rapid expansion of production without regard to the maintenance of certain minimum quality standards. Government subsidies and the cess fund created from the tax on millowners have not been sufficient to overcome the price defect, and the larger question still remains of whether or not khadi production will ever be able to be rationalized to the point at which it can compete against large-scale, mechanized industry without government subsidy.

When we consider the matter of employment and wages, it is equally discouraging. The Working Group reported in 1959 that the principal beneficiaries of the programme are lower middle classes in both urban and rural areas. Those groups which most urgently need employment—landless labourers, harijans, and low-income peasants—have generally not benefited from the programme. Some, it is true, have taken to hand spinning, but as the Working Group indicates, "the number of such people is insignificant." Furthermore, the bulk of the spinners are women. Although the khadi programme was intended to provide gainful employment during the slack agricultural seasons, and hence to mitigate the problem of underemployment as well, it has not developed in this manner. Men who earn the bulk of their living by labour, even if in severe economic distress, have not taken to hand spinning, in part because of the low level of wages, in part because of the monotony of the work, and in part, at least in some areas, because of the widespread social prejudices against men spinning.

For those who have taken to making khadi, the remuneration has not been great. The Third Plan states that spinners working on a traditional spinning machine, the charkha, make about seven dollars per year and those using an improved appliance, the ambar charkha, about eleven dollars per year. The Plan says further that in some regions, the average for spinners on the ambar charkha has gone as high as sixteen to twenty-one dollars, comparable to the earnings of many agricultural labourers. The duration of employment, on the average, would be about 2 hours a day for about 200 days in the year. For a khadi weaver, the Working Group estimated in 1959 that the average annual income would be about fifty-eight dollars, with an employment period of about five to six months, and that neither the rates nor earnings were a material contribution to the alleviation of poverty. Although there has been an increase of considerable size, in production and sales, the fact remains that the khadi programme has not reduced unemployment substantially or raised the level of wages significantly in the villages. Even if one views hand spinning as a supplementary occupation, its value must be judged from its contribution to family income. Thus the 60 to 90 cents a month which it has added, or even based on the higher average figure cited before, an additional $1.40 to $1.75, and considering the context of low rural incomes in India, is obviously inadequate. Furthermore, the Working Group reported that khadi workers feel this level of wages cannot be raised without passing the cost on to the consumer and further pricing khadi out of the market. If, therefore, the khadi programme is to make the contribution to rural India which its founders envisaged, basic reorientation and change must occur.

One reason for this situation has certainly been organisational problems within the movement and within the Khadi Commission itself. The Working Group indicated that the planning of khadi production and development has been related neither to needs nor to potential, and has lacked even the barest essentials of careful planning. Targets have had little, if any, meaning and have been set with little attention to possibilities for fulfilling them. There has also been an overlapping of organisational effort, and the khadi people have worked at cross-purposes and in duplication both with their own internal groups and with other bodies involved in rural industrial development. A further element is that khadi has been and still is a movement rather than a programme. Its own workers have usually been motivated by kinds of incentives and goals which are difficult to transfer to those who are not already true believers. Because this process of transference has been so difficult, khadi has never become very much integrated with other development programmes, even though the prestige which it derived from Gandhi has given it perhaps disproportionate influence on over-all rural industries' efforts. The Working Group pointed out this problem with great acumen:

> "Khadi, however, in fact has remained, in its conception and implementation, an isolated programme by itself. Its social implications have not been assimilated in the approach of the Government and public mind and in practice; and the contradiction between the Khadi programme and even programmes of decentralized industries, in particular, and other programmes in general are due to the lack of this assimilation ... the programme as a whole, conceptually and empirically, remains only a fragmentary effort and has on that account developed internal stresses and strains... owing to the programme remaining more or less unrelated to the other development programmes, in spite of being taken as part of the planned development of the country, its results have not only been much below expectation, but it has not developed an impetus of its own or acquired self-sustaining and self-developing qualities."

While many khadi workers would answer this by saying that their movement has not been understood, that it has been incorrectly attacked by unsympathetic materialists, and that its true significance is yet to emerge, it is important to recognize how difficult it is to make successful a development programme which is based on so definite an ideological commitment and which expects continued support in the face of limited, if not nonexistent, economic advantage.

Concerning the question of technical improvements, the

khadi group has always been acutely concerned with the question of technological unemployment, and its relatively conservative stand has often led to charges that they were opposed to technical improvements and stood only for the preservation of traditional and often archaic techniques. This has not in fact been the case; the Commission has gone out of its way to state again and again that it favoured technical improvements, although always qualifying this with the consideration that large numbers were not to be thrown out of work by the advances which were introduced. The result has been a stress on limited measures and an ambivalence about mechanization and the use of power. The programme of improvement on which the khadi group put heavy emphasis was the ambar charkha programme, begun in 1956-57. The ambar charkha is an improved hand-spinning device, which, it was hoped, would lead to substantial output by individual spinners and a concomitant rise in incomes. Despite the great hope for this device, however, a number of problems have arisen to reduce its effectiveness: work on the ambar charkha was new to the spinners and entirely different from that of the traditional machine; the first appliances were often defective; distribution was not effective; servicing was poor; and output was below what had been predicted. As a result, large numbers of ambar charkhas have been either unutilized or under-utilized. At the same time, those which were utilized have contributed to the production increases which helped to aggravate the stock accumulation problem already mentioned. As in the case of the powerloom introduced in the handloom sector, this programme for improvement has not shown the results which had been either hoped for or expected.

Another development worth noting is the Khadi Commission's Intensive Area Scheme. This has been described as a socio-economic experiment to assess the place of khadi and village industries in total economic development while contributing to a social structure based on the welfare of all (sarvodaya). Its premises were motivated by an extension of the Gandhian concept of village self-sufficiency to include area self-sufficiency; and it has tried to demonstrate that the full employment of all available manpower in an area could not be attained unless the development of khadi and village industries formed a part of the programme for developing the entire local economy.

This Intensive Area Scheme was begun in 1954-55, usually in areas where Gandhian Constructive Work had already begun and in which there were local leaders who could organise the people for the common effort required. The areas usually consisted of a group of villages, perhaps thirty or forty, with a population of twenty to thirty thousand. The work sought to create social awareness and to encourage the participation of the people in various activities, through education, propaganda, and persuasion by leaders. In most instances, integrated plans were first prepared for one or two villages, on the basis of socio-economic surveys, and these plans delineated the role of each family in the over-all development of the village. As these were implemented, it was expected that successful results would encourage contiguous villages to follow a similar course. These plans then were integrated into an over-all area plan, which made provision for the common services and facilities required by the large-scale planning.

The content of these plans was intended to bring about balanced economic development, which almost always involved a redistribution of manpower among different occupations. In most plans, attempts were made to divert manpower from agriculture to other occupations, including khadi and village industries, as well as public works which would improve the economic infrastructure of the area. The planners tried to keep the programme flexible by making new plans every year, and adjustments were made in the light of both conditions encountered and successes and failures. The resources available for the Scheme were only those which the people could raise themselves, with some help from the Khadi and Village Industries Commission, which also provided technical assistance for the planning process and for the development of khadi and village industries.

Because of the almost complete absence of statistical data, it is difficult to tell what progress the programme has made. The Third Plan indicated that at the end of September, 1960, there were 65 "intensive" areas in operation and 18 "pre-intensive" areas, and that three main lessons have been learned thus far; first, that there is scope for introducing improved techniques and mechanical power in villages without creating difficulties about full employment of manpower; second, that through proper local planning and organisation, it is possible to convert idle manpower into a productive resource; and third, that the development of village industries, in order to be significant and lasting, must be linked to the development of the rural economy as a whole. However general these lessons may be, it is evident that the Intensive Area Scheme may hold valuable information for future development planning, although at the present time it is operating at a very low level of activity.

The Khadi Commission's efforts to develop village industries have, according to a Working Group which studied them in 1959, been "essentially exploratory" during the first six years of the programme. The attempts were in only scattered areas of various States, many of the units of production were not well located, and the actual coverage of artisans was small even in organised areas. As with the khadi programme, part of the problem was organisational. Other factors noted by the Third Plan were: inexperience in developing village industry, absence of trained and qualified staff, lack of adequate funds and organisation for procurement of raw materials in bulk, and a failure to introduce more efficient techniques of production. The Plan added that those technical improvements which were introduced did not go far enough in creating increases in productivity and, as a result, did not gain widespread acceptance.

On the whole, the work of the Khadi and Village Industries Commission has not lived up to earlier expectations. As a result, the process of re-thinking the whole programme is now under way, so that new guide lines may emerge under which more productive effort will take place. One significant development is the Commission's recent stand on the introduction of power. Although it has long opposed the introduction of power, the Commission, after exhaustive study, has now taken a cautiously-permissive stand and has outlined certain criteria under which power may be introduced in village industries. Its two principal criteria were: (1) that as a consequence of the introduction of power, there should be no displacement of labour engaged in a particular industry or specific operation; and (2) that the changes introduced should not lead to the exploitation of labour or the conversion of self-employed artisans into wage earners, taking orders from an agency not under social or community control.

The Commission went on to note that the object of permitting the use of mechanical power would be to raise the level of productivity, thereby securing an increased income for the workers engaged in that occupation or industry. It also added criteria for choosing industries in which the use of power could be introduced: (a) where a particular process in an industry involved mentally-destructive drudgery, was injurious to health, or was otherwise obnoxious to the artisans engaged in the process; (b) where, in carrying out a particular operation, there was excessive physical strain or labour, where there was a disproportionate expenditure of time and energy, or where the resulting output was inadequate to meet regularly and without loss of time the subsequent processes of production; and (c) where, after meeting the requirements of the rural population in a particular region, there was a surplus of raw materials which could be processed through power techniques (within the criteria already mentioned) and exported to the benefit of the rural economy as a whole. Finally, the Commission also noted that power was often unavailable or expensive in rural areas, and that the local, or decentralized production of power from locally-available sources of energy should be treated as a primary village industry.

These criteria should open the way to a number of advances in the village industry programme, but as in its other aspects, the details of how to abide by these criteria will be difficult to evolve. The Commission has also retained a kind of ambivalence in this matter of power introduction, which has been characteristic of much of the thinking about village industries. For example, it stated that if, "even after permission has been granted for the use of power, improvements are effected in the implements used or new patterns have been devised which serve to reduce the physical strain involved in the traditional processes, the improved or new hand-operated tools should be used by preference." The way, obviously, is not yet clear.

In addition to the various committees, commissions, boards, and study teams discussed above, the Ministry of Community Development has also played a role in the village industries programme. The decision to involve this Ministry was made in 1955, but no action occurred until after the Second Plan started, when industrial pilot projects were set up in 26 selected Community

Development Blocks. These projects were located in blocks which had been started as early as 1952-53, in the hope that they would offer a more favourable scope for intensive industrial development. The scheme was envisaged as one of co-ordinating and intensifying the programmes sponsored by the All-India Boards, and it was hoped that the experience with these projects would serve as a guide for the industrialization of rural areas. The programme was reviewed by a Study Team in 1959 which, on the whole, evinced disappointment with the general working of the scheme. Of the twelve projects it visited, only three were described as even remotely satisfactory. As its first consideration, the Team noted that only 15 of the 26 projects were well enough established to make study meaningful. The others had either done little or had not been started at all. In this connection, it was noted that not all of the people in the States who should have been giving support to the programme were at all eager for it. The Team's second point was that the location of the projects did not seem to be based on any criteria of possible industrial potential. While industrial potential surveys were to be conducted, the actual creation of the projects preceded detailed surveys by two years, only rapid preliminary surveys having been conducted prior to the establishment of the projects themselves.

The Team also criticized the administrative structure of the scheme, noting that it had been mainly carried out as a departmental activity of the Ministry of Community Development through its administrative and technical officers. Little effort had been made to attract to the venture entrepreneurs or small industrialists, or other persons engaged in industry or commerce, but in the few instances in which popular participation had been actively solicited, the projects had made excellent progress. Another administrative problem had been the extreme bureaucratization of the process of sanction and approval of projects. Proposals in the beginning would go for approval from the State governments' industries and finance departments to one of the All-India Boards for technical scrutiny, from there to the Central Ministries of Industry and Finance and to the Planning Commission, and then back to the States. The problem was that no separate financial provision had been made for the projects, despite their importance as pilot schemes. There were a number of examples in which projects were thwarted, not because they were unpromising, but because the budget for that particular type of industry had already been depleted. However, from May, 1958 on, procedures had been revised and no schemes were to come to the Central Ministries or to the Planning Commission for financial sanction, and only new schemes were to be subjected to technical scrutiny by the All-India Boards. Towards the end of the Second Plan, the procedure was further liberalized in favour of the States, and very few new schemes now come to the Central government even for technical approval.

The Team also noted that, "the broad objectives of the programme were not fully translated into concrete practical steps required for their eventual fulfilment," a flaw which we have mentioned throughout this chapter. In this respect, the Team noted training, technical improvement, credit, marketing, and co-operative organisation as areas to which lip service had been given without any significant effort to develop actual, practical programmes which would help the artisans. The Team made two other observations of some significance. The first was that,

"The experience of these projects shows that where there is no electricity and other facilities for the growth of small industries are lacking or are inadequate, and where the area is generally backward, a programme of assistance to traditional and village industries can still be undertaken. There may perhaps be some question about the long-term survival chances of some of the village industries and the wages offered by them may be low; but the relative ease, economy and speed with which they can be set up, and the large number of people to whom they can provide supplementary if not substantive income, are strong points in their favour not only for the present but, it seems to us, for many years to come."

We have quoted this in full not because it is a novel idea, but because it shows that the rural industries programme, despite experimentation and many efforts of various kinds, was finding itself between the same Scylla and Charybdis as before, and the principal dilemma was far from being resolved. The Team's other important observation was that rural industries must be co-ordinated and integrated with the general programme of village development on the one hand, and with the general industrialization programme on the other. Again, this is hardly novel, but, as the Team pointed out, despite all the agreement on this idea and all the lip service paid to it over the years, nothing resembling such a pattern had yet evolved.

Despite this slow beginning, the Community Development programme is now intensifying its rural industrialization efforts. In the "Guide for Rural Industries in Community Development Blocks," released at the beginning of the Third Plan, the Ministry agreed that,

> "The programme of development of rural industries in the First and Second Plans has been slow and it has yet to make appreciable impact on the village economy... With the introduction of Panchayati Raj and coming into existence of the various people's institutions, it is earnestly believed that a better atmosphere will be ushered in for creating a climate for rural industrialization."

The rural industries programme in Community Development blocks has a number of important points. The first is that rural industries can be developed only after careful survey and planning of the problems and potential in a given area for them. Questions such as availability of: manpower, skill and entrepreneurs, resources for processing, communications, and proximity of markets must be investigated before programmes are started. The Guide also suggests that over-all district and block plans should be made which are integrated with one another and they must take due account of both the needs and strengths that the various areas can contribute to each other. Under the programme outlined, there will be a minimum plan of assistance to traditional artisans in every Community Development block. Financial help will be given to such persons for working capital, for the purchase of tools and equipment, and similar purposes. It will be given on the basis of demand for the products of the industry, demonstration of the need of the artisans, and assurance that conditions exist in which the money may be used for the effective installation of improved techniques.

In addition, rural industrial development centres are envisaged for every ten blocks during the Third Five Year Plan. These will be common-facility centres in which equipment that individual artisans or small units cannot afford will be made available, in which there will be training facilities, and in which electric power and the services of competent technical advisers may also be secured. There are also programmes projected for the development of rural industrial estates, for khadi and village industries plans of integrated development in areas of about 5,000 people, for the training of artisans, and for the utilization of rural electrification facilities for industries.

We have mentioned that the new local institutions of Panchayati Raj will also be expected to play a considerable role in the Community Development rural industrialization programme. As the Guide says, these institutions will be expected "to see that with the assistance that is available from the Government, proper climate is created for rural industrial development and to provide fuller and additional employment to the people in the area." The Guide adds that these institutions should help to promote the sales of village industries' products and help to create a spirit of 'Swadeshi" among the people.

The Guide was quite specific in spelling out the duties and responsibilities of the Panchayati Raj institutions at the various levels in making this programme effective. The local panchayat, for example, was to be concerned with local production and consumption of cloth, processing agricultural products, and helping with the artisans' programme. At the block level, activities would include surveying resources, promoting sales of local products, organising industrial co-operative societies, seminars, exhibits, etc., granting loans and subsidies under the State Aid to Industries Act, and helping with training centres of various kinds. Other duties were outlined for higher levels of administration. This new devolution of function and responsibility may well be a source of added impetus to the rural industries programme. We should add the warning, however, that in the immediate future the new-born institutions of Panchayati Raj will have a great many other functions to learn to execute; and without expert guidance and technical supervision, it is unlikely that their own efforts will be any more successful than all the others to date.

Viewed from any angle, the rural industries programme in India has yet to live up to the hopes once held for it and has yet to make significant headway. We have mentioned certain ambivalences in policy which have not helped the programme gain impetus. But we want to emphasize again that the pre-conditions for the successful introduction of modern technology into rural industries do not yet exist in India; and until there are sufficiently widespread electrification, basic overheads, technical skills and the like, the planners will be much handicapped. Furthermore, we must add that even if the hoped-for advances could not be brought about, the employment figures cited in this chapter indicate certain over-all achievements.

At the present time, the programmes for rural industries are in a ferment; and there is much rethinking in process about how to make them viable parts of the economy that contribute significantly to the problem of rural employment and income and that help raise rural standards of living. The Third Five Year Plan seems to be moving in the right direction, and within the same basic statement of aims and goals, suggests that increased outlays, combined with progressively-lessened rebates and subsidies and increased measures of positive assistance, may help to turn the corner. Even so, the Plan's suggestions are little different from those that had come before and within the over-all positive framework there are few details that would lead to definite programmes. Perhaps from the ferment, a well-defined approach will emerge.

The Government of India, in April, 1962, appointed a "Rural Industries Planning Committee" to review the progress of industries in rural areas, advise on problems of policy and planning in this field, and recommend steps that should be taken to promote intensive development of village and small industries in rural areas, including co-ordination of area and regional development plans and pilot projects. This was a high-level committee made up of representatives of the Planning Commission, the Ministries of Commerce and Industry and Community Development, the Khadi and Village Industries Commission, the All-India Handicrafts Board, and several outstanding non-official citizens. The Committee took a close look at the whole rural industries problem and decided that it might be most effective if it actually undertook some operating—in addition to advisory—functions. Although the Committee's work is still in the first stages, the notes and agenda of its July, 1963 meeting disclose a broad, well-planned approach to the question of establishing and sustaining rural industries. It is the Committee's intention to establish "Rural Industries Projects" as an intensive demonstration of what can and should be done. Virtually every State is co-operating with the Committee in the identification of the needs and potentials of particular areas within that State. Vast surveys have been undertaken to look into such questions as: what kinds of industry would be most suitable to a given area, considering the needs, resources, and employment conditions? how can credit be made more abundantly available? is the necessary power and electricity available and, if not, how can it be improved? what must be done to insure proper marketing and communication facilities?

This Committee is expected to give further impetus to the re-thinking and re-formulating of policy needed to make the rural industries programme more effective in increasing rural incomes and mitigating rural unemployment and under-employment.

MAIN AUTHORITIES QUOTED OR CITED

Annual Report, 1955-56, All-India Khadi and Village Industries Board (Ministry of Production), Published by Khadi and Village Industries Commission, Post Box 482, Bombay.

Annual Report, 1959-60, Khadi and Village Industries Commission, Post Box 482, Bombay.

Intensive Area Scheme of Rural Development: Report of the Evaluation Committee, Khadi and Village Industries Commission, 1958.

Patel, Jhaverbhai and Patwardhan, Vithal, *Organisational Pattern for Village Industries,* Khadi and Village Industries Commission, Post Box 482, Bombay, May, 1957.

Patel, Jhaverbhai, *Towards the Oceanic Circle* (Dhanaura Regional Plan), Khadi and Village Industries Commission, Bombay, December, 1958. (Intensive Area Series—8).

Report of the Village and Small Scale Industries (Second Five Year Plan) Committee, Planning Commission, Government of India, October, 1955. (Karve Committee Report).

Report of the Village Industries Evaluation Committee, Khadi and Village Industries Commission, Bombay, 1959.

Report of the Working Group (Study Team) for the Handloom Industry, Ministry of Commerce and Industry, 1959.

Report on Small Industries in India by the International Planning Team, Ministry of Commerce and Industry, 1955.

Report of the Study Team on Community Development Industrial Pilot Projects, Ministry of Community Development and Co-operation, (Department of Co-operation), Government of India, December, 1959.

Review of the First Five Year Plan, Planning Commission, Government of India, May, 1957.

Rural Industries in Community Development Blocks: A Guide, Ministry of Commerce and Industry, New Delhi, 1961.

Second Five Year Plan, Planning Commission, Government of India, 1956.

Small Scale Industries: Programme of Work for the Third Five Year Plan, Report of the Working Group, Ministry of Commerce and Industry, Government of India, New Delhi, December, 1959.

Tekumalla, V. N., *Village Plans at Work,* Khadi and Village Industries Commission, Post Box 482, Bombay, July, 1958.

The First Five Year Plan, Planning Commission, Government of India, December, 1952.

The Sixth Evaluation Report on Working of Community Development and N.E.S. Blocks, Programme Evaluation Organisation, Planning Commission, Government of India, June, 1959. (P.E.O. Publication No. 31).

Third Five Year Plan, Planning Commission, Government of India, 1961.

Working Group on Small Scale Industries: Evaluation Report, Ministry of Commerce and Industry, Government of India, August, 1959.

CHAPTER 16

PROGRAMMES FOR EDUCATION

INDIA's leaders have consistently placed a high value on education as a necessary resource for social and economic development. Few countries in the world, however, have launched plans for building a new nation with so staggering a situation in education as India had when she achieved Independence. More than four-fifths of her people were illiterate when she determined to build a "Sovereign Democratic Republic." Her people were not only "ill-fed, ill-housed, and ill-clothed," but they were ill-prepared to undertake the duties and responsibilities of informed citizenship.

Recognizing the importance of an educated citizenry in the kind of a society India wanted to create, her Constitution contained the goal of providing free, universal and compulsory education for all children up to the age of 14 within ten years. This ambitious aim was partially incorporated in the First Five Year Plan as a first step in carrying out the Constitution's mandate. It was impossible to know whether or not this feat could be accomplished within the ten years specified in the Constitution. States were given the major responsibility for educational programmes at all pre-university levels; and therefore progress was likely to be uneven over the country as a whole, depending upon the will of the various States and the resources available. Only 7 per cent of First-Plan funds was allocated to education, out of a total of about 23 per cent for "Social Services" which included Health, Housing and various kinds of welfare programmes.

The First Five Year Plan did not, of course, restrict its planned programme in education to the elementary level, but recommended expansion also in secondary education, with greater stress to be placed on technical education. The Central government focused its attention on raising the standards and quality of higher education, but its role was largely advisory. Responsibility for teacher-training was left to the States, with the Central government making certain recommendations. Funds were to be expended by the States and to be supplemented by them from local contributions in cash or in kind where necessary and possible.

By the time the Second Five Year Plan was launched in 1956, it had become clear that the educational targets of the First Plan were very far from achieved. The enormous task of providing free primary education during this period to some forty millions in the age group 6 - 14 was impossible to accomplish even within the 10 years specified in the Constitution, much less in the First-Plan period. While substantial progress was made in getting more children into school during the First-Plan period, the Second Plan provided for a greatly modified target of about 63 per cent of the age group 6-11 and about 23 per cent of the 11-14 group to be in school by 1960-61. Thus both the time to achieve the Constitutional Directive and the age span to be encompassed had to be altered. Enrolment in schools at all levels had increased considerably but still represented a small proportion of those in the age groups who should be in school. While it was regarded essential by India's planners to increase elementary school enrolment, it had become apparent that many of the immediate manpower needs in her development programmes could be satisfied by graduates of secondary schools. Therefore heavy emphasis was placed in the Second Plan on expanding and improving the schools at this level and diversifying the curriculum so that the varied personnel requirements, at least in intermediate jobs, in agricultural, technical, and scientific fields could be met by high school graduates. Attention at the university level was directed to improvement in quality and some expansion. There was also considerable pressure for engineering and technical schools in response to the demands of the development programmes that had been launched in industry, irrigation and power, agriculture, and other fields. Approximately the same proportion of funds was allocated to education in the Second Plan as in the First, but in absolute terms it represented about twice as much money.

When the Third Plan was written, India had 10 years of planning experience and programme operation behind her. Some things in the field of education had become clearer than they had been previously. The possibility of achieving the goals of universal, free and compulsory elementary education appeared to make feasible the provision of educational facilities for the entire

6-11 age group by the end of the Third Five Year Plan period, to be followed by coverage of the age group 11-14 during the Fourth and Fifth Plans. This does not mean that all boys and girls of these age groups would actually be in school. Providing the facilities is the first step, but there are still great numbers of children, and will be for some time to come, who will not be in a school for one reason or another. It is still especially difficult to bring girls into school in proportionate numbers because many parents are not convinced of the value of girls' education; many children drop out or are taken out of school as soon as they can become income-earners; and there are "backward areas" in which education is not valued and special problems of isolation and lack of interest make free and compulsory schooling almost impossible. By 1961 when the Third Plan was launched, only about half of the boys and girls in the 6 - 14 age group were in school, twice as many boys as girls. The target for 1966, the end of the Third Plan, is to have 60 per cent of this 6-14 group in school, embracing about three-fourths of the boys of these ages and about 46 per cent of the girls. Achievement of this target, involving nearly 20 million children, will call for a heroic job of providing trained teachers, school buildings of some sort, and teaching materials for an increased elementary school population of this size.

Due in part to a sharpened appreciation of manpower needs for development programmes of all kinds, India's Third Plan has continued to focus considerable attention on the expansion and improvement of the secondary level of education. Because this is terminal education for most high school students, because many intermediate-level jobs in development programmes can be filled by high school (matriculate) graduates, with special training in some cases, and because many new and wider social groups, with a broader range of abilities and interests are now enrolling in high schools, it is felt that education at this level must be not only expanded but diversified in its content. High school must prepare its students for jobs in the middle and lower grades in administration, rural development, commerce, industry, and semi-professional employment to meet the demands for trained manpower without taxing the already overcrowded colleges and universities. A further response to the increasing demands for more trained personnel in the development programmes, particularly in industry and agriculture, is the introduction of the 3-year degree course in colleges and universities (instead of the 2 years previously required) plus additional engineering, technological, and agricultural institutions during the Third-Plan period. Funds for general and technical education, exclusive of higher education, for the Third Plan are in about the same proportion of the total development budget as before but again, the actual amount of money has been more than doubled in the Third Plan over the Second-Plan period.

The most basic fact India had to contend with when she began planning for educational improvement programmes in 1951 was a literacy rate of 17 per cent, one of the lowest in the world. Even among the so-called literates, only a small proportion had had as much as eight years of schooling. Probably as few as 10 per cent of the literates continued into secondary education and fewer still, percentage-wise, went on to institutions of higher learning. Thus there are vast uneducated masses across the land and a very thin layer of educated people located mostly in towns and cities. They are unable to understand or communicate with each other. Education in the past had been supported by the British primarily for the upper classes who were groomed for government posts, and widespread free education in the Western sense was non-existent. The rural population, constituting the vast majority of the people of India, were especially disadvantaged in educational opportunities.

To embark on a programme of raising the educational level of such a large population meant that thousands of teachers would have to be trained, thousands of school buildings provided in some way, and text-books and other teaching materials produced. None of these elements of an educational programme was available to anything like the extent required.

Trained people, and those with at least some schooling, were needed in all kinds of development programmes in industry, agriculture, health, etc. It was difficult to meet this competition to get enough teachers for the growing school population, particularly in rural areas. Recruits for the teaching profession had to be found, teacher-training institutions had to be built, and many teachers were pressed into service who were not much older and who had very little more schooling than their students. New schools had to be built or buildings commandeered for school purposes. Many a school was, and still is, simply a shady spot under a tree or someone's sheltered courtyard. Village people were encouraged to provide their own facilities wherever possible. Even where a school was constructed and a teacher eventually located and put in charge of it, the troubles were not over because there were almost no real text-books, no blackboards, maps, or other teaching materials available. The village school teacher had little to work with and far more pupils than he could possibly hope to teach with any degree of success.

Further complicating an educational programme of this magnitude was the legacy of educational practices with which national planning had to start. It was felt that the curriculum was by and large adapted to a bygone era and that it needed to be oriented at all levels to the new demands of a growing, changing democratic society. This was a controversial issue for some time; but it was widely agreed that education needed a broader base, that is, more children in schools at elementary and secondary levels; that education must be more diversified and must be geared toward India's technical and industrial needs, as well as preparing some few for higher education; and that for the vast majority whose school life would be limited, education must be practical and oriented toward earning a living for the individual, while at the same time contributing toward the economic and social development of the country in many fields. Practices of rote-learning, memorization, heavy dependence on lectures and examinations were also heritages of the past which educators felt were inappropriate to the education required for a dynamic society.

These quantitative and qualitative problems constituted a formidable challenge to India's plans for education ten years ago, and there were giant problems still to be solved as the Third Five Year Plan was initiated. The programme experience of the past decade has revealed the need for qualitative changes in emphasis in the educational programmes at all levels, as well as constant demand for increased facilities and more and more trained teachers. Programmes in education have been modified to meet new and greater demands for education and training in all fields as the machinery of social and economic development all over India calls insistently for trained technicians, teachers, mechanics, agricultural extension specialists, nurses, doctors, engineers, and administrative people at all levels. Major changes in emphasis have therefore occurred within the field of education during the past 10 years in response to society's needs.

In India, where so much needed to be done in so many places and so many directions, all as quickly as possible, there have naturally been controversial issues about policies and programmes. A few rather broad but fundamental ideas have remained an influential part of the educational tasks undertaken. There have been some relatively minor threads of philosophy on educational matters running through the various measures tried. But at least five quite definite ideas can be pointed out here that have influenced the steps taken to try to solve educational problems and to pave the way for what lies ahead.

First, the new idea expressed in the Constitution concerning free, universal, and compulsory education opened the doors to learning, for the first time, to everyone instead of just the fortunate few. Even though it will be some time before this idea can be fully implemented, nevertheless the goal is explicitly and undeniably embedded in India's educational planning which encompasses all age groups, all levels of educational attainment, and all social and economic groups, including the backward classes and the physically handicapped; it includes rural and urban areas, girls and women as well as boys and men, those who prepare for a job early in life as well as those who will go on to institutions of higher learning. The goal is, of course, to make educational opportunity available equally to everyone, in keeping with the ideals of a democracy, and this is a new and exciting part of the educational picture in present-day India.

There has also gradually evolved over the past ten years a recognition on the part of India's educational planners that the schools at all levels must be realistically oriented to the manpower needs of her social and economic development programmes. If the society is to be dynamic and progressive, and if education is to keep pace with the changing needs of the country's economy, educational programmes must meet the challenge of the new areas of study and concern. Curricula have therefore become more job-oriented, new courses and colleges have been added in the technical, industrial, scientific, and mechanical fields to answer the demands for trained personnel in business and industry. More attention has been given to engineering, agriculture, medicine, veterinary science, etc. This is with a view to satisfying the changed manpower needs in an economy where only a very few can afford the luxury of a broad liberal arts or humanities college course which may lead to no functional part in society. However, no substantial switch away from liberal arts has yet taken place.

A third factor is that educators have been faced with the persistent and perplexing problem of having largely to choose between quantitative expansion of schools and facilities and qualitative improvement of curricula, text-books and other teaching tools, plus the raising of standards of schools, teachers, and content of courses. Both quantity and quality were obviously needed but could rarely be achieved at once with the limited resources of money, teachers, and buildings available. The first great expansion occurred at the elementary level in response to the Constitution's Directive, but enrolment has steadily and dramatically increased at all levels, having gone far beyond the capacities of the States and local areas to provide facilities. Schools at all levels have become seriously overcrowded. Efforts to expand the educational plant itself therefore could not be relaxed in the face of the pressure of mounting enrolments. Nevertheless, attention has been increasingly focused on qualitative improvement of subject matter, teaching methods, and standards of achievement from primary schools to institutions of higher learning.

Along with these efforts to improve the quality and quantity of education's offerings has come a companion attempt to adapt teaching methods to new materials and new needs. Real concern has been demonstrated for the uprooting of some traditional but outmoded methods of teaching. Special attention has been given to substituting individual and creative thinking and studying for the former practice of rote-learning and excessive dependence on memorization. A great deal of time and effort has been expended on reform of the examination system which has proved unsatisfactory in modern educational programmes. Teacher training has advocated a switch from the old lecture methods to free and open discussions. Many reforms of this kind, although still far from implemented, have nevertheless revealed a desire to modernize teaching methods and techniques as well as subject matter, to serve new purposes. It would be unrealistic to expect that reform of methods so long implanted in the educational system could be quickly accomplished.

There also has been, quite logically, a continuous and possibly increasing interest in involving the community in educational programmes. This has ranged all the way from such specific things as expecting local village communities to build or otherwise provide their own school buildings to such a vague thing as "educating public opinion" in favour of certain programmes or philosophies. Real effort has been devoted to enlisting the cooperation of parents to send their girls to school and not withdraw the boys as soon as they can become wage-earners. Community participation in school programmes, especially at the elementary level, has been earnestly sought and urgently needed for many aspects of these programmes—mid-day meals, help to poorer children, clothing for the needy. It is felt that community support of schools is not only necessary, but that it will become increasingly effective and widespread with the institution of Panchayati Raj in all States. This is undoubtedly a favourable development from the standpoint of both the community and the school since the responsibility thus shared should help to solve many difficult problems and bring the goals desired by parents, teachers, and educational leaders closer to fulfilment.

One or more of these five ideas or purposes can be found in the thinking and planning involved in the educational programmes undertaken since Independence. Some specific problems in education fall outside of these particular concerns, but most of the major purposes and achievements are encompassed within them. Peripheral issues are bound to be involved in so gigantic a programme as India has undertaken, but we deal here only with the programmes at the various educational levels that may be regarded as contributing to the solution of known problems, carrying out stated goals, and moving ahead in the big over-all job of making education meaningful and useful in India's changing society.

The Constitution which was approved in 1950 set forth several policy statements in the field of education which not only embraced purposes and objectives, but also delineated lines of authority and responsibility. In the area of policy, it stated that government-supported education would be secular, although private religious bodies would be given full freedom to teach as they wished. The division of labour in the administrative area called for primary and secondary education to remain the responsibility of the individual States, while the Central government would continue to take primarily policy responsibility for the expansion and improvement of technical and university education. State and Central governments allocated funds to both general and technical education, but the States were responsible for the expenditure of funds for primary and secondary levels. The role of the Central government was largely supporting and advisory. The Constitutional directive of over-riding importance in the sense of broad policy, however, was the provision for universal, free, and compulsory education for all children up to 14 years of age within a period of ten years.

It should perhaps be pointed out here that ambitious as the goal of universal elementary education was, the statement of this purpose implied much more than was actually spelled out. It was a dramatic reversal of the prevailing pattern of education which had left out the great mass of the people and catered to the favoured few who could afford its cost. It opened the doors to, or at least laid the foundation for, widespread educational opportunity and eventual vertical mobility to better working and living conditions for the next generation through education. It enunciated the purpose of offering schooling to the children of all social and economic groups, not just the urban elite.

The broadening of the educational base also had the correlative effect of reducing the domination of the universities over all lower levels, because an overwhelming portion of the expanded enrolment would not represent potential college and university candidates. The school-going population, when the goals were reached, would be beyond the interests and capacities of the institutions of higher learning. The Constitutional mandate was also inclusive enough to call for special programmes for the children of the socially and economically disadvantaged classes and the physically handicapped, as well as a determined effort to draw into the school-going population the girls of rural areas who were disproportionately represented in school.

At the time the objective of providing free schooling to all children up to 14 years of age was set forth in the Constitution, there were 22 million children of the 6-14 age group in school, about one third (32 per cent) of the children 6-14 in the total population. Nearly 85 per cent of these children who were in school, or about 19 million, were in the 6-11 year age group. By the end of the First-Plan period, although nearly 8 million children had been added to the school rolls, the percentage of the 6 to 14 group who were then in school had advanced from 32 to only 40 per cent. Schooling at this level was free but far from universal. It was also clear that the greater prospect of success lay with the age group 6 to 11 which had advanced from about 43 per cent to 53 per cent of the age group.

At the close of the Second-Plan period the proportion of children in the 6 to 11 age group who were attending school rose from 43 per cent (1951) to 61 per cent in 1961; the proportion in the 11-14 age group went up from 13 to 23 per cent during the same ten-year period, a total increase of some 18 million pupils 6 to 14. The Third Five Year Plan places special emphasis on total coverage of the 6-11 group, with extension of education to the 11-14 group in the Fourth and Fifth Plans. Special attention is also being given to increasing the proportion of girls in the school population, still far behind that of boys. It is estimated in the Third Plan that by 1966, about 90 per cent of the boys and 62 per cent of the girls will be in school, 76 per cent of the age group 6-11, and representing about 15.3 million additional children in this age group entering schools, about half of them girls.

Despite the not-surprising shortfall in attaining the universal coverage goal of the Constitution, school enrolments have far exceeded the expectations of many leaders and have greatly exceeded the capacities of the country to provide adequate facilities. The momentum of increasing enrolments has built up steadily over the past ten years and shows no sign of abatement. The problem is, therefore, no longer one primarily of promoting expanded enrolment, with the exception of girls who still need further encouragement, but one of providing the necessary trained teachers, school buildings, text-books and other teaching materials and of striving to improve the quality of the element-ary education offered. This is particularly important in a developing country with an enormous school population because for the great majority of pupils, elementary education will be their only schooling. It must therefore be meaningful, practical, and the basis for permanent literacy.

There are serious bottlenecks in the way of providing free and universal elementary education to the children of India. There is the tremendous problem of providing trained teachers to staff the thousands of new schools that have been opened all over the country, and to make their training adequate. The number of primary school teachers has increased from 538,000 in 1950-51 (59 per cent of them trained) to 910,000 in 1960-61, 65 per cent of them trained. It is estimated that 356,000 more will be needed during the Third-Plan period at the elementary level alone, of whom it is hoped 75 per cent will be trained. There still is need for providing the physical facilities to house the schools and for furnishing such basic teaching tools as text-books, blackboards, pencils and paper, all in extremely short supply. More than 158,000 new elementary schools were set up between 1951 and 1961 and some 91,000 more will be required during the next five years, bringing the estimated total number of elementary schools to about 473,000 by 1965-66. Some headway has been made in providing teaching materials, but both their quantity and quality are far from satisfactory. The matter of getting girls into school in proportionate numbers has remained a stubborn problem because many parents do not see the value of education for girls; in many cases, it has been necessary to provide separate schools and hostels for girls and for women teachers where co-education and men teachers are not yet acceptable. This has, of course, added to the cost of schooling for both sexes. There are still certain areas in which no local support is given to education and pupils are not forthcoming, areas in which the people are socially and economically backward and probably will not send their children to school except under compulsion. There are other people who may send their children to school for a while, but withdraw them temporarily or permanently when it is felt they can add to the family income. This wastage through dropping out before permanent literacy is achieved continues to be a problem which will require the co-operation of the parents and local communities to solve. The compulsory feature of the Constitutional mandate on elementary education has been carried into legislation in all the States, but it has been difficult to enforce and is actually effective in very few States.

The unexpected dimension of the increase in total population over the last decade has, of course, been a complicating factor in meeting educational needs, not only at the elementary level but at all stages. The addition of 18 million young people between the ages of 6 and 14, enrolled between 1951 and 1961, and the estimated increase of about 19 million in this same age group in the period 1961-66, has automatically altered the phasing of the programme to provide elementary schools, making it necessary to concentrate first on the 6 to 11 group and later, on the 11 to 14 year olds. A special effort has also been made to bring into the school population the children of the scheduled castes and other backward classes. Elementary education is not yet universal but it is mostly free, and significant strides have been made toward the goal of providing schooling to all the children in India up to 14 years of age.

The second major factor in the evolution of India's educational programmes is the somewhat increased orientation of education at all levels to the manpower needs of the country. Development programmes have created urgent demands for trained personnel, especially technical and professional, which India's system of education could not supply. These new demands and opportunities could only be met by a drastic revision of curriculum offerings at all levels, improvement in teaching methods, training of thousands of teachers, and great expansion of the physical plant itself. It is understandable that the significance of the manpower needs of the country was not fully grasped in the beginning of national planning, but as programme operation experience has matured and revealed the great deficiencies in trained personnel, educational planning has turned more and more in the direction of adjusting curricula to development needs. This gradual change has occurred from the elementary schools on through to the institutions of higher learning. The trend has been toward more technical and vocational education, greater diversification of curriculum offerings, and more self-sufficiency within the various levels of schooling; for many students primary or secondary schools will be terminal education.

At the elementary level, the matter of curriculum revision has centred on the controversial issue of so-called Basic Schools vis-a-vis non-Basic or traditional schools. The two major elements in what is known in India as Basic Education are: first, it is craft-centred, in the beginning mainly concerned with spinning; and second, it requires "correlated teaching", that is, teaching of conventional primary school subjects through the medium of the particular crafts being taught. The philosophy of Basic Education also includes the idea of learning from the physical and social environment of the students instead of altogether from books and memorization of facts, what Gandhi called "education for life through life" and the earlier Wardha scheme described as "training of the head through the training of the hands." These ideas are not new; they have been explored for more than 20 years; but they are generally credited to the Gandhian philosophy of revitalizing villages and making them self-sufficient by teaching children useful crafts and by focusing their learning on an understanding and appreciation of their local area. It was even proposed at first that these schools would be economically self-supporting through the sale of the craft products made there. This type of education was thought to be particularly suited to rural areas, although it was envisioned as adaptable also to urban areas. It called for a massive teacher-training programme in these special methods of teaching.

The First Five Year Plan stated that basic education was to be the accepted pattern of all elementary education, and that such Central government funds as were allotted to primary education were to be used to set up at the primary level complete units of basic education in each State, from the pre-basic school to the post-graduate basic training college for teachers. After five years of programme experience, the Second Plan said: "The importance of basic education for a country which seeks to develop rapidly is now well recognised. In the first five year plan basic education programmes began to be implemented effectively for the first time. ... Taken as a whole, the relative advance seems fairly rapid, but considering that the whole of elementary education has to be reorientated on basic lines, the process has not advanced very far yet. In 1955-56 the number of children going to basic schools accounted for less than 1 per cent of the total number of children in the elementary stage; the proportion increased to nearly 4 per cent by the end of first plan and is expected to rise to 11 per cent by 1960-61...." Total conversion of elementary schools to a complete system of basic education was thus somewhat modified to a reorientation of the system of education on basic lines. Considerable concern was expressed about the administrative problems involved in this programme, the heavy costs, and the immense job of training teachers in the new methods required.

The Third Plan summarized the situation by saying, "Reorganisation of school education along basic lines has been a key programme since the First Plan. During the Third Plan it is proposed to convert about 57,760 schools into basic schools, to orient the remaining schools to the basic pattern, to remodel all training institutions along basic lines, to establish basic schools in urban areas, and to link up basic education with the development activities of each local community." The principal arguments advanced in favour of retaining the non-basic or traditional, sometimes called "ordinary", type of elementary schools are that basic schools are too costly, in terms of land, equipment and materials required and the necessary re-training of teachers in the basic school methods; that marketing of the craft products made in the schools has not been economically sound or feasible; that craft training does not fit into the needs of a developing economy such as India is promoting. The facts, regardless of intent and ultimate changes of elementary school pattern, show that out of 381,600 elementary schools in 1960-61 in India only about 29 per cent are now labelled junior and senior basic. They embrace the age group 6-14 years of age, the same group covered in the non-basic or traditional elementary ("primary" and "middle") schools. They are still considered highly experimental especially in urban areas where the problems of providing suitable space and materials are even more critical than in rural areas. The proper orientation of the basic schools to the current manpower needs of the country is still considered by many to be a debatable issue.

The most significant developments at the secondary education level in terms of adapting school curricula to present-day vocational or manpower needs have occurred fairly recently. They include the upgrading of some high schools to higher secondary schools with the addition of one year of schooling, and the diversification of subject matter to include vocational as well as college-preparatory subjects. School attendance at the secondary level is of course far more restricted than at the elementary level; it has been customarily urban, mostly for boys, open only to tuition-paying students, and largely concerned with those students who expect to go on to college. While high schools in India are still not free, the number of students is increasing, and an earnest attempt is being made to improve the quality of the secondary level, both as terminal education for those needed in development jobs at intermediate or lower grades and as preparation for technical and scientific education at colleges and universities.

Following the recommendations of the Secondary Education Commission made as early as 1953, to bring about a greater diversity and comprehensiveness in educational courses including both general and vocational subjects, the Second Plan made these provisions: establishment of multipurpose schools, and of special facilities for agricultural education in rural schools. All secondary schools were to have courses in language, general science, social studies, and a craft as a common core. The Plan said, "A sound system of secondary education, which offers openings in a large number of different directions, is an essential foundation for economic development on modern lines." It was felt that this diversified offering would prepare,

"large numbers of skilled workers, technicians and specialists with a background of elementary or secondary education followed by technical and vocational training in specific vocations... (for) teachers, workers in national extension and community project areas, co-operative personnel, revenue administrators, technical and supervisory personnel in industry, agriculture and other fields of development (which) have to be met mainly from the age group 14-17 years.... It is common ground that at the secondary stage of education, there should be increasing diversification of courses, so that students could be guided and directed to secure training in courses according to their aptitudes and capacities. This object is proposed to be attained through introduction of craft and diversified courses, better facilities for science teaching, establishment of multipurpose schools and junior technical schools as well as upgrading of the high schools to higher secondary schools."

Special scholarship schemes were recommended for girls, to prepare them for already existing and growing job opportunities as gram sevikas (village workers), nurses, health visitors, and teachers.

The Third Plan continued these recommendations for diversification and enrichment of courses, with attention focused on the scientific, technical, and vocational needs of development programmes that could be met by matriculates (high school graduates). The Plan stated that secondary education must have enlarged content and be a self-contained unit in the educational process since high school would be terminal education for most of the students. It recommended continuation of the conversion of high schools to higher secondary schools begun in the Second Plan and further development of multipurpose schools with a number of elective subjects besides academic ones.

Both the number of secondary schools and the enrolment have more than doubled in the past 10 years, the number of schools having increased from about 7,000 to 16,600 and the enrolment from 1.2 million to nearly 3 million. Progress has also been made in upgrading to higher secondary schools about 3,000 of them. By 1961, the number of multipurpose schools had grown from 255 to more than 2,000, with "one or more practical courses in Technology, Agriculture, Commerce, Home Science, and Fine Arts in addition to humanities and science." Thus the effort has continued to make the secondary level curriculum more broadbased, more diversified, of better quality, and in tune with the manpower needs of the country. Along with this change in educational orientation has come a significant move on the part of the government to de-emphasize the college degree as a necessary qualification for many intermediate and lower-grade civil service and administrative jobs. This is to enable better-trained high school graduates to fill these jobs, either with or without further training.

The pattern of change at the college and university level in the last decade or so has been similar in character to that described for the lower levels of education. Here too, the trend has been in the direction of adapting and enriching the curriculum to satisfy the development programmes' needs for more and better-trained technical, professional, engineering, and agricultural personnel. Post-graduate and research programmes have likewise tended to acquire this orientation. College and university enrolments have skyrocketed and many new colleges of all kinds have been established. The primary emphasis, however, has been on attempting to satisfy the needs of industry, agriculture, and business with more adequately-trained college graduates.

Probably the two most important developments that occurred in the area of orienting higher education to present-day needs during the First-Plan period were: the recommendation for a three-year degree course in arts, science and commerce, to follow the higher secondary school examination or a year's course at the pre-university stage after the present matriculation (high school) or equivalent examination; and the establishment of the University Grants Commission. The three-year degree course also provided for other reforms such as improving the teacher-pupil ratio, introducing the tutorial system, and furnishing improved libraries, laboratories, and instructional buildings. The University Grants Commission which has considerably strengthened the advisory role of the Central government in the field of higher education, was regarded as an official agency for giving needed financial aid to colleges and universities without interfering with academic freedom. Outside limits of such aid were, however, to be set by the government. The Commission was also to concern itself with improving the quality of higher education.

Considerable attention was devoted in the First Plan to a separate category of higher education in India, designated as "Technical Education". Primary emphasis was given to the strengthening of the Indian Institute of Technology at Kharagpur and 14 other engineering institutions. Attention was directed to consolidating the work of these schools and improving and reorienting their training programmes in the light of development programme needs.

The Second Five Year Plan continued the emphasis on improving the quality of colleges and universities, particularly in the technical and professional fields, to serve current manpower requirements in many fields. The Plan proposed to establish seven new universities to help to accommodate the greatly-increased number of candidates. The University Grants Commission, which had been created in 1953 and given full statutory power in 1956, exerted a powerful force in trying to assert and maintain college standards. The Commission was given entire responsibility by the Education Ministry in 1960 to carry out the shift to the three-year degree course. Twenty-eight universities out of 46 had made the shift by the end of 1961. In the field of Technical Education, there was a great push for engineering and other technical schools to meet the increasing demands for trained men in these fields, during the Second-Plan period. Nine new engineering colleges, 21 polytechnics, and 3 more regional technological institutes similar to the Indian Institute at Kharagpur were set up. Responsibility for this technical field was held by the Central Government through the Ministry of Scientific Research and Cultural Affairs, guided by the All-India Council of Technical Education.

There was also considerable expansion during this period in medical and agricultural colleges and in such fields as veterinary science, business and industrial management, administration, statistics, social work, home economics, nursing administration, architecture, and town planning, including post-graduate education and research. A clear recognition of the need to co-ordinate higher education with anticipated manpower demands was the establishment in 1956 of a Directorate of Manpower in the Ministry of Home Affairs to work closely with the Planning Commission and the Council of Scientific and Industrial Research on all technical and other manpower needs, as well as with other Ministries and the States.

The present concern in the field of higher education, as shown in the Third Five Year Plan, relates in part to stemming the tide of, ever-increasing enrolments and, at the same time meeting manpower needs, by providing more facilities for vocational and technological education as an alternative to humanities and liberal arts courses, by better criteria for admitting students, and by starting evening and correspondence courses. Overcrowding and resultant student indiscipline, as well as the high rate of examination failure among B.A. candidates, are serious problems in the colleges and universities in India. Enrolment has risen from 360,000 students in arts, science and commerce courses in 1950-51 to about 900,000 in 1960-61; the number of colleges accommodating them has increased from 542 to 1,050 during the same ten-year period. In addition, the number of universities went from 27 to 46. It is planned to add about 12 more universities; and to add 70 to 80 colleges every year during the Third-Plan period.

Other important targets in the field of higher education for 1961-66 are: reorganising, strengthening, and expanding teacher-training institutions, including provision for pre-service and in-service training; completion of the 3-year degree course programme in arts, science and commerce colleges; special emphasis on science education with additional courses in specialized and applied science subjects, and special attention to science in post-graduate and research work.

Very marked concern is shown in the Third Plan for girls' education both because of the many fields in which job opportunities require their services and because their literacy rate and proportion of enrolment in schools at all levels rank far below boys. The Third Plan says at one point, " . . . by far the most important objective in the field of education during the Third Plan must be to expand facilities for the education of girls at various stages." Courses such as Home Science, Music, and Nursing, of special interest to women, have been introduced and special scholarships will continue to be provided, but even so, it is expected that a "massive effort" will be needed to partially close the gap between boys' and girls' enrolment and educational attainment.

Eleven Rural Institutes, established in the Second Plan to train rural youths in their own setting for specialized jobs in rural development, co-operation, social welfare, social education, and small-scale industries, are considered to be still in an experimental stage. They will, however, be continued in the Third-Plan period and will be examined to determine "the full potentialities of these Institutes and their contribution towards meeting the manpower requirements for rural development so as to equip them fully to the development needs of rural communities." Thus rural and urban institutions are being attuned as rapidly as possible to the urgent manpower requirements of the development programmes in all fields.

A third focus of attention which applies to all levels and

branches of the educational ladder, is the matter of reconciling and responding to the demands for both quantity and quality, more or less simultaneously. In India, where the literacy rate is extremely low, where the proportion of children in school in each age group is too low, where about 17 per cent of the rural population was not served by any school at all as recently as 1957, public pressure has understandably been very great for more schools, more trained teachers, more books, and more educational facilities of all kinds. When the Constitution set forth the objective of offering school opportunities to all children up to 14 years of age, priority attention had to be given in the First Plan to building or locating thousands of schools and teachers. As ever-increasing numbers of students have entered the lower schools, pressure has gradually built up for more schools at the secondary level, and similarly at the college and university level. The numerical supply of educational institutions is still far from satisfied, and with rapid population growth, this supply will remain a pressing problem. Nevertheless, considerable attention is now being given to consolidation of existing institutions and improvement in the quality of education, to better training of teachers and better teaching materials, and to problems due to overcrowding and too high pupil-teacher ratios.

It is a characteristic of developing countries, especially democracies, that once the people have faith in education and want schools for their children, schools will be demanded and somehow supplied until something close to a balance between supply and demand is achieved. In some countries this has taken generations; in India it will go on for some time to come.

Meanwhile, the very satisfaction of the quantitative demand leads to dissatisfaction with the quality of what is offered, and equally urgent demands arise for better quality of teaching and learning. This evolution takes time, but India has moved rapidly, and seems to be approaching the stage in which concerns of quality may soon supersede those of quantity. Many think that quality is a Fourth-Plan problem, but in some areas of concern at least, improvement in quality is already a Third-Plan facet of educational planning. As one educator recently said concerning the importance of elementary education in India and its place in the evolutionary process:

"It is not important to debate or determine whether or not India is now at the approximate front, broadly speaking, where other .countries began to concentrate on quality. It is more important to recognise that the evolutionary process is moving very rapidly in this country, that it will accelerate during the coming few years, and that it is strategic at this point to undertake the quality considerations."

The dilemma of the twin needs of quantity and quality in education was apparent from the beginning of post-Independence planning. Many of the problems involved had been aired and discussed over a period of 15 years before the First Plan actually adopted many of the proposals for dealing with quantitative expansion of schools and improvement in quality of performance simultaneously. Various commissions, committees, and boards had been dealing with many of the same educational problems. These discussions began with the reconstitution of the Central Advisory Board of Education in 1935, and were continued with the establishment of an Education Department at the Centre in 1945, which was raised to Ministry level 2 years later. An important All-India Educational Conference in 1948 advocated free and compulsory mass education at the primary level, plus establishment of the University Education Commission and All-India Council of Technical Education in 1948. This discussion and ferment, which reflected public demand for more and better educational facilities, plus Constitutional directives, were taken into account by the planners and leaders who formulated the programmes for education in India's First Five Year Plan.

Priority in the First Plan was given to "improvement and strengthening of existing institutions" and "expansion of facilities on a considerable scale" as and when resources became available —the latter aimed at carrying out the Constitutional directive on universal elementary education as quickly as possible. The most basic reforms, discussed earlier, undertaken at the higher levels of schooling to meet quality considerations included the proposals to upgrade the high schools to higher secondary, recommendation of the 3-year degree course in colleges of arts, science and commerce, emphasis on improving offerings in the field of technical education, expansion of teacher-training institutions by the States to improve the quality of teaching at all levels, and establishment of the University Grants Commission to set and maintain standards in higher education. A modest beginning was also made to improve educational facilities in rural areas through endorsement of the University Education Commission's proposal for rural universities.

The First-Plan period had not advanced very far when Indian educational leaders turned to other countries for assistance in improving certain programmes they wished to undertake. Following a report of the Secondary Education Commission in 1953 concerning basic reforms needed at this level, an international study team of four Indians, two Americans, one Englishman, and one Finnish educator made an extensive tour in India, Europe, the United States, and Japan. They then prepared a report which gave "implementing suggestions" for carrying out effectively the Commission's major reforms which we discussed earlier. In 1955, in preparing for the 3-year degree course for colleges, a scheme was proposed for introducing integrated "general education" courses. As a result of this proposal, in the last year of the First Plan a team of Indian educators was sent to study "general education" in the United Kingdom and the United States and to make suggestions for its application to Indian conditions.

In the field of rural higher education, a leading Danish authority on "folk schools" was invited by the Ministry of Education in 1953-54 to visit India's Rural Institutes and help to assess India's readiness to develop such folk schools or other institutions aimed at the practical and cultural self-improvement of the villagers. Subsequently, a group of eighteen Indian rural educators visited Denmark to study the folk schools, and another international committee of two Indians, one Englishman, and one American visited Indian institutions and made recommendations for a system of rural higher institutes. A Council for Rural Higher Education was set up in the last year of the First Plan to implement the programme and co-ordinate the work of rural institutions. Thus a pattern was set quite early, and has been followed many times since, of drawing on the experience of more developed countries to work out quality standards and techniques for educational programmes needed in India.

The major reforms undertaken during the First Plan to

enhance the quality of education were continued through the Second Plan, such as the upgrading programme and curriculum improvement at the secondary level, conversion to 3-year degree courses in colleges, assistance on the part of the Central Government to teacher-training institutions, and improvement as well as some expansion in universities. The University Grants Commission increased its efforts to raise the standards and quality of higher education. Considerable attention had to be given in many areas to increasing the number rather than quality of primary schools, sometimes by emphasizing compulsory attendance or increasing the pupil-teacher ratio, in order to get more children into school in response to strong public demand and to accommodate unexpectedly high enrolments in many States. A ten-year programme of examination reform at the secondary level was undertaken in 1957 to remove the stultifying effects of too much concentration on examinations by reorienting teaching with basic changes in curricula and teaching methods. At every level of education, the effort to give priority to quality rather than quantity considerations had to contend with the onrush of mounting enrolments and consequent problems of over-crowding, shortage of teachers and teaching materials, and too little money to provide the necessities of a fast-growing educational system.

After ten years of experience, the Third Plan saw more clearly the dimensions of the problem concerning quantity vis-a-vis quality. Concerning elementary education, the Plan revised the original target in order to provide schools for the entire 6-11 age group, leaving the further extension of education of the 11-14 group for the Fourth and Fifth Plans. Attention is also being given to bringing more girls into elementary school and to laying the foundation for an educational base in backward areas. It is proposed to improve the quality of teaching by extending the period of training for elementary school teachers to two years. The programme already under way at the secondary level, to enlarge the content and make it a self-contained unit within the educational process, is being continued in the Third Plan, along with "expansion and improvement of facilities for the teaching of science, provision of educational and vocational guidance, improvement of the examination and evaluation system, enlargement of facilities for vocational education, increased facilities for

the education of girls and the backward classes and encouragement to merit through scholarships." The Plan said, "Special
emphasis is ... to be given in the Third Plan to the consolidation
and improvement of quality in all aspects of secondary education
reorganisation."

Reforms instituted and discussed earlier at the level of higher
education to improve quality are being continued as a part of the
programme for 3-year degree courses. Opportunities for various
types of refresher and in-service training courses are continuing
for the teachers. The eleven Rural Institutes still lack a firm
footing, but are being reviewed as to their potentialities for serving
the development needs of rural communities for better-trained
personnel. Recognizing the need for both expansion and improvement at all levels of education, the Third Plan summarized the
aims of general education as a whole, differentiated from technical education, by saying, "At all stages of education, the aim
must be to develop both skill and knowledge and a creative outlook, a feeling of national unity which stands above region, caste
and language, and an understanding of common interests and
obligations."

A fourth consideration in the educational picture, on which
programmes have been focused, is the matter of adapting new
methods and techniques of learning and of teaching to serve new
educational purposes. The new purposes are implied in the three
foregoing reference points of discussion, namely: universal education which calls for not only a mass programme but one serving
a wider range of talents, interests, and needs; the focus of educational content on the present and anticipated manpower situation,
gearing educational programmes and curricula to the development
needs of the country for well-trained technical and professional
high school and college graduates; and the struggle for quantitative expansion and qualitative improvement simultaneously,
reaching rapidly-increasing numbers of students at all levels with
sound teaching methods and enriched curricula. Some of the
reforms requiring new methods and techniques are in response to
long-time complaints concerning the educational system, while
others are necessitated by the present orientation to educational
needs in a developing society.

One of the oldest and most persistent complaints concerning

the elementary and secondary levels of education was that it was drab, unimaginative, and of poor quality, due mainly to inadequate teaching and physical facilities. Its content failed to hold the interest of pupils because it seemed meaningless, dull, and unrelated to life. Two vivid descriptions by Tagore and Gandhi of the typical classroom help to reveal the character of this problem. Tagore, in 1906, said:

> "What we now call a school in this country is really a factory, and the teachers are part of it. At half past ten in the morning the factory opens with the ringing of a bell; then, as the teachers start talking, the machines start working. The teachers stop talking at four in the afternoon when the factory closes, and the pupils then go home carrying with them a few pages of machine-made learning. Later, this learning is tested at examinations and labelled."

Mahatma Gandhi, writing in 1921, put it equally well:

> "Almost from the commencement (of school) the text-books deal, not with things the boys and girls have always to deal with in their homes, but things to which they are perfect strangers. . . . He (a lad) is never taught to have any pride in his surroundings. The higher he goes, the farther he is removed from his home, so that at the end of his education he becomes estranged from his surroundings. He feels no poetry about the home life. The village scenes are all a sealed book to him. His own civilization is presented to him as imbecile, barbarous, superstitious and useless for all practical purposes. His education is calculated to wean him from his traditional culture. And if the mass of educated youths are not entirely denationalized, it is because the ancient culture is too deeply embedded in them to be altogether uprooted even by an education adverse to its growth."

This criticism on the part of two of India's great leaders reflected a deep-rooted objection to the so-called "de-Indianizing" influences of the educational system under the British, as well as the inadequate training of teachers and absence of teaching materials and facilities. It was in response to this situation that India embarked on the programme of Basic Education, when planning began after Independence, and also instituted a number of elementary and secondary programmes to make education more realistic and more interesting; started programmes to provide better training for teachers in new methods and techniques; and adopted measures to improve the quality and quantity of text-books and teaching materials of all kinds.

Secondary education was regarded as the "weakest link" in the Indian educational chain, and as largely dominated by the requirements of universities. A 1953 Report of the Secondary Education Commission, described education at this level as "too bookish and mechanical, stereotyped and rigidly uniform. . . . The stress of examinations, the over-crowded syllabus, the methods of teaching, and lack of proper material amenities tended to make education a burden rather than a joyous experience to the youthful mind. . . . In most cases, a rigid time-table, unsuitable text-books of poor quality and the unduly detailed syllabus prescribed did not give the teachers sufficient opportunity for self-expression or for developing self-reliance (and) independent thinking in their pupils."

The problem of sterile lectures and excessive cramming for examinations at the secondary level is being attacked by an attempt to institute open discussions, free inquiry, and original thinking on the part of students. A programme of reform to make examinations really valid measures of achievement and a diversified curriculum broad-based enough to satisfy the needs of a greatly-expanded enrolment are being promoted. Special scholarships are being introduced at the secondary level for girls to induce more of them to prepare for careers in vital occupations such as teaching, nursing, and village-level work. In some places the double-shift system is used to ease over-crowding and the shortage of teachers. It is felt that much more is needed for the secondary level by exploring new methods and techniques of teaching, upgrading the quality of teaching through seminars and workshops, and greatly improving text-books, laboratory equipment for science, and other teaching materials.

The new concepts of the role of the high school which have required revision and diversification of the curriculum have also necessitated a new orientation in the training of teachers, and special impetus toward quality-performance is provided in the Third-Plan proposal to give national awards for outstanding teaching. More attention is also to be given to educational and vocational guidance, the organisation of school libraries, and better use of audio-visual techniques in teaching. New emphasis is placed on science in the Third Plan, with general science to be made a compulsory course in all secondary schools, and with nearly half of the schools also offering an elective science course. This will require revised science syllabi in line with new materials and objectives, and it is also proposed to institute a scheme of talent search for promising high-school science students.

New departures to solve problems in the field of higher education include plans for more extensive use of the tutorial and discussion methods to replace excessive dependence on lectures and on external examinations; extension of facilities through the use of evening and correspondence courses; and diversion of students to technical and other specialized fields. Incorporation of new educational methods, techniques, and objectives is being sponsored for the training of teachers at all levels, together with additional research in this field. The Third Plan emphasizes pre-service training of teachers in science and social studies, introduction of new techniques of evaluation, provision of a variety of special subjects, such as guidance and audio-visual education, and the organisation of research. For in-service training of secondary school teachers, it is planned that a comprehensive system of extension centres, established during the Second Plan at fifty-four selected training colleges, will be extended to a larger number of colleges. This in-service training programme includes seminars, workshops, and conferences, audio-visual, library, and guidance services and publications. Each training college offers extension service to 100 or more secondary schools in the area, with intensive training for about twenty in the immediate neighbourhood.

India has also adopted the technique of offering scholarships to permit underprivileged and special groups to take advantage of educational opportunities and to assure the continuing education of talented students. In some cases scholarships serve as a kind of "perquisite", as in the case of merit scholarships for the children of elementary-and-secondary-school teachers whose salaries are still at a low level. In other cases, scholarships and fellowships, such as those provided by the University Grants Commission, are offered to stimulate preparation in fields such as agriculture and health where development programmes require more recruits. Awarding of scholarships of various kinds has increased in scope and importance since 1951 and is given considerable emphasis in the Third Plan.

Scholarships for scheduled tribes, scheduled castes and other backward classes are not new, but the Third Plan attaches particular importance to those at the post-matriculation stage which are now benefiting some 50,000 students. "At the pre-matriculation stage, 4 to 5 million children belonging to these groups received scholarships and other concessions in 1960-61 . . . ."

Among the other types of scholarships now available to encourage higher quality in education are those for meritorious science students, special scholarships to stimulate enrolment of women students at the college and university level, scholarships for handicapped students for higher education as well as technical and professional training, and the schemes undertaken by the Ministry of Education which include national scholarships for outstanding students at the post-matriculation stage, scholarships for overseas studies, and many offered to Indian students by foreign countries and by international agencies.

Community involvement in educational programmes, our fifth topic, has been of considerable importance since the beginning of national planning and has received increasing emphasis over the years. It is perhaps one of the most heartening features of the educational picture, as evidenced by village response to the government's need for help, especially at the elementary stage, by ever-increasing enrolments at all levels, and by the widespread interest in educational problems and needs in the country as a whole. Although adult literacy has made slow progress, the extent of co-operation by parents and adults generally augurs well for their children's schooling in the years ahead.

In connection with the elementary schools, there has been a good deal of preoccupation on the part of the government with the costs involved in providing buildings, teachers, and facilities for so large a number of school children, particularly in the Basic schools which require land, special teaching materials and equipment, and specially-trained teachers. The First Plan stated quite frankly that except for especially backward areas, the

Central Government could not undertake the responsibility for expansion in pre-university education, but would co-operate with States in certain activities of national significance. It said further that

" ... a larger share of responsibility for social services will have to be borne by the people themselves. In the case of education there is evidence that the people are keen to contribute in cash, kind, labour or land for creating the necessary facilities. It should be a major aim of the Central and State Governments and non-official organisations to explore this avenue and harness this urge in the people. ... Besides mobilising the help of the local community for the cause of education every attempt must be made to develop the productive aspect of basic and social education."

Concerning secondary education, the First Plan said, "In the rural areas, the local people should help by providing land, free labour in the construction of buildings etc.... Economic activities like agriculture, cottage industries, small-scale industries, etc., should be encouraged—even from the wider educational point of view—and thereby help to recover at least a part of the recurring expenditure." Central funds, on the other hand, were to be limited largely to pilot and experimental programmes. During the Second-Plan period, there was still considerable worry about costs for schools; to the plea for land, money for buildings, and labour was added the statement that, "What is now required is, in addition, a contribution towards the cost of maintenance of schools, which will be steady and recurring, not merely sporadic and occasional." States were urged to enable local communities, by appropriate legislation, to level a school tax or educational cess.

The confidence of the government in community response to sharing the burdens of educational programmes was apparently justified. It can be said that villagers, by and large, value education, want schools for their children, and are willing to contribute to them in cash and kind as well as by local taxation. There are other kinds of help the government has requested, and received, from local communities, such as co-operation in enrolment drives and in educating public opinion, particularly in rural areas, in favour of sending girls to school and of keeping both boys and girls in school at least until they gain permanent literacy. In some areas, people were urged to work for acceptance of co-education and in many areas to provide housing facilities and other amenities for women teachers who were everywhere in short supply. In a few States, local communities have contributed substantially to a school lunch programme. The Third Plan pointed out that, "In several States encouraging results have been achieved in the mobilisation of local resources, and it is expected that local support will be forthcoming in even greater measure as Panchayati Raj institutions are established in different States. . . . The movement for mid-day meals provides a special opportunity for each urban or rural community not only to participate in the educational effort, but also to improve nutrition and health in the schools and to assist the poorer students. . . ."

Local village voluntary groups and panchayats have been counted on to sponsor and assist school programmes, and village-school teachers have been increasingly drawn into local community life to teach after-school literacy classes, help to organise youth clubs, and act as secretaries in the village panchayats. The village teachers have also been stimulated to become a more integral part of their local communities through a programme aided by The Ford Foundation to orient them to the Community Development programme. This is an effort, started in 1955 and modified in 1960, to institutionalize, in the training of primary teachers, the objectives and methods of community development by including them in the syllabus of teacher-training institutions. Principals and staffs of these training institutions have met at selected community-development training centres to work out new courses of instruction for this purpose. Also, extension-type activities have been started in which the training colleges themselves, and the teachers serving in nearby areas, are to be involved in supporting the aims and activities of community service through the regular school-teaching programme. This is all oriented toward bringing the village-school teacher closer to the people and making him increasingly a part of village life.

The programme of "Social Education," described in the First Plan as "an all-comprehensive programme of community uplift through community action," rests for its success on community acceptance and participation. It includes programmes of literacy, health, recreation and home life of adults, training in citizenship, and guidance in improving economic efficiency. A great deal of money and effort have been expended on Social Education through the Community Development programme, their Social Education Organisers and block education officers, and a certain measure of success has been achieved in terms of developing community centres, reading rooms in villages, organisation of youth and women's groups, and the revitalizing of panchayats and co-operatives. But in the field of promoting adult literacy, results have been disappointing. Literacy has increased only from about 17 to 24 per cent during the 10 years, 1951 to 1961. The Third Plan said that,

"Social education and adult literacy have to be developed as extension activities undertaken by educational institutions, specially village schools, in collaboration with panchayats and co-operatives and voluntary organisations . . . . (but) it will be primarily for Panchayat Samitis, village panchayats and voluntary organisations to create and maintain popular enthusiasm and develop adult education and literacy on a continuing basis in a manner related organically to their own needs and conditions. At every step the local leadership, the teachers and the voluntary workers should be drawn into the movement for the expansion of literacy both among men and among women."

In trying to meet such a fundamental need as education in a large democracy, the problems are always formidable. Some of the problems India has faced, and is still facing, are those which are common to all countries, both developed and developing, that are trying to lay a sound educational foundation for present and future citizens. First of all, education requires heavy expenditure of public funds in every country where the goal is free and universal schooling. Second, there are usually shortages of all kinds that have to be met—shortages of trained teachers, school buildings and teaching materials, facilities for training teachers, and research in educational methods and techniques. And third, there is a continuing need for experimentation and change in educational programmes, which is reflected in the necessity to update and diversify curricula, text-books, and other teaching materials. Also required are periodic reviewing and revising of the methods of presenting subject matter to improve the quality of teaching, to extend scarce resources to ever-increasing numbers of students, and to keep pace with the changing needs of the economy of the country. These are only a few typical problems which countries, at whatever stage of development, must meet and solve. India has had all of these problems, but she also has others peculiar to her own situation and culture.

One of the most stubborn problems in India is the immense diversity of languages and dialects used by her people, plus the rather anomalous position of English as the lingua franca of her officialdom, but regarded as a foreign language by the vast majority of the population. While education in India was under the aegis of the British, highly restricted and private, English was taught to the relatively few who went to school and who were being prepared for civil service and administrative posts in government. India's Constitution, however, called for the gradual replacement of English by Hindi over a period of 15 years.

Since Independence, the language used at the elementary and secondary levels is generally Hindi, or the mother tongue in non-Hindi-speaking areas, while English has been retained for most higher and technical education. Even where English is used as the second language, it generally has been so poorly taught that students are at a disadvantage when they reach college and university levels. There are problems also in the use of Hindi and thirteen other major Indian languages in the lower schools. Teaching materials must be in the local language in each area, and teachers must be found who are familiar with them. Text-books and other materials in these languages are in short supply. Although an effort has been made to develop Hindi and other local language materials, a uniform, all-India educational system embracing text-books, curricula, and teacher training programmes, is impossible with the present multilingual situation.

The problem of text-books is particularly acute in higher education because the relatively few books available to the students are in English. College-level text-books are generally not available in the local languages, and even the languages themselves are not adequate to handle most modern scientific and technical terminology. College students are thus singularly handicapped in that their elementary and secondary education is in a local language, but college-level work is in English, a poorly-taught second or foreign language. A further complication is the fact that the "mother tongue" in one area may be Hindi while in another area it may be Urdu or Tamil or some other regional language. This makes the transfer of students from a Hindi-speaking area, for example, to a Tamil-speaking area difficult at the elementary and secondary levels.

At training institutions of college or post-graduate level serving all of India, the common language at present is generally English. This is also true for other all-India activities—research, regional and inter-state business and administration, in professional, technical, and scientific fields of all kinds. A common language is necessary, too, for the exchange of students and teachers both within India and with foreign countries.

A second major problem in educational programmes in India is the necessary special concern for opening educational opportunities to a large number of socially and economically disadvantaged people. This segment of the population represents about 82 million people designated as scheduled tribes (22.5 million), scheduled castes (55 million), and "denotified" tribes (4 million). To plan and to finance special educational programmes for this large group is a heavy burden. Assistance since the First Plan has been in the form of scholarships at various levels, grants to students to buy text-books or pay boarding fees, and the establishment of thousands of special schools for the children of these backward classes. About 4,000 schools were established during the First-Plan period for the children of scheduled tribes, and about 450,000 received grants for books, scholarships, boarding fees etc.; more than 8,000 scholarships were granted to tribal students, nearly 37,000 to harijans (untouchables), and about 28,000 to students from other backward classes. The scope of assistance, enlarged during the Second Plan, is being continued in the Third Plan as a supplement to the development programmes for these disadvantaged groups. The Third Plan includes special scholarships, residential facilities at educational institutions, exemption from school fees, and financial assistance to needy students.

Educational and other programmes for the backward classes were India's response to Article 46 of the Constitution which laid down "the Directive Principle that the State shall promote with special care the educational and economic interests of the weaker sections of the people and, in particular, of scheduled castes and scheduled tribes, and shall protect them from social injustice and all forms of exploitation." The educational programmes were also viewed as necessary preparation for certain reservations of government posts guaranteed by the Constitution for a period of ten years and later extended for another ten years. These people who are socially and economically disadvantaged, many of them in extreme poverty, many in isolated tribal areas, require special assistance in education, as well as all other fields, to come up to the level of living of the larger communities in which they live.

Of continuing concern to educators in India are the unsolved problems of: a low level of literacy, only very slowly improving; wastage of educational effort because students drop out of school or remain year after year in the same grade; a disproportionately small number of girls in school compared to boys, at a time when women as well as men are needed in development programmes. As in many other newly-developing countries, there is also a hiatus between the relatively few educated elite and the great mass of unschooled villagers. This is peculiarly the case in an agricultural society in which the college-trained are also urban-oriented and largely out of tune with the development needs of an overwhelmingly rural economy. Many of the educational problems such as the excessive importance attached to college degrees, overcrowding of institutions of higher learning, student indiscipline and unemployment of urban college graduates concurrent with unfulfilled demand for trained technicians in rural areas are rooted in this imbalance between urban supply and rural demands.

How well India has handled her education problems is a judgment only her own people can render. Although there is still a long road ahead to fulfilment of many of her goals, solid advance has been made in some directions and the aims have generally been altered or adjusted, not abandoned. India's national planners have stated their convictions concerning the role of education in national development in these words in the Third Five Year Plan:

"Education is the most important single factor in achieving rapid economic development and technological progress and in creating a social order founded on the values of freedom, social justice and equal opportunity. Programmes of education lie at the base of the effort to forge the bonds of common citizenship, to harness the energies of the people, and to develop the natural and human resources of every part of the country."

MAIN AUTHORITIES QUOTED OR CITED

Gandhi, Mahatma, *Young India*, 1 September, 1921, cited in *Selections from Gandhi*, by N. K. Bose, Navajivan Publishing House, Ahmedabad, India, 1948.

Kabir, Humayun, *Education in New India*, George Allen & Unwin, London, 1956.

Post-War Educational Development in India, Report of the Central Advisory Board of Education, Bureau of Education, Government of India, January, 1944.

"Progress of Basic Education in India since the First Five Year Plan," National Institute of Basic Education, Mimeo.

Report 1960-61 of the Ministry of Education, Annual Report, Ministry of Education, Government of India, 1961.

Report of the Secondary Education Commission, Ministry of Education, Government of India, (October, 1952-June, 1953).

Review of the First Five Year Plan, Planning Commission, Government of India, May, 1957.

Review of Education in India (1947-61), First Year Book of Education, National Council of Educational Research and Training, Ministry of Education, New Delhi, 1961.

Second Five Year Plan, Planning Commission, Government of India, 1956.

Tagore, Rabindranath, *Towards Universal Man*, Asia Publishing House, Bombay, 1961.

The First Five Year Plan, Planning Commission, Government of India, December, 1952.

Third Five Year Plan, Planning Commission, Government of India, 1961.

Woodman, Dr. Everett M., "Improving the Education of Primary Teachers in India," The Ford Foundation Programme Letter, Report No. 123, 12 October, 1961, Mimeo.

CHAPTER 17

HEALTH PROGRAMMES

THE magnitude of the health problem which the new Government of India faced in 1951 was almost incomprehensible. The progress made in the first ten years of national development, measured in terms of steadily-increasing accomplishments, has been praiseworthy. But the distance India still has to go to establish even a minimum modern, well-staffed health programme, is one of the indexes to the heroic tasks required of all underdeveloped countries. Adequate care for the physical well-being of their people has lagged behind the economic and educational programmes in practically all nations. This has been true in India, and for good reason.

A decade ago, life expectancy was only about 32 years; *per capita* income was about $52 per year. Some 100 million persons suffered from malaria and some one million died of it each year. Annual deaths from tuberculosis were a half million. Smallpox, dysentery, and diarrhoea killed perhaps a quarter million a year. Nearly forty per cent of all deaths were of children under ten years of age. These gross figures measure only a small portion of the disability suffered from these diseases, and no figures can aptly measure the results of malnutrition, poverty, and insanitation. Probably most forbidding of all in the situation was the validity of the statement made by the Bhore Committee that, "The people view with apathy the large amount of preventive sickness and mortality which exist."

As we view the accomplishments of the various health programmes proposed in the First and Second Plans, and some of their shortfalls and inadequacies, it should be kept in mind that health was but one of the enormous problems with which India had to deal that indirectly or directly would benefit health standards. The expenditures allocated for health were in competition with those for educational and economic development projects, and both of these would also influence the physical well-being of the people. Probably no developing country has demonstrated

better than India that programmes in even so vital a field as
health are made most effective by a co-ordinated attack on all
socio-economic problems.

Moreover, a direct attack on major causes of illness, except
in such communicable diseases as malaria, cholera, and smallpox,
is financially impossible in economically underdeveloped countries. Neither medical nor health service personnel is yet available
even if there were adequate funds. It is clear that India soon
discovered this. Her health programme has become more and
more a preventive one, including an attack on the problem of
insanitation, a programme of health education, and promotion of
family planning. Her administration of health programmes has
become more and more an integral component of local-area
Community Development programmes.

Health conditions in pre-Independence India were vividly
portrayed in the Bhore Committee's report, presented in 1946,
which formulated proposals for both long-and-short-term approaches to improving health in India. Soon after taking office
in 1946, the interim government, in spite of its great political
preoccupations, called the Health Ministers of the various provinces to a conference with Central health authorities. Using the
Bhore report as a basis for discussion, the interim government
endorsed the objectives of the Bhore Committee and used them
as the starting point for programmes of health development in
independent India. Furthermore, the incoming government stated
its own views on health development. Health, it declared, is a
gift of life to which man has a right, and like education, health
services must become a function of the State. Jawaharlal Nehru,
inaugurating the conference, emphasized the need for special
attention to village health and for extension of the benefits of
health to the entire countryside.

Ideas for the development of health services evolved rapidly
as soon as Independence was achieved. The new government, on
the very day of Independence, established a separate Ministry of
Health, under a Minister of Cabinet rank. A Directorate-General
of Health Services was appointed to have charge of both medical
and public health services. In most of the States, separate Health
Ministries were created, and in all States except four, the Medical
and Public Health Services were integrated under a Director of

Health Services. In addition, soon after Independence, WHO and UNICEF, two United Nations' agencies that were to assist significantly in India's health development, established liaison with the Indian government and began to provide both funds and technical personnel.

Because of the problems of Partition and other immediate political preoccupations, however, in the years immediately preceding the First Five Year Plan, there was no strong direction from the Central Government, and plans for over-all health development made little progress. A promising start was made, to be sure, on malaria and tuberculosis control. Safe water supply and sanitation were emphasized early. Expansion of medical education was immediately begun. State expenditures on health, and particularly on public health, were increased. But despite these beginnings, provisions for rural health services lagged.

The First Five Year Plan was essentially a preliminary step toward planning for rapid future development of health programmes. The targets were modest when compared to the achievements needed ahead, but they were high in comparison to the past. The financial allotment initially was 210 million dollars, about five per cent of the total Plan, or two and a half times as much, on a yearly average, as was being spent on health in 1950-51. This amount was later increased. Although modest, the First Plan mirrored the careful efforts, studies, and recommendations of the special committees of the immediate pre-and post-Independence years. It reflected, in addition, important new trends in policy; a tendency to stronger Central government leadership, a growing emphasis on public health, and a recognition of family planning as a programme of national importance. It stressed the importance of health as a fundamental factor in national progress and reiterated the need for government participation in health development. Furthermore, it delineated Central and State responsibilities.

Health being primarily a State responsibility, Central participation was, according to the First Plan, to be limited to higher education and research, and specific national control schemes such as the one for malaria. At the same time, the Centre reiterated the need to have direction of policy for health development in the nation as a whole. The Centre also evinced its interest by providing aid of unprecedented scale in the few areas in which it was to operate. The most significant contribution of the First Plan, however, was the designation of its priorities for national health development in the five years ahead. Although funds were not always allocated which would make these priorities effective, their very designation in the Plan set the stage for considerable future development. The following priorities were set forth:

Malaria Control: Designating malaria as the most important public health problem in India, the First Plan gave it a "topmost priority". It set forth a comprehensive nationwide control programme to replace the various Central and State programmes which had been begun earlier. A total of some $32 million was to be spent during the five-year period, principally by the Central government. The United States Technical Co-operation Mission, then just beginning its "Point Four" programme in India, offered to finance and provide technical assistance for a large part of this programme.

Water Supply and Sanitation: The Plan called safe and adequate water supply a basic requirement and gave this programme highest priority and about $48 million to be spent by the States, supplemented by $21 million in loans from the Centre for the five-year period. The planners hoped that government funds would be supplemented by voluntary labour and money from the people.

Preventive Health Care of the Rural Population: The Plan said that health services should "consist of peripheral primary health units catering to both preventive and curative care of the people with secondary health units and district units providing better and more complete facilities and supervision." Though some minimal Central funds were provided for these centres, the Plan made clear that virtually the whole burden of rural health services should be on the States. A significant new step was taken, however, when it was proposed that the primary health centres be associated with the Community Development projects then being contemplated. Thus the principle was established that rural health services would be part of, and would be spread with, the Community Development programme.

Health services for mothers and children: Few funds were allocated for this programme, but some definite principles were enunciated. The Plan suggested that maternal and child health services be integrated into the activities of the contemplated primary health centres. But it also recognized that the development of such all-round services would take many years and that specific maternal and child health centres would have to be developed in the interim. The Plan also stressed the need for personnel trained for such centres and recommended a nine months' practical training course. Finally, the Plan recommended that each State Director of Health Services should have a specially-trained woman medical officer on his staff to supervise maternal and child care services.

Medical education and training and health education: High priority was to be given to training health personnel, but the Plan's projection emphasized medical rather than public health personnel. It was proposed that medical education facilities be increased to provide 1,500 more doctors annually, or a total of 4,000 a year by 1955-56. The Plan also recognized a growing need for auxiliary health personnel. But virtually no Central funds were initially allocated for training. The government admitted it might not be able to deal with the problem fully and stressed the need for help from voluntary agencies. The targets set initially for auxiliary health personnel were woefully inadequate.

Self-sufficiency in drugs and equipment: Because India was importing essential drugs and raw materials with a value of at least $21 million annually, the Plan gave high priority to Indian manufacture of anti-malarial drugs, penicillin, streptomycin and other antibiotics, sulpha drugs, gland products, vitamins, anti-leprosy drugs, and insecticides.

Family planning and population control: The First Plan spoke of the importance and urgency of family planning, but neither in funds (only 1.3 million dollars) nor in planning did it give this programme effective priority treatment. It did, however, open the way for demographic studies, for research on birth control methods and their acceptability, for research on problems of human fertility and reproduction, and for education of the people on the need for and methods of family planning.

Health Education: A significant new proposal, although there were scant funds to implement it, was for a Central Health Education Bureau, with the strong recommendation that the States create similar bureaus. The Plan emphasized that the eventual success of all public health programmes would depend upon public participation and support. Widespread and intensive efforts for health education were therefore needed.

Despite the proposals of the First Plan, it was evident by 1954, two years later, that successful measures for health development required far more vigorous and positive planning and a far stronger lead from the Central government than had been forthcoming. The newly-established Central Council of Health, meeting for the first time in 1953, began to exert its influence as an agency for stimulating and co-ordinating health efforts; and from then on, major revisions were made in the original Plan proposals and fund allocations largely in the field of public health. A good example was the decision, in 1954, to intensify water supply and sanitation efforts. To give this programme impetus, the Central government, with the assistance of US-TCM, inaugurated a National Water Supply and Sanitation Programme in which $39.3 million were provided by the Centre, almost a third of it for rural areas.

In 1954-55, the rural primary health centres, a priority item, were given practical shape. The Community Projects Administration had begun to include health centres in their development blocks; and in 1954, the Ministry of Health made the major decision to sponsor this programme in other rural development areas as well. The Ministry encouraged State governments to establish health centres in selected National Extension Service blocks and offered Central government assistance to meet the costs of equipment and a portion of operating expenditures. Although the Ministry provided only $1 million, or enough for about one hundred health centres, a significant new policy had been enunciated. Now, instead of having to go it alone, the health programmes were to be wedded to the agency and resources being mobilized for Community Development.

Other national programmes were also initiated at this time. The outstanding success of the malaria programme helped to create a filaria control programme in 1954-55; a decision was made to institute a national leprosy-control programme in the last year of the Plan; it was decided to intensify the malaria and tuberculosis control programmes; a long range programme of supplementary feeding with milk powder was begun with the help of UNICEF; and national committees on nursing and medical education, created early in the Plan period, made their recommendations during the later Plan years. During the First-Plan period, the actual expenditures were just about what was initially planned, rather than the stepped-up allocation later proposed. Nevertheless, the Central government and States had tripled their rate of expenditure for health in the last years of the Plan, as compared with 1950-51. These expenditures were for new programmes alone, and not for the continuation and execution of those already begun.

There were noticeable health gains even by the end of the First Plan. The death rate had dropped markedly. So, too, had infant mortality which declined in the eight post-Independence years almost as much as it had during the preceding thirty-six years. Maternal mortality in urban areas had dropped from 20 per 1000 live births to 2 per 1000 in two decades. Life expectancy, which had been twenty-nine years in 1936 and thirty-two in 1947, was forty-two years in 1956. The national malaria-control programme had, after only one year of operation, cut the incidence of malaria in half. By the end of the Plan period, incidence dropped to nearly a fourth of its former level—from 75 million cases in 1952-53 to 19.3 million in 1955-56. By late 1956, it was possible to think of shifting the goal from control to complete eradication.

The BCG inoculation plan had expanded to become one of the largest in the world—over 72 million people had been tuberculin-tested and 30 million people vaccinated. In the last year of the Plan, the rate of vaccination and testing was ten times that of the first year. The Government also progressed in producing some of the needed modern drugs and insecticides. Public sector enterprises to produce Antigen, penicillin, and DDT were all initiated during this period.

Medical education facilities were rapidly expanded—from 30 medical colleges in 1950-51 to 40 in 1956, making it possible for a thousand more students to be admitted each year. At the same time, in an attempt to raise the quality of medical education, the All-India Institute of Medical Sciences opened with two hundred selected students in August, 1956, in Delhi, under the sponsorship and control of the Central government. Training of auxiliary health personnel exceeded the First Plan's modest targets. The number of nurses increased by a third, to a total of approximately twenty-four thousand; the number of trained midwives by fifty per cent to a total of some twenty-six thousand. This number was, of course, still only a fraction of the needs; and for other types of health personnel, very little advance had been made.

By the end of the First-Plan period, only 725 rural centres had been set up. Many, if not most, of these were only partially staffed, not only because of an absolute shortage of health personnel, but because doctors and other health personnel were reluctant to serve in rural areas. Moreover, it was quickly evident that the training of health personnel at all levels was geared primarily to urban conditions and facilities. In 1953, three centres were established to give orientation courses in rural health work to all health staff assigned to the development blocks. There was also a recommendation, from the national committees on nursing and medical education, to include public health in the basic curriculum for all health personnel.

The high-priority programme of sanitation and supply of safe drinking water, in operation for only eighteen months before the end of the First-Plan period, had by then moved only a small way toward its goal. In a frank appraisal, the Planning Commission admitted that during the First-Plan period only about two and one-half per cent of the total projected piped-water-supply programme for rural areas had been implemented, although the urban programme had been somewhat more successful. The reasons for such slow progress were primarily the lack of materials, technically-trained personnel, and technical organisation.

To help offset these handicaps, however, measures were taken to strengthen health organisations and facilities both in the Central government and in the States, in addition to a small public health engineering division in the Centre. Further, a Central Health Education Bureau was created. Although inevitably neither adequately-staffed nor effective, these new divisions were a beginning; and the States, urged to set up similar bureaus, also made a start. In the States, divisions of maternal and child welfare were also established. In the Central government, a Health Survey Unit was set up to improve the gathering and processing of health statistics, a problem long neglected.

As a result of the experiences of the First Plan, India's planners were in a position to view health development during the Second-Plan period with greater realism and to take for the first time an objective and perspective view of both what was necessary and what was possible. Confronted by the financial limitations imposed by the other demands of national planning, the health experts of the government considered carefully the question of how much they could achieve with how little. The Second Plan, in its final proposals, allocated somewhat more to health than the First Plan had—5.7 per cent of the total Plan budget as compared with 5 per cent. Moreover, since the Second Plan budget was about double the size of the First, the actual Second Plan allocations were almost twice as large—$575 million, as compared with $294 million in the First Plan. To achieve the most with this amount, the planners earmarked more than half of the funds for preventive public health measures—the control of communicable diseases, and safe water supply and sanitation. Just under a quarter of the funds was for other health services, such as the development of hospitals and common dispensaries and health units. Sixteen per cent was earmarked for health education and training.

The Second Plan, unlike the First, named as highest priority the need to establish primary health centres and a regional system of district and secondary hospitals. The Plan called the provision of adequate health services for the rural population "by far the most urgent need" in the five years ahead. It was proposed that more than 3,000 rural health centres be established in National Extension and Community Projects and other areas in the next five years. Also accorded a high priority was the development of para-medical manpower through appropriate training programmes. The Second Plan, now aware of inadequate staffing of every health programme, outlined the need for training nurses, midwives, pharmacists, laboratory and all types of auxiliary medical and health personnel. It also made important recommendations for strengthening training and allocated $12.6 million to create, expand, and improve training centres.

A third important programme was control of communicable diseases. The Second Plan stated clearly that, as a principle, there should be nationwide programmes for the control of tuberculosis, malaria, filaria, leprosy, and venereal disease. Of the total health budget, twenty-one per cent was designated for such control programmes, with more than half of this to go for malaria eradication. Considerable emphasis was given to a campaign for environmental hygiene, concentrated principally on a safe water supply and sanitation programme, with thirty per cent of the entire health budget allocated to it.

The Second Plan pointed to the problem of control of the size and quality of India's population through family planning and provided for further development of this programme "on systematic lines". With more than seven times the funds allocated in the First Plan, the Second Plan made a number of new suggestions: it proposed a Central Board to co-ordinate activities; it stressed the creation of family planning centres; and it repeated the need for a research programme. Twenty-three hundred family planning centres were proposed, two thousand of them for rural areas. Other important programmes outlined for the Second-Plan period included maternal and child health, nutrition, medical education and research, and the broader field of health education.

As the Third Plan was written it was both possible and necessary to assess the health achievements of the first decade—the period of India's first planned attack on its Himalaya-sized health problems. The record of these achievements is one of steady progress, although in the case of malaria there has been spectacular progress, and in the case of some other fields, such as training, some serious shortfalls.

One of the earliest programmes in the health field dealt with the problem of rural water supply. Since 1954, India has had two programmes with the objective of providing safe water, one a part of Community Development and the other an independent National Water Supply and Sanitation Programme, begun late in the First-Plan period and intensified throughout the Second. The Central government gave long-term loans and subsidies to State governments for urban and rural water supply schemes. The programme under Community Development has concentrated on building and improving wells, the main source of drinking water in most villages, because they nearly everywhere have contaminated water, partly at least because of the traditional customs involved in using them. The usual unimproved well is uncovered, has no parapet to prevent slops and dirt from falling back in. The water can be contaminated when each woman drawing water immerses her own bucket however unclean. In addition, cattle are often watered near the well, male villagers frequently bathe alongside it, and there is often seepage or run-off into it of monsoon rains.

Under the Community Development programme, drinking water wells have been built and renovated, usually with a protecting parapet and a pulley system with an attached bucket from which each woman can fill her own container. In some areas, a tubewell with a handpump has been installed. Up to 1 April, 1960 this programme had, according to official figures, built or renovated 4,570 drinking water wells. But despite this very sizeable achievement, the problem of safe drinking water remains largely unsolved. A 1960 survey by the Programme Evaluation Organisation of eighteen development blocks found that in ten of them, in nearly all of which considerable well and water-supply construction had taken place, shortage of safe drinking water was the primary health problem.

Under the National Water Supply and Sanitation Programme, approximately 11,000 villages were provided with piped water during the First and Second Plans. By the end of the Second Plan, 16 million people in rural areas had benefited from this programme; 13 million additional people in urban areas had a protected water supply, and 3 million had drainage facilities. Nevertheless, progress has not been satisfactory, chiefly because the funds provided have not been fully utilized. The principal reasons are the scarcity of public health engineering organisations and competent agencies handling the problem, and the policy of limiting national help for villages to only piped-water supplies.

The Third Plan allocated $73.5 million to this programme for piped water and $141 million to the entire problem of rural water supplies. This is considerably less than the $210 million recommended by the Planning Commission's Working Group and leaves some question about the way in which this key rural objective will be achieved. According to a recent comprehensive health survey by the so-called Mudaliar Committee, the urban situation on safe water supply is also exceedingly critical. The Committee reports that about 75 per cent of urban areas lack a protected water supply, and 85 per cent lack a sewerage system. Out of nearly 2,000 municipalities with a population ranging from 10,000 to 100,000, only about 220 had an adequate, protected water supply. The Committee stated further that at the present rate of progress, it will take 50 to 100 years to take care of the water supply and sanitation problems in the country, whereas its importance would dictate that it be solved at least within 25 years. The Planning Commission, however, believes that funds from the various water supply and sanitation programmes, if used together with fullest stress on local initiative, if carried out in the most efficient manner possible, and if integrated into block and village programmes, will make available adequate supplies of safe drinking water to the vast majority of India's villages by the end of the Third Plan. People working in public health and public health engineering, on the other hand, feel that it will require an extraordinary degree of organisation and leadership to reach this goal.

Before 1956, another basic problem, environmental sanitation, and particularly the sanitary disposal of excreta, was left principally to the Community Development programme. Included in its village projects was the building of public latrines as well as village drains and soak pits. A few public latrines were built in a number of the development blocks, but there remained the difficult problem of educating the people in the use and maintenance of them. In 1956, a pilot programme of research and action was begun by the Ministry of Health, with assistance from The Ford Foundation, to find practical solutions, at the village level, for the problem of sanitary disposal of excreta, and more specifically, to encourage the use of latrines. The work in the three centres established under this programme has had a number of objectives: to design a sanitary, cheap, and acceptable latrine; to develop health education techniques, so that villagers would accept, maintain, and use latrines; and to work out an organisational structure for improving rural environmental sanitation. The multi-disciplinary teams which have worked on these projects have included social scientists who at once began to explore the social factors involved.

One study, made at Najafgarh near Delhi, included the following observations: Almost all of the villagers interviewed have no knowledge of what germs are; they believe in the "evil eye" as being associated with disease (although only half believe in "evil spirits"); they believe that mosquitoes cause malaria and that there is value in vaccination against smallpox (although only a few have faith in immunization against other diseases). The villagers have no knowledge about the causes and prevention of tuberculosis; they have access to wells which are improved, but which still have poor sanitary conditions for drinking water; they know that "medicine" can be put into wells to make water good for drinking and think that it kills worms and insects; and they desire paving of village streets and a drainage system for disposal of waste water in the village. About one-half of the villagers interviewed believe that heat is the cause of cholera and typhoid and that "anger" is the cause of smallpox and typhoid; they think that bad food and cold food are the cause of dysentery and diarrhoea and that feces and filth are responsible for many kinds of diseases; they believe that the village headman is the proper person to look after the cleanliness of their village and that filth breeds worms and insects; they wash themselves in the village ponds which are generally used for washing clothes and from which cattle drink water.

The research team discovered that there were no religious or superstitious beliefs that precluded the use of latrines, but rather certain attitudes and long-standing social customs. The survey also showed that almost all of the interviewees did not wish to have latrines because they said they remain filthy and give a bad odour. Fresh air and avoidance of odour were the main reasons given for preferring to go to the fields for defecation. Women most often indicated that they go after sunset, in groups, thereby providing themselves an opportunity to gossip. Of the total respondents, about three-fourths said that they would refuse to have a latrine even if it were installed for them without cost.

At the same time, the project showed that customs could be changed by concentrated and skilful educational methods. When a practical latrine design was achieved, nationally accepted, and recommended in 1958, pilot educational programmes tested methods of encouraging its use and acceptance in individual homes. These tests indicated that the creation of widespread acceptance of latrines would require every kind of educational method, touching on every kind of motivation. It was also apparent that the Community Development blocks offered the most promising administrative framework for this kind of effort. Such a programme will require a full-time sanitary inspector in each block who has the close support of other members of the block team and of District and State officials. Considerable specialized training and orientation for all Community Development personnel will evidently be necessary. Furthermore, the project has demonstrated that a subsidy of about $4 for each latrine will probably be required to guarantee acceptance. With the type of organisation proposed, it is now believed that the funds available for sanitation in State Health and Community Development budgets can yield substantial results. Madras, Punjab, and West Bengal have already made arrangements to organise all their resources in this manner; and a national recommendation for such programmes has just been made by the Central government. In all, while it seems evident that it will take considerable time and effort for rural India to adopt, nationwide, new sanitary practices, the pattern of how to bring about a change is now both clear and promising.

The Second Plan decided to give comprehensive rural health service priority emphasis, a decision which emerged from the experience of placing primary health centres in Community Development blocks and utilizing their administrative structure and developmental personnel. It was this decision which launched India in establishing what is now believed to be the world's largest rural health service. The programme began on a small scale in 1954 when the Ministry of Health first established primary health centres in selected development blocks, but only 74 centres were opened, and Community Development's contribution brought the total to 725 by the end of the First Plan. Then, in 1956, it was decided to place these centres in all of the development blocks, in short, to blanket India with primary health centres. The Second Plan expressed the hope that 3,000 additional primary health centres would open during the Plan period.

Many of India's health planners feared that this spread would result in only quantity, without sufficient quality. They also were concerned that the population to be covered by each centre would be too large to be handled effectively. Nevertheless, recommendations for the centres were made, in the hope that quality would come later, and that the dissemination of a basic organisation would provide the elements of a health system for the entire country. With these problems in mind, the Second Plan suggested certain basic strategies. Knowing that the quality and pattern of health services provided by the centres would vary widely, the Plan urged that a broad uniform pattern for the structure and function of these health units be accepted throughout the country. It stated that new dispensaries should not be started along old lines, and existing dispensaries should be converted into health units; in short, that the primary health centre must become the basic health unit.

The Second Plan also noted which "essential services" the primary health centre was to provide, namely: (1) institutional and domiciliary care, with adequate emphasis on its preventive aspects, including maternal and child health, school health, and control of communicable diseases; (2) environmental sanitation; (3) health education; (4) improving vital and health statistics; and (5) family planning. Communicable-disease control, for major programmes, was to be handled at first by a special staff under national auspices. But the Plan also recommended that these programmes be integrated with other activities of the primary centres, once adequate control had been established on a national basis. A shortfall was almost inherent in so obviously heroic an attempt. By the end of the Second Plan, approximately 2,800 primary units were established, about 1,000 less than had been hoped for. The lag was due partially to shortage of personnel and partly to delays in construction of both the centres and staff quarters. Nevertheless, the programme continues to grow; and during the Third-Plan period, primary health centres are projected for every development block in the country, which will mean a total of 5,000 centres by 1966.

As expected, a principal problem has been the maintenance of quality in the services the primary centres give. First, the population to be covered is much too large for the staff available. The population effectively reached is usually about ten to fifteen thousand, whereas the block population expected to be covered is anywhere from sixty to seventy thousand. Furthermore, the staff designated for the health centres is at present minimal: one medical officer, one lady health visitor, four trained midwives, one compounder (drug-dispenser), one sanitary inspector, and a small ancillary staff. Even many of these positions remain unfilled. In March, 1960, for example, nearly 400, or 20 per cent, of the centres then functioning were without doctors. Similarly, lady health visitors, midwives, and public health nurses are in short supply. Nor is the effectiveness of the trained staff members enhanced by the burden of clerical and reporting work currently required of them.

In the recruitment of doctors, the primary health centres have been handicapped less by an absolute shortage of doctors than by the doctors' reluctance to serve in rural areas. Here the principal reason is a lack of amenities—schools, housing, and the like for the doctor's family—and the lack of financial inducement which would compensate for the loss of private practice and urban amenities. Some States now pay special rural allowances for doctors in primary centres, varying all the way from $3.15 to $32.55 per month. The States have repeatedly, at annual meetings of the Central Council of Health, asked the Central government to assist in providing both amenities and financial inducements for primary health personnel, so far without success.

The problem of staffing is made even more complicated by the fact that urban-trained doctors often have neither understanding nor sympathy for rural health problems. To combat this, work in rural clinics is gradually being introduced into the medical colleges, but as yet the number of such programmes is small. It has also been urged that more health personnel for the centres be oriented to rural health work and the problems of teamwork in the field. Three orientation centres were started for this purpose in 1953, but thus far, only about 5 per cent of all health personnel posted to primary health centres has had this training. Another handicap for the staff of primary centres is the absence of a co-ordinated plan for providing rural health services. While general guidebooks have been prepared, no coherent plan of action has been devised. Thus, a doctor who arrives at the primary centre has, in effect, no specific programme of action before him, and there is little or nothing in his urban-oriented training relevant to the staggering job he faces.

Despite all of these problems, however, India continues to

extend and strengthen this new system of rural health centres in the development areas. Almost all of the health planners feel that with proper organisation and imaginative, creative use of the minimum primary health centre staff, a far better health job than at present can be done. It is with this thought in mind, plus the realization that difficulties are inevitable in establishing an effective service for the second largest population in the world, that the programmes continue to expand and improve.

In the control of communicable diseases, India shows one of her most successful achievements and one of her most illuminating shortfalls. The success is the national malaria-control effort. Begun in 1953, this programme has become one of the most popular, as well as the most successful, of India's health efforts. Annual incidence of malaria has dropped spectacularly, from seventy-five million cases a year in 1952-53 to ten million cases in 1960-61. Indeed, the programme has been so successful that a National Eradication Programme begun in 1958 was phased over an eight-year period, with a target date of 1966 set for total eradication of the disease, a possibility not even contemplated at the time of the Bhore Committee report in 1946.

With malaria control in hand, tuberculosis remains the greatest single communicable-disease problem. Recent surveys indicate that while deaths from tuberculosis are declining, the incidence remains more or less the same, and is as much a problem in rural as in urban areas. Under a mass BCG vaccination campaign, it was estimated that at the end of the decade about 120 million people had been tuberculin-tested and about 60 million vaccinated. Both the First and Second Plans have proposed increases in clinics, in domiciliary services, and in the number of hospital beds available to tuberculosis patients. Delays in construction, shortages of State funds, and lack of trained staff have slowed down this programme, however, and progress has been well below expectations, even though Central government funds have been available.

Leprosy also remains a problem, particularly in rural areas. It is estimated that there are about two million actual cases, with a hundred million people living in endemic leprosy areas. To alleviate this, the national leprosy-control programme was begun in 1955-56 to provide clinical care and treatment, and the Second

Plan continued and intensified the programme. About one hundred and ten control-unit clinics have been set up. Another hundred are projected for the Third-Plan period. In addition, the Third Plan suggests that every hospital and primary health unit in endemic areas be organised as a nucleus for leprosy-control work. Voluntary organisations have played an important role in leprosy programmes.

Because preventive measures for both smallpox and cholera had long been part of State health programmes, and because the incidence of both had long been declining, neither was mentioned in the First and Second Plans. In early 1958, however, there was a marked rise in smallpox cases and there were sporadic outbreaks of cholera. As a result, an expert committee was appointed; reporting in mid-1959, it recommended that a national smallpox eradication campaign be undertaken, that there be compulsory vaccination and re-vaccination, and that twenty thousand vaccinators be trained for the programme. The Committee also recommended studies to determine the effectiveness of various educational and technical problems of mass vaccination; to assess cost, staff, and organisation required; and to investigate the social and cultural factors that have thus far impeded smallpox-control efforts. The failure to control smallpox is, we might add here, a striking example of how availability of a cheap, easy, and specific technique for prevention can be virtually useless and ineffective unless health education methods and proper organisational tactics are developed to implement the technique.

The Third Plan has proposed the launching of a national smallpox eradication campaign, based on the Committee's recommendations. A recent study has given added urgency to this programme. It shows that, while there has been a substantial decrease in the deaths caused by smallpox, one of the major epidemic diseases of India, there has been no significant reduction in its incidence in the past 15 years. For cholera, the committee recommended an eradication campaign in West Bengal and Orissa, and constant attention to purity of water supply in other areas that have had sporadic outbreaks. Since the disease is confined primarily to Bay of Bengal deltaic regions, a cholera-control programme on a nationwide basis was not proposed.

Basic to all health problems in India is the lack of good

nutrition. The Indian diet, of which roughly 90 per cent is cereals, is deficient in proteins, protective foods, and important minerals and vitamins. There has been, however, admittedly no concentrated effort during the first two Plans to improve nutrition, change food habits, or create greater awareness of the problem except among pre-school and school children. Although the First Plan called the Indian diet as a whole defective in quality, its only proposals were to urge school-feeding programmes and to create nutrition sections in State public health departments. Funds allocated were minimal and virtually nothing was done.

The Second Plan stated that, "Nutrition is the most important single factor in the maintenance of health." But it went on to say, "As it will not be possible to provide nutrition at optimum level to every body, priority in improving nutrition should be given to vulnerable groups of the population, namely, expectant and nursing mothers, infants, toddlers, pre-school children and children of school-going age." UNICEF, the principal agency and agitator for better nutrition, began providing, as early as 1953, skimmed milk-powder and other food supplements to various school-feeding and maternal and child care programmes. Thus far, however, coverage has necessarily been limited. There is some, though not precise, evidence, that while with the rise in food-grain production diets may contain more nearly enough calories, the supply of protective foods may not be much better, in some cases even worse, than at the time of the Bhore report in 1946.

The Third Plan again emphasizes the importance of nutrition, but it does not expect significant results in the period ahead. Nor is there an effective nutrition department in the State or Central governments. The Third Plan, however, expresses the hope that through emphasis on educational methods, which stress the importance of better nutrition, and through limited programmes aimed at school children, it should be possible to lay a solid foundation for a popular and steadily-growing effort to improve nutrition.

Progress in maternal and child care has been slow but steady. When it was decided to integrate rural health service during the Second Plan, maternal and child care became part of the primary health centre's job. To plan this aspect of the health centre's programmes, all States now have a division of maternal and child welfare whose head, a "lady doctor", has been given special training under UNICEF and other programmes. There were at the end of the decade some 4,500 maternal and child welfare centres, apart from primary health centres. One-third of these centres was in urban areas. There were about 20,000 maternity beds and a very few—about 2,000—paediatric beds throughout the country.

The scope and quality of care, however, are still very limited. There are almost no women doctors in rural areas, and the present plans for the primary health centres do not include them. Very few doctors, women or men, have as yet been trained in paediatrics. Almost all rural births are attended only by a midwife, trained or untrained; and the number of trained midwives falls far short of even minimal needs. More than 90 per cent of births in rural areas are in homes, only 20 per cent of them covered by the staff of health centres. It is not surprising, therefore, that the latest available figures indicate that infant mortality is still as high as 135 per thousand live births, and that the deaths of children below fifteen years of age are half of the total deaths in the country, and half of these are under the age of one. This is an improvement over the situation in 1951 when infant mortality was about 155 per thousand, and half of all deaths were children under ten. Maternal mortality has also dropped from 20 per 1000 in 1938 to 12.4 per thousand in 1961. Clearly, then, there has been some progress, but India has yet a long way to go.

It has been recognized for some time that the progress of all these schemes depends upon the availability of trained personnel. Despite considerable progress since the inception of the First Plan, however, it is generally agreed that India has not yet been able to make an all-out effort to solve the crucial problem of manpower for health. Not only the primary health centre programme, but the malaria, leprosy, and tuberculosis control programmes, and the environmental sanitation effort as well, are hampered by the shortage of trained personnel, possibly as much as by any other factor. It was only after the early experience of the First Plan that the training of health personnel was given high priority. Even then, the target set and the funds allotted were not adequate for the enormous job in hand. Except for village midwives, no provision was made to train personnel with limited skills for jobs as health assistants.

Furthermore, the problem of distribution of personnel between urban and rural areas has not, except perhaps in a few States, been solved, and it is an overwhelming national problem. The case of doctors well illustrates this. During the decade ending in 1961, the number actively engaged in the profession increased from fifty-six to seventy thousand. By the end of the Third Plan, the number is expected to be eighty-one thousand, but because of population increases, the population-per-doctor ratio will remain at 6,000 : 1, the same as in 1950-51. Even these figures are deceptive. Of the doctors estimated to be residing in India in 1956, only about half were full-fledged M.D.s; the rest were licentiates. Moreover, about half of all the doctors are in private practice; only thirty thousand were estimated to be in government health services. Finally, only a small fraction of all doctors, eleven per cent, were working in rural areas, and most of these, eighty-two per cent, were licentiates. Very few women doctors were working in villages. A provisional estimate was made that there were only 6,900 doctors of all kinds in all of rural India in 1954.

The Third Plan estimates that the patient-to-doctor ratio in rural areas is now about five times that of urban areas. To attempt a solution for this problem, it listed a number of proposals, such as: required service in rural areas for members of State medical cadres; provision of better accommodations and amenities as well as incentive pay; scholarships to be made available for medical education with the stipulation that graduates must serve in rural areas for a certain minimum period; the use on a part-time basis of private practitioners; and the use of practitioners of indigenous systems of medicine in primary health units and sub-centres in addition to the medical officer. The Plan also suggested that training of "medical assistants" in a short-term course be started. But the recent comprehensive "Mudaliar Report" has recommended against the revival of short-term courses for doctors in the belief that trained para-medical personnel could satisfy emergency requirements.

For other health personnel in rural areas, shortages are equally acute, especially among women workers such as midwives. It was decided late in the First-Plan period to train a new category of worker, "auxiliary nurse midwives", who would be given less training than a nurse, but more than a registered midwife. These workers are now given a two-year course to enable them to assist with general nursing as well as midwifery, both to relieve the shortage of nurses and to upgrade the quality of midwives. Eventually, it is hoped, auxiliary nurse midwives will replace midwives in primary health units and other centres. During both the First and Second Plans, the Central Government gave funds for this programme and an estimated 130 training centres have so far been established. Shortage of quarters for teaching staff and students has held back recruitment. Training facilities for this programme are, however, being considerably expanded during the Third Plan. The annual output of regular nurses more than doubled during the decade. By 1956, the target is 4,500 nurses graduating every year, and 7,000 auxiliary nurse midwives.

The quality of nurses' training has consistently improved under the guidance of the Indian Nursing Council and with technical advice and material assistance from WHO and UNICEF. But again, as with doctors, the crucial problem is to get trained nursing personnel to work in the rural areas. Bombay State has adopted what may be one solution—setting up a Statewide nursing service for which all nurses will be required to spend a specified period in rural areas. Training of rural midwives has not made enough progress to make up, even in part, for the shortage of modern nurses and midwives. By the end of 1960, India had only thirty-six thousand registered or trained rural midwives, despite a decision made during the Second-Plan period to train and utilize the traditional midwife of the villages, by teaching her modern techniques of asepsis. A stipend of up to $10.50 per month per trainee, a midwifery kit, and small fee for each delivery were used as incentives. But the programme has not been going well, primarily because the training centres have not been located in the primary health centres, and the health centres themselves are so badly understaffed.

On the whole, then, the inescapable conclusion in reviewing the training and distribution of both medical and auxiliary health workers, is that the current efforts and proposed facilities are far from adequate for India's enormous needs. Measures to provide the necessary personnel have as yet been fragmented and unco-ordinated; no all-out vigorous effort has been made. Certainly the problem of staffing rural health programmes has yet to be solved.

Family planning activities in India had started in the early 1930's, but in only a limited way, and almost entirely through voluntary agencies. For the next two decades, religious orthodoxy, reinforced by Gandhi's views on abstinence, forestalled the possibility of an effective national planning policy, or a frank appraisal of the economic results of uncontrolled population growth. The First Plan reflected this prevailing attitude, although it did recognize family planning as a national problem for the first time and did put it on the list of health priorities. The Plan advocated the rhythm method, saying that, "From the point of view of avoiding enormous expenditure as well as that of securing the ethical values that community life would gain by the self-imposed restraint which the rhythm method involves, it would seem desirable to try out this method fully and thus ascertain its practicability."

A sum of $1.3 million was allocated to provide family planning advice in hospitals and health centres, to collect and co-ordinate demographic and related data, and to do medical and biological studies. While, therefore, the Government did set up a family planning committee in 1953, there was as yet no vigorous leadership or official enthusiasm for the programme. By the end of the First Plan, only 147 family planning centres, 21 of them in rural areas, had been set up; and a large part of the First Plan funds remained unspent.

The Second Plan faced the problem with a greater sense of urgency. It called for development of a family planning programme on systematic lines under a Central Family Planning Board, and allocated about $10.5 million for the programme. It proposed to make available during this period a total of 500 urban and 2,000 rural clinics, and to do further demographic and biological studies. By the end of the decade, some 550 clinics had been set up in urban areas, and 1,100 rural centres had been established. By January, 1963, there were more than 8,000 Family Planning Service Centres (including medical institutions distributing contraceptives). Of these, 80 per cent were in rural areas. Also, more than 20,000 persons had attended one or more training courses in family planning education and service. In addition, Family Planning has been incorporated into the normal training programme of a number of teaching institutions for doctors and medical auxiliaries.

In addition to increasing the distribution of contraceptives, sterilization has been an important part of India's family planning programme. Some States are advocating sterilization for men by vasectomy, and this method is believed to offer one of the most important means of birth control until an effective low-cost contraceptive is devised. Two years into the Third Plan, approximately 125,000 women and 210,000 men have been sterilized; these figures are expected to increase considerably in the years ahead.

The Third Five Year Plan contemplates significant expansion of family planning activities, with an allocation of $56.7 million in funds. The number of family planning clinics will, it is hoped, increase from about 1,800 at the end of the Second Plan to about 8,200 by 1966. About 6,100 of these clinics may be in rural areas and 2,100 in urban areas. The problems during the five years ahead will not be ones primarily of finance, but of organisation and personnel, and it is these which will affect the scale and intensity of the programme. Furthermore, as the Third Plan notes, studies have suggested that "there is already considerable awareness of the need for family limitation and desire for practical help and guidance." The Plan goes on to say, however, "This does not mean that the difficult problems of communication and motivation have been overcome or that in terms of advice and organisation much more than a beginning has been made, in particular, in approaching rural communities." Thus, the Plan stresses the importance of education for the family planning programme and indicates that it is this which is "crucial to the success of the entire movement."

When, in the fall of 1962, government agencies were forced to re-evaluate their priorities as a result of the Chinese invasion, the Third Plan's emphasis on the need for education in family planning became prophetic. The 1962-63 Report on the Family Planning Programme indicates the change in its orientation by emphasizing the "need for family planning programme in the emergency; especially to extend the community extension education aspect of the programme, and to increase the use of non-clinical approaches to the promotion of family planning." Further, "the 'clinic approach' could be expected to reach only a relatively small fraction of the people, and could not be expected to make much impact on birth-rates. Ultimately, clinics would be viewed as a 'second echelon' resource, for providing special services."

The Report sets out the "Basic Goals and Principles" to be sought in the newly-oriented programme. "The proposed main goal from now on is to accelerate the rate of adoption of family planning so as to reduce the birth rate in India to 25 births per 1000 population by 1973. (The rate is presently 40 births per 1000.).... Achievement of this goal could approximately double the speed of over-all economic development of India, and profoundly influence India's future history." To achieve this position, the Report recommends certain "operational goals" to which an intensive application of current relevant knowledge must be applied. "The 'operational goals' of the programme will be to create, for 90 per cent of the married adult population of India, the three basic conditions needed for accelerating the adoption of family planning by couples: Group acceptance, knowledge about family planning, and available supplies."

Clearly, there is a new vitality to the family planning programme in India. Organised opposition is virtually non-existent. Where stop-gap clinical methods have proved useful as short-term and special remedies, it is now widely recognized that a new programme on a vast scale is both desirable and tenable. Through the districts, blocks, villages, and panchayats, a new group of dedicated men and women are at work, firm in the conviction that, together with their counterparts in agricultural programmes, they hold one of the two keys to the eventual prosperity and self-sustenance of India: control of her massive population.

One of the results of health programmes in India has been a tremendous increase in population. Stated the other way around, the major cause for the rapid increase in population is the rapidly falling death rate. As other developing countries have found, the results of family planning, or birth control measures, cannot for some time be expected to lower birth rates as rapidly as health measures increase life expectancy. The Planning Commission's statement that "health is a gift of life to which man has a right" is the only acceptable humanitarian conviction. But life means more than mere physical survival. Apathy concerning life is a greater tragedy than apathy concerning disease and death, and apathy concerning life will be dispelled only by over-all economic and social development, not merely by health measures. Much about healthful living can be learned, and will be learned, when general education becomes universal and when millions of persons are no longer condemned by poverty to live not only in ignorance but in squalor. India's over-all attack on the causes of poverty, on environmental sanitation, on health education, and on family planning will in the long run yield greater results in general physical and social well-being than will curative medicine.

India is travelling in this direction. She has followed the normal development trend of first attacking her most killing and debilitating diseases, followed up as rapidly as she could, if still not rapidly enough, with an increase in health personnel, and is now institutionalizing her health programme from local villages to higher centres of research. In addition to this, she now includes health, especially sanitation, in her general Community Development programme. In her Third Five Year Plan she provides for a greatly expanded programme of family planning. This programme is to be implemented not only by all that is known and can be learned about effective methods of birth control, but is to be backstopped by investigations in human genetics and studies in the physiology of reproduction. It may very well be that India, just because she must wrestle so heroically with such immense problems, will, as she is doing in some other fields, make major contributions to the growing sciences of health.

MAIN AUTHORITIES QUOTED OR CITED

Development Volume on Health Programmes in India, Planning Commission, Government of India, 1957.

Family Planning Programme Report for 1962-63, by Lieut.-Colonel B. L. Raina, Director, Family Planning, Directorate General of Health Services, Ministry of Health, New Delhi, February, 1964.

Report of the Health Survey and Development Committee (Sir Joseph Bhore, Chairman), Vol. 1, Manager of Publications, Delhi, Government of India Press, Calcutta, 1946.

Report of The Health Survey and Planning Committee (August, 1959-October, 1961), Vol. I, Ministry of Health, Government of India. (Printed at the Jupiter Press Private Ltd., Madras 18). (Dr. A. Lakshmanaswami Mudaliar, Vice-Chancellor, Madras University, Chairman of Committee).

Review of the First Five Year Plan, Planning Commission, Government of India, May, 1957.

Second Five Year Plan, Planning Commission, Government of India, 1956.

Seventh Evaluation Report on Community Development and Some Allied Fields, Programme Evaluation Organisation, Planning Commission, Government of India. 1960. (P.E.O. Publication, No. 32).

Summary of Proceedings of the Centre/Provincial Health Conference, New Delhi, October, 1946, Interim Government of India, Department of Health, April, 1947.

Summary Record of Fourth Development Commissioners' Conference on Community Projects, Simla, May, 1955, Community Projects Administration, Government of India, August, 1955.

The First Five Year Plan, Planning Commission, Government of India, December, 1952.

Third Five Year Plan, Planning Commission, Government of India, 1961.

CHAPTER 18

SOCIAL WELFARE PROGRAMMES

ONE may say correctly that almost all of India's plans and projects for development were, in essence, "welfare" programmes. Enough food, minimal health services, the spread of primary education, the raising of incomes and living standards—all these efforts had a welfare importance far exceeding, indeed far overshadowing, any possible effort at social welfare in the usual, restricted sense. Yet independent India, reflecting its long history of social work and reform, very early singled out those particularly vulnerable groups of its society which should have some special attention and welfare services under any rounded programme of development.

The new Constitution of India in 1950 not only asserted the equality of women, but also embodied in its "Directive Principles of State Policy" an important broad approach to public welfare. These principles, while not "enforceable by any Court . . . are nevertheless fundamental in the governance of the country and it shall be the duty of the State to apply these principles in making laws." Among those Directive Principles of special interest are the following:

"The State shall, in particular, direct its policy towards securing . . . that the health and strength of workers, men and women, and the tender age of children are not abused . . . that childhood and youth are protected against exploitation and against moral and material abandonment. . . . The State shall, within the limits of its economic capacity and development, make effective provision for securing the right to work, to education and to public assistance in cases of unemployment, old age, sickness and disablement, and in other cases of undeserved want . . . just and humane conditions of work and for maternity relief . . . and promote with special care the educational and economic interests of the weaker sections of the people, and, in particular, of the Scheduled Castes and the Scheduled Tribes, and shall protect them from social injustice and all forms of exploitation."

In general it is upon these principles that social welfare programmes and the newer social legislation of independent India
have been based.

As India drew up its First Five Year Plan it had a favourable
climate for social welfare work as well as social reform, a Constitution which asserted broad welfare principles, some start on social
legislation in the States, a considerable number of voluntary
welfare organisations, a rising involvement of women in welfare
activities and strong public acceptance of their role in this sphere,
and at least a good beginning in formal social work training. The
Plan recognized, for the first time on an official national level, the
importance of social welfare services to the community and to
economic development. Conceding that the broader social problems are poverty, ignorance, backwardness, and ill-health, which
the First Plan's economic programmes would help "mitigate", the
Plan nevertheless asserted that "the gains of economic development have to be maintained and consolidated by well-conceived
and organised social welfare programmes spread over the entire
country.... As the social structure becomes more complex, the
State is called upon to play an increasing role in providing services
for the welfare of the people..." that both State and Central
governments, and also local self-governing bodies, should assure
that they have "at least the minimum administrative machinery
for dealing with social problems." Among the important functions and duties conceived for State and Central governments
were: to study social legislation; to carry out social welfare
programmes; to assist social agencies not only with funds and
guidance but with pilot experiments, information and educational
materials; and to help create a body of trained welfare personnel.

The Plan recognized that, "A major responsibility for
organising activities in different fields of social welfare...falls
naturally on private voluntary agencies"...and "the State should
give them the maximum co-operation in strengthening their
efforts." The Plan added however, that, "While the State may
assist suitable voluntary agencies, the principle of self-help should
be applied to social welfare, and the resources needed should, as
far as possible, be obtained from the local communities".

The most notable proposal of the First Plan was not only
that it allotted Rs. 4 crores (about $8 million) to aid voluntary

agencies, but that it urged formation of a central non-official board to administer the Government funds. This Board "to which a great deal of administrative authority will be devolved ... should be predominantly composed of non-officials who have actual experience of field work in promoting voluntary welfare activities." While the Plan stated the need for trained social workers, it earmarked no specific funds for training, other than what was being contemplated by the States, and stated simply, "It is not possible for many voluntary organisations in the country to employ highly trained personnel for their ordinary programmes and activities." The Plan recommended training "at the community level for field workers, instructors and supervisors," and suggested that agricultural colleges introduce intensive social welfare courses and field work programmes as part of their curricula.

The specific welfare programmes proposed in the Plan were suggestive and fragmentary at best, in part because so little was known about exact welfare needs, or about the work voluntary agencies already in the field were actually doing. "One of the most important tasks of the State is to conduct a survey of the nature, quality and extent of service rendered by voluntary agencies ... to assess the extent of financial and other aid that they are in need of in order to develop their programmes of work, and to co-ordinate their activities." But some definite lines of work were proposed which set a pattern of action that has since been generally followed. "The principal social welfare problems relate to women, children, youth, the family, under-privileged groups and social vice."

What was proposed for women's welfare was stimulating "activities at the community level, both in rural and urban areas, ... by community centres, social education agencies," through organisation of women's groups, "mothers' clubs or unions", maternity clinics, milk distribution centres and the like. To deal with the problem of prostitution, stress was put on review of legislation, enforcement, homes for rescued women, and preventive welfare services. For child welfare, the main suggestion was for distribution centres for milk and other nutrients, some tentative proposals for providing recreational facilities, and child guidance clinics (at least one in every State). For handicapped children (including the destitute and orphaned) who constitute "one of the most difficult problems", more special institutions, "children's villages", boys' towns, etc., were recommended, as were closer regulation and supervision of all children's institutions to prevent abuses. The Plan stressed the need for greater co-ordination and leadership among the then-existing several hundred child welfare organisations. For juvenile delinquency, no pro-gramme was proposed, except a general encouragement for passage or amendment of Children's Acts in the States, setting up suitable enforcement and juvenile services. For the physically handicapped, no programme whatever was laid down, except for what small efforts were being made by the States and private agencies. The only positive suggestion was that sample surveys be undertaken in selected urban and rural areas to get some estimate of those afflicted.

At best, the Plan's proposals for social welfare were modest in the extreme and the funds allocated decidedly meagre. What is significant in the Plan is that here, for the first time, the State acknowledged its obligation for such services and established the principle that the major responsibility lay with the voluntary agencies. Even with this modest approach, and although only half the small funds allotted to social welfare were actually used, an "earnest beginning" was made in the First Plan. The most important development was the setting up, by government resolu-tion, of the Central Social Welfare Board in 1953 "as an auto-nomous organisation under the general administrative control of the Ministry of Education." The Board's functions were: (1) to survey the needs of welfare organisations, (2) to evaluate the programmes and projects of aided agencies, (3) to co-ordinate all government assistance given by both State and Central minis-tries to voluntary agencies, (4) to promote the setting up of new voluntary agencies where necessary, (5) to render financial aid to deserving organisations and institutions on prescribed terms. Within a year, Social Welfare Advisory Boards were set up in the States to help decentralize the work and serve as a channel for receiving and recommending applications of local welfare agencies to the Central Board.

The formation of the Central Board with its State network was, and is, considered a landmark in the social welfare scene in

India. It gave the local agencies not only opportunity for financial support for their welfare services, but provided at the Centre a strong voice on social welfare issues and a centralized medium for stimulation, guidance, and co-ordinated analysis of welfare services that had hitherto been lacking. One of the Central Board's most important functions in practice was to provide grants-in-aid to voluntary agencies. Originally these grants were on a matching basis, although this rule was later changed. To receive a grant, the agency had to employ adequately trained personnel, be open to inspection, and render financial statements. While some agencies were initially fearful of having government "controls" over their work, and did not originally seek grants, there was not in fact "any inordinate amount of government control...beyond the necessary requirements." From the Board's beginning in 1953 to the end of the First Plan, it aided 2174 voluntary agencies with Rs. 7.5 million in grants. The majority of these agencies handled problems of women and children, most of the rest (765) "general welfare". Only a few (150) dealt with handicapped persons, although virtually the only care available for the handicapped formerly was voluntary care.

Surveys made early in the First Plan had shown that most of the existing welfare agencies were in urban areas. By 1954, therefore, the Central Board took the initiative to introduce a welfare programme for women and children in rural areas. By this time the Central Government, specifically the Community Projects Administration and the Ministry of Food and Agriculture, had not yet accepted the need for women's rural extension work. Rural health services had also barely made their scant beginning. Except for a scattering of voluntary agencies (notably in Madras and UP) which reached specifically to rural women, few efforts had been made to help village women rise out of their historic isolation and poverty, and provide them with new opportunities and even elementary social services.

The Central Board's "Welfare Extension Projects" (WEPs) were designed to cover 25 villages each and offer a programme of minimum basic welfare services for women and children and the physically handicapped. The programme, which was not itself new, but resembled those already initiated in various rural welfare programmes, included pre-primary and play-schools for children, maternity and elementary health services, literacy classes, crafts and sewing classes. One welfare centre with its own building was to be set up for about every five villages. At this centre a gram sevika, a craft instructor, and a dai (local midwife with some training) were posted, and at each project centre, a trained midwife and a mukhiya sevika. Staff for these projects was trained largely by the Kasturba Gandhi National Memorial Trust, although the training was never very carefully planned. (This was a fund established as a memorial to Kasturba, the revered wife of Mahatma Gandhi). By 1950, the Trust operated 18 training centres for women welfare workers, 57 medical centres, and 200 rural welfare centres.

The first "WEPs" were established outside the community project areas and often outside the NES blocks as well, so that the villagers could be brought, during the First-Plan period, in direct contact with one programme or the other in as wide an area as possible. This policy was later changed. The initial target was 330, or one project per district by the end of the First Plan; actually about 300 were set up. The budget for each welfare project was small, Rs. 25,000 a year, half of this met by the Central Board, a fourth by the States, a fourth from local contributions by the villagers themselves. Administration of the projects was placed entirely in the hands of voluntary local workers formed into a "Project Implementing Committee". All the paid staff ("employed on the lowest rung") worked under the supervision of these volunteers. Admittedly it was not easy to find enough such voluntary workers in every district, and "the building up of a team of over 10,000 honorary workers who can devote all their time to the work" was bound to be a gradual process. Nonetheless, the scant two years' experience with these projects before the First Plan closed was promising enough to urge their continuance and expansion.

There were gradual accomplishments in other social welfare fields during the First-Plan period. Under the auspices of the Central Board, an inventory of voluntary welfare agencies was made for the first time, so that there could be some picture of what services were in fact provided and available. Also under the Central Board's auspices, comprehensive reviews of social welfare work (and of social legislation) in India were prepared for the

Planning Commission for general publication. These offered the first broad assessment of work in these fields. In 1955, the Ministry of Education set up a National Advisory Council for the Education of the Handicapped to advise on problems of education, training, and employment for this long-neglected group. A study showed that for all of India, there were in 1956 only 60 schools for the blind, 44 for deaf mutes, 9 for crippled and diseased, and 5 for the mentally handicapped. Most of these schools were government-aided. Also during the First Plan, a special committee had worked out with UNESCO guidance a Common Braille Code for all Indian languages known as Bharati Braille and a central Braille press was set up at Dehra Dun to produce books. More schools of social work and advanced or degree courses at universities were being established. A large number of voluntary organisations, aided by funds from the Central Board, were giving limited and specialized training to auxiliary welfare personnel to meet their own needs. This training varied from "quite an intensive study of theory relating to a specialized field to just a smattering of the subjects concerned."

The First-Plan period then, saw the founding of the Central Social Welfare Board as a means to promote new assistance and stimulation to voluntary agencies, described as the "conversion of the potential of voluntary effort into a dynamic force" which has been able to take part actively and constructively in a programme of national development, the wholly new departure of a government-initiated and supported rural welfare programme administered by volunteer workers on a national scale. The First-Plan period saw some, if very modest, efforts started to deal with the handicapped and to gain a more perspective view of welfare needs and agencies to serve them. But in relation to the vast welfare needs of the country, both the programmes proposed and the results accomplished had been meagre in the extreme. We can only say that although it is not possible to measure the results of welfare programmes initiated during the First Five Year Plan, in several ways, new and important steps have been taken.

The Second Plan's proposals were far less tentative and modest than those of the First Plan, in terms of funds if not in specific programmes. The funds allocated were increased more than seven-fold (Rs. 29 crores against Rs. 4 crores as in the First Plan

—very roughly, $58 million as compared with $8 million). The immediate reason for this substantial increase was "that the building up of the organisational network (the Central Social Welfare Board with the State Welfare Boards) makes it possible to embark upon larger programmes." Nearly all of the Central government's funds, and about half of the total allocated to welfare, were to go through the Central Social Welfare Board to assist voluntary organisations, and to enlarge the rural Welfare Extension Projects.

Discretion as to where the funds should go, and as to what types of welfare activities, was left entirely to the Board with its State Welfare Board network. For the first time, moreover, the States themselves showed substantial allocations—Rs. 10 crores (roughly $20 million) in all—for social welfare activities. Some funds, not inconsiderable, were allocated to what India calls social and moral hygiene—for prevention of prostitution and social vice, for youth welfare, and for measures to deal with juvenile delinquency, beggary, and probation. Some social welfare activities, such as prison reform, probationary care, labour welfare, and welfare of backward classes were carried on by the Central and State Ministries of Health, Education and Labour and Home Affairs. Many of the States were also setting up social welfare departments, although these were largely concerned with the welfare of backward classes.

The Second Plan reaffirmed the potential value and strength of voluntary organisations as an instrument for providing social welfare services, and the Government's reliance upon them, and said:

> "... personnel provided by the Government or by public authorities generally represent only a nucleus for drawing into the service of the community the voluntary labours of large numbers of private individuals ... (but) The growth of social services is necessarily a slow process ... (limited principally by) the financial resources available, ... lack of trained personnel and of organisations devoted to social welfare and lack of reliable data pertaining to social problems. These factors tend to limit the immediate objects of social welfare services to groups which are in a vulnerable position or need special assistance."

No specific attention was paid to the problems of training for social welfare work, other than to cite the proposals of the Board to train its staff for Welfare Extension Projects "at the lowest rung," for which the Second Plan presumed existing and proposed training institutions to be sufficient.

Although available data are scant, appraisal of the achievements and development in social welfare over the Second Plan, in fact over India's first decade of planned development, is now possible. The Third Plan admits that progress has been slow, and that only three fourths of the limited Second Plan social welfare funds were actually spent. Moreover, in the light of the staggering welfare problems of India, the decade's specific achievements have been but a drop in a vast ocean of need.

It is, however, known that over the decade 6,000 voluntary welfare organisations—about half of them for women's welfare, half of them for children—have been aided with government grants through the Central Social Welfare Board. It is known that there were, by early 1961, (the end of the Second Plan), some 725 women's Welfare Extension Projects, which were conducting about 3,500-4,000 individual welfare centres in the villages. Through the Central Social Welfare Board, about $15 million in the Second Plan alone was spent on these two main welfare efforts, exclusive of funds provided by the States and by voluntary contributors. It should be remembered that the voluntary agencies aided by the Central Board get financial assistance from the Board on the condition that they keep up their normal programme, using their normal contributions. The Central Board's funds thus are intended to supplement, not replace, private contributions. Village contributions for rural welfare work centres have been readily forthcoming, although the large contributors of the past, the Princes and the big landlords, are said to be less generous today.

Little, however, was done over the decade to improve facilities for the handicapped. There has been some increase in the number of institutions for the blind (100 today as compared with 60 five years ago) and more schools for the deaf. For the first time, the Central government, through a specifically-designated wing of the Ministry of Education, began to assist agencies and institutions working in this field. The Central government also, for the first time, is providing special scholarships for the education of handicapped young people (about 660 of these were awarded over the Second-Plan period). It also began, after consultation with the International Labour Organisation, to set up a series of special employment offices for the handicapped. There is increasing realization that education and training of the handicapped must be related to employment possibilities. India finds itself, even after 10 years, however, without any reliable or even reasonably comprehensive data on the number of handicapped, a very serious barrier to assessing and planning programmes. Even without these data, it is recognized now that the majority of handicapped are in rural areas, and that present programmes reach few, if any, of these.

Over the decade, the State governments have also become more aware of their responsibilities toward social welfare programmes. They now feel the need to establish the institutions and services necessary for the proper enforcement of the growing body of social legislation on their books and to carry out the new programmes on juvenile delinquency, probationary and rehabilitation care which are being stressed in the Third Plan. In general, however, although some of both national and State social legislation may be more utopian than enforceable, India has not followed, to the excess common among many newly-developing countries, the attempt to provide welfare services to its people by a plethora of social legislation which could not be implemented. Her legislation is largely confined to basic social reforms which government action can enforce. The new Constitution specified a number of such reforms, as did the First and Second Five Year Plans.

The decade saw some new trends in the approach to child welfare. Besides the work of voluntary agencies, and various milk distribution schemes, the new emphasis is on non-institutional care, and preventive work. The Third Plan is sponsoring, on a pilot basis, India's first effort to integrate existing child welfare services and stimulate new services in a few selected areas, using both official agencies and voluntary direction. This programme is intended for normal as well as deprived or handicapped children up to 16 years of age, and will include health and education, recreational, welfare, and vocational services. In the Third Plan, more stress is also being put on measures to deal with child beggary and juvenile delinquency. A Co-ordination Committee on Child Welfare has been set up in the Central Cabinet Secretariat to achieve better co-ordination of child welfare programmes conducted by the various Ministries.

The need for professional training for social work is now widely recognized and training facilities have been expanding and taking on a more professional character. Increasing efforts have been made to develop more professional and more specialized types of training, and to provide what had long been missing from curricula—opportunities for supervised field work. There are now 12 post-graduate schools of social work in India, turning out about 400 trained men and women a year. The majority of these schools, however, are concentrated in certain areas, such as Bombay, Madras, Bangalore, and Coimbatore, while some States like Assam, Madhya Pradesh, and Orissa have no schools of this kind at all. This is an important problem because of language barriers to inter-State transfers.

There is still a serious shortage of trained personnel for many welfare agencies. One of the important reasons for this is lack of well-defined and suitable terms and conditions of service in the agencies. Nearly half of the 400 yearly graduates of the schools of social work go into labour welfare work where pay, pension schemes, and working conditions are prescribed and protected by law; the largest number and best-calibre students, therefore, tend to specialize in this field. There have been discussions of developing State and Central cadres at least for the higher levels of welfare personnel, so that they might have the benefit of government pay scales and working conditions. It has also been clearly recognized that special and yet professional training should be provided for welfare personnel below the post-graduate or administrative level—i.e., for intermediate posts (like mukhiya sevikas, superintendents of welfare organisations) and for junior posts (gram sevikas, playground workers, etc.) There are shortages of such personnel particularly at the lower level, chiefly because there are not enough women "of an older age" who have the educational background to take training, especially in rural areas. "Condensed courses" for women which permit them to complete the five years of elementary school in two intensive years are being pushed, with help from the Central Social Welfare

Board. Since the quality and content of training vary widely, the need for standardization of social work training at all levels is also now receiving attention.

The rural Welfare Extension Projects were, as noted above, started because an early survey showed that few welfare agencies extended their work to the villages. Initiated at first largely outside of block development areas, from 1957 onward all new projects were "co-ordinated" with the community development movement. Central Social Welfare Board funds were pooled with the funds available for women's work in the block budgets. Supervision of the women's work in these new blocks was shared jointly by voluntary Project Implementing Committees and by elected members of the Block Development Advisory Committees. In the co-ordinated blocks, the area covered is now 100 villages instead of 25 as in the original pattern of welfare projects. Up to 10 welfare centres are provided in each block of this kind. These welfare projects, although they have offered valuable services, have not been without their problems, and have been the subject of considerable study and evaluation. Originally, most of the village-level staff in these projects had been hastily and inadequately trained and had drawn upon women who had had little previous education. As the projects merged with the development blocks, the disparity between the welfare project workers and the more formally trained gram sevikas and women Social Education Organisers of the blocks became evident. Following several very careful studies by the Programme Evaluation Organisation, and the Committee on Plan Projects, it was urged that the training of the staff, especially of the gram sevikas and mukhiya sevikas, be brought into consonance with that of the women workers of the formal block staff. A common syllabus has now been prepared and put into use, although there is still disparity in training.

Furthermore, study has shown that, not unexpectedly, the organising of so many volunteer welfare workers on Project Implementing Committees had led to some of the common problems experienced everywhere in organisations relying so heavily on volunteers—inexperience and lack of professional standards, personal rivalries, lack of consistent and regular supervision and the like. The working conditions and regularity of pay of the staff were not always administered properly and the jeep allocated to the project was frequently pre-empted by the volunteers rather than being available to the paid staff. But the fact remains that these welfare projects have brought about 15 to 20,000 women into voluntary rural welfare work, many of them for the first time, and considerable new leadership has been awakened and developed in a field formerly largely untouched, except in a few States and a few areas. The Central Board felt that the chief success of the scheme was to bring out a large number of women to work in projects in their own areas in a common programme.

The general assessment of the Welfare Extension Projects, made principally by the two studies cited and by welfare workers familiar with them, is that, "the basic idea . . . is a sound one and in spite of numerous short-comings the centres are working well." It has, for the first time, brought on a consistent basis some attention to rural women's needs, provided them with opportunities for learning crafts, for elementary maternity and child care, for a common social meeting place, development of community and club activities, and for some nursery school-kindergarten type of activity for their children. Literacy work in general has not been a significant part of the programme nor particularly popular. All studies urged that more attention be paid to young girls 14 to 20 years of age in the programme, especially to make them literate, and to the introduction of economically useful crafts, since some of the crafts originally taught were chiefly "fancy work". Another result of the rural welfare work has been to offer some means to discover deserted women and widows in the villages and send them to "reception" homes or to be trained for useful work. While the work of these Welfare Projects has been "sound" and useful, it should be kept in view that it has in fact had a limited range. In all, by the end of the Second Plan, there were some 400 Welfare Extension Projects of the "original" unintegrated pattern, and some 300 more co-ordinated with the community development blocks, which have been started since 1957. Altogether, at most about 4,000 individual welfare centres were envisaged under this programme; possibly some 3,500 of the centres actually opened. Although theoretically these centres are to serve 5 or 10 villages each, in actual practice the work of the WEP welfare centres does "not normally extend to villages other than the ones where the centres are located." We can thus assume that in fact only about 3,500 to 4,000 villages have been directly affected by the programme, less than seven-tenths per cent of the villages of India.

According to present plans, about 350 of the later, co-ordinated-pattern projects will continue to be run over the Third Plan by the Central Social Welfare Board, with the expectation that after five years their work will be taken over by properly-developed "mahila mandals" (village women's groups) made up of the local village women themselves. The earlier "original-pattern" projects (WEPs) are now being turned over entirely to the management of private voluntary agencies—some all-India agencies such as the Red Cross, the Indian Council of Child Welfare, the Kasturba Memorial Trust, etc. In several States, such as Mysore, West Bengal, and Bihar, the local mahila mandals have already developed to such a strong point that these women's groups themselves have taken over the running of the projects. The Central Board will make direct grants to all these voluntary agencies, including the local village women's groups—a very interesting decision.

The growth of mahila mandals is one of the notable developments of the past five years, under both the WEPs and the community development programmes. There are now said to be some 42,800 of them throughout India. While in some blocks, these groups are weak, fragmentary, and uncertainly guided, and some are only paper organisations set up by gram sevikas and mukhiya sevikas for show or to achieve "targets", in many areas they are now becoming a growing force and focus of women's emancipation from the obscurity and subservience of the past. According to many social workers in the field, village women are now coming forward to join these groups to such an extent that "there is now no stopping them." The Third Plan is to put increasing stress upon mahila mandals.

We cannot assess the achievements in social welfare since Independence by citing either targets or expenditures. As the Third Plan says, "Development over the past decade of social welfare activities ... has a significance which extends beyond the range of services established or the extent of resources utilised." Rather, the experience of this past decade in social welfare, as it is assessed today, has brought about two particularly important developments and three important realizations. The important developments are the extension of welfare services to the villages, and the drawing out of large numbers of volunteer women workers, most of them urban, into rural welfare service. Of the three significant realizations, one is that voluntary agencies must still carry the main burden of social services, but that government assistance and guidance are essential to supplement them and tie them into national needs. Government action, it is now felt, is also necessary to enforce social legislation and participate in programmes requiring larger resources. Further, it is now clear that the organisational and administrative arrangements for handling social welfare services must be regularized and co-ordinated through the Central Social Welfare Board to assure smooth functioning and to avoid overlapping among the voluntary agencies, for the government services, possibly through co-ordinated social welfare departments in the States and in the Central government. Third, there is far stronger realization today of the need for professionalization in welfare standards of performance. in supervision of welfare work and institutions, in the calibre of training of welfare workers, and in the specialization of welfare agencies in limited areas of activity.

Looking back over these past years at India's enormous problem of promoting the general welfare, of providing elementary education, health, even food for its vast population, as the basic "welfare" services needed by all its people, we must feel encouraged that India has at least made some gains and some beginnings, however small and marginal, in accepting and stimulating both private and governmental responsibility for the welfare of especially vulnerable groups.

MAIN AUTHORITIES QUOTED OR CITED

Basu, Durga Das, *Commentary on the Constitution of India,* Third Edition, S. C. Sarkar & Sons Ltd., 1-C College Square, Calcutta, Vol. I, June, 1955.

Estimates Committee, *1957-58 Report on Central Social Welfare Board,* Lok Sabha Secretariat, New Delhi, April, 1958.

Evaluation Report on the Working of the Welfare Extension Projects of the Central Social Welfare Board, Programme Evaluation Organisation, Planning Commission, Government of India, April, 1959. (P.E.O. Publication, No. 29).

Hersey, Evelyn, *Voluntary and Private Welfare Agencies in India*, TCM, American Embassy, June, 1955.

Natarajan, S., *A Century of Social Reform in India*, Asia Publishing House, Bombay, 1959.

Progress Report: 1953-55, (and 1955-57), Central Social Welfare Board.

Report of the Study Team on Social Welfare and Welfare of Backward Classes, Vol. 1, Committee on Plan Projects, Government of India Press, New Delhi, July, 1959.

Review of the First Five Year Plan, Planning Commission, Government of India, May, 1957.

Second Five Year Plan, Planning Commission, Government of India, 1956.

Social Legislation—Its Role in Social Welfare, Issued on behalf of the Planning Commission, Government of India, New Delhi, 1956.

Social Welfare in India, Planning Commission, Government of India, 1955.

The First Five Year Plan, Planning Commission, Government of India, December, 1952.

Third Five Year Plan, Planning Commission, Government of India, 1961.

Chapter 19

THE CONTRIBUTION OF SOCIOLOGY
TO DEVELOPMENT

Social scientists everywhere are interested in the processes and problems of national social and economic development. Because of this, a real impetus has been given to inter-disciplinary research and investigation, especially in the newly-developing countries. As Willem Brand has said, "In order to indicate not only what happened but also how and why it happened, the collaboration of many social sciences is necessary. Only thus may we understand the course of events and the interplay of economic and social phenomena which together weave the pattern of economic change." It is our purpose, in this and the remaining chapters, to contribute to this collaboration.

Economists have literally called upon the sociologist to play his due role in social science teamwork when they say, as do Buchanan and Ellis, that, " . . . to assume, as is sometimes done, that one may proceed from a strictly economic analysis of the development problem to a prescription of a program for development without careful attention to the socio-cultural environment within which this program will have to be undertaken is to proceed in ignorance toward almost certain disillusionment and possibly outright disaster." It should be the unique contribution of the sociologist to give primary attention to the social and cultural factors. In the development of economies which start largely from the basis of subsistence agriculture, there needs to be considerable emphasis on the fact that social development is essential before what Rostow calls the "take-off stage" in economic development can be reached.

To the extent that this is true, it would seem to be the obligation of the sociologist to analyze what has been done and what can be done by way of manipulating and developing non-economic factors, and even non-economic motives, toward the end of developing people to the point where they have what might be called some new economic motives. That this can be done, in fact must be done, is no small part of the objectives of the community development programmes of underdeveloped countries. An oft-repeated statement of the elite and educated members of underdeveloped countries is that the masses do not want to change, that they are apathetic. Statements are made by persons deeply interested in the development of the masses that the villages of their society are stagnant, not only physically and economically but psychologically.

Human well-being, generally stated in terms of improved standards of living of the masses, is the stated objective of development in practically all underdeveloped countries. In the view of the leaders of developing countries, all other elements in, or components of, their development programmes are essential to the attainment of this central objective. The sociologist's contributions to the analysis of the problems and processes inherent in the accomplishment of this objective are: first, to assist in an analysis of the historic, cultural, and societal causes of the present status of the masses; second, together with other social scientists, to make analyses of the processes or stages of development; and third, most importantly, to analyze the means, that is the social processes, by which higher levels of living have been and can be obtained.

Middlemen between social scientists and the planners and directors of social action assume a difficult, and in a number of ways precarious, responsibility. Systematic social theory, built out of a great accumulation of knowledge about both the systems and diversities of social relationships, must be a body of generalizations. The broader, that is the more abstract, these generalizations are the more valid they can be, but the less applicable to any specific social situation. Planners of programmes, especially of planned action programmes, require explicit and cogent understanding of specific units of action. The social scientist cannot be made responsible for the administrative direction of action, but he should not shun the responsibility of fairly specifically pointing out, or even predicting, the consequences of alternative lines of action. He is able to do this, however, only to the extent that he knows, not only the validity of the broad or abstract generalizations which constitute systematic social theory, but also knows the specific research findings which social theory generalizes. If he would be helpful to action programme planners and directors he must, so to speak, dissemble social theory into more specific knowledge about components of social situations out of which social theory is built. We do this only to the extent of identifying the cultural, social, and psychological phenomena which are bound to condition the behaviour, the thinking, and the sentiments of persons whose participation in development programmes is necessary and, in fact, inevitable.

The sociologist and the social psychologist should make fairly acceptable analyses and be able to provide reasonably adequate explanations of why so many members of the masses are apathetic or lethargic. They can analyze the socio-cultural environment out of which apathy and socio-economic stagnation grow. While this is not an easy task, there are probably enough historical or anthropological data available to make it possible of accomplishment. An analysis of the standard of living of individuals and groups requires a study of not only their physical condition but of their expectations or hopes. Anthropological and sociological studies have thus far given this little attention, but need to give the same attention to standards of living as they have given to the levels of living of individuals and groups.

While the socio-cultural environment is too global a body of behaviour cogently to analyze, it is possible to analyze such components of this environment as levels of living, social institutions, class structures, traditions and value systems. It is possible to know not only literacy rates but also to construct communication indices. It is possible, by health status indices, to know much about levels of health, and it is fairly easy to measure the degree of physical and economic poverty. Measurements or descriptions of all of these provide information on the benchmarks from which development programmes start. More importantly, they describe the resident or indigenous human situations with which most underdeveloped countries must start their upward climb. It is recognized that economic growth is desired, and is planned, by all developing countries, but it must also be recognized that hundreds of millions of persons constitute the masses of these countries, that as living human beings they are teachable, capable of growth, and that how to help them as individuals and groups to grow is part of the process and task of development.

Fairly detailed analyses of the socio-cultural environment need to be made in terms of the specific elements which constitute that environment and with which development must start. Foremost among them is the class structure of the society. It not only reflects the socio-economic status of all levels of the population and explains the wide gap between the masses and the elite, but it explains why, in the early stages of development, leadership must come from the top down, rather than from the bottom up. This in turn sets the administrative structure of development programmes and creates many human relations problems on or in the administrative assembly line. In India, for instance, classes or echelons in administration are as much a reflection of the class structure of Indian society as they are a carry-over from colonial rule. Administrators are by tradition members of the elite and are recognized as such by themselves and by those below them.

In the progress from relative stagnation to relative dynamics, many new roles must be and are created. Whether these roles are assumed and played by members of the old elite or are played by new leaders who have transcended socio-cultural class boundaries will depend more upon the extent to which traditional class structures are modified in the functional operation of development programmes than it will upon constitutional declarations or legislative enactments. The institutional structure of underdeveloped societies is rigid because of the past long period of relative absence of change. The inelasticity of institutional structure is automatically a brake on the dynamics of development.

The social institutions of most underdeveloped countries range from those derived from simple folk societies to those which have been imposed by feudal and colonial rule. In tribal areas and in many isolated villages, old folk institutions, based primarily on kinship relations, still prevail. In less isolated villages and at national, State and often district levels, relatively new institutions have been created for revenue and law and order administration. Not only interplay, but practically always conflicts, between these two systems of institutions are inevitable. The process of synthesis of old folk institutions and the secular institutions of State and national societies is a necessity of economic, social, and political development.

It is not difficult to catalogue those elements in the socio-cultural environment which are manifest in social class and institutional structures. It is difficult, however, to know the rigidity or flexibility of these structures unless we also know the rigidity and flexibility of the value systems which sustain them. Value systems are not easily analyzed, and sometimes not easily identified because the values people hold rest more on sentiment than on reason. Because of this, they are sometimes displayed as inhibitions to action when there is no overt proof there is danger in it. At other times, they do not come to the surface when action is proposed, but silently sabotage a programme when it is initiated. Both of these types of behaviour, more often observed by anthropologists than others, have often led to what we might call the "fundamentalist" doctrine that "simple people" are so tradition-bound that they automatically resist change. Some studies show, however, that rejection as well as acceptance of borrowed traits is selective; that there are "soft spots" as well as hard spots in the wall of cultural resistance. The laboratories of development now in existence offer opportunities to learn much more than we now know about these rigidities and flexibilities, the hard and soft spots, in the defence against change. Social scientists, if they are alert and diligent in observing development in action, will probably learn more from these observations than they can bring by way of solutions to the problems of change.

For immediate use, considerable understanding can be developed by comparative studies of social structures, value systems, and extent of change. A large number of countries which, fifty years ago, were as underdeveloped as those which have only recently initiated development programmes have provided experience which social scientists can and should analyze. The innovations initiated, the processes used in the initiation and follow-up, the degree of success and failure, and something about the causes of each, can be studied. Such analyses have been made of the stages or gradients of economic growth. To some extent, similar studies can be made of the factors and processes of social growth.

In economic growth, it is well known that cultural borrowing has played a great role. Major assets upon which a developing country can and does draw are the great variety and types of technologies and techniques which are the end-products of accomplished development in so-called advanced countries. Borrowing can and does telescope the period of evolution by which underdeveloped countries can and will accomplish development. Techniques, however, are not as easily borrowed as are technologies, and skills are more difficult to borrow than either of these. It can be seriously questioned whether or not values and standards can be borrowed at all.

A standard is a model for perfection. It is a value projected into the future rather than being inherited from the past. To help implement a forward value, actual performance on the job requires an understanding which goes beyond a mere mechanical performance of one's task. It requires a pride in one's share in the workmanship which produces a perfect end-product, in which each individual workman has only a small part. Thousands of giant, but jerry-built, structures and millions of home and small-shop buildings, which do not meet consumers' requirements, attest to the fact that standard products are not quickly or easily produced by workmen who have never reaped the dividends in terms of superior social status, much less economic rewards, because of taking pride in their workmanship. Pride in workmanship, like the knowledge and meticulous practice of science, is a cult which develops only in those societies in which workmen take pride in producing quality products for a large public which demands, and is able and willing to pay for, quality products. Many standards which prevail in affluent societies cannot be borrowed or expected to prevail in poverty-ridden societies for the simple reason that there is no effective demand for standard products. This is to say that standards are as truly, but differently, socially conditioned in economically poor societies as they are in affluent societies. To borrow standards which are elevated too high above the standard of living of a people is to forget, or not to know, that standards, too, are products of growth.

Old values and standards which are end-products of centuries of social experience of a people are not quickly abandoned. Without them, a people would not have a culture or a society. It is therefore inevitable that they should be cherished and safeguarded. Because they grow out of the past, they look backward rather than forward. They are therefore conservative and are brakes against change. They, however, are products of social evolution which means they have experienced change from their earliest beginnings to the present. They are not like rocks which change their shape and texture only by processes of erosion, although they have done this; they have also changed by growth. They have had to grow in order to maintain their role of sanctioning those forms of behaviour which people have evolved in their ever-expanding and diversifying experiences in life. There is every reason to expect them to continue to do so. The finding of sociological science is that old values, especially old taboos, quite silently but constantly give way under the impact of activities which enhance the day-by-day living of people who engage in these activities. But there is probably as much error in the belief that no innovations can be introduced into a tradition-ridden society as there is in the belief that any material, or mechanical, cultural object can be detached from its roots and easily transplanted in any and every cultural or societal environment.

We need not here point to evidence that values, even whole value systems, like religious beliefs and doctrines, have filtered in or been consciously transmitted from one culture to others. It is germane to present some of the many evidences that it is not easy to transmit the material, even the purely mechanical, objects and techniques from so-called advanced societies to so-called underdeveloped or developing countries. Old cultural values will always condition the thinking and even the practical behaviour of the masses of people in underdeveloped countries. Not all of them will influence this behaviour adversely. Social scientists should accept the responsibility of developing more precise analyses of the content of the value systems of underdeveloped countries. If and when this is done, all persons planning for, or working in, development programmes can move with greater surety. In some situations, they will move with greater dispatch and in other situations, they will, if wise, move with less dispatch.

Ideals are in some ways more difficult, and in some ways easier, to observe and analyze than values. They are important because they state the goals which people set for themselves and seek to gain. They are much more often expressed in newly-developing countries than in old, settled, or stable countries where they are pretty much taken for granted and come to the surface in vocal expression only in times of crisis. In newly-independent countries, they generally have to do with national unity, the nation's status in the world's family of nations, and nearly always include the expressed desire to preserve and develop some cultural or social ideas which the new nation believes it can and should contribute to the other nations of the world. These ideals or stated goals, in most underdeveloped countries, at first are held only by national leaders, but these national leaders attempt, by development processes, to make them the possessions of all the people. In countries which are utilizing totalitarian methods of mobilizing not only the physical strength but the minds of the masses, these goals are so definitely patterned that they are fairly easy to observe and analyze. They are not so patterned in countries whose leaders are dedicated to democratic methods.

Sociological analysis of ideas is not easy, but it is essential if the methods of democratic development are to be understood. Even more important than the sociologist's need to understand these methods is the need for leaders and directors of development programmes to understand them. The roles which leaders must play are so great, and the need for them so imperative, that such leaders can very easily fall into the use of totalitarian methods in trying to lead their people as rapidly as possible to accept the nation's newly-stated ideals, and to work with effectiveness and expedition on carrying out development programmes. It is believed by the national leaders of most developing countries that some single great cause is essential as a stimulus to developing morale, engendering pride, and inducing dedication of the masses to development objectives. A single great objective, however, is used to mobilize democracies only in periods of national crisis, and in such periods, democratic methods are quite generally compromised at many points. It is not, therefore, too surprising to see them violated in developing countries which are, so to speak, working in a continuous emergency or crisis. The laboratory for studying these things is in those developing countries whose leaders are dedicated to the development of democracies, but whose people, and who themselves, have never before had experience with democratic procedures and methods.

Two significant social phenomena for analyses in these countries are the development of national public opinion, with relative absence of mass means of communication, and the unique roles of national leaders. Developing effective mass communication in underdeveloped countries depends more on the literacy of the masses, their opportunities to participate freely in local group and community decision-making, and their opportunities, even necessity, for participating in wider than purely local group and community activities, than it does on the development of mass communication technologies. These technologies are well developed in advanced countries and not only can but will be quickly borrowed at the appropriate time. A level of literacy which will make the use of the technologies effective, the habits and practices of wider than local group participation, and the opportunities for and habits of participating in decision-making cannot be borrowed. They must be developed in thousands of local communities where the millions of potential participants in public affairs live.

Notwithstanding the difficulty of analyzing ideals, the playing of effective roles by national leaders who are dedicated to clearly-stated national ideals is one of the most easily identifiable differences between those underdeveloped countries which have moved forward with development programmes and those which have not. It would be precarious to analyze the motives of those leaders, but their methods or techniques of leadership are readily observable and can be fairly precisely described. These leaders are not persons whose day-by-day behaviour and expressions are entrusted with legendary characteristics of traditionalism. They are under the klieg lights of a national as well as an international stage. What roles they play and how they play them are as observable as they are important.

More is known about the techniques, if not the personalities, of national leaders in countries using totalitarian methods than about the techniques of national leaders who eschew totalitarian methods, but who must exercise more dominant leadership than is necessary, or would be permitted, in long and well-established democracies. To persons born and reared in one of the old democracies, not only the methods of leaders in new democracies, but some of the things they publicly say and do appear incongruous with democracy. Such observers are mistrustful of the charismatic leadership which is practised, and is probably necessary, in newly-developing countries.

It is undoubtedly true that such charismatic leaders come nearer making than following public opinion, and this seems to smack of totalitarianism. But the development of public opinion-making processes, and even the development of the means and instruments of communication through which public opinion can be developed and registered, are as yet only partially in being in underdeveloped countries. Types of leaders and techniques of leadership are undoubtedly conditioned by these facts. Leadership, even of national scope, both in terms of the personality of leaders and their techniques, is undoubtedly a reflection of a stage of development or underdevelopment. Whether or not this phenomenon can be precisely analyzed, it must be considered by social scientists if they would make their maximum contribution to the sociology of development.

Social scientists have, for a long while, accepted the responsibility for making a major contribution to an understanding of the socially and culturally conditioning factors in development. They are only beginning to accept a similar responsibility for the dynamic processes of development. Only recently have they undertaken the task of studying societies which have moved a considerable distance away from tribal and folk society, which all the present, so-called developing societies have done. Some sociological scientists have attempted to characterize the differences between folk societies and peasant societies, but very few of them have attempted to analyze the processes of change which accomplish this transition. With the diverse laboratories now existing in developing countries, where induced or stimulated change is the main purpose of the development programme, social scientists have outstanding opportunities not only to add a considerable amount of precise knowledge to their own body of scientific knowledge, but they also have opportunities to render service to present and future development plans and programmes.

Among the contributions which the sociologist should make to a knowledge of development processes and programmes, the greatest should be to those of community development. These are not typical "welfare" programmes for raising the level of living of the masses. They are programmes which consist of all possible methods or ways by which the masses may effectively participate in the total economic, social, and political development of their countries. Stated forthrightly, they consist of all known methods by which the greatest underdeveloped natural resource of underdeveloped countries—the masses of the population—can and will be developed. These methods and programmes are, of course, also concerned with the development of physical and economic resources. It is the obligation of the sociologist to describe and analyze the means, processes, methods, and skills by which individuals and local groups can be catalyzed and organised effectively to play their necessarily immense roles in these undertakings. Community development methods are being used primarily in underdeveloped countries. Analyses of the current experiences of the development programmes in these countries, plus all the knowledge that sociological research has built up, are probably the greatest contribution sociologists have to make to the processes and programmes of development in underdeveloped countries.

Of course, not all development programmes use community development methods. Some underdeveloped countries which claim to have community development programmes do not use these methods. A number of national leaders seem only to recognize that they need the support of the masses if they are to retain political power, but the methods they are employing serve to diversify the laboratory experience which social scientists can study. Furthermore, such diversity provides the opportunity for these scientists to define and analyze community development methods more precisely as they are used or not used as components of development programmes.

In the remaining chapters, we do not abandon our objective of focusing our observations on the objectives or goals which Indian planners and leaders have postulated and seek to reach in their rural development programme. As sociologists, students of human relationships, we have observed systems of human relations of all kinds on all levels of social action, ranging from attempts to motivate individuals and groups of various kinds to human relationships on the assembly line of programme administration. Our critical analysis is primarily of the means employed in gaining ends or goals stated by Indian planners.

"The Problems and Processes of Planned Change" focuses on the means employed to motivate hundreds of millions of persons who are said to be "apathetic" and hundreds of thousands of village communities which are said to be "stagnant". We analyze in that chapter the processes and the means by which largely unplanned change has occurred in societies in the past and utilize the research findings of sociological scientists who have studied so-called traditional societies in transition. India can and has, at least to some extent, utilized this type of knowledge in an attempt, by planning, to expedite change, but greater use could have been made of the knowledge gained from sociological studies.

The chapter on "Catalyzing An Upward Socio-Economic Cycle", is in essence an effort to relate what is sociologically and psychologically known about motivation of individuals and groups of various kinds, and to employ what is known about motivation to catalyze widespread change in the minds, attitudes, and practices of hundreds of millions of India's village masses. The chief critical assessment is that an adequate knowledge of the psychology and sociology of motivation is not yet evident, and that, in the past, some fallacious methods of motivation have been used. "The Development of Means and Methods of Communication" discusses what Indian leaders have recognized from the beginning of national planning, namely, the tremendous task of developing effective two-way communication between the planners and entrepreneurs of change and the hundreds of millions of villagers who must adopt improved or changed practices in various areas of their day-by-day life and living.

"Role and Status Relationships in Programme Administration" is in some ways the most sociologically-oriented chapter in this book. It deals with the two most deeply-rooted social structures in India, the social class structure and the bureaucratic administrative structure. In our judgment, the planned blueprint for the implementation of India's community development-extension programme provided for the functional roles to be played by each cadre of programme personnel and the functional relationships between them. By implication, the blueprint provided for two-way channels of inter-personal communication, from national and State programme directors to village-level workers, and through them from villages to all the higher cadres of programme personnel. Our observations, from the beginning, have been that the programme was very quickly, and probably inevitably, influenced by the age-old class structures, especially the class status, of the majority of the various programme personnel who sabotaged the necessary practice of fluid and thus effective communication and co-operation between joint role-players in day-by-day programme operation. Programme personnel gradually became aware that their day-by-day activities were more and more directed by administrative regulations, if not edicts, and less and less by their originally-described and assigned functional roles. We have related our analyses to the findings of research studies of bureaucratic administration on the one hand and those of functional programme role-playing on the other hand. The assessment is analytically critical but not entirely negative in its exposition of India's bureaucracy. It does point out the inevitable fact that not only hundreds of millions of Indian villagers and tens of thousands of village-level workers, but thousands of persons who by necessity are engaged in bureaucratic administration must learn how to lead in the evolution of a giant people's programme.

The two chapters on the Community Development-Extension Programme utilize far more than our observations of India's programme. Our analyses of the origin and evolution of community development methods are based on the study and personal observation of this type of programmes in more than twenty so-called developing countries, and on information obtained in our personal discussions with the national leaders who instituted, and those now directing, such programmes. The experiences, plans, and even the stated objectives of these programmes are different in some ways from each other. But in spite of, and in some ways because of, this fact, we have found it possible to identify the functional common denominators of the most successful of these programmes. The lack of success in some of them makes as great a contribution to our understanding as do their successes. Because, however, it has been our objective to formulate a model construct out of the most successful experiences in community development, we give major attention to relative successes in community development undertakings. We use the model community development construct as an instrument to assess relative successes and failures of India's programme.

"The Role of Technical Assistance" is based on observations of more than a decade of experience in both developing countries which receive assistance of all kinds and the so-called advanced countries which are furnishing it on a very wide front. There are problems inherent in this process for both donors and recipients. These pitfalls, as well as some suggestions for avoiding them, are discussed in the framework of technical assistance being an outstanding phenomenon of our age about which both givers and receivers must gain greater understanding.

"The Problems and Processes of Building a National Democratic Society" describes the task of building the kind of society which India's leaders declared in their Constitution it was their nation's intention to evolve. This new society would be represented by a national government which would be not only politically but economically and socially viable. It would be a national society which was a political, but also an economic and social democracy. We have not formulated a model construct in order to assess the progress India has made in building the kind of society she described in her Constitution. We have utilized the analyses of sociological scientists to formulate the basic characteristics of this kind of society, namely, an open class society, in which vertical mobility is easy and widespread; a communicative society in order to be a national society; a pluralistic society, that it may have diversity and thus dynamics at various levels of social action; and a mass consumption society if it is to approximate an economic and social democracy.

When India gained her independence, adopted her Constitution, and launched her First Five Year Plan, she had a long way to go to gain her stated national objectives. While it is the chief purpose of the final chapter to reveal the problems inherent in consistently and persistently following the path toward objectives, and while we recognize that sixteen years is a very short span of time in the life of a national society, the authors who have, over the past twelve years, closely observed her rural development, have no doubt they have witnessed the planting of many roots of democracy in Indian rural society. They are equally confident that in their attempts and some failures to bring India's rural masses into the bloodstream of national life, both national administrative and political leaders have become ever more deeply convinced about the dynamic forces for both development and democracy which reside in their country's hundreds of millions of village people.

MAIN AUTHORITIES QUOTED OR CITED

Brand, Willem, *The Struggle For A Higher Standard of Living*, The Problem of the Underdeveloped Countries, The Free Press, Glencoe, Illinois, 1958.

Buchanan, Norman S. and Ellis, Howard S., *Approaches to Economic Development*, The Twentieth Century Fund, New York, 1955.

Rostow, W. W., *The Stages of Economic Growth*, Cambridge University Press, New York, 1960.

CHAPTER 20

THE PROBLEMS AND PROCESSES OF PLANNED CHANGE

To formulate strategies for change is the task of planning. To formulate and execute the tactics for implementing these strategies is the responsibility of programme administrators. The problem of planned change is not so much how to initiate as how to expedite change, not so much the direction as the implementation of change. While it is not too difficult to know, observe, and assess the basic strategies of planned change, it is easier to observe and assess the day-by-day tactics which are employed in carrying out these strategies than to formulate these strategies. Here we do little more than identify the types and sources of information about social change which are available to and usable by planners of change. In the chapters which follow we discuss the major problems which have been revealed in India's experience of implementing change.

The paths of economic development are fairly well documented by economic historians, ranging all the way from descriptions of societies whose economy depends upon "hunting and fishing" or "direct appropriation" of resources, to settled occupancy, and on to societies which have reached what Rostow calls "economic take-off" in development. Sociological scientists, chiefly anthropologists, have provided most of the information by which economic historians have described the stages of economic growth. Anthropologists, however, are chary about prescribing, or even describing, stages or steps in social and cultural evolution.

Rostow describes "economic take-off" as the "great watershed in the life of modern societies" and says, "The take-off is the interval when the old blocks and resistances to steady growth are finally overcome. The forces making for economic progress, which yielded limited bursts and enclaves of modern activity, expand and come to dominate the society. Growth becomes its normal condition." He lists the stages of economic activity which provide evidence that take-off is in operation. Industries expand rapidly and yield profits. New techniques spread in agriculture. Agriculture is commercialized. The stages through which advanced societies have passed after they have reached and passed the take-off stage are characterized by Rostow as "the drive for maturity" and "the age of high mass consumption".

We need not review Rostow's discussion of the behaviour of societies after they have accomplished high mass consumption because India, and other underdeveloped countries are not yet even in reach of mass consumption. Most of them still are in the take-off or pre-take-off stage. We do, however, cite some of his statements which should challenge sociological scientists as well as development planners and leaders. He says, in general, " ... the creation of the preconditions for take-off required fundamental changes in a well-established traditional society: changes which touched and substantially altered the social structure and political system as well as techniques of production. ... the horizon of expectations must lift; and men must become prepared for a life of change and specialized function." He adds that something like this group of sociological and psychological changes would now be agreed to be at the heart of the creation of the pre-take-off conditions to take-off.

The information yielded by such *post mortem* analyses, however, is insufficient to provide the development of the necessary pre-take-off conditions. To these must be added the contributions which sociological scientists have made or are capable of making. Many of the contributions these social scientists have made are not sufficiently precise to provide specifications for planning, but they do provide the frame, or points, of reference which can be profitably employed by persons attempting to currently observe change in developing countries. Some of their broad, but we believe valid, generalizations on change, which assist observers of attempts in developing countries to induce change in the habits and thinking of the people of so-called traditional societies will be followed by the findings of some detailed studies of societies in transition.

Spicer says that "people resist changes that appear to threaten basic securities; they resist proposed changes they do not understand; they resist being forced to change." Herskovits says, "From an empirical point of view, it is apparent that much more of any single culture has been borrowed than has been invented. . . . Fundamental in the diffusion process is the manner in which cultural borrowings are reworked as they move from people to people." But "the acceptance of what comes from the outside is never a total acceptance. . . . "

The relevance to planned induced change of what these quotations state is that the types of change which any cultural group will accept is more largely determined by that group than it is by the agents of change, and whatever traits of another culture are borrowed or accepted are always reworked in such ways as to be assimilated without greatly disturbing the equanimity of the behaviour of the members of a group. Anthropologists have given increasing attention to a study of the assimilation of borrowed traits into so-called traditional societies and communities. Sociologists have made many studies of the adoption and spread of new practices in so-called modern societies. The findings of anthropologists have shown that there is no great resistance to innovation which is as Linton says, "compatible with existing cultural patterns." They show that if and when such an innovation or new way of doing some specific thing, or accomplishing some already accepted objective, is readily accepted, it is easily assimilated and generally spreads rapidly. Herskovits calls this the process of "re-enculturation".

All the generalizations of sociological scientists and historians thus far cited concern long-term change. While we must accept the validity of these generalizations, we have not found them sufficiently definitive to provide focus for day-by-day, or even year-by-year, observations of a society in transition. The same is true of broad generalizations about the evolution from folk to urban culture, or the evolution from sacred to secular values. We, however, have found that the findings of actual studies of societies in transition have provided us eyes and ears with which to see and hear, and offer assessment of changes which we have observed in India.

So-called peasant societies are at some stage in transition between folk and urban culture, between subsistence and monetized economies, and have a mixture of sacred and secular values. We present the findings of four fairly recent detailed studies of four different peasant communities, each studied by a different analyst. The four communities were in China, Egypt, Colombia, and India. Each of the communities studied was only a few decades past a folk society. The frame of their old folk organisations is still there and is buttressed by their old folk values. But the outside world has moved in on them. The findings of the four community studies fairly adequately describe the changes which have occurred and how, if not why, they have occurred.

Trade or commerce had entered these villages. In the Egyptian village the first trading shop came to the village about 60 years ago. In China a market town developed not too far from the village, which town also served a number of other villages. In Colombia some large public works furnished outside employment for village persons whose employment previously had been restricted to the village economy. In India the same sorts of things happened. As contact developed with trade centres, either with merchants located in the village or with trade towns, more and more village people developed a knowledge of the outside world in terms of activities about which they had previously known very little. What they learned naturally became matters of gossip within the village and, therefore, some understanding of marketing, prices, and other things developed on the part of all village people.

Government personnel had entered all of these villages many years back, but modern government of the type which brings services and assistance to villagers was fairly new in all of the villages. Agents of the government were now promoting development and welfare activities. When this happened there was a basis for forming new groups in the village; sometimes new parties, and often new factions, developed. Government's servants, located in or serving villages, were seldom local villagers themselves. They generally had more education and were receiving higher incomes than the villagers. This new type of person tended to introduce new social status groups among the other statuses of the villages. Government in all cases, sooner or later, established and helped to maintain schools. School teachers were new citizens of the community and, in some cases, played roles quite different from any that an outsider had ever played in the village. As some youth of the village received considerable education, they became capable of making contacts and did make contacts, outside the village. Some of them accepted employment outside the village and thus became a channel of cultural traffic in and out of it. In a few cases, persons with a degree of education took up new occupations different from those which they had traditionally followed, and moved away from the village.

As the price and market economy entered the village, some persons began making more money. Some of those who had made more money or had better contacts with outside agencies became money-lenders. In three of the four villages money-lenders began to accumulate land that had previously been held by peasants who now lost the ownership of their land. A whole new elite developed in the village—sometimes a quite powerful group. In the Chinese village new leaders arose—lay leaders—who, while they had not yet challenged the status of the old folk leaders, were looked up to by other villagers. Under their leadership some new things were undertaken in the village. In Egypt there was a quite distinct tendency for those who had received a degree of education to exercise a type of leadership which had previously not been in the village. In India, government servants began to be looked up to rather than feared.

In all the villages a degree of individualism developed. Some persons did not feel so bound to their family groups as in the past. Some new smaller groups developed. In Colombia, actual new local neighbourhoods grew up within the village. In all the villages the lower classes, that is, the lower income people, tended to form a group which protested against the large owners. It would appear from the findings that the same old reverence for elders, and for the set class structure, and even for the village values, had been considerably diluted.

These peasant communities have modified but have not completely lost their old folk characteristics. The elders, while they no longer constitute the village government, are highly respected and are still counsellors on many types of issues. The village community's organisation is perpetuated by each new generation's tendency to follow the family occupations of previous generations. There is in all of these villages still some division of labour between the families, which is fixed by the traditions of the community. Sentiment for the land, pride and tenacity in the ownership of it, is still very strong. Families, generally extended families, are more integral social groups than are the villages as a whole.

There is still relatively little tolerance for new ways of thinking and doing. To quote Professor Dube in *Indian Village*, "If people are asked to choose between tradition and progress, tradition would perhaps be their instinctive choice, although a second thought might induce them to take a few hesitating steps in the direction of change."

Studies of a number of other peasant communities have been made, some of them European villages, where the people and the economy have moved quite far toward what may be called secular societies. Probably, however, what was discovered by the analysts in these four villages will suffice to indicate that the great differences which exist between highly secularized societies and folk societies were a long while in developing, but that in their development they travelled steadily away from the old folk cultures and steadily in the direction of more highly secular organisations and value systems.

The findings of field studies of the members of peasant societies, who as individual persons are in transition from traditionalism to modernity, are doubly valuable to the would-be observer because they focus on the psychological and sociological processes of current change. Such a study is that of Daniel Lerner, who in his book, *The Passing of Traditional Society*, reports a sophisticated analysis of studies made in six Middle East societies. He classifies the more than two thousand persons interviewed as "traditionals", "transitionals", and "moderns". He meticulously defined in advance the type of individual response which would cause him to classify each individual in one or another of these classes, mainly interpreting the meaning of responses in terms of the readiness of individuals for change. He found that the major difference in responses to carefully reasoned questions was empathy, the capacity of the respondent to imagine himself playing roles of persons differently positioned than he in the society in which he lived. He found many persons who did not expect, and could not imagine, themselves living in some other locality, doing things in a different way, or being any other kinds of persons than they now are. These are the types of persons Lerner classified as "traditionals".

We have listened to many persons in India who gave these same responses, and we have in many cases had parents tell us that they had no expectations that their children, or even grand-children, would be different from them. We have also interviewed many village persons whom Lerner would classify as "moderns". It was easy to elicit responses from them because they believed they knew about different or better ways of doing things than had in the past been their practices. As was true of some of Lerner's respondents, their beliefs about what they might some-time do were too highly imaginative ever to be validated. Others were increasingly practising what they were preaching to them-selves. It was more difficult to obtain or interpret responses from "transitionals". Even when they said they had heard of new practices, and knew other persons who had adopted them, they were equivocal about their intentions to do so. We have not interviewed the same persons repeatedly, as did Lerner. We are, however, better able to interpret what Indian villagers have said in response to questions we have asked them because of the meaning Lerner has given to typical responses.

Indian development planners and leaders have undoubtedly meant somewhat the same thing as Lerner meant by empathy in their frequent assertions that the need is to "change the outlook of village people." Rostow probably means the same thing when he says that "their horizons must be lifted." Lerner systematically documents the correlates if not the causes of increasing empathy, of wider horizons and "outlook of village people". By doing so his data provide a knowledge of conditions, even facilities, which need to be provided if the "outlook of village people" is to be broadened, and their desires for and intentions to change catalyzed and increased. He found that the main correlates of empathy are literacy, urbanization, greater participation in media of com-munication, and greater political participation. All of these except political participation (which is more likely a resultant of the others) are probably causative.

In Lerner's multiple correlation of these variables, literacy ranks highest and urbanization lowest, but he makes the point "that the relationship between the four sectors is systemic." In another table he shows that in "opinion rank", the breadth of the area in which the various types of persons have any opinion, the moderns rank first and the traditionals last. Typically traditionals either refuse to express opinions on issues which have to do with areas of national, State, or even wider local community action, or they are hesitant and equivocal in their responses to questions about these wider areas of action.

To the extent that planners are aware of this type of research findings, they attempt to utilize such information in two ways in planning change. They attempt to develop conditions conducive to change and develop facilities which will induce change. Their plans provide for increasing literacy; they provide for as rapid as possible industrial development, which automatically means increased urbanism; they plan for the development of greater means of transportation and communication; and they plan for wider political participation. In addition to all of these, Indian planners, and especially development programme leaders, have made systematic efforts to directly "motivate" village people to change. In doing so they do not, however, counsel primarily with the issues of whether they will create a more secular society and thereby lessen the influence of old folk values. They give little heed to the retarding influence of old folkways and the pall of old traditions. The objective of their planning is to catalyze or induce modernism in all areas of action and thought. They attempt to help more and more traditionals to become transitionals and more transitionals to become moderns. They are in the business of catalyzing the passing of a traditional society.

Probably the most difficult problem is in making decisions about what development will most quickly and directly accomplish change, and induce development or change in other areas. These decisions need to be based on two calculations, or predictions: the known or probable effect that the accomplishment of first priorities will have in catalyzing other areas of needed accomplishment, and how long it will take for these resulting effects to become operative. Because the development of industries, for instance, takes time, it is necessary to start the process of industrial development as soon as possible in order that its benefits may be manifest within a decade or so. The major benefits of increased literacy will almost certainly not be manifest for two decades, when a majority of all citizens are literate and thus capable of participating in mass media of communication. A major problem in planning and directing change is therefore how to calculate and time the conjunction of the effects of two such high priority long-term developments as industrialization and education with the effects of short-term priorities, and thus assure that each will fructify the other.

It is difficult to observe with any precision the degree of success with which this has been accomplished in India, but on the basis of their own experiences, Indian planners are now seriously attempting to accomplish this; for example, "In the Third Plan stress is being placed on the careful phasing of projects in relation to one another. At each stage in development, there should be a series of projects under execution, ensuring continuity both in planning and in the flow of benefits. Some measure of balance must be preserved between projects with long gestation periods and those which can be completed over relatively short periods." The Plan also mentions the need for and intention to promote programmes of research, the findings of which will provide guidance for future planning. There is a failure, however, to mention research needed to provide guidance to the great masses of Indian village people, most of whom are still "traditionals", or "transitionals", this notwithstanding the fact that more precise research findings in this field of behaviour are available than in many other areas of change with which development programme directors must deal.

In terms of the applicability to India's programme of rural development, it is fortunate that the largest bodies of research findings are concerning the adoption and diffusion of agricultural practices. These findings are important because many of them are immediately applicable in India's attempt to accelerate the adoption and diffusion of improved agricultural practices; and because there is every reason why such studies could be immediately initiated in India as part of her programme of intelligently planning and initiating change among millions of agricultural producers. These studies have sought to answer such questions as: why persons adopt new practices; what are the stages in the thinking or experiences of persons which lead them to adopt new practices; what are the characteristics of the persons who may be expected to be innovators or early adopters; and, what are the social or cultural conditions which cause others, even laggards, to ultimately adopt new practices.

In simple language, it can be said that a cultivator adopts a new practice because he expects to profit more by doing so than if he follows his old customary practices. Answers to the question of what steps or stages in thinking a person takes, and probably must take, in arriving at the decision to adopt new practices have been classified as follows: First, he must hear about the new practice which it is said could be substituted for a practice which he is now using. Only if it is a substitute for an old practice is he likely to be interested in it. If and when he is interested in it, he attempts to learn all he can about it. Seldom does he adopt it without this evaluation. Such studies have been made of a sufficiently large number of adopters of new practices that the stages or steps in the experience and mental processes of adopters or innovators have been listed as follows: (1) awareness, (2) interest, (3) evaluation, (4) trial, (5) adoption.

These studies have revealed who or what type of person is most likely to be an innovator or an early adopter of new agricultural practices. The broadest conclusions which can be drawn from these findings are that innovators, or early adopters, are the better educated members of the local community; they are persons in middle-age groups; and, they are persons who are aware of the fact that their neighbours count on their initiative in agricultural improvements. Education has widened their horizons of knowledge and provided them a greater and truer body of knowledge with which to evaluate alternatives. Persons in the middle-age groups are in the period of their greatest responsibility. They are no longer beholden to their elders and more conservative parents. They have already attained a degree of leadership and are looked to by others for leadership. A number of studies have shown that even though such persons have not been called leaders, they respond to the opportunities to gain prestige and status which their neighbours offer to them. Neighbouring cultivators watch them closely and follow their lead. Later adopters, especially laggards in adoption, are those who identify more closely with kinship groups. They are those who less often converse with other than their kinsmen or very close neighbours. They seldom seek out and visit with agents of change. But they observe the effects or results of change which others have adopted and in due time, though they are the last to change, help to thoroughly establish the new practices as a local behaviour norm, or the widely accepted way of doing some important thing.

From what we have been able to observe, and have learned from the observations of others, we would say that development leaders in India have made little or no attempt to understand the typology of change in local communities. They have accepted the belief that the social or group structure of villages is sufficiently well known that those capable of local leadership are also well known. Most of such persons have, however, been leaders of status quo, not leaders of change. They are old, not new, leaders. Most of them have been leaders of highly-stratified status groups, not leaders of dynamic action groups.

There is no organisational change of greater significance than that of forming hundreds of thousands of local groups. Probably the most required change in Indian society, if the objectives set forth in the Constitution are to be reached, is the realignment of groups and the formulation of new groups. It is the intention of rural development programme directors to count on local groups to initiate and accept major responsibility for all kinds of local development undertakings. If these undertakings, or purposes, are to be fulfilled, then hundreds of thousands of new small groups will need to be formed. There are not only well-documented accounts of why new groups have been formed, but there have been detailed analytical studies of the ways in which they are formed, how they select and utilize their leaders, and how they develop group cohesion and competence.

To the extent that planning for the utilization of local groups to initiate and accomplish change is possible, some of the studies of small groups could be utilized in India. These findings make major contributions to the answers of such questions as: why persons join groups, join some groups but not others; how membership in a group influences and even changes a person's behaviour and thinking; what factors or processes develop group solidarity or cohesion, and what factors and processes develop group disturbances and disruptions; how does leadership develop, and what are the conditions for its successful functioning?

Persons join groups because they are interested in the objectives for which the group was organised and which it seeks to gain. They join with others with whom they have common purposes. Studies have found that individuals all working at the same task accomplish more if they are in the physical presence of others who are working at the same task. Moreover, individual performances are heightened when the same individuals work together in small groups. The performance of those who had been lowest when working alone was raised more than others in the group, but the performance of those who had ranked highest in the individual test was not lowered, but was in fact heightened.

These studies showed that a member's loyalty to his group is in direct relation to the extent of his participation in group discussions and activities. The zest and constancy with which an individual played his role in a group depended upon the degree of honourable recognition the group gave to the role he played. Each individual lowered or heightened his participation in a group's activities in accordance with his own conception of the status he himself had in the group. Group cohesion and solidarity increased with each succeeding objective or goal the group reached. Optimum adjustment to outside forces, directions, or situations was made at the cost of a degree of internal solidarity of the group. The greater the solidarity, the more capable it was to withstand outside pressure and to triumph over incipient internal factions. But group solidarity on different and new levels of thinking and action could not be attained too quickly, or the change be too great, without weakening the group's cohesion. This cohesion was most easily accomplished by elaborate, democratic group discussion of what would be gained and what lost by some new objective. The more cohesive a group was, the more it influenced the opinions and behaviour of its members.

Each member played or participated in some group role. Some members had greater influence, were listened to, were imitated and followed more than others. The nature of the group's tasks determined the role each individual played and thus determined the function which leadership and leaders performed. There were, however, group roles other than leadership which were essential to group functioning. Everyone in a group influenced its behaviour. No one was disregarded. If anyone was disregarded, the group's solidarity suffered. The nature and amount of leadership or number of leaders depend upon the complexity and diversity of the things undertaken by the group; quite frequently a number of sub-leaders were required to carry out its objectives. Added to all of these specific findings is the quite general knowledge that a large portion of all that individuals accomplish they accomplish as members of one or another group.

We present social research findings on the ways by which the behaviour and attitudes of masses of so-called common people are changed, because it is clearly recognized in India that one of the most crucial tasks of planned change is "changing the outlook" of hundreds of millions of village people. Indian development programme planners and leaders have from the beginning recognized this as a giant task. They have formulated and been operating a community development-extension programme to accomplish it. They have not, as they have in other areas of planned change, made something approaching maximum use of the findings and tools of the sociological sciences. This palpably obvious fact leads us to a discussion of the logic, or strategy, of planned social change.

Although planners of programmes of change probably do not and should not counsel too much with theories of societal and cultural change, they must formulate some strategy for social change. Probably the core rationale of planning change is that priority must be given to those undertakings which, if successfully carried out, will catalyze the greatest number of other changes which are believed to be essential to development. Our observations of planning in India are that there have been much clearer evidences of strategy in planning economic than social change, and that there has been no planning for cultural change. There was clear strategy in the early allocation of funds for development of heavy industries and irrigation projects, the contributions of which to other areas of development would require considerable time. We assume that this strategy was to so calculate and time the expected effects of development projects which require long periods of gestation that they would fructify the effects of development projects which require shorter periods of gestation. The construction of steel mills would not only produce needed steel products, but would create a great deal of needed employment. Large irrigation projects would furnish water to millions of acres of land and thus increase agricultural production, stimulate trade and commerce, and raise the level of living of cultivator families.

It was recognized from the beginning that one of the greatest needs was that the hundreds of millions of village people become desirous of change, and even more important, become aware of the possibilities of change. An agricultural extension programme was launched to help cultivators in all phases of better farming, and a community development programme to encourage and assist local villagers to initiate and accept responsibility, not only for improvement in agricultural production, but in all aspects of life and living in their local areas. These, together with programmes of education and health, were to be the main programmes for developing the human resources of rural areas. If there was a strategy for the development of these resources, it was far more pragmatic than planned. The major problems were identified as those of motivating "apathetic villagers" and "strengthening the self-reliance" of village and other local groups. But we have been unable to observe any systematic use or much awareness of the large body of existent knowledge on how these desirable objectives have been and are being accomplished in other countries.

It was fairly clear that Indian planners and directors of change did not, and could not, make much use of the broad generalized findings of sociological scientists who, by post mortem analyses of long-term trends in change have validated universal trends from subsistence to monetized economies, from small folk societies to urbanized societies, and from sacred to secular values. It is, of course, more than probable that over centuries, and even decades, these trends will become manifest in India. But it is to be doubted that they can be manipulated, and planners of programmes for change must deal with factors and forces which can be assumed to be susceptible of manipulation. But because they are in the business of catalyzing change, they must presume that what they promote and manipulate will lead from some present, clearly-identified situations toward some clearly-identified, desired situations.

Lerner aptly characterized this trend from the past to the

future in developing countries in terms of the differences in the degree of empathy of individuals. In terms used by Indian promoters of change, this was expressed in the need "to change the outlook of village people." Some research findings would indicate that the lack of desire for change on the part of the traditional person is due to the fact he has never been confronted with the possibility, much less the probability, of change. It is, however, almost certain that it would be possible for Indian programme planners and directors to manipulate situations and employ processes which would gradually, but surely, change a steadily increasing number of what Lerner calls "traditionals" into "transitionals," and gradually into "moderns."

Notwithstanding the large body of accumulated information about long-term social change, provided by sociological scientists and historians, planners for change find that they can employ little of this information to catalyze, or induce, short-term social change. At least partially because of this fact, they are far more specific in their prescriptions for physical and economic change than for psychological and social change. They do, however, project large programmes for accomplishing social, and even psychological, change as quickly as possible. In planning and directing these programmes, they fail to employ, and by and large appear not to know about the existence of, a substantial body of validated technical know-how for the initiation of change among traditional people who must adopt change in practices and lead in the diffusion of these practices among thousands of local groups which exist or can be organised in local areas. They fail also to counsel with the fact that, in addition to change in the behaviour and attitudes of village people, there is an imperative need for change in the behaviour and attitudes of those who assume the responsibility for administering programmes for change.

In spite of the complexity of planning for different areas of change, each interacting with the other, the most basic strategy is clear. It is to so time the desired effect in each area of change that it will fructify the effects in other areas. The strategy is as applicable to social change as it is to physical and economic change. Even though changes in all areas are concomitant, they do not all progress at the same pace. Furthermore, there are differences in the extent or degree of interaction between the various areas of change. Where the relationships between two different areas are causal, that is, one of them cannot occur until the other has occurred, priority in planning must be given to that area of change which will fructify the effects and the progress of the greatest number of other areas of change.

Priority needs to be given to those areas of change which require the longest period of gestation, in order that their results may be available at approximately the same time as the results of projects with shorter periods of gestation. From the beginning of planning in India, it was recognized that industrialization would increase employment and thus relieve unemployment in rural areas. There are, however, few illustrations of precisely predictable causative effects of the development of human resources on physical and economic development; and partly because of this, the strategy for the development of human resources has been either murky or equivocal.

However, a community development-extension programme was launched to develop the human resources of rural areas. There was bound to be a great difference in the tactics required to implement this type of programme rather than so-called construction programmes. The tactics for implementing construction projects require primarily the employment of engineering skills; for implementing human resources, social skills. This was recognized from the beginning of national planning in India. It was assumed that a major social problem in the rural development programme would be that of "motivating" millions of tradition-bound village people, requiring the employment of social skills. But apparently it was not for a long time recognized, and may not yet be recognized, that there is a basic difference between social and administrative skills.

The technical know-how of administrative skills is how to manage men, materials, and money. The technical know-how of social skills is how to develop and inspire human beings and human groups. The pay-off for the effective use of administrative skills is the orderly and timely dispatch and surety of every action taken. The pay-off for the effective use of social skills is evidence that action can no longer be surely timed because it is constantly accelerating. It will not be orderly because it is constantly taking new directions and setting new goals. It is our judgment that social skills have not as yet been effectively employed in the operation of India's community development-extension programme.

MAIN AUTHORITIES QUOTED OR CITED

Ammar, Hamed, *Growing Up In An Egyptian Village*, Routledge and Kegan Paul, Ltd., London, 1954.

Becker, Howard and Boskoff, Alvin, (Ed.) *Modern Sociological Theory in Continuity and Change*, The Dryden Press, New York, 1957, Chap. 9.

Dube, S. C., *Indian Village*, Routledge and Kegan Paul, Ltd., London, 1956.

Herskovits, Melville J., "The Processes of Cultural Change," in Linton, Ralph (Ed.), *The Science of Man in the World Crisis*, Columbia University Press, New York, 1945.

Herskovits, Melville J., "The Problem of Adapting Societies to New Tasks," in Hoselitz, Bert F. (Ed.), *The Progress of Underdeveloped Areas*, The University of Chicago Press, Chicago, 1952.

Holmberg, A. R., in *Human Organisation*, "Experimental Intervention in a Field Situation," Vol. XIV, No. 1, 1955; "From Paternalism to Democracy," Vol. XV. No. 3, 1956, (with Dobyns, H. F.) "The Process of Accelerating Community Change," Vol. XXI, No. 2, 1962; Society for Applied Anthropology, Ithaca, N. Y.

Lerner, Daniel, *The Passing of Traditional Society : Modernizing the Middle East*, The Free Press, Glencoe, Ill., 1958.

Rostow, W. W., *The Stages of Economic Growth*, Cambridge University Press, New York, 1960.

Spicer, Edward H., *Human Problems in Technological Change*, A Casebook, Russell Sage Foundation, New York, 1952.

Third Five Year Plan, Planning Commission, Government of India, 1961.

Yang, Martin C., *A Chinese Village*, Columbia University Press, New York, 1950.

CHAPTER 21

CATALYZING AN UPWARD SOCIO-ECONOMIC CYCLE

ON the development continuum from underdeveloped to developed countries, Gunnar Myrdal makes, and validates by a number of statistical measurements and wide personal observation, the three following generalizations: (1) that in the processes of economic and social development, the gap between the "have" and "have-not" countries has widened; (2) that within developing countries, the gap has widened between the have and have-not sectors of the country's population; and (3) that in many countries, there has been an absolute downward cycle in the status of the traditional "have-nots"; that today they have less of the wherewithal to satisfy the basic needs of life than they had when they lived in isolated but relatively self-sufficient local communities.

A knowledge and employment of ways to reverse a downward cycle, if such there has been, and to generate an upward social cycle, are essential to the development of the capacities of the hundreds of millions of underdeveloped people who now constitute the overwhelming majority of those who live in underdeveloped countries. Quite common statements of programme planners and leaders in developing countries are that the members of the masses are "apathetic". Sociological scientists characterize the great mass of isolated peasants in underdeveloped countries as tradition-bound and conservative. But development leaders have had a quite unquestioned belief that the masses could "be motivated" and all development programmes have utilized methods which these leaders believed would accomplish this objective. Most of them have sooner or later been disappointed with the results they have obtained. It is the purpose of this chapter to analyze their experiences by the use of sociological knowledge and theory about motivation.

To be motivated means to be stimulated to action. Persons are moved to act by both internal and external stimuli. Acts which are essential to physical survival, whether they be called instincts, drives, or predispositions, are guaranteed to men as a part of the physiological functioning of their bodies. All persons respond positively, almost tropistically, to hunger, sex, and fear. They respond negatively to anything which, according to their past experiences, threatens their survival. But in even the most primitive human society, these internal, unlearned drives become sublimated and overlaid by learned behaviour, and purely individual responses are conditioned by the imperatives of group life. With further social and cultural development, persons are motivated by purposes, by stimuli which pull them from in front rather than merely push them from behind. The vast portion of learned behaviour, from learned skills of the simplest kinds to purposes of the most complex types, provides external stimulation or motivation to action.

These oversimplified generalizations are validated by the findings of biological, psychological, and sociological research, notwithstanding the fact that no one has ever seen a motive, and no one ever will. The knowledge of motives must be inferred by what has been and can be learned by studying action. Nothing can be learned about motivation by attempting to study passivity, much less will leaders of development start an upward cycle in human development by assuming they must start with a great mass of apathetic villagers. "Villagers' apathy" and "village stagnation" are not, however, inappropriate terms to apply to conditions which are readily observable in practically all underdeveloped countries. These are conditions the overcoming of which requires an understanding and skilful use of all that is known about motivation. While, therefore, the research findings of sociological scientists are less precise in this than in some other fields of human behaviour, there is no field to which such scientists have dedicated more consistent effort than to the field of motivation. They can therefore make some contribution to the problems which developing countries face. And they themselves can learn much by dedicating their talents to a study of the conditions which exist in underdeveloped countries.

The physical stagnation of the vast majority of villages in underdeveloped countries is so palpably evident to the casual visitor that it scarcely needs documentation. Not only lack of sanitation, but widespread insanitation; not only poor and uncomfortable houses, but lack of heat, light, and ventilation in houses; not only universal poverty, but actual squalor are conditions which could be eliminated or greatly alleviated by individual or group effort of the villagers themselves. But there are enough findings from interviews with persons living under these conditions to reveal their apathy toward changing the conditions, and there is nothing more frustrating and more discouraging to development programme personnel, who are dedicated to improving the lot of villagers, than to be confronted with lack of concern on the part of the people who, they have believed, would be motivated by their proffered assistance.

The fact that neither programme planners nor leaders in India foresaw this phenomenon is not because they have not attempted to use methods of motivating village people, but largely because the findings of sociological scientists have not been sufficiently precise or sufficiently prescriptive to be made easily usable by action programme directors. We therefore assume the role of sociological middlemen between sociologists and development programme planners and directors. We know full well the precariousness of playing this role. Researchers will quarrel with our generalizations because they do not include all the ifs, ands, and buts with which they have safeguarded their conclusions, and will probably aver that we do not thoroughly understand their theories. Directors of action programmes will quarrel with us if we do not so categorize the findings of research as to make it possible for them to convert these findings into prescriptions for action, which they can hand to subordinates for execution. We shall do little of either, but shall do our best to relate sociological science know-how about motivation to the imperative problems of motivating masses of seemingly apathetic persons.

Our short synopsis of what is known, or accepted, by sociological scientists will run the gamut of what may be called the levels of motivation, starting with internally initiated actions and concluding with actions directed by purpose. That the individual human being, like any other animal, is urged by internal stimuli to satisfy hunger and sex needs no exposition. That his fears start with sensations of physical disequilibrium, and in early childhood are enlarged by things which his parents teach him are dangerous, is documented by both detailed research and common observation.

That long before he has grown to maturity, his responses to hunger and sex have become conditioned by sanctions and taboos of the groups of which he is by necessity a part, is witnessed in both simple and complex societies. The problem of understanding all the stimuli involved in a given action becomes difficult, however, when it is known that the individual is attempting to direct his action toward goals, because it then becomes necessary to analyze the social and cultural origins of these goals. Purposes or goals are social ideas or values, derived not from the mere imperatives for survival, and quite often not derived from one's immediate social environment, but derived from and stimulated by images of conditions which transcend present day-by-day conditions of life and living. Such envisioned goals may be mere fantasies, but if and when they are more than this and are not only hopes but expectations, they become aspirations which provide real motivations to those who possess them.

Few, if any, experiments in motivation have been conducted on the scale which development programmes are required to use. In these programmes, the immediate necessity is not a matter of the kind of understanding and use of methods that is developed and used in fields of child guidance, although some of the best research in motivation has been done in this field. Nor are the findings of psychiatrists, who have made major contributions to the understanding of motivation and who habitually seek for and manipulate stimuli to action, directly applicable to mass use. The great mass of adults who are said to be apathetic are not disturbed or confused personalities, but such stable personalities as to be called static or stagnant. There is much, however, which these two fields of research and practice have learned that can and should be employed by directors in the operation of programmes which require an understanding of the motivation of individuals and local groups.

If motives were concrete entities, composed of discrete, isolable components, it would be possible to determine the position which any person, at any moment of time, occupies on the continuum of motivation from animal drives to motivation from farseeing purposes. But such is not and cannot be the case. What can be known are the dominant and dominating conditions of life which drive some persons and groups, by sheer necessity, quite habitually and systematically to give major attention to the imperatives of mere survival. If and when such groups have, for generations, lived under such conditions, it can be inferred, from their habitual and systematic behaviour, that their motives are dominantly survival motives. They respond with diligence and arduous, even painful, labour, to provide for their felt needs of food, whether by means of the hunt and chase or by wresting it from small plots of land with the use of very primitive tools. It is more than probable that a better explanation than that such persons are inherently apathetic, that is, lack motives, is that they neither know nor believe that they have any alternatives to their custom-old and tested ways of doing the things they know they must do, and which they do with dedicated thought and action. Just as it would be well for economists and planners and directors of economic development to analyze and understand, as best they can, the economics of poverty, so it would be well for sociological scientists and the planners and directors of pro-grammes of social development to analyze and understand, as best they can, the psychology or social psychology of survival. But the fact that sociological scientists have not provided the assistance which the findings of such studies could provide has not relieved development programme planners and directors of the necessity of doing everything they can to motivate the masses whose more effective labours and increasing zest are prime essentials for their own and their country's development.

No matter what their scientific or technical know-how is, the leaders of development programmes must and do attempt to motivate the masses of their people. In an appraisal of the methods they most frequently use, it is freely admitted that it is far easier to identify the weaknesses of these methods than it is to offer prescriptions for more effective methods. One of the weaknesses is inherent in a condition or situation over which development leaders, for the time being, have no control. Those who have knowledge about proven superior, alternative practices are far removed both intellectually and socially from those who must adopt these practices. They, therefore, have no choice other than to attempt to communicate to the masses both a knowledge of better practices and a desire to adopt these practices. While awaiting the slow development of widespread formal education, the method or means of motivation they must frequently use is that of propaganda or preachment. The second most prevalent method by use of which attempts are made to catalyze into action "apathetic" villagers and "stagnant" local communities is to guarantee to them some of the amenities of life and living, the absence of which is the chief index to, or measure of, their underdeveloped status. The assumption upon which this second theory of motivation is based is that by making it possible for disadvantaged villagers to taste and enjoy some of the amenities which more fortunate persons enjoy, a hunger for more amenities will be created, and in order to satisfy this hunger villagers will be inspired to produce the wherewithal to pay for an increasing number of them. The efficacy of the first of these methods (propaganda or preachment) may be seriously questioned. The theory of motivation of the second method rests on sound sociological assumptions.

The weakness of propaganda or preachment is not that most of the things which leaders exhort villagers to do are not important to development, but that their importance does not fall within the mental and emotional horizons of most villagers. The masses are told that they must take greater responsibility for that sector of the nation's life, generally the production of raw products, for which they alone can be made responsible; that they must feed the nation, urban as well as rural people; that they must produce for export, in order that their country may have international exchange with which to promote heavy industry and other lines of development which require great amounts of capital. They are told that they must evince and exercise more initiative and must work harder.

The focus and content of our observations of the effectiveness of propaganda and preachment as methods of motivation are based upon a knowledge that motives are not entities, not like something which can be handed by one person to another or one group to another. They are not some sort of elixir which, if presented to a person or a group, will catalyze that person or that group into dynamic action. Our analysis is based upon a knowledge that all persons are living organisms and as such possess motives which they habitually try to implement, and habitually do implement, by following those paths of behaviour which are open to them. Analysis of motivation is always an analysis of the alternatives which confront a person, and of the conditioning factors which influence his choice of one or another of his alternatives.

It may legitimately be argued by those who use preachment and propaganda that they always present alternatives to the masses. Broadly speaking, one alternative is the continuance of old practices and their known results. The other alternative is change to different practices and their promised results. But these alternatives must be presented in terms readily comprehensible to villagers. Furthermore, they must be alternatives between which villagers themselves choose.

There is ample evidence that if and when a new alternative and its results are presented in terms that are comprehensible and meaningful to even the most custom and tradition-ridden members of the masses, they are not apathetic, but manifest interest and act with alertness. They do not, however, react with alertness to the attempts of leaders to motivate them with preachments about the necessity that they work harder, produce more in order that others may have more to consume, or that the nation may have a greater amount of exportable commodities. These pleas, or exhortations, do not promise results which are meaningful to persons whose mental horizons do not comprehend such broad objectives.

There are plenty of evidences that the masses in underdeveloped countries are stimulated by preachment about national objectives only in periods, and on issues, of national crisis. At such times and on such issues, they are motivated by charismatic leaders. But to the humdrum and necessitous tasks of making a living day-by-day, for a number of reasons charismatic leaders make little contribution. Furthermore, most of the exhorters do not have charismatic status with the masses. What they propose does not present comprehensible alternatives to villagers, and furthermore, most of what they say is never effectively communicated to villagers.

Propaganda is, however, one of the legitimate means of motivation by external stimulation. The problem of such external stimulation is the problem of how to communicate the stimulus to would-be or desired responders. Even the rapid development of mass means of communication does not by itself solve the problem because some of the chief hurdles in the paths of communication are social and psychological as well as physical. Newspapers, radios, moving pictures, film strips, and other visual aids are media through which those attempting to catalyze change in behaviour communicate with those whom they seek to motivate. Furthermore, anyone who closely observes efforts in communication between the originators of proposals for changes and those who must adopt changes may legitimately question whether the promoters of change may not have more to learn about interpersonal communication than do adopters of change. They are so far removed, both mentally and emotionally, from those whom they seek to stimulate (or motivate) that they cannot communicate with them. The villager does not understand what the spokesman for change says, and the spokesman does not have sufficient understanding of the percepts of villagers to attach what he says to what the villager knows, thinks, and feels.

To raise the villager's understanding to a level where he can perceive the images which the spokesman presents awaits the slow development of formal education and the growth and multiplication of mass means of communication. In the meantime, communication must be largely oral. The spokesman must not only speak personally to the villager, but must make his appeal on the level of the villager's comprehension. This requires that he understand the percepts of the villager. Being an educated person, to gain this understanding is within his capabilities. Such understanding, however, requires that he know what a considerable body of social science research has revealed about tradition-bound peasants.

No more vivid analysis of the peasant's traditional and custom-bound world in an underdeveloped country is available than Father Ayrout's account of the Egyptian peasants, the fellahin. The Egyptian fellah is by no means as tradition-bound as the Bedouin. He is a member of a society that is quite developed in many ways, a society in which the educated elite is on a level comparable with, or above, the leaders of a number of other developing countries. The following quotations from Father Ayrout's book will, however, reveal how far this Egyptian peasant is from being a member of what is often called a communicative society:

" ... the fellahin owe their astonishing stability and uniformity to their association with the soil of Egypt, an element no less stable and uniform. Between these two there has grown up a bond both firm and elastic; a balanced self-sufficient interdependence which neither crises nor governments can disturb. ... This unbroken contact of people and land has brought about a continual process, a play of action and reaction, likeness and difference, which strengthens the indissoluble union of the two...

" ... The family is a group for working the soil. It bears children to work the soil. Domestic life is regulated by traditions, which bind it to the soil.

"Let us consider the village as a whole. With its land, it forms a whole, outside which even its neighbours are alien and dangerous. It lives its own self-centred life, regulated by customs, manners and prohibitions handed down from the past, immemorial laws which govern the acts and pleasures of every inhabitant.

" ... Everyone knows everyone else in the village, and no one would ever be allowed to die of hunger. Men help each other readily in the fields, and women help each other in housework. The solidarity shown by the fellahin when working for a common interest, and not under orders or outside interference, can be striking, if it is rare.

"The fellah preserves and repeats, but does not originate or create. What improvements and inventions have been introduced into agriculture, health and housing are imposed upon him from outside. By dint of accepting, receiving, repeating and enduring, his intelligence has become atrophied and passive. And because it is kept in leading strings, it is not stimulated to innovate, for that would mean running risks and disturbing the torpor which protects him from unnecessary suffering. What one knows is better than what one does not know.

"The truth is that the fellah does not think outside the immediate present; he is fettered to the moment. No time and place except the present have much effect on his mind, because they have none on his senses. He is like a primitive or a child; his intellect is controlled by the things he is feeling and doing. He looks for causes and effects not in the rational, but in the visible order. Life is a succession of todays. And this is why he seems to us illogical.

"*Kayf* is a word of profound significance, meaning a kind of waking passivity, of doing, saying and thinking nothing. It is a state of perfect patience, taught by the soil. To wait without movement, to keep the mind half asleep, to drown activity in private fantasy, in his humming which lulls his work and all his movements, in a mental languor which softens all human shocks and contacts—that is *kayf*, the fellah's most characteristic attitude, a semi-consciousness which abates suffering. . .

"Because he lives in the present, he is neither in a hurry, nor ambitious, nor curious. He is mild and peaceful because he is patient, and patient because he is subject to men and events, and for these very reasons he has become like the Nile, indifferent rather than idle. He feels no need for constant activity. His mind is passive and fatalistic; he accepts things as they are."

These descriptions by Father Ayrout help to explain the "apathy" and "fatalism" of millions of physically and mentally isolated peasants throughout the world.

Lerner's study of six countries presents data which show that there are in many countries which are said to be on the move large residues of the narrow and institutionalized world which Father Ayrout so vividly describes. The persons interviewed in these six countries are typed as "traditional", "transitional", or "modern", by criteria of the extent to which, and the ways in which, they respond to various media of communication. To illustrate, a person is classified as a "modern" by facts ascertained about his behaviour: he has moved from a small to a larger population centre; he reads newspapers and/or listens to the radio; he finds satisfaction in such reading and listening; he goes to moving picture shows; the news he reads or listens to is of wider than local community interest; he is informed on such news; he feels he should or can do something about public issues which are revealed in the news; and he can imagine himself playing roles which are more important or of wider scope than any he has ever played.

The "traditional" person is one who seldom responds favourably to these media of communication, who responds with disdain, or who responds negatively. The transitional is naturally the person who acts partially like a modern, but who retains many of the types of behaviour and attitudes of the traditional. It is important to know that in societies where a large percentage of the population have become modern, and even a larger percentage are in transition, that there are definite, isolated islands of traditionalists.

Planners and directors of programmes of change specify or assign goals which assume that at some future time, if not the majority, then some large portion of their people, will be what Lerner and his colleagues call "moderns". They therefore must, or should, know all they can about the processes by which that evolution has been and is being accomplished. There are two sociological imperatives to this knowledge; first, a clear recognition of the present differences between traditionals and moderns, in general, and especially in their own countries; and second, the processes by which traditionals become first transitionals and then moderns. The following statements are selected from Lerner's report on Turkey, a country which in many ways is in transition, and a fairly large number of whose people are moderns.

"In villages that remain Traditional, no voices need be raised to defend traditional ways because no other ways are on the agenda. It is a distinctive trait of Traditional society that it promotes no alternatives to itself; hence the corresponding psychic trait of the Traditional villager is that he lacks 'curiosity'....

"At different points in the Turkish interviews, respondents were asked what they would like to know about the world, about various countries, about specific events they had heard of only vaguely. The Moderns, with the Transitionals just behind them, demonstrated an abundant curiosity; there were all sorts of questions they wanted to have answered. The Traditionals, typically, could find few questions to ask. Most of them said that there wasn't anything they cared to know....

"... Only one of twelve Traditionals was able to connect his personal economic problems with those on the national level. It is fair to say 'able' rather than 'willing', for most Traditionals simply did not name *any* alternative problem before the nation. Confronted with so awesome a demand upon their capacities, they fell silent altogether....

" ... What our study underscores is that Modernity and Tradition are even more radically different from each other than is commonly acknowledged, that bridging the difference hinges upon a transformation of personality along with a remaking of institutions. ... "

Information on, or understanding of, the processes by which a number of persons in traditional societies have become transitional, and some of them modern, can be summarized in the generalization that communication with those persons who are markedly traditional must be confined almost altogether to oral media. Lerner says, " ... two observations appear to hold for all countries, regardless of continent, culture, or creed. First the direction of change is always from oral to media system," that is, first by use of the personally-spoken word and only later by use of mass means of communication. "Secondly, the degree of change toward media system appears to correlate significantly with changes in other key sectors of the social system." A further statement about word-of-mouth communication is that, "For outside news, the Beduin ... depends mainly on known persons who can be 'faced and placed,' such as tribesmen returning from trips with gossip." This in essence says, and there is evidence from many other sources to corroborate it, that even the spoken word is not thoroughly trusted by isolated persons unless they know well the one who speaks.

Because our chief laboratory for observation is India, it is fortunate that a substantial study by Bower of "Communication of Ideas in India" is available, from which we cite only the information on communication of ideas at the village level. In this study, the city of Lucknow must represent the modern; two villages represent the transitional and one village the traditional. Findings concerning the percepts, behaviour, and attitudes of respondents in the traditional village are not unlike those reported by Lerner about Turkey and by Father Ayrout concerning the Egyptian fellaheen. The medium by which news comes to villages is chiefly word of mouth, and the institutional life of the villager quite often circumscribes the information which reaches him from beyond the boundaries of the village. As Bower says, "The outside world is seen not through the press, radio, and film, but through the eyes of beggars, traveling troops of actors and storytellers, villagers returning from a city visit, and the local socialist leader.... The chief source of information, opinion, wisdom and advice is a sabhapti (council head or leader)."

Data on how well respondents in India were informed on events which had wider than local interest showed the extreme extent to which the mental horizons of tradition-bound villagers are limited. Only 16 per cent of the respondents in the traditional village knew the correct day and year of national independence; the data for the respondents of two transitional villages showed 36 per cent and 50 per cent, and for Lucknow college-educated, 93 per cent. When asked about leaders, practically no respondents in the traditional village mentioned a national leader, and only 6 per cent "appeared to have heard of Rajendra Prasad, India's President." Some persons named as "national leaders" turned out to be "local leaders". Only 6 of the 248 respondents in all three villages knew anything about a nationally important Act of Parliament which had been widely discussed in the national press.

Adherence and loyalty to traditional institutions is evidenced by the following facts: In the traditional village, 99 per cent averred that they preferred to have "disputes settled by the panchayat (ancient and revered village council of elders) than in a court of law." Only 60 per cent in the transitional village, 43 per cent of Lucknow uneducated, and 17 per cent of Lucknow college-educated respondents selected this alternative. The percentage of all respondents who would limit marriage to their own caste was approximately 85 per cent in all three villages studied, whereas it was only slightly over 50 per cent in the city of Lucknow, 37 per cent for college-educated persons over 40 years of age, and only 34 per cent for college-educated persons under 40 years of age.

These research findings are not given to belittle the intelligence of village people. On many, if not most, issues of their own family and village life, they are more intelligent than the vast majority of the college graduates in their own country. We have, rather, presented the problems of communication which confront development programme personnel in their attempts effectively to reach village people with ideas, an acceptance of which they believe will motivate these people to undertake many kinds of changes in individual family and village practices. Our repeated inferences have been that methods of propaganda and preachment are not likely to be adequate to this undertaking.

We stated earlier that the second most prevalent method of motivation used by development programme directors is to guarantee to disadvantaged village people some of the amenities which they so sorely lack. Because it is known that village people do strive to improve and increase amenities, many developing countries seek to use this factor in motivation as a first phase of an upward cycle of change. The main, stated objective of most development plans and programmes is "to raise the standard of living of the masses." This is proposed to be done by guaranteeing to village people that if they will mobilize their manpower, make maximum use of their existent physical resources, and organise themselves for effectively undertaking various types of community improvement, their government will aid them with technical and financial assistance. National programme leaders thus use villagers' desires for amenities as a motive force to crack the "cake of custom" which they say has sabotaged personal dynamics, and to induce local community initiative and responsibility and thereby to catalyze an upward cycle of improvement in all areas of village life and living. Their theory about the self-perpetuation and self-generating tendency of a process which, step by step, yields obvious and desired results is verified by countless examples of both personal and group development. It is verified by the universally-observed fact that persons and families are stimulated to strive hard to obtain the wherewithal to guarantee to themselves those higher levels of living which they know that others enjoy. The standard of living is sociologically defined as that level of living which a person envisions and has expectations of securing.

In their own terms, in countries which have made something approaching maximum use of amenities guaranteed to local communities, it has been assumed that the zest created by the immediate, or quick, securing of amenities, which require financial outlays as well as work, would motivate local community groups to work harder and organise more effectively to earn money to pay for additional amenities. It has also been assumed that the personalities of the individuals, and the spirit of community pride and teamwork, would be so fundamentally changed by these fruitful experiences that they would continue to catalyze change. There are, however, many evidences that the providing of amenities, with minimum contributions from local communities, has failed to validate the assumption that the securing of community amenities is an adequate or self-generating motive for community development. Much less is it a stimulant to increase production, the responsibility for which rests more upon individual or family or small special-interest-group action than it does on total local community action. There is almost universal evidence that when amenities such as community halls or other physical structures are provided solely, or even mainly, as free gifts from government, these amenities fail to stimulate communities to greater effort, or even to stimulate them to make constructive use of the facilities which have been given to them.

When programme planners and programme leaders observe these things, as they always do sooner or later, they begin to ask why the universal phenomenon of each higher level of living acting as a stimulant to a yet higher level has not repeated itself in so many of the places where the first step in this psycho-social process has been guaranteed by making available improved and increased amenities. Their reactions are not only disappointment but frustration. From the observations of the frustrations which programme planners and leaders have suffered; from the experiences of programmes which have not assumed that either preachment of national leaders or easily-secured amenities are stimulants to community action; and out of what has been learned from the findings of sociological scientific research, we shall analyze what sociological technical know-how can contribute to the imperative, but overwhelming, task of catalyzing an upward cycle in the lives and expectations of the masses. It should be said forthwith that the first contribution is the knowledge that in social processes, as well as in physical or mechanical processes, there is a causal relation between each preceding step in progress and all succeeding steps, and this causal relationship cannot be eliminated or annulled.

The common sense observation of many persons who are not social scientists, in highly-developed societies as well as in underdeveloped societies, is that when persons suddenly find themselves today in possession of the means for a level of living for which yesterday they had no expectations, confusion results. The sociological explanation is that the upward cycle of either an individual personality or a human group is a process, a sequence of steps or stages in evolution or growth, and that each succeeding step or stage in that evolution depends upon each previous step or stage. Furthermore, that each preceding stage must itself approximate maturity before it can be a sound stepping-stone or springboard for the next step. If, in order to reap the reward or reach the target òf the whole process quickly, an attempt is made to omit one or more intermediate steps, the process is actually destroyed. If any of the preceding steps are not consolidated, all succeeding steps are jeopardized. A blueprint of the last stage of a mechanical process can quite often be borrowed, and if faithfully followed, all stages by which the blueprint was evolved are relatively unimportant. But this is not the case with either personal or group growth.

It cannot be emphasized too often that all development programmes in underdeveloped countries face the task of changing the habits, the day-by-day practices, and the attitudes of hundreds of thousands, in some cases hundreds of millions of persons. The immensity of this task has been reported in some of the information assembled from sociological studies concerning the habits, beliefs, and attitudes of tradition-bound persons. The knowledge that cultural, socio-economic, and even national development has moved forward and will continue slowly to move forward does not satisfy the leaders of development programmes. That social analysts, and the leaders themselves, are able to identify the weaknesses, even the misfirings, of some of the methods they have used in an attempt to motivate the masses is not enough. What are needed are, if not prescriptions for, then descriptions of methods of motivation which are validated by analytical observations and scientific research. We, therefore, as sociological middlemen, assume the precarious task of making that necessary contribution. We offer generalizations on problems and methods of motivating individuals and groups, because it is these two units for action which must be successfully catalyzed if millions of so-called "apathetic villagers" and hundreds of thousands of so-called "stagnant local communities" are to become dynamic units of development.

The findings of research on "group dynamics" provide more prescriptive information than do the findings on the motivation of individuals. This is due to the fact that the behaviour of groups can be more easily manipulated than the behaviour of individuals and because the tricky concept of motivation need not be employed in group dynamics. It is only in psychotherapy and child guidance, and even there not always, that the analyst seeks for or infers motives. It is hardly possible to employ psychiatric and personal guidance methods in the problem of catalyzing millions of adult villagers. We therefore confine our discussion of motivating individuals to facts which are so readily observable that they are known by anyone whose perceptions are not clouded by the vague concept of motivation.

There are some tremendously important observations of the behaviour of isolated and disadvantaged persons which will be effectively utilized by development leaders only if they understand them in terms of their psychological and sociological significance. Father Ayrout's study of *The Egyptian Peasant*, Lerner's study of *The Passing of Traditional Society*, and Bower's study of "*The Communication of Ideas in India*" have been presented. We shall here relate both the findings of sociological research and theory to the practical problems which face development leaders who attempt to "motivate" a great number of persons and groups.

We believe that the following eight categorical statements are validated by social science research and theory, and that they can provide valuable guidance for development personnel: (1) Human beings, like all biological organisms, are internally stimulated to action. The task of agents of change is not that of providing motives to villagers but that of implementing, utilizing, and conditioning their built-in drives to act. (2) In all human groups, the automatic responses of individuals to internal stimuli are from birth conditioned by the groups into which they are born. Even their animal impulses are channelled into the established and sanctioned practices of family and local community life. (3) To conform to these practices is so necessary for both the group's and the individual's survival, and the practices are adopted by the individual so completely, that they literally become his "second nature". (4) As the individual grows to maturity, he learns so many other sanctioned forms of human behaviour that what he has learned provides an ever-increasing explanation of why he acts as he does. He responds relatively more and more to external stimuli and relatively less and less to internal stimuli. (5) There is apparently no limit to what may be learned, but there are limits to what any given person has learned. There are, therefore, limits to his capacity to respond to new ideas. This is another way of saying that he cannot respond to percepts or ideas which he does not comprehend. To do so would be to destroy the integrity of his own personality. This, however, does not mean that he lives a purposeless life or lacks goals which pull him from in front as certainly as internal stimuli push him from behind. (6) Other persons who would influence his behaviour, motivate him, in any direction, must start by providing him with possible alternative ways to reach his goals or accomplish his purposes. (7) As his mental horizons expand, and his social participation experiences are increased, his goals of life rise, and his purposes in life become less centred in personal, family, and local community concerns. (8) No matter on what level in this personality growth he is at any given moment, any agent of change can effectively reach him only on that level.

Here we only point out the most obviously necessary use of these known facts about motivation in dealing with the types of persons described by Ayrout, Lerner, and Bower. They are much nearer the levels of motivation on which the imperatives of survival are dominant than they are on those of thought and purpose which motivate national planners and leaders. Most villagers can and will be effectively reached, for the time being, only where motivation has to do with desires for levels of living only slightly above those of survival. Means and methods of motivation must be employed which offer them immediate, superior alternatives to ways of doing those things which are, day by day and year by year, the dominating concerns of their lives. To attempt to reach them on any other level and by any other than demonstrably better practices will leave them noticeably apathetic. The spell of apathy cannot be broken by attempting to use the motives which inspire national leaders. It can be dispelled by more effectively implementing the motives which drive millions of persons and hundreds of thousands of families to literally, day by day, struggle to survive and maintain their ineffective but cherished local institutions.

That the necessity of knowing all they can about group motivation is equally important to knowing all they can about individual motivation is not always thoroughly recognized by development programme planners and leaders. Many such leaders do not recognize the inevitable fact that new group formation and old group alignment are major elements in programmes of pronounced and rapid change. Knowledge about groups is literally the heart of sociology. Social scientists, from anthropologists to specialists in group dynamics, have for many decades studied groups of all kinds. But there are some difficulties in attempting to apply their research findings to the problems of planned change. Relatively little anthropological research has been focused on change, and practically no detailed studies of, and experiments in, group dynamics have been conducted in highly stratified societies.

What has been, and can be, learned from the findings of research in the field of group dynamics is more precise than what is known about individual motivation. Even so, there are the following reasons why there are difficulties in the application of research findings on the behaviour of groups to the problems which face development personnel in most underdeveloped countries: (1) All the findings of research and experiments in group dynamics have been in highly communicative and loosely stratified societies, whereas the opposite conditions prevail in most underdeveloped countries. (2) Social distance is far wider than physical distance between the different classes of people who constitute the population of local communities. Social strata are so rigid that even most local gossip does not cross class boundaries. (3) Even discussion between the leaders of the different class groups in the community is governed by custom, sometimes even by regulations. Leadership in most local groups is determined by inheritance, not by democratic action. (4) Participation in total community action is directed, and regulated, by traditionally-established divisions of labour between the highly stratified sub-groups which constitute the village social organisation. Anything approaching reciprocal communication between persons is within, not between groups.

Because of these facts, the task of formulating prescriptions for changing or alleviating these long-established conditions is both difficult and precarious. It is difficult because the practical sociologist knows that organising new groups, in ways validated by experiments in group dynamics in highly-communicative societies, has not started with the task of removing the hurdles in the paths of inter-personal communication which exist in local communities in practically all underdeveloped countries. It is precarious because his obligation is not merely to do research, and let the chips from his findings fall where they will, but to utilize research findings to help development leaders formulate prescriptions for action.

The growth of widespread felt need for development in practically all underdeveloped countries is a phenomenon of the past few decades. It can correctly be described as "the rising expectations of the masses". It is the springboard for mobilizing the masses, but they won't be mobilized en masse; they will be mobilized effectively only in hundreds of thousands of local groups. Many of these will need to be new groups to accomplish new undertakings. Local communities in underdeveloped countries are highly organised; that they have for so long been highly organised is a major part of the cause for their stagnation. New group alignments are essential to break, or dispel, that stagnation. It will, in many situations, be easier to form new groups than it will be to eliminate or combine old groups. The sociological scientist knows the adamancy of old group structures in local communities in underdeveloped countries. And he knows that few development personnel, either those who work face to face with village people or those who issue the directions for what shall be done in villages, understand the sociology and psychology of group dynamics. It is our observation that few of them understand the difference between what Homans calls real "human groups" and others which are not human groups at all but organisations, as he says in his study:

"In this book we shall study the most familiar features of the most familiar thing in the world—the human group. We mean by a group a number of persons who communicate with one another often over a span of time, and who are few enough so that each person is able to communicate with all the others, not at secondhand, through other people, but face-to-face. Sociologists call this the primary group. A chance meeting of casual acquaintances does not count as a group for us."

In the face of the typical, almost universal, existence of highly-stratified groups in the villages of underdeveloped countries, we should add that highly-stratified groups are seldom "human groups", and that "human groups" are not highly stratified.

Homans' criteria for the identification of human groups are: first, that they are composed of a small number of persons who have common interests; second, that there are frequent face-to-face interactions between all of them; and third, that they develop group sentiments and norms. These are not only the prerequisites of the group integrity, but they describe the stages, or the sequence of stages or steps, in the process of group formation.

Our analytical observations of a fairly large number of effective, newly-formed local groups in the presently-operating community development programmes in underdeveloped countries so nearly replicate Homans' more sophisticated analysis that we can, with considerable confidence, prescribe the sequence of the stages in group formation which must be followed if such new groups are to be formed.

The first necessary step in most local communities in underdeveloped countries is to help persons and families in local communities to become aware that there are other persons and families in the community who have many of the same dominant interests as they. The second step is to urge and assist these families to meet together to discuss their common interests, problems, and felt needs. Third, out of their interactions, the participants will develop group sentiments, compounded out of their common desires. Even though they do not at the moment foresee anything they can do to solve their commonly-recognized problems, they have, through these three stages, become sociologically and psychologically a human group. Their group sentiments will not only be the cement which holds the group together, but also the basic ingredients of its motivation.

Not until these groups have been formed does the agent of development have something to which he can tie in the same sure way he ties to the urge to satisfy the physical hunger of an individual or a family. As in the case of tying on to the springs of action of an individual, the development agent must tie his suggestions to the group for changes on to its dominating interests. He does this by providing the members fruitful alternatives, ways of doing specific things which are superior to what they are now doing. If he does this, he facilitates the next step in its growth, the decision to launch a group undertaking or enterprise.

Human groups, like persons, grow in both competence and confidence through decision-making and action, and especially by successfully completing what they decide to do. What the change agent encourages the group to undertake as a first enterprise must therefore be within its present competence. Failure in the first undertaking would weaken the emerging group. Too much material assistance, or even too much technical assistance, can also weaken it, or at least sabotage its growth. On the contrary, the new group will experience a great step in growth itself by threshing out the decision of what its first undertaking will be.

By increased, intensified, and focused interaction between the members of the group, it will not only uncover or discover the capabilities or capacities of its individual members, but it will discover to what extent each member is committed to its undertaking. If the group is not interfered with in this evaluating and decision-making process, it will, in all probability, be prepared to accomplish what it sets out to do. In this fourth sequential step in growth, it is no longer a group cemented merely by sentiment, but one galvanized for action.

The fifth step is the group's growth in both competence and confidence by the accomplishment of its first undertaking. In its determined effort to do a group job, it will discover the special competence of each of its members, who can and will do what. Its confidence in itself is therefore surer, because it now knows what to expect from each of its members, and each member knows what the group expects of him, both of which are prime requisites of undertaking other and larger enterprises. The sixth step or stage is incipient at the successful completion of the group's first undertaking; it becomes an established characteristic after it has successfully completed a number of its projects. At this stage, it becomes an aspiring group. It seeks new undertakings to prove to itself, and to others, what kind of a group it is. It now has what in others is called *esprit de corps* or teamwork, not only faith but pride in itself. It expects others to have faith in it.

What we have just said implies that primary or human groups sharply condition the behaviour of their individual members and can thus be said to influence their motives. Membership and participation in a primary group influence the behaviour of a person whether it is an old, traditional group or a newly-formed one. In old, established groups, a person is, so to speak, compelled to conform to their norms and values, and is thus strongly conditioned against individual innovations. In a new group, formed for the purpose of initiating change, doing something about commonly-felt needs, not only are suggested innovations solicited in its discussions, but once a group decision is made, its ideals and sentiments strengthen the wills of the weaker members. This is not only verified by a number of detailed studies, but corroborated by everyone who constantly experiences the tendency to do what other members of his family or his intimate friends expect of him.

It is these types of groups which leaders of development programmes would like to see emerge and grow; it is these which must be permitted and stimulated to form and grow by the tens of thousands in developing countries if the members of the masses, most of them living in local rural communities, are to be stimulated and assisted to make their potential, and essential, contribution to the development programmes of their countries.

One of the greatest problems of developing countries is how to motivate hundreds of millions of individuals who are said to be apathetic, and hundreds of thousands of local communities which are said to be stagnant. We have indicated the usable contributions of the knowledge which social scientists bring to a solution of this problem. We mean by usable knowledge prescriptive means and methods which development programme personnel can learn and employ in motivating individuals and small groups. Having tried, as have many others, to be middlemen between social scientists and action programme planners, we have felt the need to translate the findings of science into prescriptions for action. This is a difficult undertaking in the field of motivation because a motive cannot be seen. Any director of motives, whether a psychiatrist or a national development leader, has had to infer motives from observable actions. Any stimulator of

motives has had to do so by catalyzing action by one means or
another.

We do not know of any findings of science which should
lead any agent of development or change to believe he can give
to another person some entity called a motive. Nor do we know
of any psychotherapist or man of practical affairs who assumes
anything other than that all persons have within them internal
stimuli which can be triggered into action. Development personnel need to know this, instead of counselling with the idea that
they need to or can, per se, motivate other human beings. What
they need to do is to offer the seemingly apathetic person alternatives and superior opportunities to respond to and implement
his impulses to action.

There is a large body of sociological research which shows
the extent to which, and the ways in which, the customs (ways
of doing) and traditions (ways of thinking) of the groups in
which persons are born and reared channel their responses to
their internal organised drives into ways of doing and thinking.
We need to emphasize that what is so often called social stagnation of local groups and communities in underdeveloped countries
is primarily due to their attempt to preserve ways and values of
life which they cherish. This is to imply that most development
programme planners and leaders are not adequately aware of how
much they need to know about the psychology and sociology
of individual and group behaviour, gradually to dispel successfully
the restraints which control, and if we must say motivate, the
behaviour of relatively isolated individuals and local groups.

These very generalized findings of sociological research and
theory show the universality of human groups, the processes by
which they evolve, and the ways by which they become aspiring,
dynamic social units of action. Development personnel need to
understand the necessity of the growth of such groups if locally-
environed persons are to organise successfully, purposefully and
enthusiastically, to make their maximum contribution to their
own and their country's upward cycle in social development.

However much national growth may be measured in terms
of economic growth, especially in the early stages, this growth
depends tremendously on the social growth of the nation's rural
masses. Because leaders almost universally declare that this growth

will occur only to the extent that the masses can be motivated, we have assumed that the sociology of development should make a contribution by way of analysis of the sociology and psychology of motivation.

It is a fallacy to assume that because villagers are seemingly apathetic to change that they do not have motives. They have deep and abiding concerns about providing for those who depend upon them, whether these persons be members of their immediate family, their joint family, or their larger kinship group. Because of the conditions under which such people live and work, they probably drive themselves harder in trying to implement their motives than do any other groups in their society. They follow the best alternatives they know to accomplish the goals for which they strive. They do not respond favourably to suggestions offered by persons whom they do not know intimately, and they do not accept alternatives which they do not understand. Conversely, they do accept suggestions from those whom they know and trust and do adopt practices the superiority of which they have seen demonstrated.

Community development methods are presumed to discover, or uncover, the felt needs which local people strive to meet by employment of the best means they understand. Community development methods also attempt to provide these people with an awareness of alternatives superior to many of their present ways of attempting to meet their needs. They do this through local village workers who try to demonstrate the superiority of these alternatives in one local community after another. The effectiveness of these methods does not depend on preachment but upon demonstration, and is jeopardized by a plethora of material aid. The methods rest upon the assumption that village people and groups cherish self-reliance, and furthermore, that they become increasingly eager to change just as rapidly as they become intelligently aware of alternatives superior to their present practices. The various community development programmes of the world provide excellent laboratories for studying methods by which to "motivate" millions of persons who have been said to be apathetic, and to rebuild hundreds of thousands of village communities which have been said to be stagnant.

MAIN AUTHORITIES QUOTED OR CITED

Ayrout, Henry H., *The Egyptian Peasant*, Beacon Press, Inc., Boston, Mass., 1963.

Berlo, David K., *The Process of Communication*, Holt, Rinehart and Winston, Inc., New York, 1960.

Bower, Robert T., "Communication of Ideas in India," Bureau of Social Research, American University, Washington, D. C., 1960. (Mimeo.)

Homans, George C., *The Human Group*, Harcourt, Brace and Co., New York, 1950.

Katz, Elihu and Lazarsfeld, Paul F., *Personal Influence*, The Part Played by People in the Flow of Mass Communications, The Free Press, Glencoe, Illinois, 1955.

Kelly, George A., "Man's Construction of His Alternatives", in Lindzey, Gardner (Ed.), *Assessment of Human Motives*, Rinehart and Co., Inc., New York, 1958.

Lerner, Daniel, *The Passing of Traditional Society : Modernizing the Middle East*, The Free Press, Glencoe, Illinois, 1958.

Monthly Public Opinion Survey, Indian Institute of Public Opinion, Vols. I, II, V, New Delhi.

Myrdal, Gunnar, *Rich Lands and Poor*, The Road to World Prosperity, Harper and Bros. Publishers, New York, (World Perspectives Series, Volume Sixteen), 1957.

Young, Kimball, *Handbook of Social Psychology*, Routledge and Kegan Paul, Ltd., London, (Revised edition), 1957.

Zinkin, Maurice, *Development For Free Asia*, Essential Books, Inc., Fair Lawn, N. J., 1956.

CHAPTER 22

DEVELOPMENT OF MEANS AND METHODS OF COMMUNICATION

IN Chapter 8 we presented a brief discussion of the comparative status of India among other nations in terms of her transportation and communication facilities. Using such data as were available, it was clear that India in 1950 had a relatively ample railway system and what could be called a nationwide trunk highway system, but that she lagged in most other fields of communication. Our interpretation of the basic historic causes of these conditions was that railways and roads had been built primarily to serve the economic interests of a colonial power, primarily to carry raw products to ports for shipment to British factories. When the national development programme was launched, improved transportation facilities, and especially improved communication facilities, were needed to serve two other national government purposes. The first was to provide means by which millions of relatively isolated village people could be reached and their participation in economic and social development elicited. The second purpose was gradually to weld national unity out of the great diversity of people who were to build a national democratic, and therefore by necessity a communicative, society.

Because the construction of a network of communications to serve the masses would not have directly implemented the purposes of a colonial regime, India lagged behind countries in communication facilities which she outranked in transportation facilities. But now that she was launching a giant development programme, designed to reach millions of relatively isolated people, she would need to utilize every possible type of communication. Here, as in so many other areas, India's experiences constitute a giant laboratory in which to observe the utilization of the type of knowledge which the sociological sciences have developed in the field of communication. We look first at the use made of this knowledge in planning.

Whatever Indian planners for development, in 1950-51, knew

about the status and methods of communication with village people, it was their purpose greatly to increase communication between agents of change and the millions of people who live in villages. There was a substantial chapter in the First Five Year Plan dedicated to an analysis of "Transport and Communications". The analyses of problems and prescriptions for solutions dealt chiefly with transportation—railroads, highways, ports, and civil aviation. The Plan said that the growth of postal and telegraph facilities had been inadequate to meet increasing demands and that, "the absence of a sufficient mileage of village roads is a serious drawback in the system of communication;" and it indicated that village road development would be an important element in local community development programmes. The only statement in the Plan which evinced an appreciation of the problems and processes of communication between village-level workers, local agents of change, and village people was that these workers would need to "understand rural problems, the psychology of the farmer, and offer solutions to his various difficulties;" that, "The confidence of the villager is gained with difficulty and lost easily" and that village leaders would need to be found, developed, and utilized in the mobilization of village people.

There was thus a recognition of the fact that a knowledge and use of inter-personal communication would be vital in the day-by-day operation of the rural development programme. But there was no discussion in the Plan of the technical know-how of this type of communication. The same has been the case in the development plans of other developing countries. We can only guess that the reason it has not been done is either because planners have not thought it important or they have thought it was easy. It seems to have been assumed that if and when governments·had made technical aid in agriculture, health, sanitation, and so forth available to villagers and had provided funds to them to implement improvements in these fields, villagers' responses would be readily forthcoming. A better knowledge, not only of the inertia of isolated village people, but of their relationships with each other would have cast doubt upon this assumption.

It was not, in India, impossible to have secured this better knowledge, but to obtain such knowledge would have required the same sort of study and analysis of the problems of communication as was made of a number of other development resources. If such a working paper had been prepared for Indian planners, it would undoubtedly have encountered the historic fact that there had never been much communication from those in the top layers of the socio-economic structure of Indian society to the masses; that government administrators and landlords had reached the common people through various echelons of intermediaries and on missions which were most often not welcomed by the common people. It would probably have made programme planners and directors aware of the fact that their mere acceptance by villagers was not proof of actual rapport with villagers. It would have forewarned programme directors of what they later discovered out of operating experience, namely, that the acceptance by village leaders of financial assistance was not proof that village people, or even village leaders, would accept suggestions from outsiders for change in their mode of behaviour and thinking.

Whether or not development programme directors yet recognize that inadequate or incomplete communication with village people has been a major weakness in programme operation, they have gradually become convinced that they must have suggestions from villagers as well as make them to villagers. To the extent that this is the case, they have gone further than they did in the First Five Year Plan when they said, "A democracy working for social ends has to base itself on willing assent of the people. . . . " They have approached the maxim of Maurice Zinkin that the peasant cannot "farm in a modern way unless he can both get at the wider world, and be got at by it." This is also a maxim for communication, which to be complete must be reciprocal. That it never is reciprocal in the day-by-day operation of development programmes in newly-developing countries must be the testimony of any observer who has travelled up and down the assembly line of administration of a number of these programmes.

We emphasize here the fact that in national development plans there are generally clear-cut plans for communication from programme leaders down to local communities, but never adequate plans for communication from village people to top programme directors. There is, however, one thing that is clear, namely, that such plans would have to be formulated in a knowledge of the fact that persons as far removed from village people as are those who must formulate national plans, and those who must be assigned the responsibility for directing national development programmes, cannot know the reactions of villagers to their communications unless there is some mechanism or facility by which villagers can communicate with them. We have observed no greater block to the establishing of such a mechanism or facility than the belief on the part of development leaders that they already know the ideas of villagers and how to communicate ideas to them.

If it be asked how, in the light of these facts, it might have been expected that programme planners or directors would be alert, in advance, to some of the things they have learned from programme operation experience, the answer is that there were persons who knew a great deal about Indian villages and villagers. In no developing country of the world, other than India, have more village studies been made, by anthropologists, each of whom lived for a year or more in a particular village for the specific purpose of studying its social structure and system of human relationships. While the focus of all of these studies was not specifically on communication, the analyses made by them yield information which is more precise than the ideas planners themselves had.

One cannot read these descriptions of the day-by-day social behaviour of villagers without arriving at the conclusion that it is very seldom that the whole village moves in unison or under the leadership of one village-wide leader. In the vast majority of villages, persons and families function in sub-village groups of various kinds—joint families, castes, and factions—to which they are more loyal than they are to the village as a whole. Their primary social contacts are within these groups. Leadership in the village is not only multiple, but compartmentalized.

Alan Beals classified leaders in a Mysore village according to the nature and characteristics of their followers, as leadership (1) organised on the basis of kinship; (2) enforced through economic dominance; (3) unorganised or atomistic; and (4) organised by voluntary affiliation through common interests. Other studies have found that in one district "informal leadership" was chiefly based upon the respect such leaders inspired in others or the power they exercised over others and that the "pattern of leadership" is not continuous. Morris Opler discovered that quite often new, or prospective, leaders do not hesitate to challenge the traditional leaders. Others have found that young men from 25 to 30 years of age are more and more frequently being elected to panchayats. All of this information does not say that Indian village social structure is rapidly becoming amorphous. It does seem to say that from the multiplied evidence of these findings, the easy assumption that the behaviour pattern of Indian villages is so completely traditional, so completely well known that it can be taken for granted, is not true; that once entree into the village is accomplished, there need be no concern about the effective diffusion of ideas throughout the total population of the village is not true either.

These village studies were not focused on change, or the diffusion of innovations within villages, but an analysis of their findings reveals some of the ways in which, and some of the channels through which, diffusion within villages takes place. They show further that, as various types of change take place, change in traditional patterns of social relationships and organisation also takes place. The introduction of irrigation and irrigation farming changes old jajmani relationships. The acceptance of new ideas by even a few villagers may weaken old caste, and even old joint-family, relationships. When some member of an old village circle of human relationships has established, and especially when he is maintaining, contacts with persons outside the village, he becomes an ambassador of change within the village circle to which he belongs. When school teachers or government officials come to reside in villages and are counsellors to villagers, in even a small portion of their concerns, the role and power of traditional leaders are weakened. Business positions and the possession of wealth and education become the channels of vertical mobility. As Dube points out, these types of changes, and others, were in process before development programmes were launched. He provides considerable information on the methods by which change is diffused.

No one of the village studies, nor all of them combined, presents such a systematic description of the channels of village communication as to provide a method by which these channels can be quickly revealed to programme personnel who seek to introduce and diffuse information throughout the whole village population. Each study, however, validated two types of information which, if utilized, would make it possible to design and use a method by which these channels could be quickly known. Each of them provided precise information on the structure, the channels, and the patterns of communication between the different sectors of the population of a given village. Each of them revealed that these patterns had become different from traditional stereotypes.

Any person who had rapport with a village, and possessed a relatively minor understanding of what these anthropologists learned from their village studies, could discover and plot the basic channels of communication of any given village in less time than was spent in the benchmark surveys which attempted to assess physical, economic, and social needs of villages. Furthermore, the information secured by such a channel of communication study would have been more valuable for programme operation than was the information revealed by the benchmark surveys. We believe that programme operators have gradually discovered this fact as they have tried to establish effective communication with, that is to reach and alert the people who live in the hundreds of thousands of villages, concerning the availability of various government services.

What has thus far been observed about the problems and the processes of communication in the planning and first ten years of India's rural development programme, would be about as follows: There had been, in the past, practically no communication between administrators of government programmes and the people whom they governed. Therefore, lines of communication would have to be established de novo. There was not adequate recognition of the difficulties which would inhere in establishing effective lines of communication between village people and programme directors nor of the existent body of technical know-how about the kinds of communication most useful in attempting to reach isolated, largely illiterate, village people. There is not yet, among Indian programme planners and directors, an adequate appreciation of the need for communication from villagers, or of how such communication can be initiated and channelled up the assembly line of programme administration. Nor is there yet an adequate understanding of the vital need for such communication. But something like such an understanding and appreciation has evolved out of India's own analysis of her ten years of programme experience.

As we have said before, the Programme Evaluation Organisation was established early, and began fairly quickly to report on what was happening and what programme operation was revealing. In its report covering the first 18 months of programme operation, it said, "The prospects of interesting the villagers themselves in planning their development becomes dim if information regarding their life and prospects is not carefully collected for being discussed by and with them ... (that) to be realistic ... targets (for village accomplishment) must result from a process of observation, discussion and common agreement. In the absence of this process the targets are either non-existent or they are unrealistic."

In its second annual report, the Organisation said, "... the programme has to be popular, with officials participating, ... (not) an official programme in which the people are exhorted to participate, and in a few cases, are almost dragged in." Two years later, it said, "While there has been considerable increase in rural consciousness of economic, and to a smaller extent, of social needs, the objective of stimulating continuing and positive effort based on self-help for promoting economic or social development has been comparatively unsuccessful." A year later, this Organisation's report included a fairly detailed analysis of the people's participation. While the only statistical measure of participation was expenditures, the report was that the proportion of the people's participation in block expenditures had tended to decline. It made a plea for types of investigations which would explain why this was the case.

None of the statements quoted from the Programme Evaluation Organisation's reports used the term "communication". They did point to the lack of response of village people and the disappointing record of village people's voluntary involvement in programme undertakings, the fact that reciprocity between village people and programme personnel was not what had been hoped for. Communication is not only always a reciprocal process, but is the most universal and complete process of reciprocity. The

Programme Evaluation reports, therefore, did in essence discuss the issue of inadequate communication between programme personnel and villagers.

The same conclusion can be drawn from what was reported by the Parliament's Estimates Committee and the Team for the Study of Community Projects and National Extension Service. This Team cited shortcomings in villager and village organisation participation, pointed out weaknesses, and said that local opinion could probably be usefully harnessed. It recommended that the government divest itself completely of certain duties and responsibilities and delegate them to a body which would have in its charge all development work within its jurisdiction, keeping only the functions of guidance, supervision, and higher planning. It has been the implementation of this programme of "democratic decentralization" (now Panchayati Raj) which will undoubtedly go far to remedy the great weakness in communication between government and other outside agencies and village people, namely, the relative absence of positive participation of village people in programme planning and execution, or even in discussion of what programmes should be undertaken in their villages.

The Study Team of Community Projects expressed the belief that village public opinion could be harnessed, which was to imply that this had not been done successfully in the past. It could not be harnessed, however, unless a village public opinion actually existed, and was known and understood by programme personnel. From various sources, there are evidences that such public opinion, on development programmes, did not always exist. Furthermore, the best methods by which it could be brought into existence and developed were seldom used. All development programme personnel undoubtedly attempted to explain the programme to villagers, and special Social Education Officers were assigned the duty of making the programme and its purposes known to village people. But preachment about, and exposition of programmes to villagers are not methods by which the opinion of listeners becomes known. Much less are they the basic methods by which public opinion is formed. Such formation must be accomplished by ready and repeated communication between the persons who themselves constitute a village group. Among persons a great many of whom are illiterate, the only method of communication is by word of mouth, which means discussion. The necessity for this was recognized, and its practice planned and promoted on every level of planning and operation except at the village level. It was not systematically, or even frequently, practised at the village level until the programme of democratic decentralization was introduced.

It was only when democratic decentralization was introduced that programme personnel began to learn what village people thought and felt. Many of them were astonished and exhilarated by the willingness and manifest desire of village people, especially village leaders, to make their ideas and feelings known. Many programme personnel were also surprised to learn that villagers had been inhibited in their participation in projects because some projects had not met with their favour, had in fact run counter to their judgments and desires. This need never have been the case had those programme personnel who worked directly with village people made discussion among the villagers one of their chief methods of programme promotion. And, it might be added, had they been expected by those higher up in programme administration to do this, and to relay up the channels of communication what they learned from village people about their desires and their opinions.

It would, of course, not have been possible to plan such communication in terms of target dates, specifying that a given amount of public opinion should be evolved or that the content of that opinion should be this or that. But it is possible to measure the effectiveness of both an upward and a downward flow of communication. This is regularly done by experts in the field of communication, such as in the fields of advertising and radio broadcasting. It has been done by fairly well-standardized social research methods.

It could have been done in India had those who had planned, and were trying effectively to reach, village people clearly recognized that it was important to know quite accurately how ideas entered villages from the outside, and how they flowed through constantly-operating communication channels once they were inside village boundaries. But no systematic attempts were made to do this. The result was that the only measure obtained of the effectiveness of communication was the extent to which the planned targets of physical production were accomplished. Even this measure or assessment gradually revealed that communications with villagers had not been adequately effective. What could have been learned quickly, by the use of practical social study methods very early in the programme, was ultimately learned from unsatisfactory programme results. It was the clear awareness of what these results indicated that led to an attempt completely to reverse communications from the flow downward to a flow upward.

As would be expected, even the ineffectiveness of the downward flow of communication would reveal itself slowly if it had to do so only by waiting for end-products in behaviour, such as inadequate increased agricultural production. During the period of programme operation, there have, however, been some attempts to measure this downward flow of communication, not so much by programme operators as by others. The Indian Institute of Public Opinion, during its first year, attempted to measure the awareness of various village population groups of actions which were being taken beyond the boundaries of their local communities. The studies made by this Institute seldom bore directly upon the development programmes, but their findings revealed things which persons operating programmes intended to reach village people needed very much to know. The first Public Opinion Survey was of a Congress Party resolution which had been passed some year and a half previous to the time of the survey. The most important findings of the survey were that 95 per cent of all illiterates, and 46 per cent of all persons with less than matriculation education, had never heard of the resolution.

Another survey during the same year asked respondents the question, "Do you think India was right in voting against the resolutions on Hungary in the Central Assembly?" (United Nations). In the Calcutta sample, 21 per cent of all respondents, and 90 per cent of all illiterate respondents said they had never heard of the United Nations. As late as 1959, an all-India, urban-rural survey included inquiries about what respondents knew and thought about a number of national leaders. More than 60 per cent of all respondents, and more than 90 per cent of all illiterate respondents, said they had no opinion. In the same issue, responses were obtained to the question, "Have you kept yourself well informed on the progress of the community development programme in India?" Only a little over 28 per cent said yes. Almost 38 per cent said no; the others would express no opinion.

During the year 1960, surveys were made on the important issues of newspaper readership and radio listening. The findings on newspapers were that 34 per cent of all respondents claimed that they read newpapers; an additional 4 per cent had newspapers read to them, and an additional 8 per cent had news told to them. Thus, 46 per cent said they got news directly or indirectly from newspapers. No illiterates, of course, read newspapers. Only 14 per cent of them said they had news read or told to them.

The radio-listening survey covered only a sample of those who possessed radio licences. More than 95 per cent of all respondents had radios in their own homes. The survey therefore provides no data on the percentage of all families who possess radios or of those who listen to radios which they themselves do not possess. The chief value of the findings of the survey is on listening preferences. Almost 75 per cent of all respondents said they had listened to the radio on the day before the interview, illiterates less than others. News bulletins ranked far above all other alternatives except among the illiterates and the undergraduates, both of whom preferred Indian film songs. Probably the most significant generalization that can be drawn from this study can be stated in the words of the editors, namely, "While broadcasting has a role in providing entertainment, it is also evidenced from the present study that educational programmes can also be made interesting."

We have presented the only evidence of an effort in India to measure systematically the flow of communications, and these have been attempts to measure the flow downward. The findings are important not only because they show the extent to which communications flowing downward do or do not reach the people at the bottom, but because they give some information on how they reach these people and why they do not reach certain segments of the village population. The findings of these studies, together with those of Bower's study of "Communication of Ideas in India", and Lerner's and colleagues' studies of six Middle East countries, make it possible to prescribe the order of usefulness of the various means of communication in India's rural deve-

lopment programme. Clearly it is necessary to give first priority
to face-to-face, word-of-mouth communication. This is the only
means by which far more than half of the rural people can or
will be reached. It is, of course, also one of the means by which
those who read and listen to the radio can be reached. There
should be added to this tremendously important fact another
conclusion, derived from research findings, namely, that those
who would be agents of change by talking with villagers must
be persons whom villagers know and have reason to trust.

Nothing we have said discounts the utility of mass media of
communication. Some of the information we have presented
shows that many village persons who cannot, or do not, read
newspapers receive the news from friends who do read. There are
many examples of village groups which meet regularly to listen
to those who have read the newspapers. It is a fairly common
practice for clusters of persons in villages to gather together to
hear radio broadcasts, and the radio has become widely and
effectively utilized in a number of developing countries. The
utility of these two means of mass communication is not, however,
sufficient if they are the chief, or only, media of communication.
Their utility is raised, if not in direct proportion, at least greatly,
by the extent to which they are supplemented, or preceded, by a
great deal of face-to-face communication. This fact has special
significance in countries where the majority of rural people are
still traditional, not greatly concerned about, and even suspicious
of, ideas presented by persons with whom they are not personally
acquainted. It is worth emphasizing that speeches by State and
national leaders to large audiences are also a type of mass communication, not an example of inter-personal communication. The
utility of speeches to large audiences is also raised to the extent
that members of the audience have previously been engaged in
inter-personal communication concerning the same topic as the
address to which they are listening.

We mentioned previously that in the newly-developing
countries, ample and ready means of communication serve a
major purpose other than that of development programme administration; that widespread and diverse types of communication
are facilities for creating national unity or integration. In this
field, mass means of communication for a number of reasons rise

to their highest degree of usefulness. By their use, not only is the same content of communication channelled to millions of persons, but class and caste status need not be hurdles to equality in participation. All who are able to read have opportunities to read the same news. All who have chances to listen to radios are informed simultaneously of events and ideas. No one is excluded from large audiences. Even low-status classes are not excluded from entering cinema theatres, except sometimes by the cost of admission. But in development programme operation all, or most, mass means of communication become anything like fully operative only after the boundaries of tradition-bound local people have been breached by face-to-face communication between persons who enter, or frequently move in and out of, local communities. This role is ordinarily played by traders, travelling troubadours, or other types of habitual itinerants. In development programmes, however, it is played by government programme personnel who are consciously attempting to be agents of change.

In India, national leaders are trying to reach and communicate with hundreds of millions of village people in hundreds of thousands of villages. We have said that these leaders, from various evaluation studies, became convinced that villagers were not responding to programme appeals and assistance as readily as had been expected. We have implied that leaders had identified the chief difficulty as failure not only positively to seek village responses to appeals and assistance, but failure to stimulate village initiative. In terms of processes of communication, we have interpreted this experience as a failure to develop two-way channels of communication with village people.

All during the period of development programme operation, there have been sporadic attempts to improve the volume and effectiveness of the downward flow of communication through mass media. There has been increasing attention to radio broadcasting beamed at village problems. Newspapers and other printed materials have been steadily more widely distributed. Motion picture films, slides, exhibits, and posters on development topics have been increasingly utilized. These have been improvements for the purpose of implementing the downward flow of communication, but little has been done to increase or even facilitate an upward flow of communication. As a matter of fact, there has seemed to be no awareness on the part of development programme planners and directors that village people had impulses for, or ideas about, improvement of the conditions under which they lived; this was notwithstanding the fact that they extolled, and expected to build on, the self-reliance of villagers. This viewpoint was subsequently reversed in the light of programme experience.

There are development programmes in which the vital importance of two-way communication is recognized and implemented. In the first few years of Puerto Rico's Community Education Programme, approximately one-half of the total budget was allocated to production of stories about what was happening in local communities. Film strips and even whole dramas were produced to enlighten the general public, national leaders included, about the creative things local communities were doing. These were circulated in other communities upon the assumption that they would be inspired by what others had accomplished. It was, and is, the conviction of the directors of this programme that not too much can be accomplished by preachments, or for that matter directives, from above, but that a great deal can be accomplished by informing local communities about what others have done. Probably more important is the fact that national leaders learn what local communities think needs to be done.

We pointed out earlier the low status of India, even among underdeveloped countries, in terms of those mass media of communication which reach villages from the outside. Data show that there was great need to improve both ends of the line of communication and the channels between them. India's rate of literacy was so low that millions of peasants could not utilize or receive written communications. India met this situation forthrightly when she planned for a programme which, when it was in full operation, would have more than 50,000 programme employees living among village people and communicating face-to-face with them. It has been her experience in this type of inter-personal communication that should make a major contribution to the solution of the communication problem in many other underdeveloped countries.

But at the end of six or seven years of programme experience, she became convinced that her elaborate system of inter-personal communication, as measured by changed village practices and thinking, had been deficient. Having observed this system at all levels of operation, from the Central and State governments downward and from villages upward, it is our judgment that the most basic causes of this deficiency were: *First*, that village-level workers and those next above them, in block offices, were not apt in inter-personal communication with village people; and *second*, that the whole operation was geared far more to the task of relaying communications downward than it was to eliciting personal ideas and attitudes from villagers and communicating them upward.

The one thing that makes inter-personal communication potentially the only method of complete communication is that it alone can be reciprocal. Communication by mass media is entirely or largely one-way communication. The messages transmitted are received, but no response is made. In inter-personal communication—conversations and discussions—the receivers of messages can respond, and will respond, if not inhibited by the initiator of the conversation or discussion. It is important to emphasize that unless there is response, there is no proof that what was presumed to be communicated has actually registered. Thousands of persons in India have presented hundreds of ideas, most of them undoubtedly good ideas, to rural people and large gatherings of village people, and have believed they have communicated these ideas simply because their audience listened, and even treated the speaker with great deference.

Reciprocal communication does not occur merely by one person asking another person what he thinks about what was said. It occurs when each person desires to know, and by conversation or discussion finds out, what the other person thinks about a situation. In this, each must depend as much on the other as he does on himself. Only when this is the case is real communication accomplished. It is accomplished because empathy between the two parties has been accomplished. Each has been able to think and feel himself into the other's position. One can do this only if and when the other person states his thinking and reveals his feeling.

The Panchayati Raj organisation provides for and invites village people to reveal their ideas and attitudes on every problem related to the improvement of their own life and work. To the extent that this programme works as it is now designed, development planners and leaders will for the first time communicate with village people, and village people will be able to communicate their ideas, step by step, up the channels of administrative communication to all levels of programme administration and planning. Programme leaders will be able, as they have always said was their desire, to change their programme from a government one which has sought the assistance of village people, to a people's programme in which villagers would seek the assistance of the government in helping them to complete undertakings which they themselves had initiated.

A study of the operation of Panchayati Raj was initiated almost simultaneously with the launching of that programme. The Central Institute of Study and Research in Community Organisation stated that the purpose of its study was "to relate the formal theoretical structure of the Panchayati Raj as officially planned to the present degree of involvement of the villagers." The study was made in the first two States to initiate the Panchayati Raj programme. The main body of the interviews was with villagers, but members of the block staff and other higher officers were also interviewed. The methods of the study were of the highest order and, while the sample of villagers interviewed was small, the findings highlight some significant observations on the problem of communication with village people in the first years of the Panchayati Raj programme.

The "formal theoretical structure" referred to in the purpose of this research, was based upon the communication system of the typical Indian village. It consists of the gram sabha, an organisation similar to the New England town meeting in which every family is represented. The gram sabha is, so to speak, a village assembly of which the village panchayat is its executive committee. There are also ward meetings in which neighbours can meet, discuss their problems, formulate and express their opinions. The study did not seek information on the actual participation of villagers in the gram sabha and ward meetings, but tried to discover to what extent villagers were aware of opportunities to participate. The findings of the study, therefore, bear directly on the effectiveness of communication and indicate that the mere existence of such people's organisations as the village panchayat, gram sabha, and wards, does not in and of itself guarantee communication from villagers upward.

In one of the States, less than one-fifth of the respondents knew of a recent pertinent decision made by their village panchayat, and only ten per cent of them indicated that a gram sabha meeting had been held during the past year. More than 78 per cent of them averred that they knew of no recent ward meeting. In the other State, 66 per cent of the respondents indicated that a gram sabha meeting had been held during the past year, and 60 per cent of them indicated that there had been a recent ward meeting. Some 70 per cent of them knew of a recent pertinent decision made by their village panchayats. The study did not report what would have been a significant finding, namely, why villagers were better informed in one State than in the other, except to note that a tom-tom which all could hear had always announced the convening of the gram sabha in the one State where a majority of the villagers knew that a meeting had been held during the last year.

The researchers made a rather definitive analysis of the comprehension which respondents had of the programme. In one State, slightly less than 60 per cent had a general awareness of the programme, slightly less than 17 per cent had comprehension of its organisation, and only 35 per cent of all respondents indicated complete ignorance of the programme. Because Panchayati Raj will, within a short time, be operative throughout India, and because it, as a people's organisation, together with village-level workers and extension personnel, are the main avenues or channels of communication between village people and their State and national development programme leaders, every possible effort should be exerted to learn why these channels are effective, where they are ineffective, and why and how. Only on the basis of such definitive information can the means of effective communication be learned from actual programme experiences.

The basic means for bringing the masses of the rural people of India into the bloodstream of national life is to bring them into communication with those in their own society who desire that India as a whole, and every sector of its population, move from traditionalism to modernity. It is as important that the leaders of the nation who plan and attempt to direct this transition know what the millions of members of the rural masses think and why, as it is that the rural masses know what the leaders think and plan. The channels of communication, especially of upward communication, have literally had to be created de novo. Indian planners, from the beginning of India's programme of planned development, have recognized the need to understand the minds of rural or village people. We have attempted to explain why, for historic reasons, national leaders do not adequately understand either the ways of doing or thinking of village people and that they never will, or can, until upward means of communication have been provided and are fully operative. The rapid development of literacy is, of course, a requisite for both effective downward and upward communication. But India need not wait for the full impact of complete literacy of her people. The formal administrative organisation of her rural development programme provides the means not only for downward communication to rural people, but for upward communication from them. The Panchayati Raj hierarchical organisation is hopefully and definitely planned to stimulate the upward flow of communication.

There are, however, two possible, and we would say probable, reasons why what is assumed will happen may not happen to the extent hoped for. First is the possibility that the panchayats will develop primarily into government administrative units, and thus look upward to higher units of organisation for guidance rather than downward for guidance from the people whom they are presumed to represent. This is not only a tradition but a deep-seated practice in India. Its reversal, however, is the only way which is consonant with either the means for developing a democratic social order or an effective means for capturing, utilizing, and developing the giant potential dynamic which resides in her millions of rural people. The second reason is the possibility, even the probability, that in attempting to arouse the rural people to dynamic thought and action, major emphasis will not be placed on the necessity of utilizing every known effective means of word-of-mouth, or inter-personal communication; that various levels and groups of people will not be urged to discuss among themselves the things they would like to do and desire that their government help them to do; and that they will not be facilitated in the organisation of special local-interest or special-purpose groups to enable them to make their maximum contribution to their own and their nation's development.

Mention should be made of the 1963 report of the Mass Communications Study Team sponsored by The Ford Foundation at the invitation of the Government of India. Submitted to the Ministry of Information and Broadcasting, it recommends the establishment of "A Centre for Advanced Study in Mass Communication". This centre would provide both training (via basic and refresher courses for communications personnel) and research into the problems confronting the dissemination and utilization of information. Such a "research-cum-action" role will necessarily probe the questions raised here regarding the two-way exchange of information and opinion; as such, it can only be welcomed by those who recognize the vital nature of the problem and who wish to enhance and hasten the nation's development.

MAIN AUTHORITIES QUOTED OR CITED

Berlo, David K., *The Process of Communication*, Holt, Rinehart and Winston, Inc., New York, 1960.

Dube, S. C., *Some Problems of Communication in Rural Community Development*, Cornell University, Ithaca, N. Y., 1956. (Mimeo.)

Evaluation Report on First Year's Working of Community Projects, Programme Evaluation Organisation, Planning Commission, Government of India, May, 1954.

Evaluation Report on Second Year's Working of Community Projects, Vol. I, Programme Evaluation Organisation, Planning Commission, Government of India, April, 1955.

Evaluation Report on Working of Community Projects and N.E.S. Blocks, Vol. I, Programme Evaluation Organisation, Planning Commission, Government of India, April, 1957.

Hoffsommer, H. and Dubey, D. C., *A Sociological Study of Panchayati Raj*, Central Institute of Study and Research in Community Development, Ministry of Community Development and Co-operation, Government of India, 1961.

Katz, Elihu and Lazarsfeld, Paul F., *Personal Influence*, The Part Played by People in the Flow of Mass Communications, The Free Press, Glencoe, Illinois, 1955.

Monthly Public Opinion Survey, Vol. II, Nos. 12, 14; Vol. V. Nos. 7 and 8, Indian Institute of Public Opinion, New Delhi.

Nair, Kusum, *Blossoms in the Dust*, The Human Element in Indian Development, Gerald Duckworth and Co. Ltd., London, 1961.

Report of the Study Team, sponsored by The Ford Foundation, Ministry of Information and Broadcasting, Government of India, 1963.

Report of the Team for the Study of Community Projects and National Extension Service, Committee on Plan Projects (COPP), New Delhi, November, 1957.

Seminar on South Asia Studies, University of Chicago, 1956, Working Papers on Leadership in Indian Villages (Beals, A. R., Opler, M., et al).

Shannon, L. W., *Underdeveloped Areas,* Harper and Brothers Publishers, New York, 1957.

The First Five Year Plan, Planning Commission, Government of India, December, 1952. (Chapter XV).

Zinkin, Maurice, *Development For Free Asia,* Essential Books, Inc., Fair Lawn, N. J., 1956. (especially Chapters 4 and 18).

CHAPTER 23

ROLE AND STATUS RELATIONSHIPS IN PROGRAMME ADMINISTRATION

THE magnitude and diversity of change initiated by a planned programme of change automatically require the creation of many action roles which have never previously been a part of government programme operation. A planned programme of change also requires a great expansion in government personnel. New roles to be played are dictated by the new jobs which the programme creates, and many persons who, previously, have never played official roles in the operation of government are now required to do so. Many old government employees are required to play roles which they never before have played.

In the past, stability and cohesiveness in government administration have been easily maintained because each person employed in programme administration knew the patterns of behaviour or action which were expected of him. In a planned development programme, whether or not it is foreseen, the relationships between the old status groups will be changed, and the emergence of new expectations will engender social dynamics, and thus instability. In this process, old high-status groups will have to play programme roles which are beneath their old social status. Some formerly low-status groups will have to play roles for which they have had no expectations, that is, have had no psychological preparation. India's vast programme of development provides an opportunity to observe the influence which an old, stable social status of both high- and low-status groups has in the operation of a programme which is geared to change.

Attempts to understand the whys and wherefores of status have always been one of the chief objectives of sociological scientists, and of philosophers before them. Studies of roles, which are the behaviour or action components or correlates of statuses, are of more recent origin. As was the case with the psychology and sociology of motivation, we shall here present a brief exposition of the basic sociological knowledge about roles and statuses, and the inter-relationships between them. We recognize that to do this by use of sociological knowledge validated by research, and to apply that knowledge to the problems involved in the day-by-day operation of India's community development programme is not easy. The research findings, and the theories which derive from them, were made in more static societies than those of developing countries. The anthropologist's view is that status in simple societies is determined chiefly by age, sex, and occupation and that whatever prestige an individual enjoys is determined by the status group to which he belongs. Not only his rights, but his obligations are functions of the level of prestige which his status grants.

More important is the fact that the few groups which enjoy the highest prestige constitute what in modern society are called power groups. It is expected by all others that the members of these groups will direct the community, clan, or society which accord them this prestige and power. An understanding of these facts is important to development programme planners and leaders, for the simple reason that there are large carry-overs of all of these ways of doing and thinking in underdeveloped countries. The social structure of most underdeveloped countries is still highly and rigidly stratified. Therefore, whatever is known about the functional or dysfunctional conditioning influence of rigidly-set status groups should be useful to development programme planners and directors who seek to change many status relationships. No matter in what field a national programme operates, it is conditioned by the general social structure of the society in which it operates.

What is known about role and status is more readily applicable in the administration of programme operation than it is in local community life. Therefore, information about roles, statuses, and relationships between the two, which has been gained by studies of the operation of large action programmes, is exceedingly valuable in observing and analyzing the influence of administration in India's community development programme. Even though most, if not all, of the recent studies of role and status in programme administration have been made in open class societies, the functional and dysfunctional relationships between roles and statuses reveal themselves on all levels of life. But more important in what these studies reveal are the essential type and kind of relationships which must prevail if both efficiency and morale are to develop and prevail in programme operation.

In our attempt to apply sociological research findings and the theories which derive from research, and to use our analytical observations, we shall show the conditioning influence of status carry-overs from the past in those areas of day-by-day programme operation in which members of two different status groups must play co-operative roles in doing a single job. But for the most part, we shall delay discussion of the carry-overs of ways of doing and thinking of the past until we come to a discussion of the role of bureaucracies in national development programmes. To arrive at this point in our analysis, we need first to present the areas of day-by-day programme operation in which experts in role analysis have made detailed observations, in order to determine the necessary inter-relationships of individual roles in total programme operation. Only then can we illustrate the usefulness of making this same kind of observations of day-by-day programme operation of India's community development programme.

The total work of any organisation gets done by division of labour between the role-players who do the various and differing jobs. Because effective programme operation depends not only on each person in the organisation knowing what his role is, but also knowing what the roles of other persons are, analysts attempt to discover to what extent this understanding prevails; in other words, to what extent does role consensus prevail among the personnel of the whole organisation?

The first two questions to which the analyst seeks answers about each individual role are: (1) what precisely is the division of labour which this role-player is supposed to play; and (2) where is he located functionally, on the organisation chart and physically, in order to do his job. The analyst seeks answers to two further questions: (3) what are the expectations of the person who is assigned or elected to play this role, what satisfactions does he expect to enjoy, and what frustrations does he encounter; and (4) what do other role-players in the programme think his job is and what do they expect of him. Some of the major findings of social scientists in this field are presented here primarily for the purpose of understanding all roles and role-players in an organisation the operation of which depends, at least to some extent, upon an understanding by all role-players of the roles of others.

The extent to which consensus of or among those playing all roles is necessary depends upon the kind of group or organisation in operation. In small groups, it is probably necessary that all persons in the group or organisation understand all of the roles, and that there be some consensus within the organisation as to what the rights and responsibilities of all role-players are. In a large, hierarchical, very rationalized organisation, it is desirable but not imperative, and probably not possible, that all persons in the organisation understand the day-by-day necessities and conditions of all the roles which are to be played. But in either case, it is necessary that there be common understanding and agreement between persons who play two roles which, because of the job to be done, make the skills and physical presence of both of them essential. This is repeatedly and systematically the case with any two role-players who occupy adjacent locations in the organisation structure.

In a large, hierarchically-organised programme, day-by-day operation is carried on chiefly by the co-operation of pairs of role-players. Each role-player joins a person playing another role, who is located adjacent to him in one direction, and joins a person playing a still different role, who is located adjacent to him in the other direction. Thus, all roles, all divisions of labour of the programme, are linked from bottom to top and top to bottom by joint roles in a programme-operating organisation. Our inquiry will be, at the moment, about what happens when adjacent-position roles are not understood and appreciated by both adjacent role-players. This is important because in all such situations, the behaviour of either one fructifies or sabotages the playing of the other's role.

Furthermore, it is not enough for one of this pair merely to know what the other's job is. He is both personally and professionally concerned about how well the other role is played. In other words, he must, for the sake of the organisation of which he is a part, for the sake of the morale of the other role-player, and for his own sake, respect the importance of the other role;

if he downgrades it, that fact is relatively apparent to the person who must play that role. If he assumes that the other role is subordinate to his own role, and therefore the other person should be subordinate to him, he sullies the playing of the joint role. Not only is the efficiency of a necessarily-hierarchical organisation promoted, but its soul is saved by the opportunity to employ and practise the types of inter-personal relationships which nurture and sustain the social values inherent in co-operative human relations. It is in these paired, role-playing situations that the personal behaviour of individual role-players, and their inter-personal relations with other role-players, are exceedingly important.

Not only group situations, but the behaviour and attitudes of individual role-players have been objects of analysis of researchers in the field of role and status. Their findings corroborate what is obvious to the close observer of any action programme operation, namely, that the dynamics or lack of dynamics of programme operation inhere in the expectations, that is, the motivations, of individual role-players. If an individual role-player believes, and has evidence, that others, especially his adjacent role-player, believe his role is important, he has real zest in doing his job. If he is in doubt about what others think about the importance of his role, he is bound to have anxiety; if he knows that his companion in paired role-playing discounts the importance of his role in their necessarily co-operative undertakings, he suffers continuous frustration. Under the first set of conditions, he has zest in his job and does it with satisfaction and enthusiasm. Under the second set of conditions, he is not only frustrated in doing his work, but has doubts about his own usefulness. If a whole cadre of programme personnel, to which a vital programme role has been assigned, is compelled to work with anxieties about the degree of recognition accorded them by other cadres of programme personnel, if each or any large number of them is downgraded by another cadre of personnel with whom they must work daily, the very foundation of programme dynamics is undermined. If, on the other hand, and in spite of the fact that they hold positions of relatively low programme status, it is obvious to them every day of their lives that others believe that their role is vital, and they are constantly seeking ways to emphasize and strengthen their capacity to play that role effectively, then programme operation is dynamic from the bottom up.

It is our opinion that India's community development programme is so structured that it lends itself to the same system of analysis which has been employed in the studies of other hierarchically-structured organisations. Each echelon of programme operation is logically related to the echelons above it and below it in programme administration. The role of each cadre of programme personnel is clearly delineated. Each role-player is repeatedly paired with an adjacent person who is playing a different but supporting role. It is therefore possible to observe all the types of role behaviour, the effectiveness or ineffectiveness of which has been observed in carefully-designed research studies.

In the presentation of our observations of India's programme in action, we shall first show that the programme personnel of the organisation are so located that all roles, if effectively played and properly related to supporting roles, would not only guarantee effective and efficient programme operation, but develop good teamwork and high morale in the whole programme organisation. We shall then discuss the ways in which the different statuses of the various cadres of personnel, statuses not gained by meritorious playing of development programme roles, adversely condition the effective functioning of an excellently-designed programme.

India's community development programme organisation chart is a quite symmetrical pyramid. Since the programme has blanketed the entire country (in 1963) there are more than 50,000 workers located at the village level, at least 25,000 extension specialists located at the block level, and approximately 3,000 more mature specialists and administrators located at the district level. There are more than 300 administrative districts, and there will be, in due time, 5,000 blocks. Above the districts are the State Governments, and below the blocks there are the panchayats. There are 550,000 villages.

The village-level worker works, on the one hand, with villagers and village groups, and on the other hand, with the programme personnel located in the block. The programme persons located at block headquarters work, on the one hand, with the village-level workers, and on the other hand with pro-gramme personnel located at district or sub-district headquarters. All persons located in district offices are members of one of the State Ministries, called nation-building departments, or are members of some State corps of administrators.

We shall first describe the stated roles of the two largest echelons of programme personnel—village-level workers and block extension specialists—and their functional relationships each with the other, in terms of a model which students of roles would prescribe, and a model which India's planners and directors did prescribe. We shall then discuss the playing of roles of these two levels and their relationships to each other, and to all other pro-gramme roles, chiefly those played by the persons who constitute the administrative bureaucracy of the State and national governments.

The village-level worker is, as we know, a village-born and reared person, who has at least a secondary school education, and who now spend two years in an institute where he receives special training in the skills his job requires. His most intensive training has been in agriculture because the majority of villagers with whom he is to work are cultivators and because increased agricultural production is one of the outstanding needs of his country. He lives in one of the villages he serves. His role in the total development programme includes the jobs of making village people aware of improved ways of living and working, and rendering them first-aid assistance in learning these new ways; acting as liaison, a channel of communication, between villagers and block specialists in various fields of improvement; and helping village people effectively to organise for accomplishing improvements of any and all kinds. The playing of this role, as was said above, requires that he work with the players of each of two other roles, the village people and the block specialists.

Notwithstanding the fact that the role of the village people is not, cannot and need not be, a role assigned by programme administrators, their co-operation in everything the village-level worker seeks to accomplish is vitally important. Their role, however, cannot be aptly discussed in the frame of reference of this chapter. The role of the block extension specialist can and needs to be described here, in order that we may portray the programme's prescribed relationships between his role and the role of the village-level worker. He is located at the headquarters office of the block, which has responsibility for total development of an area which includes 100 villages. He works with from 10 to 20 village-level workers. He is a college-trained man, a specialist in some one field of technical knowledge. His job is to provide technical assistance to village-level workers and to the villagers whom they serve. No small part of his role is continuous in-service training of village-level workers with whom he works, in order that they may be better technical assisters. His role is also to render direct technical assistance to groups which village-level workers have catalyzed and mobilized. It is a part of his role to secure for himself, for village-level workers, and for villagers the superior technical information which a higher cadre of programme personnel, located in the districts, can provide.

Located at block headquarters are a number of other specialists, and also the chief Block Development Officer, who is the administrative and programme director or coach of all block personnel, those living and working in villages, and those located at, and working out of, the block development headquarters. We shall, for the moment, confine our observations and descriptions to the role-relations of the village-level workers and block agricultural-extension specialists, in the specific task of increasing agricultural production in one after another of the more than 550,000 villages in India.

We assume, properly we believe, that every cultivator in every village desires to increase his agricultural production. We therefore begin with the first job in the role of the village-level worker which is making village cultivators aware of the fact that there are known and proven agricultural practices superior to those now being employed in the village. Because of his training, the village-level worker is competent to play this role. Because he is village-born and reared, possibly the son of a cultivator, he is accepted. In the eyes of the village, he is an educated person and therefore is accorded status. He has had intensive training in agriculture and can talk not only the language of the cultivators, but can tell them about improved agricultural practices. He can even render considerable technical assistance to them in their learning to practise improved methods of agricultural production;

and he can promise them that he can, if they will mobilize for a meeting with the block agricultural specialist, secure for them more and surer advice on how to improve agricultural production than he, the village-level worker, is able to provide. The design of the programme provided for the needed supporting role of the agricultural specialist who was expected at this point to be sought and provided. The village-level worker therefore asks for, and is assured of, the assistance of the block agricultural specialist.

We turn now to what each of the two programme role-players must do, and what the village cultivators do, in launching and carrying out a project of improvement in agricultural production in one village. In addition to the things the village-level worker has already done in preparing villagers for a meeting with the block agricultural specialist, he must arrange for a place to meet, and he must assemble the cultivators at that place at the time agreed upon. Knowing the cultivators of the village, he will have exerted special effort to see that those cultivators who are most trusted by all the rest, and the leaders of any special groups of cultivators, are present at the meeting. He has thus done all the jobs essential to the playing of his role. But the agricultural specialist may request the privilege of visiting, and may want the assembled cultivators to visit, different types of farms in the village area. The village-level worker responds to this request by making arrangements for such visits.

By the time the first visit of the agricultural specialist has concluded, it has been agreed that certain improved practices will be undertaken in the village. Almost certainly, they will be undertaken by only a few cultivators, maybe by only one cultivator who has volunteered to have the effectiveness of the new methods demonstrated on his farm. From there on, three roles must be played jointly, the role of the demonstrating cultivator, of the village-level worker, and of the block agricultural specialist. The demonstrating cultivator will agree to carry out each phase of the demonstration, from preparing the ground for planting to harvesting the crop. The village-level worker can provide some of this assistance, but the superior technical knowledge and greater maturity of judgment of the agricultural specialist will be needed from time to time, so he must return on pre-arranged dates. At all such times, it is the role of the demonstrator to invite all the cultivators in the village to be present. It is the role of the village-level worker to mobilize as many village cultivators as possible to hear what the agricultural specialist and the demonstrator have to say about what has been done and what needs to be done at this stage in the employment of the new practice.

This is India's design for the effective operation of her community development-extension programme at the village level. We could report from our many observations of its operation, and observations of similar programmes in other countries, examples of almost perfect joint or co-operative functioning of the three programme roles just described. To do so, however, would be to repeat the above model. We could report examples in which some one of the roles was played ineffectively, and far more examples where improvement undertakings failed, or were far from satisfactorily completed, because of the absence or ineffectual playing of one or more of these essential roles; and still more examples where there were ineffectual relations between roles and role-players.

Our observations are that the first programme job in the village-level worker's role is quite well played by about one-half of the village extension workers in India. Once a programme worker has come to live and work among them, villagers not only become aware of the existence of practices superior to some of those they are now employing, but they develop expectations that they will be helped to learn how to use these practices. They also testify in increasing number, by word and deed, that they are willing to join hands to undertake various types of organised self-help projects, the need of which they already knew, but which they had neglected.

Generally village-level workers believe their greatest opportunity is to assist in agricultural improvements because the great majority of village families are cultivators. Increasingly, however, village extension workers are expressing discouragement because they cannot secure needed technical assistance from block agricultural specialists. They also complain that they do not obtain needed materials which they had been promised would be forthcoming if and when they had induced cultivators to use better seeds, plants, breeding stock, etc. To these could be added so many other evidences of ineffectual role relationships in day-by-day programme operation that we venture an analysis of the reasons for these observed facts. Sometimes, of course, the cause was the sheer ignorance of some persons about how to do their assigned jobs, and/or lack of dedication to their work. But even these were quite often manifestations of latent dissatisfactions induced by experience in playing their roles under conditions created by the way one or more other necessary programme roles had been played. Detailed sociological research has discovered that such dissatisfactions, and frustrations, most often result from the treatment a person experiences because some adjacent role-player, consciously or unconsciously, has sabotaged the fulfilment of the role expectations this person had when he accepted or was assigned to his job.

It would, of course, not be possible precisely to analyze the ineffectual functioning of role relationships in the operation of a programme the size of India's community development programme except by a carefully-designed, detailed research study. But because each programme role was clearly delineated in the plan for the programme, and each role-player was presumably taught in a training centre the skills essential to the effective playing of his role, it is probably correct to conclude that there exists a weakness in role relationships in day-by-day development programme operation. Furthermore, it is possible, from repeated field observations, clearly to identify the major weaknesses in these role relationships. As precarious, therefore, as it may appear, we offer a few illustrations of almost countless other similar observations of the absence of helpful human relationships between various role-players in the development programmes of under-developed countries.

The illustrations we are looking for, and looking at, are human relationships between role-players in day-by-day programme operation which do not square with the types represented in the description above, of the co-operative relationships between villagers, the village-level worker, and the block agricultural specialist in a village agricultural improvement project. Most, but not all, of the illustrations are from India's community development programme. All others are from very similar programmes in other developing countries. These few examples could be multiplied a hundredfold.

A Block Development Officer, in one instance, extols his corps of village workers as the best in India, but all his personal contacts with them are very formal, as from a superordinate to a subordinate. In a block staff meeting, the Block Development Officer and block specialists instruct the village-level workers, seldom solicit suggestions from them. A block specialist visits a village, unaccompanied by the village-level worker who is resident in that area. He makes no inquiry about the village-level worker while he is in the village. A regional officer in Ghana pilots a foreign visitor to a local village project, hunts up the village worker and severely criticizes him for not being present at the meeting, about which the worker had not been informed. He discovers later that the local worker was at another place, doing the job required to be done that day and at that place. The regional man makes no apology. An area development officer in Pakistan, accompanied by VIPs, holds a meeting in a village and assumes the task of explaining a local project. The only village-level workers present were assigned the role of serving a meal to the VIPs. Numerous observations were made of work done or being done in a village, where the local village workers and the villagers had done some laudable job, but some higher official—a block specialist, a Block Development Officer, or even a district officer—assumed the role of explaining what was done and how it was done. The village-level worker was asked no questions and volunteered no comments. In each of these examples, the pride of the village level role-player in his role had no opportunity to manifest itself, and the role-player himself was either ignored or compromised. We think it is fair to say that we doubt that the programme associate who compromised or ignored him was aware of what he had done in each case. In each instance, the associate was exercising what he consciously or unconsciously thought was behaviour becoming to, and even expected of, a person of his status.

Because a person's status is proof to others and to himself of who he is, he is almost certain to, consciously or unconsciously, exhibit his status in all except his primary group relationships. This tendency is certain to be especially strong in countries where the class structure has, for a long time, been rigid, and the status of every individual is known and accepted. In such societies, the status, or station, a person occupies not only determines his superior or inferior rank among others, but also determines the nature and amount of his responsibility. This is the case in open-class societies as well as in closed-class ones. The difference between the two is that in open-class societies, the movement of an individual from one class, and therefore one status, to another is permitted, expected, and encouraged, whereas, in the other, no such movement is encouraged or expected and, in fact in many cases, is forbidden by public sentiment and sometimes by law. Even if it be taken for granted that the national leaders of most countries which have launched development programmes do not sanction either the laws or the public sentiments which tend to perpetuate old class structures, no group of national leaders can obviate the inevitable carry-overs of yesterday's social practices and sanctions into many of today's practices.

The operation of a nationwide development programme requires a large number of personnel. From the numbers cited earlier as required in the operation of India's community development programme, it should be evident that thousands of persons must play roles which are beneath the rank which, in their society, their old statuses accorded to them. Many more thousands are given the opportunity to play roles which are far more honorific than they have aspired to before. Only those who have had opportunities to learn the meaning of status in India, or some other Asian society, can appreciate the many and great frustrations involved in these changed roles. These frustrations are far deeper than the average person born and reared in an open-class society can imagine. It is even difficult for dedicated, intellectually-objective national leaders who were, so to speak, born to status to appreciate what required changes in status demand in personal adjustments.

A status-role, in a highly class-structured society, is what is required of each person who is a member of one of the many status groups. Many of the roles he plays are functions of his social status. Complete behaviour performance is not, however, so constantly and repeatedly required of him as a member of a status group as is required of him as a member of such a primary group as the family. In both cases, status or position determines both the role he plays and the degree of his dedication to that role. In his family duties, a father's duties to his children are so completely internalized that dedicated performance is literally the passion of his life. In his societal status group, he, in many instances, may play his status role or roles only because the maintenance of his reputation requires it. On many occasions, he can and does maintain his reputation by little more than symbolic role gestures. He is present at places where he is expected to be seen, speaks up if it is assumed by others that he should, and says the things which persons with his status ought to say. To do these things may not at all be the passion, but only the style, of his life.

In a large, rationalized organisation, roles are assigned in terms of jobs to be done. Emphasis is placed on the proven performance, not the social status, of those to whom specific roles are assigned. In a society where there are many such large rationalized organisations, there are many persons with proven performance records who can be recruited to play any and all of the roles essential to the operation of any new organisation which is to be launched. In India at the time the rural development programme was launched, government was almost the only large, rationally-organised structure from which experienced personnel could be recruited. It was therefore necessary to assign persons from government administration to the various roles essential to the operation of development programmes, notwithstanding the fact that most of them had never before played the roles to which they were now assigned. Naturally each person was assigned to that level of programme responsibility to which his status in government administration entitled him. When this was done, it was almost inevitable that his old administrative status would condition his behaviour and attitudes in the playing of his new role. Furthermore, it was inevitable that many persons thus assigned to new roles would be at least as much dedicated to the maintenance of their status as to the performance of their new roles.

Status is a phenomenon of all societies. In societies which have for centuries been traditionally stratified, the origins of statuses cannot be precisely known. But from all that has been learned from studies of a number of such societies, there seems to be agreement that division of labour between different sectors of the population, whether in tribal or village economies, was a major, if not the first, step into or toward social stratification. If this assumption, and the evidence to support it, are correct, the social roles a person or a group played determined social status. This is another way of saying that the old status systems, at some time in the past, had been validated by the meritorious playing of the roles necessary to each society's survival and continuance.

In Indian society, and probably in all others, each status group came in due time to have roles other than those required by the economic system. The playing of some of these roles was more honorific than others, and thus there was status differentiation, or rank, within each status group. It is partly because of this that rank, as a measure of who a person is, is highly magnified in Indian society. One is impressed by its universality, as portrayed in folk tales and also its practice in highly secular organisations. It prevails among any corps of house servants, where it is based on divisions of labour between caste occupations. But it also prevails among occupational equals, where there is always at least a number one and a number two. High-ranking persons may not be permitted to exercise any authority over their occupational equals, but they advertise their rank at every opportunity, and in the presence of others. Their colleagues honour their rank. It is probably inevitable that it also prevails in India's rural development programme. It prevails especially strongly among the various cadres of administrative personnel, that is, in the hierarchical administration of the community development programme, as well as in all other government programmes.

It is not possible precisely to relate caste status to development programme status even though it is clearly evident in all societies that such institutions, in fact all types and kinds of organisations within a society, are conditioned not only in their functioning, but in their structure, by the organisation of the society in which they operate. It is possible to relate bureaucratic status to programme status in India, and to observe, at all levels of programme operation, how administrative or bureaucratic status conditions vitally important inter-personal relations, and adversely conditions the dynamics of day-by-day programme operation.

The dynamics of a community development programme are developed at the bottom, not at the top of programme operation. Bureaucratic administration always operates, and must, from the top down. India had an efficient bureaucracy when she launched her community development programme. Since this was to be nationwide, it was necessary that she make maximum use of this efficient bureaucracy. This same necessity exists in all under-developed countries, even though few, if any others, have developed as efficient an administrative bureaucracy as has India. It is because her administrative structure is so thoroughly representative of efficient bureaucracies that it is possible to describe the roles this structure plays in the nation's community development programme, and to understand how it plays these roles. We shall, therefore, report our observations, and the observations of others, on the influences of bureaucratic direction on the dynamic playing of vital roles in total programme operation.

In sociological analyses, many conflicts or ineffective accommodations are observed between status positions and status persons and their assigned roles. Many village-level workers, on the lowest rung of the hierarchical programme organisation, lack satisfactions in performing their roles and are disappointed in their expectations. There is also considerable disappointment and disillusionment on the part of bureaucratic programme directors over the lack of fulfilment of goals. There is criticism of, and a demand for a reappraisal by, national leaders and to some extent by makers of public opinion. There is not yet a consciousness of the contribution that the analysis and understanding of roles and role relationships could make to more efficient programme administration.

No better analysis has been made than by Max Weber of the processes involved in the development of bureaucracy as society evolved out of tribal societies into modern States, and steadily shifted from charismatic to bureaucratic leadership. Weber states six basic characteristics of bureaucracy as follows: (1) there are jurisdictional areas fixed by rules and regulations; (2) the levels of graded authority are a system of superordination and subordination; (3) office managing is based upon written documents, and therefore the care and manipulation of files require a staff of subaltern officials; (4) office management, because it is specialized, can be learned; (5) because it can be learned, persons can be trained as specialists in administration; and (6) such management is not on a personal or inter-personal basis, but is governed by "abstract" or non-personal rules and regulations.

These characteristics are easily observed in the operation of the central office of any large organisation. They are replicated in the lower administrative offices of any large hierarchical organisation. The essential components of each of the major characteristics of bureaucracy, or major elements in the day-by-day administrative behaviour of administrative personnel, are not so easily observed. But here also, Weber's description helps an analyst to see, understand, and interpret what he observes in terms of inter-personal relationships between persons of different statuses. Persons assigned to fixed jurisdictional areas are assigned fixed official duties, and these duties are spelled out in rules and regulations. Authority of officials to give commands is strictly delimited by rules. Only persons qualified by regulations and specifications are employed. Appeal from a lower office to a higher authority must be in a regulated manner.

This very brief summary of Weber's description of a bureaucracy helps one to see how bureaucratic office-holding can be a vocation, which it is in India, and which it is in every government whose employees are members of the civil service. The high, almost sacrosanct status of those in the Indian Administrative Service can be understood only in the light of historic development of which there were two facets. In terms of long-time development, bureaucratic administration and leadership superseded charismatic and semi-charismatic administration and leadership. This undoubtedly took place gradually as India moved steadily away from tribal government toward a modern State, and from numerous and diverse States ruled by semi-charismatic princes toward a unitary government. In short terms, the development was under the guidance of Great Britain's elite corps of civil servants. Added to the firm mores, or high standards, promoted and maintained by British civil servants, was the fact that Britain was a colonial power, operating in a foreign society, which made it imperative that its civil servants behave quite impersonally. This civil service was participated in by Indians, who are now in command of the Indian Administrative Service. That these persons act arbitrarily, or objectively, within the framework of fixed jurisdictions, specified rights and duties, grades or ranks of authority, superordination and subordination, means that they are acting as all efficient bureaucrats act.

Those who man India's bureaucracy are not only trained and competent, but proud of their role of upholding the integrity of government management. If they are accused of acting like "high priests", it is because they insist not only on efficiency but integrity or morality on the part of those who manage and direct day-by-day government operation. In the face of casteism, and especially familism, which tend to foster nepotism, Indian bureaucrats insist upon objective, arbitrarily-applied and administered rules and standards. As in all underdeveloped countries, and many others, trained bureaucrats overtly or covertly wage war against the forces of nepotism, communalism, and politics. In most developing countries, they are still being defeated in these struggles. In India, the struggle was widely successful well before national Independence was achieved and was consolidated immediately afterward.

Weber's generalizations about the automatic, conservative influence of bureaucratic administration are germane to a discussion of the problem which arises in a country that has a highly competent bureaucracy, but is operating a vast programme of change. His generalizations about the influence of bureaucracy on change were based on his observations of bureaucracy in Germany at the time he wrote rather than on bureaucratic behaviour in predominantly democratic societies. They, however, probably apply fairly accurately to developing countries, none of which in the past has had democratic administration.

Blau cites two writers as saying:

"Nobody can be at the same time a correct bureaucrat and an innovator. Progress is precisely that which the rules and regulations did not foresee; it is necessarily outside the field of bureaucratic activities." "Adherence to the rules, originally conceived as a means, becomes transformed into an end-in-itself; there occurs the familiar process of *dis-*

placement of goals whereby 'an instrumental value becomes a terminal value'. Discipline, readily interpreted as conformance with regulations, whatever the situation, is seen not as a measure designed for specific purposes but becomes an immediate value in the life-organization of the bureaucrat. This emphasis, resulting from the displacement of the original goals, develops into rigidities and an inability to adjust readily. Formalism, even ritualism ensues with an unchallenged insistence upon punctilious adherence to formalized procedures.... Thus, the very elements which conduce toward efficiency in general produce inefficiency in specific instances."

It is these characteristics of bureaucracy, from insistence on conformity to rules and regulations to the ritualistic adherence to formalized procedures which caused India's programme planners and leaders seriously to question to what extent they could turn over the administration of the community development programme to the various cadres of the Indian Administrative Service. They never completely did so. A single concrete example of how they wrestled with this issue will illustrate a problem which has been with them from the inception of the programme to the present. It had been decided to introduce a block development office located in the government's administrative structure between the district and all the units of local action which it was expected would be necessary to the operation of the new programme of change. The issues debated were: (1) whether the block should be identical with, or actually be, the old sub-district unit of administration; and (2) whether the old cadre of sub-district officers or a new cadre of personnel should be placed in charge of these block offices. The first of these issues was largely resolved by a geographic-population equation; that is, the number of people to be served, and the geographic factors which conditioned the capacity of programme personnel to reach and serve that population. It was the second decision which the following example documents. A communication from the Secretary of the Planning Commission to all State Governments, dated 25 March, 1952, stated that, "For appointment to these posts (Executive Officers), therefore, it will be desirable to select the best available persons, whether from official cadres or otherwise."

This communication was followed in April by a communication to all State Governments saying, "It is intended that the Project Executive Officer will have the same status as that of a Sub-Divisional Officer (or Sub-Collector), being either a junior officer of the I.A.S. (Indian Administrative Service) or a fairly senior Deputy Collector ... Assistant Project Officers will (be) approximately in status to junior Deputy Collectors.... In case there is difficulty in securing the required number of suitable Project Executive Officers in a particular State, the Establishment Officer to the Government of India, Ministry of Home Affairs, would be prepared to assist in securing the services of suitable junior I.A.S. Officers."

The above is a citation to only one of the many types of situations which programme planners and directors have faced because they must seek the best qualified persons for each development task, but at the same time, in practically every instance, must give consideration to persons or classes of persons who have established status in the elite civil service (I.A.S.) and who, by that status, have preferred rights to employment. The problems of meeting the needs for development personnel and of respecting the rights to employment of civil servants were resolved in two ways. Persons already in the I.A.S. were assigned to new development programme positions, and other persons were qualified to fill these positions by I.A.S. examinations. In addition, thousands of persons have been recruited and trained but not granted civil service status. It is mainly in the relations between persons with and without civil service status that the behaviour of bureaucrats has influenced the day-by-day operation of the community development programme.

In pursuing an analysis of that influence, we turn again to Weber's generalizations, but use in addition the findings of more recent and more detailed studies of large formal organisations, some of them studies of bureaucracies. Weber's generalizations have been fairly well validated by considerable detailed research in recent years. Most often, the frame of reference in recent studies of bureaucracies has been a continuum from primary or human groups to secondary or secular groups. Since all types of groups have and seek to maintain their integrity by norms of behaviour, the studies have submitted these types of behaviour to analyses of their norms.

. Bureaucracies are, of course, secondary or secular, not primary groups. This means that their integrity is, and must be, guaranteed by rules and regulations. It means that their members must live by the norms essential to maintenance of rules and regulations, and this in turn means that employees must have sentiments which sustain these norms. To have sentiments means that the norms of the group have been internalized, are reflected in the attitudes of the members of the organisation. If this were not true, the organisation would not be integral. To the extent that it is not true, the integrity of the organisation is jeopardized.

These few sociological statements, we believe, explain why conformity is held in such high esteem in bureaucracies, and why rules, regulations, and procedures are instituted to induce, if possible to guarantee, conformity. In Weber's terms, anyone who questions these imperatives, wants to change them, is not a good bureaucrat. It may be questioned, however, whether or not Weber's conclusion is correct that the more fully a bureaucracy is developed, "the more completely it succeeds in eliminating from official business love, hatred, and all purely personal, irrational, and emotional elements which escape calculation." We believe the answer derived from recent sociological research is no. Chester Barnard, himself the head of a large bureaucracy, out of his broad observation and own personal experience, says, " . . . informal organizations are necessary to the operation of formal organizations as a means of communication, of cohesion, and of protecting the integrity of the individual." It is not having to conform too rigidly to rules and regulations, but treatment by fellow bureaucrats of higher rank which compromises or violates the integrity of individuals, and it is lack of inter-personal communication between persons with different ranks that sabotages cohesion in organisation behaviour.

It is not possible to present the findings in detail of the studies of large formal organisations, some of them bureaucracies, which validate the statement of Barnard quoted above. It is possible, and we believe essential, to summarize or generalize these findings, in order to justify our judgment that the Indian Administrative Service can perform its necessary role as an efficient bureaucracy and play its necessary role in the giant, fast-moving community development programme, if it will practise, if necessary require, inter-personal communication or inter-action between all programme personnel who by necessity must work together in face-to-face role positions. This art, or indeed this science (in the sense of knowing what needs to be done and how to do it), has been validated by studies of inter-personal relations in all types of groups and organisations.

The elimination, or at least dilution, of the dire influences of status and rank which are so often dysfunctional in day-by-day programme operation, requires the introduction of the practice of inter-personal relations into the assembly-line of administration. The identification and analysis of the characteristics of inter-personal relations in administration have constituted one of the great contributions of sociological studies. Kropotkin described these characteristics as practice of "mutual aid and mutual support". Cooley described them as the basic characteristics of primary groups, and said that among these characteristics were what he called primary group values—love, loyalty, etc, the very characteristics which Weber says bureaucracy disregards. Homans, in discussing "The Human Group", says:

> " ... the first and most immediate social experience of mankind is small group experience. From infancy onward we are members of families, childhood gangs, school and college cliques, clubs and teams—all small groups. When, as grownups, we get jobs, we still find ourselves working with a few persons and not with the whole firm, association, or government department. We are members of these larger social organizations, but the people we deal with regularly are always few. They mediate between us and the leviathans. The group is the commonest, as it is the most familiar, of social units...."

Homans describes one study, of a factory work group, which was begun as a study of production efficiency. The analysts manipulated every known physical factor, but had been unable to increase productivity per person or lessen turn-over in factory employment. They concluded that there was in the situation an unknown factor which they called "x". When this factor was identified and analysed in detail, it was discovered to be the tendency of previously unrelated persons to develop primary group relationships and sentiments among the individuals of a group whose jobs necessitated that they work day-by-day in face-to-face relationships. The findings of this early study, followed by many others, warrant the generalization that, whether persons are members of traditional primary groups such as the family, or of relatively temporal groups, primary group relations arise for the same reasons and have many of the same characteristics. Because of the constant inter-actions between a relatively few persons, they develop either co-operation or hostility. If necessity requires that the relationships be co-operative, they develop primary group norms and sentiments.

Necessity requires, in India's community development programme, that the relations of programme personnel be co-operative at every point in this nationwide programme where two different cadres of programme personnel meet; where village-level workers meet village leaders; where members of the block staff meet village-level workers; and where higher-ranking programme officers meet block officers. We, and others, have observed that in the great majority of cases there is an absence of this type of relationships in Indian administration. In the face of a great deal of dedication on the part of most programme personnel, we are impelled to believe that this is due to a lack of understanding, or even knowledge, of the "x" factor.

More recent studies of bureaucracies than Weber's justify the conclusion that all human relations on the assembly line of communication need not be impersonal. We interpolate the findings of only one of these studies, the specific objective of which was to analyze the inter-personal relationships of the members of two government bureaucracies. The findings of Blau's analysis were based upon daily observations, over a period of three months, of the activities of officials and are directly germane to the issue we are discussing at this point. Furthermore, he permits himself to generalize the import of his findings to wider areas than those organisations which he specifically studied. A few of his findings preface our discussion of how bureaucracies are different in two countries which have quite different historical and social milieux.

Because of his findings, Blau refused to accept the fatalistic conclusion that, "Nobody can be at the same time a correct bureaucrat and an innovator." He said that his findings suggested that ritual resulted not so much from over-identification with rules and strong habituation to established practices as it did from lack of security in important social relationships in the organisation; and further, that social insecurity breeds rigidity. He found that when and where officials were afraid of possible negative reactions from superiors, "overconformity" ensued. A careful reading of his research findings would lead one to conclude that he discovered many of the characteristics of bureaucratic behaviour which Weber generalized about, but he found many situations in which Weber's characteristics of bureaucratic behaviour did not prevail. Two of Blau's generalizations are in essence prescriptive; that is, they suggest the way out for bureaucracies which tend to develop characteristics which Weber asserted were inevitable. He said,

"Treatment of associates as unique individuals rather than as social types develops primarily among peers, and such an approach is a prerequisite for social interaction that is intrinsically gratifying and thereby produces strong social ties. To perpetuate group cohesion, the orientation in interpersonal relations should disallow quantitative differentiations of status but stress qualitative differentiation of persons. This orientation toward equals whose particular qualities merit consideration is also likely to enhance identification with the purposes of the group and its standards of behaviour at least in a culture where submission to authoritarian commands is negatively valued.

Maximum rationality in the organization, ... depends on the ability of operating officials to assume the initiative in establishing informal relations and instituting unofficial practices that eliminate operational difficulties as they occur. This ability, in turn, presupposes the absence of acute feelings of inequality among the members of the bureaucracy."

Anyone who studies the findings of this research and who has had opportunities to observe government bureaucracy in open-class democratic societies as well as Indian government bureaucracy can identify many similarities. Both are dedicated to the service of a great number of persons. Each operates in a period of rapid change. Each provides its employees with the basic prerequisites of a government bureaucracy: job security, promotion, and retirement annuities. Each has a pyramidal administrative structure, many employees in the low-salaried cadres of personnel, few in its high-salaried cadres. But there are also differences. All bureaucracies in open-class democratic societies are relatively young; Indian bureaucracy is old. New bureaucracies have had to prove their right to exist in every stage of their growth; the efficiency of a bureaucracy is an established tradition in India. High bureaucratic rank in open-class societies is no guarantee of high, general social status; in India, it is. The specifications for gaining rank in Indian bureaucracy are highly rationalized, by I.A.S. examinations, to pass which requires long periods of arduous study. In the United States, it is taken for granted that routine college or university studies, and/or accumulated practical experience, prepare many candidates for meeting civil service standards.

All of this is to say that the inadequacies of Indian bureaucracy are not due to the fact that it is a bureaucracy, but due, to a considerable extent, to the fact that it carries too much baggage from the past. It is due primarily, however, to the fact that it places relatively too much emphasis on surety, one of the imperatives of action programme administration, and relatively too little emphasis on dispatch, the other imperative of an action programme. It not only wastes many administrative man-hours on checking and double-checking sanctions for action, in order to guarantee surety, but in doing so, destroys its own capacity to move with dispatch. Its undue concern for surety leads persons in top positions to hold within their own hands decisions which need to be made quickly and at different levels of administration in a fast-moving community development programme. When top-level administrators attempt to make decisions for all levels of programme operation, they assume a responsibility for decisions which can be sound only if and when they are made by those who live and work at the various levels of day-by-day programme operation.

It is because these are our observations, and the observations of many Indian community development programme leaders, that we have pointed out some of the major findings of sociological research which prove that it is necessary and possible for a bureau-cracy to be dynamic. Those bureaucracies are dynamic which not only permit but promote change, which welcome and reward innovations at any level of programme action where either pro-gramme personnel, or the people whom they serve, have evolved better ways of doing their jobs than those prescribed in manuals of bureaucratic instruction. That the programme personnel in 5,000 development blocks and some 50,000 village level circles will, if permitted and encouraged to do so, evolve many better ways of doing their jobs than top bureaucrats can prescribe is almost certain. But to permit and encourage this requires decen-tralization of decision-making, a thing that runs counter to tradi-tion-bound bureaucracies.

Tradition is, however, a global term. To assess its functional and dysfunctional influence at any moment of time and on any specific situation is difficult unless that influence is assessed in terms of concrete forms of personal behaviour and readily identified personal attitudes or sentiments. These sentiments are related to status. In India, statuses are spelled out in systems of rank which pervade the whole society, from small groups of house servants to government bureaucracy. In day-by-day community development programme operation, feeling about, and practice of, status-ranking are inimical to fluid inter-personal communication between programme personnel who must co-operate daily in programme operation. Only by such co-operation will each person, no matter what his role, do his job with personal satisfac-tion and zest, which is the sine qua non of widespread programme dynamics.

If such inter-personal co-operation is practised between the various cadres of programme personnel, there is nothing inherent in programme organisation structure which will keep a bureau-cracy from being dynamic. Nor is it difficult to prescribe the means and methods for the development of this dynamic. It does not require such an improbability or impossibility as State Deve-lopment Commissioners or District Officers practising daily inter-personal relations with all, or even any, village-level workers. It does require that any two cadres of personnel, or any two persons, who must constantly play joint roles in day-by-day programme tasks, must have fluid, that is uninhibited inter-personal relations, and must develop common sentiments. These are essentials, represented in the model illustration presented earlier, of increasing agricultural production in a single village.

This is to say clearly what Barnard implied, that primary group practices and attitudes constitute the rationale of a dynamic bureaucracy. Nor should it be assumed that the sole accomplishment would be that each adjacently-placed role-player would come to understand and appreciate the role, and honour the person, of his closest associate in daily programme operation. Because each role-player is, on each programme task, paired with a person below him, and on another, is paired with a person above him, a chain of such linked role-relationships develops a system of programme communication and co-ordination, which cannot be guaranteed by prescribed rules and regulations or by directions issued from State or national organisation headquarters.

Because the general social structure of a society conditions the behaviour of all levels of government, as well as all other kinds of groups and organisations which function within that society, we have analyzed some of the conditioning factors which influence the operation of India's community development programme. Although it is inevitable that each of the three most basic social structures of Indian society—the village, the caste system, and the joint family—would influence any and all action programmes, we have described only the types of social structure here which are common to all societies. In this discussion, we have subsumed under "status" an analysis of rank which everywhere in India allocates not only the relative position between but within status groups; and we have included a discussion of bureaucratic status because the community development programme is, and must be, administered by State and Central government bureaucracies.

A large part of the genius of a government bureaucracy is its stability; if it is not stable, government itself is not stable. But to be stable means to be conservative in action, and the problems we have been talking about have arisen from the inevitable conflict between conservatism and change. India's community development programme is one of the most extensive and diversified programmes of change in the world. To carry out that programme, many new jobs have to be done, many new programme roles instituted and played. Even if India had not set out to build an egalitarian social order, many persons to whom some of these new roles were assigned were bound to enhance their status, and the old rights and privileges which many other persons had were bound not to be appropriate to the new roles they were asked to play. Because both of these were necessary, accommodations between new roles and old statuses were imperative. The story of day-by-day development programme experiences has therefore been the story of the successes, partial successes, or failures in making these accommodations. In the process of accommodation, neither party surrenders its identity or integrity. It is not only a process by which conflict is reduced or eliminated, but a process by which the integrity of each party is enhanced because the talents, the ideas, and the will of each party fructify the talents, enlarge the ideas, and strengthen the will of the other.

What we have observed in India at all levels of day-by-day programme operation comes much nearer to being compromise than accommodation. Each programme person with a higher status tends to dominate each person with a lower status, and each person with a higher rank tends to dominate all persons with a lower rank. This phenomenon of unhealthy inter-personal relationships sabotages the zests of persons with lower status and rank, because it automatically downgrades the vital roles of lower-ranking persons, and thus sabotages the dynamics of day-by-day programme operation. The significance of this inevitable fact cannot be too explicitly stated. Differences in status, of course, prevail in all societies. Rank, even among equals, arises naturally in all groups, large and small. Differences in administrative status provide the essential structure in any large formal organisation. But the efficient operation of any type of organisation, even an army, is not enhanced by attaching feelings of personal superiority to either status or rank. To permit such feelings to exhibit themselves in necessary inter-actions among action programme personnel not only inhibits the upward and downward flow of communication which is essential to programme co-ordination, but thwarts the mutual or reciprocal support which each cadre of programme personnel can supply to every other cadre.

To tens of thousands of persons with low organisation rank and status, each playing a vital programme role, the personal satisfaction each has in doing his job is the basic incentive for doing that job well. If the person next above him in programme status does not understand how vital his role is, downgrades his role, and downgrades him as a person, whether conscious of it or not, this lessens the incentive of the largest cadre of development personnel and reduces programme dynamics at the grass roots. The same is, of course, true in every link of programme operation where the members of two cadres of personnel must work face-to-face in day-by-day programme operation. We have, however, placed special emphasis on the basic role of the village-level worker because it is believed the dynamics of the community development-extension programme will, in due time, induce dynamics in government bureaucracy and will help to develop dynamics from the bottom up.

MAIN AUTHORITIES QUOTED OR CITED

Appleby, Paul H., *Public Administration in India*, Manager of Publications, Government of India, New Delhi, 1955; and *Public Administration for a Welfare State*, Asia Publishing House, Bombay, 1962.

Barnard, Chester I., *The Functions of the Executive*, Harvard University Press, Cambridge, Mass., 1956.

Blau, Peter M., *The Dynamics of Bureaucracy*, University of Chicago Press, Chicago, Illinois, 1955.

Cooley, Charles Horton, *Human Nature and the Social Order*, Charles Scribner's Sons, New York, 1902; also with *Social Organization* (2 vols. in one), The Free Press, Glencoe, Illinois, 1956.

Gerth, H. H. and Mills, C. Wright, *From Max Weber: Essays in Sociology*, Routledge and Kegan Paul, Ltd., London, 1961. (Chapter VIII).

Homans, George C., *The Human Group*, Harcourt, Brace and Co., New York, 1950.

Important Letters Issued by Community Projects Administration, (Period April, 1952 to October, 1953), Community Projects Administration, Government of India, March, 1955. (C.P.A. Series 35).

Kropotkin, Peter, *Mutual Aid*, Porter Sargent Publisher, 11 Beacon St., Boston 8, Mass., 1955.

Roethlisberger, F. J. and Dickson, W. J., *Management and the Worker*, Harvard University Presss, Cambridge, 1950.

CHAPTER 24

A COMMUNITY DEVELOPMENT-EXTENSION PROGRAMME AS A VEHICLE FOR INITIATING CHANGE

WHAT has come to be called "extension", most often "agricultural extension", is a method, or a series of methods, by which the technical know-how of science is carried to and inculcated into the practices of cultivators. Although not called "extension", the technical know-how of health, sanitation, nutrition, and even welfare have also employed extension methods and increased the knowledge of the contributions of science to the masses. What have come to be called "community development" methods have also evolved out of attempts to extend the contributions of science to the masses, and to combine with these contributions what organised local groups can contribute to the improvement of their own life and living.

There has accumulated a vast and diverse body of experience in the development, or evolution, of these two bodies of methods. These experiences have varied all the way from those of agents of change attempting to catalyze change in isolated local areas, but having no systematically-established and effectively-operating channels of contact with the sources of technical know-how, to agencies and institutions of science and technical know-how which establish systematic channels from themselves into local areas but fail to utilize already-organised self-help local groups. Because India in her community development-extension programme consciously and logically planned to combine community development-extension methods into one programme, and because in the following chapter we shall attempt critically to assess her experiences of more than a decade of operating that programme, we shall attempt here to develop criteria by means of which to make that assessment.

We assume that our chief contribution will be an analysis of the community development components of a combined community development-extension programme. We are convinced that there has been enough programme experience in a sufficient number of countries that, based on this experience, a model for a community development programme can be constructed. We believe it is only by the use of such an empirically formulated model that we can practically, and justifiably, assess critically India's experience.

The common denominators of successfully-operating community development programmes will be used as components of a model community development programme. A model is an ideal construct, formulated out of a combination of validated facts. No one of the programmes out of which our community development model is constructed has exemplified the ideal construct as a whole. Each of the programmes' experiences has, however, validated one or more components of that model. Each was selected for citation and some exposition because it has provided such validation. The rationale for the employment of a model thus constructed as a tool for programme analysis is the same as the rationale for programme planning. Both do and must reckon with proven possibilities.

It would be impossible to specify the exact time or place where what have come to be called "community development methods" were first used. It is clear, however, that these methods evolved out of the experiences of agencies which were attempting to carry into isolated areas a knowledge of improved practices in agriculture, health and sanitation, and education. Persons from national centres of so-called higher culture and from technically more advanced countries, attempting to reach isolated rural groups, were thus the first agents of extension. In citing some of the known facts about the evolution of the term "community development", we in no sense are attempting to allocate credit for the origin of this now much-used term, but instead to show why what had been learned from practical field experiences was formulated in prescriptions for future programme guidance.

The British Colonial Office undoubtedly was one of the first to make something approaching a definitive analysis of its own elaborate experiences in this field. A conference held in Cambridge in August, 1948, while it dealt only with the African colonies and chiefly with its experience with development programmes in African territories, had at its command a record of much greater and longer experience than that upon which this conference was focused. It is because of this larger experience that we mention its proposal to change the term "Mass Education" to "Community Development". This term was intended to represent community-wide activities of many kinds, including agriculture, health, education, etc. It was also at this 1948 conference that it was decided to establish the Community Development Clearing House in the University of London.

This may have been the first time that the term "community development" was specifically used to represent the types of action which are now pretty generally recognized as essential to community development processes. There are, however, what may be called elements in, or components of, this process which were earlier identified by others. Harold B. Allen records that one of his Near East Foundation colleagues, in 1933, said that "he intended to confine his efforts to helping the peasant help himself." He also records significant examples of groups of local people who, by joining hands to accomplish one task, developed the social know-how and the group zest essential to undertaking other tasks. Numerous quotations might be taken from this remarkable document entitled *Come Over Into Macedonia* and its sequel, *Rural Reconstruction in Action,* which continues the detailed story of the experiences of the Near East Foundation over a period of almost thirty years. It is from documents of this type, of which there are very few, and the Wisers' book *Behind Mud Walls,* that one is able to analyze community development processes and programmes from their initiation and for a considerable period of time. Analyses can also be made from the published documents of other community development programmes which have been in operation for a long time, such as the work of the Jamaican Welfare Commission, the Mass Education programme in Ghana, and the Community Education programme in Puerto Rico.

Statements made by those who have worked in programmes or projects out of which the community development processes have evolved indicate that there has been a long, vast, and varied body of experiences upon which to draw in attempting to assess the comparative experiences of community development programmes. We shall add the knowledge gained from personal observations of a number of these programmes to the observations and analyses of others who have watched some of the same and other programmes in action.

In order to identify types or patterns of human behaviour, or of social organisation, the common denominators of seemingly diverse types of action must always be sought, and minor differences or variations must always be disregarded. The diversities are quite marked among what would now be called community development projects or programmes, described by various persons, each with his own frame of reference for observation and analysis. It is, however, the task of a social analyst, utilizing such data as are available, to identify and formulate the common denominators in these diversities. We recognize that, in order analytically to summarize the multiplied and diverse known experiences of so-called community development undertakings, we must describe them in terms of patterns which in fact have not been as discrete as our descriptions will indicate. Our characterizations will not, however, be invalid as historical accounts of the various stages in the evolution of community development methods and programmes.

In the practice of community development methods, programmes have been called "mass education", "social education", "community education", "rural welfare", "local community organisation", "rural welfare centres", "village services", "village uplift", etc. Some of these so-called community development programmes have been in operation for more than thirty years, a number of them from ten to twenty years. An analysis of their experiences provides the only empirical information available for an objective discussion of how and why community development has come to be one of the major components of rural development programmes of a number of developing countries; what the role of community development programmes has been in total development; the inter-relationships of the role of community development with the other necessary roles or components of a rural development programme; and the type of rural development programme administration or administrative organisation which will best guarantee that the various elements in, or components of, an over-all development programme will each fructify the other.

Community development as a body of activities and methods

grew out of the experiences of rural development programmes in underdeveloped countries, where conditions prevailed which do not exist in developed countries. Chief among these conditions is the isolation of millions of village people and the consequent great social distance between the illiterate masses and the intelligentsia. Illiteracy among the rural masses, of course, contributes to their isolation. The elite status of the intelligentsia is also an obstacle to their communication with, or even their understanding of, the masses. Probably the greatest contribution community development-type programmes have made to a solution of the problems of development is their discovery of how to cross or breach these boundaries of local isolation and establish communication between areas of so-called progress and areas of so-called stagnation. They have done this by appointing carefully selected persons who are not too different from traditionally isolated rural people and posting them in local communities, that is within the boundary of local isolation.

These locally-posted persons have been agents of change in local communities, and have acted as liaison between these communities and those who live outside, some of them far outside, the boundaries of local, isolated communities. These local agents of change have learned how to catalyze change in the traditional practices and attitudes of isolated individuals, families, groups, and whole local communities. They have learned that this can best be done by helping local groups to test the validity of new practices of various kinds of programmes. The success of such groups has been great enough, under sufficiently diverse conditions, to have led their sponsors to aver that to catalyze and effectively organise local self-help groups is the sole contribution that so-called community development methods have made to rural development programmes in newly-developing countries.

There is, however, repeated—we might say universal—evidence from the experience of these programmes that isolated, poverty-stricken villagers cannot lift themselves solely by their own bootstraps. They must have technical assistance and, at times, material assistance. Some vital lessons have been learned from what various countries have done when they came to recognize this imperative. Few newly-developing countries are now operating programmes of technical and material assistance to only self-help local groups; nor are they rendering this assistance in such a way as to exemplify a model for a community development programme which would require the providing of enough aid, and the right kind, to always fructify but never sabotage the dynamics of local self-help accomplishment.

To establish empirically the validity of the components of a model for a community development programme, we present observations on only those programmes which have been planned and directed, and by means of which outside groups or organisations have attempted to reach and influence persons or groups who live in simple societies or in isolated sectors of sophisticated societies. To thus confine our analyses to planned programmes has greatly reduced the amount of programme experience out of which our model is constructed. To do so, however, sharply reduces the confusion about what community development is, confusion which has arisen because it has been so often used as a slogan to promote programmes which in fact do not employ community development methods. The number of examples is further reduced if only those programmes which have been analyzed with some relatively high degree of objectivity are used.

These limitations, however, have a number of advantages. In the last dozen years, during which the term "community development" has been employed, the sponsors of a great many programmes have called them community development programmes, although a fair number of them have been primarily agriculture, health, or education programmes which have employed community development methods. A number of so-called community development programmes, about which a great deal has been written, are as yet only planned, not in operation. The leaders and directors of many, if not most, of the programmes which are in operation are far from objective in their reports about results, or even in their reports about methods. For these reasons, we shall utilize only information about programmes which have had a sufficiently long experience to yield observable results and of which objective analyses have been made.

We have already mentioned the comments of Dr. Harold Allen of the Near East Foundation and the action taken by the British Colonial Office in the summer of 1948. Subsequent to this, the British Colonial Office published a report on the Ashridge Conference on Social Development in August of 1954. It was this Conference which adopted a definition of community development and formulated a model for a governmental community development organisation which was widely used in many British overseas territories. Three years later (September, 1957), a study conference prepared a manual entitled "Community Development: A Handbook", which was used extensively overseas. This guide placed emphasis on the idea of developing the initiative of local communities to see and to solve their own problems, as far as possible with their local community resources, but calling on expert advice and assistance from the outside if necessary.

This seminar group which reviewed the practical programme experience of many British colonies can be said to have put the word "community" solidly into the term "community development" by saying that the sine qua non of community development is that "the local community appreciates its social obligations and responsibilities for measures to better the conditions of the community as a whole."

The British Colonial Office, and over recent years the Community Development Clearing House, University of London Institute of Education, have for more than a decade persistently studied community development projects. T. R. Batten, a British social scientist, who has probably as consistently studied such programmes and projects in action as any person in the world, drives a point with which practical analysts would agree when he says:

> " Agencies and workers who themselves decide the specific form development should take, assume, of course, that they know better than the people what the people want. ... Most governments want quick results, and this means specific targets within a given time.... Directive methods are in the government administrative tradition and are temporarily straightforward and easy to apply."

He states as one of the basic "principles of agency work" that "agencies must reach agreement with the people on what the changes should be."

One of the United States missions which studied a great

variety of programmes in five different countries, and visited projects or programmes where government had heavily subsidized, and in one country paid the whole cost of, community halls or community centre buildings, contrasts two cases in the same country in the following way:

> "Of these two community centres one has an ample community building for which the government contributed $4,500. It is located in an area where, according to the community council, the people to be served 'have no community feeling,' and where community consciousness was not developed in the process of constructing the building. A formal council composed of representatives from five different organisations manages the program, but the allegation is 'that there are no leaders,' and that their chief worry is how to get the organisations and the people to use the community hall. In the other community, the local, self-organised groups joined hands to construct a small building in which they and the whole neighborhood-community can and do meet. The government contributed $500, but has helped the local group by means of community advice and assistance."

There was no question in the judgment of the members of the mission that community development had taken place in the second case, but that it had not in the first case. This mission stated, however, that it "saw no outstanding examples of community development which were not stimulated and assisted by some outside agency or institution." It said, "This stimulation and assistance most often has come from some government agency"; and that it was most effective when a community was helped by a specialist in community education or community organisation, whether or not with material assistance.

We think this mission fairly well summarized what has been learned from programme experiences about how isolated groups can be effectively reached and aided to make continuous progress toward both organised self-help accomplishments and effective utilization of the technical and material assistance which their governments attempt to provide to them. It said:

> "The mission is convinced that the following principles and practices are valid and effective in all cases of community

education and development: (1) Maximum self-help effort must be developed in all cases, and, for this development, specialists in community organisation are required; (2) if such an agent or person must work alone, he must be first of all a group organiser or specialist, and secondly, must be thoroughly aware of where he and the community can go to obtain the various types of special technical assistance required; (3) the person or persons working with a community must reside and work in that community for a substantial period of time; (4) locally-recruited technical assistants must be trained to assume some of the functions exercised by technical agents; and (5) regardless of the adequacy that welfare centers and their services may achieve, they should never be left without at least one paid community specialist readily available to assist these centers in their self-help efforts and to act as a bridge between them and the specialized services which the communities will be progressively more ready to use."

We have thus far identified only the need for initiating change within the boundaries of local isolation and the need for effective channels of communication between local agents of change and agencies upon which they, and the local people whom they seek to assist, must depend for technical, and often material, assistance. But a great deal has also been learned from community development programmes about the recruitment and training of local agents of change and assistance, about the roles they must play, and the ways in which they can be implemented, or thwarted, in accomplishing the things they need to do. A great deal has been learned about the effective establishment and operation of the channels of communication between local communities and local agents of change and the agencies which render technical and material assistance.

The selection and training of local agents of change need to accord with the roles which they are presumed to play. The chief role is that of catalyzing self-help effort, and organisation, among the people who live within the boundaries of local isolation. Not all the agents of change who have attempted to induce local communities to organise their efforts have used methods which are consonant with good community or group organisation. It can be said, however, that organised local self-help has been something approaching a universal method employed in all community development programmes, no matter by what title or designation the programme is described.

The second role of these local agents of change is to act as liaison between organised local self-help groups and those agencies, institutions, or organisations located outside the local community which can render them technical, and in some cases material, assistance. There have been elaborate and diversified experiences in the kinds of assistance rendered to self-help local groups, and the methods by which such assistance has been provided. In a number of cases, outside agencies have provided so much material assistance that they have dulled the customary self-reliance of village people. The maps of underdeveloped countries are pockmarked with decaying structures which governments have provided to local communities, but of which rural people have made no constructive use.

Some countries which have assumed that local self-help groups needed only technical assistance have attempted to borrow or adopt the pattern of the extension programmes of advanced countries. Egypt and a number of other countries have established pilot projects in isolated rural areas and staffed these projects with trained technical personnel from one or more government technical departments. Each such pilot project in Egypt was equipped with seed and animal breeding units, the purpose of which was to demonstrate good farming methods. In this and similar pilot projects the technical personnel have spent their time and effort on these breeding units, but generally were unable to reach the mass of cultivators. What was done at these stations did not spread outward from the demonstration centres, with the result that very little was accomplished by way of increased agricultural production even in the adjacent areas, much less among the mass of cultivators.

Other countries which have recognized the vital need for technical assistance have spent much time and money in attempting to recruit and train a large enough corps of technically-trained personnel to blanket rural areas with direct technical assistance to the masses of rural people. All of them have quickly discovered that they could not recruit enough educated persons for such training; or if they could, that these educated persons, because they were not born and reared in rural families, or even in rural communities, were not successful in their attempts to influence rural people. In such cases, the functions of would-be agents of change have usually degenerated into the task of distributing free seed, fertilizer, insecticides, etc. To the extent that this has been true, they have contributed considerable material assistance but very little technical assistance to rural people.

Other newly-developing countries have attempted to develop *in toto* the agricultural extension system of the United States or European countries. They have had to recruit largely city-born and reared persons as candidates to be trained as agricultural agents. They have not only subsidized the training of these recruits, but guaranteed the candidates jobs when they had completed their training. Iran, for instance, had little difficulty in recruiting candidates for such training, but for two reasons had great difficulties in channelling these trainees into rural areas. There had been no preparation of local communities to want, and thus request, or even welcome the services of technically trained persons, and the trainees being urban-born and reared did not want to work—especially did not want to live—in rural areas.

These are examples, however, of only minor difficulties in the establishment of extension systems which have been developed in so-called advanced countries. The chief difficulties have been due to the great difference between the countries where such systems have been developed and where they work excellently, and developing countries which have sought to adapt them to their own economic and social situations. The most important difference has been, and is, that in the United States and northern European countries, where modern agricultural extension systems have evolved, not only are all farmers literate, but a high percentage of them know of and accept the fact that agricultural scientific knowledge is superior to most traditional farming know-how. In the majority of cases, all the agricultural extension agent needs to do in these advanced countries is, so to speak, to walk through the gates which are open to him by the cultivators' knowledge of these facts. In many cases the agent needs do no more, and is asked to do no more, than assist the cultivator to secure some agricultural experiment station bulletin and the cultivator will study and apply the practice or practices which the bulletin recommends. In most, if not all, underdeveloped countries the average cultivator has moved so slightly up the scale of technical know-how, to meet the proffered assistance of the agricultural extension agent, that the agent's first task is merely to make cultivators aware that there are agricultural practices superior to those they are now employing.

The second great difference is the far greater cultural distance which exists between the technically trained persons in underdeveloped countries and those who live in rural communities. In the United States and western Europe, practically all technically trained agriculturalists were born and reared on farms and thus understand and appreciate the traditional know-how of farming. They can and do meet the farmer on his own familiar ground. This is seldom the case with academically trained agricultural specialists in underdeveloped countries.

A third substantial difference between underdeveloped countries and developed societies is that in so-called developed societies many types of technical assistance are rendered to persons living in local communities through an ample set of service institutions; not only schools, but hospitals and clinics and service agencies provide institutional assistance. In most developing countries, all these agencies must be provided by a government extension programme.

There would be no reason to expect even adequately trained agricultural agents to possess the technical know-how to render assistance in all of these fields. There is less reason to expect, even if the funds were available, that an adequate corps of extension agents in all types of needed technical assistance could be mobilized in any underdeveloped country. It is primarily for this reason, above all others, that multi-purpose local community development workers must attempt to provide extension services, and is why India in her First Five Year Plan says that, while extension will be the agency, community development will be the method by which the agencies of technical and material assistance will attempt to reach and serve people living in isolated areas.

The countries from whose experiences we construct our model for community development extension programmes may not have rationalized their problems as did India, and so far as we

know did not, but they have provided a great volume of experience from which India can draw a good deal of information to
assist her in operating her rationalized community development-
extension programme.

We, in essence, named the basic elements in, or components
of, a model community development programme when we earlier
identified what we called the "common denominators" in the
experiences of a number of successfully-operated programmes.
They are as follows: The first essential component is location of
personal agents of change within the boundaries of isolated communities. The second is having effectively organised self-help
groups within local communities. The third is technical and material aid to such groups. And the fourth is the operation of organised and systematic channels of communication and administration between agencies of technical and material assistance and
organised, self-help, local community groups.

No one of the countries, which has operated a community
development or extension programme over a sufficiently long
period of time to have demonstrated the essential role of one or
more of these elements, has demonstrated or validated all of them.
An analysis of the best that has been learned about each of the
four basic components, even if it is exemplified by only one programme, is presented here. It is thus that model constructs are
formulated as both instruments of description and tools of analysis.
They are ideal blueprints constructed from the best that is known
about each of the elements or components out of which the blueprint or model is constructed.

As an example of the first essential element of local community workers within the boundaries of local isolation we might
—and to some extent will—use the experiences of Mexico, Jamaica,
Puerto Rico, Ghana, the Philippines, and Egypt. We use primarily
the experiences of Puerto Rico because we have more thoroughly
followed the developments of that programme, and because its
directors have favoured us with detailed descriptions of the selection and training of its local workers. We quote at some length
from the directors of that programme on what was sought for
in the person of a "group organiser", the title carried by their
local field worker. Queries to which interviewers of candidates
for employment sought answers, by long and repeated visits with

each applicant who was seriously considered for appointment and by long interviews with those who were intimately acquainted with the applicant, were as follows:

"Was he a man of the people," tested by "how he felt about himself and his fellow man?" "Could he work in his own community?" "What concerns had he shown for the problems of his community?" "What were his attitudes toward authoritarianism?" "Was he a secure person?" "Did he have a set of moral values which he used on all situations and all people indiscriminately?" "What was his attitude toward the opinions of others?" "Was he a static personality or did he possess the capacity for growth?"

Mr. and Mrs. Wale (the directors of the programme) say that,

"In the light of these qualifications, such matters as whether the candidate was a man or a woman, the level of his formal education, whether he had a profession or a trade, his age, whether he was married or single, were of secondary importance. . . . " Candidates were "visited by a committee of three staff members. The interview was conducted in the candidate's home area, in a place he was most at ease; on a hillside near his home, under a tree on the grounds of his school, or beside a river in the barrio he had known since childhood. The interview was held without pressure of time. As often as possible he was observed in relationship to his family and his neighbors. In this way, the forty group organisers now in the field were interviewed three or more times before coming into training." The directors of the programme describe the sources from which persons were selected in the following words:
" . . . Of the forty, one was a country peddler, one a fisherman, one the manager of a large co-operative store, one a clerk at the Army Air Base, and one temporarily unemployed though he had recently left the management of an experimental farm. Two had been clergymen and two policemen. Seven were teachers; seven others were small farmers. Seven were former municipal employees in such jobs as auditor, school director-treasurer, hospital administrator. Ten others were employed in the commonwealth government in such agencies as the Department of Public Works, the Land Authority, as a cooperative instructor in the Social Programs Admi-

nistration, as an inspector for the Department of Health. A small number had ended their formal education at the eighth grade, a larger number below the twelfth grade, and a small group had spent some time at the University. One of the forty had a college degree. The youngest was twenty-eight, the oldest fifty-three. The average age was thirty-eight. All forty were born and brought up in the country and with a few exceptions all lived in the country when selected. All came from the area they now serve with connections since boyhood in most of their barrios. All were men, for the few women who applied soon withdrew when they learned the full demands of the position."[1]

Some of those selected for three months of training were screened out during, or at the end of, the training period. Thus the more mature judgment about the personal fitness of trainees, and the trainees' performance during the training period, are part of the selection process. The training is almost wholly in group methods and processes because this is the only field in which the field worker must have special aptitudes and skills. During the training period, he is informed by other agencies of the government, and by leaders of voluntary associations, of the services they are prepared to render to self-organised local groups who request their services. The purpose of this portion of a candidate's training is not to make him competent in any field of technical assistance, because his job is not that of an extension agent but of a group organiser. Once he is in the field, he does not even act as a go-between for organised local groups and extension agencies. All he does is to help groups to organise for self-help undertakings and to make them aware that they can, as citizens, request assistance from established agencies. The group organiser insists that the groups themselves make the necessary contacts and, as citizens, present their requests.

The type of training provided, the methods of training, and who gives the instruction, reflect the concept of programme planners and directors of the roles which local community workers are expected to play. In Jamaica, Ghana, Puerto Rico, and the

---

[1] See Carmen Isales and Fred J. Wale, "The Field Program of the Puerto Rican Division of Community Education" in *Underdeveloped Areas* by Lyle W. Shannon, Harper and Bros., New York, 1957, pp. 350-60.

Philippines, training is primarily to prepare trainees for the role of helping local communities to organise for self-help undertakings. In Jamaica and Puerto Rico, there is something approaching an ample set of government extension agencies in such technical fields as agriculture, health, and public works. In Ghana, these technical services are not so readily available. But as in Puerto Rico, in Jamaica and Ghana community development government field workers are not trained in technical extension skills.

In the Jamaica programme, which has been operating for more than twenty years, all presently-salaried workers have been selected from among those who have, as residents of local communities, been voluntary workers in organised self-help projects. Therefore, no small part of their training has been the practical experience they have had in serving their own local communities purely as volunteers. As such, they have received considerable training provided by the Jamaica Welfare Commission in group methods, leadership, etc. Even after they are accepted as applicants for paid employment, they are required to serve for six months, carrying the full responsibilities of their assigned jobs, before they are finally accepted and placed on the pay-roll. The Jamaica Welfare Commission can thus assert that there is no one in its official family who has come to his or her present job except through a very elaborate school of practical experience.

In Ghana, it has not been possible to recruit all needed local workers from among rural people, but included in the training programme is field work in rural areas. No field worker is assigned full responsibility for a local area until he has gone through a series of stages of in-service experience. Thus he becomes qualified as a full-fledged "mass education officer" only by passing through a fairly long period of actual field experience, in the early stages accompanied by a more mature field worker, and later, on his own responsibility.

We have chosen our illustrations of criteria from programmes which have selected and trained persons as group organisers, as entrepreneurs of community development methods, so to speak, not as agents of technical assistance. They illustrate the personal characteristics believed to be crucial and the kinds of training experience that will induce or maximize these characteristics. No matter how trite it may sound, the conviction is that the needed characteristics must be a concern for, and sympathy with, persons whose lot in life is hard and whose mental and even emotional horizons are narrow. One who has no sympathy with such persons, who cannot, so to speak, imagine himself in their situations, probably cannot easily be trained in these attitudes. He can be taught "how to make friends and influence people," but he will not thereby develop everlasting and undeviating faith in the capacities of local, seemingly ignorant people for development. Without these personality characteristics, he will not be deeply dedicated to the tasks he has been assigned and will not have real joy in doing them. It is because of these socio-psychological facts that the programmes we have used as illustrations have, in so far as possible, recruited local workers from among the types of people with whom they would work; and, when this was not possible, have required successful demonstration of the required personality characteristics, through in-service training, before they were assigned the roles of full-fledged local area workers.

In the programmes of these countries, the heart of the training has been in group methods, because it has been assumed that the most basic role of local workers is to help their communities become aware of their capacities, if effectively organised, to improve many of the conditions of their own lives. This is to say that effectively organised self-help is the chief conditioning factor of the success of local community workers. It is also a strong conditioning factor of the capacities of local communities to utilize whatever technical and material assistance is, or may become, available from government agencies. It is because of this that organised local self-help is the second element in our component of a model community development programme. Needless to say, if local community workers, and those who trained them, do not know the type of improvement undertakings for which local people will mobilize, or can be most readily mobilized, they are not in a position to easily catalyze them to organised self-effort. We believe that information from the experiences of the most successful community development programmes is not only available and convincing, but that an understanding of the importance of this imperative should also be clear. Local communities can quite readily be mobilized and organised to work on local community projects. They cannot be easily mobilized to work on State-wide or nationwide projects because in economically underdeveloped countries they are physically and culturally isolated from the stream of State and national events; their chief concerns are about local needs and local affairs. It is relatively easy to enlist their interest in local improvements, but it is difficult to do so in national development programmes.

The validity of these statements has been so well attested by experience in a great enough number of underdeveloped countries, where sound practical methods of community development are being used, that it is possible to specify the steps in the methods of successful local-self-help group development. This is not, of course, to say that these steps can be blueprinted and precisely followed like the steps in building a house, or that the members of local communities can, like an army platoon, be commanded to take them. They are, however, steps which any group of people, if permitted and assisted, will take to meet needs which are common to all or a large portion of them. We present the sequence of steps which constitutes the process by which persons living in local communities move from apathy about even their obvious common needs to an awareness of them, an awareness of their capacities to meet at least some of these needs, and ultimately, to aspirations to solve, or help solve, all of their local problems.

The first step in local group or community development is systematic discussion of commonly-felt needs by members of the community. Unsystematic discussions of various kinds are continuously going on among people who literally live, as they do in rural villages, all the time in each other's presence. They may, however, be concerned with mere gossip or with complaints. It is only when discussions about common problems are systematic, even though among a relatively few representative persons or families, that important commonly-felt needs are revealed. Such discussion is readily induced when local villagers have cause to believe that any organised self-help efforts on their part will be encouraged and assisted by their government or some other dependable agency. This simple, but necessary, first step is not taken when community councils or other village bodies are created by law or overhead administrative directives. It is not taken when some technical agency or welfare organisation decides to initiate some improvement just because it has the consent, or even the invitation, of some one self-appointed, would-be, local leader. It is not taken by finding one willing innovator who will try out one improved practice. Sound community development programmes, now in operation in a number of underdeveloped countries, insist that the first role played by the local worker be to stimulate systematic discussions among villagers of what their most common needs are and what they can, or might by organised effort, do to meet these needs.

The second step is systematic planning by local people to carry out the first self-help undertaking which has been selected by the method of sustained and systematic discussion. The most important thing learned by the community in taking this step is that nothing by way of community development occurs if a project is nominated which is totally beyond the local community's own self-help capacity to carry out. The community may think its greatest need is canal water for irrigation, which can be provided only by constructing a great dam a hundred miles from the village. This it cannot do or even help to do. Or it may think that its greatest need is for more commercial fertilizers which would require the construction of a factory and the development of a market distribution system. The first of these is an undertaking for national or State governments, and the other an undertaking for government or some business entrepreneur. Systematic planning for a self-help community undertaking leads to the selection of the type of first project which, because it is practical and feasible, will mobilize the local manpower and ingenuity of those living in the community. It leads to the actual task of enlisting persons who will contribute their labour and talents, and often materials and money, to carry out the project. It accomplishes realistic and responsible thinking about what should be done and what can be done. It is a step that starts to mobilize the community to do something for itself.

The third step in community development is the mobilization and harnessing of the physical, economic, and social potentialities of local community groups to accomplish the first task which local people have assigned to themselves. Once a fair-sized, organised local group starts working on a project which, if completed, will yield obvious and early benefits to the whole community, members of the community who have thus far been only mildly interested, or even sceptical, start contributing to its successful completion. One of the authors listened to a national leader's dedication speech of a recently-completed self-help local community improvement project, in which the speaker quite aptly described this step in the community development process when he spoke approximately as follows: "Three years ago some of your most progressive people decided you needed a new road. Not all of you helped to build that road, but many of you did. There is the road and everybody uses it." He followed this with a description of three additional projects, completed one per year, and then concluded about as follows: "Only a relative few helped with the first project, more helped with the second, more with the third, and even more with this project, the completion of which we dedicate today. It may be that some of you have not helped with any of these projects and won't help with the next one. But because an increasing number has helped with each new project, you are building a new community."

The fourth step is the development of group aspirations. Until this step is taken, the universal problem of how to get local villages to desire and to initiate one improvement project after another is not solved. Many community organisations promoted by outsiders never take this step. But there are both good physical and good sociological reasons why the majority of community groups, which have come into existence and progressed by taking the three previous steps described here, do take this fourth step. The physical reason is that there are other improvements which need to be undertaken that are within the now-increased competence of the group. The sociological reason is that every human group that has successfully accomplished worthwhile undertakings is proud of itself, and tends to seek out and do other things to justify and feed its group pride. It has developed team spirit, esprit de corps, patriotism, or, in simpler terms, group sentiments.

All kinds of experiences have been and are being gained in attempts to mobilize local communities for effectively organised self-help. There are cases in which the third step has been attempted without the second step having been accomplished. There are examples of local communities which have mobilized, or been mobilized, to undertake some community improvement and have done so in a spectacular fashion, by furious and seemingly successful campaigns. But after the improvement project was successfully completed, it was found that no local community group had been developed in the process. There are examples even of the third step seeming to have been taken when neither the first nor the second step had preceded it. The physical and economic resources had been mobilized and utilized, and practically every family in the community pressured, in some way to make its maximum contribution, but the fourth step did not follow. When the undertaking in hand was completed, there was no carry-over into other improvement undertakings. Instead of being inspired to help with additional projects, many persons who had helped on the one just completed, lapsed into lethargy, exhausted by the super-stimulated effort which it had taken to accomplish the first project. No ample, self-stimulating, self-directive group had been built by the methods employed in completing the improvement project. The fourth step in the community development process was, therefore, never taken.

The group development process, like any other process, is a sequence of steps or stages, each preceding step providing the springboard or impulse for the next step or stage. Each succeeding stage grows out of the ways by which each of the preceding steps was taken or previous stages accomplished. There are many examples of outside agencies, governments or others, whose leaders, having witnessed one or more local communities mobilize to accomplish some improvement project, have jumped to the conclusion that a whirlwind, nationwide propaganda campaign, or some other mass stimulation in mobilization technique, can be used to start a rash of community development activities. Such experiences teach almost as much as do sound community development methods, because they teach that there is no substitute for the first and second steps or stages in the community development process. Even more important, they teach the lesson that the most important and final step in developing self-generating, aspiring local groups grows primarily out of the group's own creative experiences, not from outside direction nor even from outside technical and/or material assistance.

Community development programmes have had a variety of experiences, and have experimented in different ways in an attempt to supply needed assistance to self-help local groups, the third component of our model. A few of those experiences have been very carefully studied for their effectiveness. There have been a large number of cases in which assistance agencies have assumed that the chief, if not the universal, need of local self-help groups was material assistance. This idea has probably derived from two sources. First is the very widely held belief of persons with relatively high material levels of living that persons who have low material levels of living yearn for amenities. The second reason is that it is much easier for isolated, illiterate persons to accept material assistance than to accept technical assistance. They can and do accept many types of material assistance for the simple reason that they thereby can enjoy a higher material level of living than they by themselves can afford, and because their acceptance of amenities does not require much if any change in their deeply-rooted practices; the acceptance of most types of technical assistance does.

There is a great deal of information on what may be called successful and unsuccessful methods of granting material assistance to local groups or communities. The criterion of unsuccessful methods is whether or not a higher material level of living, which persons or groups obtain by means other than by their own efforts, breeds confusion in their ways of doing and thinking. If it does, it can be taken for granted that it is inimical to the growth of their faith and confidence in their own capacities for self-help. The criterion for success in providing material assistance is whether or not a local group or community will undertake some self-selected improvement project for the completion of which it does not have some essential material resource; therefore, it cannot and will not mobilize either the human or material resources which it does possess. The project may be only a cement culvert without which the construction of a needed road would prove to be unfeasible; the project therefore would not be undertaken, or if it were undertaken it would fail.

There are all kinds of illustrations of both effective and ineffective material assistance. By and large, programmes in which an aid agency, generally government, assures any local community that it will provide all or most of the outside material assistance needed to accomplish types of projects which the aid agencies specify, have not served to develop either the faith or competence of local self-help groups. There are, on the other hand, quite a number of examples in which local communities have constructed school buildings, and even built health centres, on the promise of their government to provide teachers and health personnel to staff these local institutions. Some of the buildings provided by local financial support and labour have been pretty crude, but they are tokens of aroused and dedicated organised local interest and self-help. We quote the director of health in Jamica who said he welcomed the requests for nurses and physicians by groups who had even crude physical accommodation for them, and added, "A thousand such requests would do more than all other things combined to build an adequate insular department of health."

In the early days of the Egyptian rural centres, the promoters and directors of that programme discouraged, and in some cases refused, the gifts of land on which to construct community centre buildings, if these gifts came from single donors. They insisted that the local community, by organised effort, provide the funds to purchase such land, and then the government would assist in providing the necessary materials for the buildings. A different example is in Iraq, where large landlords provided not only the land but the building materials for schools and health centres, and the government paid wages to any and all members of the local community who helped to construct the buildings. A number of schools and health centres were built and staffed by government personnel. But nothing was accomplished by way of developing self-help local groups, much less in the development of the faith of local people in their competence for self-help undertakings, or the feeling that they could, and should, be volunteer partners in improving their own conditions.

Concerning the fourth component of the model for a community development-extension programme, viz. the establishment and operation of a responsible and responsive system of communication between national technical and material assistance agencies and local self-help groups, it must be said that there are no integrated community development-extension programmes which can provide India with a neat pattern to follow.

Because the technical know-how of science is a free good,

it can be borrowed from the ends of the world and applied wherever it is needed. The potentials of rural people must be developed where they are. Because local communities and other local groups in most so-called underdeveloped countries have not been utilized in national programmes, in fact in many countries have not been permitted to assume any responsibility for the conduct of national affairs, and often been denied the privilege of organising for their own development, newly formed governments have, over the last two decades, recognized the necessity for bringing these groups into the blood-stream of national development. It is out of their attempts to do this that community development programmes or projects have been instituted in many countries. The types or kinds of programmes or projects they have instituted vary greatly, but they have all had some common objectives.

Each of the community development programmes whose experiences we have employed to construct a model for a community development extension programme seeks to stimulate and to help local self-help groups, and seeks to open or create channels of effective communication between these groups and the agencies of government which exist to serve them. In all cases, there has prevailed the faith that there is inherent in local community groups the capacity to do many things to improve their own conditions of life and living. But there has also prevailed the judgment on the part of national leaders that local groups need assistance if they are to develop their highest potential for doing this. The first element in this assistance has most often been to make local communities aware of the fact that they are henceforth going to be counted on to play a basic and dynamic role in their own and their country's social and economic development.

Community development, as a term to describe what has been attempted, and accomplished, has been used ambivalently. In some national leaders' minds, it has meant developing local communities as such. In others' minds, it has meant any and all types of local, organised activities, whether organised by local people themselves or by outside agencies, which will help these agencies to carry out their specialized programmes in local areas. The common denominators of all these programmes are that they all seek to catalyze organised local self-help undertakings; they seek to create channels of communication between organised local groups and agencies designed to serve them; and they believe that by combining the contributions of self-help groups and agencies rendering assistance to these groups, both maximum local area and maximum national development will result. Thus community development is not a programme apart from other components of rural development programmes, or apart from rural extension programmes. It is one of the methods by which the potential natural resources for development are maximized and utilized. Its basic role is the development of the human resources of local areas.

Over the past few decades, community development has become a widely used term, so widely used as to have become a stereotype. We have not utilized any of the stereotypes formulated by either academic discussion or by planning groups. Rather we have utilized the empirical experiences of functioning rural development programmes as our frame of reference, and out of a knowledge of these experiences constructed what we have called a model for community development programmes.

Community development has no role to play in building trunk highways, railroads, or large irrigation works. It has roles to play in every improvement programme which requires the willing and organised co-operation of the masses of rural people. Furthermore, these roles in rural development are played, and can be played by no means other than what are now called community development methods. Based on the experiences of those countries which have made most effective use of these methods, their effective use does not require that all the members of a local community join hands to work on any and all improvement projects which will benefit any segment of its population. It quite often means the organisation of a number of local special-purpose groups composed of all or a fair number of those members of a local community who have one or many recognised common needs. It does not require, although it is desirable, that all families in a local community join hands in working on projects which will benefit all members of the community. But a number of countries have thwarted the maximum use of community development methods by insisting that all families in all local communities help on any and all development projects which will improve the conditions under which any sector of a local community lives and works.

The genius of community development methods is indexed by the enthusiastic co-operation of any number of persons who are willing to join hands to solve some problem or meet some need which is recognized as common to all of them. There are countries which do not call the methods employed "community development", by which they accomplish this willing and enthusiastic co-operation of groups of local people. The methods they use do, however, catalyze and mobilize many effective local groups, and in some cases do it better than other countries which have attempted to stereotype the ways in which local people shall organise for undertaking various types of local improvements. There are many cases in which the utopian idea that all members of local communities must participate in every local improvement undertaking has sabotaged the carrying out of legitimate and essential improvements, just because their stereotyped ideas of what constitutes community development have caused them to insist on complete community participation.

To guarantee total participation of all the members of all local communities in a community development programme would require the use of totalitarian methods, whereas, to repeat, the genius of community development methods is willing and enthusiastic participation of local groups in undertakings which these groups deem worth while. It is by means of stimulating, encouraging, and assisting hundreds of thousands of these local groups, some of them total community groups, but many more of them special-purpose groups, that the potential human resources of local areas are developed and utilized in local area and national development. The basic role of community development methods is, therefore, to develop these human resources of a country, by involving groups of local people in, and to as large a degree as possible, making them responsible for, the improvement of all facets of their own conditions of life and living.

CHAPTER 25

A CRITICAL ANALYSIS OF INDIA'S COMMUNITY DEVELOPMENT-EXTENSION PROGRAMME EXPERIENCES

INDIA's planned community development-extension programme quite completely replicated the model presented in the preceding chapter. It provided for: selecting, training, and posting village-level workers in local areas, to catalyze and help organise local community self-help improvement undertakings; both technical and material assistance to such self-help groups; and an assembly line of administration and communication between the sources, or agencies, of assistance and the local self-help groups. The more than ten years of operating experience of this programme provide an unparalleled opportunity for analyzing the processes and the problems involved in the effective use of community development methods on a giant scale. The model we presented was constructed out of what in our judgment had been the combined successes of the community development experiences of a number of countries, but no one of them had made its community development programme the chief agent or agency for total rural development.

We do not confine our assessment to what the use of this model makes possible, for we have personally observed the programme from the day it was initiated to the present time. Hence, even if we had tried, we could not have foregone constant analysis of the programme which we were closely observing. We assume that other social scientists, as well as development programme planners and directors, will be interested in the fact that our analysis to some extent justifies the conviction that all social analysis need not be post mortem in order to be valid. It is possible in many cases to predict events which will follow as a result of the use or lack of use of certain methods.

It is necessary here to make two statements, the validity of which to us is obvious. The first is that there was great wisdom in the decision of Indian planners to as definitely formulate methods by which to develop the human resources as to develop the physical and economic resources of rural areas. The second statement is that models, or blueprints, for the manipulation of human behaviour and social organisation, are not static like blueprints for irrigation and reclamation projects which, once placed on the drawing boards, dictate what the structure must and will be. Blueprints for human behaviour and social organisation must be ideal, to which accommodation but not conformity can and should be expected.

Some persons outside of India and probably some within India, would have counselled that going more slowly was an alternative to launching such a giant programme. We are convinced that there were impelling reasons why such an alternative was not feasible. The long struggle for national independence had led millions of Indian people to expect immediate change in their conditions of life and living once Independence was won. It was therefore essential that the new government have a programme or programmes which would as nearly as possible serve all its various peoples and geographic areas, and in which great numbers of people could be made conscious of their personal participation. It was believed that a community development programme which would as rapidly as possible reach all villages would be this type of programme.

It should, of course, be clear that there would be difficulties and problems involved in the launching and carrying out of such a programme. There were 550,000 villages in India, many of them highly isolated physically and socially from higher units of government. At least 90 per cent of all villagers were illiterate. Colonial and feudal governments in the past had never established and operated adequate systems of extension in agriculture, health, welfare, or even education. There had not been, under these governments, any organic relationship between local village folk organisations and the central government. There was a vast social distance between the relatively few who planned and would have to direct programmes and processes of change and the millions of village people who would need to adopt the changes which the programme was designed to activate.

From a knowledge of these facts it should be apparent that a programme which would require at least 50,000 village workers, each part and parcel of village life and culture but each with at least a high school education, could not possibly be immediately implemented. The same was the case for the corps of personnel needed to train village-level workers. It was true even for the block extension agents who were to provide the staffs of the development blocks and whose role it was to backstop and assist village-level workers. Because these problems were recognized, it was decided there would be no attempt to immediately blanket the country with community development-extension blocks, but an attempt would be made to do so during the next few years.

The first obvious, and clearly recognized, problem was that of selecting and training personnel to staff the programme. A correlative problem was what kind of training the largest cadre of programme personnel—village-level workers—would need in order to play their assigned roles, which, of course, also involved a question of what these roles should be. Our interpretation of the answers given to these questions is in terms of what we reported to be the most successful experiences of other countries in the use of community development methods. The first criterion was that those who were selected to work with relatively isolated village people should be persons who were not socially and culturally too different from villagers themselves. The decision in India was in keeping with this criterion. Those selected to be trained as village-level workers were to be young persons who themselves were born and reared in villages. This met a criterion validated by successful community development experiences, viz., that those selected to work in local communities should have had experience which had given them a wider mental horizon than that of the vast majority of villagers.

Definition of the roles of village-level workers was not so clear-cut, and reflected a viewpoint which was not so thoroughly in keeping with successful community development experience. They were told that they were to be "philosophers, friends, and guides" of village people. There could be no question that they should be friends in order to establish rapport with village people. That they could and would be philosophers was asking a great deal of persons of their age. That they would be accepted by mature village persons as guides should have been doubted. Another prescribed element in their qualifications and training was undoubtedly very perceptive. It was that they should be willing to do, and capable of doing, many of the things which villagers must necessarily do. This was called the "philosophy and practice of dirty hands". It meant that a village-level worker would be capable, for instance, of helping a villager or village group to dig compost pits, build roads, construct drains, etc. There was, however, very little in the prescribed training which would help village-level workers in the important community development task of organising local groups to undertake local improvements.

From observations of village-level workers at work in villages, and from visits with those above them, one of our early conclusions was that there was a considerable absence of understanding of the role which voluntary local groups have to play in community development methods. Another question in our minds at the time the programme was being launched was to what extent those who would supervise, in fact direct, village-level workers when they were posted in the field would have an adequate understanding of community development methods, or would have the same altruistic dedication to the tasks at hand that was being instilled in village-level workers in their training centres. Those who were to be supervisors and directors of village-level workers were to be selected largely from cadres trained in bureaucratic administration and there was, in the beginning, no programme which provided these supervisors any training in community development methods. There was therefore the possibility, even the probability, that supervisors and directors of village-level workers would unknowingly sabotage the community development methods in the use of which village-level workers had been trained.

During the early years of the programme, one of the authors was invited to address an audience of development planners and leaders. His address was published in *Kurukshetra*, the Monthly Organ of the Ministry of Community Development (October 1956). He said in part:

"An evaluation of the adequacy of the training in Extension Methods ... can best be made from a critical look at the inner working of Community Development and National

Extension programmes over the past four years. This evaluation reveals among other things that far greater progress has been made on the building of physical targets than has been made in penetrating the inner minds of the village people. Village people have been mobilized to build roads but few have been educated to place enough value on the roads to have an organized plan to maintain them. Thousands of village homes and streets have been cleaned but in few is it considered important to have an organized plan to keep the village clean. Thousands of village wells have been dug but few are the villages where the people see the relationship between maintaining pure clean water and good health. Thousands of compost pits have been dug but few are the people who fully understand the purpose to be served by the compost pit. Thousands of schools have been built to meet the villagers' inner urge for educating their children away from the drudgery of the village life. In all too few cases, however, do village people visualize any possible relationship between the village school, education and improved village life. Too many village people look upon the village improvement programmes as being of Government origin and direction. . . .

It is shocking to note that after four years of training and work in the Community Development programme that the Evaluation Organization for the Community Development programme has paid so little attention to evaluation of the training programme. After four years, India can do little more than generalize about what makes for a successful Gram Sevak either from the point of view of background, experience or training. . . .

What is now required is the same devoted leadership and sense of urgency once felt by all who were responsible for the early establishment of these centres (training centres) in the beginning. Now, however, all effort should be focussed on turning out Gram Sevaks and Gram Sevikas who will (a) understand the objectives and philosophy and inner working of the Community Development programme; (b) be trained to understand family and village values and group relationships; (c) be skilled in the use of Extension methods to guide village people in focussing their attention on their problems and assist village people to grow, through self-education, in self-confidence and competence in solving of family and village problems; (d) have the essential grounding in agriculture but be trained to serve as a multi-purpose village Extension worker possessing 'first-aid' knowledge and skills which will be helpful to village people in improving their agriculture, health, education and family and village life."

Another one of the authors was invited by the Administrator of Community Projects to spend a year, July, 1955—July, 1956, in making a Critical Analysis of India's Community Development Programme. He visited all levels of programme operation from village to block, to district, to State and Central government administrations, recording day-by-day what he saw and heard. He was requested not only to be critical in his analysis, but also to make suggestions for improvement in programme operation. Excerpts from that report follow:

"In my assigned undertaking, to critically evaluate India's Community Development Programme, I have found it necessary to focus my attention sharply on those aspects of the Community Development Programme which permitted me to take a bifocal or stereoptic view. One focus has been what I was presently seeing and hearing in India, the other was what I had seen of a similar character in a fairly large number of other countries. . .

Community Development is the method by which people who live in local villages or communities are involved in helping to improve their own economic and social conditions and thereby become effective working groups in programmes of national development. The adoption of this method is based upon a knowledge that villagers who in the past have seemed to be lethargic and not interested in change, will become dynamic if they are permitted to take decisions concerning, exercise responsibility for, and are helped to carry out projects and programmes for improvements in their own villages.

They (villagers) definitely have higher standards of living, that is they have visions, hopes, and expectations for better things. But they give the Government great credit for what has been done, and they apparently expect much from the Government in the future. How much their outlook about their own capacities has changed I do not know. How much they trust their own initiative is not evident. How much they have become self-starting and self-perpetuating groups it is impossible to discover because they seldom do anything in which the Government does not have a big hand.

Voluntary group effort is a part of the deepest values and traditions of India. . . . Voluntary organizations cannot, however, be assigned tasks as if they were a part of a bureaucracy. Their efforts cannot be turned off and on, like the flow of water, with a spigot. But if it is recognized by everyone that they and they alone are expected to be responsible for certain types of action they will systematically organize and direct their efforts toward these ends. If no such responsibility is expected of them, their efforts are often episodic, spasmodic, and even disruptive, and their purposes likely to be selfish. Not only does initiative inhere in the volunteerism of such groups but additional initiative, and leaders, grow out of the responsibility such groups are willing to assume."

The above quotations were from statements made by the authors during the year 1956, after three years of programme operation and just as the First-Plan period was coming to an end. Indian programme planners and leaders requested that we not only be critical but suggest remedies for programme weaknesses. We, as observers, were at that time convinced that community development methods were in many ways not being effectively employed, and that because of this certain effects which could be expected to flow from their full and correct use would not result.

In our judgment India's planned programme clearly replicated the model community development-extension programme which we presented in the preceding chapter. Statements made in the First Five Year Plan and elsewhere gave cause to believe that community development methods were understood. The Plan had said, "The Community Development Programme aims at the establishment of a suitable organ to ensure participation of the villagers at the planning stage," and that local talent should be used as far as possible in selecting village-level workers, in order to stimulate the enthusiasm of the people of the local areas.

Our observation of village-level workers at work in the villages in the early days of the programme had led us to believe that this cadre of personnel understood these objectives well and were having considerable success in stimulating behaviour which would implement them. They were patient during the period required to convince villagers that they were sent to help them. It was the testimony of village people that village-level workers had stimulated a great deal of local co-operative effort and had thereby reduced village dissensions and factions. We believe that anyone observing villages in 1954 would have been impressed by the teeming activities which he witnessed at that time: village roads being built, schools, clinics, and community centres being constructed, village lanes being paved, wells and tanks being dug. There was great enthusiasm on the part of villagers and on the part of all programme personnel from development blocks to State and Central governments. To us, like everyone who saw the immense improvements which were being carried out, in village after village, it appeared that community development was being accomplished on a wide front.

From observations of these enthusiasms and activities in village after village, and an awareness that many villages not yet included in the programme were eagerly asking when they could expect to be included, it appeared that the only issue was how rapidly the coverage of all villages could be assured. It was only after we had sat for hours with a great many village groups and their spokesmen that we began to discover that a more important issue was whether the faith of villagers in their own competence was increasing and whether their traditional self-reliance was being strengthened. Their repeated, almost universal, answer to our question of why they were for the first time doing this, that, or another thing to meet needs which they had had for generations was, "Because the government helped us." Their answer to our question, "What are you going to do next," was to name a great variety of improvement projects, practically all of which would require increasing grants of government funds. We also observed that in construction types of projects, which had come to constitute the major improvement projects in villages, and for which village contributions of manual labour were required, it was the less affluent members of village communities who provided this labour. We could not help but wonder whether this co-operation of the poorer members of the community was always willing and eager, or whether it was provided merely because it had always been expected of them.

When (in 1956) we were requested by the Ministry of Community Development to study the programme in action, we asked the Minister what his worries about the programme were and thus for what questions he wanted us to seek answers. His statement was, "We need to know whether the outlook of villagers is being changed, and whether the programme which was initiated by the government but has sought participation of the people, is gradually changing to a people's programme which is seeking government participation." Recognizing that answers to these questions would be difficult, we focused our observations and our questions to villagers directly on these issues. Our answer to the first question, after a year's intensive study, was that whether or not the outlook of villagers was changing, their expectation of what material assistance they would receive from the government was far beyond what the government would be able to provide. This provided part of the answer to the second question, namely, that there was little observable evidence that the programme was becoming a people's programme in the sense that villagers were developing greater initiative and taking, or being permitted to assume, greater responsibility for local village improvement projects.

From the testimony of village-level workers, we were disturbed about the fact that, over the first few years of programme operation, no systematic methods had been used to discover the most commonly felt needs of villagers. Village-level workers said they had been taught no such methods and had not been requested to try to discover villagers' felt needs. It had been expected by programme planners that local village pride and self-reliance would guarantee that village people would mobilize to meet their clearly recognized common needs if they were assured that they would be permitted, expected, and assisted to do so. This expectation was based on the experiences of some of the most successful community development programmes of other countries, in which members of local communities had been assisted to become aware of their common needs, and which of them they could most successfully tackle.

There is considerable fiction in the notion that persons and families who live physically adjacent to each other always know what each other's felt needs are. There is far greater fiction in the belief that an outsider can easily identify these commonly felt needs. Such highly successful community development programmes as Puerto Rico's, Jamaica's, and Ghana's, the success of which has depended primarily upon maximized, organised local self-help to accomplish local improvements, have utilized methods by which to discover what the greatest felt needs of each separate community are. It has been found that the only way the members of local communities have been able to agree upon their most commonly felt needs is through sustained and systematic discussion among themselves. The discussions have needed to be sustained because various persons have named their individual felt needs only to discover that other persons did not feel these same needs. By sustained or repeated discussions, all these individualistic needs were winnowed out, and in due time those needs which were most nearly common became the focus of discussions. If and when such groups understood that a part of their objective was to discuss only those needs which they themselves by organised effort could meet, even some of their commonly felt needs were, so to speak, removed from the agenda for discussion, because it became clear that to meet some of these needs was beyond their capacities.

From the experiences of these programmes, and from a large number of experiments in group dynamics, a great deal is now known about ways in which local communities are most easily and most completely mobilized for local action. Each of the most successful community development programmes on whose experiences we have drawn stimulates the widest possible discussion, and generally over a very long period of time, in street gossip, in inter-family visiting, and almost every place or occasion where two or more persons meet. The decision of a community to do something about its most commonly felt needs, and what to do, is practically always taken at a well-organised and generally well-attended community meeting.

Government personnel in India have not only assumed major responsibility for determining what the needs of the villagers were, but assumed the responsibility for prescribing how these needs could and should be met. Village workers were taught how to make surveys of these needs. They were not taught how to induce and help local villagers to make self-surveys of their needs. Even if the findings of the surveys made by government personnel and of self-surveys of villagers themselves were to discover the same felt needs there would be, in terms of initiating community group formations, something which happened in the self-survey that could not happen from a survey by outside personnel. A self-survey would have built upon a traditional self-reliance of village people and the almost certain potential capacities of village groups to know for what sort of improvement undertakings the greatest number of their local community would contribute their manpower, their ingenuity, and their enthusiasm. Contrary to this having happened, we and other observers, who over the early years of programme operation talked with hundreds of village leaders and with a great many dedicated national and State programme planners and leaders, are convinced that the maximum growth of organised self-help has quite generally been thwarted by those who decided for what types of self-help projects technical and material assistance from the government would be granted. We are also convinced that there need be no conflict between the responsibility of those who determine for what national project limited government funds will be expended and the responsibility of organised village groups who alone can and will determine for what improvement projects they can and will mobilize the greatest amount of self-help village resources and enthusiasm.

National planners and leaders are, of course, duty-bound to decide for what types of nationwide projects necessarily limited government assistance will be provided. It could, however, have been made known by national programme planners and directors that maximum available funds would be granted, let us say, for improving domestic water supplies, increasing agricultural production, improving environmental sanitation, and that for certain types of projects nothing but technical assistance would be provided. The scale or schedule of grants could have been made known to all villages, and each village could have decided which among the shelf of cafeteria projects it desired to undertake, ranging from those for which it can mobilize the greatest amount of local material and human resources to those for which it could receive the greatest amount of government assistance. We have listened to the testimony in village after village, and from village leaders themselves, that they have had difficulty in mobilizing their people to undertake projects which they themselves had not selected. We are convinced that, had the programme procedure which we have just described been used, many more locally-initiated village improvements would have been undertaken; that many more self-generative local village groups would have been organised, and consequently more village leaders would have been developed; almost of equal importance, local village under-takings, which national and State planners were convinced quite correctly were of great importance to national social and economic development, would have been more actively carried out, supported, and maintained locally.

Probably the reason that little, if any, use was made of the processes of helping villagers to analyze their most commonly felt needs and to organise for self-help improvement undertakings was that there was an absence of understanding that the basic purpose of helping local village people to come to an agreement on their most commonly felt needs was not that higher pro-gramme officials might decide what technical and material assis-tance they would provide to local improvement projects, but was for the purpose of generating local group dynamics.

The primary role prescribed for village-level workers was to assist villagers and village groups to take the first steps in technical improvement, whether in the field of economic production, health and sanitation, or education. The workers were better trained in agriculture than in any other technical field because increased agricultural production was given first priority in the rural deve-lopment programme. We interviewed at least one hundred village-level workers during the years 1954-55 and 1955-56, the period in which the programme was developing rapidly and being backed by unquestioned national enthusiasm. We practically always started our questions to village-level workers about as follows: "Now that you have had some experience on the job, for which of your tasks do you believe you were best trained; for what tasks least well trained; which assigned tasks have you found easiest to do; and, which most difficult to perform?" The answers they gave were, of course, not unanimous, but by and large were that they felt they were best prepared to render assistance in the field of agriculture and least prepared to stimulate group action; that aid to cultivators was easiest because most of the villagers were cultivators, and a number of these cultivators sought, or at least accepted, their assistance. They said they were not very successful in mobilizing or catalyzing local village groups because they had not received much training in this field, and the only groups they found already organised were castes and factions. Because of this they had made little use of already organised local groups and had done even less in attempting to organise new groups.

The chief complaint of village-level workers was about the amount of time they were compelled to give to record keeping and reports. They testified to the Committee on Plan Projects, and to us, that these demands sharply reduced the time they could give to extension and community development work. Those workers whom we met in villages and whose activities we were able to observe were very much more often participating in some construction project than they were in economic production projects. Our conclusion at the time was that the village-level workers were well accepted—in most cases enthusiastically—by village people, but because of the diversity of things they were supposed to do and the demands made upon them by higher authorities, they were not sure what their main roles were. A year later we felt they had largely become the errand boys of programme administrators rather than catalyzers and servants of village people and organised village groups. Even though we quite often asked these village workers leading questions, we seldom elicited the response that one of their roles was to relay up the assembly line of communication and programme administration a knowledge or awareness of what they, as grass roots echelon of programme personnel, were learning about the response or lack of response of village people to the programme in which their enthusiastic participation was vital.

We were able to visit with fewer development block personnel, who constituted the first link in the chain of communication up to higher officials. We did question a large number of block staffs as groups at block headquarters and quite often we were piloted in our tours of blocks by Block Development Officers. Our over-all impressions at that time (1954-56) were about as follows:

That block specialists in agriculture and health had fairly good conceptions of their assigned roles and they themselves felt that they were effective in their work. The social education organisers, whose role was originally described as being specialists in community organisation, very often appeared to have no clear-cut concept of their roles, and quite often said their chief accomplishments were organising and staging social or cultural programmes. The block specialists in the field of co-operation were enthusiastic and indicated that they were promoting a great deal of propaganda, but were able to report few concrete results of their efforts.

We visited in the offices and travelled in the field with a large number of Block Development Officers and chief Project Officers. Our conclusions at that time were that a majority of them conceived their job to be chiefly that of administration, managing funds, and directing their subordinates. However, we recorded that if there could be combined in one Block Development Officer the best types of behaviour and attitudes we had observed in the best of all of them, he would be an ideal entrepreneur of rural development. In summary, we quote from our Critical Analysis, the field work of which was done during the year 1955-56:

> Block Development Officers—"Men who had looked forward to being Tax Collectors have seen a new vision, developed new zest, and testify that they never imagined they could be so dedicated as they now are to their new jobs... Not all Block Development Officers are, however, these types of persons. I have not observed one of them that I thought was not diligent. Some of them seem to be utterly smothered with details and some of them are trying to be specialists in all fields, which they are not. Some of them seem not to recognize how much more technical know-how the members of their staff possess than they do...
>
> The whole Block staff, including Village-Level Workers, should constitute a development team. The Block Development Officer should be the captain of that team. He should be an entrepreneur of development in his Block, not an administrator in the common meaning of the term. He has no responsibility for law and order or revenue administration. He has a maximum of twenty-seven persons on his staff, counting the Village-Level Workers, in the most intensive

Blocks. His job is to get coordinated teamwork among that staff, to spend much time helping development groups and leaders in villages, and to educate all members of his staff and as many village groups and village leaders as possible on the whole development programme and process. I have seen Block Development Officers doing all of these things well. I have seen others doing some of these things well but failing badly in one or two others. My description of the role and genius of the Block Development Officer, and my characterisation of him as a key man in the whole Community Development Programme, is based on the best I have seen in Development Blocks in India. But the Block Development Officer because he is a key man should be better trained in community development methods."

Dr. Howard Beers, as Ford Foundation consultant in Community Development, spent a large part of the year 1958-59 in making a much more thorough analysis of block operation and block personnel than we were able to make a few years earlier. He interviewed block personnel separately and often at length. By and large, he found about the same things we have reported; that Block Development Officers felt greatly beholden to those above them in programme administration; that they were chiefly administrators and behaved as such; that they did not conceive of themselves as entrepreneurs of local development or leaders of closely-knit block development teams.

Commissions and study teams, composed wholly of Indians, identified and discussed many of the problems identified in our analysis of each of the components of programme operation. We turn our attention now to more purely sociological analyses of problems which were inherent in this planned and directed programme, the most basic objective of which was to change the practices and attitudes of millions of traditionalized persons. The vast majority of them could not be expected, for some time to come at least, to share in or comprehend the aspirations of national planners and leaders. Our focus will be primarily on social problems and sociological processes.

There were repeated statements by planners and leaders that one of the most important, and probably most difficult, problems would be that of "changing the outlook" of village people. But

it has been our judgment, based, we believe, on a sound understanding of the psychology of motivation, that not only ineffective
but, for at least a considerable period of time, fallacious theories
of motivation were employed by programme directors.

The most basic problem involved in motivation was undoubtedly stated when planners said the main task of development
was to raise the *standard* of living of the vast rural masses of
India. Sociologically there is a difference between a *standard* of
living and a *level* of living. The level of living of individuals or
families consists of the volume and quality of goods and services
which they consume or use. A standard of living is that level of
living to which they aspire, a target they set for themselves and
strive to reach. There is always a dynamic relationship between
what a family has and a target which it sets for itself. That dynamic
may never develop if someone else attempts to set the target. In
fact, targets set by others may be dysfunctional rather than functional. This is very likely to be the case if attempts are made to
provide levels of living which are not the conscious standards of
those to whom the levels of living are provided.

The greatest dynamic of those societies which have moved
rapidly from widespread low levels of living to widespread high
levels of living, has been the opportunity of a steadily increasing
percentage of all their people, generation after generation, to
attain today that level of living which yesterday was only their
target or standard of living. If they have legitimized expectations
today that they can, by diligent effort, attain that level of living
tomorrow to which they today aspire, it can be taken for granted
that an upward spiral in their life is pretty well guaranteed. This
upward spiral was what Indian leaders meant when they said it
was necessary to change the outlook of village people. It appears
to us, however, that they did not foresee, and probably did not
understand, the possibility of a dysfunctional relationship between
a level of living obtained by outside material assistance and one
to which millions of villagers had never in the past aspired.

Most persons in so-called advanced societies, which are also
affluent societies, will have difficulty in realizing how impossible it
is that any large part of the village population of India will or can
make a great leap upward in their levels of living. Few leaders
in India recognize that this is not necessary in order to convert

"apathetic villagers" into aspiring persons, and to convert "stagnant village communities" into dynamic units of social and economic action. The level of living of village people has been low for so long that the majority of them have no higher standards of living than their present levels of living. Their expectations are so low that it would not be difficult to help the majority of them exceed their own expectations. The dynamics which such experiences generate everywhere in the evolution of human societies could happen in India by thoroughgoing and consistent use of community development methods.

The "rising tide of expectations", which is said to be frustrating development planners and directors, has been largely stimulated by Indian programme directors. Our observations indicate that it is not so much the lack of motives but the lack of legitimized expectations which causes apathy on the part of hundreds of thousands of village people in India. Indian villagers are, and always have been, motivated to stay alive, to avoid sickness, and to provide clothing and shelter for their families. What is primarily needed is that the community development-extension programme provide them with an understanding of validated knowledge of superior methods by which they can implement these motives. In all too many cases, development leaders have been more successful in attempting to arouse unwarranted expectations than they have in implementing those that are warranted. To arouse unwarranted expectations is not a sound method of motivation. To provide struggling village people with unsolicited material assistance is not to use sound community development methods and interrupts the sequence of steps by which self-generative local groups gain strength and confidence. This sequence is that such groups shall be stimulated to undertake self-help local improvement projects; then supplied with all possible technical assistance to carry out these projects, and only enough material assistance to keep self-help projects from failing.

To help village groups in this way generates widespread social dynamics, which is a prime objective of community development methods. The creation, or generation, of widespread social dynamics, and not some great leap forward, provides the explanation of the progress of those societies which have experienced steadily rising standards and levels of living. The obverse of these experiences is the well-known frustration which has resulted from unfulfilled, and unwarranted expectations. It is our judgment that Indian development leaders have stimulated this frustration by providing types and amounts of material assistance which were unsolicited by local self-help groups, instead of working consistently and effectively at the task of gradually developing aspiring local groups and then helping these groups to implement their aspirations.

There is also the problem of developing flexibility and dynamics in higher levels of programme administration. There was, from the beginning, some recognition of the problem of introducing flexibility into programme roles, especially in the behaviour and attitudes of those who by necessity would have to administer the various levels of programme operation. The chief problem was whether or not district officers could be expected to change from the practices and attitudes required in playing the roles of tax collectors and magistrates to those of development entrepreneurs. By placing development planning officers on district staffs and introducing development blocks between districts and villages, it was assumed that an assembly line, through which aid could flow from State governments to village people, was fairly well assured.

Because the assigned role of each of the components of India's community development-extension programme so nearly replicates one of the roles which the successful programmes of other countries has demonstrated, we arrive at the following conclusions as to why India's programme has not worked more successfully: *first*, her programme was validly conceived but because of its magnitude, it has been difficult to recruit and train enough persons to play all of the essential roles to adequately staff the many local areas where the programme is now operating; *second*, it has proved to be not only impossible, but not feasible, to attempt to compensate for these inevitable weaknesses by administrative direction from above; *third*, the only remedy for these weaknesses is to reorient the programme and begin strengthening its grass roots foundation component, work at the village level. This would mean doing everything possible to more effectively implement the role, or roles, of the village-level workers and the block development staff. We suggest how this can, and we believe ultimately will, be done. Our rationale is not different from that expressed in the initial plans for the programme.

It was assumed from the beginning of rural development planning that the potential of the rural masses to contribute to their own local area's and their country's development was probably the greatest undeveloped natural resource of the nation, and that this resource could and would be developed by community development methods. Tens of thousands of village-level workers have been trained in these methods and are now posted in local areas. Two Social Education Organisers whose originally assigned role was that of community organisation, are posted in each block.

The voluntary testimony of village-level workers themselves is that they have had minimal success in mobilizing or even catalyzing, much less developing, the human resources of the areas in which they work. Social Education Organisers, because they are not village-born and reared, have not been able to exercise leadership or even adequate guidance to rural groups. The Programme Evaluation Organisation has not found, even when it tried, any great number of self-generative dynamic local groups functioning in local areas. But all this time there have been various kinds of local leaders better prepared and better positioned than either village-level workers or Social Education Organisers to mobilize groups of persons who are especially interested in some one area of improvement, but their talents have not been effectively employed.

This is not to imply that local area rural development personnel—village-level workers, Social Education Organisers, block specialists and Block Development Officers—have made no use of persons who have proved themselves to be leaders of local groups. But we have, in India and in other countries, seen such persons lifted, so to speak, out of their self-created ways of doing things and made official agents of some official programme. In practically all cases, their normal status of leadership among their neighbours was destroyed. When they were made official agents, they were assigned official tasks and told when and how to do them. This need not have been. There is a better way to utilize and increase the influence of persons with special talents who live in local communities, a way that is consonant with community development methods. An illustration of this better way would be for village-level workers and block agricultural specialists to help the known progressive farmers of a local community to constitute themselves a progressive farmers' group, which would discuss their experiences, learn from each other, and invite others who are, so to speak, "near-progressive" farmers. Such groups are not only purposive types of association, but the many studies of adoption and spread of improved agricultural practices show that a knowledge of the improved practices of neighbouring farmers provides the chief motivation for change in the practices of other farmers; also, that those farmers who, on their own initiative have made the greatest improvement, most readily seek and accept assistance from official agricultural extension agents.

Organised progressive farmers' groups are only one illustration of the proven effectiveness of local special-interest and special-purpose groups. School teachers have no administrative authority in the field of educational development, but they can organise parents of the children whom they teach, and others, not only to promote improvement of local schools but improvement of all aspects of life in the local communities in which they work. Welfare leaders, unofficial as well as official, can do the same thing. Such groups are self-motivated, and need only to be permitted and encouraged to develop local leaders. They need not, and ought not to be assigned tasks by official programme directors nor be made beholden to government officials, but only to the local people whom they seek to serve. They can and will, if permitted and encouraged, mobilize the talents and enthusiasm of local people as no official programme personnel can.

A multiplicity of such groups is essential for mobilizing and developing the interest and purposes of any great number of people. Some special-interest and special-purpose groups concern themselves with only local improvements in their own communities. Some of them join hands with similar groups in adjacent communities. Some are associated with groups which are concerned primarily with State and national problems. Here we are referring only to the need for and potentialities of such groups in a block or a samiti area, encouraged not only by village-level workers but by Block Development Officers and their staffs.

Following successful performance of the primary function of local group formation, the second role of village-level workers, illustrated and validated by the most successful community development programmes in other countries, is one which has never been assigned to India's village workers. This is the role of acting as ambassadors of organised local groups to the government and other agencies which are prepared to assist local self-help groups. This has not been because it was assumed by development programme leaders that local self-help groups would not need both technical and material assistance. Development blocks were organised to render such assistance and make it available near at hand. As the programme developed, however, it was higher programme officials and not organised self-help village groups who determined what type of assistance and how much would be made available. Higher programme officials have made these decisions and relayed them down, through Block Development Officials to village-level workers, with the result that village-level workers have come nearer to being messengers from high officials to village groups than from village groups to higher officials.

It is clear that this was not the intention of those who planned the programme. In setting up the block organisation, the first communication sent to "All State Governments" from the Secretary of the Planning Commission said that in selecting Executive Officers (later given the title, "Block Development Officers") to be in charge of individual projects, special attention should be given to experience, general outlook, understanding of the methods of community development, capacity for leadership, and ability to win official and non-official co-operation. For these posts, therefore, it would be wise to select the best available persons whether from official cadres or not. A little later, the chief role of the Block Development Officer was described as captain of a local development team, this team to be composed of from ten to twenty village-level workers in his block and some seven to nine specialists to work out of the Block Development Office. The role of the Block Development Officer was described again and again as "the key man in the whole rural development programme," probably best described as an entrepreneur of local area development, the local area to be a block of some one hundred villages.

In order for the Block Development Officer to play this role effectively, his attention must be primarily directed downward toward the people, not upward toward his superiors in the line of administrative authority. It is not merely that he and his staff are physically closer to the masses which the rural development programme is designed to serve and can therefore more effectively tailor aid to their needs, though this is both true and important. It is also that they are physically in a position to assess, mobilize, and develop the potential human resources of a local area. If they do not envision this as their task, are not capable of doing it, or because of tasks assigned from above are not permitted to do it, then of course they cannot effectively play the role of local area development entrepreneurs. The development of local resources, including human resources, is the sole unique contribution which community development methods have to make to the total rural development programme. This contribution cannot be made unless a great deal of autonomy is granted to the block or local development team.

If it be said that there are not four thousand or more trained or experienced men in India to fill the positions of local area development entrepreneurs, then the same can be said concerning every other cadre of programme personnel, from village-level workers to top civil servant. More important, it should be said that if a lack of expected results from the ten years of programme operation experience have led to a nationwide decentralization of government, which the Panchayati Raj contemplates, then this ten years of experience should have also led to a conviction that there is need for decentralization of programme administrative responsibility.

If the block development staff is to promote community development as well as to implement the extension work of the "nation building departments" of government, and also in every way possible to assist samitis to become not only viable but integral social and economic entities, the two main tasks will be to create opportunities for, in every way possible to encourage and assist, a great variety of local special-purpose groups; and through these groups and others, help to develop a fabric of group-conscious social structures. In order to encourage and assist local special-purpose groups, the Block Development Officer and all members of his staff will need superior training in community development methods.

The Block Development Officer, above all other programme officials, needs to know that he and his block staff cannot, in and of themselves, get very far in promoting the adoption and spread of improved practices unless they have the genuine co-operation of a great many organised local groups, the members of which will themselves adopt these practices and take some responsibility for the diffusion of them among their neighbours. The Block Development Officer, all members of his staff, and all those above him in programme administration, should know that they cannot wish or decree such local, aspiring, dynamic groups into being. They undoubtedly now recognize that the failure to bring such groups into existence has encouraged higher programme officials to grant government money solely or chiefly for projects which could be planned and carried out by administrative direction and procedures. But good extension work, unlike construction projects, cannot be done in this way. It must be done by community development methods in which both extension agents and organised local groups work together and thus fructify or supplement each other.

Now that Panchayati Raj has been instituted, not only local village special-purpose groups but samiti special-purpose groups should be organised and catalyzed and made responsible for local area development. Local initiative will not automatically spring forth just because Panchayati Raj laws have been passed by State governments. The method by which such initiative can be stimulated is not through administrative procedures but is a part of the methods of community development. The tasks of the samiti and the tasks of the block development staff are parallel and complementary. Neither can effectively perform his tasks without the assistance of the other. No small part of the task of the block development staff is to help all of the people of samiti areas to become self-conscious local area groups.

During ten years of development programme experience, nothing has been done to make those who live in a given block area a group-conscious social entity. It is not only because the samiti is now a political entity, but because it is expected to be a unit of development activities, that steps need to be taken to make it a group-conscious entity. How this can be done, and has been done in the evolution of societies, is documented by the experience of other countries which have inevitably traversed this path. People who live in newly-created political areas become new self-conscious action groups to the extent that the various persons who live in those areas recognize the need, and are provided the opportunity, to meet their needs by joint action. This is accomplished by creating opportunities for, and facilitating systematic interaction between, persons who live in various sub-sections of the block or samiti area. It cannot be accomplished solely by mass meetings of all those who reside in the samiti area. It can be accomplished only by purposeful, functioning organisations of various kinds, among persons and groups from the different subsections and communities of the samiti area.

Community development methods can be employed to hasten this evolution or development and it is only those programme personnel who are posted within the block who can effectively employ these methods. They have not done so in the past, at least partially because, no matter what the original plan provided, they have either themselves envisioned their roles as, or been forced to play the roles of, administrators. Even those Block Development Officers who have demonstrated genius as block area development entrepreneurs have not only been overburdened by administrative tasks handed to them by their superior administrative officers, but have quite often been second-guessed by their superior officers as to what should be done in their blocks.

Now that the block, previously only a development programme administrative unit, has been made a statutory unit of government, it is feasible and desirable that the role of the block officer should be redefined. To define his role as block area development entrepreneur would best describe what he most needs to do. To assign him merely the position of executive officer of the samiti will make him even more an administrator than he has been in the past. To make him a block area development entrepreneur will place him in a position to work creatively not only with the samiti officials but with every type of existent organised group in the block area, and with every type of special-purpose group which can be brought into existence in the block area. It will, of course, still be his and his staff's special function to provide all possible outside technical aid to those who live in the block, but it will also be his function to develop the resident potential resources of the area, chiefly the human resources.

It is not too much to expect that in due time a sufficient number of competent block area development entrepreneurs will be available, through experience, training, and promotion from lower cadres of programme personnel, to entrepreneur all aspects of development in all the samiti areas of India, and that the steadily increasing confidence and competence of both village panchayat and samiti officers will make it possible to transfer development initiative to the block development staff. Nor is it too much to expect under Panchayati Raj that hundreds of thousands of local special-purpose groups, tens of thousands of village panchayats and more than 5,000 samitis, will not only convert India's community development-extension programme from a purely government programme seeking the participation of village people, but also to a people's programme which all levels of government will seek and be adequately prepared to serve.

It is not possible or necessary to predict how long this will take. It is enough to know that while development leaders have at times been disappointed with programme results, there are evidences of steady progress in programme improvement. Equally or more significant is the fact that there has been no deviation from the original stated objectives. There has been constant endeavour to learn from experience how to improve both planning and programme organisation and operation.

To these optimistic notes we must, however, add some critical comments about failures on the part of programme administrators effectively to implement or carry forward certain tasks which are essential to real community development. The authors, along with many others who have observed and evaluated the community development programme over the past ten years, have expressed repeated concern over the lack of emphasis on strengthening the economic base of village communities. From its inception, India's leaders have conceived of the community development programme as being organised self-help by village people. There have been repeated references in official literature to the fact that village people must learn to solve their own problems and not continue to assume that government could or should do all the things that the people over time would feel needed to be done. Self-help, from the beginning, was and must be understood both by village people and the block staff who seek to serve village people. For the individual family whose wants are expressed in terms of desiring more and better health services and facilities, more and better education, better housing, etc., there is no alternative to helping the people to understand that the only reasonable way they can assure having the things they want is to give attention to increasing their agricultural production. Carrying out improved agricultural practices can, through community development, have real meaning to the people, in that they can succeed through their own efforts in providing, by increased production, the financial resources they need for the things they want.

There has been considerable failure on the part of the programme administration to make shifts to administrative procedures, practices, and attitudes which are essential to the success of field operation. There still continues the practice of shifting administrative persons to one assignment after the other, which has been particularly detrimental to the community development-extension programme. Because both community development and extension methods require the systematic involvement of local people in all phases of development, it is clear, and has been from the inception of the programme, that those who work as block development and extension officers, as well as the village-level workers, must, if they are to understand local problems, gain rapport with and be trusted by local groups and leaders, and must remain in one location for a considerable period of time. For village people, the continuous transfer of block staff has meant a continued, or repeated, detachment of the staff from the people, with the result that the relations between programme officials and the people continue to be more formal than is desirable in community development-extension work, and to this extent automatically less effective.

In our critical analysis of India's community development programme, by use of a model construct and our own continuous observation of India's programme in action, we are aware that we have counselled with standards of perfection. Indian leaders have both too narrowly and too broadly conceived the role of community development methods, too broadly when they assume that no matter by what method local community improvements were accomplished, community development had been accomplished. They have conceived of community development methods too narrowly when they assumed that they required only the mobilization of all members of local communities. The methods of community development are equally effective in developing smaller than entire community groups, and in developing some larger than local community groups.

We have emphasized the need to employ community development methods in helping the people of the samiti area to become self-conscious groups. We have in other places said that these methods have not been effectively employed in the past for mobilizing special-purpose groups, for instance, in mobilizing cultivators for the adoption and diffusion of improved agricultural practices. At a number of places we have stated that community development methods are not administrative procedures which can be meticulously prescribed and administratively directed; they consist of a sequence of steps in group development, starting with the people where they are and with what they want to do. Only in succeeding steps do community development methods involve other than local groups. When they do involve them, the function of these groups is, in every way possible, to aid and implement the growing dynamics of local groups.

We have critically analyzed weaknesses in the operation of India's community development programme, not its planned design. Having personally observed a large number of other community development programmes in operation, we again emphasize that India is operating what, by any and all measures, is the greatest planned programme of this type that any nation in the world has ever attempted to plan and operate. She has sought and welcomed the criticism of her programme by many persons and agencies and has constantly evaluated it and adopted correctives for the future whenever convinced that the criticisms of past performances were valid. She has never departed from her originally-stated objectives; and although she has not always effectively employed community development methods, and in some ways sabotaged those methods by administrative procedures and attitudes, she has recently taken revolutionary steps to correct these shortcomings.

Maybe it would have been too much to expect that persons with socially-isolated elite administrative status would understand how important it was that they learn about the felt needs of villagers, their systems of local social relationships, and the influence of these vitally important things in the day-by-day life of village people. They were more than once warned by the then Deputy Chairman of the Planning Commission about how much they needed to learn, but it was not until the programme had drifted from the objectives of community development and had become a "construction" and "amenities" and as some said, "an administrator's" programme, that revolutionary action was taken to return the programme to its original focus or objectives. Now that two new steps have been taken—establishment of the Panchayati Raj, which permits and encourages local planning, local group initiative, and responsibility; and promotion of the Intensive Agricultural Districts Programme, which demonstrates under controlled conditions complete and effective agricultural extension methods—the whole rural development programme is evolving back toward the well-conceived plan with which it started.

As the programme travels these redirected paths, it will for some time be handicapped by too few adequately-trained technical personnel. Those who constitute the lower tiers of local government will only slowly learn the difficult task of local planning, responsibility, and initiative. But it is quite certain that out of this giant laboratory of rural development, by use of community development methods, India will gradually move in the direction which her plans have described; and by trial, error, and success will make a great contribution to other countries which are attempting to develop democratic, dynamic societies through democratic methods.

CHAPTER 26

THE ROLE OF TECHNICAL ASSISTANCE

TECHNICAL assistance is the symbol and product of great humanitarian ideals. To the newly-developing countries in ferment around the world, it is the hope of a better day. To all countries it offers the prospect of building a better and more peaceful world. Thus, the assistance movement holds out an opportunity and a challenge for both givers and receivers of assistance—an opportunity to achieve new levels of human well-being and a challenge to overcome the problems involved.

The technical assistance movement is essentially new. It is new in its present and growing scale; new in terms of its orientation, purpose, and problems; new in its vast potentialities. World experience in it thus far, though still limited, is sufficient to reveal its power for substantial progress. This experience also gives a clearer picture of the role of technical assistance in development, and of its problems, than could be seen earlier.

In this broad movement, the more advanced nations and their institutions, as well as various international bodies, are supplying resources and technical guidance to help less advanced countries achieve economic and social improvements in the depressed condition of their people. Virtually all nations are participating in this work to some degree as either donors or recipients of assistance, or both.

The assistance movement is rooted in the so-called "revolution of rising expectations", the current worldwide upsurge of depressed people to gain their freedom and abolish their old conditions of poverty, hunger, and misery. In this ferment, attended by the breaking up of numerous colonial empires, peoples not yet free are seeking independence, while those newly-free are struggling to build their economies, raise their standards of living, and become a part of the modern world. The response of the more advanced nations is their recognition that this world-wide drive for freedom and better living cannot be ignored without disregard of their own ideals and without exposing the world to chaos and disorder. Thus, many of the aid-receiving countries are the newly-free nations. Technical assistance is seeking to help them overcome their widespread poverty, lack of technological progress, inadequate administration, low productivity, poor education, poor health, and mass unemployment and underemployment.

Economic aid and technical assistance together inject into the economies of these countries essential investments in new productive activities, impart to them technical know-how for carrying forward this work, and help develop the educational and institutional services that are required to foster continuing improvement in the years ahead. The assistance is focused upon development work which will feed continuous progress. In each case the aim is to help set in motion the processes of self-generating advance. Most of the recipient countries, including India, conduct and manage their own foreign-assisted projects, frequently with technical assistance from foreign consultants.

The world's physical and economic resources are adequate for bringing the less-developed nations into a position of self-sustaining growth, if the advanced nations apply their will and ingenuity to the job. Apparently they have decided to do this. A number of governments, singly and through the United Nations, have committed funds and many technical experts and other workers to this task over the past fifteen years. The volume of these efforts has grown steadily. Worldwide thought is now being given to how to apply science and technology to the problems of agriculture, health, education, and industrial growth in the less advanced countries. National and international conferences are held to create firmer ground for plans and programmes in this field, and there is an increasing exchange of persons and ideas between East and West, North and South.

Reflecting the world concern with technical assistance is the designation of the 1960's as the "Development Decade". This was formally endorsed by the U.N. General Assembly in a resolution of 19 December, 1961, after being suggested by President Kennedy in a foreign aid message to the U.S. Congress in March of that year. The Development Decade embraces an effort by all nations to achieve "a substantial increase in the rate of growth, with each country setting its own target, taking as the objective a minimum annual rate of growth of aggregate national income of five per cent at the end of the Decade". This is an attempt to combine the resources of science and technology with the political goodwill of all nations.

The emphasis on science and technology in assistance was highlighted by a meeting in Geneva in February, 1963 which 1,800 delegates attended from 80 countries. This was a two-week United Nations Conference on the Application of Science and Technology for the Benefit of the Less Developed Countries. The conference was called by the United Nations Economic and Social Council to implement the objectives of the Development Decade. It was described by the National Planning Association of the United States as: "the first major international effort to link the tools of science and technology with the development requirements of the striving peoples of the emerging countries and to match the recent advances in science and technology to their specialized needs."

Paul G. Hoffman, from his wide experience in administering national and international aid programmes, has listed these six common denominators of underdevelopment: (1) Shortage of capital, (2) lack of knowledge of physical resources, (3) lack of trained people, (4) lack of organised programming and planning for development, (5) lack of productivity, and (6) rapidly expanding population.

Technical assistance and related aid have already resulted in substantial economic and social gains in many parts of the world—in India, South and Central America, the Middle East, Africa, and elsewhere. Dramatic results were demonstrated, of course, in the post-World War II reconstruction of European and other countries.

The opportunities are compelling and their realization is amply possible, though the job will not be easy nor quickly completed. Experience shows we must expect to encounter many difficulties and unfamiliar conditions in this work. Moreover, it is predictable that new problems will unfold as the work proceeds.

Much more is involved in technological advance than the placement of structures and equipment or the training of workers to use better tools and practices. Rendering and accepting expert technical assistance is a social process heavily dependent on human relationships and institutional factors. In every project, it involves bridging of the cultural and institutional gaps that stretch between the donor and receiver of assistance. It is concerned with imparting technical know-how to officials and peoples whose society, laws, governmental machinery, economic and social orientations, languages, customs and attitudes differ widely from those of the donor. Development of fuller experience, more research knowledge, and greater mutual understanding are major requirements for dealing with these problems.

Dispensing and accepting technical assistance are always a delicate matter for both participants. The roles of administrators and technicians share this condition, beginning with the earliest negotiations and continuing throughout the operational phases. A very high level of sympathy and understanding is required of the assistance-giving personnel in all attitudes and relationships with the receiving countries, their officials, and the peoples as a whole.

The sensitivity of nations in receiving outside help always colours the assistance picture. Many of the emergent countries are still wary of colonialism and are actively on guard against possible undue influence by other nations. They are rightly jealous of their hard-won opportunity to carve out their own destinies. Urgent need now compels them to seek help in speeding up their economic growth, but they are determined to safeguard their independence. Deeper understanding of these conditions is required of the givers of assistance and, at the same time, the basic requirements of technological improvement work need to be more adequately appreciated by the recipients. Mutual understanding and consideration are essential if these needs are to be met. They are of special concern to sociologists, of course, as scholars and workers in the field of human relationships. By appropriate attention to requirements in this field, they can do much to enable the necessary composition of interests, viewpoints, attitudes, and goals. There are also other major problems such as establishing of priorities, determining the size and pace of commitments, and finding enough resources and trained personnel in donor and receiving countries to carry forward their work.

Any programme of technical assistance carries with it certain problems for both donors and receivers. Since most scientific knowledge is in the public domain—a part of humanity's heritage from the past—developing countries may feel that they have a right to have it made available to them by countries in a position to do so—indeed, that this must be done if their growth is to be as rapid as necessary. Often, however, the would-be receivers of scientific know-how do not fully understand the many-sided actions that are involved in technological improvement. Some of their officials may feel that their old ways are best and that they need no help with know-how. Others may believe it best to create their own by research and experience and cultural borrowing. However, the countries' leaders want the help to speed up progress to the maximum. Too slow advance, they fear, would be disastrous.

The above facts are part of the background of development work everywhere and they apply to India, of course. We shall focus our discussion upon the assistance experience in India by illustrating from three fields in which technical assistance has been given there—agriculture, education, and administration. Necessarily, the role of foreign consultants will be given consideration.

India's case would seem to meet all six of the criteria laid down by Hoffman as evidences of underdevelopment. After the nation's successful struggle for Independence, her leaders saw immediately that assistance would be necessary to put the country on a stable modern footing, and that science and technology were essential aids to this end. Therefore, India's leaders early accepted the assistance of the United States and later of other countries. As a result, technical assistance in India now has a history of a full decade and more. We record some of the problems observed over these years as India has gradually enlarged the character and scope of outside help, and also certain recommendations looking toward improvement in assistance efforts.

Beginning with the Third Five Year Plan, India has accorded a place of highest priority to the increasing of agricultural production. Many outside agencies, public and private, have been rendering technical assistance in this field for some time. A predominantly agricultural country, India has the pressing task of growing more food for her expanding population and more fibre for her increasing industrial plant.

Foreign technical advisers have been asked to help in the agricultural development task. India has many highly-trained theoretical scientists, but they are rarely products of rural village

life or concerned with the use of technical know-how by cultivators. Even well-qualified agricultural scientists may have had
little if any experience in practical farming and in dealing with
farm people. Most such scientists are primarily concerned with
science rather than farming. Their training in colleges and universities in the past has often been lacking in field experience,
laboratory work, and certain experimental types of research. A
number of institutions are now giving more emphasis to farming.
But generally, the educated and non-village Indians have inhibitions against doing manual farm work such as is often required of
the good agricultural extension agent or teacher. There is a great
social distance between the educated agriculturalists and the
cultivators who need to learn better farming practices. These
factors make the rendering of technical assistance in agriculture
difficult for Indians, as well as outsiders.

In addition, the foreign consultant in agriculture has problems stemming from his own earlier environment. All too often,
he may wish to approach the problems of an unfamiliar culture
with ready-made solutions from back home, without adjusting
them to fit the conditions. For example, an American agricultural
technician might visualize the American extension structure in
agriculture and home economics as the precise mould and model
of what is needed for extension work in India. The fact that the
Stateside system of agricultural colleges, experiment stations, and
county agents is not now available in India nor will be possible
in the very near future, is surely something he should take into
account. This is an instance of non-feasible cultural borrowing.
India's agricultural institutions must first be planted in their own
context, and its agents of agricultural extension must be trained
to do the jobs that are needed and possible in India where agricultural extension education is carried to the village cultivators
through the community development programme.

If invited, the foreign consultant can advise on agricultural
curricula, practical applications of scientific know-how, training
of agricultural workers, and development of village institutions,
but he must also know and understand the Indian scene. He must
see that the Indian cultivator has to start where he is and gradually
adopt the improved practices he believes will help him up the
economic ladder.

The outsider must exercise both sympathy and patience. The task of increasing agricultural production is tremendous, urgent, and complex. As pointed out elsewhere, the barriers to change have deep foundations. Basic reforms in institutions, administration, land tenure, taxation, and management of physical resources are needed, as well as the growth and spread of scientific and technical knowledge. Although the consultant can help and can advise on these problems, he cannot interfere in or dictate the host country's solutions. He can help design simple agricultural implements; he can help establish soils laboratories; he can recommend the use of improved seeds, fertilizers, insecticides, and methods of planting and cultivation; he can assist in getting the message of better practices to cultivators; he can help demonstrate improved practices in the fields, and help get needed supplies to the farmers at the right times and in the right amounts. But the ultimate responsibility for the agricultural programme in India rests with the host country. The foreign consultant must learn to play his role in the light of this fact. He must have enough sympathy, understanding, and patience to do his work without overstepping the bounds of his assignment and his invitation to help.

In a democracy such as India is building, education is of over-riding importance. In education, as in agriculture, technical assistance is necessary. Although universal education, even at the primary level, is still a long way off, India has made progress in building more schools, training more teachers, and adapting curricula to development needs. These improvements are serving India increasingly well and hold rich promise for the future. In this broad effort, technical assistance in education can widen and hasten progress.

Technical and even material assistance to enlarge the quantitative side of education—more buildings, more teachers, more text-books—is far easier to provide than improving its quality. Quality improvements depend not only on resources, but also upon the intensity of education's motivation or will to change, to move to meet new needs, and to adopt methods and techniques that meet these needs. The old pattern of education which simply hands down the learning of the past by memorization, rote imitation, lectures and examinations simply cannot do the job required in a scientific and technical age. To be able to do their part in

India's advancement, her people must be taught to meet their problems, new and old, by learning to think for themselves, find answers, and make decisions that are fitted to their problems. India, like most developing countries, has an acute shortage of trained technicians. The most urgent short-term needs for technical people can probably be met by external assistance. However, all developing countries should endeavour to lay an adequate base immediately for training their own technicians and workers for development. This is probably the only way the long-run needs can be met.

India has accomplished a good deal in providing new and better educational opportunities in engineering and medicine, as well as in technical training at the secondary level. A better job has been done in this area than in providing quality education on a broad base or in providing adequate specialized training in the crucial field of agriculture. Much closer attention needs to be paid to the training and use of manpower to meet urgent development needs and to mitigate the existing problems of great numbers of "educated unemployed"—too many young people "educated" inadequately or for unspecialized occupations. Also, far more effort should go into education of adults to enable them to contribute to the development of the country.

Max Millikan, in a recent symposium entitled *Restless Nations*, has said on this aspect of development, "... For economic development to proceed rapidly, the underdeveloped countries must, as a matter of national policy, devote much more attention to adult education than is necessary in the United States and Western Europe. In the underdeveloped countries an exceedingly small fraction of the labor force possesses the education necessary to operate a modern economy.... If we were to rely exclusively on the education of school-age children to change our capital stock of educated human beings, an underdeveloped country with little education in the past, which adopted today universal primary education and extensive secondary education, would require thirty or forty years to bring its entire labor force up to the educational levels needed to operate a modern economy. This is too long to wait. Clearly special measures are needed to raise the educational level of the existing labor force..."

This matter of "special measures" in education has particular relevance to the responsibilities of educational advisers and consultants. It is not only in the field of adult education that special measures, or imaginative new techniques, are needed; new methods of teaching are needed in all levels and branches of education. Foreign educators, if they are to render fruitful assistance, must be able to develop and employ teaching methods and techniques which have direct usefulness to the people. They must also be well trained and truly anxious to meet the demands of an assignment that requires all the energy, skill, ingenuity, and determination they can muster. Donor countries offering technical assistance in education should make sure that the educators they recruit have these attributes.

Administration is one of the weak spots in many developing countries. Contributing factors in this are the past colonial status, deficiencies in educational systems, and the magnitude of the problem of expanding slow-paced economies by means of fast-moving programmes.

India, more fortunate than most of the others, made her start on the road of independence with a well-trained cadre of civil servants and an on-going administrative structure. These have been great assets. However, it is also true that the needs and purposes for which this administrative system was created originally are different in many respects from those of a development-seeking society. Her administrative people are largely those trained for law enforcement and revenue collection. Very few are trained or experienced in implementing planned programmes of economic and social improvement. As a result, although programmes are carefully planned, there is a serious lack of follow-through in administration. Technical assistance is needed in this field to help reduce the rigidity of the structure, smooth out operating procedures, and encourage bolder and speedier decision-making at the policy levels. There is need also for training of administrators for effective communication with personnel who are responsible for carrying out specific activities.

Foreign technicians in public administration can advise on efficient operating procedures and provide counsel on the training of administrative personnel. They can also help Indians look ahead to the needs of the future, so that enough trained people will then be available. They cannot administer the programmes, but can help smooth the road their hosts must take to carry out programmes faster and more efficiently.

The first big hurdle the Western consultant in any field of assistance encounters in India is in understanding and adjusting to a very different culture. No matter how learned and skilled he may be in his field, he must acquire different ways of doing and thinking before he can find common ground with those he is to serve. For the technician new on the scene, it takes time to perceive the difference between the India that is an old culture bound by age-old rigidities and the India that is a new republic with more than a decade of expanding experience in development. As he begins to understand the universe of his operations, he realizes that he has much to learn before he can be an effective teacher or consultant. He needs to understand what changes are desirable and seek ways of obtaining them that make sense to India.

In the field of social relationships, the job of the foreign specialist is especially difficult. While most leaders of developing countries freely admit that social development is necessary to catalyze economic development, is in fact an integral part of total development, and that modern technical know-how must accompany the modern technology they seek, few realize that validated knowledge exists in the area of human relationships. Some simply fail to recognize that they need this specialized know-how, or they feel that they already possess it. While rapport and real understanding are frequently hard to establish for the specialist in human relationships, nevertheless the field is one in which known methods and techniques can be borrowed by those willing to use them, while technologies cannot easily be borrowed. Social skills can be learned and applied as well as engineering or accounting skills and methods, but factors such as status, sensitivity, misunderstanding due to incomplete communication often intervene in their successful adoption by recipients of social technical assistance.

For some reason, few social scientists are sent abroad for training in the field of social skills. Even those who do receive this training are rarely given an opportunity to use it after they return. This is sometimes due to the fact that positions needing these skills are already filled by people of high status who will not or cannot be replaced or shifted to other jobs. The training is therefore wasted and the skills are not transmitted and diffused to others needing them. It is our judgment that the kind of social skills developed in dynamic, democratic societies, where individuals and groups through free communication and widespread vertical mobility, participate actively in local and national affairs, can be learned and can be used to advantage in India.

Because most technicians are assigned to India for initial periods of two years, they arrive with a sense of urgency in advancing their areas of work. Many undergo an initial shock when they find that the ground has not been well prepared for them or that they are not enthusiastically received by the Indians they are to assist. It usually takes time for a maturing of viewpoint that permits the adviser to recognize he is in India because the country has far-reaching plans for development; that the individuals to whom he is assigned may or may not yet be oriented to change; that his role is quietly to assist the Indian officials and technical staff in development work whenever possible, despite the difficulties; and that helping overcome these difficulties is a part of his task.

Foreign advisers may not be effective immediately on arrival. The successful ones have often had to "sell" themselves and to "prove" first that they had a contribution to make. Too frequently, the burden of creating positive collaboration has rested on the foreigners and their countries, agencies, and institutions. The experts have been forced to explore their own ways to contribute to programme development and execution, often encountering officials who are not change-oriented and who view change as threatening their security and status.

The skilled consultant must move slowly and carefully while he sizes up the work that is needed, the special conditions in India, and his position in the scheme of things. If he sees that his Indian associates are thinking of "business as usual", instead of improvement, he does some rethinking. He does not immediately conclude that, since he cannot do all he had hoped on a rapid and orderly schedule, he should go back home. Neither does he give up trying and merely live out his assignment in uselessness. Instead, he realizes he is simply meeting with some of the difficulties of a tradition-bound society, and that his assignment is to thread his way through these to assist with the improvements which are possible and to improve the climate for change. He sees this job as tough and challenging, involving many problems and stresses outside of his field of specialization, as well as inside.

Viewing his role thus, he sees that he will succeed in it only to the extent he helps his Indian co-workers develop, promote, and carry out constructive action. He will welcome their reshaping his suggestions and advancing them as their own. He will push ahead in seeking progress, doing so with tactful self-effacement. He will know that it is his job to assist India's development, not to build up a score of personal touchdowns. The desire for personal recognition on an item-by-item basis has little place. The consultant must plant and cultivate ideas in the minds of others, help them gain recognition for these ideas, and assist them in organising and implementing the needed action. Adequate credit for his own services will come in due time and in broad terms. His greatest contribution may well turn out to be not a specific plan or programme but the in-service training of his co-workers through the patient and tactful imparting of new ideas and skills.

India's Planning Commission and the Five Year Plans have provided the means for deciding whether technical assistance is to be requested, the kinds needed, the Ministry that will receive and utilize it. The Planning Commission's aim has always been to apply foreign technical assistance either to specific items in the Plan or to pioneering of certain work for inclusion in the next one. It has continuously tried to channel technical assistance toward priority programmes, and to assure that each of the assisting countries, agencies, or institutions works in its areas of competence. Little duplication of effort by the givers of assistance has occurred. Usually, India's desire for help in implementing the Plans has been greater than the outside resources available. The work of the Planning Commission has been of extraordinary value in guiding the effective use of foreign assistance.

There are several reasons why better use has not been made of assistance. Importantly, there has been inadequate realization that the acceptance of foreign assistance implies that administrative effectiveness will be provided and that, through it, policies and personnel will be dynamically oriented.

Sensitivity concerning expert counsel by foreigners has often been observed. Both officials and workers have been sensitive about being the direct recipients of expert help. Many have seemed to feel that being assigned such assistance implied that, in the eyes of their superiors and colleagues, they were inadequate for their jobs, rather than regarding it as signifying a privileged opportunity to work with colleagues of recognized competence and stature.

Care to select development-minded officials, as well as those who are conscious of the opportunity given, is necessary for new activities. However, in the absence of advance explanation and orientation for the officials of a new programme, narrow reactions are all too understandable. Only in rare instances has such an official been asked about his feelings *before* a consultant arrived. Even more rarely has he been given an adequate explanation of the role of the adviser and of the pioneering nature of the new work. Often he is simply informed that a foreign expert will be assigned to him and his programme, under terms of an appointment made at higher levels. Under these circumstances, the official may merely accept the adviser and make no effort to use him to best advantage. Experience emphasizes that it is essential for the official to be adequately oriented in advance as to the importance of his programme, his leadership role in assuring its success, the function of the consultant in helping him, and the opportunity given him for advancing his own effectiveness.

It is possible that the services of technical advisers are accepted in some cases only because India's leaders sense a possibility of political or economic embarrassment in declining. We believe this is a factor more frequently than either of the participants would care to admit. In some cases, it would explain a lack of high-level concern for creating the conditions for effective work.

Paralleling the need for proper orientation of the advisers, Indian programme officials also need training and orienting in the philosophy, requirements, and techniques of change, as well as in the purposes of their programmes. Those who are to work with foreign consultants need this particularly. The officials know their administrative mechanisms and procedures and are able to make sound decisions, but may not be aware of the new requirements of new programmes. Also, they are likely to be relatively unfamiliar with the processes of building public understanding and participation in development, of effectively communicating ideas and recommendations to the people, of helping them to adopt changes widely and voluntarily, and of then working with them to bring about programme changes which the people want.

Along with a general policy of accepting technical assistance, India has always agreed in principle that she should assign one or more co-workers to each foreign adviser. The idea behind this has been that official decisions must be made by the Indians, and that the direct association of designated officials with the consultants will help transmit to India the techniques and skills of the foreigner. But long delays have occurred in designating some of the counterpart workers. In some instances, appropriate officials could not be freed from existing posts and, in others, the designated counterparts have been transferred to other work in the middle or at the end of the foreign consultant's assignment.

Over-all, it should be realized that the concept of development is still relatively new to India. Its officials have limited experience in development work and therefore have few benchmarks to go by in using technical assistance. In the long run, further experience by the officials, with increasing orientation to development purposes, can be expected to bring improvements.

Growth of public understanding and support for developmental change will also help. This growth is under way, in all probability. Also, the thousands of Indian students studying abroad, and the several hundred specialists and officials going abroad each year for training are potentially valuable channels for dissemination of new ideas and aspirations, as well as scientific knowledge. Means are needed now to assure that ideas and information brought in by these people are adequately aired and discussed. This is part, of course, of the over-all task of opening more windows to the winds of knowledge.

Based on observations in India during the past decade, we suggest that constructive, collaborative thought is in order for both donors and recipients of assistance. Their mutual commitment to certain basic points is recommended. Some of these are indicated below:

Recognizing that India and all newly-developing nations need foreign technical assistance, each new project should be looked at closely in terms of whether such assistance is really desired. If it is not, it should be withheld or re-channelled to projects where it is wanted and will be used effectively. There are enough projects for which technical guidance is truly wanted that this would pose little problem for either of the parties in assistance undertakings. Technical assistance resources are too scarce and valuable for either party to sanction their unwanted and ineffective use. It should be possible to concentrate assistance in the areas of mutual and thorough agreement.

Next, all should recognize that technical assistance succeeds or founders on the basis of the human relationships on both sides. High quality personnel, properly oriented and well trained for the purposes of the individual programmes, should be selected as foreign consultants and as their counterparts. As the host country conducts and administers each programme, it has a strong interest in selecting high quality programme leaders and administrators.

Avoidance of delays in staffing should be provided for and agreed upon. There should be agreement that all key staff members, project by project, will be recruited and actually placed on the job at the right locations before the programme starts. Without some such approach, the staffing up of key workers can drag along interminably and do lasting harm to the programme.

Also, the donor needs to work out specific agreements with the recipient country to assure that each project will have an administrative structure which will use the project's technical experts efficiently. Without adequate administrative support and without the help of development-oriented administrative and operating personnel, the services of advisers can be substantially nullified. If the assistance negotiators were correct in the first place, such failure can be expected to diminish or prevent the success of the project. New programmes in new fields can seldom be piloted into modern channels and given technical vigour and soundness without effective expert guidance.

Agreement on project goals is another need. A memorandum of agreement and understanding should be jointly formulated and approved by the participants, fully outlining the purposes and methods of operation for each project. The responsibilities of the aid-giving and aid-receiving countries, agencies, and institutions should be set forth in detail. In light of the wide differences in culture, attitudes, and procedures of the agreeing parties, little of importance should be left undefined. The qualifications and job descriptions for the staffs of Indian programmes should also be specified, as well as the methods to be used in programme evaluation. In India, some governmental unit should be assigned the responsibility of making sure that the Ministry implementing the programme will, in fact, meet the government's commitments.

The agreement should embody a realistic understanding as to the length of time the programme will take to achieve its objectives and the period for which foreign technicians will be required. The agreement should also spell out the priority of each project among the total and give some indication of priorities within the programme. Too many programmes are retarded by undertaking too many things at once, or by not doing enough at the appropriate times. Outlining of specific steps in the beginning can eliminate confusion, delay, and dispersion of effort.

Experience shows that the personnel assigned to projects will not always be action-minded or change-oriented. Therefore, the principals concerned in assistance should agree in advance upon the major-action steps which are anticipated. The needed changes should be highlighted. Such agreement can help to lessen early tensions and foster effective work from the start.

In India, the joint commitments for development work should guarantee that key programme workers at the Centre, State, and district levels will remain on the job for specified periods of time. Advance arrangements should prevent such assignments from penalizing staff members in status, promotions, pay allowances, travel pay, and amenities of family living. Also, there should be agreement that administrative responsibility for each programme will be so placed as to assure that decisions can be made and implemented promptly, and that the programme will be integrated into the administrative bureaucracy. Provision should be made for an annual review of the year's work and a projection of work for the year ahead. Each year's review report should indicate the major problems which must be solved to ensure the programme's success. The report should be subjected to an annual policy review by the Government of India and the aid-giving agency, as agreed upon.

Both donor and recipient of technical assistance should feel convinced that each project undertaken is necessary, feasible, and

a key part of the over-all strategy of development. This consideration should be weighed carefully by both parties and the views
of both should receive careful attention. Both are seeking progress, both want to maximize the fruitfulness of the resources used.
In assessing the importance of project proposals, due weight
should be given to the recipient's need for projects which can
catalyze the interest of its people. Programmes for awakening
popular support for change should not be avoided or unduly
discounted.

A further point is that assistance should be projectable in
advance. Nearly everyone agrees that assistance is maximized
when it is based on specific, continuing periods of time. As
Barbara Ward has pointed out, " 'On again, off again' assistance,
on an indeterminate and inadequate scale, has no chance of either
stimulating or underpinning a properly conceived economic
strategy and a coherent body of reform." Present patterns of
assistance are not immutable. Responsible people have urged
greater emphasis on multilateral assistance, instead of the usual
bilateral aid programmes. Others have suggested that, instead of
assisting specific projects, it would be better to support "country
plans," or regionwide plans. But if changes are to be made, they
should be known far ahead of time.

A further suggestion has been made by Dr. C. D. Deshmukh
of India and is supported by others. Dr. Deshmukh has said: "It is
essential that each recipient country should become a donor country, at least in a small way, as soon as it can. This is necessary not
only to enable the lesser developed countries to get the benefit
of a bigger pool of aid, but also to enable the recipient country
to understand the attitudes and dealings of a donor country."

A great deal has been learned in recent years about how to
spread the know-how of technicians. This knowledge is shared
by donor and receiving governments, agencies, and institutions.
Proper evaluation of this experience, with consequent improvements in operations, can contribute much to the speed of development.

As Barbara Ward has said: " . . . the concept of an international effort to hasten and complete the world-wide revolution of
modernization is new. It contradicts imperialism in the most

precise sense. Its aim is to make the local community not more but less dependent upon outside support. . . "

A further element is involved in the worldwide agreement and determination that assistance is to be given to newly-developing countries. John Lindeman, in discussing "The Magnitude and Complexity of Technical Assistance," says . . . "for the first time, there is a consensus that the transfer of technical knowledge and skills should be purposefully arranged by the governments of the more advanced countries (whether acting bilaterally or multi-laterally) so as to contribute to realizing the economic and social development aspirations of the less advanced ones—the aspirations being defined, by and large, by the governments of the less advanced countries themselves. The purpose is broad; the relationship is one of government-to-government (or international agency to government)." These new elements of urgency and magnitude make it imperative that donors and recipients of technical assistance, whether public or private, take a hard look at the problems involved and renew their efforts to make this necessary flow of technical assistance a significant and fruitful contribution to the "Development Decade".

Underlying many of the situations described here are key uncertainties in the field of human relationships. India, as in the case of other recipient countries, seems slow to trust the outsider's role and skills in this field, either in administration or agricultural development. The donors, for their part, are convinced from their experience that skills in creating understanding, teamwork, and enthusiasm in developmental endeavour are essential to its success. That these problems have their present importance in technical assistance is a strong indication, no doubt, of the need for much greater mutual concern with them, supported by fuller consultations and more operations-oriented research.

MAIN AUTHORITIES QUOTED OR CITED

Restless Nations, A Study of World Tensions and Development, (Symposium), Geo. Allen and Unwin Ltd., London, 1962.

Looking Ahead, Vol. 10, No. 8, November, 1962, National Planning Association, Washington, D.C., "The Magnitude and Complexity of Technical Assistance" by John Lindeman.

Looking Ahead, Vol. 11, No. 2, March, 1963, National Planning Association, Washington, D.C., "World Mobilization for Growth".

CHAPTER 27

PROBLEMS AND PROCESSES OF BUILDING A NATIONAL DEMOCRATIC SOCIETY

WE have discussed at various points in this book the ways in which India was, in 1950, an underdeveloped country. She was in some ways less developed, and in some ways more developed, than would be indicated by her rank among other nations in the array of statistics compiled to show the comparative status of the nations of the world. We have not attempted, by use of these statistics, to place India on a continuum running from underdeveloped to developed status, because many culturally and socially significant factors valued by a people cannot be portrayed in statistics. Furthermore, where India may rank by any statistical measurement among the other nations of the world is not among the main concerns of those leaders of India who drafted her Constitution and who are formulating and guiding her future development. There are, however, important facts of life and living revealed by such statistical measurements which not only condition the path India has planned to follow, but which, unless altered, will make it impossible for her to evolve the kind of society she has clearly stated her intention to become.

Of all of the many goals toward which India's development programmes are pointed, the supreme goal is the type of society she is attempting to build or evolve. That goal was clearly stated in the Constitution she adopted in 1949, in which it was declared that the "people of India" had "solemnly resolved to constitute India a Sovereign Democratic Republic." The First Five Year Plan declaring that only democratic methods would be employed in national development programmes, and describing the methods by which this would be done, said:

"An underdeveloped economy is characterised by the co-existence, in greater or less degree, of unutilised or under-utilised manpower on the one hand and of the unexploited natural resources on the other.... But the basic premise of democratic planning is that society can develop as an integral whole and that the position which particular classes occupy at any given time—a product of various historical forces for which no individual or class as such can be held responsible—can be altered without reliance on class hatreds or the use of violence. . . . If the people are to be trained to be the builders of the future, the works have to be entrusted, even at certain risks, to the people themselves through their representative agencies. . . "

We shall only delineate and analyze the social problems which in 1950 were inherent in the conditions existing at that time and the social processes which would need to be employed to transform those conditions into ones that would be prime requisites of the type of society envisioned and prescribed by the Constitution.

In the early part of this book we described some of the most obvious benchmarks from which India launched her planned development programme. Apart from a description of India's social structure and a discussion of planned change, we have not provided any clue to the deeper social and cultural problems which would be inherent in a programme of vast and diverse change. Had we attempted to give exposition to these problems, we would have assumed the task of answering the questions which Jawaharlal Nehru, a number of years before India gained her Independence, sought to answer, namely:

"What is this India, apart from her physical and geographical aspects? What did she represent in the past? What gave strength to her then? How did she lose that old strength? And has she lost it completely? Does she represent anything vital now, apart from being the home of a vast number of human beings? How does she fit into the modern world?"

It would be presumptuous for us to describe in any detail the type of society which India desires to build. It is neither presumptuous nor audacious, however, to identify and discuss the problems inherent in India's task of moving from the social conditions prevailing at the time she gained Independence to the time when she hopes to approximate the model for a democratic society portrayed in her Constitution, and to which she has dedicated all her development programmes. All that is required to indicate the inherent problems is to describe the most basic social characteristics and the principal imperatives in the development of that model-type democratic society.

All democratic societies are *open-class* societies, in which no person is denied the right to change his class status. Diversified economies and social opportunities help him to do so. Millions of persons by vertical mobility change social status to the extent they become aware of these opportunities. Large numbers of those who become aware of these opportunities grasp them eagerly. Widespread, successful vertical mobility thus depends as much on the development of a *communicative society* as it does on the development of an open-class society. It becomes a truly democratic society only to the extent that it also becomes a *mass consumption society*, and it can become a mass consumption society only to the extent that economic and social opportunities are many and diversified. It must, therefore, also be a pluralistic or a *pluralist society*, in which many persons can move in various directions and participate in different types of undertakings and achievements. All modern truly democratic societies are open-class societies in which vertical mobility is widespread. They are also communicative, pluralistic, and mass consumption societies.

In an open-class society, social status is most often symbolized either by the possession of wealth or by demonstrated merit in the performance of economic, social, and political services. Because of this, some persons during their lifetime move up the status ladder and, over generations of time, some drift down the ladder or lose high social status. Such movements provide evidence that inherited social status is not a sine qua non for holding positions in the day-by-day operation of the social order. The opportunity for upward mobility of millions of persons, however, creates and maintains the dynamics of open-class societies. It is not only the multiplied zests of those who enjoy the social and economic dividends of steadily-improving status, but the expectations of practically all others that they can enjoy these dividends, which automatically create dynamics in the whole social order. Even though no social order is ever completely egalitarian, the fact that no social position in society is foreclosed to any person is a prerequisite for the continuous but increasing dynamics of democratic societies.

Theoretically, it is impossible for any person to change his status, in a closed, class-structured society. Theoretically, it is possible for any person to change his status in an open-class society. But neither of these absolutes maintains in any society. There are persons in open-class societies whose capabilities to climb the status ladder are adversely conditioned by circumstances created by others, and it is definitely known that there are cases of change in status and even changes in caste in Indian society. The major differences in these two situations are the means by which status is changed and the assumption, even expectation, that the status of many individuals will change during their life-time. Furthermore, in an open-class society even the criteria of status change. In a caste society, they change infrequently and in many cases not at all. The chief means for change in status of most persons in an open-class society are education and increased economic income.

Vertical mobility is the means, or the process, by which persons change their relative position in the status structure or on the status ladder in their society. If millions of relatively socially-isolated persons in India are to be vertically mobile, they must be helped to be capable of vertical mobility. The problem is not only one of education but of communication. This is the problem of how to make all, or a great majority, of the people aware of the opportunities which their evolving society is creating and will increasingly create. The mental horizons of these people must be widened and they must be given higher expectations than they now have. The opportunities for vertical mobility must be known to them and they must be assisted to grasp these opportunities successfully. How great the task of creating these opportunities is in India can be at least partially portrayed by an assessment of what portion of the population is now in each status class. Even without any precise quantitative measurement, it is universally known that the vast majority of the people of India are in what Lloyd Warner describes as the "lower-lower" class in American society. India will not become even nominally an egalitarian society until the majority of her people are, and know that they are, in the middle class.

In most cases in India, vertical mobility of members of the lower class is accomplished only by horizontal mobility. A person seldom changes social status if he remains in the local community where he was born and where his caste status is known by everyone. If and when, however, he moves to a larger community, especially to a large urban centre, and when he changes his occupation, he is measured as a person more by what he can do than who he is. The fabric of these human relationships in which he participates is more impersonal but more conducive to his demonstrating his personal merit. A person's opportunity to advance in social status by horizontal mobility is greatly enhanced if he has enough education to prepare him to play one of the many new roles required in an increasingly industrialized and commercialized economy. If he has no such training, and moves to an urban centre, he only swells the number of slum dwellers, lives in a ghetto populated by lower class people, and although his wages have increased, his social status has not. Even if an urban-dwelling rural migrant has had some schooling in his village, he may not be capable of competing successfully with better-trained urban persons for a more honorific clerical position; his school training alone does not prepare him to advance very many steps up the ladder of social status. Capacity for entrepreneurship does. Thus in India's increasingly industrialized and commercialized economy, entrepreneurship shares with education the continuing capacity for advancing one step after another upward in social status.

In open-class societies, entrepreneurs, small and large, constitute the middle class, the status attained by those who move up from the lower class. This has been the case in India. But those in India's middle class are few in comparison to those still remaining in the lower class, whereas in an open-class society the majority of persons and families are members of the middle class, and furthermore are proud to claim middle-class status. There probably will be no better index in the future to India's progress toward the objective of developing a democratic social order than the progress made in increasing the percentage of her people who can legitimately claim to be members of the middle class.

Good communication between all classes and all sectors of the national population, and especially between the leaders and the masses, is a prerequisite not only for a functioning democracy but for a development programme which operates concurrently on all levels of society. In an open-class society this is not too difficult. Some of the many persons, who in a single generation have moved upward in social status, are distributed on each level of society; or at least a number of persons, who were born on lower levels, are now on some one of the higher levels. There is thus a chain of inter-personal relationships, and there can be a chain of inter-personal communication, connecting all levels of society. Whether communication is from the bottom up or from the top down, each person is able to communicate with someone who is not too socially and culturally distant from him. At the present time, this is not the case in India. Because of this, effective communication between the two classes is difficult. It is, therefore, necessary for development programme leaders to attempt to travel downward over the great social distance which exists between them and the lower classes whom they seek to serve.

This matter of social distance is not appreciated, or even believed, by most of India's top and intermediate leaders. Due to no fault of their own, they have never participated in a society in which relatively uninhibited and free conversation is frequent between those living at different levels of society. It is, of course, not often, in even the most open-class societies, that persons from the top of the social status ladder are in actual conversation with some member of a group on one of the lowest rungs of that status ladder. But there are almost countless rungs on that ladder of vertical mobility and almost imperceptible differences between persons who occupy adjacent rungs. Such persons are by and large on common ground. It is not only that there is uninhibited and free conversation between them, but neither participant talks up or down to the other and communication is thus reciprocal. While such communication is not frequent between the members of the highest and lowest classes, what may be called a chain of this type of conversation runs from top to bottom and from bottom to top of the whole society. A society functioning in this way is truly a communicative society.

A prerequisite to becoming a communicative society is that all members of the society become literate as nearly and as quickly as possible. Mass literacy and mass means of communication are necessary to a communicative society and also to a truly national society functioning as a social entity. In some developing countries, means of ready communication, or even a national system of transportation, may be as great a need as mass literacy. Without all three, national integration is bound to be tenuous; with all three, there can be national unity in the face of great social diversities.

In the final analysis, justification for recognizing that a democratic or dynamic society must be a communicative society is the well-known general tendency of traditional societies to conformity, which is due largely to the unawareness of the masses that there are alternatives to their present ways of living and making a living. These masses, living in relative isolation, not in communication with the larger sectors of the society in which they also live, do not know all the ways in which national developments are opening new opportunities to them. This must be effectively communicated to them. At the moment, the prime means of communication is face-to-face, inter-personal communication. Rather than to assume that the first major step in this direction awaits the development of mass means of communication, a more valid assumption is that the effective employment of mass means of communication awaits the contribution of the great volume of face-to-face, word-of-mouth communication which can, and should, be made in the effective, day-by-day operation of the rural development programme.

The reasons why a large democratic society must be pluralistic are very different from the reasons why it must be a communicative one. Mass communication which effectively reaches all the people of a nation could be as effectively employed to build a totalitarian society as it could be to build a democratic society. It is in fact employed by totalitarian regimes to develop mass national sentiment and nationalistic societies. In doing so, these regimes disregard and, by design sabotage, all diversities of both sentiments and social organisations. A democratic society attempts to build a national society out of a great diversity of social groups functioning on all levels of society. A society of great diversity of groups and diversity of sentiments can be a national society only by being a pluralistic society. It is only through the self-organised efforts of a great variety of groups that the manpower and dedicated interests of the many persons who constitute the population of a great society can be effectively mobilized. It is, therefore, an asset, not a liability in the task of building a democratic national society, to have some, in fact a great many, groups whose primary interest is that of local community or local area improvement. It is an advantage that many of these groups are voluntarily organised, not organised by directives from government, or assigned tasks by some higher authority.

A pluralistically-structured society, with a great number and many different kinds of groups operating at all levels of social action, does not function as a hierarchy and cannot be directed as such, but pluralism is a characteristic of the structure of all free societies. That structure is a concatenation of various kinds and levels of associated persons, each level of association having objectives of its own, but all levels functionally linked in a greater association which constitutes a national society. It most effectively generates maximum individual and group initiative and responsibility, and thus mobilizes the manpower and the interests, of approximately all those who compose the society. Local groups develop and effectively utilize self-chosen leaders on all levels of social action. They undertake many improvement projects at various levels of social action. Numerous persons, even though they live in local communities, also participate in wider group action. Some of them participate in State-wide and nationwide group action. It is primarily through such persons, coming from the bottom up, not through governmental official administration, that a democratic national society is evolved.

Not only small but large special-interest groups have evolved in every free society which has evolved a price-market economy. They have developed because communication is possible between persons who are engaged in the same enterprises and occupations, although living in many different local areas, and because they have become aware of their common interests and purposes. It probably is inevitable that some of these groups are "vested interest" groups, their purposes confined largely to promoting selfish interests. But in a pluralistic, communicative society, the purposes of many special-interest groups are altruistic. In such a society, there is at least one such group or association voluntarily and effectively seeking to implement practically every interest and purpose which government seeks to promote and implement. The groups are composed of persons from many local areas who form associations to promote and implement education, health, or welfare programmes. Historically, they have pioneered in programmes which governments have been slow to undertake, or have not had funds to implement.

It is true that such State and national special-interest groups very often, if not always, become pressure groups. But it has been through their pressure, lobbying for State and national legislation and popular propaganda, that so-called open-class, pluralistic societies have become progressively more and more welfare societies, and governments have tended to become welfare States. At this moment in India's development programmes, we would say that the two issues are: first, the capacity of national and State plans progressively to meet the felt needs of the various sectors of the national population; and second, the capacity of members of the elite corps of programme administration to share the responsibility for development with voluntarily-organised groups on all levels of development.

The final test of the economic viability, and thus the social and political viability, of a national society is its capacity to produce consumer goods and services, and thus be a mass consumption society. Measures of this capacity are gross national product and *per capita* income. In a democratic society, there is the added measure of how nearly equally the *per capita* income is distributed. There are evidences over the last few decades that the attempt to guarantee something approaching equality of income has not been successful in totalitarian societies, even though they have considerably increased their gross national product. There are many evidences that democratic societies can come much closer to being mass consumption societies. One reason is that the economic as well as social organisation of democratic societies is pluralistic, composed of hundreds of types of enterprises and thousands of entrepreneurs.

If Indian society is to evolve in the direction of the democratic goal stated in her Constitution and toward which all her planning aims, she will develop the major characteristics, or requisites, of a dynamic society, briefly discussed above. India has already moved a considerable distance out of a subsistence agriculture and village economy toward and into a price-market national economy. As she moves further in this direction, the inevitable concomitants of such an economy will evolve. Agriculture will become more commercialized. Industrially-employed persons will provide larger markets for farm products and industrially-produced goods will be purchased by village people. Many new occupations will develop and specialization in them will proliferate. Many of the new occupations, which will be recognized as essential to the economy, will be valuable and recognized as such, and therefore honorific. This will create opportunity for economic and social vertical mobility. Migration of rural persons to urban areas will not only make it possible for them to learn new skills and enter new occupations, but will establish many personal contacts between rural and urban people, including market contacts which will rapidly multiply the opportunity for, and practice of, communication. Diversified and specialized occupational and economic interest groups will evolve for mutual support and protection. Economic communalism will increase, and isolated, locality communalism will be relatively less dominant. All these things are concomitants of the evolution from a simple to a complex economy.

It is relatively easy to observe the still spotted, but gradual, shift in India's rural economy away from the "jajmani" system by which the various tasks in a village were divided between the different occupational groups, and the economic and social dividends were distributed among the various families in the community. It is not yet so easy to observe with any precision the way in which the economic and social dividends of the steadily-increasing price-market economy are being divided. The patterns which India will build may not identically follow those of other now-advanced democratic societies. Indeed the patterns of all well-developed democratic societies are not identical, but each such society does have the four basic characteristics we have been discussing.

None of the advanced democratic societies is completely classless, but their classes are not castes. Vertical mobility is prevalent. They are all communicative, pluralistic, mass consumption societies. We believe India is making progress in the direction of developing all of these proven requisites of a dynamic democratic society. Evidences are that this is true, but there are also many evidences that it is not yet entirely true.

It would be easy to start our consideration of the basic problems and processes of social and economic programmes of change with two broad generalizations, both of them valid, but neither of them prescriptive for the future. The first generalization would be that the caste structure of Indian society is the chief hurdle in the path of developing a democratic, dynamic society. A caste structure is the direct opposite of an open-class structure and likewise the chief hurdle in the path of vertical mobility. It is bound to sabotage the rapidity of group realignment which is essential in the development of a pluralistic social order. It even dampens free communication between persons and classes, and thus thwarts the development of a freely-communicative society. The other broad generalization would be that the most basic social constant in the evolution of societies is change from traditionalism to modernism, from sacred to secular values, and from drifting to planning. But neither of these broad generalizations is very diagnostic. What is needed is an analysis of the ways in which "traditional values" and old forms of social structure condition the processes which are necessary to change.

We have pointed out the benchmarks from which planned change in India had to start, and we have stated what we believe are the basic characteristics, even the requisites, of the type of society India plans to evolve. We have listed categorically these four requisites in the following order—an open-class society, (one in which vertical mobility is easy and therefore widely prevalent), a pluralistic society, a communicative, and a mass consumption society. We are willing to hypothesize that India's programme of planned change, in its attempt to develop this kind of society, will prove that the order in which to promote development will be almost the reverse of the order in which we have listed the characteristics and prerequisites of a dynamic society.

The first task should be, and is, an attack on the problems of developing a mass consumption society. In pursuing this basic problem, India will learn how to do successfully the sorts of things which will speed up the development of the other three characteristics of a dynamic society. She will develop a pluralistic society in order to catalyze and use effectively the potential capabilities of hundreds of millions of her citizens, and hundreds of thousands of groups. It will become steadily more evident that the need for trained and skilled manpower cannot be met unless a rapidly-increasing number of her local citizens, by vertical mobility, move up to supply this ever-growing need. Everything possible will be done, in legal and other frontal attacks on the caste system, as an inevitable concomitant and consequence of purely practical processes essential to developing mass consumption. These efforts will steadily dilute, and probably ultimately destroy, the present closed caste system of Indian society. In the process by which India's economy shifts from its numerous little, relatively-isolated, subsistence agricultural enterprises to a national and world price-market economy, the whole society will develop the major characteristics and prerequisites of a dynamic society.

What is meant by purely practical processes in promoting mass consumption may be illustrated by India's experiences in her attempt to provide the first requisite, namely, an adequate food supply. Her practical attack on this problem was initiated in the multiple-purpose, community development programme in 1951. Among its purposes, an increase in agricultural production, to be accomplished by technical assistance in agricultural extension, was given the highest priority. The First Five Year Plan said it is:

> "of the essence of extension that the initial start is made with items whose usefulness to the cultivator in increasing agricultural production has been well established. It is only after sufficient confidence is gained that comparatively untried measures can be put forward, and even these should be held out as experiments until the people have found the answer for themselves."

The basic objective of the agricultural extension programme was to increase the nation's food supply, the first necessary step toward mass consumption. The experiences described earlier revealed that the programme was, for a number of years, far off the track because of attempts to provide amenities rather than to maintain emphasis on increasing agricultural production. Lessons learned from practical operating experience have now corrected many of these mistakes. At no time since the rural development programme was launched has the drive for increased agricultural production been so highly focused as at present.

This is not the only illustration of what India has learned from practical development experiences about moving steadily in the direction of evolving a dynamic and democratic society. The initiation of the Panchayati Raj programme was a direct result of accumulated experience which showed that the need for rapidly increasing food and other agricultural products was not being guaranteed under the sole directive of government administration. What is now called Panchayati Raj was at first called democratic decentralization, the objective of which was to decentralize responsibility, utilize and develop local area and local group initiative.

What we are saying is that the evidences are that India is moving in the direction of the development of a democratic society. This is partly because she is discovering, through experiences in her rural development programme, that neither logical planning which has been done, nor efficient bureaucratic administration which she has, accomplishes the basic task of increasing the food supply rapidly enough to greatly improve mass consumption.

This is not to say that planning has not been necessary, or that Indian planning has been illogical. It is not to deny that the rural development programme had to be initiated by Central government action and be directed by State and Central government administrators. It is to say that it has become evident that neither logical planning nor high-level bureaucratic administration engenders dynamics in the hundreds of millions of Indian people, nor intelligent and enthusiastic organisation of hundreds of thousands of organised, local-action groups. Only the willing and enthusiastic endeavour of each cultivator family to farm more efficiently will create widespread dynamics in rural areas. The development of hundreds of thousands of largely self-directed local groups will provide the foundation stones of a basic democracy. No matter how great the shortcomings of India's rural development programme, she has established the framework of a community development-extension programme which provides a vehicle, or machinery, by means of which rural progress can be carried forward by democratic methods and procedures. The building of this framework is an accomplished fact. Its effective utilization to increase agricultural production can and probably will make a major contribution, if not *the* major contribution, to the development of a democratic society in India.

The trained personnel now available through this framework to assist in the development of increased agricultural production, and to assist organised local self-help groups, consists of some fifty thousand local village workers and more than half of that number of technically trained persons located in development blocks. Now that the primary task of increasing agricultural production is clearly recognized, and the Panchayati Raj programme is being rapidly initiated, it should be taken for granted that the primary tasks of both village-level workers and the block programme personnel will be to work with the locally-initiated and planned improvement programmes.

In the Panchayati Raj programme, all programme personnel presumably will be working on projects which local groups have initiated and will be working with local bodies. To the extent that their activities are confined to extension work, local group formation, and local group assistance, and to the extent that they are released from carrying out tasks assigned by Central and State administrators, fifty thousand village workers and twenty-five thousand block employees can make a tremendous and increasingly-important contribution to both increased agricultural production and organised local group action. In addition to these major contributions, they will be agents of much needed communication between village people and official programme administrators and planners. The village-level workers' most immediate and most frequent upward contact will, of course, be with official programme personnel located in development blocks. Because the contacts of block development personnel will be not only with village-level workers but also with local people's organisations, they too will be in a favourable position to facilitate effective communication between rural people and overhead programme administration.

The favourable outlooks for development programme operation will not in and of themselves guarantee that Indian society will quickly develop all the characteristics, or requirements, of a democratic, and thus a dynamic, society. The carry-over of old cultural values and attitudes, of old class structures, and old practices of government bureaucracy will probably present more hurdles than facilities to rapid social change.

Development programme leaders and the rural people of India are learning about democratic methods from the trials, errors, and corrections in the operation of their rural development programme. The major correction they have made is to move away from too much dependence on the capacity of State and Central government administrators to mobilize and organise the co-operation of the millions of people who live in villages, and toward greater reliance on local initiative and local responsibility. National leaders have, from their own experience, become convinced of the great contributions that the hundreds of millions of villagers can, and must, make to the building of a viable national society; and believe that these contributions will be willingly and enthusiastically made only if and when local groups and local leaders are given major responsibility for the planning and direction of local economic and social improvement.

In addition to being a society of many villages, India, in 1950, was a society of many cultures. Out of these diversities, India is in the process of developing one national society. There is no complete correlation between the social order and the government of a nation. There are a number of large societies whose members belong to different cultural groups. There are a number of national governments which blanket several cultural areas and cultural groups. The only societies of which this is not true are small village or tribal ones concerning which it can be said that their culture, their society, and their government constitute one unity. In large national societies, culture or cultures induce one type of unity, the social structure another type, and government still another. Whatever unity each represents or induces is a different type of unity from the others. The only way a person on the ground can observe the existence and influence of any one of these unifying factors is to observe extensively and intensively how attitudes or values affect the behaviour of persons and groups. We add "groups" because they tend to perpetuate and enforce cultural values. In very small, isolated groups, enforcement is imperious; in very large groups, it is tenuous. In great national societies, enforcement is little more than symbolic.

This is not to say that what various erudite scholars have

written about India's culture has no validity, but that we have not, in our observation of behaviour, and in our conversations with persons on all levels of Indian society, been able to identify cultural values which will either facilitate or impede the development of national unity. The same cannot be said, however, of the social structure of Indian society.

The social structure of Indian society can be most easily observed in terms of caste, joint families, and village community institutions. Each of these is ancient. It is not only the deep loyalty which the joint family requires of its members, but the obligation which it imposes on them that makes it difficult for many persons to exercise their rights and obligations as citizens of a national society. The caste structure is not only a divisive influence in India, but the higher castes tend to constitute a power group on all levels of society and government. Even the super-loyalty to one's local village, while it does not inhibit a person's loyalty to his State and nation, does dilute his recognition of obligations to the national society.

The effective functioning of a national democratic government does not require that loyalties to all other levels of government and to all other social groups be abrogated. It does require that no element in the social structure subvert the principles and practices of democracy. A democratic government, like all kinds of national governments, is supposed to be an organ of society. But it can be an organ of a national society only if there *is* a national society. A new national government must, therefore, act as an agent and even an entrepreneur for the development of a national society. A national democratic government must be an entrepreneur for the development of a democratic society.

If and when the people of a given geographic area seek to organise a government, that is to be or to become a State, they grant to that government the authority to safeguard the integrity and harmony in the society whose organ or agent the State is. In exercising this authority, totalitarian governments and many colonial powers have attempted to force the various societies which they seek to govern into conformity with the will of those who govern. In such cases, the State, instead of being the agent of society, attempts to make society the agent of the State. This is the tendency of many newly-formed national governments.

Those who have formulated and founded the new governments were necessarily a corps of intellectuals, not the elected representatives of the masses. Once the new State is formed, even though its constitution provides for a democracy, there still remains the task of developing a democratic society. Only as rapidly as this is accomplished can or will the State be a democratic government.

One unique difference between government (a sovereign State) and a society or a culture, is that the State exercises the power of authority. No society or culture maintains itself and guarantees its continuity or even its integrity by authority. A State does. But there are sharp differences between a government which feels impelled to assume and exercise excessive authority not only as its right but as its bounden duty, and a government which recognizes that it is an organ or agent of society. The basis of these differences is from whence and from whom comes the grant of authority to the State. It is an historically significant fact that the founders of India's present national government, even though by necessity the intellectual elite of Indian society, decided that India would be a "Sovereign Democratic Republic," not a totalitarian State; that the authority which the State must necessarily exercise would be granted by the people themselves. Because of ineffective communication between the masses and the intellectual elite who framed the Constitution, this grant of authority by the people in India was bound to be only permissive. The processes by which it will become positively active are part and parcel of the processes of not only political but social and even economic development.

We have pointed out the differences between the nature of cultures, societies, and governments, and the interrelations between them, as a preface to our observations in India which have been chiefly of India's rural development programme. If we are to assess the problems of, and the processes by which, India will evolve a "Sovereign Democratic Republic", we must perforce attempt to assess the relationships of, and the interplay between culture, society, and the government, or the State. An analysis of these relationships cannot be meticulously or precisely made. We have found it difficult to observe, in the day-by-day operation of the rural development programme, the influence of either the power of old traditions or the purely social structure of Indian society. We are inclined to doubt that, as conditioning factors in India's transition from a "traditional" toward a "modern" society, these two are independent variables. We have, however, found it useful to attempt to observe them separately as they influence the problems and the processes of change.

India is an old civilization and as such has inherited the cultural products of a long past. She cannot disregard this heritage. She has had to start her planned development from where and what she was in 1950 as a culture, and as a society. It might seem easy to analyze her experiences by simply describing her culture and her society as of 1950 and then assessing her first ten years' experience in development in terms of the progress she has made in moving toward the type of society she is dedicated to evolving.

We have chosen to undertake this task of assessment by first presenting, as we did, the major benchmarks from which national development in 1950 began, followed by some observations on the problems posed by old social structures and, in some cases, by old traditions and values. We have also dealt directly with social and cultural factors as they have conditioned development programme action as, for example, the influence of social status on programme administration and some of the ways in which traditional practices of government have affected programme dynamics. Our observations are that India has, over the past decade, in a number of ways, progressed steadily in the direction of developing a democratic society, and by the use of democratic methods. We must, however, call attention to the ways in which old social structures have, and are, negatively influencing this progress. We cannot so clearly identify either the positive or negative effect of old cultural values.

The first important step India took toward building a democratic society was the formulation and adoption of a Constitution which guarantees that the national government and all State governments would be representative governments. It is sociologically significant that it was India's elite upper class who framed the national Constitution and formulated her First Five Year Plan. It is this elite class that administers her development programmes.

The next most obvious evidence of progress in building a democratic society is what is now happening at the other end of the social status scale. The Panchayati Raj programme has been launched and is spreading throughout the country. It is a daring experiment in raw democracy. Hundreds of thousands of village communities, and millions of village-chosen leaders, are not only being permitted but urged to accept responsibility for initiating and carrying out local development programmes. The training programme being conducted for members of panchayats is the largest adult education programme in any developing country in the world. For the first time, the lower classes of rural people are being requested to give free expression to their felt needs and are being counselled about what they can do, and what they think their government can and should do, to help them meet these needs. This programme, too, was initiated by State and national leaders, but has prospects of becoming a real people's movement. The extent and speed of development of this movement will dictate the speed with which a new pyramid of Indian social structure is built from the bottom up, and ultimately the extent to which India's government personnel are recruited by the process of vertical mobility, steadily but surely rising from lower to higher social status.

In addition to the Constitution's provisions for a democratic form of government, and the substantial progress already made in establishing people's units of local government, the guarantee of universal suffrage has made possible the staging of three great national elections, in each of which more persons have participated than in any other country in the world. In each succeeding election, there has been increasing evidence of discriminating, or at least selective, voting. Because of this, persons seeking elective office have felt impelled to campaign, openly seeking the support of their constituents. In doing so, they have discussed public issues before them. They have also felt impelled to learn from the citizens their felt needs and desires and, like all good politicians, have promised to respond to them. Because they must periodically stand for re-election, it can be taken for granted that as lawmakers they try effectively to respond to their constituents' needs and desires.

If we are correct in our assumptions, warranted in our faith, and justified by our own personal observations, we would say that the greatest evidence that democracy is taking root in India comes from what is being learned from more than ten years of experience in operating her giant rural development programme. In this experience, both programme leaders and the masses of village people are developing democracy by practising it. Not least among the things they have learned is that the roots of democracy were not firmly planted by either the declarations of the Constitution or the provisions of the national Plans, but that some roots of democracy are not only being firmly planted but nourished by the practices of democratic methods in development programme operation, and now even in programme planning.

There are experiences other than those gained in the operation of the community development-extension programme which have also induced the practice of democratic methods, and prepared citizens for intelligent and effective participation in a democratic society and a democratic polity. First are the provisions of the Third Five Year Plan for rapid improvement in the education of the masses; second, the persistent drive for the development of co-operative societies of all kinds; and third, the steady growth of what can be called public opinion.

The Constitution directed that there should be free compulsory education for all children six to fourteen years of age by 1960. As was pointed out in Chapter 16, this target was by no means reached by the end of the Second Five Year Plan in 1961. But in the Third Five Year Plan, the nation squarely faced the necessity of laying the base for a universally literate population. It said, "The programme for extending education to all children in the age-group 6-11 is of such crucial importance that financial considerations as such should not be allowed to come in the way of its successful execution in any State."

It can be presumed that the critical significance of a literate citizenry has become steadily and increasingly revealed not only by the programme experience of the community development-extension programme, but by the realization that in a planned programme of national economic and social development, there will be great need and demand for skilled manpower in a great many fields. Efforts to meet the demand for, and provide this imperative of, national development will also provide the outstanding basic requisite of political democracy—a literate electorate. The fact that the target date for providing universal education for the eleven to fourteen age-group has been extended fifteen years beyond the originally-stated target date is a recognition by Indian planners and leaders that planting the basic roots of democracy is a long, tedious, and costly undertaking.

The faith of Indian leaders in co-operatives is based not only on a conviction that co-operatives are, or can be, efficient business organisations, but also that they are a modern expression of old methods of mutual aid and support which for centuries have been practised in Indian villages. Furthermore, there is the conviction that co-operatives reflect and perpetuate a basic value in Indian culture. However historically justified this faith in co-operatives may be, the persistent drive for the development of co-operatives is a drive for direct, not delayed, democratic action. Progress has been slow, but the experiences and consistent experimentation in the development of co-operatives are contributing a vast amount of learning and practice in the use and value of democratic methods.

The development of what may be called public opinion, or public opinions, is difficult to observe or document. It is observable in the extent to which government action or proposed action is subjected to public debate. Such debate in newspaper editorials and columns has increased markedly in the last decade. Public opinion is reflected in debates in Parliament, between representatives of different geographical areas and groups. It is not yet as readily observable in the expressions and concerns of village people as it is in countries where all or the vast majority are literate, and where millions of persons read newspapers and listen to radio or television. We have attempted, in meeting after meeting with village groups, to ascertain their awareness that they are citizens of a national society. They have said almost universally, "We are now citizens." When queried as to what difference "Independence" has made to them, they have quite generally said two things: "We are now free," and "Now our government will help us." In no instance has any one of them said, "We are now participants in government," or "We can influence and help our government."

It can be expected that this will change, in fact we have some evidence that it is changing, under Panchayati Raj. It will develop and become manifest as not only village panchayats but larger groups become self-conscious civic organisations. They will automatically become locality special-interest groups, each seeking to influence higher-than-local levels of government action. They will even become legitimate pressure groups, each seeking to secure its share, or more than its share, of government assistance. This will be a frightening process, but it will manifest clearly the difference between a democracy and a monolithic or totalitarian society and government. Only when opinions on various topics are focused and freely expressed can the voice of the people be said to govern.

A prerequisite to the development of public opinion is that the masses of the people be informed on public issues. A requisite to being informed is the development of means of communication and the education of the masses. There are some promising evidences of fairly rapid development of education in India. The amount of funds allocated for the improvement of communication is relatively small. The total allocations for the improvement of communication and transportation are reported together in the Plan; in all three of the Five Year Plans, more than ninety per cent of these combined funds have been allocated to transportation. There can be no justification for great expenditures for various media of communication until a large percentage of the population is not only literate but intelligently aware of public issues, and especially aware of those issues which have become a legitimate and real concern of the masses of people. Simply stated, any great growth in communications, especially in rural areas, awaits the development of a literate rural population. The development of an intelligent public opinion, on the part of the rural people of India, will not come until something like the majority of them are effectively and practically literate.

The influence of the people on either those who make the laws or those who direct the day-by-day affairs of government is in a broad way guaranteed by universal suffrage. But in exercising their suffrage, the people have no opportunity to influence the officials for whom they have voted except to wait usually for five years, at which time they can sanction or censor by their vote what the persons they have helped to elect have done over the previous five years. However, when the phenomenon called public opinion, sometimes called a myth, becomes an instrument in the hands, minds, and judgments of the masses of the people, and through established channels of communication the people can express their opinions, it is then possible for them not only to make their government aware of their needs, their desires, and their judgments, but it is possible, and fairly imperative, for both the lawmakers and the government bureaucracy to respond to and thus represent the will of the people.

In discussing specific aspects of the rural development programme, we have identified the ways in which India's government bureaucracy has handicapped the dynamics of programme operation. We know that an efficient bureaucracy cannot cater to political whims, that in fact it must be freed from political meddling. But unless there are ways by which the bureaucratic establishment may become aware that it must respond effectively not only to public needs but to public opinion, the administrative machinery of a government can be autocratic and almost totalitarian. It is only in a democratic society with a democratic government that the people, through public opinion, have any influence on the conduct of day-by-day government administration.

In simple terms, a bureaucratic establishment must be the administrative agency of a national government in its day-by-day operation and services. The members of the bureaucracy must of necessity interpret and carry out government policies. But the elected representatives of government, the members of legislatures and parliaments, must be held accountable to the people for the operation of the government bureaucracy. Thus, legislative bodies serve as the go-between for the electorate and bureaucracy and hold every Minister responsible for that sector of the government bureaucracy which is located in his Ministry; legislators hold themselves responsible to those who elected them. It is through this machinery of democratic government that people make their desires, and sometimes their demands, known and that bureaucracy responds to the will of the people.

Our most critical judgment, broadly stated but firmly based on many years of observation, is that under national planning and bureaucratic administration, adequate attention has not been given to social relationships and an adequate understanding of them has not yet developed. The results of this shortcoming are revealed in the failure to mobilize effectively the willing co-operation of village people in improving their own conditions of life and living.

The most obvious result of this comparative failure is that practically none of the agricultural production targets has been reached. An equal, though less easily measured, comparative failure has been the small growth in organised community groups which would initiate and accept responsibility for local development programmes. Practically no progress has been made in group realignment and organisation of new special-purpose groups on the various levels of social action.

We believe we are also warranted in saying that adequate effort has not been made to learn why village people do not readily and rapidly accept new agricultural practices, the superiority of which has been validated by scientific research. Little effort has been made to discover and to understand the most effective means of spreading or diffusing information about superior methods of agricultural production. Literally no effort has been made to analyze, and thus effectively utilize, the indigenous communication system or network of communications in village communities. The need for studies of these kinds is clearly recognized elsewhere, and the findings of such studies have been found useful in extension work in even the most technically advanced countries of the world. In India, there still seems to prevail the tacit assumption that the social structure of village communities is simple, uniform, and well understood by programme planners and directors.

It has been in the operation of the community development-extension programme that we have been able to observe these things. The basic cause for these shortcomings has not been inadequate planning, or the unavailability of technical knowledge needed to improve agricultural production. It has been insufficient understanding and use of social skills in the motivation of village people plus an inadequate understanding of the network of human relationships in villages, and the ways by which both technical assistants and administrators can effectively communicate with those whom they seek to serve.

At least part of the resolution of these shortcomings must be the development of knowledge and understanding by the various levels of personnel in India's bureaucracy of why village people do or do not adopt improved practices, why and how new practices, once introduced into a village community, do or do not spread widely among other villages, and whether or not, or how, the well-established network of communication in village societies can be utilized to diffuse these improved practices. Answers to these questions will be found only if Indian bureaucracy assumes responsibility for the relatively simple types of research by which these answers can be found, as is done in well-established democratic societies. The assumption of this responsibility by India's bureaucracy would do more than anything else to change that bureaucracy from the practice of, and pride in, "guiding" village people to an understanding of how to "motivate" village people, and how to utilize the long-established social structure of village communities as a vehicle for promoting both development and democracy.

We have pointed out the major shortcomings in the operation of the rural development programme because it is in this, of all development programmes, that the Indian bureaucracy, through its lower echelons of personnel, must work in close co-operation with village people's organisations, and can thus be directly responsive to people's needs, desires, and opinions. It is in this programme under Panchayati Raj that India's bureaucracy will, by necessity, learn how to respond to these desires and opinions, and will gradually learn that it need not sacrifice its administrative integrity, even though it loses some of its elite social status. The bureaucracy will no longer tend to perpetuate social distance between its personnel and the masses.

Our most favourable comment is that under the impact of experience in operating the rural development programme, and as a result of the studies made by the Planning Commission's Programme Evaluation Organisation, every shortcoming mentioned above is being rectified by Indian leaders and planners who are heeding its findings. They have appointed special commissions and have invited outside agencies and individuals to study the operation of the programme, and even to study the operation of their bureaucratic administration. They have sent dozens of missions and many individuals to so-called democratic societies to learn not only the practices of their governments but to observe and study democracy, in terms of both the behaviour and the attitudes of persons living on all levels of these societies. We believe we can report valid observation of the steadily-increasing influence accorded to members of the far-flung government bureaucracy who, from the initiation of the rural development programme, have pleaded for less "supervision" and more training of subordinates in that bureaucracy; more recognition of the responsibility and role of voluntary groups and associations; and even more dependence on the opinions, and more faith in the knowledge and wisdom, of the so-called common people.

Our analysis of the community development-extension programme, the largest development programme in India in terms of the number of people being served and the number of official employees engaged in serving them, is different in many ways from the analyses of anthropologists who have briefly studied local communities and cultures. It is different from those of both political and economic historians who have depended on post mortem analyses. Our study has been more similar to, (though necessarily not so sophisticated nor so precise as), that of Daniel Lerner and his colleagues in *The Passing of Traditional Society*. We have not tried so much to compare measurable facts about the past with measurable facts of the present as we have attempted to observe what is happening in the present which will be preface and preparation for the future. We have not, as Lerner and his colleagues did, restricted our analyses to an observation of change in the beliefs, attitudes, and behaviour of individuals. We have sought to observe any progress made in the development of a democratic society. In order to do this, we began with the benchmark institutions and conditions with which India had to start her development toward the goal of building a democracy. We have not only described various rural development programmes, but have critically analyzed the use of democratic objectives and methods in programme planning and operation. We suspect that the greatest test of whether or not democracy is taking root in Indian society has been made in the operation of the rural development programme.

The surest proof that this great design is indeed being implemented in India is probably to be found in what is occurring in her rural life. For some time to come, it will be an increase in the productive capacity of Indian farms and village industries which will provide the goods for the first stages in the development of a mass consumption society. It will be migrants from rural to urban areas who will experience the greatest volume of vertical mobility. The rapidity with which the hundreds of millions of rural people are brought into effective communication with each other, and with other sectors of Indian society, will measure how rapidly India is becoming a communicative society. To the extent that the majority of the most illiterate sector of Indian population becomes literate, rural people will become aware of their common interests, will organise in all kinds of common-purpose groups and associations, and by doing so will evolve a pluralistic society. All such developments will be evidence that India is developing the characteristics, and the requisites, of a democratic society.

We did not start, and have not pursued our observations of India's rural development programme, with the idea of determining whether or not, or in what ways, democracy was being promoted or practised. But as we approached the consummation of our analyses, we became convinced that probably the most significant thing we had witnessed, over more than a decade of that programme's operation, was a steady growth in both the practice of, and dedication to, the methods of democracy. It was only then that we chose the title which this book bears. The title is not an assertion that democracy has taken root in, or under, all the foundations and superstructures of Indian society. It is meant to imply that we have observed the problems inherent in planting the roots of democracy in what was probably the most highly socially-stratified society in the world. We believe many roots of democracy have been planted in the operation of the rural community development-extension programme.

We trust that our account of the difficulties encountered in programme operation and the continuous efforts of programme leaders to eliminate shortcomings in the use of democratic methods warrants the faith of the people of India, and the people of all democratic societies, that this great country will make steady and consistent progress in the building of a democratic society, and by the use of democratic methods.

India is only one of the many newly-developing countries of the world whose leaders have declared their intentions to develop democratic governments and democratic societies. India is the second most populous newly-developing society in the world. She is by far the most populous newly-developing country which has declared her intentions to build a democratic national society and is bending all her efforts to that end. All of the governments of newly-developing countries can profit from the trials and experiences of India's rural development programme. The three most basic things they can learn are: first, that their national constitutions must permit and provide for a democratic government; second, that a class of intellectually elite, dedicated leaders is a basic essential to initiating and promoting democratic ideologies and ideals; and third, that a development programme must from the start and continuously involve great and increasing numbers of individuals and organised groups in the processes of developing democracy at the grass roots of society.

That India has all of the geographic, physical, and human resources to be one of the great nations of the world is obvious. That she is dedicated to the objective of becoming a democracy cannot be questioned. We have here emphasized the importance of these facts to the people of India, but they are also important to the rest of the world. Not least important to the society of nations is what kind of a society India is becoming. And not least important to any national society is what its posture and influence are among the other national societies of the world.

The evidences we have already noted are that India is painfully but steadily becoming a more democratic society. Our analyses will make their greatest contribution if they provide to the leaders of other developing countries an understanding and appreciation of the importance of the experience gained in operating India's giant community development-extension programme. This experience is of great value because: first, Indian leaders have demonstrated a deep dedication to the task of planting and nurturing the roots of democracy in Indian rural society and in programme planning and administration; and second, there has been a willingness to learn, and a great deal has been learned, about the need for and the practical efficiencies of democratic methods in a programme that requires the co-operation of hundreds of millions of persons and hundreds of thousands of organised groups. These are the firm roots from which a democratic society grows. That these roots are being planted in India's rural development programme is probably the chief story this book has, more or less inadvertently, related. That she will continue to make progress in developing a national democratic society is and should be of major concern not only to the leaders and people of India but to the leaders and people of all other nations.

MAIN AUTHORITIES QUOTED OR CITED

Bowles, Chester, *Ambassador's Report*, Harper and Bros., New York, 1954.

Foster, George M., *Traditional Cultures: and the Impact of Technological Change*, Harper and Row, Publishers, New York, 1962.

Fisher M. W. and Bondrivant, J. V., *The Indian Experience with Democratic Elections*, Institute of International Studies, University of California, Berkeley, 1956.

Krishnamachari, V. T., *Planning in India*, Orient Longmans, Calcutta, 1961.

Lerner, Daniel, *The Passing of Traditional Society: Modernizing the Middle East*, The Free Press, Glencoe, Illinois, 1958.

Nehru, Jawaharlal, *The Discovery of India*, Signet Press, Calcutta, Sixth Edition, April, 1956.

Pye, Lucian W., *Politics, Personality and Nation Building: Burma's Search for Identity*, Yale University Press, New Haven and London, 1962.

Warner, Wm. Lloyd, *Social Classes in America*, Science Research Associates Inc., Chicago, 1949; and *The Social Life of a Modern Community*, Yale University Press, New Haven; London, H. Milford, Oxford University Press, 1941.

Weiner, Myron, *The Politics of Scarcity: Public Pressure and Political Response in India*, University of Chicago Press, 1962, and Asia Publishing House, Bombay, 1963.

Yinger, M., "Cultural Values in India's Development," Annals of American Academy of Political and Social Science, Philadelphia, May, 1956.

Yinger, M., *Economic Development and Cultural Change*, Vol. VIII, No. 1, 1959, University of Chicago, Chicago, Illinois.

INDEX